Content Area Reading

Literacy and Learning Across the Curriculum

Thirteenth Edition

Richard T. Vacca
Emeritus, Kent State University

Maryann Mraz
University of North Carolina at Charlotte

Jo Anne L. Vacca
Emerita, Kent State University

 Pearson

Please contact https://support.pearson.com/getsupport/s/contactsupport with any queries on this content.

Library of Congress Cataloging-in-Publication Data

Names: Vacca, Richard T., author. | Mraz, Maryann, author. | Vacca, Jo Anne L., author.
Title: Content area reading : literacy and learning across the curriculum / Richard T. Vacca, Maryann Mraz, Jo Anne L. Vacca.
Description: 13th edition. | Hoboken, NJ : Pearson, 2021. | Includes bibliographical references and index.
Identifiers: LCCN 2019037444 (print) | LCCN 2019037445 (ebook) | ISBN 9780135760963 (paperback) | ISBN 9780135761076 (ebook)
Subjects: LCSH: Content area reading.
Classification: LCC LB1050.455 .V33 2021 (print) | LCC LB1050.455 (ebook) | DDC 372.47/6—dc23
LC record available at https://lccn.loc.gov/2019037444
LC ebook record available at https://lccn.loc.gov/2019037445

1 2020

Access Code Card
ISBN-10: 0-13-576087-9
ISBN-13: 978-0-13-576087-1

Rental
ISBN-10: 0-13-576096-8
ISBN-13: 978-0-13-576096-3

Instructor's Review Copy
ISBN-10: 0-13-576129-8
ISBN-13: 978-0-13-576129-8

To teachers
You did not choose your profession to make a world of money, but instead
to make a world of difference in the lives of your students.
Thank you!
—*Rich and Jo Anne Vacca*

To my family
who departed the Old Country for Ellis Island and the hope of a new life in America:
Janko, Marko, Jela, Toma, Barbara, William, Helen, Anthon, Ursula, and Nikola.
They are remembered here with gratitude and love.
—*Maryann Mraz*

About the Authors

Richard and Jo Anne Vacca are Professors Emeriti in the School of Teaching, Learning, and Curriculum Studies in the College of Education, Health, and Human Services at Kent State University. They have published numerous books, chapters, and articles. They met as undergraduate English majors at SUNY Albany and have been partners ever since. Jo Anne taught language arts in middle schools in New York and Illinois and received her doctorate from Boston University. Rich taught high school English and earned his doctorate at Syracuse University. He is a past president of the International Reading Association.

The Vaccas live in Vero Beach, Florida, where they keep active professionally, golf, volunteer, and walk their toy poodles, Tiger, Gigi, and Joely. They especially enjoy visiting and traveling with their daughter, Courtney; son-in-law, Gary; and grandsons, Simon, Max, and Joe.

Maryann Mraz is a Professor in the Reading and Elementary Education Department at the University of North Carolina at Charlotte (UNCC). She earned her Ph.D. from Kent State University and her B.A. and M.Ed. from John Carroll University, where she was awarded the Distinguished Alumni Educator Award in 2014. Maryann has served as a board member of the Association of Literacy Educators and Researchers (ALER) and as the Doctoral Program Director for Curriculum and Instruction at UNCC. She is the author of more than 70 books, articles, chapters, and instructional materials on literacy education. Maryann teaches bachelors, masters, and doctoral courses in literacy education and provides professional development programs to teachers and literacy coaches.

Brief Contents

Contents

Part II Instructional Practices and Strategies 152

Preface

About this Book

The 13th edition of *Content Area Reading: Literacy and Learning across the Curriculum* continues to reflect an ever-expanding knowledge base grounded in research and practice in the areas of content literacy, instructional scaffolding, differentiated instruction, student diversity, and new literacies. It continues to emphasize a contemporary, functional approach to content literacy instruction. In a functional approach, content area teachers learn how to integrate literacy-related strategies into instructional routines without sacrificing the teaching of content. Our intent is not to morph a content teacher into a reading specialist or writing instructor. Rather, our goal has always been, and shall continue to be, to improve the overall coverage of instructional strategies and practices that remain at the heart of this book.

New to This Edition

In this edition, chapter content has been rigorously updated to reflect current theory, research, and practice related to literacy and learning across the curriculum. New and updated content and features of this text include the following:

- Expanded emphasis on what it means to be literate in an age of ever-increasing **new literacies**. See Chapters 2, 9, and 10.

- New suggestions for supporting **English Learners** in comprehending content area vocabulary and texts. See Chapter 6, Box 6.1: "Evidence-Based Practices: The Intersections of Literacy and Culture"; Chapter 7, Box 7.2: "Supporting English Learners"; and in Chapter 8, Box 8.1: "Voices from the Field" on the challenges of differentiating instruction and Box 8.5: "Supporting English Learners."

- Attention to the use of **formative assessment** to support data-based instructional decision making. See Chapter 4.

- An expanded emphasis on and new examples of **learning with multiple texts**, including both classic and contemporary adolescent literature. See Chapters 5 and 11.

- Updated **disciplinary literacy** features in many chapters to show how teachers adapt various aspects of content literacy instruction to meet the demands and peculiarities of their disciplines. See Chapter 7, Box 7.4: "Using Discipline Literacy with Project Planning in a Business Classroom," and Chapter 9, Box 9.4: "Using Disciplinary Literacy to Explore the Real-Life Tasks of a Multimedia Story Teller."

- Updated **Voices from the Field** features in many chapters. This feature captures the challenges that instructional team members have encountered relative to chapter topics and the strategies used to address those challenges. See Chapters 1, 2, 3, 6, and 8. Many **instructional examples** have been replaced and updated throughout the text.

Key Content Updates by Chapter

Updates of new research and ways of thinking about literacy, learning, and instructional practice appear throughout the chapters. Updated content and features by chapter include the following:

- **Chapter 1, Literacy Matters,** is updated to reflect changes in education policy and standards. A new Voices from the Field segment presents the perspective of an instructional coach supporting content area teachers as they respond to these changes. The chapter discusses using technology integration to support collaborative learning across content areas.

- **Chapter 2, Learning with New Literacies,** reflects the prevalence of technology in schools and provides numerous new strategies and models, such as SAMR and the TPACK Framework, for integrating technology into content area classrooms. We offer suggestions for integrating social media tools in ways that increase digital citizenship and responsibility among students.

- **Chapter 3, Culturally Responsive Teaching in Diverse Classrooms,** is expanded to include a more detailed analysis of culturally relevant pedagogy and teaching for cultural understanding. We have included new strategies for supporting culturally and linguistically diverse students and have added a new Voices from the Field segment on using technology to support literacy development.

- **Chapter 4, Assessing Students and Texts,** discusses emergent content standards and their impact on assessment and data-driven instruction. The chapter is enhanced with new strategies for information assessment, a discussion of a formative assessment teaching cycle, and a framework for integrating data collection and instructional decision making.

- **Chapter 5, Planning Instruction for Content Literacy,** contains updated information on incorporating academic vocabulary in lesson planning and offers numerous updating strategy applications, including those for collaborative interactions and group investigations.

- **Chapter 6, Activating Prior Knowledge and Interest,** contains a new Evidence-Based Practices box on "The Intersections of Literacy and Culture" as well as a new Voices from the Field segment from the perspective of a first-year teacher who applies multimedia methods to activate students' prior knowledge and interest.

- **Chapter 7, Guided Reading Comprehension,** offers new suggestions for supporting English Learners and a new Disciplinary Literacy Box that applies disciplinary literacy principles to project planning in a business class. New, updated examples are offered for the QAR strategy.

- **Chapter 8, Developing Vocabulary and Concepts,** includes new content for supporting English Learners, a New Voices from the Field segment from the perspective of a high school English teacher working to meet the diverse vocabulary needs of her students, and new strategy application examples.

- **Chapter 9, Writing Across the Curriculum,** includes new information on applying disciplinary literacy principles to real-life tasks through multimedia story telling. Updated strategy examples are offered throughout the chapter.

- **Chapter 10, Studying Text,** contains many new examples of literacy applications across content areas. It includes a discussion of electronic text structure as it relates to studying text.

- **Chapter 11, Learning with Multiple Texts,** incorporates updated, research-based strategies for teaching with contemporary literature that addresses complex topics. The chapter broadens its emphasis to include multiple texts, graphic nonfiction, e-books, and databases. It includes expanded suggestions for strategy applications, especially with new technologies.

MyLab Education

One of the most visible changes, and one of the most significant in the 13th edition, is the expansion of the digital learning and assessment resources embedded in the e-text and the inclusion of MyLab Education in the text. MyLab Education is an online homework, tutorial, and assessment program designed to engage learners and improve learning. Within its structured environment, learners see key concepts demonstrated through real classroom video footage, practice what they learn, test their understanding, and receive feedback to guide their learning and to ensure their mastery of key learning outcomes. Designed to bring learners more directly into the world of content area classrooms and to help them see the real and powerful impact of ideas covered in this book, the online resources in MyLab Education with the Enhanced eText include:

- **Video Examples.** Three or four times per chapter, an embedded video provides an illustration of important ideas in action. These video examples illustrate students and teachers working in classrooms and also describe how students and their teachers wrestle with challenges and dilemmas they encounter in classrooms.

- **Self-Checks.** In each chapter, self-check quizzes help assess how well learners have mastered the content. The self-checks are made up of self-grading, multiple-choice items that not only provide feedback on whether questions are answered correctly or incorrectly but also provide rationales for both correct and incorrect answers.

- **Application Exercises.** These exercises give learners opportunities to practice applying the content from the chapters. The questions in these exercises are usually constructed responses. Once learners provide their own answers to the questions, they receive feedback in the form of model answers written by experts.

Organization and Features of This Edition

As part of the revision process for this edition, we decided to keep the same structure as the previous edition by organizing chapters into two main parts. Part I, "Learners, Literacies, and Texts," places the focus on the cultural, linguistic, and academic diversity of today's learners, their personal and academic literacies, and the kinds of texts that are integral to their lives in and out of school. Part II, "Instructional Practices and Strategies," contains a multitude of evidence-based instructional strategies waiting to be adapted to meet the conceptual demands inherent in disciplinary learning.

Changes are interwoven throughout the e-text and the traditional print edition in the form of new disciplinary literacy boxes, new Voices from the Field segments, updated content in many of the chapters, updated references, and new examples of instructional strategies. This edition is enhanced by new online resources in the MyLab Education in the Enhanced E-text, including video examples, self-check assessments, and application exercises. These activities and strategies are powerful tools for supporting students as they think and learn with text.

This edition of *Content Area Reading* retains many of the features of the previous edition while improving its overall coverage of content literacy topics. In every chapter, special pedagogical features are provided to aid in this effort.

Features at the beginning of each chapter include the following:

Part I   Learners, Literacies, and Texts

Chapter 1
Literacy Matters
Written in collaboration with Melissa Sykes

▼ **Chapter Overview and Learning Outcomes**

After reading this chapter, you should be able to:

1.1 Explain the characteristics of effective teachers and effective teaching, the difference between the two, and their impact on students and learning.

1.2 Explain how *literacy* has evolved and the classroom implications of 21st-century literacy.

1.3 Describe the factors influencing reading to learn in a discipline.

◀ **Learning Outcomes** reflect the major objectives of the chapter under study.

▼ **Graphic organizer** depicts the relationships among ideas presented in the chapter.

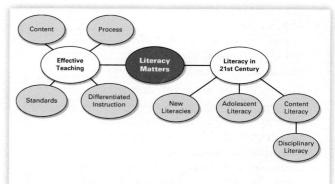

The **Organizing Principle** provides ▶ readers with a "heads-up" by introducing the rationale for the chapter and highlighting its underlying theme.

Organizing Principle

New literacies have transformed the way we read, write, think, communicate, and make meaning.

In many ways, the universe serves as a metaphor for the human mind. It is never ending, ever expanding, and unfathomable. So is the human mind. Literacy has a powerful impact on the

Frame of Mind ▶ questions get readers thinking about chapter topics.

This need not be the case. The organizing principle of this chapter underscores the dynamic relationship between literacy and learning: Effective teachers show students how to think, learn, and communicate with all kinds of texts.

Study the Chapter Overview. It's your map to the major ideas that you will encounter in the chapter. The graphic display shows the relationships that exist among the concepts you will study. Use it as an organizer. What is the chapter about? What do you know already about the content to be presented in the chapter? What do you need to learn more about? How will you implement the presented information and concepts in your own practice?

In conjunction with the Chapter Overview, take a moment or two to study the Frame of Mind questions. This feature uses key questions to help you think about the ideas that you will read about. When you finish reading, you should be able to respond fully to the Frame of Mind questions.

MyLab Education
Response Journal 1.1
Write a "five-minute essay" in your response journal on your initial reaction to standards-based planning, instruction, and learning.

Frame of Mind

1. What is the difference between content and process knowledge?
2. What are the characteristics of effective teaching?
3. How do content standards and content-driven planning and instruction affect literacy and learning in content areas?
4. Why is differentiated instruction an important aspect of content literacy and learning?
5. What are new literacies, and how are they changing the way we think about learning and literacy in the 21st century?
6. In what ways can technology aid instruction and support student literacy and learning?
7. What is adolescent literacy, and why is it important to 21st-century society?
8. How are content literacy and disciplinary literacy alike? How are they different?
9. What comprehension strategies are critical to reading? What role does prior knowledge play in comprehension?
10. What literacy strategies specifically target the challenges struggling and English Learners (ELs) readers face?

Teaching is an exercise in observation and response; there are no definitive formulas for teachers who want students to develop core concepts and good habits of thinking within a discipline. Nor are there magic potions in the form of instructional strategies that will make a difference with all students, all the time. Teaching is a problem-solving activity: There's just you; the academic texts and instructional strategies that you use; and the students whose lives you briefly and, hopefully, positively impact. Teaching is a daunting but immensely rewarding enterprise for those who are up to the challenge.

Effective Teaching In Content Areas

1.1   Explain the characteristics of effective teachers and effective teaching, the difference between the two, and their impact on students and learning.

Highly effective content area teachers plan lessons that are engaging and purposeful. These teachers recognize that "engaging the disengaged" is an essential, but difficult, task. Yet continually striving to make learning intellectually challenging and relevant for students makes teaching more effective and learning more stimulating. A top instructional priority, therefore, is to involve students actively in learning the important ideas and concepts of the *content* they are studying. But the effective teacher also knows that an intellectually challenging instructional environment engages students not only in the acquisition of content but also in the *thinking processes* by which they learn that content.

In-text features include the following:

Videos in each chapter help readers approach the text in a critical frame of mind as they analyze and interpret the information presented. ▶

Chapter 3 Culturally Responsive Teaching in Diverse Classrooms 71

MyLab Education **Self-Check 3.2**

MyLab Education **Application Exercise 3.2:**
Valuing Students' Funds of Knowledge in a Content Area Classroom

Linguistic Differences in Today's Schools

3.3 Explain the impact of linguistic diversity on content area instruction.

Linguistic differences among today's student population are strikingly evident in many school districts throughout the United States. From the East Coast to the West Coast and from the Gulf to the northern Great Lakes, the increasingly large number of immigrants from non-European nations is influencing how content area teachers approach instruction. It is no exaggeration to suggest that in some large urban school districts, more than 175 different languages are spoken (Charlotte-Mecklenburg Schools, 2014).

When immigrant students maintain a strong identification with their culture and native language, they are more likely to succeed academically, and they have more positive self-concepts about their ability to learn (Banks, 2001; Diaz, 2001; Garcia, 2002). Schools, however, tend to view linguistically diverse students whose first language is one other than English from a deficit model, not a difference model. For these English Learners, instructional practices currently are compensatory in nature: "That is, they are premised on the assumption that language diversity is an illness that needs to be cured" (Diaz, 2001, p. 159).

In addition, regional variations in language usage, commonly known as dialects, are a complicated issue for teachers. In truth, as explained in Box 3.3, all English language users speak a dialect of English, which is rooted in such factors as age, gender, socioeconomic status, and the region of the country where one was born and grew up. Even presidents of the United States speak dialects! The difficulty with dialect differences in the classroom is the *value* assigned to dialects—the perceived goodness or badness of one language variation over another. Linguists explain that language variations are neither good nor bad and that such judgments are often about the people who make them rather than about clarity or precision (Ahearn, 2012). Gee (2012) argues quite convincingly that teachers need to respect and recognize the strengths of diverse learners who use dialects in the classroom.

MyLab Education Video Example 3.2: How Can Educators Help Students to Learn English
Watch this video to hear one educator's advice on helping students learn English.

Box 3.3 Evidence-Based Practices

Standard English Is Not the Only English

Scholars have long disagreed on the actual number of dialects in the United States, but one point they agree on is that everyone speaks a *dialect* of English. In the companion website for PBS's series "Do You Speak American?," Fought (2005) writes: "Do you think because I'm a professor, I don't speak a dialect? I do. I speak Valley Girl! My native dialect is 'Valley Girl' English,

changes. The people who live in an area as well as those who enter an area influence dialect. African American Vernacular English (AAVE), Ebonics, or Black English Vernacular, as it is also known, may have evolved as a fusion of West African languages and English. What is most interesting about AAVE is that while other dialects are typically defined by the regions

▼ **Voices from the Field** include interviews with teachers, administrators, and curriculum specialists related to instructional practices and policies.

Box 6.3 Voices from the Field

Drew, Mathematics Coach

Challenge

During a unit on area and perimeter, a fifth-grade classroom teacher, Mrs. Little, and I posed a real-world mathematical task to students to allow them to explore these concepts more deeply. Here is the task they were given:

You have 12 yards of fencing to build a rectangular cage for your rabbit. Which dimensions give you the most space inside the cage?

Students often struggle with solving these types of mathematical tasks for a couple reasons: They struggle to read and make sense of the mathematical situation, and, sometimes, they don't know where to begin. In this case, students struggled to distinguish between the concepts of perimeter (the amount of fencing) and area (the space inside).

Strategy

To support the students, Mrs. Little and I spent time at the beginning of the lesson activating their prior knowledge by asking them about real-life examples of area and perimeter. We posed questions such as:

- If we needed to build a fence, how would we determine how much fencing we would need?
- Can you think of other examples where we would need to figure out the distance around something?
- If we needed to put carpet down on the floor of a house, how would we determine how much carpet we would need?
- Can you think of other examples where we would need to figure out how much material we will need to cover a flat surface?

We posed the task to students and provided them with plastic square tiles to begin exploring the task. Initially, students connected the number 12 in the task with the need to grab 12 square tiles. Nearly every student did this and immediately made rectangles. Some students made a rectangle that was 6 tiles wide and 2 tiles tall, while others made one that was 4 tiles wide and 3 tiles tall. While both used 12 tiles, neither rectangle had a perimeter of 12.

Seeing this misconception, Mrs. Little and I revisited students' understanding of perimeter by asking them a few questions:

Mrs. Little: Do we know the amount of fencing that we have or the space that we have inside of our pen?

Polly: If we know that we have 12 yards of fencing, how can we use our tiles to help us?

Jimmy: We can look at the rectangles that we made and then count the distance around each shape.

Mrs. Little: Go ahead and do that.

As students counted the distance around, they realized that neither rectangle had a perimeter of 12 units. Rather, the 6 · 2 rectangle had a perimeter of 16 units, and the 4 · 3 rectangle had a perimeter of 14 units. Students were confused about how to find a rectangle with a perimeter of 12 units. Mrs. Little asked, "How can we find a rectangle that has a perimeter of 12?" Students started to manipulate the 12 tiles and counted the perimeter of their representations. No students were able to find a rectangle that used 12 tiles and also had a perimeter of 12.

Mrs. Little then asked, "Do we have to use exactly 12 tiles, or can we use a different number?" The students all responded, "A different number."

When Mrs. Little asked why that was the case, Samuel commented, "The only thing given to us is that the fencing or perimeter had to be 12. The number of tiles could be different."

Students worked for the next 15 minutes making rectangles out of their tiles that had a perimeter of 12. The teacher then asked students to share their solutions on the SMART Board by drawing a picture of their rectangle and writing the dimensions. The use of a visual helped struggling students to make sense of their classmates' answers. Table 1 shows the students' solutions.

During the discussion, Mrs. Little had made Table 1 on the SMART Board and asked students to talk with their table groups about observations that they had. Tyrone mentioned, "There are two rectangles that have an area of 5 and two that have an area of 8." After Mrs. Little asked him to explain the difference between the two rectangles that had an area of 5, Tyrone said, "One rectangle is 5 by 1 and the other is 1 by 5. When we draw them, they have the same dimensions, but one is just twisted around." Tyrone drew a visual up on the SMART Board of the two rectangles to match his explanation.

Lastly, the entire class was able to explain that the pen with the largest amount of space was a 3 by 3 rectangle, which students called a square. The discussion of this part of the task allowed students to discuss the relationship between squares and rectangles.

Reflection

This lesson allowed fifth-grade students to build on their prior knowledge of fencing and carpets to explore a real-world mathematical task about the area and perimeter of rectangles. The

136 PART 1 Learners, Literacies, and Texts

- *Present findings of research in a variety of products and formats*, including charts, graphs, and visual or performing arts.
- *Discuss possible sources for information* presented in the class or for answering questions posed by the teacher or students (e.g., personal interviews, diaries, experiments).

The teacher must carefully plan inquiry-centered projects, giving just the right amount of direction to allow students to explore and discover ideas on their own. The research process isn't a do-your-own-thing proposition; budding researchers need structure. The trick is to strike a balance between teacher guidance and student self-reliance. A research project must have just enough structure to give students (1) a problem focus, (2) physical and intellectual freedom, (3) an environment in which they can obtain data, and (4) feedback situations in which to report the results of their research.

Box 5.2 Evidence-Based Best Practices

Procedures for Guiding Inquiry/Research Projects

I. Raise questions, identify interests, organize information.
  A. Discuss interest areas related to the unit of study.
  B. Engage in goal setting.
    1. Arouse curiosities.
    2. Create awareness of present levels of knowledge.
  C. Pose questions relating to each area and/or subarea.
    1. "What do you want to find out?"
    2. "What do you want to know about?"
    3. Record the questions or topics.
    4. "What do you already know about?"
  D. Organize information; have students make predictions about likely answers to gaps in knowledge.
    1. Accept all predictions as possible answers.
    2. Encourage thoughtful speculations in a nonthreatening way.

II. Select materials.
  A. Use visual materials.
    1. Trade books
    2. Magazines, catalogs, directories
    3. Newspapers and comics
    4. Indexes, atlases, almanacs, dictionaries, readers' guides, computer catalogs
    5. Films, slides
    6. Online videos, television programs
    7. Digital texts: CD-ROMs, website documents, online articles and databases, webinars, virtual field trips
  B. Use nonvisual materials.
    1. Audio files
    2. Recorded music or talk
    3. Radio programs or webcasts
    4. Field trips
  C. Use human resources.
    1. Interviews
    2. Letters
    3. On-site visits
    4. Discussion groups
    5. E-mail
    6. Listservs
  D. Encourage self-selection of materials.
    1. "What can I understand?"
    2. "What gives me the best answers?"

III. Guide the information search.
  A. Encourage active research.
    1. Reading
    2. Listening
    3. Observing
    4. Talking
    5. Writing
  B. Facilitate with questions.
    1. "How are you doing?"
    2. "Can I help you?"
    3. "Do you have all the materials you need?"
    4. "Can I help you with ideas you don't understand?"
  C. Have students keep records.
    1. Learning log that includes plans, procedures, notes, and rough drafts
    2. Book record cards
    3. Record of conferences with the teacher

IV. Consider different forms of writing.
  A. Initiate a discussion of sharing techniques.
  B. Encourage a variety of writing forms.
    1. Essay or paper
    2. Lecture to a specific audience
    3. Case study
    4. Story: adventure, science fiction, another genre
    5. Dialogue, conversation, interview
    6. Dramatization through scripts
    7. Commentary or editorial
    8. Thumbnail sketch

V. Guide the writing process.
  A. Help students organize information.
  B. Guide first-draft writing.
  C. Encourage responding, revising, and rewriting.
  D. "Publish" finished products.
    1. Individual presentations
    2. Classroom arrangement
    3. Class interaction

Chapter 7 Guiding Reading Comprehension 205

Box 7.4 Disciplinary Literacy

Using Disciplinary Literacy With Project Planning in a Business Classroom

As we learned in Chapter 1, disciplinary literacy is becoming increasingly important in content classrooms due to the textual demands associated with discipline-specific content. As a reminder, each discipline requires students to read, write, think, and speak in order to acquire knowledge in the discipline itself (Shanahan & Shanahan, 2008). Thus, when students have opportunities to engage in specific discipline practices, they can begin to see themselves as engineers, mathematicians, scientists, poets and authors, and future entrepreneurs (Buehl, 2009). Put another way, teachers become the facilitators and scaffold learning so their students "develop the capacity to read disciplinary specific texts through an insider perspective" (Buehl, 2011, p. 10).

High school business classes provide an ideal setting for the application of disciplinary literacy. After all, the primary purpose of these classes should be to allow students to dip their toes into business practices to get a feel for their personal fit. Unfortunately, the purpose often gets lost in prolonged projects, outdated software applications, and job descriptions that no longer apply to real positions. The question then becomes: What guidelines should content area classroom teachers consider when implementing disciplinary literacy practices and still teaching the content curriculum?

To assist classroom teachers, the Southwest Educational Development Laboratory (SEDL) provides recommendations or "insights" to consider when planning to initiate disciplinary literacy practices into their content areas (Chauvin & Theodore, 2015, p. 1):

1. Provide an approach to content instruction that cultivates the skills for 21st-century literacy: critical thinking, communication, collaboration, and creativity;
2. Take charge of designing authentic, real-word experiences and assessments;
3. Commit to a conceptual framework of learning by doing;
4. Provide opportunities for students to use inquiry, key habits of practice, and academic language; and
5. Implement ongoing, job-embedded professional development and collaboration by discipline with teachers as designers and facilitators.

3) to develop the academic language critical to the role of a project manager. The ultimate goal was to engage his students in one facet of a real-world business practice.

To begin, he chose the career path of the project manager. Not only does this job exist in almost every industry, but it also encompasses the basic skills necessary to be successful in the management of a business. He planned a 6-week project to be accomplished in three parts. For Part One, the students would conduct in-depth research on the knowledge, skills, and education required to be a project manager. During Part Two, the students would engage in actual project planning; and for Part Three, the students would prepare a presentation for an employer.

On day one, he had his business students scour the Internet for project manager job descriptions because he wanted his students to formulate an understanding of the words **project** and **project management**. It was essential that his students understand that every project is engineered by goal-minded individuals who are trained in leadership and management practices. Additionally, the students looked up college programs to identify the course of study associated with the training and development of a project manager. Over the course of 2 weeks, the students chose where they would ideally like to work and which salary was most appealing. Under the guidance of the teacher, they made their lists of required knowledge, skills, and education needed for project management that matched the job descriptions geographically and their preferences by salary for prospective employment.

To initiate Part Two, the teacher rolled out the sample project plan – the next great sneaker. To set the course for the project, he showed a power point on project management to highlight the essential project management techniques, the organizational, assessment, and software tools, and the project management process in order for his students to achieve the next great sneaker. In order for his students to fully understand the job of project management, he knew this could best be achieved if he created planning teams. He believed the jigsaw strategy (discussed in Chapter 5) would provide each member of the planning team the opportunity to become an expert. As a result, he divided his class into five teams, consisting of five members to a team, and each member of a team was assigned a critical element of the **five stages of project management**:

▲ **Disciplinary Literacy** features show how teachers in a particular discipline adapt various aspects of content literacy instruction to meet the demands and peculiarities of their disciplines.

◀ **Evidence-Based Best Practices** highlight the steps and procedures involved in using high-visibility strategies that are supported by theoretically sound rationales and/or evidence-based, scientific research.

Special marginal notations and callouts provide opportunities to enhance the basic instruction within the chapters:

learning tasks and activities for students to complete using Internet resources. WebQuests are typically organized around several components: introduction, task, process, resources, learning advice, and conclusion.

The introduction to a WebQuest provides an overview of the learning opportunity available to the students. Often the introduction places the learner(s) in a hypothetical situation somewhat similar to RAFT writing activities (see Chapter 9). As a result, students are assigned a role and a purpose for engaging in the learning activity. The task component of the WebQuest describes the task(s) students will complete and lists the questions that guide the information search. The process component outlines the steps and procedures students will follow to complete the learning task. The resources component of a WebQuest provides links to information resources on the Internet that students will need to access to complete the learning task. The "learning advice" component provides directions to students on how to organize information, whether in outlines, time lines, graphic organizers (see Chapter 10), notebook entries such as the double-entry journal format (see Chapter 5), or I-charts. And, finally, the conclusion to the WebQuest brings closure to the activity and summarizes what students should have learned from participation in the WebQuest.

Adapting Learning Strategies with Technology

Computers and digital technologies are both a "facilitator of knowledge and medium for literacy" (Biancarosa & Snow, 2004). Technology allows teachers to plan higher levels of differentiation and to meet the academic needs of a greater number of students during instruction. Electronic databases, such as EBSCO and ProQuest, provide middle and high school students a wealth of information at various degrees of reading difficulty, allowing teachers to find multiple texts related to course content.

MyLab Education
Response Journal 2.2
Consider how technology has evolved throughout your educational experience as a student and, perhaps, as a teacher. How has technology impacted your experiences in classrooms and schools and changed learning for you?

For example, ProQuest has created the ProQuest Central and STEM Database and EBSCO has Explora, search engines designed for middle and high school students. Explora and ProQuest Central provide adolescent learners with appropriate research tools for easily obtaining the information that they seek from these databases, including electronic magazines, newspapers, biographies, and videos. Students can also search databases by topic and limit their searches according to appropriate *Lexile reading levels* (see Chapter 4 for a discussion of Lexile reading levels and other tools for determining the readability or difficulty level of texts).

Using electronic texts, content area teachers can create flexible groups within their classes that allow all students access to text appropriate to their needs and relevant to course objectives. In addition, interactive computer programs, such as Newsela and CommonLit, offer a range of textual material adapted to students' reading levels, while ReadWorks provides a range of nonfiction material for teachers to use with K–12 students. Many of these texts and websites adapt to a student's reading performance by providing text passages that are written at a level consistent with the student's needs. Doing so increases the comprehensibility of the text for the student. Additionally, such programs provide students with immediate feedback on assignments and allow teachers to track student progress toward goals outlined in intervention plans. Some programs that include voice recognition software allow students to record themselves while reading so that miscues can be tracked and appropriate feedback provided. These resources can be useful for providing students with multiple interactions with texts and for offering independent practice (Biancarosa & Snow, 2004).

Many learning strategies such as KWL and RAFT can be adapted using Web 2.0 technologies. For example, comprehension strategies such as KWL and 3-2-1 can be created in shared document sites like Google Drive. Teachers can post research and writing tools, such as I-charts and RAFT, to a Dropbox folder or their class wiki. Twitter can be used in place of question cards to generate questions for a class discussion.

Here is a chart with digital adaptations of some of the strategies presented in this book.

◀ **Response Journal** marginal icons signal readers to use a "response journal" while reading to make personal and professional connections as they react to ideas presented in each chapter.

Classroom Artifact figures ▶ throughout the book illustrate instructional procedures and materials developed by teachers for authentic teaching situations.

Figure 9.5 Entries from a Double-Entry Journal Assignment for *The Call of the Wild*

Classroom Artifact

What did you learn from the demonstration?	How did the demonstration help you better understand the novel?
I learned that although dogs just look big and cuddly they really can work. When people take the time they can teach their dog anything. Yet that saying also applies to life. [Alex]	I never realized how hard it was for Buck to pull the sled. It takes a lot of work.
It was excellent. I learned that the owners and the dogs were a family and extremely hard workers. I learned how hard a race could be and the risk involved. I'm glad I got to see the dogs and their personalities. [Marcus]	It proved to me how Buck needed to be treated with praise and discipline and equality. That way you get a wonderful dog and a companion for life.
I learned about how they trained their dogs and that they need as much or more love and attention as they do discipline. [Jennifer]	It helped me understand the book better because it showed how unique Buck is compared to the other dogs. Also what a dog sled looks like and what Buck might have looked like. It made the story come alive more.

Box 9.3 Evidence-Based Practices

Authentic Writing With English Learners

Daniel (2017) reminds writing instructors that English Learners benefit from authentic writing experiences that are connected to their experiences. For example, an eighth-grade science class engaged in a unit study on the spread of disease. One of their writing assignments was to imagine that they worked for the Centers for Disease Control and Prevention (CDC). Their task was to catalog and categorize the diseases, their symptoms, and their cures. This class included several Hmong students who had limited proficiency with English. The teacher created sight word cards and corresponding picture cards of disease symptoms. Capitalizing not only on the eighth-grade fascination with all things gruesome but also picture/word associations, the Hmong students worked with their English-speaking counterparts to learn the vocabulary as they matched the sight word cards with the pictures. Next, they worked in small groups to dramatize symptoms that corresponded to a disease. The experience of playing these roles helped all students to understand the nature of the diseases they were studying. This activity supports

Chapters conclude with additional features that help readers review and practice the concepts introduced in the chapter:

Texted Reading Guides

An engaged classroom provides an opportunity to learn and practice in authentic ways. One way to do this is to encourage students to use technology that usually resides outside of the classroom, inside the classroom (Crawley, 2015). Texted reading guides are one way to allow students to use their texting skills academically. An activity that is best done in groups of two, texted reading guides can either be an e-mail exchange or, more ideally, a text exchange. The learners work together to text or e-mail each other their notes. Just like an outline, they should organize their writing so that, when read back, it can reflect the structure of the texts. This process starts with one reader texting a title and the other texting the main point. This continues until all the main points have been explored.

Here is an excerpt from an exchange about *The Outsiders*. The students were given the assignment to discuss how they felt about Ponyboy.

> Student One: *I like Ponyboy, but I think he is really naïve.*
> Student Two: *Why do you think that?*
> Student One: *I think he trusts people too much. Like when he is trusting his brothers to take care of everything. I think he looks at them like they can do no wrong. That is naïve. Don't you think.*
> Student Two: *Yes I guess, but they are also family. Sometimes you have to believe in something, right? If you can't believe in your family, what else do you have. I don't call that naïve, I call that loyal.*

Then the process begins again with a new title and new points. Not only does this assignment allow students to express their opinions and points of comprehension authentically, but also their conversation is saved digitally. They can look back at their notes to study, ask questions, and recall important points. They can read and revise it in real time, and through the revision, it becomes a living document.

MyLab Education **Self-Check 10.4**

MyLab Education **Application Exercise 10.4:**
Using Text Annotations in Content Area Classrooms

Looking Back Looking Forward

Teaching students how and why to study texts involves showing them how to become independent learners. In this chapter, we used the role that text structure plays to illustrate how you can teach students to use learner-directed strategies that involve constructing graphic organizers, writing summaries, and making and taking notes. We also emphasized the importance to connecting studying to authentic tasks and technologies.

Understanding how authors organize their ideas is a powerful factor in learning with texts. Because authors write to communicate, they organize ideas to make them accessible to readers. A well-organized text is a considerate one. The text patterns that authors use to organize their ideas revolve around description, sequence, comparison and contrast, cause and effect, and problem and solution. The more students perceive text patterns, the more likely they are to remember and interpret the ideas they encounter in reading as they connect them with their cultural backgrounds and life experiences.

Graphic organizers help students outline important information that is reflected in the text patterns that authors use to organize ideas. The construction of graphic organizers allows students to map the relationships that exist among the ideas presented in text. This strategy is a valuable tool for comprehending, retaining, and expressing information.

Students who engage in summarizing what they have read often gain greater understanding and retention of the main ideas in text. Students need to become aware of summarization rules and to receive instruction in how to use these rules to write and polish a summary.

◀ **Looking Back, Looking Forward** sections at the end of each chapter offer a summative review of the concepts introduced and a perspective on where the discussion will lead to next.

eResources

Explore topics on content area literacy presented on the Reading Rockets website. Consider how you might apply concepts presented there to enhance instruction in your discipline.

The National Reading Panel's focus on research-based strategies serves as a landmark in reading education. Review the panel's findings on text comprehension.

Use the keywords "QtA" or "questioning the author" and "KWL" or "KWL strategies" to search for these two powerful comprehension strategies. Consider how you might use these strategies in your content area. Reading Quest provides examples of how to apply strategies such as KWL and QtA in the discipline of social studies. If you teach social studies, consider how you might adapt these strategies for use in your classes.

eResources signal readers to ▶ investigate online resources to enrich and extend the topics presented.

Acknowledgments

We are grateful to the many colleagues, alumni, and graduate students of UNCC who helped to make this edition possible. Thank you to those who collaborated with us on writing chapters: Erin Donovan, Ph.D.; Elena King, Ph.D.; Lina Soares, Ph.D.; Melissa Sykes; Bruce Taylor, Ph.D.; and Jean Vintinner, Ph.D. A well-deserved "shout-out" is due to Susan Green, Ph.D., for her contributions to supporting English Learners in content area classrooms. Special thanks goes to Jean Vintinner for her exemplary work developing the MyLab Education materials for this edition. We are grateful for new Voices from the Field contributions from Nicole Lipp; Alyson MacDonald; and Brian Williams, Ph.D. We would like to thank the reviewers of this edition for their helpful suggestions: Chyllis Elayne Scott, University of Nevada, Las Vegas; Dr. J. Kris Rodenberg, San Diego State University; Rebecca L. Perini, University of Virginia; Sharon D. Matthews, Texas A&M University. We thank our outstanding editorial team of Drew Bennett, Rebecca Fox-Gieg, Jeff Johnson, Yagnesh Jani, and Denise Forlow, who offered helpful insights and expert guidance every step of the way.

Part I Learners, Literacies, and Texts

Chapter 1
Literacy Matters

Written in collaboration with Melissa Sykes

Shutterstock

 ## Chapter Overview and Learning Outcomes

After reading this chapter, you should be able to:

1.1 Explain the characteristics of effective teachers and effective teaching, the difference between the two, and their impact on students and learning.

1.2 Explain how *literacy* has evolved and the classroom implications of 21st-century literacy.

1.3 Describe the factors influencing reading to learn in a discipline.

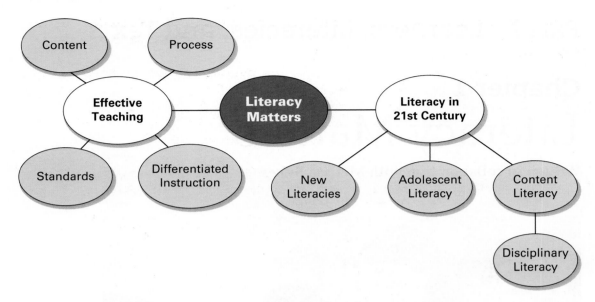

Organizing Principle

New literacies have transformed the way we read, write, think, communicate, and make meaning.

In many ways, the universe serves as a metaphor for the human mind. It is never ending, ever expanding, and unfathomable. So is the human mind. Literacy has a powerful impact on the meaning-making and learning that take place in the universe of our minds. Through literacy, we begin to see, to imagine, to comprehend, and to think more deeply about images and ideas encountered in all kinds of texts. When it comes to learning in content areas, literacy matters. All teachers have a critical role and powerful opportunity to make a difference in the literate lives of their students. In this chapter, we explore what that role requires for effective teaching in the content areas. And in the process of doing so, we clarify several core concepts related to literacy, teaching, and learning: *teacher effectiveness, standards-based planning, differentiated instruction, new literacies, adolescent literacy, content/disciplinary literacy, reading to learn*, and *strategies to support high-needs learners*.

Though both preservice and content area teachers may question the need for a course that has the terms *reading* and/or *literacy* in its title, all teachers have an important role to play in showing students how to use literacy skills and strategies regardless of discipline or context. While many view their primary role as teaching the core ideas and concepts of their discipline, literacy is an evolving concept that changes with society over time. Content counts, but literacy is the foundation for content-specific comprehension! Perhaps it's best to think of literacy in terms of the *multiple literacies* that we use to make and communicate meaning. In this book, we explore how to support students' literacies by helping them make and communicate meaning with the various kinds of texts—both print and digital—they use in content areas.

Our primary emphasis throughout this book is on reading and writing to learn in middle and high school. Unfortunately, many adolescent learners struggle with academic texts. Teachers across all content areas will be faced with the task of supporting students' understanding and use of reading and writing as tools for thinking and learning. Many students either read or write on a superficial level or find ways to circumvent literacy tasks altogether; and all too often, adolescent learners give up on reading with the expectation that teachers will impart information through lecture, demonstration, and class discussion. When students become too dependent on teachers as their primary source of information, they are rarely in a position to engage in active literacy for learning.

This need not be the case. The organizing principle of this chapter underscores the dynamic relationship between literacy and learning: Effective teachers show students how to think, learn, and communicate with all kinds of texts.

Study the Chapter Overview. It's your map to the major ideas that you will encounter in the chapter. The graphic display shows the relationships that exist among the concepts you will study. Use it as an organizer. What is the chapter about? What do you know already about the content to be presented in the chapter? What do you need to learn more about? How will you implement the presented information and concepts in your own practice?

In conjunction with the Chapter Overview, take a moment or two to study the Frame of Mind questions. This feature uses key questions to help you think about the ideas that you will read about. When you finish reading, you should be able to respond fully to the Frame of Mind questions.

MyLab Education
Response Journal 1.1
Write a "five-minute essay" in your response journal on your initial reaction to standards-based planning, instruction, and learning.

Frame of Mind

1. What is the difference between content and process knowledge?
2. What are the characteristics of effective teaching?
3. How do content standards and content-driven planning and instruction affect literacy and learning in content areas?
4. Why is differentiated instruction an important aspect of content literacy and learning?
5. What are new literacies, and how are they changing the way we think about learning and literacy in the 21st century?
6. In what ways can technology aid instruction and support student literacy and learning?
7. What is adolescent literacy, and why is it important to 21st-century society?
8. How are content literacy and disciplinary literacy alike? How are they different?
9. What comprehension strategies are critical to reading? What role does prior knowledge play in comprehension?
10. What literacy strategies specifically target the challenges struggling and English Learners (ELs) readers face?

Teaching is an exercise in observation and response; there are no definitive formulas for teachers who want students to develop core concepts and good habits of thinking within a discipline. Nor are there magic potions in the form of instructional strategies that will make a difference with all students, all the time. Teaching is a problem-solving activity: There's just you; the academic texts and instructional strategies that you use; and the students whose lives you briefly and, hopefully, positively impact. Teaching is a daunting but immensely rewarding enterprise for those who are up to the challenge.

Effective Teaching in Content Areas

1.1   Explain the characteristics of effective teachers and effective teaching, the difference between the two, and their impact on students and learning.

Highly effective content area teachers plan lessons that are engaging and purposeful. These teachers recognize that "engaging the disengaged" is an essential, but difficult, task. Yet continually striving to make learning intellectually challenging and relevant for students makes teaching more effective and learning more stimulating. A top instructional priority, therefore, is to involve students actively in learning the important ideas and concepts of the *content* they are studying. But the effective teacher also knows that an intellectually challenging instructional environment engages students not only in the acquisition of content but also in the *thinking processes* by which they learn that content.

No wonder the classroom is like a crucible, a place where the special mix of teacher, student, and text come together to create wonderfully complex human interactions that stir the minds of learners. Some days, of course, are better than others. The things that you thought about doing and the classroom surprises that you didn't expect fall into place. A creative energy imbues teaching and learning.

Sometimes, however, lessons limp along. Others simply bomb—so you cut them short. The four or so remaining minutes before the class ends are a kind of self-inflicted wound. Nothing is more unnerving than waiting for class to end when students don't have anything meaningful to do. During this time the silence can be deafening, and behavior management can become overwhelming.

Consider a high school science teacher's reflection on the way things went in one of her chemistry classes. "Something was missing," she explains. "The students aren't usually as quiet and passive as they were today. Excuse the pun, but the chemistry wasn't there. Maybe the text assignment was too hard. Maybe I could have done something differently. Any suggestions?"

This teacher's spirit of inquiry is admirable. She shows she knows her students and wants them to succeed; she also wants to know how to improve her teaching—how to engage students in learning the important concepts of her chemistry course and how to involve them in thinking like scientists.

Like all good teachers, the chemistry teacher in the preceding example cares about *what* she does and *how* she does it. **Content** and *process*, after all, are two sides of the same instructional coin. She knows a lot about the *what* of instruction—the content of chemistry—and how to teach that content in ways that develop important ideas and concepts in an intellectually challenging instructional environment. A strong attraction to academic content is one of the reasons teachers are wedded to a particular discipline. Yet it is often much more difficult to teach something than to know that something: "The teacher of the American Revolution must know both a great deal about the American Revolution and a variety of ways of communicating the essence of the American Revolution to a wide variety of students, in a pedagogically interesting way" (Shulman, 1987, p. 5). While a teacher's passion may lie with the content, the instruction of that content requires more skill and finesse.

Teaching is complicated. There are no shortcuts to effective teaching in content areas. Often, what to teach (content) and how to teach it (process) represent nagging problems for today's teachers. Despite pacing guides and standardized programs, the specific what and how of teaching is dependent on individual student needs, and quality instruction of the content is vital. On one hand, researchers have shown that subject matter mastery is essential for effective teaching (Allen, 2003; Sanders, 2004; Walsh & Snyder, 2004). Indeed, a strong connection exists between teachers' content knowledge preparation and higher student achievement.

The Educational Testing Service (ETS) study *How Teaching Matters* (Wenglinski, 2000) concluded, not surprisingly, that teachers' content knowledge is an important factor in student achievement. Content counts! Student achievement, for example, increases by 40% of a grade level in both mathematics and science when teachers have a major or minor in the subject. However, the study also concluded that content knowledge alone is not the only factor necessary to help increase student achievement. Indeed, the classroom instructional practices and strategies of teachers significantly influence student achievement. The study found that students who engage in active, hands-on learning activities and respond to higher-order thinking questions outperform their peers by more than 70% of a grade level in mathematics and 40% in science. In addition, the study showed that students whose teachers have received professional development training in working with special populations outperform their peers by more than a full grade level. The findings of the ETS study indicate that greater attention, not less, needs to be paid to improving the pedagogical knowledge of teachers and the classroom aspects of teacher effectiveness.

What Makes a Teacher Effective?

The U.S. Department of Education (2010), readily acknowledges that the "most important factor" in student success is the teacher. When students have access to effective teachers in the classroom, not only can achievement gaps narrow, but students will approach literacy and learning tasks with purpose and enthusiasm. Realistically, however, even in classrooms where teachers are practicing their craft effectively, some students will zone out from time to time or become sidetracked with other matters. Ball and Forzani (2010) put it this way in describing the difference between a tutor working one on one with a learner and a teacher working with an entire class of learners:

> Not only do teachers have more learners to understand and interact with, but they also must design and manage a productive environment in which all are able to learn. One student requires a firm hand and a great deal of direction whereas another works best when left to puzzle further on his own. One student is active—tapping her pen, doodling, and rocking on her chair—even while deeply engaged whereas a second is easily distracted. (p. 42)

Yet in the presence of an effective teacher most learners will tune in to what they are studying in the classroom—and stay tuned in.

With today's focus on educational reform, teacher effectiveness is closely tied to student achievement. An effective teacher has been defined as one whose students' growth is equivalent to at least one grade level in an academic year (U.S. Department of Education, 2009). Linda Darling-Hammond (2006) expands the notion of teacher effectiveness beyond how well students perform on achievement measures. She suggests that it is important to keep in mind the distinction between *teacher quality* and *teaching quality*. She defines teacher quality as the traits, understandings, and characteristics an effective teacher brings to instruction, including the following:

- Strong general intelligence and verbal ability that help teachers organize and explain ideas as well as observe and think diagnostically

- Strong content knowledge

- Knowledge of how to teach others; how to use hands-on learning techniques and how to develop higher-order thinking skills

- An understanding of learners and their learning and development—including how to assess and scaffold learning, how to support students who have learning differences or difficulties, and how to support the learning of language and content for those who are not already proficient in the language of instruction

- Adaptive expertise that allows teachers to make judgments about what it is like to work in a given context in response to student needs (Darling-Hammond, 2006, p. 2)

Teaching quality, on the other hand, has more to do with the context of instruction. Quality teaching enables a teacher to meet the demands of a discipline and to provide "strong instruction" that allows a wide range of students to learn.

Pearson and Hoffman (2011) also discuss teaching quality and strong instruction from the perspective of what it means to be a practicing teacher. They describe practicing teachers as *thoughtful, effective, pragmatic,* and *reflective.* In the classroom, the actions of a practicing teacher are guided by ten general "principles of practice" associated with teaching quality. Effective teachers reflect and are guided by these principles in their daily work in the classroom. These principles of practice are summarized in Table 1.1.

Higher levels of student achievement, Pearson and Hoffman (2011) contend, will not result from mandated standards or high-stakes testing alone. While standards and high-stakes assessment are an integral part of today's educational landscape, practicing teachers, who know how to balance content and process in a standards-based curriculum, are the real game changers in the education of 21st-century learners.

Table 1.1 Ten General Principles of Practice Associated With Quality Teaching

1. ***Principle of Praxis:*** Effective teachers act on the understanding that education has the power to transform the individual and society.	6. ***Principle of Community:*** Effective teachers share their classroom knowledge and experiences within and across multiple professional communities as a means of growing professionally and giving back.
2. ***Principle of Purpose:*** Effective teachers operate in the moment guided by a clear understanding of *why* they are doing *what* they are doing. There is always a purpose behind their actions in the classroom.	7. ***Principle of Service:*** Effective teachers serve the learners in their classrooms and their parents.
3. ***Principle of Serendipity:*** Although effective teachers engage in a variety of instructional practices, they "expect the unexpected" and are open to learning opportunities that may occur within the context of instruction.	8. ***Principle of Flexibility:*** Effective teachers plan instruction but are flexible in the implementation of lessons. They adapt to unanticipated events or responses in ways that make learning possible.
4. ***Principle of Exploration:*** Effective teachers are continually exploring new practices and making changes in their practices based on their exploration of instructional possibilities in the classroom.	9. ***Principle of Caring:*** Effective teachers care about the learners in their classroom, the disciplinary content that they teach, and the literacy processes they use to make a difference in the lives of students. Caring is necessary to build relationships essential to the teaching/learning transaction.
5. ***Principle of Reflection:*** Effective teachers think about the *what, how*, and *why* of instruction during and after each teaching activity. They engage in the process of reflection to solve instructional problems and set goals.	10. ***Principle of Reward:*** Effective teachers find satisfaction and reward in what they do for their students; they value the spontaneity of classroom life, the immediacy of the classroom, the learning they are a part of, and the autonomy of making instructional decisions.

Effective Teachers and the Standards-Driven Classroom

Literacy and learning are challenges in today's classrooms, where the demands inherent in the teaching of content standards can easily lead to "covering" information without much attention given to *how* students with a wide range of skills and abilities acquire core concepts. Schools continue to question the curriculum choices made in their classrooms. Curriculum refers to the content taught, which resources and strategies are used, and the learning activities in which students are engaged (Dunkle, 2012). Building or employing a curriculum that balances content and process in a standards-based curriculum means at the very least:

- Knowing the standards for your content area and grade level
- Making instructional decisions based on authentic assessments throughout the school year about students' abilities to use reading and writing to learn
- Integrating content literacy practices and strategies into instructional plans and units of study

MyLab Education
Response Journal 1.2
Did you have many teachers who were effective in the classroom? Why were they effective?

Standards, in a nutshell, are expected academic consequences defining what students should learn and how they should learn it at designated grade levels and in content areas. Since the mid-1990s, a proliferation of state standards have provided a road map to what students *should know* and *be able to do* at each grade level and for each content area.

The underlying rationale for the creation of standards is that high learning expectations—clearly stated and specific in nature—will lead to dramatic changes in student achievement. With high learning expectations comes an accountability system based on "high-stakes" testing to determine how well students meet the standards formulated in each content area. The goal is purposeful instruction with clear data points that allow teachers to identify if students have learned what they aimed to teach and to determine what their students know. Some states tie high-stakes assessment to the threat of grade-level retention for students who perform below predetermined levels of proficiency in critical areas such as reading. We explore in more detail the nature of high-stakes assessment, and the types of authentic assessments to improve learning, in Chapter 4.

The United States, unlike most countries, does not have a set of national education standards. Individual states have sole responsibility for determining what teachers should teach and students learn. However, to unite the nation around standards-based teaching, in 2010 the National Governors Association and the Council of Chief State School Officers released the **Common Core State Standards (CCSS)** for literacy and mathematics. The Common Core State Standards Initiative (2010) defined the Common Core State Standards as a way to

> provide a consistent, clear understanding of what students are expected to learn, so teachers and parents know what they need to do to help them. The standards are designed to be robust and relevant to the real world, reflecting the knowledge that our young people need for success in college and careers. With American students fully prepared for the future, our communities will be best positioned to compete successfully in the global economy. (p. 11)

Proponents of the CCSS argued that a standardized curriculum would facilitate the following:

- Increased collaboration between teachers in a subject area, a grade level, a district, and even across state lines
- Increased teacher readiness to teach content regardless of assignment
- Standardized texts and resources focused on the most relevant concepts that relate most directly to student learning
- Increased depth of instruction that explores concepts substantially rather than working to cover many disparate topics that may be inadequately developed (Dunkle, 2012)

Initially adopted by 45 of the 50 states in 2010, Common Core standards implementation has been controversial. Though the standards are the closest the United States has come as a country to adopting a national curriculum, since the initial proposal of the standards, "24 of those states have reviewed and revised their English language arts (ELA) and mathematics standards. In most states, the review process was triggered in response to mounting political opposition to the Common Core or associated testing and accountability policies" (Achieve, 2017). Despite Common Core politics and state-specific standards reforms, the push for teachers to work from the same core standards, and the possibility for broad-based sharing of what works in the classroom, has never been greater. Because the Common Core does not come with rigid guidelines concerning implementation, it provides local school flexibility to decide how best to implement the standards at various grade levels (Phillips & Wong, 2011).

In addition, state-specific revisions of Common Core standards have shifted the focus toward "the characteristics of high-quality college- and career-ready (CCR) standards" that aim to develop students "to enter and succeed in entry-level, credit-bearing courses in postsecondary institutions and to have access to careers" (Achieve, 2017). Even the Common Core standards reference and recognize that CCR anchor standards and grade-specific standards "work in tandem to define college and career readiness expectations—the former providing broad standards, the latter providing additional specificity" (National Governors Association, 2018).

Several important shifts resulted from the implementation of the Common Core standards and have continued throughout states' revisions of the core standards. In order to focus on CCR teaching that "reflect[s] the skills and knowledge students will need to succeed in college, career, and life," most literacy standards now require the tenets of CCSS, including:

- Regular practice with complex texts and their academic language
- Reading, writing, and speaking grounded in evidence from texts, both literary and informational
- Building knowledge through content-rich nonfiction (National Governors Association, 2018).

Through an increased exposure to nonfiction resources, students may build their background knowledge, or schema (to be discussed more fully later in this chapter); cultivate their cognitive learning and critical thinking skills; learn to read and write in a real-world, authentic manner; and read writing that more clearly links to the content area (Dunkle, 2012).

A greater emphasis on helping students build thinking habits rather than memorize content facts and figures is now the focus; the intention of standards-based teaching is to help students develop an inquiry mind-set that can be utilized across the curriculum. Learning the skill of perseverance, for example, would help a student stick with a difficult math problem as well as complete a difficult text. Accordingly, these mind-sets are meant not to help a student pass a test but to prepare that student to enter university or succeed in his or her chosen career.

Finally, the emphasis placed on texts and text-based answers (McLaughlin & Overturf, 2012), requires students to comprehend, evaluate, articulate, and form an argument based on evidence in the text (National Governors Association, 2018). Nonfiction, content-heavy texts are employed to help students learn how to use the text to answer questions while backing up their thoughts through understanding the author's arguments and logic. These thinking skills can then be transferred to any text the students are given, the ultimate goal being the understanding not of the text but of how to use the text as a means to answer questions.

One of the important dimensions of standards-based instruction is the emphasis on literacy in all content areas. Phillips and Wong (2011) put it this way: "Think of literacy as the spine; it holds everything together. The branches of learning connect to it, meaning that all core content teachers have a responsibility to teach literacy (pp. 40–41)." The real potential of standards-driven planning, instruction, and assessment from a literacy perspective is that it positions students to become more active in their use of literacy skills by discovering concepts and processes that lead to independent learning. To become literate in a content area, students must learn how to learn with texts. Integrating these thinking/learning processes into content instruction helps learners to better understand what they are reading about, writing about, talking about in classroom discussion, or viewing on a computer screen or video monitor. Weaving literacy into the fabric of disciplinary study does not diminish the teacher's role as a subject matter specialist. Instead, reading, writing, talking, and viewing are tools that students use to learn with texts in content areas. Who's in a better, more strategic position to show students how to learn with texts in a content area and grade level than the teacher who guides *what* students are expected to learn and *how* they are to learn it?

A social studies middle school teacher working to integrate the literacy goals in his or her practice might consider teaching content as follows:

The teacher's goal is to teach the divisive societal conflicts that led to the French Revolution.

- The teacher would first collect a variety of nonfiction, content-rich texts that would describe those conflicts. Students would have their choice of text that best fits their learning needs and reading style.
- The students would then have time to collaborate and use the key tenets of literacy to analyze and engage with the text during lessons, working both individually and collectively to connect with, explore, and reflect on the concepts presented.
- The teacher would act as facilitator, pushing students to think deeper through purposeful questioning and providing guidance through pointed student monitoring and reflective feedback.

- The students would be given a writing task, such as those described in Chapter 9. Basing their writing on the provided text, they would complete their nonfiction writing task.

The intention of this instruction would be the creation of a student-centered, independent learning environment that allows students the space to develop their own understanding of the conflicts through an in-depth understanding of the information presented in the texts. It is indeed a departure from the teacher/lecturer model or the fact-based instruction often seen in the social studies classroom.

A standards-based approach creates high expectations for students to develop their ability to use literacy and language skills to learn in content areas. One of the ultimate goals is that students will develop independent learning habits to more adequately develop a college-ready mind-set:

> Students must read widely and deeply from among a broad range of high-quality, increasingly challenging literary and informational texts. Through extensive reading of stories, dramas, poems, and myths from diverse cultures and different time periods, students gain literary and cultural knowledge as well as familiarity with various text structures and elements. By reading texts in history/social studies, science, and other disciplines, students build a foundation of knowledge in these fields that will also give them the background to be better readers in all content areas. Students can only gain this foundation when the curriculum is intentionally and coherently structured to develop rich content knowledge within and across grades. Students also acquire the habits of reading independently and closely, which are essential to their future success. (Common Core State Standards Initiative, 2010, p. 35)

Another major goal is that all learners will develop a strong knowledge base across the curriculum:

> Students establish a base of knowledge across a wide range of subject matter by engaging with works of quality and substance. They become proficient in new areas through research and study. They read purposefully and listen attentively to gain both general knowledge and discipline-specific expertise.
>
> They refine and share their knowledge through writing and speaking. They respond to the varying demands of audience, task, purpose, and discipline. (Common Core State Standards Initiative, 2010, p. 35)

CCSS has not progressed without its critics; even standards-based instruction (and its frequent assessments) has been challenged as limiting for certain student populations, including ESL and special needs learners. Tienken (2011), for example, fears that standardization of the curriculum may not meet the needs of a diverse population of U.S. students. Some critics argue that top-down mandates for curriculum change are often only vaguely related to day-to-day instruction. Such mandates ignore the professional expertise and thinking of teachers to determine the most effective instructional strategies and methods to teach their students (Lee, 2011). Successful implementation of standards-based instruction requires ongoing professional development to support teachers as they learn how to integrate literacy strategies into their regular instructional routines. This requires a long-term time commitment in school districts where funding for professional development may be limited.

Despite some of the criticism leveled toward CCSS and standards-based learning, many educators are hopeful that these approaches will make a difference in the content knowledge and skills that learners will develop to be successful in college or in careers. Box 1.1, Voices from the Field, captures an instructional coach's perspective on how standards-based instruction affects the planning process for teachers.

Given the wide range of students that teachers encounter daily, *differentiating instruction* will be one of the keys to ensuring the successful implementation of standards-based approaches to learning.

Box 1.1 Voices from the Field

Melissa, Instructional Coach

Challenge

Standards-based instruction has a clear impact on teacher lesson planning and student assessment. It can be particularly challenging for new teachers entering the classroom for the first time because it requires an analysis of the standards to determine what skills to teach and an understanding of the framework for assessment and student outcomes. Sometimes just understanding what a standard means can be difficult and confusing; in addition, standards-based learning requires data analysis and assessment check points to determine if mastery has been obtained.

Teaching and lesson planning around standards can be challenging, especially as state-driven standards reforms keep learning objectives in flux. Teachers must be able to identify, understand, and implement district policies, content curriculum, and school improvement goals and initiatives and also function within the daily realities of a school filled with students and teachers who must be respected and considered as individuals. As an instructional coach, my job is to help teachers navigate these realities while providing support for quality planning, instruction, and assessment to ensure teacher effectiveness and student achievement.

The key areas I work on with teachers is knowing what they need to teach, how they should present content so learning happens, and identifying what their students know. This is a challenge, to say the least. Standards-based teaching affects teachers' daily instruction in a substantial way. Teachers must be able to understand and use the standards to teach conceptually and deeply; critical thinking and problem solving do not just happen in the classroom naturally—opportunities for this to occur must be planned, instructional strategies that support student learning must be utilized, and assessment and feedback must be implemented correctly for students to learn and generalize their learning across content areas and to future experiences.

To complement a district's vision of how standards should be implemented and to encourage teacher and student growth, I support teachers to ensure they have a solid grasp on unpacking standards, which leads to quality lesson planning and assessment analysis to ensure standards-based learning and student mastery occur.

Strategy

The first step in solid lesson planning is knowing what skills are associated with a standard. For example, after selecting a standard, a teacher must break it down into the following categories:

- What does it say?
- What does it mean?
- What material/text could be used to help students access this skill/meaning?

This then must be broken down into a learning objective, a student-friendly I Can statement, and essential question(s) that you want students to master. A question as simple as, "What do students need to know before leaving my classroom today?" may help to support the unpacking of the standard.

Next, assessment points, rubrics, and an assessment for the end of the unit must be determined, in addition to considering what end product will demonstrate students have met the standard with mastery. A combination of both authentic and traditional assessments must be used, as standards-based instruction requires a constant process of teaching and reteaching to ensure depth of learning and mastery occurs.

Finally, daily lesson objectives, lesson planning and incorporation of best practices must be determined to ensure all students can access the standard and demonstrate understanding in a way that makes sense for them. Active engagement and monitored feedback must be implemented; purpose in practice is essential for student learning outcomes.

While the planning process for providing students with purposeful, quality, standards-driven learning opportunities can be time consuming; it will result in clearer goals for student achievement and increased comprehension.

Reflection

Even with standards to guide instruction, knowing what to teach and articulating clear skills and learning objectives can be difficult. You cannot provide authentic learning for students without knowing what it is you want them to master. Many times, teachers can feel overwhelmed with this process and never take the time to fully understand what they are being asked to teach. Without a definite end point and understanding of the concepts, skills, and progressions of content, instruction can never be purposeful. In fact, once a teacher unpacks their standards and considers essential learning targets, planning becomes easier and instruction more beneficial, resulting in more student achievement and a greater sense of accomplishment that students are better prepared for future challenges as a result of your teaching and daily influence.

Effective Teachers Differentiate Instruction for a Wide Range of Students

Although texts come with the territory, using them to help students acquire content doesn't work well for many teachers. Teaching with texts is more complex than it appears on the surface. As we discuss in Chapter 3, today's classrooms are more diverse than ever before. The wide range of differences is evident in the skills, interests, languages, cultural backgrounds, and funds of knowledge that learners bring to the classroom. Whether you're a novice or a veteran teacher, effective instruction requires the use of *differentiated learning* strategies and a willingness to move beyond *assigning* and *telling* when using texts in the classroom.

Think back to when you were a middle or high school student. You probably had teachers who used an instructional strategy for teaching with text that consisted of the following: *assign* a text to read (usually with questions to be answered for homework); then, in subsequent lessons, *tell* students what the material they read was about, explaining and elaborating on the ideas and information in the text through lecture and question-and-answer routines. The interaction between teacher and students no doubt involved calling on a student to answer a question, listening to the student's response, and then evaluating or modifying the student's response. An assign-and-tell instructional strategy, more often than not, squelches active involvement in learning and denies students ownership of and responsibility for the development of core concepts and processes. Teachers place themselves, either by design or by circumstance, in the unenviable position of dispensing knowledge rather than helping learners to construct knowledge. When teachers become dispensers of knowledge with little attention given to how learners acquire that knowledge, students soon become nonparticipants in the academic life of the classroom. There is no place for students to learn in a classroom where their voices, experiences, and presence are not recognized.

An effective teacher plans instruction and organizes learning opportunities for students so that they will engage actively in developing the core concepts and processes underlying a discipline. Planning is the key to differentiated learning. Tomlinson (2017) characterizes differentiation as "responsive teaching." She explains that it involves preparing in advance for a variety of student needs in order to maximize student learning.

Ongoing formative assessment, a topic we discuss in Chapter 4, allows teachers to adjust in their instructional approaches to meet the skill needs, interests, and learning styles of their students. Planning instruction, as we show in Chapter 5, allows teachers to organize learning in ways that will meet the needs of a wide range of students. Differentiating learning through a variety of texts and instructional strategies, which is the main thrust of this book, will actively engage all students in literacy and learning. To use texts and instructional strategies effectively in mixed-ability classrooms, we must first be aware of the powerful bonds that link literacy and learning in a discipline. Let's begin by taking a closer look at some of the meanings attached to the term *literacy*.

> **MyLab Education Self-Check 1.1**
>
> **MyLab Education Application Exercise 1.1:**
> Effective Teachers and the Standards-Driven Classroom

MyLab Education
Response Journal 1.3
What do you do as a reader to make meaning and construct knowledge as you interact with a text?

MyLab Education
Video Example 1.1:
What is differentiated instruction?
This video provides a succinct overview of what it means to differentiate instruction.

Literacy in a 21st-Century World

1.2   Explain how *literacy* has evolved and the implications of 21st-century literacy.

To better understand what it means to be literate in a discipline, we need to first examine some of the ways the term *literacy* has been used in our 21st-century, techno-savvy, media-driven world. Literacy is a dynamic concept that is continually evolving. In the United States and other technologically advanced countries, becoming literate carries with it strong cultural expectations. Society places a premium on literate behavior and demands that its citizens acquire literacy for personal, social, academic, and economic success. However, in many developing countries, individuals still struggle to become literate with tasks that require reading, writing, and communicating with digital texts.

In Box 1.2, Charles Robinson, an international educator who has worked with teachers and students in both technologically advanced and less developed countries, provides a unique perspective on what it means to be literate in the 21st century.

What, then, does it mean to be literate in a 21st-century world? The meaning of *literacy* often fluctuates from one social context to another and from one group to another. For example, the term *computer literacy* has been used in recent times to describe the level of expertise and familiarity someone has with computers and computer applications. *Digital literacy* is often defined as the ability to use digital technology, communication tools, or networks to locate, evaluate, use, and create information. In today's multimedia world, *information literacy* denotes the ability to identify, locate, and access appropriate sources of information to meet one's needs. The broad definition of *media literacy* is even more encompassing in that it refers to someone's ability to access, analyze, evaluate, and produce communication and information in a variety of media modes, genres, and forms. And in the health and wellness field, *health literacy* is a more specific type of information-based competence denoting someone's ability to obtain, process, and understand the basic health information and services needed to make appropriate health decisions.

Box 1.2 Voices from the Field

Charles Robinson, International Educator

That was the beginning of the real revolution—teaching Nicaraguans to read.

(Belli, 2003, p. 288)

In my nearly 30 years of teaching teachers in international schools around the world, I've come to realize that the value of literacy and learning is universal. From the crowded subways of Seoul, South Korea, to the poor neighborhoods of Managua, Nicaragua, individuals see literacy as a key to improving their lives. A few examples of the importance of literacy in these two very different countries follow.

In Seoul today, it seems that everyone on the subway is reading. While some may be responding to social media, students and young professionals are studying and others are reading newspapers or books. It is not uncommon for Korean elementary and secondary students to spend two to three hours each night at "hagwons" getting extra tutoring or learning English or Mandarin. This is in addition to the two to three hours of homework all students have daily. There is a shared belief here that hard work leads to success. The growth of the Korean economy in the past 20 years is due in large part to the emphasis on literacy and learning.

In February 1980, the National Literacy Crusade began in Nicaragua. Thousands of teenagers left their comfortable homes to go out into the countryside to teach reading because 70% of their countrymen were illiterate (Belli, 2003). The teachings of Brazilian educator Paulo Freire served as the foundation for this initiative. Freire believed that literacy would enable the poor to overcome the oppression of the wealthy landowners that kept them poor (Oakes & Lipton, 2007).

Despite the ensuing years of revolution, political instability, and natural disasters, education remains the key to opportunity in Nicaragua. In 2013, I saw this firsthand in the start of a new school dedicated to educating the lower middle class in Managua. While the tuition was low, many families had to make financial sacrifices so that their children could attend. The teachers and staff that I worked with are passionately committed to improving the lives of their students, and I look forward to continuing to work with them.

Technology and social media have had a major impact on education worldwide. In America today, literacy is "cool"; or, to put it another way, the inability to read and write is not so cool. How can you be in constant contact with your peers if you can't read and write (or come up with creative spelling)? We no longer need to teach keyboarding, as most kids seem to be born with these skills. Three-year-olds now have their own tablets. In a sense, we have created a "pass-back generation" so that when children are unruly in their car seats, we pass back a mobile device to soothe them—an electronic pacifier!

In the '80s, I would not assign homework involving computers because not all my students had computers at home. Today, we assume that all homes have digital access, and laptops are being replaced with "smartphones" with unbelievable capabilities. A professor friend of mine told me that her students no longer take notes; they just use their phones to take photos of the information on the whiteboard. She also said that she no longer uses e-mail, as nearly all her students use only texting.

Does literacy change the world, or is our constantly evolving world changing literacy? Literacy continues to be the key to success for individuals and countries committed to improving the lives of their people. Costa Rica is a perfect example of the impact of literacy on a country's social and economic growth. In 1948, Costa Rica eliminated its military and developed a plan to improve literacy through access to education for all its citizens. Today, Costa Rica has become one of the most stable countries in Central America, if not the world, with an economy that is dependent on a literate population providing the skills necessary to support tourism, which is one of the country's major sources of revenue. I strongly believe that literacy remains a universal value regardless of developments in technology or political and economic shifts.

Charles Robinson currently teaches in the International Education Program at Framingham (MA) State University.

The above examples are but a few ways the term *literacy* has morphed to characterize someone's level of knowledge or competence in a particular area or subject in a multimodal society. For centuries, the most common use of the term *literacy* had been to denote one's ability to read and write a language with competence. Today, however, the dynamic nature of literacy is such that it encompasses more than the ability to read and write black marks on a printed page. Literacy has come to represent a synthesis of language, thinking, and contextual practices through which people make and communicate meaning. Yet the more society evolves, the more complex and multidimensional the concept of literacy becomes. To be literate in today's world means so much more than decoding existing messages; it means being able to comprehend, dissect, and contribute additional meanings instantly:

> Today information about the world around us comes to us not only by words on a piece of paper but more and more through the powerful images and sounds of our multi-media culture. Although mediated messages appear to be self-evident, in truth, they use a complex audio/visual "language" which has its own rules (grammar) and which can be used to express many-layered concepts and ideas about the world. Not everything may be obvious at first; and images go by so fast! If our children are to be able to navigate their lives through this multi-media culture, they need to be fluent in "reading" and "writing" the language of images and sounds just as we have always taught them to "read" and "write" the language of printed communications. (Thoman & Jolls, 2005, p. 8)

As notions of literacy expand with the times, so does the concept of *text*. Literate activity is no longer limited by conventional notions of text (Neilsen, 2006). Texts include not only print forms of communication but also nonprint forms that are digital, aural, or visual in nature. Texts in content area classrooms represent sets of potential meanings and signifying practices, whether the text is a novel in an English class, the instructional conversation that takes place about the novel, or the made-for-television movie based on the novel. Helping students to *think* and *learn* with all kinds of texts is an important responsibility of the content area teacher. It is the responsibility of educators to adequately represent in the classroom the texts that students are encountering, working with, and creating outside of the school walls. Johannes Gutenberg's invention of movable type in the 15th century resulted in a revolution of ideas. Printed texts in the hands of the masses changed the face of literacy and learning in much the same way that multimodal information and communication technologies (ICT) are creating new literacies and new ways of learning.

New Literacies, New Ways of Learning

The potential for media and technology to make a difference in students' literacy development and learning was evident in the early 1980s, when computers began to play an increasingly important role in classrooms. However, the digital technologies available three decades ago were primitive compared to today's powerful technologies. Today's adolescents represent the first generation of youth who have grown up since the emergence of digital technologies, video games, cell phones, instant messaging, and the World Wide Web. Because they are the first generation to be immersed in ICT for their entire lives, they have at their fingertips more information than any generation in history (Considine, Horton, & Moorman, 2009). Teachers compete every minute of every lesson for the engagement of students who can access the world with one click on their iPhone.

With continuously emerging ICT a reality in the 21st century, **new literacies** are necessary to use ICT effectively and to fully exploit their potential for learning (Kist, 2005; Leu, 2000). Teachers are now preparing students for occupations and careers that may not currently exist—a constant among all future developments is the concept of being a literate thinker. The new literacies are grounded in students' abilities to use reading and writing to learn but require new strategic knowledge, skills, and insights to meet the conceptual and technological demands inherent in complexly networked environments. To be sure, the Internet is one of the most powerful extant ICTs, and it depends on literacy.

Nevertheless, there are real differences between reading printed texts and reading texts in a digital medium. As Kist (2005, p. 5) explains, printed texts such as books are written for the reader to proceed from the front of the book to the back of the book, reading from left to right, "and most readers of a book will read the text with the order of the words coming in the same order for him or her as for every other reader of that book." However, one reader on the Internet might click on a hyperlink that another online reader would not. As a result, the first online reader would then process the text in a completely different sequence from that of the second reader.

Reading texts in a digital environment is not a linear activity. Recognizing literacy as defined by ever-expanding delineations, therefore, is crucial in the search for content area information on the Internet and other ICT. As Leu, Leu, and Coiro (2006, p. 1) point out, rapidly developing new literacies allow readers "to *identify* important questions, *navigate* complex information networks to locate important information, *critically evaluate* that information, *synthesize* it to address those questions, and then *communicate* the answers to others. These five functions help to define the new literacies that your students need to be successful with the Internet and other information and communication technologies (ICT)."

What, then, are some of the classroom implications for the development of new literacies? First and foremost, teachers need to help students "learn how to learn" new technologies. From a new literacies perspective, knowing how to learn continuously changing technologies is more critical than learning any particular ICT. Moreover, teachers need to provide instructional support in the development and use of strategies that, among other things, help students critically read and evaluate information. According to Leu (2002, p. 314), learners will need to know how to put into play

> new forms of strategic knowledge necessary to locate, evaluate, and effectively use the extensive resources available within complexly networked ICT such as the Internet. The extent and complexity of this information is staggering.... How do we best search for information in these complex worlds? How do we design a Web page to be useful to people who are likely to visit? How do we communicate effectively with videoconference technologies? Strategic knowledge is central to the new literacies.

A teacher should not automatically assume that today's adolescents already are strategic in their use of ICT for academic purposes. The extensive use of ICT by adolescents in social and personal contexts often creates a false sense of competence in an academic context. As Considine, Horton, and Moorman (2009, p. 472) put it, "hands-on is not the same as heads-on" when it comes to making assumptions about how effectively adolescents use ICT to learn.

One of the key considerations teachers face to support student literacy in a 21st-century world is to determine where technology and ICT fits in their classroom. It is a gross negligence for teachers to assume that students should not utilize technology during instruction; in fact, technology can enhance instruction and support student literacy and learning. As the need to create more powerful learning environments increases, teachers must seek out those supports that entice student engagement. Purposeful use of technology in planning and instructional processes provides teachers new ways of learning while reinforcing new literacies that students need to master.

It is understood that students learn better when they are able to work, think, and discuss; technology is one way to support collaborative learning using both group and individual contributions. Blended learning, a mix of traditional teaching and online learning, is "an area of design and inquiry that combines face-to-face and online modalities" (Halverson, Graham, Spring, & Drysdale, 2012, p. 381). Flipped classrooms and virtual learning environments allow students to experience concepts and interact with content in a way that goes beyond the walls of the classroom and the boundaries of their environment. Incorporation of technology provides an immediacy to the lesson that forces students to be active, allows the teacher to take on the role of facilitator rather than "sage on the stage," and provides opportunities for students to share in the learning process together. In addition, digitizing activities and ways for students to write and respond gives students agency over their learning; collaborative websites provide a space for students to reflect on the assumptions and thought processes of others and publishes their messages and meaning for audiences larger than the classroom community (Resta & Laferrière, 2007).

Print resources, such as textbooks and trade books, in combination with digital texts, sounds, images, and collaborative discussions, create powerful learning environments in an academic discipline. Learning with new literacies, which we will explore in Chapter 2, involves many of the same thinking processes that print forms of texts involve. However, teachers who work with adolescent learners in middle and high school may find that some, if not many, of their students struggle with assignments that require thinking and learning with academic texts in print or nonprint forms. No wonder *adolescent literacy* is a hot topic in education today (Cassidy & Cassidy, 2009). Let's take a closer look at the concept of adolescent literacy and its implications for thinking and learning with texts.

Adolescent Literacy

Now more than ever, adolescent literacy is continuously evolving; there has never been a time in history when information has been more accessible or critical reading skills more important than in today's world. From the moment they awake to the minutes before sleep, adolescents are continuously experiencing literacy in the form of text messages, Internet searches, social media posts, GPS maps, streaming video services, and digital and print texts. In 1999, the Commission on Adolescent Literacy of the International Reading Association (IRA) asserted that

> adolescents entering the adult world in the 21st century will read and write more than at any other time in human history. They will need advanced levels of literacy to perform their jobs, run their households, act as citizens, and conduct their personal lives. They will need literacy to cope with the flood of information they will find everywhere they turn. They will need literacy to feed their imaginations, so they can create the world of the future. In a complex and sometimes even dangerous world, their ability to read will be crucial. Continual instruction beyond the early grades is needed. (Moore, Bean, Birdyshaw, & Rycik, 1999, p. 3)

In 2012, the IRA built upon Moore, et al.'s position to reflect the increasingly complex and varied "range of print and non-print materials available in the 21st century" (International Reading Association, 2012). Furthermore, a multitude of research now demonstrates that discipline-specific learning and strategy-based support is essential. As stated by the IRA, it is essential

> to include an expanded understanding of the multiple literacy strategies adolescents need to successfully engage with the range of print and nonprint materials available in the 21st century. Adolescents who engage with these appropriate strategies to mine the content for meaning and understand how the different print and nonprint structures influence understanding. (International Reading Association, 2012)

In the early grades of elementary school, many students learn basic skills related to reading and writing; however, by fourth grade and on, they need to continue to develop skill and sophistication in the use of literacy strategies and practices specific to different disciplines, texts, and situations. As the emphasis on disciplinary learning increases in middle and high schools, adolescents must develop both confidence in themselves and the thinking processes necessary for academic success in various content areas. This is a challenge for many students, as developmental readiness; appropriateness of text; and, many times, a lack of "access to teachers with the deep understanding that facilitates the successful implementation of disciplinary literacy" (Duhaylongsod et al., 2015 p. 589) hinder achievement.

Since 1992, when periodic National Assessment of Educational Progress (NAEP) surveys in reading began for students in Grades 4, 8, and 12, it has become evident that there is an adolescent literacy crisis in the United States (Alliance for Excellent Education, 2006; Kamil, 2003; Vacca, 1998; Vacca & Alvermann, 1998). Not only have test scores remained relatively stagnant over the years of implementation, but it has become evident that the achievement gap is widening (Sparks, 2018). Few would argue with the importance of early reading development, and "although students in grade 4 score among the best in the world, by grade 10 U.S. students place close to the bottom among developed nations" (Haynes, 2011, p. 10). While an emphasis on learning to read in the primary grades in the United States has served to magnify the lack of attention and commitment given to adolescent learners and their literacy needs, "the literacy performance of 13- and 17-year olds on the National Assessment of Educational Progress (NAEP) has remained stunningly low, revealing that nearly 6 million of the 22 million American secondary students struggle to read and write" (Haynes, 2011, p. 10).

From a historical perspective, the literacy needs of middle and high school students have received marginal attention by policy makers and curriculum planners. In the latter half of the 20th century, students who struggled with reading often were identified as "remedial readers" and were assigned to "reading labs" or "remedial reading" classes, where they typically received piecemeal instruction apart from the content areas. The statistics confirm this lack of growth, as NAEP results have remained flat for decades, with trends illustrating achievement gaps between high achievers, struggling students, minority students, and those students impacted by socio-economic status (Carnoy & Garcia, 2017). For fourth- and eighth-grade math, "the average scores from 2017 were identical to the average scores from 2009" (Hansen et al., 2018, p. 4), and reading scores "were more modest than the gains in math scores" (Hansen et al., 2018, p. 4).

However, there have been positive initiatives taking place focusing on the literacy needs of adolescents. In an effort to prepare students "to use reading to gain access to the world of knowledge, to synthesize information from different sources, to evaluate arguments, and to learn totally new subjects" (Murnane, Sawhill, & Snow, 2012, p. 3), educators are seeking out instruction that promotes 21st-century reading skills that will results in career- and college-ready learners. Some trends include strategy-based instruction that encourages a "shift toward interventions that focused on multiple strategies and their coordination" (Goldman, 2012, p. 94); discussion-based instruction that encourages students to articulate meaning and interpret comprehension; and disciplinary content-based instruction, which promotes knowing about a subject, problem solving and questioning (Goldman, 2012, p. 98–105).

In 2004, a landmark report titled *Reading Next* identified 15 critical elements of effective adolescent literacy programs, presenting key fundamentals that are now more relevant than ever. These elements are highlighted in Box 1.3 and complement the 2008 What Works Clearinghouse report recommendations for effective classroom and intervention practices to improve adolescent literacy, including to provide explicit vocabulary instruction, to provide direct and explicit comprehension strategy instruction, to provide opportunities for extended discussion of text meaning and interpretation, to increase student motivation and engagement in literacy learning, and to make available intensive and individualized interventions for struggling readers that can be provided by trained specialists (Institute of Education Sciences, 2008).

Teaching adolescents is no easy task. Their lives are complex. Not only are they undergoing great physical changes, but they also are faced with ongoing cognitive, emotional, and social challenges. Adolescents who struggle with literacy in academic disciplines often go through the motions of reading without engaging in the process. Living in such a fast-paced, immediately gratifying digital world distracts struggling readers and encourages their preference for skimming and desire for bite-sized texts. Even skilled

Box 1.3 Evidence-Based Best Practices

Fifteen Elements of Effective Adolescent Literacy Programs

Reading Next, a report to the Carnegie Corporation of New York, provides a "vision for action and research" in the development of adolescent literacy programs. The report delineates 15 elements for improving middle and high school literacy achievement:

1. *Direct, explicit comprehension instruction,* which is instruction in the strategies and processes that proficient readers use to understand what they read, including summarizing, keeping track of one's own understanding, and a host of other practices
2. *Effective instructional principles embedded in content,* including language arts teachers using content-area texts and content-area teachers providing instruction and practice in reading and writing skills specific to their subject area
3. *Motivation and self-directed learning,* which includes building motivation to read and learn and providing students with the instruction and supports needed for independent learning tasks they will face after graduation
4. *Text-based collaborative learning,* which involves students interacting with one another around a variety of texts
5. *Strategic tutoring,* which provides students with intense individualized reading, writing, and content instruction as needed
6. *Diverse texts,* which are texts at a variety of difficulty levels and on a variety of topics
7. *Intensive writing,* including instruction connected to the kinds of writing tasks students will have to perform well in high school and beyond

8. *A technology component,* which includes technology as a tool for and a topic of literacy instruction
9. *Ongoing formative assessment of students,* which is informal, often daily assessment of how students are progressing under current instructional practices
10. *Extended time for literacy,* which includes approximately two to four hours of literacy instruction and practice that takes place in language arts and content-area classes.
11. *Professional development* that is both long-term and ongoing
12. *Ongoing summative assessment of students and programs,* which is more formal and provides data that are reported for accountability and research purposes
13. *Teacher teams,* which are interdisciplinary teams that meet regularly to discuss students and align instruction
14. *Leadership,* which can come from principals and teachers who have a solid understanding of how to teach reading and writing to the full array of students present in schools
15. *A comprehensive and coordinated literacy program,* which is interdisciplinary and interdepartmental and may even coordinate with out-of-school organizations and the local community

SOURCE: *Reading Next: A Vision for Action and Research in Middle and High School Literacy* (2004). https://all4ed.org/reports-factsheets/reading-next-a-vision-for-action-and-research-in-middle-and-high-school-literacy/, pp. 12–13.

---

adolescent readers will struggle with reading sometimes, in some places, with some texts. Some students may lack the prior knowledge needed to connect to important ideas in the text. Others may get lost in the author's line of reasoning, become confused by the way the text is organized, or run into unknown words that are difficult to pronounce, let alone define. Often comprehension problems are only temporary. However, the difference between proficient adolescent readers and those who struggle all the time is this: When proficient readers struggle with text, they know what to do to get out of trouble. They have confidence in themselves as readers and learners. When a text becomes confusing or doesn't make sense, good readers recognize that they have an array of skills and strategies that they can use to work themselves out of difficulty.

Average and above-average adolescent learners, who are usually on track to go to college, might also struggle with reading without their teachers being cognizant of it. Often these students feel helpless about their ability to engage in academic literacy tasks but go through the motions of "doing" school. Since 1992, periodic national assessments of reading conducted by the National Center for Education Statistics (NCES) show that the majority of U.S. students in Grades 4, 8, and 12 have obtained, at best, only "basic" levels of literacy. These NCES (2007) surveys for reading reveal that the vast majority of adolescent learners in Grades 4 and 8 have difficulty with complex literacy tasks. For example, they may be able to read with some degree of fluency and accuracy but might not know what to do with a text beyond saying the words and comprehending at what is essentially a literal level of performance. In the classroom, these students may appear *skillful* in the mechanics of reading but aren't *strategic* enough in their abilities to handle reading tasks that require interpretation and critical thinking—the essential skills necessary to succeed in the technologically advanced, text-rich global community in which students will work and live. Throughout this book, we explore the role of motivation in the academic lives of adolescents who struggle with school-based literacy even though they are likely to use new literacies *outside* of school for personal and social purposes (Lenters, 2006; Moje, 2007; Moje, Overby, Tysvaer, & Morris, 2008).

The terms *content literacy* and *disciplinary literacy* are frequently used to describe a discipline-centered instructional approach to literacy and learning in content area classrooms. From our perspective, content literacy and disciplinary literacy reflect many of the same instructional attributes, although critics of content literacy pedagogy claim some real differences between the two approaches to literacy and learning (Draper, 2008; Moje, 2007, 2008). In the next section, we explore the common ground between content literacy and disciplinary literacy and discuss how the two concepts may differ in terms of teaching practices.

MyLab Education **Self-Check 1.2**

MyLab Education **Application Exercise 1.2:**
Using New Literacies as a Tool for Learning and Engagement

Disciplinary Literacy in Perspective

1.3 Describe the factors influencing reading to learn in a discipline.

For many years, the term *content area reading* was associated with helping students better understand what they read across the curriculum. However, the concept of content area reading was broadened in the 1990s to reflect the inclusive role language plays in learning with texts. Hence, the relatively new construct of *content literacy* refers to the ability to use reading, writing, talking, listening, and viewing to learn subject matter in a given discipline (Vacca, 2002a). Content literacy involves the use of research-based cognitive learning strategies designed to support reading, writing, thinking, and learning with text. Most recently, *disciplinary literacy* is having an impact on the way researchers and educators think about literacy and learning in content areas (Buehl & Moore, 2009; Lee, 2004; Moje, 2007, 2008; Shanahan & Shanahan, 2008). Box 1.4 provides a succinct explanation of the concept of disciplinary literacy.

Box 1.4 What Is Disciplinary Literacy?

Disciplinary literacy practices challenge the way students approach texts by providing the skills necessary for students to adapt a mind-set that allows them to think like the real people, in the real world, who work in the respective content areas. Disciplinary literacy seeks to help students read, write, and think in a way that is aligned with the methods that professionals utilize in their respective fields. As a result, disciplinary literacy practices refer to shared methods of reading, writing, thinking, and reasoning within each academic field (Rainey & Moje, 2012). Changing the way students approach texts and react to what they learn challenges them to work beyond telling to knowing. Providing them with real-world tasks to which they can relate also helps students build and access their background knowledge (Achugara & Carpenter, 2012; Girard, & Harris, 2012; Pytash, 2012).

For example, in *social studies* classes students must look at a text from the point of view of a historian. To do this, they may connect facts, understand cause and effect, and organize and categorize people and events while they write to help their readers understand why historical occurrences are significant.

In *mathematics* classes, students must be problem solvers. They must take a text and connect it to numbers and pictorial representations, such as graphs, charts, and geometric figures, to understand relationships, patterns, and numerical significance. In an *English* classroom, students must learn how to be effective readers and writers, understanding and demonstrating how readers move with fluidity from different genres and how their writing then mirrors the original intent of the author. In *science*, students must experiment. They must use very specific language and notation in which very small mistakes cause very different outcomes. They should be able to group, solve, and predict in a way that is different from any other content area.

The practices of disciplinary literacy teach students to think differently in each content area. As readers and writers, we change the way we look at a text according to the skills that are necessary in the daily lives of historians, mathematicians, scientists, and literary scholars. Disciplinary literacies provide not only a method for understanding texts but also a means of expression that authentically replicates real-world practices.

Disciplinary Literacy: A Brief Historical View

William S. Gray, one of the early titans in the field of reading, articulated the relationship between reading and learning that remains today the underlying rationale for reading in content areas. Not only did he forge the beginnings of content area reading, but he also is credited with what has become an often-used, and often-confused, mantra in education: "Every teacher is a teacher of reading." More than 85 years ago, Gray (1925) published one of the first descriptive studies to identify reading and study skills by content area. He determined that each content area requires different sets of skills for the effective reading and study of text material. These different skill sets are related to one's purpose for reading and the conceptual demands of the text.

Many other researchers in the 1940s, 1950s, and 1960s designed "content-centered" studies to investigate the effectiveness of guiding students' reading within the context of disciplinary instruction. Harold Herber (1964), for example, developed "guide materials" to assist high school physics students in the development of core concepts in their textbook. He found that the students who used "study guides" to read a physics text significantly outperformed those students who did not use guides to read the content under study. Herber (1970) later wrote the first comprehensive textbook, *Teaching Reading in Content Areas,* exclusively devoted to content area reading instruction. The guiding principle underlying Herber's book is as powerful today as it was more than 40 years ago: *Content determines process.* Even though the majority of students learn how to read in elementary school with some degree of proficiency, they must learn how to adapt reading and thinking strategies to meet the peculiarities and conceptual demands of each discipline they study.

Content literacy and disciplinary literacy are extensions of the concept of content area reading, where "content determines process" in a given discipline. The underlying goal of a discipline-specific approach to literacy is to show students how to think and learn with text as they develop a deep understanding of concepts and ideas encountered in texts. Each discipline poses its own challenges in terms of purposes for reading, vocabulary, concepts, texts, themes, and topics. How students read, think, and learn with text more than likely varies from content area to content area: "Even casual observation shows that students who struggle with reading a physics text may be excellent readers of poetry; the student who has difficulty with word problems in math may be very comfortable with historical narratives" (National Council of Teachers of English, 2006).

Doug Buehl (2009, p. 535), a longtime advocate of adolescent literacy and a former social studies teacher and literacy coach in Madison, Wisconsin, argues that middle and high school curricula must focus not only on what students should know and be able to do but also on how "experts within a discipline read, write, and think." He contends that content area teachers are sometimes frustrated by "generic literacy practices" encountered in professional development workshops that are not relevant to reading and learning in their disciplines.

Buehl (2009, p. 537) advocates for continued research on discipline-specific literacy practices, which seem "to be an especially fertile ground for determining how to mentor students to read, write, and think through the lens of a mathematician, biologist, musician, historian, artist, novelist, and so forth." He cites a statewide project in Wisconsin called Thinking Like a Historian in which history teachers are encouraged to engage in questioning routines around five core themes crucial to thinking and learning with historical text:

1. Cause and effect: "What happened and why?"
2. Change and continuity: "What changed and what remained the same?"
3. Turning points: "How did events of the past affect the future?"

4. Through their eyes: "How did people in the past view their lives and world?"
5. Using the past: "How does studying the past help us understand our lives and world?" (Wisconsin Historical Society, 2009)

In a similar vein, Lee (2004, p. 14) describes disciplinary literacy as "the ability to understand, critique, and use knowledge from texts in content areas." She links disciplinary literacy directly to the needs of culturally diverse adolescent readers who struggle with academic texts and suggests that an important dimension of a discipline-specific approach to literacy is to draw on adolescent learners' "cultural funds of knowledge"— that is, the kinds of knowledge that culturally diverse students bring to learning situations. As we explain in Chapter 3, how teachers adjust instruction to the sociocultural strengths of students in diverse classrooms is an important aspect of literacy and learning in a discipline.

Moje (2007) provides a complex view of disciplinary literacy as she discusses some of the theory, research, and pedagogical practices supporting instructional approaches to disciplinary literacy. She describes one such approach found on the website of the Institute for Learning at the University of Pittsburgh:

> This approach to teaching and learning integrates academically rigorous content with discipline-appropriate habits of thinking. The driving idea is that knowledge and thinking must go hand in hand. To develop deep conceptual knowledge in a discipline, one needs to use the habits of thinking that are valued and used by that discipline.... The ultimate goal of Disciplinary Literacy is that all students will develop deep content knowledge and literate habits of thinking in the context of academically rigorous learning in individual disciplines. (Quoted in Moje, 2007, p. 10)

Others have called for a rethinking of the way literacy is embedded within various disciplinary-specific learning situations. For example, Shanahan and Shanahan (2008) conducted a descriptive research project in which they studied how disciplinary experts (university professors and classroom teachers) from mathematics, history, and chemistry engaged in reading to learn. In the first year of the project, the researchers adapted a pedagogical practice called "think-alouds" to identify the "specialized reading skills" used by the experts to comprehend texts in their respective disciplines. During the think-aloud sessions, the researchers discovered that "each of the disciplinary experts emphasized a different array of reading processes, suggesting the focused and highly specialized nature of literacy at these levels" (Shanahan & Shanahan, 2008, p. 49).

In the second year of the project, the teams of disciplinary experts studied the viability of generic literacy strategies and explored ways to develop instructional strategies that were discipline specific. These strategies are similar in intent to the kinds of cognitive-based strategies found in this and other books dealing with literacy and learning across the curriculum. However, the teams of discipline-specific experts modified and adapted generic literacy strategies to meet the textual and conceptual demands inherent in their specific disciplines.

Whether you call it *content area reading, content literacy*, or *disciplinary literacy*, the guiding principle behind each instructional approach remains as powerful today as it has for nearly a century. *Content determines process.* The conceptual demands and structure of a discipline-specific text determine how a reader will interact with that text, make sense of it, and learn from it. As Kamil (2003) concluded, teaching literacy strategies has value for all teachers. However, a disciplinary literacy perspective reminds us that teachers, as subject matter specialists, must also have a solid understanding of the reading, writing, and thinking processes necessary to adapt and modify literacy strategies, tailoring them to meet the conceptual and textual demands of the content under study.

Reading to Learn in a Discipline

A variety of classroom-related factors influence reading to learn in a given discipline, including:

- The learner's prior knowledge of, attitude toward, and interest in the subject
- The learner's purpose for engaging in reading, writing, and discussion
- The vocabulary and conceptual difficulty of the text material
- The assumptions that the text writers make about their audience of readers
- The text structures that writers use to organize ideas and information
- The teacher's beliefs about and attitude toward the use of texts in learning situations

Writers of texts communicate with readers in the same way that speakers use language to communicate with listeners or filmmakers use sound and moving images to tell a story or communicate meaning to viewers. Teaching with written text involves more than assigning pages to be read, lecturing, or using questions to check whether students have read the material the night before. To use written texts strategically and effectively, you must first be aware of the powerful bonds between reading and knowledge construction. With this in mind, consider how reading to learn relates to meaning-making and text comprehension.

The Role of Prior Knowledge in Reading

In their book *A Good Teacher in Every Classroom*, Darling-Hammond and Baratz-Snowden (2005, pp. 2–3) argue that the conventional view of teaching is simplistic in that teaching is viewed as proceeding through a set curriculum in a manner that *transmits* information from teacher to student. Moreover, they contend that there is much more to teaching than knowing the subject matter that students should learn. Among the many classroom practices characteristic of effective teachers, they "carefully organize activities, materials, and instruction based on students' prior knowledge ... and engage students in active learning."

Many of the literacy practices and strategies that you will learn about in this book will help you organize instruction around students' prior knowledge and their active engagement in text-related activities. As a result, students will be in a better position to understand the structure of your discipline and the important ideas and concepts underlying the subject matter that you teach. We no longer teach students who want to receive information; instead, we are working with learners who bring previous knowledge to the learning environment and who seek to experience content and concepts, not just be told about them.

Not only do readers activate prior knowledge *before* reading, but they also use prior knowledge *during* and *after* reading to infer meaning and elaborate on the text content. Good readers don't just read to get the gist of what they are reading unless that is their specific purpose. Good teachers help students to work from their schema and provide purposeful schematic connections between students and content. Students must use prior knowledge, as well as what they know (or think they know) about the text, to make inferences, to evaluate, and to elaborate on the content. Why is this the case?

Cognitive scientists use the technical term *schema* to describe how people use prior knowledge to organize and store information in their heads. Furthermore, *schema activation* is the mechanism by which people access what they know and match it to the information in a text. In doing so, they build on the meaning they already bring to a learning situation. Indeed, *schemata* (the plural of *schema*) have been called "the building blocks of cognition" (Rumelhart, 1982) because they represent elaborate networks of information that people use to make sense of new stimuli, events, and situations. When a match occurs between students' prior knowledge and text material, a schema functions in at least three ways.

First, a schema provides a framework for learning that allows readers to *seek and select* information that is relevant to their purposes for reading. In the process of searching and selecting, readers are more likely to *make inferences* about the text. You make inferences when you *anticipate* content and *make predictions* about upcoming material or when you *fill in gaps* in the material during reading.

Second, a schema helps readers *organize* text information. The process by which you organize and integrate new information into old facilitates the ability to *retain and remember* what you read. A poorly organized text is difficult for readers to comprehend. We illustrate this point in more detail when we discuss the influences of text structure on comprehension and retention in later chapters.

Third, a schema helps readers *elaborate* information. When you elaborate what you have read, you engage in a cognitive process that involves deeper levels of insight, judgment, and evaluation. You are inclined to ask, "So what?" as you engage in conversation with an author.

Reading as a Meaning-Making Process

Language helps a learner to make sense of the world, to understand, and to be understood. As a result, language and meaning cannot be severed from one another. Language isn't language unless meaning-making is involved. Oral language without meaning is mere prattle—a string of senseless, meaningless speech sounds. Written language without meaning is a cipher of mysterious markings on paper.

To be literate in content area classrooms, students must learn how to use reading and the many forms of literacy previously discussed to construct knowledge in the company of authors, other learners, and teachers. Using reading in the classroom to help students to learn doesn't require specialized training on the part of content teachers, although many of today's middle and high schools employ *literacy coaches* (a topic discussed in Chapter 12) to develop, support, and extend content area teachers' use of literacy strategies. Content literacy practices do not diminish the teacher's role as a subject matter specialist. Instead, reading is a tool students use to construct, clarify, and extend meaning in a given discipline.

Why are you able to read a text such as Lewis Carroll's "Jabberwocky" with little trouble, even though Carroll invents words such as *chortled* and *toves* throughout the poem? Try reading "Jabberwocky" aloud:

JABBERWOCKY

'Twas brillig, and the slithy toves
   Did gyre and gimble in the wabe;
All mimsy were the borogoves,
   And the mome raths outgrabe.

"Beware the Jabberwock, my son!
   The jaws that bite, the claws that catch!
Beware the Jubjub bird and shun
   The frumious Bandersnatch!"

He took his vorpal sword in hand:
   Long time the manxome foe he sought—
So rested he by the Tumtum tree,
   And stood awhile in thought.

And, as in uffish thought he stood,
   The Jabberwock, with eyes of flame,
Came whiffling through the tulgey wood,
   And burbled as it came!

One, two! One, two! And through and through
   The vorpal blade went snicker-snack!
He left it dead, and with its head
   He went galumphing back.

"And hast thou slain the Jabberwock?
    Come to my arms, my beamish boy!
O frabjous day! Callooh! Callay!"
    He chortled in his joy.

'Twas brillig, and the slithy toves
    Did gyre and gimble in the wabe;
All mimsy were the borogoves,
    And the mome raths outgrabe.

What is quickly apparent from your reading of the poem is that going from print to speech is a hollow act unless meaning-making is involved in the transaction.

Try rewriting the poem using your own words. If you and a colleague or two were to compare your rewrites, you undoubtedly would find similarities in meaning, but also important differences. These differences undoubtedly reflect the knowledge of the world—*prior knowledge*—that you as a reader bring to the text as well as the *strategies* you used to make meaning.

Reading as a Strategic Process

Throughout this book, we argue that the real value of reading lies in its uses. Whether we use reading to enter into the imaginative world of fiction; learn with academic texts; meet workplace demands; acquire insight and knowledge about people, places, and things; or understand a graphic on a website, readers, to be successful, must use strategies to meet the demands of the task at hand.

For example, a skilled reader will approach the following passage as a challenge and use a repertoire of reading strategies to construct meaning.

A PLAN FOR THE IMPROVEMENT OF ENGLISH SPELLING*

For example, in Year 1 that useless letter "c" would be dropped to be replased either by "k" or "s," and likewise "x" would no longer be part of the alphabet. The only kase in which "c" would be retained would be the "ch" formation, which will be dealt with later. Year 2 might reform "w" spelling, so that "which" and "one" would take the same konsonant, wile Year 3 might well abolish "y" replasing it with "i" and Iear 4 might fiks the "g/j" anomali wonse and for all.

Jenerally, then, the improvement would kontinue iear bai iear with Iear 5 doing awai with useless double konsonants, and Iears 6–12 or so modifaiing vowlz and the rimeining voist and unvoist konsonants. Bai Iear 15 or sou, it wud fainali bi posibl tu meik ius ov thi ridandant letez "c," "y" and "x"—bai now jast a memori in the maindz ov ould doderez—tu riplais "ch," "sh," and "th" rispektivli.

Fainali, xen, aafte sam 20 iers ov orxogrefkl riform, wi wud hev a lojikl, kohirnt speling in ius xrewawt xe Ingliy-spiking werld.

In order to comprehend text successfully, skilled readers must be able to *decode* or pronounce words quickly and accurately, read with *fluency*, activate *vocabulary knowledge* in relation to the language of the text, and put into play *text comprehension* strategies to understand what they are reading. As Figure 1.1 suggests, decoding, reading fluency, vocabulary, and comprehension are interrelated processes. If readers have trouble decoding words quickly and accurately (e.g., analyzing and recognizing sound–letter relationships), it will slow down their ability to read fluently in a smooth, conversational manner. Moreover, if they struggle to decode words accurately, various reading errors (e.g., mispronunciations, word omissions, and substitutions), if significant, will cause cognitive confusion and limit readers' abilities to bring meaning and conceptual understanding to the words in the text.

---

*Although on the Internet this passage is widely attributed to Mark Twain, there is uncertainty as to its actual author.

Figure 1.1 Reading Involves the Use of Decoding, Fluency, Vocabulary, and Comprehension Strategies

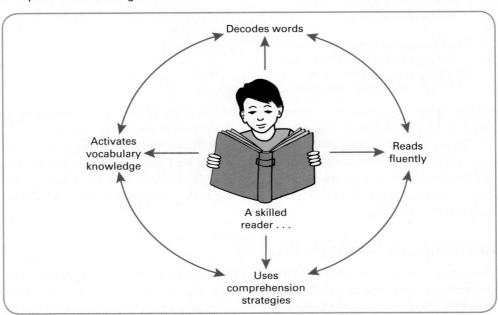

When students lack decoding and fluency skills, the act of reading no longer becomes automatic. As you read "A Plan for the Improvement of English Spelling," did the letter substitutions cause you to struggle as a reader? Perhaps. The progressive substitution of letters undoubtedly slowed down your ability to read in a smooth, conversational manner and may even have affected your accuracy in recognizing some words. Just think about some of the students in classrooms today who lack the ability to decode words accurately and read fluently. They may experience difficulty because they read in a slow and halting manner, word by word, and have trouble pronouncing words quickly and accurately. They spend so much time and attention on trying to "say the words" that comprehension suffers and, as a result, the reading process breaks down for them. Such students will benefit from *direct, explicit* instruction in decoding and fluency strategies from trained literacy specialists.

Our guess is that the reading process did not break down for you as you read the passage. Even though the substitution of letters slowed down your reading, chances are you were still able to comprehend the passage and construct meaning from it. This is because skilled readers do not use a single strategy to comprehend text. They know how to "think with print" as they search for and construct meaning from text. Skilled readers have at their command *multiple strategies* for comprehending text.

This exercise highlights the challenges struggling and hesitant readers and ELs face. For competent readers, strategies come easily—sometimes students don't even realize they are doing them! Other students lack these processes, and though ELs and hesitant readers may have the commonality of struggling with reading in common, "they differ significantly from one another in their levels of reading difficulty, [and] they also differ from one another in the nature of their reading problems" (Torgesen et al., 2007, p. 67).

Reading can be a difficult task, and many students need literacy support regardless of grade level and content area. When reading processes break down, behavior issues may emerge, frustration may occur, and even the best of readers may want to disengage with the content due to feelings of defeat or inadequacy. In addition, many teachers struggle with knowing how to support learners who struggle with texts, content vocabulary, and literacy:

> All these students, as adolescents, face the dual challenges of dramatically improving their reading skills while also keeping pace with grade-level expectations in the content areas, where reading is often the primary means of acquiring new information. Many of these students will require instructional support beyond that which content-area teachers can provide, both in the intensity of the instruction and in the focus and skill with which it is delivered. (Torgesen et al., 2007, p. 67)

While additional supports may be necessary outside of teacher competencies, there are some strategies that can aid literacy development in struggling and EL students. Interventions for students reading below grade level or struggling with literacy that have shown to improve the instructional needs of these types of readers include those focused on word-reading accuracy and fluency and on vocabulary and reading comprehension strategies (Torgesen et al., 2007). These strategies also are helpful for students' on-grade-level peers. For ELs who are "simultaneously acquir[ing] literacy skills, content knowledge, academic vocabulary, command of language structures, and strategic thinking skills," academic oral language instruction and direct, explicit comprehension instruction are targeted interventions that can support vocabulary development and reading comprehension (Torgesen et al., 2007).

Preparing all students to succeed in literacy- and content-rich environments is important, but it is essential to support those students for whom disciplinary literacy and meaning-making is a challenge. Teachers must try to learn about their students and seek out opportunities to support their varied literacies across texts and media. Strategic and purposeful interventions can help to change the trajectory of students' literacy skills. Teachers must be the catalyst for this change.

Reading Comprehension

When skilled readers have difficulty comprehending what they are reading, they often become *strategic* in the way they approach challenging and difficult text. Good readers develop *skills* and *strategies* that they use to understand what they are reading. In essence, they engage in strategic reading. As Duke and Pearson (2002, p. 205) explain, we know a great deal about what good readers do when they read: "Reading comprehension research has a long and rich history … much work on the process of reading comprehension has been grounded in studies of good readers." Table 1.2 delineates what good readers do when they engage in the process of comprehending text.

The research-based findings of two influential reports, *Report of the National Reading Panel* (National Reading Panel, 2000) and the *RAND Report on Reading Comprehension* (RAND Reading Study Group, 2002), indicate that much is known about comprehension instruction. These reports, for example, draw several conclusions about effective comprehension instruction, including the following:

- Instruction can be effective in helping students develop a repertoire of strategies that promotes and fosters comprehension.
- Strategy instruction, when integrated into subject matter learning, improves students' comprehension of text.
- Struggling readers benefit from *explicit instruction* in the use of strategies.
- Vocabulary knowledge is strongly related to text comprehension and is especially important in teaching English Learners.
- Effective comprehension strategies include *question generation, question answering routines, comprehension monitoring, cooperative learning, summarizing,* visual displays known as *graphic organizers,* and knowledge of different *text structures.*

Table 1.2 What Do Good Readers Do When They Comprehend Text?

Characteristics of Good Readers	Strategies of Good Readers
Good readers are	**Good readers**
• Active • Purposeful • Evaluative • Thoughtful • Strategic • Persistent • Productive	• Have clear *goals* in mind for their reading and evaluate whether the text, and their reading of it, is meeting their goals. • *Look over* the text before they read, noting such things as the *structure* of the text and text sections that might be most relevant to their reading goals. • *Make predictions* about what is to come. • Read *selectively*, continually making decisions about their reading—what to read carefully, what to read quickly, what not to read, what to reread, and so on. • *Construct, revise,* and *question* the meanings they make as they read. • Try to determine the meanings of *unfamiliar words and concepts* in the text. • Draw from, compare, and *integrate their prior knowledge* with material in the text. • Think about the *authors* of the text and their styles, beliefs, intentions, historical milieu, and so on. • *Monitor their understanding* of the text, making adjustments in their reading as necessary. • *Evaluate the text's quality and value* and react to the text in a range of ways, both intellectually and emotionally. • *Read different kinds of text differently.* • *Attend closely* to the setting and characters when reading narrative. • Frequently *construct* and *revise summaries* of what they have read when reading an expository text. • Think about the text before, during, and after reading.

- Students benefit from exposure to different types, or *genres,* of texts (e.g., informational and narrative texts).

- Teachers who provide choices, challenging tasks, and collaborative learning experiences increase students' motivation to read and comprehend texts.

Throughout Part Two of this book, we will explore a variety of instructional practices that will help students comprehend discipline-specific texts more effectively. Some of these strategies will be useful and highly effective in your specific discipline; some may not. *Content determines process.* How teachers adapt instructional strategies to meet the conceptual demands and peculiarities of their disciplines will be the difference-maker in the literate lives of their students.

> MyLab Education **Self-Check 1.3**
>
> MyLab Education **Application Exercises 1.3:**
> Supporting Students in Reading to Learn

Looking Back Looking Forward

In this chapter, we invited you to begin an examination of content literacy practices and the assumptions underlying those practices. Teachers play a critical role in helping students use literacy strategies to think and learn with text. Effective teachers make a difference in the literate lives of their students. Therefore, we made a distinction between *teacher qualities* and *teaching quality.* Teacher qualities are the characteristics associated with an effective teacher. Teaching quality, on the other hand, refers to the instructional context and the dynamics underpinning effective teaching in content areas. Effective teachers, for example, differentiate instruction for a wide range of students. Learning with all kinds of text, whether print or digital in nature, is an active process. In today's standards-based educational environment, the pressure to teach content standards well can easily lead to content-only instruction with little attention paid to how students acquire information and develop concepts. The standards-based instruction, however, is a step in the right direction. The Common Core acknowledges that teachers must balance content (what they teach) and process (how they teach) as they engage students in thinking and learning with all kinds of texts.

To this end, we explored the role that literacy plays in the acquisition of content knowledge. The concept of literacy must be viewed from a 21st-century perspective. In an era of digital media, many of today's adolescents have developed "new literacies" that they use for personal and social purposes. New literacies are having a major influence on learning in academic contexts. To shift the burden of learning from teacher to student requires an understanding of the relationships among literacies, texts, and learning across the curriculum. As a result, we attempted to put content literacy and disciplinary literacy practices into perspective, contending that the two approaches to instruction share much common ground. Our emphasis throughout this book is on reading and writing to learn. Learning how to comprehend text across disciplines is what content area reading is all about.

The next chapter puts the spotlight on new literacies in the adolescent lives of 21st-century learners. Digital texts are highly engaging and interactive. New literacies make it possible to interact with text in ways not imaginable even a short while ago. Literacy-related learning opportunities in multimodal environments are interactive, enhance communication, engage students in multimedia, create opportunities for inquiry, and support socially mediated learning. Whether students are navigating the Internet or interacting with popular media such as video games, an array of learning experiences awaits them.

eResources

Take a closer look at standards for your content area by visiting your State Department of Public Instruction website.

Examine how states such as Wisconsin and Illinois have created initiatives related to disciplinary literacy by visiting their Department of Education websites.

Connect to the Reading Online website to study the International Reading Association's position statement on new literacies in a 21st-century world.

Chapter 2
Learning with New Literacies

Written in collaboration with Bruce Taylor, Ph.D.

Shutterstock

Chapter Overview and Learning Outcomes

After reading this chapter, you should be able to:

2.1 Explain new literacies and multiliteracies and the changing expectations of literacy in and out of the classroom.

2.2 Describe the strategies for writing to learn in content area classes, including how they incorporate multiliteracies.

2.3 Describe several multimodal learning practices and explain how learning strategies have been impacted by the use of technology in classrooms.

Organizing Principle

New literacies have transformed the way we read, write, think, communicate, and make meaning.

Our understandings of literacy and text have undergone significant change since John Willinsky coined the term "new literacy" (Willinsky, 1990), the New London Group published its article on "multiliteracies" (1996), and Paul Gilster popularized the term "digital literacy" in his 1997 book of that name (Gilster, 1997). In a 21st-century digital culture, what counts as text has blurred, as have our technologies for reading and writing (New Media Consortium, 2005). The digital devices that allow us to read, write, and communicate virtually any time or place have moved into schools and classrooms. *Education Week*'s Technology Counts reports widespread adoption of digital learning tools in K–12 classrooms and schools (Bushwell, 2017), while the National Center for Education Statistics reports data from 2015 show that 94% of children ages 3 to 18 had a computer at home and 61% had Internet access at home. As the idea of new literacies approaches the quarter-century mark, there's still much that is "new" in the way technology impacts literacy teaching and learning.

Today's students have been described as digital natives, but some scholars have begun to challenge this notion (boyd, 2014). It is indisputable that students today have grown up surrounded by technologies. Consequently, many learners have developed social media skills and "new literacies" that some parents, described as "digital immigrants," struggle to learn. Many of today's youth are fluent at exchanging e-mails, texts, messages, and posts to a changing array of social networking sites that include Twitter, Instagram, and Facebook. Although youth have access to and experience with information and communication technologies (ICT), as danah boyd argues in *It's Complicated: The Social Lives of Networked Teens* (2014), we can't take for granted that this immersion means that they have mastered the academic and social nuances of these technologies. What does this mean for literacy and learning across the curriculum? First and foremost, it signifies in a very public way that we live in a new media age, where technological advances brought on by the digital forces of electronic devices are transforming the way we communicate, collect information, make meaning, and construct knowledge. It also means that teachers and schools have much work to do to scaffold learning across a more complex array of texts and technologies for students who are savvy users of technology but who may lack experience using that savvy in academic contexts.

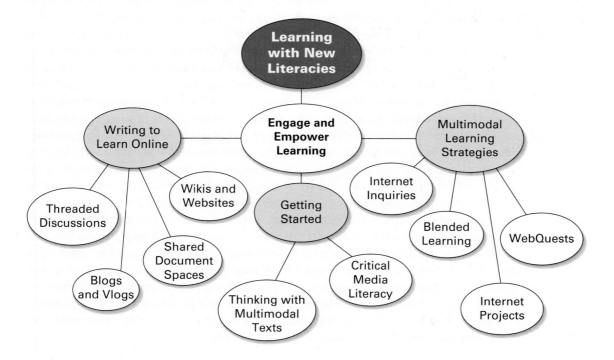

Walk into any middle or high school classroom today, and you may see students using laptops, iPads, or smartphones to look up information, access teacher-created documents, or turn in homework. Listen to students, and you are likely to hear them talk about "Googling" for information or posting comments in a class discussion to a blog or online Padlet page. These exchanges reflect the types of information gathering students typically engage in as they interact with digital texts in and out of today's content area classrooms. Obviously, the ways in which we find information, no matter what the topic, have transformed radically in just a few short years. The Internet has made information accessible to a degree never imagined. Yet it is best to heed the advice of Karchmer-Klein and Shinas (2012, p. 291): "As teachers it is necessary to suspend assumptions regarding the technological knowledge and experience students bring to the classroom and instead develop instruction designed to address curriculum goals and students' individual needs."

The challenges are no less daunting for teachers than for their students. Computers are nearly ubiquitous tools in most schools. *Education Week* reported in its first-ever "Tech Confidence Index" (Education Week Research Center, 2016) that its survey of 700 classroom teachers resulted in an overall confidence score of 49 out of 100. While the overall score was at the midrange, a majority of teachers had scores between 26 and 50 with only about a third of teachers earning higher scores between 51 and 75. The impact of these levels of confidence impact classroom technology use, with students of teachers with higher levels of confidence spending nearly twice as much time using digital learning tools as students of teachers with lower levels of confidence. In its 2017 *National Education Technology Plan* update, the U.S. Department of Education indicated that about half of teachers request more professional development than they currently receive and call for more preservice and in-service training to "develop a teaching forces skilled in online and blended instruction" (Office of Educational Technology, 2017, p. 88). Indeed, despite the widespread use of computers, research suggests that classrooms remain "book-centric" in many ways (Bialostok, 2014) and that teacher professional development is vital to meaningful integration and use of technology in schools and classrooms.

Yet, more schools and classrooms are becoming 1:1 where students are assigned a laptop or digital tablet to use throughout their classes and, in many cases, at home. More teachers are being asked to create hybrid or blended learning environments or "flipped" classrooms using learning management systems like Canvas, Schoology, and Edmodo. Research on these blended learning models is emergent but shows some promise across content areas including science, math and with EL students (Duffy, 2016; Graziano & Hall, 2017; Murphy, Chang & Suaray, 2016). Research by Winter (2018) at the middle school level suggests that flipped learning may lead to increased motivation and improvement in academic performance.

Therein lies the challenge for teachers in this era of "new literacies": As schools adopt an increasing assortment of technology, how can we help our students be effective readers and writers when our concept of "literacy" is evolving so rapidly? Even though students may have developed social networking skills, how will we help them find, make meaning of, and evaluate the information available to them via digital media? How do we help young people keep up with the immense changes occurring in digital media when we may have trouble keeping up with these changes ourselves? It simply is not possible to adequately prepare students for reading and writing in the 21st century without integrating new literacies into the everyday life of today's classrooms. We've moved from using technology to access information (Web 1.0) to a world in which teachers and students read, write, and respond to information (Web 2.0). Discussions of Web 3.0 (whatever that may be) may have become a reality by the time you read this book. Are today's schools up to the challenge? While it is important for teachers to show students how to comprehend texts that are page based, the organizing principle for this chapter suggests that students are also going to need to be interacting more with texts that are screen based—texts that include not only print but also images, motion, and sound—if they are going to be able to lead fully realized literate lives: New literacies have transformed the way we read, write, communicate, and make meaning.

Frame of Mind

1. What are new literacies?
2. What is different about learning with new literacies? What is the same?
3. Why is learning with new literacies essential for students?
4. What are some instructional strategies and approaches that can be used to engage and empower learning using new literacies?
5. How do the roles of teachers change when they make new literacies an integral part of subject matter learning?

Literacy has evolved from a traditional view of print-based reading and writing to one that recognizes the multiplicity of literacies that vary across time and space. Although skilled readers use many of the same strategies online as they do offline, there are also new skill sets and strategies that learners must develop to use new literacies effectively (Coiro & Moore, 2012). The comprehension strategies that we discussed in Chapter 1, for example, are used by learners both online and offline depending on their purposes for reading. When they go online, however, some of the new literacy strategies that learners are likely to use may include generating digital questions, examining search engine results, and making sense of the multimodal aspects of digital text. As Sweeny (2010, p. 122) noted, "Schools need to embrace ICTs so that students are prepared to function in a world where new literacies are the expectation and the norm." No wonder new literacies are changing the instructional landscape for learning in today's classrooms.

New Literacies and Multiliteracies: an Overview

2.1   Explain new literacies and multiliteracies and the changing expectations of literacy in and out of the classroom.

Technology has always played an integral role in literacy and learning. Ancient technologies, such as clay tablets and papyrus scrolls, gave way to paper and pencil and changed the landscape of literacy and what it meant to be literate in ages past. However, over the past few decades, ICT have not just expanded the kinds and quantity of text but also accelerated the pace of that change—a "big bang" of literacy and learning. The impact of this change has been likened to the revolutionary invention of the printing press (McLuhan, 1962). As we've moved from "new literacy" to "multiliteracies" to "digital literacy," these changes have affected the way we think about teaching and learning. Willinsky's idea of a "new" literacy revolved more around a different mind-set for approaching reading and writing in the classroom than around technological advances. He describes classrooms that are driven not by textbooks and teacher talk but instead by inquiry and student choice—a "new" literacy that wasn't dependent on students regurgitating "right" answers. Of course, the roots of a student-centered concept of curriculum, literacy, and learning can be traced back to the groundbreaking work of John Dewey (1899–1980) and many other educational pioneers and literacy researchers who followed in his footsteps.

Multiliteracies, a term coined by a group of scholars under the name the New London Group (1996), captures this shifting notion of literacy: The "multiplicity of communications channels and increasing cultural and linguistic diversity in the world today call for a much broader view of literacy than portrayed by traditional language-based approaches." The changes in thinking about literacy are seen by some as a radical shift away from long-held traditions of what it means to read and write and have given rise to new literacy communities not imagined two decades ago. Communicative practices associated with new literacies are described by some scholars as new mind-sets, signaling the ways in which information communication technologies (ICT) have influenced communication in and out of the classroom (Lankshear & Knobel, 2006).

This work by Willinsky, the New London Group, and others gave rise to a more recent line of research—the **New Literacy Studies**—that underscores the importance of "a specific sociocultural approach to understanding and researching literacy" (Lankshear & Knobel, 2003, p. 16). A sociocultural approach views literacy as social practice. That is to say, New Literacy Studies examine literacy as situated in the way people use it in their lives as they act at work, at school, within the family, and in any social situation (Gee, 1996). This thinking is seen as providing important insights into students' everyday literacy practices with the potential to create instruction that connects in- and out-of-school literacy practices (Knobel & Lankshear, 2014).

These ideas have been echoed by organizations including the International Literacy Association (ILA) and the National Council of Teachers of English (NCTE). The NCTE's policy statement on **21st-Century Literacies** states that "as society and technology change, so does literacy" (National Council of Teachers of English, 2010). In short, this statement lays out the case that in the 21st-century, people possess not one but multiple literacies and that schools need to equip students to be literate across many contexts using different kinds of texts and tools. New Literacies is not just the domain of reading and English language arts. Allison and Goldston (2018) state that the Next Generation Science Standards, adopted in many states, emphasize the interconnectedness between multiliteracies and scientific practices with implications for the student development of scientific literacy. Research in the use of text in mathematics classrooms shows that early-career math teachers favor the use of digital text because of its presumed interactive qualities (Barry, Gay, Pelkey & Rothrock, 2017).

Digital Literacies has become a key focus of new literacies. Dowell (2018) states that digital literacies "is a broad, umbrella term that pertains to the use of literacy skills defined as reading, writing, listening, speaking, composing, communicating, and interacting within digital environments" (p. 2326). Digital literacies is a term more often associated with older students and adults (Kazakoff, 2013). Recent studies show promising outcomes of using digital texts and technologies with English Learners and immigrant students (Crosby, 2018; Featro & DiGregorio, 2016).

As new media became more and more a part of our lives, teachers learned how to surf the Internet and bookmark; in today's classrooms, they're learning how to blog, create video content and podcasts, and tweet information. Being a literate person today involves more than being able to construct meaning from a printed text. A literate person needs to be able to "read" and "write" and learn with texts that have *multimodal* elements such as print, graphic design, audio, video, gesture, and nonstop interaction. In a 21st-century, media-driven society, a teacher needs to be knowledgeable of reading and writing using modes of communication that were previously left to the art, music, theater, and film teachers.

MyLab Education
Video Example 2.1:
Teaching Content with
Technology
Watch this video to review the importance of digital literacy in today's classrooms.

From the Creative to the Critical

Technology is often associated with sciences, an alignment highlighted in the emergence of STEM (science, technology, engineering, and mathematics) education; however, as Wynn and Harris (2013) suggest, the term has more recently evolved to include arts, becoming STEAM education. Furman further suggests that this acronym needs to be updated to include reading or, as he writes, "Science and Technology, interpreted through Engineering and the Arts, conveyed through reading and writing, all based in elements of Mathematics" (Furman, 2017).

Research documents the creative uses and connections among digital technologies, digital literacies, and the creative process (Frydenberg & Andone, 2016; Schmidt & Beucher, 2018). Over the past few decades, many educators have advocated for more inclusion of the arts in classrooms. Arts integration advocate Elliot Eisner (1997) has urged teachers to bring into every classroom multiple forms of representation, such as painting, music, and theater. Leland and Harste (1994) discuss these forms of representation as "ways of knowing" that need to be honored in our classrooms regardless of whether the Internet has brought these arts elements into the everyday lives of readers and writers. Those who have described what arts-integrated classrooms can look like have given us a glimpse into what all classrooms may need to look like when all reading and writing are done in a multimodal environment.

While the computers and the technologies that make digital literacy possible do not bring to mind creativity for some, they are used by some teachers and students in highly creative ways. STEAM education brings together the digital, technological, and scientific literacies with artistic and creative problem solving in what Gess (2017) argues is needed in order to become a globally literate citizen. Cortés et al. (2018) examined the creative and critical processes employed by a community of teenagers participating in developing entertainment workshops designed to create digital literacies. Ribeiro (2015) documents how digital storytelling can be used in the English language arts to what she describes as an integrated language arts approach to teaching and learning.

The digital turn in literacy and learning can include creative, but also critical, elements. At the same time that some educators were urging arts integration (Lemon, 2015), television had already been an impetus to the development of another key strand of the new literacies movement. Many educators, particularly from the United Kingdom and Australia, called for young people to be educated about the ways of television and all media (Bazalgette & Buckingham, 2013), arguing that all students should be exposed to at least the basics of media education. Along with the work of media educators are the critical literacy theorists who have urged educators to help students explore and examine the power dynamics in the discourses that surround us (Morrell, 2013; Freire, 1970, 2000). Talib (2018) argues for digital media literacy education through the inclusion of a critical, multimodal, and interdisciplinary approach that includes the use and analysis of social media. Baker-Doyle (2018) suggests instruction that links the teaching of computer coding to critical literacy can help foster greater civic literacy and engagement.

Taken a step further, digital technologies provide teachers and students with tools to speak back and create counternarratives. Work by Burwell (2013) using digital video remix technology allowed the teacher to introduce critical conversations with students about representation, appropriation, creativity, and copyright, and recent work by Leent and Mills (2018) proposes a new pedagogical model of a queer critical media literacy with a focus on addressing inequalities for LGBTQ+ youth. However, as Vickery (2017) notes in her book, *Worried About the Wrong Things*, not all children have opportunities for participation in a digital culture. Technical and material barriers create inequalities for low-income and other marginalized young people from the community-building and creative experiences that are possible online.

Nonlinear Characteristics of New Literacies

Along with the multimodal aspects of the new literacies, there are additional characteristics of reading on the screen that differentiate new literacies from print-based literacy. For example, new media are usually read in a nonlinear fashion. The reader may jump from element to element within a digital text in a completely random way. Traditional printed texts, such as books, are written for readers to proceed from front to back, reading from left to right. However, readers of electronic texts have the option of clicking on any one of several hyperlinks that can take them on a path that digresses completely from the path other readers might take. Linear reading, of course, still occurs. Though many adolescents have probably read the *Harry Potter* or *Hunger Games* books, and perhaps even last night's assignments in their textbooks, much of their personal reading now is done with digital texts. As a result, reading is individualized and proceeds in nonlinear fashion, based on the immediate interests and characteristics of the reader (Reinking, 1997).

In addition, a reader can now interact with other readers and even the author of the text being read. With several keystrokes, the reader can find a community of readers via a bookselling site, Facebook, or Goodreads with whom to engage in some social networking revolving around the text. If there were ever a doubt that reading is a socially constructed activity, these characteristics of new media completely negate the stereotype of the lonely reader being "shushed" by the librarian. Though individualized, reading is becoming a truly social and interactive experience.

The nonlinear aspects of text are reshaping teaching and learning in other ways as well. Scholarship suggests that digital learning environments have the potential to change traditional teaching functions in areas including assessment, explicit instruction, and classroom discussion to provide more opportunities to differentiate based on individual students' needs (Pandya, 2012; Shaffer, Nash & Ruis, 2015).

In-School and Out-of-School Literacies

The literacies that students have access to outside of school continue to evolve. As adolescent learners develop their use of new literacies for personal and social purposes, there seems to be more of a gap between students' in-school literacies and their out-of-school literacies as well as changes to teens' reading habits. Data from the Pew Research Center show that in 2016, 73% of Americans as a whole read a book, with 65% reading a print book and 28% sharing that they read an e-book (Perrin, 2016), and further reported that 18% of Americans listen to audiobooks. For teens, the story is different. A recent study showed that of the American teens surveyed, less than 20% reported reading a book, magazine, or newspaper daily for pleasure, but 80% said they use social media daily (Twenge, Martin & Spitzberg, 2018). The authors share that in the mid-2010s, "the average American 12th grader reported spending approximately 2 hours a day texting, just over 2 hours a day on the Internet (which includes gaming), and just under 2 hours a day on social media and thus about 6 hours a day in total on three digital media activities," (p. 9). The report further states that adolescents are spending less time with legacy media (books, magazines, newspapers, TV, and movies). These changes have implications for teachers and students. Scholar and author Maryanne Wolf (2018) raises questions about the way digital texts and reading may be changing the reading brain and that the prevalence of digital text may be the cause in a decline of what she calls *deep reading*. Wolf does not argue against the use of digital text but suggests that further research is needed to understand how readers interact differently with digital and print text and calls for teaching children how to read the different formats.

While these reports raise questions and concerns about digital media, there's no slowing the digital progression. The Pew Research Center (2018) reported that 89% of American adults use the Internet. However, for 18- to 29-year-olds, Internet usage is nearly ubiquitous at 98%. This points to a practical and economic argument for using new literacies in the classroom: Helping students to learn with new literacies is part of making sure that they are prepared for life in the 21st century.

Using activities that involve visual art—another form of text in the classroom, such as the "sketch-to-stretch" activity—has been shown to further students' comprehension of print and learning in general (Bustle, 2004; Short, Harste, & Burke, 1996). The sketch-to-stretch activity involves asking students to take a break from reading by stretching and then sketch what is being visualized while reading, thus linking print literacy with visual literacy. (See Chapter 9 for a detailed discussion.)

Many teachers are embracing new literacies, in combination with printed texts, as motivational tools in their classrooms; new literacies become "the spoonful of sugar to help the print go down" (Kist, 2005). Read about the journey of a high school earth science teacher, Sarah, and the evolution of teaching and learning in her classroom involving the use of new literacies and technologies in Voices from the Field (see Box 2.1).

Box 2.1 Voices from the Field

Erika, a Middle School Mathematics Teacher in a 1:1 School

Challenge

Two years ago, our school became a 1:1 school, and every student received a laptop to use. Students bring their laptops to class and take them home with them. They've become an important part of teaching and learning at our school. The challenge for teachers has been learning how to use them. I'm "old school" and was used to using textbooks and worksheets and doing problems on the dry-erase board. Graphing calculators were the only obvious piece of technology we used in my class. Computers just weren't something we used much in math class. But now they are!

Our district provided us with professional development and with programs that have helped us flip teaching and learning. I've moved beyond textbooks and worksheets! I have a digital SMART Board and a document camera. My students and I use Canvas, the learning management system our school district provides, to post assignments and quizzes and turn in homework. It's a blended learning environment.

Technology isn't just a graphing calculator—something that sits to the side that we use from time to time. Technology is part of the fabric of how I teach and help my students learn, but we are all still figuring out how to use these tools. One of the things I've noticed more since we've become a 1:1 school is how literacy is woven into learning math. I guess I knew that before, but it wasn't as visible. Now with kids on computers, writing out answers, recording video responses, and joining in online discussions about how they solved a problem, you can see the way literacy is a part of teaching and learning math.

Strategy

I've been on a steep learning curve the past couple of years as we moved from a mostly paper environment to more of a digital environment for teaching and learning. The year before we adopted the laptops for all students, we did intensive planning. Our district offered quite a bit of professional development for our teachers, and that was helpful, but there's a piece of this you just have to learn through the process. I'm the math department chair and this year had to mentor two new teachers on using technology. Here's some things I've shared with them.

- Change the way you think. First, learning math is about learning how to think, read, write, and talk math. It's about becoming mathematically literate. Build in those opportunities for students to discuss and share ideas in person and online. Help them use writing and discussion as a way to engage in problem solving and reflect on their learning. Second, the technology we have can't teach your students but can help you and your students learn together. It can help you engage students in learning the math and take that learning beyond the classroom walls at times. For example, I use a website called Flipgrid to post problems in the form of a short video screencast I create. In class, I then have my students post video responses where they show how they solved the problem. What emerges is a rich discussion about solving problems in different ways. Students are teaching and talking with each other through Flipgrid; and then, if they have Internet access at home, they can go back and review that discussion.

In the past, I'd call a student up to the dry-erase board to solve a problem, then we'd talk a bit and move to the next problem. Using Flipgrid allows more students to share ideas and comment on the process. I have several EL students in my class at different stages of learning English. They share a first language and post comments and videos in Spanish and English, depending on their knowledge of English. This allows all of these students—many of whom are not comfortable speaking up in class—to engage in the learning.

- Build a foundation and establish routines. This is big to me! Good teachers develop routines for teaching. That helps make planning more manageable for the teacher and helps students know what to expect. The technology is no different. You have to build a foundation by using some core programs and establishing routines. For us, Canvas is our learning platform. All the assignments go up in our class Canvas site. We teach students how to access and turn in assignments there and take quizzes and tests. We add links to additional materials there as well—websites and video content. Khan Academy has some good videos that students can use when they need some help when they are at home. I also use a few other tools, such as Flipgrid for interactive discussions, Google Docs for written reflections, and Google Forms and Sheets for setting up and grading quizzes. I've found a program called Flubaroo that works with Google Forms and Sheets to automate the grading and create reports to show me and my students where we need to do more work. My students know how to use the technology, and we've established a routine for how we work together.

- Be willing to try new things. While I have my core set of programs and routines, you also have to be willing to try new things. That includes trying something new and finding out they don't fit with how you teach and how your students learn, but that's okay! Right now, the math teachers at my school are looking at social media platforms as a way to connect our students to students. We are in a rural area, and we want our students to interact with students from other places around the U.S. and world in learning math but also about others who are different from yourself. We are piloting a project using a Facebook group with students in an urban middle school. We haven't worked out all the challenges yet, but we hope we can continue this collaboration. We tried using Twitter at first, but it wasn't the right tool. It's a process that involves trial and error.

- Anticipate and work around challenges. Technology creates its own set of challenges, and you must learn to anticipate those and work around them. In class, you have to have a backup plan for when a computer or projector is down or a website or program isn't working. I also work to keep my students focused and engaged in learning the math and not off checking their e-mail or Instagram. One way I do that is to give two-minute personal tech breaks, so students can check e-mail or social media. One big challenge is that not all students have Internet access at home, so we've had to help them work around that by finding libraries or places near their homes with wireless hot spots to connect. I'm careful about what I require students to do from home that requires Internet access. However, the technology also has benefits. I mentioned the instructional videos that help students when they are not in school. There's also a website called Desmos that has a good graphing calculator program. That's been a big help for students whose families can't afford to purchase a graphing calculator.

Reflection

Technology is part of the fabric of "doing school" and learning math. I am learning with and from my students as we try new

things and find new tools. That allows them to see me as a student learning new things as well as the teacher who is supposed to have the answers. The technology also allows me to engage students in different ways. My shy or quiet kids can post comments or share through the technology, which for many is more comfortable for them. It also allows teaching and learning to move beyond the walls of our classroom. We can connect with other students in learning and have access to tools to help students learn when we are not in class together. I am not so "old school" that I can't see the power in that!

MyLab Education
Response Journal 2.1
As we've seen, information communication technologies (ICT) have emerged and changed the nature of literacy to include multiple forms of text, including digital texts and ways of reading, writing, and communicating. Reflect on how these changes have impacted the ways you read, write, and communicate with others.

New Literacies and Content Standards

Knowing how to use new literacies is integral to the strategic knowledge and skills that every student in all content areas will need to develop to be discipline-literate in the 21st century. For example, the Common Core State Standards (National Governors Association Center for Best Practices, n.d.), which emerged in 2010, integrate technology into its standards for reading literacy (Standard 7), reading information text (Standard 5), and writing (Standard 8) as well into the standards for literacy in history/social studies, science, and technical subjects. These standards, which have had an impact on technology integration, have evolved and been integrated into standards in many states.

Practically all the national education associations in the various academic disciplines have developed content standards or statements of principle that implicitly or explicitly acknowledge the use of technologies for information and communication. New literacies are embedded in more state and national standards than many people assume. Though the term *new literacies* is absent from most state standards within the United States, *technology, media*, and *media literacy* are more than likely mentioned. And as Baker (2009) points out, regardless of whether states use the term **media literacy** in their state standards, the topics related to media are present in many subject areas:

- Propaganda and persuasion
- The vocabulary of film and video
- Advertising and marketing
- Bias and objectivity

One of the more comprehensive set of standards for the proficient use of technologies in schools was developed in 2007 and updated in 2016 by the International Society for Technology in Education (ISTE). The ISTE standards acknowledge the rapidly evolving role of technology in classrooms as tools for collaboration as well as personalized learning. While the ISTE standards focused on strategic skills initially they now highlight the role of technology in learning that is student-centered. The standards focus on student roles including empowered learning, digital citizen, knowledge constructor, innovative designer, computational thinker, creative communicator and global collaborator. The standards for each of these areas are outlined in Box 2.2.

Engage and Empower Learning: Getting Started

Technology has changed the way we think, inquire, communicate, read, and write. This revolutionary way of communicating includes elements of print, visual art, sound, video, social media, and advertising. Based on a review of new literacies research and a

Box 2.2 ISTE Educational Technology Standards for Students*

1. **Empowered Learner.** Students leverage technology to take an active role in choosing, achieving and demonstrating competency in their learning goals, informed by the learning sciences.

   - Students articulate and set personal learning goals, develop strategies leveraging technology to achieve them and reflect on the learning process itself to improve learning out-comes.
   - Students build networks and customize their learning environments in ways that support the learning process.
   - Students use technology to seek feedback that informs and improves their practice and to demonstrate their learning in a variety of ways.
   - Students understand the fundamental concepts of technology operations, demonstrate the ability to choose, use and troubleshoot current technologies and are able to transfer their knowledge to explore emerging technologies.

2. **Digital Citizen.** Students recognize the rights, responsibilities and opportunities of living, learning and working in an interconnected digital world, and they act and model in ways that are safe, legal and ethical.

   - Students cultivate and manage their digital identity and reputation and are aware of the permanence of their actions in the digital world.
   - Students engage in positive, safe, legal and ethical behavior when using technology, including social interactions online or when using networked devices.
   - Students demonstrate an understanding of and respect for the rights and obligations of using and sharing intellectual property.
   - Students manage their personal data to maintain digital privacy and security and are aware of data-collection technology used to track their navigation online.

3. **Knowledge Constructor.** Students critically curate a variety of resources using digital tools to construct knowledge, produce creative artifacts and make meaningful learning experiences for themselves and others.

   - Students plan and employ effective research strategies to locate information and other resources for their intellectual or creative pursuits.
   - Students evaluate the accuracy, perspective, credibility and relevance of information, media, data or other resources.
   - Students curate information from digital resources using a variety of tools and methods to create collections of artifacts that demonstrate meaningful connections or conclusions.
   - Students build knowledge by actively exploring real-world issues and problems, developing ideas and theories and pursuing answers and solutions.

4. **Innovative Designer.** Students use a variety of technologies within a design process to identify and solve problems by creating new, useful or imaginative solutions.

   - Students know and use a deliberate design process for generating ideas, testing theories, creating innovative artifacts or solving authentic problems.
   - Students select and use digital tools to plan and manage a design process that considers design constraints and calculated risks.
   - Students develop, test and refine prototypes as part of a cyclical design process.
   - Students exhibit a tolerance for ambiguity, perseverance and the capacity to work with open-ended problems.

5. **Computational Thinker.** Students develop and employ strategies for understanding and solving problems in ways that leverage the power of technological methods to develop and test solutions.

   - Students formulate problem definitions suited for technology-assisted methods such as data analysis, abstract models and algorithmic thinking in exploring and finding solutions.
   - Students collect data or identify relevant data sets, use digital tools to analyze them, and represent data in various ways to facilitate problem-solving and decision-making.
   - Students break problems into component parts, extract key information, and develop descriptive models to understand complex systems or facilitate problem-solving.
   - Students understand how automation works and use algorithmic thinking to develop a sequence of steps to create and test automated solutions.

6. **Creative Communicator.** Students communicate clearly and express themselves creatively for a variety of purposes using the platforms, tools, styles, formats and digital media appropriate to their goals.

   - Students choose the appropriate platforms and tools for meeting the desired objectives of their creation or communication.
   - Students create original works or responsibly repurpose or remix digital resources into new creations.
   - Students communicate complex ideas clearly and effectively by creating or using a variety of digital objects such as visualizations, models or simulations.
   - Students publish or present content that customizes the message and medium for their intended audiences.

7. **Global Collaborator.** Students use digital tools to broaden their perspectives and enrich their learning by collaborating with others and working effectively in teams locally and globally.

   - Students use digital tools to connect with learners from a variety of backgrounds and cultures, engaging with them in ways that broaden mutual understanding and learning.
   - Students use collaborative technologies to work with others, including peers, experts or community members, to examine issues and problems from multiple viewpoints.
   - Students contribute constructively to project teams, assuming various roles and responsibilities to work effectively toward a common goal.
   - Students explore local and global issues and use collaborative technologies to work with others to investigate solutions.

* International Society for Technology in Education (2016). *ISTE's Educational Technology Standards for Students*. Retrieved August 2, 2019, from https://www.iste.org/standards/for-students.

long-term study of classrooms that are embracing new literacies, Kist (2003, 2012) has proposed some characteristics of new literacies classrooms:

- New literacies classrooms feature daily work in multiple forms of representation.
- In new literacies classrooms, there are explicit discussions of the merits of using certain symbol systems in certain situations with much choice.
- In new literacies classrooms, there are metadialogues, such as think-alouds, by teachers who model working through problems using certain symbol systems.
- In new literacies classrooms, students take part in a mix of individual and collaborative activities.
- New literacies classrooms are places of student engagement in which students report achieving a "flow" state.

There are numerous instructional tools and strategies for using new literacies in content area classrooms. Given the multiplicity of possibilities for online learning, it is reasonable for a teacher to ask, "Where do I begin?" A good starting point is to demonstrate to students how to think critically in a multimodal environment.

Literacy and Learning in Multimodal Environments

The nature of digital and multimodal text is long familiar to teachers and students. There is little or no mystery to the nonlinear, interactive nature of websites and other digital media. Many students are raised with computers, cell phones, and Internet access at home. The U.S. Census Bureau reports for 2016 that 68% of households had mobile broadband access (Bauman, 2018) while 89% had a computer (Ryan, 2018). However, as danah boyd (2014) has argued, the exposure to computers, the Internet, and social media tools does not mean that students are savvy in using them. The focus of the New London Group's (1996) work on multiliteracies was to help educators envision pedagogies that consider diverse and changing texts and contexts for literacy and learning.

Research on teaching and learning that draws on digital and print-based texts and technologies suggests that digital technologies have come to complement other resources rather than replacing them or being used as alternatives (Yelland, 2018). Other research documents the ways digital and touch-screen devices, for example, engage and motivate students in reading and writing activities that foster co-construction and collaboration (Cordero et al., 2018) and serve as a vehicle to apprentice students into diverse disciplinary literacies including literacy practices in mathematics (Taylor, 2018). As noted earlier, multimodal texts, including graphic novels, can foster critical literacy skills with second-language learners (Kang, 2017) and support the engagement and learning of struggling readers (Pacheco, 2017).

A social studies teacher and her students are working through a unit about civil rights and the systemic effects of segregation. Students use their laptops to study digital exhibits at the National Civil Rights Museum website and document their learning using a double-entry journal format, writing out key points in their journals then adding to these notes in discussion with other students. The teacher gives the students some guiding questions but encourages them to follow links to multiple pages within the museum's website. Next, while viewing a documentary, *Mighty Times: The Children's March* (Houston et al., 2005) from Teaching Tolerance, students write additional notes in their journals using an IEPC (**I**magine, **E**laborate, **P**redict, **C**onfirm) format. As the unit progresses, the teacher assigns some readings from their textbook but also has students read the graphic novel, *March*, co-authored by Congressman John Lewis (Lewis, Aydin & Powell, 2013). She has students respond to online discussions in small groups but also submit a RAFT (**R**ole of the writer, **A**udience, **F**ormat, **T**opic) writing assignment. The unit culminates with students creating audio and video podcasts that allow them to share their learning with each other and taking a test that allows the teacher to determine student mastery of learning objectives.

Throughout this social studies unit we see students using multiple forms of text, including video and websites, but also a textbook and a graphic novel. Literacy is multimodal and includes writing in traditional forms (journals and tests) as well as in digital formats on blogs and in audio and video podcasts. These traditional literacies and new literacies are interwoven and, as Yelland (2018) suggests, complement each other.

Developing a Framework for New Literacies

Since terms like *multiliteracies* and *new literacies* have come into use, much thought has been given to ways teachers and students can use new and emerging technologies. While traditional literacies still have a prominent role in classrooms (Burnett & Merchant, 2015), teachers at the elementary level, middle grades, and high school level have developed numerous applications of technology for teaching and learning (Buckley-Marudas, 2016; Cardullo, Zygouris-Coe & Wilson, 2017; Chen, 2017; Graziano & Hall, 2017). Teachers have found ways to use technology to help students with the writing process (Hicks, 2013) as well as teaching specific reading skills (Castek & Coiro, 2015) and higher-order thinking skills (Zawlinski, 2009). Research also documents the use of digital literacies with reluctant and struggling readers and with English Learners (Crosby, 2018; Gunter & Kenny, 2008). New literacies cut across content areas as well, with research documenting their use not only in English language arts (Herrera & Kidwell, 2018; Zoch, Myers, & Belcher, 2017) but in a range of other subject areas, including math, science, social studies, and arts (Hilton, 2016; Lemon, 2015; Riley, 2016; Wang & Hsu, 2017).

The development of theories (for example: New London Group, 1996) and practices has helped teachers consider how they might use ICT in the classroom. However, scholarship suggests that technology integration runs a spectrum. Some scholars have pointed out that one drawback is that technology is often added to and not integrated with classroom instruction (Collins, 2017; Collins & Halverson, 2009), while others see evidence of greater integration of technology with traditional texts, tools, and pedagogies (Yelland, 2018).

A middle ground between theory and practice has been suggested to help teachers consider the ways technologies can be woven into instruction to support student learning (Taylor, 2012; Taylor & Yearta, 2013). These authors have developed categories to organize different digital- and Web-based applications and tools that have found their way into classrooms into learning actions undertaking by students, including researching, communicating, collaborating, exploring, creating, and sharing.

While tools and technologies change—new ones emerging and others fading away—this structure offers a way to organize and use new applications.

Engaging Teachers and Students in Evaluating Technology Use

Teachers make decisions about technology use in their classrooms but, as has been shared, many lack confidence in their use of technology (Education Week Research Center, 2016) and/or the training (Office of Educational Technology, 2017). Technological Pedagogical Content Knowledge (TPACK) offers a framework for teachers to consider the interconnections between content knowledge (CK), pedagogic knowledge (PK), and technological knowledge (TK). The diagram from TPACK.org illustrates that framework.

The SAMR Model (Puentedura, 2009) offers teachers a tool to help them evaluate technology use. The SAMR Model is a framework that places classroom technology use into four categories, following the SAMR acronym: substitution, augmentation, modification, and redefinition. The model can help teachers think about how they

SOURCE: http://tpack.org/ The below rights-free image is the only one hosted by TPACK.ORG.

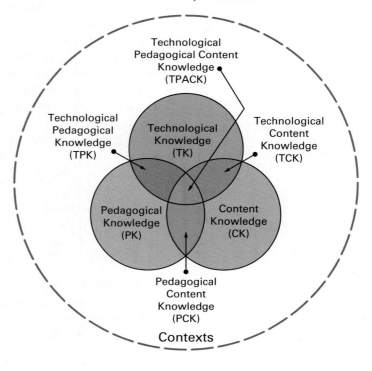

are using technology across a spectrum from substitution with no functional change in teaching and learning to redefinition of teaching and learning tasks due to the use of technology. Puentedura (2009) sees *substitution* and *augmentation* as uses of technology that enhance learning, while *modification* and *redefinition* are uses of technology that can transform learning. He defines the four categories of technology use in his model this way:

- **Enhancement**
  - *Substitution:* Tech acts as a direct tool substitute, with no functional change
  - *Augmentation:* Tech acts as a direct tool substitute, with functional improvement

- **Transformation**
  - *Modification:* Tech allows for significant task redesign
  - *Redefinition:* Tech allows for the creation of new tasks, previously inconceivable

We can apply the SAMR Model to an example of students in a middle school science classroom who are working on a writing up a lab report on water quality samples they have taken from a stream that runs by their school. After analyzing the samples, students could write down their findings in a report using paper and pen or pencil but could, alternatively, use a word processing program on a computer (*substitution*) or write it up with team members in a Google Docs document, thus allowing for others to comment and collaborate on the report (*augmentation*). Taking this further, the teacher could work with students to create a website or blog for the project so that students could post a series of short reports and digital images of their work (*modification*). Students could create digital videos of their work and post them to YouTube or another video streaming site and could use them to engage students in other schools in a discussion of their work or share with community members to brainstorm solutions and generate action around improving water quality (*redefinition*).

Cummings (2012) stated that the SAMR Model is meant to "facilitate the acquisition of proficiency in modern consumer technologies and software for both staff and students with the hope of promoting 21st century skills." Research suggests that teacher knowledge and use of the SAMR Model can help to change teaching practices by encouraging them to integrate technology at higher levels—moving beyond substitution and augmentation (Savignano, 2017). In an analysis of SAMR and TPACK models, Hilton (2016) found that both models have value but differ in orientation of technology. The SAMR Model seems to "place greater emphasis on students as the primary subjects, whereas TPACK focuses on the teacher" (Hilton, 2016, p. 72).

Along with the benefits of interactive Web texts come the risks of quality control. Because a hyperlink can take the reader to potentially untested sites, students need to be taught from an early age how to evaluate the links they come across and how to use them wisely. There are many models for helping students to search effectively online. Don Leu and his New Literacies Research Team at the University of Connecticut have come up with a framework for student practice that uses four different lenses when evaluating online resources: (1) examining what bias the site may contain; (2) determining how reliable the site is; (3) determining the accuracy of information on the site; and (4) synthesizing the information presented on the site in a meaningful way (see Figure 2.1).

Tools such as the CRAAP test (Blakeslee, 2004) provide students with structured options for evaluating information obtained from Internet searches.

The CRAAP test is an acronym that stands for *currency, relevance, authority, accuracy,* and *purpose.* It is particularly well suited to helping students evaluate Web-based information in and outside of an academic setting (Lewis, 2018). The CRAAP test can help students consider the following when evaluating sources of information:

- **Currency**: the timeliness of information
  - When was the information produced or published?
  - Is the information up to date?
  - Has the information been revised?

Figure 2.1 A Framework for Critically Evaluating Websites

Bias and Stance

- Identify, evaluate, and recognize that all websites have an agenda, perspective, or bias.
- Identify and evaluate bias, given a website with a clear bias.
- Identify and evaluate the author of a website whenever visiting an important new site.
- Use information about the author of a site to evaluate how information will be biased at that site.

Reliability

- Investigate multiple sources to compare and contrast the reliability of information. Identify several markers that may affect reliability such as:

  Is this a commercial site?
  Is the author an authoritative source (e.g., professor, scientist, librarian, etc.)?
  Does the website have links that are broken?
  Does the information make sense?
  Does the author include links to other reliable websites?
  Does the website contain numerous typos?
  Does the URL provide any clues to reliability?
  Do the images or videos appear to be altered?

- Understand that Wikipedia is a reasonable, but imperfect, portal of information.
- Identify the general purpose of a website (entertainment, educational, commercial, persuasive, exchange of information, social, etc.).

- Identify the form of a website (e.g., blog, forum, advertisement, informational website, commercial website, government website, etc.) and use this information when considering reliability.

Accuracy

- Evaluate information based on the degree to which it is likely to be accurate by verifying and consulting alternative and/or especially reliable sources.

Synthesize Information

- Understand both the specific information related to the task as well as the broader context within which that information is located.
- Synthesize information from multiple media sources, including written prose, audio, visual, video, and/or tables and graphs.
- Separate relevant information from irrelevant information.
- Organize information effectively.
- Manage multiple sources both on- and offline, including:

  Choose tools to meet the needs of managing information, including file folders, electronic file folders, notebooks, e-mail, and so on.
  Cite sources.
  Take notes with paper and pencil, when appropriate.
  Take notes with a word processor, when appropriate.
  Type notes using shortcut strokes such as highlight/cut/copy/paste.

SOURCE: Leu, D. J., Coiro, J., Castek, J., Hartman, D. K., Henry, L. A., & Reinking, D. (2008). Research on instruction and assessment in the new literacies of online reading comprehension. In C. C. Block, S. Parris, & P. Afflerbach (Eds.), *Comprehension instruction: Research-based best practices.* New York: Guilford Press. Reprinted by permission of Guilford Press.

- **Relevance**: the importance of the information
  - Does the information relate to your topic?
  - Is the information at an appropriate level for your audience?
  - Have you looked at a variety of sources in addition to this one?

- **Authority**: the source of the information
  - Who is the author or publisher of the information?
  - Is this a credible source for this information?
  - Do the URL or site reveal anything about the author or source? (.com = commercial, .edu = educational, .gov = U.S. government)
  - Is there contact information, such as an address or e-mail?

- **Accuracy**: the truthfulness and correctness of the content
  - Where does the information come from?
  - Are credible sources cited?
  - Can the information be verified by other sources?
  - Does the tone and language seem free of bias and emotion?

- **Purpose**: the reason the information exists
  - What is the purpose of the information (to inform, teach, sell, or entertain)?
  - Do the authors make clear their purposes or intent?
  - Does the information seem impartial and objective?
  - Are there political, personal, religious, cultural, or other biases?

	Title of page you are evaluating:	Title of page you are evaluating:
1. Look at the URL:		
Personal page or site?		
What type of domain is it? Appropriate for the content?	__ .com __ .org/.net __ .edu __ .gov/mil/us __ non-U.S.____ __ other:	__ .com __ .org/.net __ .edu __ .gov/mil/us __ non-U.S.____ __ other:
Who is the publisher? Does the publisher make sense? Does it correspond to the name of the site?	Publisher or domain name:	Publisher or domain name:
2. Scan the page, looking for answers to these questions:		
Who wrote the page?	__ Email __ Name:	__ Email __ Name:
Is there a date? Is it current or old?	Date _____ Current enough?	Date _____ Current enough?
Credentials on this subject?	Evidence?	Evidence?
3. Look for these indicators of quality:		
Are sources well documented?		
Is the information complete? Is it altered or made up?		
Are there links to other sources? Do they work?		
Are other viewpoints included? Is the information biased?		
4. What do others say about the site?		
Who links to this site? Check search engines.	Many or few? Opinions of it?	Many or few? Opinions of it?
Is this page rated in a directory? http://about.com		
Look up the author on a search engine.		
5. Does it all add up?		
Why was this page put out on the Web?	__ Inform, facts, data __ Explain __ Persuade __ Sell __ Entice __ Share __ Other:	__ Inform, facts, data __ Explain __ Persuade __ Sell __ Entice __ Share __ Other:
Possibly ironic? Satire or parody?		
Is the information as good as other sources?		

An entertaining and instructive way to help students see how easily readers of the Internet can be misled is to show them some of the well-known hoax sites, such as the Male Pregnancy site that purports to follow a man through the first recorded male pregnancy. Students can list and discuss design elements of the hoax sites that make them seem as if they are presenting legitimate information. Hoax sites, such as Mind Control Deflector, The Dog Island, and Northwest Tree Octopus, can be used to teach students the principle that not all sites that appear to be valid are, in fact, valid.

Lubniewski, McArthur, and Harriott (2018) have developed the App Checklist for Educators (ACE), which provides teachers with a tool to evaluate instructional apps available for iPads and other digital tablets. ACE considers student interest, design features, connections to curriculum, instruction features, and ratings and reviews.

However, in a post-truth, "fake news" era in which social media plays a greater role in information and news dissemination, some scholars suggest that students need more than checklists or rubrics to evaluate websites (Breakstone et al., 2018). They argue that we need to help students do more than review fact-checking websites but develop the skills to fact check on their own. Scholars suggest that students need to gain media literacy skills (Little, 2018).

MyLab Education **Self-Check 2.1**

MyLab Education **Application Exercises 2.1:**
Using Technology to Support Content Area Instruction

Strategies for Writing to Learn

2.2 Describe the strategies for writing to learn in content area classes, including how they incorporate multiliteracies.

Writing is an essential tool in a new literacies classroom. Many of the instructional strategies associated with multimodal learning feature writing in one form or another. As we explain in Chapter 9, writing to learn is an essential component of literacy and learning across all disciplines because students are often expected to represent their knowledge through writing. What makes the new literacies applications different is that the concept of "writing" has expanded to include creating multimodal texts such as audio, video, images, and texts that blend these elements together with print. Authorship has become more fluid; with tools that foster greater collaboration across both time and space and texts, the use of digital mixing and remixing has blurred the boundaries of authorship.

There are many applications for writing with multiple representations of text. Student representations of content in a Google Slides presentation and Prezi are types of writing activities that allow them to think about and share core ideas and concepts with classmates and others. However, with new literacies, students have at their command the ability to think and learn with content not only using print but also graphics, sound, and video. A common project, for example, in social studies classrooms is to have students do historical research and share their findings in a digital format. For example, a group of students in a high school civics class learning about the Gilded Age in the United States came across the photographs of Jacob Riis, who documented the squalid living conditions in New York City slums in the late 1800s. The students, many of whom lived in a low-income urban neighborhood, read about Riis's book *How the Other Half Lives* (Riis & Museum of the City of New York, 1971), published in 1890. They worked with their teacher to create a video exposé exploring how "the other half" lived in their community. They videotaped interviews with members of the community and created their own video. Students in a middle-grades science class studied the ecosystems around their school using a crowdsourcing app called iNaturalist that allowed them to photograph and identify species of plants and animals and add their finds to the database of flora and fauna on iNaturalist. Students in the class used this information to create a website and blog to document their work and share it with members of the community.

For additional ideas and lessons for multimodal writing, explore the lesson ideas described in Figure 2.2.

Although we live in a new media age, some educators are concerned that technology is "degrading" literacy: that today's students are so tuned in to their smartphones and social media that written communication will come to look more like Instagram posts and phone texts. Some fear that student writing will include emojis and text shorthand such as LOL and BRB ("laugh out loud" and "be right back"). It's clear, however, that what many people are doing on their digital devices is a form of reading and writing and that these new literacies are shaping our communication in ways we never could have envisioned just 20 years ago. A Pew Research Center report (Purcell, Buchanan & Friedrich, 2013) based on results of a survey of 2,462 Advanced Placement (AP) and National Writing Project (NWP) teachers suggests that educators worry that students' use of digital writing tools has some undesirable effects, including making their writing less formal. However, they also cite positive benefits, including:

- 96% agree (including 52% who strongly agree) that digital technologies "allow students to share their work with a wider and more varied audience"
- 79% agree (23% strongly agree) that these tools "encourage greater collaboration among students"
- 78% agree (26% strongly agree) that digital technologies "encourage student creativity and personal expression"

Figure 2.2 Related Read/Write/Think Lesson Plans

These lesson plans elaborate on ideas suggested in this chapter. ReadWriteThink is a joint project of the International Reading Association and the National Council of Teachers of English. See the ReadWriteThink website for more ideas.

Expressing Understanding of Content Through Photography and Reflection

Students choose photographs from websites and use those to create two-minute scripts in which they explore the facts and their feelings about the topic. They use presentation software like PowerPoint or Prezi to record their narrative using the images as illustrations.

Blogging About Utopian Societies

As part of the study of utopian literature, students create their own vision for a utopian society and describe it in a blog. As they work on the details describing their world, other students provide feedback. The final product is evaluated using a rubric.

Critical Media Literacy: Commercial Advertising

This unit provides students with the opportunity to look at mass media and advertising through a critical lens that helps them become more aware of the quantity of mass media and mass media's impact on their lives.

Collaborative Internet Research: A Local Research Project

This project immerses students in a decade of history in their local community. Small groups of students work together researching different topics within that period of time. Specific roles are suggested for the students, which helps foster collaboration and distribute the work fairly.

Defining Literacy in a Digital World

Students create an inventory of personal texts they use in their lives, which helps them recognize the rich and varied formats (print, visual, audio) that text takes. Students redefine literacy in their own lives as they share their lists and discuss the importance of multiple text forms.

Using Wikis to Catalog Protest Songs

Protest songs have long been a way to combat racism, sexism, poverty, war, and homophobia. In this lesson, students pair up to research and analyze both contemporary and historical protest songs, posting their ideas to a class wiki.

Teachers have found ways to use technology to help students with the writing process (Davis & McGrail, 2009; Hicks, 2013). This includes the use of digital tools such as blogs, wikis, and websites (de Ramirez, 2013; West, 2013), digital tablets and e-readers (Chambers et al., 2018; McCrea, 2013), and social media (Martin et al., 2018; Snow, 2017). See Figure 2.3.

Clearly, educators around the world see the reality and potential of new reading and writing forms; and as research suggests (Cordero et al., 2018; Yelland, 2018), these digital tools (texts and technologies) have become integrated into teaching and learning in many classrooms. Learners will need to have practice in navigating the rich sources of communication that are available in greater abundance and in more alternative forms than ever before. Writing provides many opportunities to learn in a new literacies-centered classroom. Let's take a closer look at some of the communication tools that teachers can use to engage and empower writing to learn.

Figure 2.3 *Writing, Technology, and Teens:* Summary of Findings

- Even though teens are heavily embedded in a tech-rich world, they do not believe that communication over the Internet or text messaging is writing.
- The impact of technology on writing is hardly a frivolous issue because most believe that good writing is important to teens' future success.
- Teens are motivated to write by relevant topics, high expectations, an interested audience, and opportunities to write creatively.
- Writing for school is a nearly everyday activity for teens, but most assignments are short.
- Teens believe that the writing instruction they receive in school could be improved.
- Nonschool writing, while less common than school writing, is still widespread among teens.
- Multichannel teens and gadget owners do not write any more—or less—than their counterparts, but bloggers are more prolific.
- Teens more often write by hand for both out-of-school writing and schoolwork.
- As tech savvy as they are, teens do not believe that writing with computers makes a big difference in the quality of their writing.
- Parents are generally more positive than their teen children about the effect of computers and text-based communication tools on their child's writing.
- Teens enjoy nonschool writing and, to a lesser extent, the writing they do for school.

SOURCE: Lenhart, A., Arafeh, S., Smith, A., & Rankin Macgill, A. (2008). *Writing, technology, and teens.* Washington, DC: Pew Internet & American Life Project. Retrieved May 2009 from http://www.pewinternet.org/~media/Files/Reports/2008/PIP_Writing_Report_FINAL3.pdf. Reprinted by permission.

Blogs, Websites, and Wikis

Readers frequently access information from collaborative texts found online in the form of *blogs* and *websites* or *wikis*.

BLOGS AND VLOGS   **Blogs**, short for *weblogs,* are essentially online journals or diaries that often include personal accounts of life experiences, such as narrative accounts of travel, interests, hobbies, and how-to information. Blogs can range from stream-of-consciousness accounts to serious information about politics, social issues, beliefs, and experiences using text, photos, GIFs, video, and audio. Video blogs, or **vlogs**, are common on platforms such as YouTube, Vimeo, Facebook, and Instagram. Some teachers assign students to read preselected blogs related to class projects and make comments on the blogs, and then report back to the class, perhaps in the form of their own student blogs. A class can set up its own blog to post and share academic content or communicate with parents and families, and students can create personal blogs for projects or to document writing. Commonly used sites to host blogs are WordPress, Blogger, Kidblog and Edublogs.

Blogs can be set up so that only members of the class can access them and only the blog owner can post entries. The teacher can be notified via e-mail each time an entry is posted or a comment is made so that appropriateness of content can be monitored. Teachers are using blogs for such functions as classroom management, learning logs and online notebooks, class discussions, and, of course, personal expression (Echlin, 2007). Blogs can also be used as e-portfolios. When introducing blogs, it's important to establish guidelines for blogging, such as those suggested in Figure 2.4.

An interesting blogging project called Youth Voices attempts to bring together schools from around the world as students write blog entries and collaborate on various writing activities. The project represents a school-based social network that was started in 2003 by a group of teachers participating in the National Writing Project. Students are also allowed and encouraged to create their own groups about topics as diverse as rap music and world peace.

As they communicate with each other online about their various topics of inquiry, students are expected to adhere to some simple, but direct, rules of conduct:

- Speak directly to the student or teacher whose post you are responding to.
- Quote from the post or describe specific details (of an image or video).
- Relate the work to your own experiences or to another text, image, video, or audio that this one reminds you of.
- Be encouraging and generous with your remarks; end on a positive note.

Figure 2.4 Student Blogging Guidelines

1. Avoid inappropriate language. When engaging in online discussions of a classroom topic, comments should be related to the content of the post and should not involve gossiping, bullying, "chat talk," or non-content-related explanations or observations.

2. Blog posts should be respectful, constructive, and on-topic and add meaningful content to the online discussion. The goal of classroom-related blogging is to share knowledge of the topic and to advance the online discussion. Whenever possible, end a post with a question so your readers will have something to think about as they prepare their responses.

3. Approach blogging as an activity that leads to a "published" piece of writing. Resist reacting to a post without first thinking about the topic, what you already know about the topic, or what questions you might raise to advance the discussion. Then respond to the post, but also take the time to proofread, revise, and edit your comments before you submit them for others to read. Check also for correct spelling and grammar.

4. Avoid providing personal information, photos, or videos with your image in your blogs. Classroom-related sites for blogging may be open to the public to view. You never know who will read your posts.

5. Reply to all or most of your comments. Use references and resources, but do not plagiarize.

Following these guidelines leads to a greater citizenship potential for students, as they will increasingly have to collaborate and interact with people online over the course of their lives.

WEBSITES AND WIKIS Wikis are websites that foster collaboration. Readers and contributors seek to build knowledge on a specific topic and upload the text to a common environment. *Wiki* is a Hawaiian word meaning "fast" and has come to signify a collaboratively built text in which volunteers contribute facts and help to edit and shape the presentation of the information. Some teachers use sites such as PBworks to host wikis that they build with their students, but many use websites created with webhosting sites such as WordPress, Google Sites, Wix, Weebly, and iPage. Most of these have free options but also subscription (paid) options with more features. These website-building platforms offer the collaborative nature of wikis but with the aesthetic appeal of a website. Students and teachers can select from an array of themes and upload images, post videos, and write text. Such website building can also serve to facilitate a discussion about the advantages and pitfalls of using wikis and websites for information: When anyone and everyone can contribute information to a wiki or website, readers need to make sure the information being read is accurate.

Online Discussions

The use of class discussion blogs and, more recently, learning management systems (LMS) such as Canvas, Schoology, and Edmodo have made online discussion a part of learning in many classrooms. These digital writing and communication tools allow students to participate in *threaded discussions* in and out of class. **Threaded discussions** are designed to involve students in the exploration of texts and topics under study. In the process of doing so, learners are often engaged in problem solving, reflection, and critical thinking.

In an online discussion, small groups of students in a class are connected through a digital medium such as an Internet-based forum or discussion board. *Google Hangouts* is another popular, free option that teachers have used for discussion forums, while other teachers use social media tools such as Facebook, Twitter, and Instagram. Whatever platform is used to establish an online discussion, it is important that the site used is secure and can be accessed only with a password. It should also be easy to navigate and have instructions on how to use and participate in discussions.

When used for instructional purposes, online discussions allow a teacher or students to post questions or introduce a topic for students to read about from various sources and reflect upon. The teacher can create small groups with each getting a different question or topic for discussion. Within their small groups, learners then respond to the question with their own posts over time.

Online discussion groups may be selected by the teacher or self-selected by the students themselves. Each learner in a group works individually to inquire into the topic (or respond to a question) and gather information using online and/or offline informational sources. In a literature class, for example, online discussion may be involved in a discussion of a short story or novel; in an American history class, threaded or online discussions may be used for gathering information online, from a textbook, and/or from supplementary texts in order to respond to a question posted by the teacher; in an eighth-grade science class, students may be studying global warming by searching for information on the Internet and discussing it in a blog. These discussions are *asynchronous*; in other words, discussion is not simultaneous as in face-to-face exchanges among participants in FaceTime or Skype discussions. Asynchronous online discussions allow students the time to search for and gather information as well as read, think, and reflect on the topic or question before responding. Within the framework of an asynchronous online discussion, a teacher can participate in every group and monitor several groups at once because discussions are not occurring in real time.

Research shows that online discussion can serve to provide students with a safe space for discussion that fosters community (Chadha, 2018) and can help build disciplinary or content knowledge (Nachowitz, 2018). Research also suggests that online discussions can help to build critical-thinking skills in students (Gokhale & Machina, 2018).

NETIQUETTE IN ONLINE DISCUSSIONS   The idea behind online discussion is to be collaborative, not combative. Before beginning an online discussion as a classroom activity, a teacher should review and emphasize the rules of *netiquette* when posting a response online. **Netiquette**—a "cyber word"—refers to the social code and rules of network communication. The term is derived from the words *network* and *etiquette*. When students are engaged in online discussions and other forms of online communication, it is imperative that they follow netiquette rules. First and foremost, they are to treat other students in online discussions with respect and courtesy. They shouldn't attack another student for his or her ideas. This is not to say they can't disagree with another's comments, but they should be respectful of the student who made them. Moreover, no one student should dominate a discussion with multiple posts.

Consider the following netiquette suggestions for student interactions in online forums, adapted from Online Student Expectations (2012):

- Respect the privacy of classmates and what they share.
- Ask for clarification if a posting is difficult to understand.
- Recognize that exposure to another group member's response and comments is part of the learning experience, even though you may personally disagree with the comments.
- Before posting a comment, ask whether you would make the same comment in a face-to-face discussion.
- Keep in mind that something that would be inappropriate in a face-to-face classroom discussion is also inappropriate in an online discussion.

GUIDELINES FOR ONLINE DISCUSSIONS   Planning instruction, a topic we discuss in detail in Chapter 5, is essential to the success of online discussions in the classroom. McVerry (2007) suggests following four stages of implementation that include organizing online discussions, modeling the skills students need to effectively post online, facilitating and managing the group discussions as they take place online, and assessing the quality of students' posts. When organizing an online discussion, teachers need to ask themselves:

- What are the goals and objectives of the online discussion?
- What are the rules and conventions students should follow in making a post?
- How many posts will students be required to make? How long should a post be?
- Will small groups in the class receive the same question or different questions?
- How much choice should students have in how the discussion unfolds?

Providing explicit instruction that models what is expected of students when making posts online is another important instructional component that will help to ensure the success of online discussions. Begin by walking students through the use of the technology needed to engage in discussions. Also model and discuss models of high-quality posts from past classes. Once the online discussions begin, continue to model the process by participating in the online discussion with teacher posts that help facilitate the conversations occurring among students.

Facilitating online discussions is especially important, especially if students lack confidence, are unsure of themselves, or do not participate fully in the discussions. Some students may lack prior knowledge or interest in the subject under discussion. Others may fear being wrong or lack experience with online communication. Whatever the case, the teacher needs to guide and manage online discussions on an ongoing basis to ensure that students participate successfully and are engaged in higher levels of thinking than merely regurgitating a fact or two.

Several well-established guidelines to facilitate online discussions are suggested below:

- Use one question or topic to begin an online discussion.
- Assign a different question or topic to each group in the class.
- Vary the writing approach for responding to questions. For example, students can respond to topics with comments or opinions supported by text study, they can engage in role-play according to assigned roles, or they can raise reflective questions for further response and study.
- Lead the conversation in order to model effective posting, set the tone for discussion, and keep students focused on the topic.

Allow students to disagree with a post in a collaborative, not combative, manner. In addition to these suggestions, it is important to be specific with instructions. For example, you might instruct students to respond to a posted question with a paragraph of at least five to eight sentences or more, depending on the purpose of the discussion. Also, you might ask students to respond to other student posts with a minimum of two or three sentences. Research on netiquette suggests that it plays an important role in addressing cyberbullying in schools (Tate, 2017) and is important in the implementation of effective online learning environments (Farmer & Ramsdale, 2016).

When assessing, the quality of students' writings in an online discussion should be viewed as a culminating learning experience, not a paper-and-pencil test of students' ability to write in this particular medium. In other words, assessment is *authentic*. Engaging in authentic assessment, as we discuss in detail in Chapter 4, is a collaborative experience between teacher and students. The use of a *rubric* is one way to have students play a role in judging the quality of their writing and participation in an online discussion. A rubric provides students with a detailed framework and guidelines about what is expected of them in online discussions.

The design of the rubric depends on the instructional objective(s) for student engagement and learning in the online discussion. The teacher develops performance criteria that are directly tied to the lesson's objectives. Each criterion is then judged along several dimensions. Teachers use rubrics to rate student performance; however, students may also use a rubric as a self-assessment tool to improve performance. Figure 2.5 contains a sample rubric that covers the basic criteria for an online discussion.

SHARED DOCUMENT SPACES Many teachers have leveraged shared document spaces like Google Drive and Dropbox to allow their students to share content and collaborate in learning. Google Drive (formerly Google Docs) features word processing, presentation, and spreadsheet software that is accessible from the Web or the "cloud." Students can create a document in one of these formats and invite others as coauthors or readers. Teachers and students can access these documents from virtually any computer that has an Internet connection to comment, contribute, or edit. These documents can be pulled up on computers at school or from home (or a coffee shop). Other kinds of files can also be shared through Google Drive. Other file-sharing sites, like Dropbox, OneDrive, and iCloud, allow teachers and students to post files to an online folder with secure access to only those who have permission.

The advantage of having students document their process via a blog, wiki, collaborative website, and/or shared document space is that teachers and students have a running record of the journey taken. Research by Krishnan, Cusimano, Wang & Yim (2018) suggests that students value collaborative writing using tools like Google Docs and may be willing to write longer essays than those they author alone. Research with English language learners supports the value of collaborative and individual writing using Google Docs (Alsubaie & Ashuraidah, 2017). Moreover, a teacher can guide and redirect student

Figure 2.5 Rubric Example for an Online Discussion

Category	1	2	3	4
Participation and Timeliness	Does not respond to posts in a timely manner	Occasionally responds to posts in a timely manner	Frequently responds to posts within a 24-hour period	Consistently responds to posts within a 24-hour period
Relevance	Comments and opinions do not relate to discussion of content	Most posts are off-topic or offer little insight into discussion content	Frequently posts comments related to topic and prompts further discussion of content	Consistently posts comments related to topic and prompts further discussion of content
Content Quality	Does not express ideas clearly; posts are not supported with specific ideas or examples	Minimal development of topic; posts are occasionally supported with specific ideas and examples	Posts are frequently supported with specific ideas and examples	Ideas are fully developed and consistently supported by ideas and examples
Writing Mechanics	Poor spelling and grammar in most posts; posts are hastily written with noticeable errors	Errors in spelling and grammar in some posts	Few spelling or grammatical errors	Consistently uses grammatically correct language with correct spelling

TOTAL

COMMENTS:

thinking, if necessary, via a well-placed blog comment or comment in a wiki forum. The fact that the teacher's comment appears alongside the students' gives a clear visual representation that the teacher and students are colearners.

MyLab Education **Self-Check 2.2**

MyLab Education **Application Exercise 2.2:**
Using Multimodal Writing in Content Area Classrooms

Approaches to Multimodal Learning

2.3   Describe several multimodal learning practices and explain how learning strategies have been impacted by the use of technology in classrooms.

New literacies and new technologies have ushered in new approaches to teaching and learning. Teachers and students are using hybrid learning formats that bring together, or blend, traditional literacies and learning with new literacies and learning. Along the spectrum of blended learning approaches is the flipped-classroom model, which reverses or "flips" the traditional paradigm for teaching and learning by delivering content outside the classroom using technology to share readings, lectures, and notes so that activities often used as homework are done in class. These blended learning approaches provide students with opportunities to think and learn in multimodal environments, participate in online discussions, and use tools such as blogs, wikis, websites and apps.

Blended and Hybrid Learning

While technology is a key component of blended learning, Linder (2017) writes that in hybrid classroom settings, "face-to-face activities are often combined with technology-mediated activities so that there is more active learning in the face-to-face setting as well as more intentional guidance when students are learning outside the classroom" (p. 11). Imbriale (2013) argues that it is not a fundamental redesign of the classroom but of time outside the classroom. He suggests that blended learning is a way to personalize learning and offer more control to students in and out of the classroom. Staker and Horn suggest models for blended learning (Staker, Horn & Innosight Institute, 2012) including:

- The **Rotation model** allows students to rotate on a fixed schedule or at the teacher's discretion between learning modalities, at least one of which is online learning. The flipped classroom is one type of rotation model.

- The **Flex model** is a program in which content and instruction are delivered primarily by the Internet; students move on an individually customized, fluid schedule among learning modalities; and the teacher of record is on-site.

- The **Self-blend model** describes a scenario in which students choose to take one or more courses entirely online to supplement their traditional courses and the teacher of record is the online teacher. This is used in many high schools where students take online courses through universities and community colleges as part of their high school experience.

These models span a range from more traditional brick-and-mortar learning (rotation and flex) to more fully online (self-blend) and allow teachers to draw on tools and technologies such as shared documents (Google Docs); blogs and online discussions; digital texts, including audio and video; websites; and learning apps on tablets and laptops.

An English language arts teacher can create a blended reading and writing workshop to allow students to discuss and work collaboratively. In some respects, it is similar in purpose to a writing workshop or a reading workshop in an English language arts classroom (Atwell, 2014). In writing and reading workshops, teachers who use a workshop model in their classrooms set aside regularly scheduled time for students to engage in reading and writing activities. In the process of doing so, students share their reading and writing with others in the class, typically in small-group book discussions or writing response groups. During workshop time, teachers often conduct "minilessons" to respond to content- and process-related issues and problems students are having during reading or writing sessions. Minilessons may also be designed for strategy instruction. In these explicit instructional situations, a teacher may take several minutes or more of workshop time to show students how to use a set of procedures that will help them become more skillful as readers and writers.

In the blended approach to the reading and writing workshop, the teacher can draw on traditional print texts as well as online sources texts on e-readers or through websites, such as myON, that offer libraries of digital texts that schools can subscribe to. The teacher can have students discuss books in small groups in person in class but also through a class blog or in an online discussion on the class learning management system, such as Canvas or Schoology. For writing, students can draft ideas in class in their notebooks but extend those ideas to a Google Docs document where the group can collaborate in class and from outside of class. The group can use any of a number of digital tools, such as Prezi or ThingLink, to create multimedia reports to document what they are learning.

In a biology class that is studying population ecology, the teacher has students read articles from websites, including the *National Geographic* and *Smithsonian Magazine* websites, to supplement information from their textbook. Students post notes in a shared Padlet created by the teacher and then use an online graphing calculator at Desmos to graph different predictions based on data from the World Health Organization and United Nations to explore different possible human population growth patterns. The teacher then has the students work in teams on a lab, using the Virtual Biology Lab website, and share their findings in class using Google Slides so that all students can see the results and findings. Before taking an exam in class, the teacher posts links to Khan Academy videos on her class Schoology page as a source of out-of-class review.

In blended learning, teachers and students draw on traditional and online resources to foster engagement during class and extend learning beyond the classroom. Depending on the level of access students have to the Internet, teachers may be able flip elements of learning and have students view informational and how-to videos, read online texts, or conduct virtual experiments outside of class so that class time can be used in other ways.

Internet Inquiries

The Internet inquiry engages students in research using information sources on the Internet. Inquiries can be conducted individually or collaboratively and often take one or more weeks to complete. **Internet inquiries** are typically part of larger thematic units and are used in conjunction with Internet workshops. The Internet inquiry broadly follows the tenets of a discovery model for investigating hypotheses or questions. Students are invited to (1) generate questions about a topic or theme under discussion in class, (2) search for information on the Internet to answer the questions, (3) analyze the information, (4) compose a report or some other form of dissemination related to findings, and (5) share findings with the whole class.

Question generation is one of the keys to conducting a successful Internet inquiry. Many teachers use the KWL strategy (what I **K**now, what I **W**ant to learn, and what I did **L**earn) (see Chapter 7) to help students raise questions. Others use brainstorming techniques to generate a list of questions. Whatever strategy is used for generating questions, the questions should come from the students rather than the teacher whenever possible. An Internet workshop minilesson might focus on asking good questions to guide the information search. A teacher may also use workshop time to scaffold instruction on how to use search engines effectively or how to record and analyze information using "inquiry charts" (I-charts) and other tools for recording and analyzing findings.

AN INTERNET INQUIRY IN ELEMENTARY SCIENCE   Students in a third-grade classroom have been engaged in a thematic unit related to the study of monarch butterflies. As part of the unit, the class developed a plan for raising monarch butterflies and visited several websites on the Internet related to specific workshop activities that the teacher had planned. The students also read trade books such as *Discovering Butterflies* by Douglas Florian, *Monarch Butterfly* by Gail Gibbons, and *Butterflies (Animal World)* by Donna Bailey. As a result of these classroom learning experiences, the class embarked on an Internet inquiry designed around the students' "personal questions" regarding monarch butterflies. The class first brainstormed a list of questions that the teacher recorded on chart paper. Some of the questions included: "Do monarch butterflies eat anything besides milkweed?," "Are monarch butterflies found all over the world?," "How long do monarch butterflies live?," and "How many eggs can one monarch butterfly lay?" Using the list of questions on chart paper as a guide, each student selected three questions to research. The questions did not have to come from the brainstormed list, but could be generated by students as they engaged in their information search on the Internet and in trade books that were available in the classroom.

The teacher explained to students how to use I-charts to record information they found on individual websites or in trade books related to each of their questions. Across the top of the I-chart, each student recorded his or her name and a personal question about monarch butterflies. The remainder of the I-chart was divided into two columns. The left column provided space for a student to record the name of the website or trade book that was used to gather information. The right column was used to record information that students found to answer their questions. Across the bottom of the I-chart was space for students to record "new questions" based on their research.

When students completed their information searches, they collected their I-charts and began analyzing the information to answer their questions. The teacher facilitated the analysis by walking around the room, helping individuals as needs arose. Students used the analysis to create a poster portraying the answers to their questions. The inquiry culminated with a "poster session" in which students shared the information related to their questions.

WEBQUESTS   WebQuests have been a popular instructional model for engaging learners on the Internet. A **WebQuest** is a teacher-designed webpage that packages various learning tasks and activities for students to complete using Internet resources. WebQuests are typically organized around several components: introduction, task, process, resources, learning advice, and conclusion.

The introduction to a WebQuest provides an overview of the learning opportunity available to the students. Often the introduction places the learner(s) in a hypothetical situation somewhat similar to RAFT writing activities (see Chapter 9). As a result, students are assigned a role and a purpose for engaging in the learning activity. The task component of the WebQuest describes the task(s) students will complete and lists the questions that guide the information search. The process component outlines the steps and procedures students will follow to complete the learning task. The resources component of a WebQuest provides links to information resources on the Internet that students will need to access to complete the learning task. The "learning advice" component provides directions to students on how to organize information, whether in outlines, time lines, graphic organizers (see Chapter 10), notebook entries such as the double-entry journal format (see Chapter 5), or I-charts. And, finally, the conclusion to the WebQuest brings closure to the activity and summarizes what students should have learned from participation in the WebQuest.

Adapting Learning Strategies with Technology

Computers and digital technologies are both a "facilitator of knowledge and medium for literacy" (Biancarosa & Snow, 2004). Technology allows teachers to plan higher levels of differentiation and to meet the academic needs of a greater number of students during instruction. Electronic databases, such as EBSCO and ProQuest, provide middle and high school students a wealth of information at various degrees of reading difficulty, allowing teachers to find multiple texts related to course content.

MyLab Education
Response Journal 2.2
Consider how technology has evolved throughout your educational experience as a student and, perhaps, as a teacher. How has technology impacted your experiences in classrooms and schools and changed learning for you?

For example, ProQuest has created the ProQuest Central and STEM Database and EBSCO has Explora, search engines designed for middle and high school students. Explora and ProQuest Central provide adolescent learners with appropriate research tools for easily obtaining the information that they seek from these databases, including electronic magazines, newspapers, biographies, and videos. Students can also search databases by topic and limit their searches according to appropriate *Lexile reading levels* (see Chapter 4 for a discussion of Lexile reading levels and other tools for determining the readability or difficulty level of texts).

Using electronic texts, content area teachers can create flexible groups within their classes that allow all students access to text appropriate to their needs and relevant to course objectives. In addition, interactive computer programs, such as Newsela and CommonLit, offer a range of textual material adapted to students' reading levels, while ReadWorks provides a range of nonfiction material for teachers to use with K–12 students. Many of these texts and websites adapt to a student's reading performance by providing text passages that are written at a level consistent with the student's needs. Doing so increases the comprehensibility of the text for the student. Additionally, such programs provide students with immediate feedback on assignments and allow teachers to track student progress toward goals outlined in intervention plans. Some programs that include voice recognition software allow students to record themselves while reading so that miscues can be tracked and appropriate feedback provided. These resources can be useful for providing students with multiple interactions with texts and for offering independent practice (Biancarosa & Snow, 2004).

Many learning strategies such as KWL and RAFT can be adapted using Web 2.0 technologies. For example, comprehension strategies such as KWL and 3-2-1 can be created in shared document sites like Google Drive. Teachers can post research and writing tools, such as I-charts and RAFT, to a Dropbox folder or their class wiki. Twitter can be used in place of question cards to generate questions for a class discussion.

Here is a chart with digital adaptations of some of the strategies presented in this book.

Strategy and Purpose	Digital Adaptation	Benefits
IEPC: Imagine, Elaborate, Predict, and Confirm *(see Chapter 6)* Helps students who struggle with reading to create mental images.	Teacher creates the IEPC chart in Google Docs and provides link to students. This allows students to use IEPC during class and from other locations, such as the library or home.	• Extends use of IEPC beyond the classroom. • Fosters collaboration among students working in groups.
KWL Strategy *(see Chapter 7)* Engages students in active text learning.	Can be created on Google Slides or a website such as Padlet so KWL becomes a tool used by groups of students or all students in a class throughout a unit that can be accessed in and out of class using computers, tablets, or smartphones.	• Encourages active text learning throughout a unit using multiple sources of information. • Provides access to a single KWL chart to all students who collaborate in its creation.
Vocabulary Self-Collection Strategy *(see Chapter 8)* Promotes long-term acquisition of language in a subject area.	Teacher uses a "sticky note" app or website like Padlet so students can post words to a class or group digital word wall.	• Creates a document that can be accessed in and out of class by multiple students. • Provides a document that can be added to over time (no fear of "losing your homework").
Double-Entry Journal *(see Chapter 9)* Scaffolds comprehension and increases engagement in learning.	Apps like Evernote, Pages, and Notes can turn a smartphone or iPad into a digital notebook. Have students use a program or app like Pages or Evernote to create a two-column journal entry. They can take notes as they read ("What is it?") and then extend those notes through reflection and dialogue ("What does it mean to you?").	• Creates a shareable document that can be submitted electronically to the teacher and others. • Submissions can be posted to class wikis or shared document spaces so students can access the notes of other students. • Students can create a double-entry journal in an app or software that they use throughout a semester or year.

As we see through these examples, adapting learning strategies like IEPC, KWL, and double-entry journals using Web 2.0 tools extends their use beyond the classroom. It also provides an opportunity for students to use these tools collaboratively, which can further student engagement in learning.

MyLab Education **Self-Check 2.3**

MyLab Education **Application Exercise 2.3:**
Using Internet Inquiries to Support Content Knowledge
✓ Check Your Understanding

Looking Back Looking Forward

Digital texts and media are highly engaging and interactive and make it possible to interact and collaborate in the classroom and beyond. Text learning opportunities in multimodal environments are interactive, enhance communication, engage students in multimedia, create opportunities for inquiry through information searches and retrieval, and support socially mediated learning. Reading and writing with digital technologies have changed the way we think about literacy and learning. Whether students are navigating the Internet or interacting and collaborating with others through online discussions, blogs, websites, and apps, an array of electronic text learning experiences awaits them. Various instructional approaches, including blended and hybrid learning, Internet inquiries, Internet projects, and WebQuests, are approaches to online learning in various content areas.

In the next chapter, we take a closer look at one type of student who often struggles with content literacy tasks: the English Learner. With every passing year, the United States becomes more linguistically and culturally diverse. English Learners struggle with academic language and are often tracked in lower-ability classes than language majority students. The dropout rate among English Learners is alarmingly high. How can content area teachers plan instruction to account for cultural and linguistic differences in their classrooms? Let's read to find out.

eResources

Conduct an Internet inquiry of your own by going to International Literacy Association's Reading Online and Global SchoolNet's Internet Project Registry. Study reports and Internet projects in your content area.

Find out more about WebQuests by searching the Internet for sites that describe this learning strategy and offer lesson plan ideas. Explore existing WebQuests and consider how you could create a WebQuest for your content area.

Observe how a high school teacher engages students in inquiry activities in a flipped classroom.

Chapter 3
Culturally Responsive Teaching in Diverse Classrooms

Written in collaboration with Elena King, Ph.D.

Rawpixel.com/Shutterstock

 Chapter Overview and Learning Outcomes

After reading this chapter, you should be able to:

3.1 Define culturally relevant pedagogy and explain how these principles should shape instruction.

3.2 Explain funds of knowledge and how teachers' incorporation of students' funds of knowledge can impact content area learning.

3.3 Explain the impact of linguistic diversity on content area instruction.

3.4 Describe the ways in which instruction can be adapted to meet the needs of English Learners.

Organizing Principle

Teachers respond to linguistic and cultural differences by scaffolding instruction in culturally responsive classrooms.

Over the past several decades, political, social, and economic changes have brought an increasingly diverse group of students to U.S. schools from all across the globe. The National Center for Education Statistics found that, in the 2015–2016 school year, 51% of all U.S. students in public schools were non-White (Geiger, 2018). English Learners (ELs) comprised 9.4% of the total student population, nearly 4.6 million students, during the 2014–2015 school year. In urban schools, the average enrollment of ELs was 14.2% (U.S. Department of Education, 2017). Educational standards across the United States require all learners to acquire English proficiency regardless of their cultural or socioeconomic backgrounds. When it comes to teaching and learning with texts in diverse classrooms, we're all in the same boat, and the ship's captain—the teacher—is responsible for the welfare of everyone on board.

Different languages and cultures are gifts in our classrooms; they bring us fresh perspectives and vibrant new ideas that have the potential to animate classroom interactions. Yet cultural and linguistic diversity can make teaching with texts more challenging. Often, students from different backgrounds struggle with literacy and learning in traditional academic contexts. As a result, the strengths that they bring to instructional situations can go untapped. In order to make connections between the content that we teach and students' cultures and languages, teachers can draw on the ideas of *culturally responsive teaching* or **culturally relevant pedagogy** (Gay, 1995; 2000). Ladson-Billings (1995) defines this as a pedagogy "that empowers students to maintain cultural integrity, while succeeding academically." This type of pedagogy involves a thoughtfulness and reflectiveness on the part of the teacher to ensure that the ship is being steered in the right direction.

The increasing number of culturally and linguistically diverse learners (CLDs) demands literacy instruction that is strategic and culturally responsive. This includes high learning expectations so that all students have access to opportunities that will support them in meeting the college and career reading standards emphasized in schools today. The *Every Student Succeeds Act* (ESSA), a reauthorization of the Elementary and Secondary Education Act, emphasizes the importance of providing appropriate instruction, a challenging curriculum, and additional supports to meet diverse learner needs.

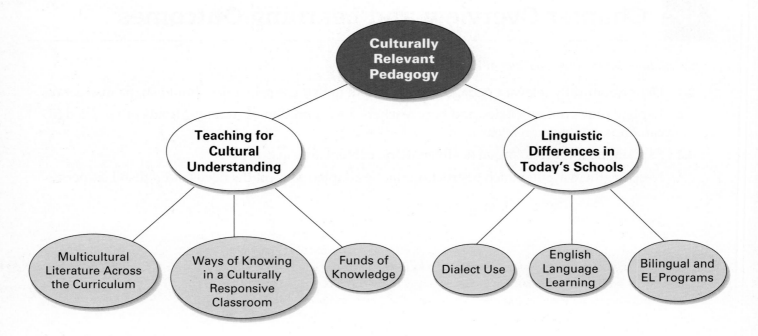

How can teachers be responsive to linguistic and cultural diversity in their classrooms while maintaining high standards for content literacy and learning? Understanding cultural and linguistic differences is an important first step, as the organizing principle of this chapter suggests: Teachers respond to linguistic and cultural differences by scaffolding instruction in culturally responsive classrooms.

Frame of Mind

1. Why are today's classrooms more diverse than they were several decades ago?
2. What are some of the cultural and linguistic differences that students from various racial and ethnic backgrounds bring to classroom learning situations?
3. What is culturally responsive instruction, and what does it look like in content area classrooms?
4. What can a teacher do to implement culturally responsive instruction in a content area classroom?
5. Why do English Learners struggle with content literacy tasks, and how does sheltered instruction make content more accessible to them while providing additional language support?

The purpose of this chapter is to help teachers successfully respond to linguistic and cultural differences in their classrooms and to promote academic achievement for all learners. In culturally responsive classrooms, teachers draw on students' backgrounds, languages, and experiences to make connections with the discipline-specific content under study while creating social-emotional connections that allow students' brains to do the hard work of thinking in sophisticated ways. In doing so, students find that academic experiences are more meaningful in their lives and therefore become more interested and focused on content area learning. This is not a simple process but one that occurs in small increments and by using a variety of strategies as teachers and students experience positive results.

Nicole, a high school civics and history teacher, describes how she fosters a learning environment that resonates with her African American students and English Learners as she works with them to develop their own civic voices. Her voice is featured in Box 3.1. Lakia, a middle school English language arts teacher, captures the essence of culturally responsive instruction by using "rap parties" to teach code-switching. Her voice is featured in Box 3.2. As diverse learners become more engaged, they are motivated to focus on topics, complete assignments, and contribute to the classroom community with thoughtful questions and appropriate comments (Izzo & Schmidt, 2006; Schmidt & Finkbeiner, 2006).

Most people, other than those who study culture, probably don't think much about what it means to be immersed in a culture, just as fish probably don't think much about what it means to be immersed in water. The term *culture* represents a complex and multidimensional concept at best. Culture has been defined by Peregoy and Boyle (2008) as the shared beliefs, values, and rule-governed patterns of behavior that define a group and are required for group membership. On one level are the surface features of a culture—its foods, dress, holidays, and celebrations. On another level are deeper elements, which include not only values and belief systems but also "family structures and child-rearing practices, language and non-verbal communication, expectations, gender roles, biases—all the fundamentals of life that affect learning" (Díaz-Rico & Weed, 2002, p. 197).

Language and culture are inextricably connected. Native speakers learn language in social settings, and in the process, they also learn their culture's norms for using language. As you might expect, different cultures have different rules that are culturally defined and culturally specific. When a student's norms differ from the teacher's expectations, communication can be hindered. It is not always easy for teachers to detect when they are using the language norms of their own culture or miscommunicating with students who have different dialects and cultural norms than they do.

MyLab Education
Response Journal 3.1
If you currently are teaching, how would you describe the cultural and linguistic differences of your students? If you are studying to be a teacher, describe the cultural and linguistic differences that existed in your school experiences.

Culturally Relevant Pedagogy

3.1 Define culturally relevant pedagogy and explain how these principles should shape instruction.

The rapidly changing demography of the United States and its schools is transforming the country into a society that is increasingly *multicultural*. Guofang Li (2009), for example, explored the extent to which cultural and linguistic diversity prevails in today's classrooms as well as the conflicts and struggles of diverse learners trying to make sense of a curriculum dominated by mainstream European American cultures. Li's book *Multicultural Families, Home Literacies, and Mainstream Schooling* provides a powerful lens for better understanding the lives and home practices of underrepresented students and their families.

In diverse classrooms, cultural and linguistic sensitivity is a crucial first step in working with students to meet academic standards. Developing and implementing culturally relevant instructional practices require that other elements be considered. Brown-Jeffy and Cooper (2011) drew on the work of Gay (1995, 2000) and Ladson-Billings (1995) to identify five essential themes in their framework for culturally relevant pedagogy:

1. Identity and achievement
2. Equity and excellence
3. Developmental appropriateness
4. Teaching the whole child
5. Student–teacher relationships

Identity and achievement considers the identity of both student and teacher. It invites teachers to consider the cultural lens through which they see themselves as well as the lens through which students view their own identities. Brown-Jeffy and Cooper (2011, p. 73) point out that "cultural awareness does not and should not include colorblindness or race-neutral policies." In American culture, it is often seen as impolite to point out any differences among race or ethnicity. However, Nieto and Bode (2012) describe colorblindness, the refusal to see racial differences, and colormuteness, the refusal to discuss those differences, as part of a larger problem because race has a strong history in American society. By opening their classrooms to discussions about the power issues embedded in race in the United States, educators can create greater equity in the classroom and help their students understand differences without seeing deficits. To this end, the home cultures of students should be acknowledged, valued, and used as a tool for learning.

Equity and excellence emphasizes that students have different learning needs. To be effective, teachers need to recognize that achieving equity doesn't mean that every student receives the same instruction or the same type of support. It means that each student receives what he or she needs to understand the concepts presented. Equity and excellence also encompasses the belief that the curriculum area content needs to make sense within those cultures represented in a classroom.

Brown-Jeffy and Cooper's theme of *developmental appropriateness* asks teachers to consider not only whether a concept or activity is appropriate for a student's developmental level, but also how the diversity of the student's culture might affect developmental appropriateness. In other words, teachers are encouraged to consider what might be considered culturally appropriate for students from diverse backgrounds.

Teaching the whole student is related to developmental appropriateness but focuses more on home–school–community collaboration and fostering a supportive learning community for students from diverse backgrounds. Family and community experiences shape the academic identity of students. Understanding these experiences and influences will help a teacher to be sensitive and responsive to diverse student needs.

Finally, *student–teacher relationships* focus on fostering a classroom atmosphere that communicates a message of genuine concern for individual students and effective interactions between teachers, students, and families.

In addition to these elements, Hammond (2015) encourages teachers seeking to develop culturally responsive teaching, to consider new developments in neuroscience. Like Brown-Jeffy and Cooper's description of culturally relevant teaching, Hammond also emphasizes the need to contextualize her students in their sociopolitical histories, establish connections, build trust and use students' cultural understandings to view school. She sees these elements as strongly tied to cognitive science as well. Our brains create new pathways as we learn, but if students do not feel that they are in a nurturing environment, the amygdala sends out signals to induce the stress hormone, cortisol. Hammond writes that "when we look at the stress some students experience in the classroom because they belong to marginalized communities because of race, class, language or gender, we have to understand their safety-threat detection system is already cued to be on the alert for social and psychological threats based on past experiences" (p. 45). If we don't build trust and rapport with students, then their brains may not be in the right frame of mind to learn. Through building trust, listening to students, and creating culturally relevant lesson plans, we can prime students' brains to be engaged.

Sensitivity to cultural and language differences, and a willingness to understand and respond to these differences, enables teachers to teach with greater effectiveness (Sharan, 2010). Similarly, teachers have found that allowing students to interact freely during class discussions is helpful in that it encourages them to explore ideas without the fear of having to speak perfect English. Doing so does not minimize the importance of learning Standard English, but rather, analogous to the writing process, it allows students from diverse backgrounds to have brainstorming and drafting time in their verbal interactions. Teaching for cultural understanding will also make a difference in the way diverse learners respond to instruction. In the following section, we will look at how to engage in culturally responsive teaching.

MyLab Education
Video Example 3.1:
Systems of Knowledge and Interaction
Watch this video to gain insight into systems of knowledge and interactions.

Teaching for Cultural Understanding

It's important to remember that cultural understanding begins with the teacher. As we have already seen at the beginning of this chapter, teachers and students may not always have the same frame of reference for language and culture. That is why the first steps to creating cultural understanding begin with the teacher. In her language and culture course, Varga-Dobai (2018), asks her preservice teachers to investigate their own cultural understandings in a way that allows them to visually connect their own sense of self to their family history through "Cultural Selfies." The cultural selfie project begins with preservice teachers reading articles about funds of knowledge and literacy. Then they collect information about their own lives, investigating four major categories of their identity: self as part of family, community, literary person, and teacher. As preservice teachers learn more about themselves and learn to question what culture and literacy mean to them, they also "become researchers who investigate, ask questions, get to know the families, and listen to the stories children tell" (p. 119). When teachers engage in this type of self-reflective activity, they develop awareness of how their own beliefs are formed by culture. Hammond (2015) describes this awareness as understanding a mental model or schema. By first understanding our own schemas, we can learn to detect how we view the world, and also uncover our own implicit biases or unconscious attitudes and stereotypes. The next step is to listen.

Students have an uncanny ability to detect authenticity. They know when a teacher genuinely cares about them, and this care can be shown by how well a teacher listens. In a busy classroom where high-stakes tests may be the culminating activity, listening and talking with students is sometimes considered a waste of time. However, trust and rapport are paramount for engaging in culturally responsive teaching. Hammond (2015) describes the need for teachers to "listen with grace" (p. 78), which includes the following:

- Give one's full attention to the speaker and to what is being said
- Understand the feeling behind the words and be sensitive to emotions being expressed
- Suspend judgment and listen with compassion
- Honor the speaker's cultural way of communicating

In Box 3.1, civics and history teacher Nicole Lipp describes how she developed a pedagogy of listening over time that helped her build rapport with her students.

Once rapport is built in the classroom, it is time to examine what is being taught and how. Various instructional perspectives reflect different belief systems related to the teaching of multicultural concepts in today's classrooms. Diaz (2001) describes these perspectives within the context of four distinct instructional approaches. In the *contributions approach,* teachers typically emphasize culturally specific celebrations and holidays within the curriculum, such as Martin Luther King Day. The contributions approach reflects the surface level of a culture but does not make provisions for in-depth study of its deeper elements.

Somewhat related to the contributions approach is an instructional perspective that is additive in nature. The *additive approach* underscores the teaching of various themes related to multicultural concepts and issues. These concepts and issues are integrated

Box 3.1 Voices from the Field

Nicole, High School Civics & History Teacher

A Pedagogy Of Listening:

My path to creating a culturally inclusive classroom that meets the needs of diverse learners has been a long one. I was unprepared to meet their needs when I first started. This has been a process, an evolution into genuinely understanding different populations and learning to incorporate their cultures into my class. I grew up in an area of the country where my entire K–12 educational experience was with peers who looked just like me: White and upper middle class. I then spent 4 years at college, where the demographics were pretty similar to where I grew up. So, when it came time to do my student teaching I asked to be placed in a low-income, diverse school so I could push myself out of my comfort zone. I had lived a life where I had very little exposure to diversity and oftentimes believed the many stereotypes and myths surrounding certain groups. I entered student teaching completely unprepared for what was about to happen. I was placed in one of the "worst" schools in the city and given a cooperating teacher who was waiting to retire. I was left alone for six classes a day with a room full of students I had nothing in common with. No matter what I did, they ate me alive. At one point, in my African American history class, a student stood up and called me out on knowing nothing about his culture. He was right. I had no idea what to do.

At 22 years old, I couldn't understand what was happening in my classroom. Now, as an experienced educator, I realize that I had lacked the knowledge needed to have authentic interactions with my students. How do you develop the ability to interact authentically with diverse learners? The first thing you do is listen. Listen to their stories of being refugees; listen to the foods they like and the music they enjoy. Listen to them tell the stories of the arduous journey they took to get here. Ask for their recommendations of restaurants that serve their native food. Research their countries and learn what is happening there. Do everything you can to be armed with information that can help you build a bridge between you and your students. Genuinely understanding their history, the issues that concern them, their culture will allow you to get the kids to move mountains.

Once I learn about their cultures and spend time understanding the issues that are important to them, I work diligently to create a space that is safe for them as soon as they walk into the classroom. Every year, I write my students a letter saying that they are protected and safe in this classroom, and I post this letter on my door. Every day, I make sure my diverse learners are represented by carefully selecting images in my PowerPoints that look like them. I wear T-shirts with messages or images that send positive messages about marginalized groups. I teach civics and history, so I require them to know who their local, state, and national representatives are, and I encourage my students to follow these representatives on Facebook and Twitter. I help them use social media, not as a platform for complaining but as a way for them to have their voices heard as part of a democratic process. We discuss current topics that are relevant to my students, and I show them how to engage in discourse, not debate. Then I listen.

into the curriculum through the development of a thematic unit of study, but overall the curriculum remains relatively the same throughout the year.

When teachers attempt to help students understand diverse ethnic and cultural perspectives by providing them with ongoing opportunities to read about concepts and events, make judgments about them, think critically, and generate their own conclusions and opinions, they are using a *transformative approach*. This approach, combined with the next one, lends itself well to content literacy strategies that emphasize critical analysis and interpretation. According to Diaz (2001), an extension of the transformative approach involves project learning. The *decision-making/social action approach* provides learners with opportunities to engage in activities and projects related to cultural concepts and issues, particularly those issues and problems dealing with social action.

Teachers need to go beyond limiting the content of instructional lessons to celebrations or one-time-only thematic units related to multicultural concepts. Today's teachers need to engage students in literacy and learning experiences that will provide them with the cross-cultural knowledge and skills they will need as future adults in a nation that has become increasingly diverse.

Ladson-Billings (2006, p. 30) explains that culturally relevant pedagogy extends beyond instructional practices: "I argue that the first problem teachers confront is believing that successful teaching for poor students of color is primarily about 'what to do.' Instead, I suggest that the problem is rooted in how we think—the social contexts, about the students, about the curriculum, and about instruction." Ladson-Billings explains that the context of the school, students, and teachers all interact in a way that is not consistent across states, schools, or even classrooms. One of the most important aspects of culturally relevant pedagogy is a critical analysis of what is happening in the classroom and why. Ladson-Billings proposes that teachers not just take on a tutorial role in teaching students the prescribed curriculum, but rather think about their students as a long-term commitment. To this end, teachers need to understand that they are nurturing students to be productive members in a democratic society. (Box 3.2 explains three components of culturally relevant pedagogy.) One way to encourage students to begin to view the world more thoughtfully is by using multicultural literature.

Box 3.2 Understanding the Components of Culturally Relevant Pedagogy

1. *Academic achievement:* In culturally relevant classrooms, teachers understand that student learning is the primary goal. Teachers should spend a significant amount of time thinking about what they ask their students to accomplish and why. This means looking at the curriculum and setting long-term goals for the semester. In the first years of teaching, this can be a difficult task, but one that is necessary so as not to fall into a complacency of assigning tasks simply based on their own past school experiences. Creating a classroom focused on academic achievement requires purposeful assignments to which students can relate and that students can apply to broader learning contexts.

2. *Cultural competence:* Cultural competence in the classroom involves instructing students to recognize and honor aspects of their own cultures while also acquiring access to wider cultures. This does not simply entail having students write reports about their home cultures, but allowing students to understand that cultural references have different meanings to different populations. An example of this was seen during a class discussion about college in an urban, majority African American, high school. A student asked if there are "White" fraternities in colleges. When asked to elaborate, the student explained that he knew several members of Sigma Pi Phi, Kappa Alpha Psi, and Omega Psi Phi—all historically Black fraternities—but did not know if fraternities accepted White students as members. In a different cultural context, fraternities may be seen as predominately White based on media images or the historical nature of fraternities in the United States. Teaching students to understand the historical background of potentially misunderstood references can support them in developing a wider worldview without sacrificing their own culture and beliefs.

3. *Sociopolitical consciousness:* This aspect of culturally relevant pedagogy asks a lot of teachers. It asks them to cross out of comfort zones and understand the structures of their school community, including decisions made by the school board and how social and political issues of housing and health care affect their students. Once teachers have a better understanding of the intersections

of race, socioeconomic status, and history in their communities, they can help guide students to critically analyze these elements as well.

4. *Putting it together:* The United Nations Educational, Scientific and Cultural Organization (UNESCO, 2005) characterizes literacy as a fundamental human right. Making

sure that students receive literacy instruction that promotes social consciousness first begins with the teacher. Teachers, as lifelong learners, must constantly strive to understand the world they live in to make sure that they can guide their students to be able to read the *world* as well as read *words*.

Integrating Multicultural Literature Across the Curriculum

When teachers use multicultural literature in the classroom, they provide students with texts that not only are engaging but also recognize the unique contributions of each culture and the similarities of the human experience across cultures. At the same time, they help nonmainstream cultures appreciate and value their heritage and give all students the benefits of understanding ways of knowing about the world that are different from their own. Choosing multicultural texts to integrate into the curriculum is no easy task. When selecting multicultural literature, Louie (2006) offers the following suggestions for effective teaching practices:

- Consider whether the story is an authentic depiction of the culture it intends to represent.
- Consider the perspectives of the diverse characters in the story.
- Identify the characters' perspectives of events and conflicts.
- Encourage students to relate their own experiences to those portrayed in the text.
- Identify values that shape the conflict–resolution strategies used by characters.
- Discuss how cultural mores and expectations may have influenced a character's decisions and viewpoints.

Braden and Rodriguez (2016) further suggest that once teachers choose a book to study, they also engage in the hard work of teaching students to question the text. In their study of Latino children's books they found that often English was privileged. The books depicted near-perfect or utopian societies, and the authors sometimes only lightly touched on controversial issues such as immigration. Teachers are encouraged to use multicultural texts as a springboard for more complex discussions of race and culture in the United States and globally.

Multicultural Books: A Closer Look

Multicultural books encompass every genre, including picture books, poetry, fiction, and nonfiction. A defining characteristic of multicultural books is their focus on people of color. These books provide diverse students with rich opportunities not only to see themselves reflected in the books they read but also to appreciate and celebrate the experiences of people of color from the past. As such, multicultural books also provide mainstream students with opportunities to learn about other cultures and peoples. For example, Suzanne Fisher Staples's (1991) *Shabanu: Daughter of the Wind* draws readers into the life of a girl growing up among camel-trading nomads in modern Pakistan. Similarly, Linda Crew's (1991) *Children of the River* portrays the challenges faced by Cambodian immigrants as they work to assimilate into the American culture.

Such books can help students understand cultural norms related to family, morality, sex roles, dress, and values of other cultures. Most importantly, however, multicultural literature brings the people of a particular group into focus and can help students realize that in spite of our differences all people share many common emotions, dreams, and hopes for the future. Through interactions with characters representing a variety of cultures, young people begin to view members of parallel cultures as individuals who are unique and yet have universal feelings and experiences. Pam Muñoz Ryan's (2000) *Esperanza Rising* is a wonderful coming-of-age novel focused on a "riches to rags" story of a wealthy young Mexican girl and her mother who end up becoming migrant workers in the fields of California. The book is based on the real-life experiences of the author's grandmother. Teenagers can relate to it because it tells a story of identity and family—common themes in all our lives.

Multicultural books portray members of a wide variety of cultures, including African and African American, Asian and Asian American, Native American, Latino, and so on. It is important to note that there is a difference between being Mexican and being Mexican American. When selecting multicultural books for the classroom, teachers must differentiate between these groups. For example, a Mexican person living in Mexico has remarkably different experiences from a Mexican American person living in the United States. Teachers cannot assume, for example, that a modern Mexican American child will be able to relate to a book about Mexico.

Studying the folklore of diverse cultures is a common practice in schools, especially in the lower grades; however, the protagonists of many folktales are adolescents who have much to say to today's young adults. The human dimension of slavery is powerfully told, for example, in Virginia Hamilton's *The People Could Fly* (1985); true multicultural understanding is also enhanced by her compilation of creation myths titled *In the Beginning* (1988). A host of folktale collections from around the world can add insight to the study of history, social studies, and geography. Folk literature is the "cement" or "mirror" of society (Sutherland & Arbuthnot, 1986, p. 163) and thus gives readers an insider's view of a culture's beliefs and attitudes that is not typically found in textbooks. That said, scholars of multicultural literature caution against using folktales exclusively, a practice that can perpetuate perceptions of exoticism and otherness. Ideally, folktales are typically studied in conjunction with contemporary, realistic depictions of the cultures in question. For example, it would be ideal to pair a substantial library of Chinese folktales about Mulan with more contemporary stories about Chinese American females such as Grace Lin's (2007) *The Year of the Dog* and/or Joyce Lee Wong's (2007) *Seeing Emily*.

Historical fiction can provide a lens into the challenges and perspectives of diverse cultures. Gary Paulsen's (1995) *Nightjohn* chronicles the perils faced by a slave who secretly teaches other slaves to read. The story encourages students to consider the empowering potential of the ability to read both for the characters in the story and for themselves. Similarly, in Helen Hughes Vick's (1998) *Walker of Time,* a Hopi Indian boy goes back in time to view the life from the perspective of the ancients. Similarly, texts that describe the narratives of marginalized groups throughout U.S. history are also important. For example, when teaching a unit on World War II, teachers could include texts about the Japanese internment such as *Looking Like the Enemy: My Story of Imprisonment in Japanese American Internment Camps* (Gruenewald, 2005) and texts about African American women during this time such as *Bitter Fruit: African American Women in World War II* (Honey, 1999). Considering and studying multiple perspectives about any given topic and/or unit only enhance and deepen the content and cultural knowledge; in this way, the lives of our students are further enriched.

While including multicultural texts is an excellent way to engage students in thinking about diverse cultures, Ehst and Hermann-Wilmarth (2014) encourage teachers and students to read critically by examining authors and publishing. To illustrate their point, they examine three multicultural texts: *In Darkness* by Nick Lake (2012), a story set in Haiti after the 2010 earthquake; *Never Fall Down* by Patricia McCormick (2012), based on the true story of Arn Chorn-Pond, a Cambodian labor camp survivor; and *My Name Is Parvana (2012),* by Deborah Ellis, about an attempt to establish a school for girls in

Afghanistan. While all three books can be used to encourage discussion about other cultures and to invite empathy with narrators suffering through horrific world events, Ehst and Hermann-Wilmarth point out that all three authors are White and from privileged societies. While this does not discount them from telling the stories of Shorty, Arn Chorn-Pond and Parvana, it does allow for conversations about the experiences and viewpoints that authors bring to the stories they tell. Ehst and Hermann-Wilmarth also point out that all three texts result in a relatively happy ending. They challenge teachers to resist what they call the "single story of triumph" (p. 28). For example, they write, "The teacher of *In Darkness* might ask her students to investigate the rebuilding efforts in Haiti that continue today." The types of conversations, analyses, and discussions about voice and larger societal injustices are at the cornerstone of culturally responsive teaching.

Many students in today's ethnically diverse urban classrooms prefer books about young people living in challenging circumstances that may parallel their own experiences. These titles describe teens' personal struggles with drugs, gangs, abuse, and similar issues. Many urban students feel a strong connection with characters in these books, for whom daily survival in today's world is often a challenge. Short story anthologies like *Big City Cool: Short Stories About Urban Youth* (Weiss & Weiss, 2002) contain selections by Walter Dean Myers, Amy Tan, and other authors familiar with what it means to grow up in urban America. Geoffrey Canada's (2010) *Fist Stick Knife Gun* chronicles the author's own experiences growing up in the South Bronx and learning the codes of the street. The book provides a vivid depiction of the violence encountered on these urban streets and offers a glimpse into the inner conflict experienced by those who navigate them.

Fran Buss's (2002) *Journey of the Sparrows* depicts the terrifying journey of Salvadoran immigrants as they seek to cross the U.S. border. The memoir *Always Running: La Vida Loca: Gang Days in L.A.* (Rodriguez, 1993) is what high school teacher Carol Jago calls a "disappearing book"—a book that mysteriously leaves the shelves of her classroom library and seldom returns, which is a clear indicator of its popularity. *Always Running* is the controversial memoir of Luis Rodriguez's life in a gang, which was written to get his son to leave gang life and create a different future for himself. Other factual books of interest to urban students include Loung Ung's (2000) *First They Killed My Father: A Daughter of Cambodia Remembers*, which graphically portrays one family's struggle to survive the horrors of the Khmer Rouge in Cambodia. In *Voices from the Fields: Children of Migrant Farm Workers Tell Their Stories* (Atkin, 1993), 10 Mexican American children of migrant farmworkers describe their lives in their own words. One of the young people featured is a gang member, one is an unmarried teenage mother, and one is making plans to attend college and become a physician. The author portrays the uncertainty of their lives, at the same time recognizing the strong bonds that bind these young people to their families.

Research suggests that despite the availability of high-quality and interesting multicultural books, many teachers are not using these books to full advantage. Teachers often cite lack of time and knowledge about these books as reasons for limiting their use (Loh, 2006). Because of the canon or other required readings dictated by the school district, teachers sometimes report that they do not have time or opportunity to expose their students to multicultural books that fall outside of the prescribed curricula.

To learn more about the many resources for identifying multicultural books for students, teachers can refer to lists and guides developed by the Cooperative Children's Book Center, the North Central Regional Educational Laboratory, the American Library Association, and so on. Other sources include magazines such as *Booklist, School Library Journal, Kirkus Review,* and the *Horn Book Magazine.* Lastly, teachers can consider books that have won awards such as the Asian/Pacific American Award for Literature, the International Board on Books for Young People (IBBY) Honour List, the Pura Belpré Award, and the Coretta Scott King Award, among others.

Teachers report that they often fear offending other cultures by choosing the "wrong" book. For this reason, some teachers opt out of using multicultural books altogether (Loh,

2006; Bishop, 2003). The resources mentioned above can help teachers select appropriate multicultural books with confidence and avoid the temptation to ignore diversity in our classroom libraries and in our curricula and instruction.

While it is important for teachers to integrate multicultural literature for their students, choosing to read multicultural texts themselves can help foster new perspectives and encourage teachers to become more sociologically mindful. Books such as Su's (2009) *I Love Yous Are for White People: A Memoir*; Grennan's (2011) *Little Princes: One Man's Promise to Bring Home the Lost Children of Nepal*; and Nazario's (2006) *Enrique's Journey: The Story of a Boy's Dangerous Odyssey to Reunite with His Mother* all have elements that help teachers understand the complicated nature of acculturation, literacy, and education. By creating their own reading lists, teachers may further understand how texts can extend conversations of diversity and the complicated history of diversity within the United States.

MyLab Education **Self-Check 3.1**

MyLab Education **Application Exercise 3.1:**
Creating a Culturally Relevant Content Area Classroom

Ways of Knowing in a Culturally Responsive Classroom

3.2 Explain funds of knowledge and how teachers' incorporation of students' funds of knowledge can impact content area learning.

It is important to be aware that students from diverse cultural backgrounds bring different ways of knowing, different styles of questioning, and different patterns of interaction to school.

For example, different cultures may place a different emphasis and value on various cognitive activities and styles of questioning. Heath (1983) discovered that African American students experienced academic difficulty in their classrooms partly because of their lack of familiarity with the kinds of questions they were expected to answer in school. Over 20 years later, Delpit (2006) described the same experiences for African American students. In the language of school, a teacher will sometimes pose a question such as "Are you supposed to sharpen your pencil while I'm speaking?" with the implication of "sit down while I'm speaking." The indirect nature of this type of question can be confusing for students who don't share the same linguistic pattern for indirect questioning. These students may respond better to a directive, such as "Sit down while I'm speaking, please."

When teachers became aware of the differences between the kinds of questions they asked and the kinds of questions familiar to the students, they were able to make adjustments in their questioning style. Likewise, when they understood the varied storytelling styles of their students, they were able to encourage and appreciate each style. As a result, the teachers noticed a marked contrast in their students' participation and interest in lessons.

Ways of knowing are intertwined with ways of interacting and learning. Rather than emphasize individual competition, some cultural groups prize group interaction, helping one another, and collaborative activity. Most European cultures emphasize independence and individual achievement over collective mind-sets (Hammond, 2015). In the classroom, this often results in a focus on individual studying and learning where competition is encouraged and self-reliance is privileged. The United States scores a 91 out of 100 points on the Cultural Dimensions Index, which makes it an extremely individualist culture. On the more collectivist side of the index are countries like Guatemala, Ecuador,

Panama, Pakistan, and Venezuela, which all scored under 15 (Hofstede, Hofstede, & Minkov, 2010). These more collectivist cultures emphasize group work, collaboration, and a focus on interdependence. These cultural mismatches can sometimes create issues in the classroom when teachers expect students to adhere to a certain norm of individualism for class learning. When teachers are aware of their students' inclinations toward collectivism, they can create spaces that emphasize group learning. Many students from diverse linguistic and cultural backgrounds are discriminated against not only because of race and language, but also because of their struggles to exist in high-poverty areas. The daily struggles to survive in poverty also yield funds of knowledge that are often overlooked in schools. It is each teacher's responsibility to develop relationships that nourish trust. By drawing on students' interests and popular culture, teachers can make connections that demonstrate a respect for students' lives (Hammond, 2015; Schmidt, 2005a; Schmidt & Lazar, 2011).

When teaching for linguistic and cultural diversity, motivational activities are based on the same principles as those learned for any successful teaching and learning situation. Teachers must draw on students' prior knowledge and interests. Therefore, family and community cultures and languages, popular culture, and individual student interests are all necessary considerations when motivating students for learning. Teachers differentiate instruction and plan for the inclusion of relevant information in their content areas. Ideas interspersed throughout this book will demonstrate and expound on these motivational principles for engaging diverse groups of students in content area classrooms.

Funds of Knowledge

The powerful role that culture plays in shaping students' behaviors and their knowledge of the world often goes unnoticed in classrooms. The concept of *funds of knowledge* provides a framework to recognize a student's interests and the background knowledge that he or she brings to content area concepts (Hedges, Cullen, & Jordon, 2011). Convincing students that their experiences are recognized and valued as they approach new learning situations is particularly challenging when "culturally inherited ways of knowing do not match those privileged in the school curriculum" (Zipin, 2009, p. 317).

MyLab Education
Response Journal 3.2
Think about the funds of knowledge that you possess based on your cultural background and heritage. Describe how you make use (or will make use) of such knowledge in your teaching.

Understanding the sociocultural dynamics of home and community gives us a broader perspective on the worldviews students bring to school. Culturally and linguistically diverse students typically come from working-class families where their individual lives are inseparable from the social dynamics of the household and community in which they live. A teacher who makes a point of understanding the home culture, ethnic background, and community of students is in a better position (1) to understand the kinds of knowledge that culturally diverse students bring to learning situations and (2) to adjust the curriculum to their sociocultural strengths.

Moll (1994) contends that much is to be gained from understanding the "social networks" of the households in a cultural group. These networks are crucial to families, who often engage in exchanging "funds of knowledge." These funds of knowledge may represent occupationally related skills and information that families share with one another as a means of economic survival. Moll argues that the social and cultural resources that students bring to school—their funds of knowledge—are rarely tapped in classroom learning contexts. Using the community's rich resources and funds of knowledge builds on one of students' greatest assets: the social networks established within a cultural group. One such resource is its people. Moll (1994, p. 194) puts it this way: "One has to believe that there are diverse types of people that can be helpful in the classroom even though they do not have professional credentials. Wisdom and imagination are distributed in the same way among professional and nonprofessional groups."

In a middle school classroom, Mexican American students in Tucson, Arizona, engage in a study of construction that includes inquiry into the history of dwellings and different ways of building structures. The students have access to a wide array of reading materials from the library to focus their investigation: trade books, magazines, newspapers, and reference resources, to name a few. The teacher builds on students' reading by inviting parents and community members to speak to them about their jobs in the construction industry. For example, a father visits the class to describe his work as a mason. Similarly, Cuero (2010) describes the experience of a Mexican American fifth-grade student who lacked confidence in her reading and writing abilities. For this student, a dialogue journal correspondence with her teacher in her native language of Spanish allowed her to describe her transnational experiences through vivid written expression and a strong voice. The implications of this experience support the importance of validating and including students' home language experiences and the fund of knowledge they might bring to their new academic pursuits.

Drawing on Students' Funds of Knowledge Across Content Areas

Drawing on funds of knowledge can help students to make meaningful connections between the often abstract concepts addressed in content area classes and the application of those concepts in the world outside of the classroom. Understanding how individuals in various occupations and professions use the same knowledge and concepts presented in their content area classes helps to make course material more relevant to students. This heightened relevance leads to higher levels of engagement and retention. Hearing the experiences of community and family members can help students open their minds to future occupations that may be of interest to them.

For the teacher, a first step in this process is to become aware of the experiences and backgrounds of family members and community members that may help students to better understand how content area knowledge can be used. This can be done through projects such as Family Dialogue Journals. In this type of written exchange, the teacher can create and establish relationships in which parents and students can help shape the experiences and curriculum in the class (Moll, 2015). Another way to learn about families is by sending out an electronic or paper survey to family members. Through surveys, teachers can learn about the types of jobs in which parents or other family members engage as well as their hobbies or interests that may have applicability to a particular content area. Family and community members can contribute to content area classrooms in different ways. Some, for example, may be willing to visit the classroom and to serve as a guest speaker on a topic of interest. Schmidt and Ma (2006) suggest ways in which a variety of community members can share their knowledge and talents with students in content areas such as music, art, dance, mathematics, science, culinary arts, and vocational studies. Examples include:

- A local musician can discuss the instruments he or she uses when performing and may even bring in examples of these instruments for students to see and use.

- An artist can share the different types of materials used in his or her work or hobby and can encourage students to explore different ways in which those materials can be used.

- Dancers who represent different cultures, such as Latino, African, Asian, or Arabic, can show students the dance steps used as well as the accompanying music and clothing that help to showcase the history and richness of the culture represented.

- A professional chef, cook, or baker can visit a chemistry class to demonstrate and discuss how various ingredients, such as yeast, sugar, and hot and cold water, interact with one another. Students can then predict the interactions of ingredient combinations of their own creation and conduct experiments to check the accuracy of their predictions and the connections to chemical formulas they have studied in class.

- An engineer, architect, or tradesman can visit a mathematics class to showcase some of the tools of his or her respective trade and to explain how knowledge of mathematical concepts is applied when using these tools. A contractor, for example, may discuss how the dimensions pictured on a blueprint are transformed into a full-scale structure.

- A systems engineer from a local company can visit a technology classroom to explain both the hardware and software involved in supporting such a business. In addition, someone in the field of information technology can express to students the need for ongoing professional development to stay up to date in the advancements that affect this field.

- Local small-business entrepreneurs can be motivational in the classroom. They can raise awareness for these businesses within the community. They can show students the necessity of a well-rounded education, as owners must handle many areas of the business, such as managing, accounting, and public relations. Also, entrepreneurs embody the creativity required to see what a community needs and find a way to fill that need.

For a family or community member, serving as an interviewee for students who are researching connections between a content area and a particular occupation could be an alternative to giving a full-class demonstration or presentation. Additionally, with proper planning, businesses often allow students to visit their place of employment so that they can observe the profession in action.

Whether students are interviewing people in various professions, participating in the visit of a guest speaker, or visiting a company or business, teachers can help to make these experiences meaningful by following a model similar to the Before-During-After (B-D-A) lesson model described in Chapter 5. Schmidt and Ma (2006) suggest that, before a presentation, visit, or interview, teachers and students should work together to prepare for the experience by activating students' prior knowledge about the occupation or hobby to be investigated, listing what they would like to learn about how work in that field is carried out, and compiling questions that they might pose to the guest speaker or interviewee. During the presentation, visit, or interview, it is helpful for students to be engaged in the experience by asking questions, making connections to their content area studies, and, if applicable, actively participating in appropriate aspects of the presentation. After the experience, the teacher can continue to encourage students to investigate how new content area concepts may be used in occupations about which they have learned. Through connections between units of study in school and the experiences of their family and community members, the relevance of the content area studies can become more apparent.

Another way to activate and build on students' funds of knowledge is through biography-driven instruction (BDI), or getting to know students holistically (Herrera, Holmes, & Kavimandan, 2012). BDI asks teachers to understand their students through four dimensions: sociocultural, linguistic, cognitive, and academic. Teachers develop strategies that support and draw on students learning in three phases:

- Activation: In the first phase, the teacher observes and discovers what students already know—what are their funds of knowledge from the home and community.

- Connection: In this phase, the teacher uses the students' knowledge already observed in the activation phase to connect to the new learning.

- Affirmation: Finally, the teacher uses authentic assessments rather than standardized tests to document learning and affirm the student's new learning to their original funds of knowledge.

An example of BDI in use would be through the strategy described by Herrera and Murry (2016) as Linking Language. In this strategy, the teacher begins to activate prior knowledge by posting a series of pictures around the room. Students rotate through the images in groups and use markers to write on the pictures describing anything they see, feel, or know about the images. After each group has written on the images (in either English or their home language), the groups then circle all words or ideas that are similar. The groups share out with the class, and then the teacher asks them to make predictions about the lesson based on the posters. These predictions can then be connected to the lesson. Students' engagement increases when they are actively involved in learning and believe that they have something to offer to the class.

Characteristics of Culturally Responsive Instruction

Culturally responsive instruction, as you can see, is related to students' ways of knowing, motivation for learning, and their funds of knowledge. In other words, instruction that is responsive to cultural differences in the classroom makes connections with students' backgrounds, origins, and interests to teach the required standards associated with a curriculum. Learning becomes more relevant as teachers draw on students' prior knowledge and experiences. So, how can teachers tell that culturally responsive instruction is happening in classrooms?

Schmidt (2003) used the research on culturally responsive instruction to develop seven key characteristics of culturally responsive instruction. When lessons in secondary mathematics, social studies, science, language, and English content areas incorporate the seven characteristics, students stay more focused, become invested in what is happening, and actually step onto the road of academic success and social achievement (Tatum, 2000). Additionally, literacy development is promoted because reading, writing, listening, speaking, and viewing provide the foundation for the seven characteristics of culturally responsive teaching (Schmidt, 2005a, (2005b). These characteristics, with brief definitions, follow (Schmidt, 2003):

1. *High expectations.* Supporting students as they develop the literacy appropriate to their ages and abilities.
2. *Positive relationships with families and community.* Demonstrating clear connections with student families and communities in terms of curriculum content and relationships.
3. *Cultural sensitivity.* Reshaped curriculum mediated for culturally valued knowledge, connecting with the standards-based curriculum as well as individual students' cultural backgrounds.
4. *Active teaching methods.* Involving students in a variety of reading, writing, listening, speaking, and viewing behaviors throughout the lesson plan.
5. *Teacher as facilitator.* Presenting information; giving directions; summarizing responses; and working with small groups, pairs, and individuals.
6. *Student control of portions of the lesson ("healthy hum").* Talking at conversation levels around the topic studied while completing assignments in small groups and pairs.
7. *Instruction around groups and pairs to create low anxiety.* Completing assignments individually, but usually in small groups or pairs, with time to share ideas and think critically about the work.

Culturally responsive instruction helps to create classroom learning environments that celebrate languages and cultures and encourage high academic standards (Herrera & Murry, 2016). Literacy coaches support content area teachers in the development of classroom learning environments by providing support around the following ideas and others found in this chapter:

- Label objects in the classroom, such as desk, chair, book, teacher, students, and so on, in two or three languages. Have the student or a family member assist the teacher if necessary. Labeling is common in primary classrooms. It works great in secondary classrooms too. A daily practice pronouncing the vocabulary highlights other cultures and languages. The small amount of time necessary to implement this idea not only recognizes linguistic differences but also teaches and brings an awareness to second language learning.

- Invite students or family members to present information or artifacts from their country of origin. Many students have jewelry and art objects they can share. Storytelling in some cultures is a powerful record of history.
- Use paired learning.
- Give opportunities for students to speak, read, or write in their home language each day in school.
- Include visuals wherever and whenever possible, such as videos, images projected on SMART Boards, pictures, and posters when teaching.
- Present opportunities for hands-on classroom experiences and field trips.
- Put up the daily class schedule and provide a predictable environment for learning.
- Have a map of the world or globe for students to view.
- Use choral reading for students with limited English fluency.
- Have bilingual dictionaries available.
- Use nonfiction picture books to teach key concepts in content areas.
- Include different cultures in curriculum topics (e.g., famous Latino chemists, famous Chinese artists).
- Encourage drawing and writing in both the target and home languages.
- Keep a personal journal.
- Help students keep an assignment pad.

Technology also has a place within culturally responsive instruction. Teachers can use technology in ways that will prepare students for college and careers by teaching them to interact with peers and the community in collaborative ways across multiple media and social outlets (ILA, 2018). Teachers can create lessons that allow students to explore and analyze the use of technology. For example, as part of a unit study of social justice movements, students might explore the rhetorical structure of hashtags in social networks. Similarly, video editing software may support student-created documentaries in a social studies class (ILA, 2018). Because many students already know how to use social media, the emphasis is on allowing students to make meaning from and interpret the use of technology within contexts of content area learning. The use of mobile devices and online forums in classrooms may give voice to those students who are less confident about their abilities to speak aloud in class.

Video creation can also support culturally relevant pedagogy. In one middle school, for example, students created personal videos rich in narration about their lives. Students gained important literacy skills in writing narratives and scripts, and teachers and students were able to establish a strong home–school connection through the videos (Mackay & Strickland, 2018). Blogging sites, such as Edublogs.org, can provide students with platforms for reading and responding to texts (Trumble & Mills, 2016). Blogs can be shared with families and friends, who can contribute questions and comments, thus furthering home–school connections.

Teachers or students can use screencasting programs and apps, such as Screencast-O-Matic or ShowMe, on their computers or phones to record and narrate videos (Trumble & Mills, 2016). When students use these technologies, they learn skills such as writing, revising, editing, narrating, and creating visual representation. When teachers use these to aid in instruction, they can create lectures that students can watch over again on their phones to help them study. To use technology as part of culturally responsive instruction, teachers should be aware of students' access to technologies outside of the school environment.

MyLab Education **Self-Check 3.2**

MyLab Education **Application Exercise 3.2:**
Valuing Students' Funds of Knowledge in a Content Area Classroom

Linguistic Differences in Today's Schools

3.3   Explain the impact of linguistic diversity on content area instruction.

Linguistic differences among today's student population are strikingly evident in many school districts throughout the United States. From the East Coast to the West Coast and from the Gulf to the northern Great Lakes, the increasingly large number of immigrants from non-European nations is influencing how content area teachers approach instruction. It is no exaggeration to suggest that in some large urban school districts, more than 175 different languages are spoken (Charlotte-Mecklenburg Schools, 2014).

When immigrant students maintain a strong identification with their culture and native language, they are more likely to succeed academically, and they have more positive self-concepts about their ability to learn (Banks, 2001; Diaz, 2001; Garcia, 2002). Schools, however, tend to view linguistically diverse students whose first language is one other than English from a deficit model, not a difference model. For these English Learners, instructional practices currently are compensatory in nature: "That is, they are premised on the assumption that language diversity is an illness that needs to be cured" (Diaz, 2001, p. 159).

In addition, regional variations in language usage, commonly known as dialects, are a complicated issue for teachers. In truth, as explained in Box 3.3, all English language users speak a dialect of English, which is rooted in such factors as age, gender, socioeconomic status, and the region of the country where one was born and grew up. Even presidents of the United States speak dialects! The difficulty with dialect differences in the classroom is the *value* assigned to dialects—the perceived goodness or badness of one language variation over another. Linguists explain that language variations are neither good nor bad and that such judgments are often about the people who make them rather than about clarity or precision (Ahearn, 2012). Gee (2012) argues quite convincingly that teachers need to respect and recognize the strengths of diverse learners who use dialects in the classroom.

MyLab Education
Video Example 3.2:
How Can Educators Help Students to Learn English
Watch this video to hear one educator's advice on helping students learn English.

Box 3.3 Evidence-Based Practices

Standard English Is Not the Only English

Scholars have long disagreed on the actual number of dialects in the United States, but one point they agree on is that everyone speaks a *dialect* of English. In the companion website for PBS's series "Do You Speak American?," Fought (2005) writes: "Do you think because I'm a professor, I don't speak a dialect? I do. I speak Valley Girl! My native dialect is 'Valley Girl' English, a variety of California English that shares many features with other Californian ways of speaking." Fought readily acknowledges her dialect; however, Redd and Webb (2005) explain that "much of the public wrongly assumes that the standard dialect *is* the English language because it is the dialect promoted by the people in power" (p. 8). In fact, to call it "standard" actually creates some of the bias. Dialects of English all contain their own phonological and morphological attributes. Linguists like to think of language as dynamic, meaning it constantly

changes. The people who live in an area as well as those who enter an area influence dialect. African American Vernacular English (AAVE), Ebonics, or Black English Vernacular, as it is also known, may have evolved as a fusion of West African languages and English. What is most interesting about AAVE is that while other dialects are typically defined by the regions where they are spoken, AAVE spans the geography of the United States and can be found across age and socioeconomic groups (Redd & Webb, 2005).

During their careers, educators will encounter a variety of dialects, languages, and accents on a regular basis. Exploring languages and dialects and the similarities and differences among them can be an encouraging way to both legitimize and teach students about each other and the multiple dialects used in and out of the classroom.

Dialect Use in the Classroom

Cultural variation in the use of language has a strong influence on literacy learning. Even though students whose first language is not English do not have full control of English grammatical structures, pronunciation, and vocabulary, they can engage in reading and writing activities (Peregoy & Boyle, 2008). When students use their own culturally acceptable conversational style to talk and write about ideas they read in texts, they are likely to become more content literate and to improve their literacy skills.

Language *differences* should not be mistaken for language *deficits* among culturally diverse students. National reports have found that the literacy levels of African American and Hispanic/Latino students are continually low (National Assessment of Educational Progress, 2009; National Center for Education Statistics, 2011). The rising attention on student achievement has challenged both researchers and practitioners to find innovative ways to reach and teach urban learners and, more specifically, the demographic of students who may experience academic difficulties as a result of differences between their home or native language and the academic language of the school setting.

To bridge the gap between the language forms students use at home and the academic language of school, teachers are encouraged to engage students in interacting by demonstrating *code-switching* (Landsman & Lewis, 2006; Wheeler & Swords, 2006) and linguistic dexterity (Paris, 2012). Code-switching, or register shifting, is used to explain the interplay of language structures using phonological and syntactical variations, for example, starting a conversation in one language and interspersing it with words from another language or shifting between different formalities or style of language (Ahearn, 2012). Paris (2012) describes language dexterity as "the ability to use a range of language practices in a multiethnic society" (p. 96). A teacher of a diverse group of students might welcome class members into the room by saying, "Hello," "Hola," or "What's up?" Students learn that their response to a peer might not be the same as a response to an adult. For example, a student might tell a peer, "Nope, thas wrong," versus telling the teller, "No, ma'am. That answer is incorrect." Technology tools such as blogging, digital study boards, and chat rooms can help students to learn "codes" of language and their variations as determined by the environment (Tarasiuk, 2010). Additionally, Scott (2013) created "rap parties" (explained in Box 3.4) in which students could find ways, through music and journaling, to appropriate language by understanding the differences between conversational speech and academic talk.

Similarly, Martínez (2010) states that the use of Spanglish—a blend of Spanish and English among English Learners—can be a helpful tool for supporting students' development of academic literacy. By code-switching, for example, where students begin a sentence in one language and switch to the other language, Martínez found that English Learners were better able to communicate the nuances of meaning in creative and intelligent ways. The use of Spanglish helped them to draw upon and transfer the language skills that they already possessed.

Shouldn't students from minority backgrounds learn to use Standard English? The question is a rhetorical one. As teachers, our stance toward the use of standard American English is critical. Standard English, often thought of as the "news broadcast–type" English used in the conduct of business, is the language of the dominant mainstream culture in U.S. society—the "culture of power," according to Delpit (1988). Delpit explains that the rules and codes of the culture of power, including the rules and codes for language use, are acquired by students from mainstream backgrounds through interaction with their families. Minority students, however, whose families are outside the mainstream culture, do not acquire the same rules and codes. If students are going to have access to opportunities in mainstream society, schools must acquaint students from minority backgrounds with the rules and codes of the culture of power. Not making Standard English accessible to students from minority backgrounds puts them at a disadvantage in competing with their mainstream counterparts.

Box 3.4 Voices from the Field

Lakia, Middle School English Language Arts Teacher

Rap It Out: Code-Switching for the Urban Classroom

My first 3 years of teaching were spent at an all-male middle charter school in an urban district. Most of my students were African American or Hispanic and came from homes with low or lower-middle socioeconomic backgrounds. The school in which I worked welcomed students from all campuses within the district. It was the school that one would attend after getting expelled from his home school. For this reason, my students were often labeled as the "throw-backs" of the district. In other words, it appeared to some teachers and administrators that schooling would have little influence on students because they assumed, based on students' academic and behavioral attitudes, that education was not valued by the students themselves; and as a result, they should just be "thrown back" to their urban neighborhoods and ghettoes. As a teacher, my role would be ever crucial in helping them to see education as a vehicle to their own liberation from societal circumstances as opposed to education as an imposed ideology.

As many novice educators can relate, at the start of the school year, I was overwhelmed with the instructional pacing guides, curriculum resources, and other pedagogical tools that were given to help me prepare. As the weeks went by, I found myself desperately trying to teach and "preach" the importance of subject–verb agreement and sentence structure to my students in such a way that the lessons and overall instruction became somewhat methodical and routine. And for a while, I thought I was achieving what needed to be done in my classroom; "they are learning," I said to myself, "they get it." But I soon realized these were *just* lessons and instruction to them; as quickly as they left my class, those lessons were left at the door. It was then that I decided to have an honest conversation with my sixth-, seventh-, and eighth-grade groups about what they were learning.

Students were not hesitant to share how meaningless the English language arts (ELA) lessons were because around them, the grammatical and syntactical rules of language were rarely spoken *in that way*. In other words, students expressed that they could not relate to this standard type of English because they did not speak it and did not hear it in the communities they were from. They had raised a very valid argument: Classroom or "academic talk" is vastly different from the way students speak in their homes and cultural communities. That afternoon, their comments haunted me. I began to wonder to myself: How could they be encouraged to appropriate their language to Standard English if they did not have tangible examples or models within their own cultural communities to which they could relate? It was this well-received reality check that birthed my idea to have a "rap party" in class.

For the next two weeks, I cultivated a curriculum that embraced the hip-hop culture and its rap icons. First, I asked students to think of their favorite rap song and recite the lyrics. Students were even encouraged to bring CDs of their choice of music to class. Those who were unable to bring CDs were given time on computers to find their songs on the Internet. From the CDs and website links, we were able to compile a class list and download the songs. Next, we played the songs—sometimes over and over to unlock the meanings within the raps. Afterward, in a leisurely manner, I would have the students tell me what the songs were about. Once they could articulate the narrative, then came the challenge. Students were tasked to use "classroom talk" or academic language to tell each other what occurred. Taking the lesson a step further, I asked them to write a letter to the principal to discuss the details of the song. They came to realize that they would need to "speak differently" to get their point across to the varied audiences—me, their classmate, and the principal. Aha! They were mastering the ability to appropriate their language to fit their environments; these students were code-switching.

As students became more familiar with the notion that they must appropriate their language to the context of their surroundings, they began to assess if others, such as parents and community members, who spoke their language did the same. For this reason, I did a bit of research on popular rap artists. I found video segments displaying music icons such as Jay Z, Lil Jon, 50 Cent, and LL Cool J from television interviews and other broadcasts. I played a few video excerpts for students to take heed of these rappers in "live form" away from the microphone. To their amazement, they saw the King of Crunk himself, Lil Jon, appropriating his language. They were able to witness the smooth transition of sentences and aligned subject–verb agreement in his speech. Students dropped their jaws when they realized how linguistically savvy Jay Z was when he was interviewed by a sportscaster when discussing his recent purchase of a sports team. And perhaps most revealing was hip-hop icon LL Cool J—he wasn't chanting his chart-topping "Mama Said Knock You Out," but rather speaking in poised and appropriate tense shifts when seated with Oprah Winfrey, an internationally recognized television personality and broadcast billionaire. To their shock, students saw that even rap artists (who have the ability and influence to capitalize on speech forms such as Ebonics and slang in order to sell records) code-switch to their surroundings.

Students were engaged in learning more about speaking and writing with academically appropriate language. They were inspired to see their musical idols become so well versed in speaking in multiple language codes. As a result, code-switching became a regular routine for students because they now saw the connection of their ELA lessons to their lives and their futures. I truly believe that in this one instance they felt that their linguistic diversity would serve as an agent of freedom as opposed to a limitation.

It was a transformative year both for the students and for me. The students developed a love for language and a greater appreciation for code-switching. I, on the other hand, learned to become more attuned to my students' academic needs by not only listening to them but also by seeking to understand their cultural backgrounds and academic identities.

Although it is important for culturally diverse learners to receive explicit instruction in the use of Standard English, *when* and *under what circumstances* become critical instructional issues. All students should understand how cultural contexts influence what they read, write, hear, say, and view.

English Language Learning

English Learners (ELs) are those students who speak English as a nonnative language. Because their home language is that of a minority group—for example, Spanish, Navajo, or Vietnamese—they are considered to be *language minority* students. English Learners are, for the most part, the children of immigrants who left their homelands for one reason or another. Some English Learners, however, are born in the United States. As Peregoy and Boyle (2001, p. 3) explain:

> Many recent immigrants have left countries brutally torn by war or political strife in regions such as Southeast Asia, Central America, and Eastern Europe; others have immigrated for economic reasons. Still others come to be reunited with families who are already here or because of the educational opportunities they may find in the United States. Finally, many English language learners were born in the United States and some of them, such as Native Americans of numerous tribal heritages, have roots in American soil that go back for countless generations.

Among recent immigrants, there exist various groups within this newcomer population. Some are highly schooled in their native language but need to learn academic English, vocabulary, and core concepts. Some have limited school experience in their native country, while others may have never attended a school of any kind. It is important for teachers to remember that English Learners are not a homogenous group. Calderón, Slavin, and Sánchez (2011) estimate that 80% of second-generation immigrant children are classified as long-term English Learners in middle and high school, despite having been in the United States since kindergarten. Some students are reclassified as general education students as soon as they pass the state assessment even though they may not have developed English proficiency across the domains of listening, speaking, reading, and writing. Migrant English Learners are another group of ELs who are typically born in the United States but who lack English proficiency because their families move from state to state picking crops, thus interrupting their educational experiences. Transnational English Learners return to their native countries for a portion of the school year, attend school there, and then return to U.S. schools, also creating inconsistencies in their educational experiences.

BILINGUAL AND ESL PROGRAMS   English Learners vary in their use of English. Some may have little or no proficiency in the use of English. Others may have limited English skills; still others may use English proficiently and are mainstreamed into the regular curriculum. What is language proficiency? It has been defined as "the ability to use a language effectively and appropriately throughout the range of social, personal, school, and work situations required for daily living in a given society" (Peregoy & Boyle, 2001, p. 29). Language proficiency, therefore, encompasses both oral and written language processes, including speaking, listening, reading, and writing.

To be clear, **ESL (English as a Second Language)** is the *program*; English Learners (ELs) are the *students*. Limited English Proficient (LEP) is the official subgroup used by NCLB but not ESL practitioners because of the deficit thinking in calling a student "limited." When parents bring their children to register for school, whether entering kindergarten or when joining a new district, they receive a home language survey. If the parent indicates that he or she or the child speaks a language other than English in the home, the child is administered an English language proficiency test. In more than 35 states and the District of Columbia, this test is the World-Class Instructional Design and Assessment (WIDA) Placement Test (W-APT). If determined to be Limited English Proficient based on this assessment's cut scores, the child is eligible for ESL services.

The typical programs available throughout the United States may be divided into two groups: English-only or monolingual forms of instruction and bilingual instruction. Monolingual ESL instruction includes pull-out programs, typically used in elementary schools, in which the child is removed from the mainstream class to the ESL classroom for additional language support. Sheltered or structured English immersion (SEI) or English language development (ELD) classes are often used in middle and secondary school and taught either as a substitute for English language arts classes or as an additional elective. In some regions, newcomer schools or centers are utilized to provide some language instruction before sending students to their home schools. Sheltered Instruction Observation Protocol (SIOP), developed by Jana Echevarria, Deborah Short, and MaryEllen Vogt (2008), which falls under the umbrella of SEI, is a model that offers guidance in planning, teaching, observing, and evaluating effective instruction for ELs.

Far less common in the United States are **bilingual programs**. Transitional bilingual programs, the most common type of bilingual program in the United States, provide some content instruction in the native language along with English language development. The goal is to transition students from bilingual classrooms to monolingual English classrooms as quickly as possible. Other forms of bilingual education include developmental bilingual education (DBE), dual language, and bilingual immersion. DBE targets the maintenance of the first language while learning English; dual language programs are made up of equal numbers of English speakers and speakers of another language with classes taught in both languages; and bilingual immersion programs target English speakers looking to learn a second language. Bilingual programs reach only a small percentage of students, despite a growing body of research that suggests that immigrant students who maintain a strong identification with their culture and native language are more likely to succeed academically and have more positive self-concepts about their abilities to learn (Banks, 2001; Diaz, 2001; Garcia, 2002).

The role of the ESL teacher changes based on the needs of each school. While bilingual education teachers often speak more than one language, ESL teachers are often monolingual. In most ESL classes around the country, multiple languages are spoken by the students in the class. It would be logistically impossible for ESL teachers to speak the languages of all of their students. Instead, ESL teachers are language experts, meaning that they have the skills to help their students acquire the English language across content areas. Depending on the school, ESL teachers either focus on teaching classes or pull-out groups of students or perform various levels of co-teaching. ESL teachers are a primary source for helping classroom and content area teachers modify lessons and assessments. They are also invaluable for helping teachers understand the language proficiency of the students in the school. Bilingual and ESL teachers provide invaluable compensatory services for language minority students with limited English proficiency. When these students are mainstreamed into the regular curriculum, however, they often struggle with content literacy tasks. Let's take a closer look at some of the reasons diverse learners struggle with reading and writing in content area classrooms.

WHAT MAKES CONTENT LITERACY DIFFICULT FOR ENGLISH LEARNERS?

Once they are mainstreamed into the regular curriculum, English Learners encounter numerous challenges in learning the English language. Not only must they acquire skills for social uses of English, they must acquire academic skills, across the content areas, in the domains of listening, speaking, reading, and writing. The academic language of texts is not the language of conversational speech, but rather it is word knowledge that makes it possible for students to interact with texts that are used across school subject areas (Flynt & Brozo, 2008).

Reading textbooks is one of the most cognitively demanding, context-reduced tasks that minority language students will encounter. Teachers of English Learners can support English literacy development through a series of strategies, including: teaching vocabulary and grammar, teaching phonics and phonological awareness, teaching explicit reading strategies, and teaching students to understand the text features of genres (Calderón & Minaya-Rowe, 2011). The vast variety of subject area vocabulary and the linguistic complexity of the English language make English language learning particularly challenging for many middle and secondary students. Many educators find it difficult to grasp the magnitude of learning academic English. While many students acquire informal, social English in approximately two to three years, academic English typically takes between five and 10 years to master. This can make content area instruction challenging for teachers and students alike (Flynt & Brozo, 2008). Consider the vocabulary of a native English speaker. A 5-year-old native English speaker would begin kindergarten with a vocabulary that ranges from 5,000 to 7,000 words (Manyak & Bauer, 2009)—words that a nonnative English speaker would not have in his or her vocabulary. These initial words are what we refer to as the Tier 1 words. Typically, the Tier 1 words are ones that most English speakers would know, but that must be taught explicitly to English Learners. Tier 1 words can be taught through direct translation, images, gestures, and drawings (Calderón & Minaya-Rowe, 2011). The vocabulary load of content area textbooks is particularly challenging for some English Learners. To try to understand the complexity involved in learning academic vocabulary, consider the vocabulary of the seemingly simple word *apple*. *Apple* would be considered a Tier 1 word. You can teach this easily through direct translation or through realia or images. If you were to list key words or phrases about emotional associations with apples or why you like apples, your list might include additional Tier 1 vocabulary such as:

> apple pie
>
> sweet
>
> crunchy
>
> stem
>
> cozy kitchen
>
> pleasant aroma

While the social language of *apple* may seem common and relatively simple to learn, consider what the academic language of *apple* might look like. Consider the language of *apple* from a poet's perspective, and the additional vocabulary and linguistic complexity needed to understand the opening lines of Robert Frost's poem *After Apple-Picking*.

> My long two-pointed ladder's sticking through a tree toward heaven still,
>   And there's a barrel that I didn't fill
>
> Beside it, and there may be two or three
>   Apples I didn't pick upon some bough.
>
> But I am done with apple-picking now.
>   Essence of winter sleep is on the night,
>
> The scent of apples: I am drowsing off.

While every content area teacher knows the academic language of his or her subject, we rarely have the time to consider the academic language involved in other content areas. This more difficult academic vocabulary is split between Tier 2 and Tier 3 words, with Tier 2 including general academic vocabulary and phrases. For example, Tier 2 words from the above poem would include sophisticated words like *bough* or *essence*. These words are not necessarily used in everyday language, nor are they specific to a particular content. Tier 2 words can include polysemous words, or those that have multiple meanings like *cell*, as well as connector words such as *although* and *however* (Calderón & Minaya-Rowe, 2011). That English learner who leaves poetry class still must face the academic demands of at least three other content areas. When that same student goes to mathematics class, the language of *apple* may change according to computations or to an economist's perspective: *measurements, quart, bushel, tons, yield, symmetry, circumference, crop abundance.* When that student goes to science class, the academic language may be from a biologist's perspective and may include vocabulary such as *orchard, botanical information, blossoms, pollination, deciduous, harvest,* and *pruning.* When that student goes to social studies class, the language of *apple* may be from an historian's perspective: *immigration of the apple, legend of Johnny Appleseed, John Chapman,* and *the cultivation of various apple varieties.* These content specific examples are considered Tier 3 vocabulary words (Calderón & Minaya-Rowe, 2011).

As the language of *apple* changes, the demands of academic language and vocabulary become more apparent. When we are aware of this, it is easier to empathize with the English learner who has to face this volume of academic vocabulary and complexity surrounding this single, and previously simple-sounding, concept.

Manyak and Bauer (2009) suggest that for English language vocabulary instruction to be effective, schools must implement consistent and intensive vocabulary instruction across grade levels. English Learners in particular benefit from vocabulary instruction that presents high-frequency words in phrases and short reading passages designed to improve reading fluency. Effective instruction requires teachers to strike a balance between attention to basic word concepts and the richer vocabulary instruction of their content area. One of the best ways for English Learners to learn vocabulary is by reading books that are on or slightly above their reading level. The following section outlines literature that can support ELs in their language development and vocabulary growth.

Books for English Learners

English Learners have become a recognizable force in today's classrooms. ELs face a triple challenge compared with mainstream students: They need to learn academic content, develop native-like English proficiency, and achieve comfort with American culture. It is important to note that ELs have language, not cognitive, obstacles.

One way to address these challenges is to have ELs interact with authentic trade books. In doing so, teachers can increase students' content and vocabulary knowledge, offer more practice with authentic language, and provide scenarios that describe the life of American teenagers, which will expose ELs to a variety of cultural behaviors and ways of thinking. Books, TV shows, and movies can be excellent venues for ELs to learn about real-life experiences. For example, Jeff Kinney's *Diary of a Wimpy Kid* (Kinney, 2007) can introduce ELs to the dynamics of junior high school hierarchies. The book's humor, simple vocabulary, and graphics will engage ELs, which increases their motivation to read.

Knowing that English Learners need additional support with language learning, teachers may find *graphic novels* to be a perfect alternative for these students. Graphic novels, already popular with adolescents for independent reading, combine words with pictures that can support the learning of students for whom English poses difficulties. Using graphic novels in the classroom is an increasingly popular way to scaffold ELs' understanding of content. Illustrations in graphic novels provide valuable context clues about the meaning of the written content and offer support for students who lack the ability to visualize as they read. Graphic novels are available in a variety of genres, including biographies, fiction, nonfiction, and fantasy. These texts have appeal for reluctant readers and can be used to teach a variety of literacy skills including dialogue; inferencing; story elements; literary terms like *writing, satire, irony, parody,* and many more.

Using Will Eisner's (2000) *New York: The Big City,* Kelly Faust developed a lesson for her urban English Learners, many of whom had been in this country for only one year. The purpose of the lesson was to further student understanding of story elements and encourage writing. She began the lesson by showing the students six frames of a wordless story from the book on the overhead projector. She then used the think-aloud strategy to point out the events of the story and the ways in which the visual techniques of the illustrator supported it. She reviewed the basic elements of a story with her students and asked students whether the frames represented a story. Students pointed out that these frames contained characters, setting, and a simple plot. Students then discussed the story with a partner, creating their own version of the events portrayed in the frames. At this point, one team of students dictated its story to the group. Kelly wrote this story on chart paper so other students could see the concepts recorded. She modeled for the students how to use quotation marks to designate the exact words of a speaker. At strategic points, Kelly involved specific students in recording the text on paper. Next, Kelly directed the students to identify the characters, the setting, and the events of the plot in the recorded story.

Following this, Kelly presented students with a new series of wordless frames from the Eisner book. She reviewed the think-aloud strategy, and students took turns thinking aloud with a partner about the text. Students then worked in teams to draft their own stories on notebook paper. At this point, Kelly conducted minilessons reviewing areas of need reflected in the student drafts. After revising, the students transferred their stories to chart paper and shared them with the class, pointing out the elements of story as reflected in their own writing.

Vocabulary in areas such as mathematics, social studies, and science can be overwhelming, causing content to be inaccessible for many English Learners. More vocabulary is introduced in social studies and science textbooks than in textbooks used to teach students a foreign language. Using picture books with ELs is a good practice because pictures can aid comprehension (see Box 3.5). Also, the vocabulary and language patterns of picture books are simple, which also aids comprehension. Picture books, including wordless picture books, have been found to support English Learners' facilitation with

Box 3.5 Picture Books in Mathematics

A variety of picture books may be used not only to help young adolescent English Learners develop mathematical concepts, but also to draw on their prior knowledge and experience (Schmidt & Ma, 2006). Here are several suggestions for using math picture books in middle-grade classrooms:

- To spark interest and develop an understanding of mathematical concepts, have English Learners read stories about famous mathematicians and cultures that have been mathematically oriented. The Internet provides wonderful leads on famous mathematicians from different cultures.
- Have English Learners read math-oriented picture books to younger siblings. Picture books explain in ways that help students understand mathematical concepts. In addition, students may create and design their own math books to be shared in other classrooms and with younger audiences.
- Use math picture books as a strategy for motivating interest in mathematics and providing a greater depth of understanding of mathematical concepts. Create an area in the classroom to display picture books, such as the following:

Burns, M., *The Greedy Triangle*
Heller, R., *More Geometrics*
McKellar, D., *Kiss My Math: Showing Pre-Algebra Who's Boss*
Neuschwander, C., *Sir Cumference and the First Round Table*
Schwartz, D., *How Much Is a Million?*
Scieszka, J., *Math Curse*
Seife, C., *Zero: The Biography of a Dangerous Idea*
Tang, G., *Math for All Seasons*
Tang, G., *Math-terpieces*
Tang, G., *The Grapes of Math*
Wisniewski, D., *RainPlayer*

These books enhance the study of mathematics with humor and delightful stories and illustrations, bringing added joy to the study of math while encouraging related reading, writing, listening, speaking, and viewing activities.

the English language, particularly in terms of speaking and listening, as students are invited to explain their interpretation of a story by reading the pictures. Martínez-Roldán and Newcomer (2011) suggest the following strategies for engaging students in wordless picture book reading:

- Use a small-group, rather than whole-class, format for book discussions.
- Use an assortment of books by the same author to compare techniques and messages.
- Invite open conversations about the text, using open-ended, inferential, and applied questions.
- Invite students to make text predictions.
- Invite students to create annotated pages or to create narrations to accompany their interpretations of the visual images in the book.

Additionally, chapter book series such as Mary Pope Osborne's *Magic Tree House* and Jon Scieszka's *Time Warp Trio* bring various science and social studies concepts to life in an easy-to-read but content-rich manner.

English Learners need to learn to navigate nonnarrative texts because much of secondary schooling is based on the ability to read this text type. For social studies topics, check out books by Russell Freedman. Freedman includes a lot of primary and secondary sources and illustrations in his works. Furthermore, his books are rich in content but more concise and interesting than textbooks. *Immigrant Kids* (Freedman, 1995), for example, is ideally suited for ELs, as are other books about teens who share their struggles. Shaun Tan's wordless graphic novel *The Arrival* (Tan, 2007) depicts the journey of an immigrant who grapples with loneliness and the strangeness of learning a new language and culture. There are also several anthologies that address this topic, such as *First Crossing: Stories About Teen Immigrants* (Gallo, 2007) and *Kids Like Me: Voices of the Immigrant Experience* (Blohm & Lapinsky, 2006). Series such as Ellen Levin's *If You …* (e.g., *If Your Name Was Changed at Ellis Island* [1996] and *If You Traveled West in a Covered Wagon* [1992]) and David Adler's picture book biographies are also welcome additions to content area learning for ELs.

Teaching for cultural understanding and using multicultural literature create a community of learners within the four walls of the classroom. Within such learning communities, it is important for teachers to understand the ways in which diverse learners "come to know" and to tap into students' "funds of knowledge."

MyLab Education **Self-Check 3.3**

MyLab Education **Application Exercise 3.3:**
Code-Switching to Academic Language in Content Area Classes

Sheltered Instruction for English Learners

3.4   Describe the ways in which instruction can be adapted to meet the needs of English Learners.

Sheltered instruction does not focus specifically on second language development issues. Instead, teachers often use a variety of instructional aids to let students who have limited skills in reading, writing, listening, and speaking "see" challenging, and often abstract, content visually. This may be done by contextualizing the learning tasks through hands-on cooperative activities, pictures, relevant media, artistic representations of meaning, and reading-to-learn strategies modeled for the students (Campano, 2007; Haynes, 2007). As a result, sheltered instruction often provides opportunities for nonnative students to learn

MyLab Education
**Video Example 3.2:
Strategies**
Watch this video to learn about effective instructional strategies to support English Learners.

MyLab Education
Response Journal 3.3
What does the term *sheltered* suggest to you? Why do you think it is used to describe an instructional approach for English Learners?

discipline-specific content while improving their English language skills (Díaz-Rico, 2008; Faltis & Coulter, 2008).

When English Learners struggle with content literacy tasks, instruction should be specially designed to meet their academic and linguistic needs, which often include (1) learning grade-appropriate and academically demanding content; (2) learning the language of academic English as reflected in content subjects, texts, and classroom discourse; (3) engaging in appropriate classroom behavior and understanding participation rules and expectations in small groups and whole-class instructional routines; and (4) mastering English vocabulary and grammar (Echevarria, Vogt, & Short, 2008). Sheltered instruction, also known as specially designed academic instruction in English (SDAIE), is an approach to content area learning and language development that provides the instructional support needed to make grade-level content more accessible for ELs while promoting English development (Echevarria & Graves, 2003).

Although the concept of "sheltering" English Learners is similar to the concept of scaffolding instruction for all learners who need instructional support to be successful with content literacy tasks, it has been adapted for use in two types of instructional contexts: (1) in mainstreamed, core curriculum classrooms made up of native speakers and nonnative speakers who are at an *intermediate* level of language proficiency and (2) in ESL classrooms made up of nonnative speakers who are at similar levels of language proficiency.

The SIOP Model

One model for sheltered instruction, Sheltered Instruction Observation Protocol (SIOP), provides a comprehensive instructional framework that can be used in several ways to shelter instruction for English Learners. First, the **SIOP model** serves as a blueprint for designing lessons that integrate content learning with additional language support for English Learners. Second, the SIOP model enhances instructional delivery by making teachers aware of highly effective practices and behaviors that will make a difference in the academic and language development of students. And third, the SIOP model provides an observational framework for rating teachers in sheltered classrooms. Figure 3.1 depicts the major components within the SIOP model: lesson preparation, instruction, strategies, interaction, practice/application, lesson delivery, and assessment (Echevarria, Vogt, & Short, 2008).

Sheltered instruction is a powerful approach to content area learning and language development. The literacy strategies described throughout this book may be incorporated into instructional routines for students in sheltered or nonsheltered classrooms. Many of these strategies have been recommended by English language educators for use with language minority students (Díaz-Rico & Weed, 2002; Echevarria & Graves, 2003; Echevarria, Vogt, & Short, 2008; Peregoy & Boyle, 2001). In the next section, we highlight several strategies and suggest ways to adapt instruction for diverse learners.

Adapting Instruction in Content Classrooms

Content area teachers are in a strategic position to make adaptations in the way they design and deliver instruction in classrooms with native and nonnative speakers. These adaptations in instructional design and delivery lead to additional language support for English Learners as well as increased learning opportunities in the core curriculum.

PROVIDE COMPREHENSIBLE INPUT   Support nonnative speakers in your classroom by showing sensitivity to their language needs. An important component of sheltered instruction is to provide *comprehensible input* for English Learners (Echevarria & Graves, 2003). Make content learning comprehensible by simplifying your language when giving directions, leading whole-class discussions, or facilitating small-group interactions. When

Figure 3.1 The Sheltered Instruction Observation Protocol (SIOP)

Observer: _____   Teacher: _____
Date: _____   School: _____
Grade: _____   ESL level: _____
Class: _____   Lesson: Multi-day   Single-day

I.   Preparation

1. Clearly defined *content objectives* for students
2. Clearly defined *language objectives* for students
3. *Content concepts* appropriate for age and educational background level of students
4. *Supplementary materials* used to a high degree, making the lesson clear and meaningful (graphs, models, visuals)
5. *Adaptation of content* (e.g., text, assignment) to all levels of student proficiency
6. *Meaningful activities* that integrate lesson concepts (e.g., surveys, letter writing, simulations, constructing models) with language practice opportunities for reading, writing, listening, and/or speaking

II.   Instruction

(1)   Building Background

7. *Concepts explicitly linked* to students' background experiences
8. *Links explicitly made* between past learning and new concepts
9. *Key vocabulary emphasized* (e.g., introduced, written, repeated, and highlighted for students to see)

(2)   Comprehensible

10. *Speech* appropriate for students' proficiency level (e.g., slower rate, enunciation, and simple sentence structure for beginners)
11. *Explanation* of academic tasks clear
12. Uses a variety of *techniques* to make content concepts clear (e.g., modeling, visuals, hands-on activities, demonstrations, gestures, body language)

(3)   Strategies

13. Provides ample opportunities for student to use *strategies*
14. Consistent use of *scaffolding* techniques throughout lesson, assisting and supporting student understanding
15. Teacher uses a variety of *question types throughout the lesson, including those that promote higher-order thinking skills* throughout the lesson (e.g., literal, analytical, and interpretive questions)

(4)   Interaction

16. Frequent opportunities for *interactions* and discussion between teacher/student and among students, which encourage elaborated responses about lesson concepts
17. *Grouping configurations* support language and content objectives of the lesson
18. Consistently provides sufficient *wait time for student response*
19. Ample opportunities for students to *clarify key concepts in L1*

(5)   Practice/Application

20. Provides *hands-on* materials and/or manipulatives for students to practice using new content knowledge
21. Provides activities for students to *apply content and language knowledge* in the classroom
22. Uses activities that integrate all *language skills* (i.e., reading, writing, listening, and speaking)

(6)   Lesson Delivery

23. *Content objectives* clearly supported by lesson delivery
24. *Language objectives* clearly supported by lesson delivery
25. *Students engaged* approximately 90–100% of the period
26. *Pacing* of the lesson appropriate to the students' ability level

III.   Review/Assessment

27. Comprehensive *review* of key vocabulary
28. Comprehensive *review* of key content concepts
29. Regularly provides *feedback* to students on their output (e.g., language, content, work)
30. Conducts *assessment* of student comprehension and learning of all lesson objectives (e.g., spot checking, group response) throughout the lesson

SOURCE: Echevarria, J., Vogt, M., & Short, D. (2008). *Making content comprehensible for English language learners: The SIOP model,* 3rd ed. Published by Allyn & Bacon, Boston, MA. Copyright © 2008 by Pearson Education Inc. Reprinted with permission of the publisher.

talking to a class that includes ELs, especially students at a beginning or intermediate level of language proficiency, it may be necessary to speak clearly and speak at a slightly slower rate than you normally would if you had only native speakers in your classroom. During discussions, it may also be necessary to repeat yourself, define new words in a meaningful context, or paraphrase when you use more sophisticated language than ELs can understand, and check for understanding during class conversations. Providing comprehensible input also means being aware of your use of **idiomatic expressions** and limiting them when students find idiomatic expressions difficult to understand. Moreover, keep in mind that gestures and facial expressions help to dramatize what you are saying during discussion. As we explained earlier in the chapter, scaffold instruction during discussion by supporting students in their use of home languages and their own culturally acceptable conversational styles.

USE STRATEGIES FOR VOCABULARY DEVELOPMENT Linguistically diverse learners, whether they are good or poor readers, will encounter unfamiliar content area vocabulary during reading that may pose comprehension problems for them. English Learners who struggle as readers benefit from targeted vocabulary strategy instruction (Calderón & Minaya-Rowe, 2011). Vocabulary strategy instruction is effective when a teacher helps ELs to develop a few key terms in-depth rather than attempting to have them learn many words superficially (Allen, 2007). Such instruction should consider strategies and procedures that will help students build meaning for important concept terms.

For example, whenever the opportunity presents itself, it's important to help students recognize and use the relationship between cognates and the context in which they are used. *Cognates* are words that are culturally and linguistically related in both the non-native speaker's language and in English. As part of cognitive strategy instruction for struggling readers, Latino(a) students in a middle school special education classroom were shown how to approximate word meaning through the cognate relationships they encountered in the texts that they were reading. For example, knowing the meaning of *libertad* in Spanish can help English Learners to recognize and understand the word *liberty* in English (Calderón & Minaya-Rowe, 2011).

In addition to emphasizing cognate-related vocabulary building, showing linguistically diverse learners how to approximate word meaning through *word structure* and context is another important aspect of vocabulary building. Brozo (2017) suggests seven guidelines for effective vocabulary instruction:

- Teach vocabulary in multiple language contexts.
- Reinforce word learning with repeated exposures over time.
- Emphasize students' active role in the word-learning process.
- Give students tools to expand word knowledge independently.
- Stimulate students' awareness and interest in words.
- Build a language-rich environment to support word learning.
- Encourage students to read widely. (p. 220)

In Chapter 8, we will examine in more detail how to use context and word structure in content classrooms and explore a variety of strategies for vocabulary and concept development.

DIFFERENTIATE BETWEEN INTENSIVE AND EXTENSIVE READING English Learners need to be taught that not all texts need to be read and understood at the same level of detail and that they may employ different strategies for different reading tasks. Kristin Berry, a 10th-grade global studies teacher, introduced *intensive reading* and *extensive reading* strategies to her interdisciplinary English/global studies class while working on a unit of study about World War II. She followed these four steps to help English Learners and native language speakers recognize when to use intensive reading and extensive reading strategies:

1. Kristin required her students to engage in an intensive reading of the core textbook to understand the big picture. They read about Germany's aggression in Europe, Japan's aggression in Asia, diplomacy and the Allied forces, major events and figures, and the fall of Germany and Japan, as well as the relationships among the social, political, military, and economic factors.

2. To help her students comprehend the chapters, Kristin not only worked with them on important vocabulary but also clarified the meaning of difficult sentences through rereading, paraphrasing, summarizing, group discussion, and written response. Through reading intensively, Kristin helped her students develop a solid under-standing of the textbook.

3. In collaboration with her language arts colleague, Kristin incorporated a variety of learning activities and assignments into her lessons. She required students to read extensively some of the books that addressed various aspects of the war, such as *The Diary of Anne Frank: Play and Related Readings* (Goodrich & Hackett, 2000), *Night* (Wiesel, 2006), *Rumors of Peace* (Leffland, 1979), and *Summer of My German Soldier* (Greene, 1999). Then Kristin asked her students to select one novel to read for a general understanding. They were to connect what they read with what they had learned from reading the textbook.

4. To help students cope with the large volume of reading, Kristin also gave explicit instruction in the use of two study strategies that we elaborate on in Chapter 10: *skimming* (i.e., reading quickly to grasp the main ideas of a text) and *scanning* (i.e., reading quickly to locate specific details). These varied reading experiences extended, diversified, and brought life to the textbook.

As a result of Kristin's sheltered approach to instruction, intensive reading and extensive reading helped both English Learners and mainstream students learn during the unit of study.

USE THE REPEATED READING STRATEGY   For English Learners who are still in the process of developing reading fluency, the *repeated reading strategy* may be a useful intensive reading approach to fully comprehend a content area text across varied grade levels. A three-step reading process may help students better understand a text using repeated readings of text material:

1. The first reading focuses on breaking down the linguistic barriers for the English Learners. To begin, each student is required to skim a given text and mark any language item not understood. Before explaining the terms in class, the teacher encourages responses from other students. This is useful in developing students' ability to guess the meaning of a word from its context. The teacher may call students' attention to some "key points." The teacher also helps ELs differentiate between *denotation* (the literal meaning a word has) and *connotation* (the implied or suggested meaning of a word in context). Thus, the students will not do a rigid word-for-word interpretation of every sentence in English. It is worth mentioning that because of the linguistic subtleties and intricacies of English figurative expressions, special consideration should be given to the unique difficulty of learning "language forms."

2. The next reading centers on the ideas expressed in the text. Clearly, the students should be allowed more time for this second reading so that they may dwell on the main ideas and important details in the text for in-depth comprehension. As the language form is but a vehicle for carrying meaning, the students should be encouraged to learn how the main ideas, viewpoints, and so on, are presented; how the ideas flow from beginning to end; and how all the separate sentences and paragraphs are tightly knitted semantically. In other words, now the central task is to understand the ideas that are presented and the way they are connected in the text.

3. The third stage primarily aims to help students size up how the material is organized to have an overview of the text. The organizational pattern; the effect of the style, tone, and attitude achieved; and the basic writing techniques (such as diction and rhetoric) can all be dealt with in this final reading.

After the three readings, students would better know the language forms involved in the text and the ideas these forms express. As a result, students' knowledge of the text is likely to be more comprehensive because of the text-centered method employed throughout the reading process. It is important to remember that the three steps are interchangeable. When used in combination with other group discussion and/or writing activities, the repeated reading strategy would be even more effective.

USE LEARNING STRATEGIES FOR ACTIVE ENGAGEMENT   Throughout the remainder of this book, we will be focusing on learning strategies that will engage students in comprehending texts. These strategies can be as simple and straightforward as creating posters for a chapter. This strategy allows teachers to use a variety of group and collaborative activities in different content areas. Betty, for example, uses posters with the English Learners in her middle school social studies class. She follows these three steps:

1. After her students read a chapter, Betty asks them to create a poster to visually represent the main ideas expressed by the chapter. Based on the length and complexity of the chapter, she varies the requirement for the total number of key concepts to be included in a poster from five to 12. Her students use illustrations, color, lettering, and so on, to present the chapter's information in an inviting and creative manner.
2. Betty's students share their posters in a small group consisting of three to five students (including both English Learners and mainstream learners). All members take turns sharing their posters with each other. While sharing, they are encouraged to use the ideas from the poster as "talking points." Betty asks the other students to point out at least one thing that they particularly like in the poster and to offer one suggestion about how to better interpret the chapter's content as well.
3. After the group sharing, Betty invites all students to share in a whole-class session, and each individual can share some of the highlights from his or her own reading, writing, or group sharing. Meanwhile, she provides further explanation about the main ideas, concepts, or additional background information related to the chapter under study. When needed, she also gives feedback to clarify any unclear points or misunderstandings as reflected from the students' posters or presentations.

In summary, Betty feels that asking her students to create posters for a text they read helps deepen their engagement with the text. The sharing provides further opportunities for both the English Learners and mainstream students to exchange ideas about what they thought and understood. This strategy may be easily adjusted for use in other content areas. In each case, the poster helps to support English Learners' critical engagement with a text in a socially supported context. Chapter 5 provides a more extended discussion of collaborative learning strategies.

USE WRITING STRATEGIES   English Learners sometimes get stuck while engaging in specific writing activities. By being involved in a variety of writing strategies, as emphasized in Chapter 9, students will come to view writing as a tool to understand as well as to be understood. One such strategy, "mental composition," is particularly useful in composing an essay or reflecting on a learning task. The strategy helps students, especially ELs, think about what they are going to write without having to worry about "getting it down on paper." It is helpful to introduce this strategy to students by thinking aloud with them and modeling the process. For example, after reading the young adult novel *Walk Two Moons* (Creech, 1996), a seventh-grade language arts teacher, Stephanie, used her response to the novel to model the steps of the mental composition strategy. She wanted her students to understand that a written paper would need to have an introduction, a body, and an ending, so she began the lesson by explaining that the book told the story of a young girl named Salamanca (Sal) Tree Hiddle. Next, she wanted to model for her students how to write the body of her paper. She thought aloud with them about the story structure of this novel, noting that there was a story within a story. One story was about Sal's trip with her grandparents to visit her mother's burial place, and the other story focused on her best friend. Finally, to model how to write the ending of her paper, Stephanie discussed how Sal's journey ended. She also mentioned some of the important issues raised in the novel, such as coping with the death of a family member as a young adolescent. At the end of the lesson, she pointed out that the thought process she had modeled reflected how she might approach the writing of her paper. Then she invited the students to share how they might approach a written paper based on their reading of this novel.

Stephanie models the procedures for mental composition or, in her words, "seeing a paper unfolding in one's head." She realizes the importance of engaging English Learners in actual writing as well. Therefore, in addition to mental composition, she selects some topics to involve her students in practicing brainstorming, planning, drafting, revising, and completing the writing. At the same time, she provides some concrete suggestions to help them generate ideas: journal entries, informal nongraded writing, one-page think pieces, in-class free writing, microtheme paragraphs, practice exam questions/topics, small-group discussions, rewrites, and so on. In other words, mental composition and regular writing become supplementary and complementary.

Mental composition may be adapted for helping students notice varied learning tasks. For example, students may use it to recall what was learned at various stages of reading a novel or text and review what was taught after a class. When used in combination with other writing practices, such mental composing promotes active intellectual participation through writing, reading, speaking, and listening across content areas.

When teaching writing, it is important to think of it on three levels: the discourse, sentence, and word or phrase level. Gibbons (2002) suggests teaching within the following cycle. In stage one, the teacher builds knowledge on the topic, allowing students to read, experiment, or otherwise research information and vocabulary pertinent to the writing topic. At this level, students should develop vocabulary that is pertinent to the content as well as the structure of the discourse. For example, if students will eventually be asked to write a cause and effect essay, then they should be taught additional vocabulary such as *cause* as a verb, *cause* as a noun, *effect, affect,* and so on.

In stage two, the teacher models the text, explicitly teaching the discourse, or structure, of the text. This includes demonstrating to students the organization of the writing, such as narrative, argumentative essay, cause and effect essay, or scientific report; drawing attention to the function or purpose of the writing; and describing the characteristics of the writing. For example, narratives may be written chronologically or using flashbacks. It may be in first person or third person. Scientific writing often is structured to describe a hypothesis, a process, and then a result.

The third stage, joint construction, may include a minilesson on grammatical features and mechanics. For example, academic and scientific writing is often marked by the passive voice, as in, "The reaction *was caused* by the addition of the third liquid." This type of structure can be difficult for language learners, so keep in mind when modeling texts that depending on their level that you may want to take time to teach a mini-grammar lesson on passive voice, or it may be better to use active voice: "The third liquid *caused* the reaction." Finally, the fourth stage is independent writing. In her text, Gibbons provides specific activities and games prepared to enhance students' understanding of the discourse level of writing.

Cloud, Genesee, and Hamayan (2009) express that there are five tenets for creating meaningful writing activities. First, activities must be meaningful and functional. Writing should be connected to the curriculum and have a purpose that is beyond complying with a teacher's assignment. Second, activities must be relevant and interesting to the students. Writing about topics that interest them will result in more enthusiastic students and more authentic writing, as they will care about the topics they choose. Third, activities should build on oral language. This can be accomplished by allowing students multiple opportunities to talk about the topics they will write about. Students also benefit from activities such as dictating to their peers or teacher or being involved in the *language experience approach,* in which class members experience an activity together and then collectively write a text. The teacher then works with the class to read through the text. These types of activities help students make connections between experiences, the spoken word, and writing.

Finally, writing activities must expand a student's language. Simply copying chunks of text does not help students develop an understanding of the function of language. Writing is an extremely difficult activity for both native speakers of English and non-native speakers. By explicitly teaching discourse patterns, grammatical structures and mechanics, and vocabulary related to the content as well as the discourse, and by connecting writing to reading and speaking through meaningful themes, students will soon see themselves as successful authors of multiple genres.

MyLab Education Self-Check 3.4

MyLab Education Application Exercise 3.4:
Reading for Different Purposes in Content Area Classes
✓ Check Your Understanding

Looking Back Looking Forward

The linguistic, cultural, and achievement differences of students contribute to the complexities of classroom diversity. Students of diverse backgrounds (who may be distinguished by their ethnicity, social class, language, or achievement level) often struggle in classrooms. English Learners especially challenge teachers to look for and experiment with instructional strategies that will actively involve them in the life of the classroom. Sheltered instruction makes a difference in the academic and language development of English Learners.

The achievement gap for English Learners remains prevalent and signifies the importance of teacher preparation, ongoing professional development, and community-wide support for the achievement of English Learners. Funding cuts during the economic downturn of recent years have made meeting diverse learner needs increasingly challenging. Calderón, Slavin, and Sánchez (2011) point out that collaboration among school faculty and the cultivation of home–school connections can help to address students' language, literacy, and core content needs. Teachers reach diverse learners by scaffolding instruction in ways that support content literacy and learning.

In the next chapter, we explore another dimension of standards-based curriculum as we shift our attention to different forms of assessment in the content area classroom. Concern about assessment is one of the major issues in education in the United States today. What role do standardized "high-stakes" assessments play in the lives of classroom teachers? How do authentic forms of assessment inform instructional decisions? How can teachers use portfolios and make decisions about the texts they use? The key to assessment in content areas, as we contend in the next chapter, is to make it as useful as possible. Let's find out how and why this is the case.

---

eResources

The following Google searches can lead to sites that are filled with ideas for engaging English Learners of all levels:

Colorín Colorado: Provides bilingual information for educators, administrators, librarians, families, and English Learners. Explore the starter kit on placement, instruction, special services, and assessment as well as suggestions for teaching and learning across the content areas.

Graphic Classroom Blogspot: Offers suggestions on using comics and graphic novels across the curriculum.

SIOP Central: Suggests lesson plans based on the SIOP model.

International Dialects of English Archive: Provides examples of dialect differences.

National Public Radio: Breaking Out the Broken English: Demonstrates examples of code-switching and discusses different perspectives on this subject.

Chapter 4
Assessing Students and Texts

Written in collaboration with Melissa Sykes.

Shutterstock

 ## Chapter Overview and Learning Outcomes

After reading this chapter, you should be able to:

4.1 Compare high-stakes and authentic assessments, including the essential characteristics of each.

4.2 Describe how portfolios can be used to assess student learning in content areas.

4.3 Define text complexity and compare the ways in which it can be measured.

Organizing Principle

Instructional assessment is a process of gathering and using multiple sources of relevant information about students for instructional purposes.

How effectively are students learning to use reading, writing, talking, and viewing as tools to comprehend and respond to material in content areas? Assessing students and texts to provide this kind of information means that there is a direct connection between teaching and learning and a direct influence on instructional quality and the improvement of practice. Assessment in content area classrooms means that students and teachers are actively engaged in a process of evaluation and self-evaluation. Instead of measuring learning exclusively by a score on a standardized test or proficiency exam, the learning process includes the assessment of authentic tasks that demonstrate concept mastery or areas of needed growth.

Teachers and students want useful assessment; that is, they want to make sense of how and what is taught and learned at any given time. Data collection that is purposeful and timely supports teachers' ability to make instructional decisions based on their students' content literacy skills, concepts, and performance. Yet, teachers must also deal with the very real pressure of state and federal mandates for standards-based curriculum and testing. While many educational stakeholders push goals for raised test scores, some researchers and teachers question the effect of mandated standards and assessments on student learning and on teachers' ability to meet diverse learner needs. More than ever in this high-stakes testing environment, there is a clear need to carefully consider what assessments are testing, how assessments are implemented and interpreted, and where assessments can aid teaching and learning across the content areas.

To understand assessment, you need to differentiate between two major contrasting approaches: a formal, high-stakes approach and an informal, authentic approach. When standards were initially developed by professional organizations and state governments, testing was thought to be necessary to ensure that schools would meet high standards of achievement. The goal was to have a measurement that would allow learning to be compared across students, schools, and regions. Soon, students' performances on state-mandated tests became the focus of debate among educators, policy makers, and constituency groups; and while the public's attention today is often on this formal, high-stakes approach to assessment, the value of assessing students cannot be measured by scores alone. Authentic assessment practices, combined with formal assessments, can help to inform teachers' instructional

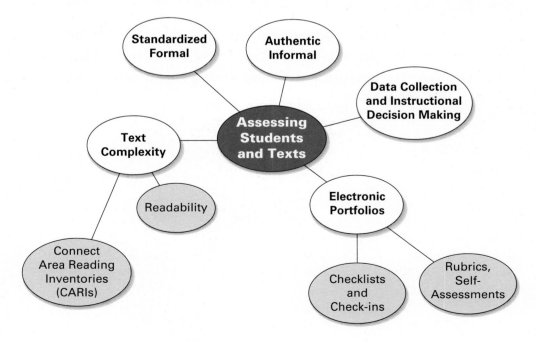

decisions in order to meet the diverse learning needs of students. Authentic assessments include graphic organizers, portfolios, observations and anecdotal records, checklists, simulations, conferences, and the production of digital artifacts.

Assessing for instruction should, first and foremost, provide the opportunity to gather and interpret useful information about students as they learn, including their prior knowledge; their attitudes toward reading, writing, and subject matter; and their ability to use content literacy to learn with texts. Through the portfolio assessment process—collecting authentic evidence of student work over time—and the formative assessment teaching cycle, teachers and students gather useful information about an individual's comprehension and response to content area material. The goal of the portfolio and all authentic assessment is that of growth based on feedback, demonstration, and application. The organizing principle of this chapter maintains that assessment should be useful, authentic, and responsive to teacher decision making: Instructional assessment creates targeted learning support based on purposeful data collection processes, using multiple demonstrations of student mastery and misconceptions.

Frame of Mind

1. How does assessment help us set instructional goals?
2. How does a formal, high-stakes approach differ from an informal, authentic approach?
3. How have state and federal policies affected assessment and student achievement?
4. What are some of the informal assessment strategies teachers use in the context of their classrooms?
5. How can content area teachers involve students in authentic assessment and self-reflection?
6. How might teachers analyze the complexity of texts?

Teachers sometimes know intuitively that what they do in class is working. More often, however, information for making decisions is best obtained through careful observation and purposeful assessment of students. Their strengths and weaknesses as they demonstrate comprehension and interact with one another and with texts can be assessed as they participate in small groups, contribute to class discussions, respond to questions, and complete assignments focused around application of content and concepts. This approach to assessment is *informal* and *authentic*; it is student centered and classroom based. This approach, however, isn't the only one operating in schools today. If teachers are in a school district guided by standards-based curricula, they need to understand the differences between *high-stakes* and *authentic* approaches to assessment.

MyLab Education
Response Journal 4.1
Write about an assessment tool you remember having to use as a student. What did you learn from using this tool?

Approaches to Assessment

4.1 **Compare high-stakes and authentic assessments, including the essential characteristics of each.**

The two major views of assessment, high-stakes and authentic, are like different sides of the same coin. They represent the almost opposite perspectives of those who believe in quantifying learning for comparison and effectiveness ratings on one side and those who believe in assessing students for knowledge check-ins and growth on the other. Policy makers are responding to the public demand for assurances that students will leave school well prepared to enter either the workforce or college. Teachers and other educators are calling for better, more authentic assessment practices that will improve instruction and result in learning. As Tierney (1998, p. 378) put it, one focuses on "something you *do to* students," and the other focuses on "something you *do with* them or help them *do for themselves*."

Authentic methods often include some combination of observations, interviews, anecdotal records, and student-selected performances and products. The information gained from an authentic assessment can be organized into a rich description or portrait of your content area classroom or into student portfolios. Concerns that emerge, whether about individual students or about the delivery of instructional strategies, are likely to make sense because they come directly from the classroom context and often result from teacher–student or student–student interaction.

Consider how an authentic approach differs from a more formal, high-stakes one. In Table 4.1, the two approaches are compared in several categories. Certainly, there are many gray areas in assessment, where the formal and informal overlap. In this table, however, differences between the two approaches are emphasized. Traditional, formal assessments are product oriented. They are more tangible and can be obtained at predetermined points in time. *Authentic assessments* are informal and process oriented. The process is ongoing, providing as much information about the student as learner as about the product. Together, they permit a more balanced approach through a combination of formal and informal practices. The result is an understanding of *why* particular results are obtained in formal assessment, which informs the *how* of the teacher decision-making process.

High-Stakes Testing

As the era of No Child Left Behind (U.S. Department of Education, 2001) came to a close, the Every Student Succeeds Act (U.S. Department of Education, 2015) emerged as a more flexible measure of school quality and offered a shift from federal intervention to more state and local control (Beachum, 2018). ESSA stated that mandatory testing must still take place at the state level in reading and math in Grades 3–8 and high school, but also required evidence-based plans for supporting struggling learners to be developed (Meibaum, 2016). With virtually every state adopting content standards in multiple content areas, such as English, mathematics, social studies, and science, standardized testing systems have been mandated, developed, and put in place throughout the United States.

As the need for accountability grows, effectiveness measurements and teacher performance assessment systems have risen in popularity. Such assessments are intended to account for high-quality teacher preparation and teaching success by using observations, videos, lesson plans, and reflections as well as student performance measures (Literacy Research Association, 2013). It is anticipated that federal policy makers will create policies requiring the use of assessment programs with a variety of measures to evaluate

Table 4.1 Comparisons of Two Approaches to Assessment

	High-Stakes/Formal	Authentic/Informal
Orientation	Formal; developed by expert committees and test publishers	Informal; developed by teachers and students
Administration	Testing one-time performance; paper-and-pencil, multiple-choice; given to groups at one seating	Continuously evolving and intermittent throughout an instructional unit; small-group, one-on-one
Methods	Objective; standardized reading achievement tests designed to measure levels of current attainment; state proficiency testing of content knowledge	Classroom tests, checklists, observations, interviews, and so on, designed to evaluate understanding of course content; real-life reading and writing tasks
Uses	Compare performance of one group with students in other schools or classrooms; determine funding, support for districts and schools; estimate range of reading ability in a class; select appropriate materials for reading; identify students who need further diagnosis; align curriculum; allocate classroom time	Make qualitative judgments about students' strengths and instructional needs in reading and learning content subjects; select appropriate materials; adjust instruction when necessary; self-assess strengths and weaknesses
Feedback Format	Reports, printouts of subtest scores; summaries of high and low areas of performance; percentiles, norms, stanines	Notes, profiles, portfolios, discussions, recommendations that evolve throughout instructional units; expansive (relate to interests, strategies, purpose for learning and reading)

teacher effectiveness. The edTPA is one example of a teacher performance assessment that is currently used to assess and, depending on the state, license new teachers. In addition, the Teacher and School Leader Incentive Program supports schools that experiment with performance pay plans and other key ways to increase teacher quality (Klein, 2016).

Although standardized testing has been used to evaluate student achievement since Thorndike developed the first standardized tests in the early part of the 20th century, mandatory testing and its significant rewards and penalties have not achieved what was intended. That has led some to lament the impact high-stakes testing has had on the role of the teacher. Teachers who entered the profession intending to inspire students and nurture curiosity often find that a disproportionate amount of their energy is spent preparing students to pass tests (Beers, 2013/2014) that do not necessarily lead to student growth.

Proponents claim that test results can help schools to identify areas of weakness and to allocate resources where they are most needed to improve their programs and the performance of individual students. While states now have more freedom to assess students using multiple measures, the need to assess through standardized measurements remains (Klein, 2016). As such, questions abound about the implications of such tests and the ever-widening gap between educational policy and actual teaching (Shanahan, 2014). One concern centers on the narrowing of the school curriculum because of the heavy emphasis placed on test preparation (Nichols & Berliner, 2007, p. 9). As Guilfoyle (2006) explains, "In this culture of 'What gets measured gets done,' the question that begs to be asked [is], 'What happens to what *doesn't* get measured?'" What doesn't get tested can include subjects such as social studies, visual arts, music, and physical education as well as school-sponsored extracurricular activities. All too often, these subjects become marginalized. In their study of social studies instruction, Fichett and Heafner (2010) found that an average of 12 minutes a day in elementary grades and 24 minutes a day in the intermediate grades were spent on social studies instruction. Teachers often used time designated for social studies instruction to teach math and reading skills that are part of mandated assessments.

No single test can meet the needs of all groups who require information about school and student performance. While data collection is essential for understanding what students know, purposeful assessment is essential. Different constituencies need different types of information, presented in different forms, and made available at different times; and while policy makers and the general public may benefit from information provided by norm-referenced tests that are administered on an annual basis, teachers need ongoing, targeted assessment that will guide their practice and give insight into whether students are "getting it." Parents, teachers, and students need information specific to individual students on a more consistent basis. Multiple methods of formative assessment about student progress are more effective than standardized tests in providing that type of information. The goal of assessment should not be just to identify the gaps in mastery, but instead identify the ways in which students "think about what they know and don't know" in order to inform teachers' next steps on the journey towards mastery (Supovitz, 2012, p. 2).

Standardized Testing: What Teachers Need to Know

Standardized reading tests are formal, usually machine-scorable instruments in which scores for the tested group are compared with standards established by an original normative population. The purpose of a standardized reading test is to show where students rank in relation to other students based on a single performance.

To make sense of test information and to determine how relevant or useful it may be, you need to be thoroughly familiar with the language, purposes, and legitimate uses of standardized tests. For example, as a test user, it is your responsibility to know about the norming and standardization of the reading test used by your school district.

MyLab Education
Response Journal 4.2
When did you take your first "big" test in school? What kind of an experience was it? How did you feel before, during, and after that assessment experience?

MyLab Education
Video Example 4.1:
Analyzing Benchmark Data to Identify Student Misconceptions
Watch this video to see how one teaching team analyzed benchmark data in order to improve instruction.

Consult a test manual or online resource for an explanation of what the test is about, the rationale behind its development, and a clear description of what the test purports to measure. Not only should test instructions for administering and scoring be clearly spelled out, but also information related to norms, reliability, and validity should be easily defined and made available.

Norms represent average scores of a sampling of students selected for testing according to factors such as age, sex, race, grade, and socioeconomic status. Once a test maker determines norm scores, those scores become the basis for comparing the test performance of individuals or groups with the performance of those who were included in the norming sample. *Representativeness,* therefore, is a key concept in understanding student scores. It's crucial to make sure that the norming sample used in devising the reading test resembles the characteristics of the students you teach.

Norms are extrapolated from raw scores. A *raw score* is the number of items a student answers correctly on a test. Raw scores are converted to other kinds of scores so that comparisons can be made among individuals or groups of students. Three such conversions—percentile scores, stanine scores, and grade-equivalent scores—are often represented by test makers as they report scores.

Percentile scores describe the relative standing of a student at a particular grade level. For example, the percentile score of 85 of a student in the fifth grade means that his or her score is equal to or higher than the scores of 85% of comparable fifth graders.

Stanine scores are raw scores that have been transformed to a common standard to permit comparison. In this respect, stanines represent one of several types of standard scores. Because standard scores have the same mean and standard deviation, they permit the direct comparison of student performance across tests and subtests. The term *stanine* refers to a *sta*ndard *nine*-point scale, in which the distribution of scores on a test is divided into nine parts. Each stanine indicates a single digit ranging from 0 to 9 in numerical value. Thus, a stanine of 5 is at the midpoint of the scale and represents average performance. Stanines 6, 7, 8, and 9 indicate increasingly better performance; stanines 4, 3, 2, and 1 represent decreasing performance. As teachers, we can use stanines effectively to view a student's approximate place above or below the average in the norming group.

Grade-equivalent scores provide information about reading-test performance as it relates to students at various grade levels. A grade-equivalent score is a questionable abstraction. It suggests that growth in reading progresses throughout a school year at a constant rate; for example, a student with a grade-equivalent score of 7.4 is supposedly performing at a level that is average for students who have completed 4 months of the seventh grade. At best, this is a silly and spurious interpretation: "Based on what is known about human development generally and language growth specifically, such an assumption [underlying grade-equivalent scores] makes little sense when applied to a human process as complex as learning to read" (Vacca et al., 2002).

Reliability refers to the consistency or stability of a student's test scores. A teacher must raise the question, "Can similar test results be achieved under different conditions?" Suppose your students were to take a reading test on Monday, their first day back from vacation, and then take an equivalent form of the same test on Thursday. Would their scores be about the same? If so, the test may indeed be reliable.

Validity, by contrast, tells the teacher whether the test is measuring what it purports to measure. Validity, without question, is one of the most important characteristics of a test. If the test purports to measure reading comprehension, what is the test maker's concept of reading comprehension? Answers to this question provide insight into the *construct validity* of a test. Other aspects of validity include *content validity* (Does the test reflect the domain or content area being examined?) and *predictive validity* (Does the test predict future performance?).

In general, information from standardized tests may help screen for students who have major difficulties in reading, compare general reading achievement levels of different classes or grades of students, assess group reading achievement, and assess the reading growth of groups of students. However, teachers also need useful information about students' text-related behavior and background knowledge. You would be guilty of misusing standardized test results if you were to extrapolate about a student's background knowledge or ability to comprehend course materials based on standardized reading-test performance. Alternatives to high-stakes, formal assessments are found in an informal, authentic approach to assessment. One of the most useful tools for inquiry into the classroom is observation.

MyLab Education
Video Example 4.2:
Standardized Tests
Watch this video to hear Gerald Bracey explain the components and purposes of standardized testing.

Authentic Assessment: The Teacher's Role

In a high-stakes approach to assessment, the *test* is the major tool; in an authentic approach, the teacher is the major tool. As such, the teacher's role moves from the owner of knowledge to that of a facilitator who uses observation, student feedback, and knowledge of instructional practice to enhance the meaning of classroom events. Teachers' collection and use of data allows for strategic response rooted in the student thinking process (Supovitz, 2012, p. 3). Consequently, the teacher moves into the role of an observer of the relevant interactive and independent behavior of students as they learn in the content area classroom.

Observation is one unobtrusive measure that ranges from the occasional noticing of unusual student behavior to frequent anecdotal jottings to regular and detailed written field notes. Besides the obvious opportunity to observe students' oral and silent reading, there are other advantages to observation. Observing students' appearance, posture, mannerisms, enthusiasm, or apathy may reveal information about self-image and aids in developing the foundation of student achievement: student–teacher relationships. However, unless there is a systematic effort to analyze student performance, valuable insights may be lost. Teachers must listen and watch with purpose. Observation should be a natural outgrowth of teaching; it increases teaching efficiency and effectiveness. Instructional decisions based on accurate observations provide teachers with the "what and how to teach" in relation to communication tasks.

Today's teachers are expected to meet the special needs of all students. Consequently, the challenges of teaching diverse learners in the classroom may cause general education teachers to feel frustrated and unprepared. Understanding and accepting that all students learn and behave differently in the classroom can, however, lead to effective instructional adaptations. Lynne, a middle school literacy coach, explains how she has used observational assessment to help address the needs of students with behavioral issues that affect their learning:

> I am often asked by teachers for advice on how to address students struggling with behavioral choices in the classroom. I begin by recommending that the teacher use a behavior frequency observation checklist as a diagnostic–prescriptive measure to record the instances of inappropriate or inattentive behaviors they observe. I've used the checklist with individual teachers and with teachers across subject areas to document student behaviors observed in different content area classes. For example, I've given teachers across content areas the same frequency observation form to document the existence of the targeted behaviors of a particular student or a group of students. This orderly observation and documentation allowed the teachers to determine if the same behaviors occurred across content area classes or if the behaviors were isolated to a specific class. The idea is that you can mesh qualitative data with quantifiable patterns or trends to develop and implement appropriate intervention strategies. After an agreed-upon period, the frequency checklist can be repeated to determine to what extent intervention strategies were effective.

There are several advantages to using a frequency observation form: The observer can identify specific target behaviors or academic skills; when completed, the form provides objective data about targeted behaviors that can be used when communicating concerns to parents or to school support personnel; data collected can be used to develop intervention strategies to enhance the learning environment for the student; and the form can serve as both a pre-assessment tool to establish a baseline for future intervention and as a post-assessment tool to judge the impact of an intervention. This data also can then be shared with the student, giving them a snapshot of their behavior, allowing for self-reflection and metacognition opportunities. In addition to the basic format for behavior frequency data, Lynne included two other sections: *other pertinent information*, where she noted the reason for the observation as well as any support the student might be receiving in or out of school, and *tentative conclusions*, where she made comments about what she just observed and what to focus on in the next observation. Figure 4.1 illustrates Lynne's observation of Thomas.

To record systematic observations, to note significant teaching–learning events, or simply to make note of classroom happenings, you need to keep a notebook on hand or develop a digital document that can be altered in the moment. In addition, some apps can be utilized via a phone or tablet so that the process becomes streamlined while the teacher is actively engaged in the classroom. Information collected purposefully aids in classifying information, inferring patterns of behavior, and making predictions about the effectiveness of innovative instructional procedures. As they accumulate, these "field notes" provide documentary evidence of students' interactions over periods of time.

Teachers and others who use informal, authentic tools to collect information almost always use more than one means of collecting data, a practice known as *triangulation*. This helps ensure that the information is valid and that what is learned from one source is corroborated by what is learned from another source. A fifth-grade science teacher recounted how he combined the taking of field notes with active listening and discussion to assess his students' current achievement and future needs in the subject:

> I briefly document on individual cards how students behave during experiments conducted individually, within a group, during reading assignments, during phases of a project, and during formal assessments. Knowing which students or what size group tends to enhance or distract a student's ability to stay on task helps me organize a more effective instructional environment. When students meet to discuss their projects and the steps they followed, I

Figure 4.1 Behavior Frequency Observation

Classroom Artifact

Student name: Thomas   Date: October 12

Start time: 10:00 A.M.   Stop time: 10:30 A.M.

School: Edison Middle School   Grade: 6

Subject: Mathematics

Other pertinent information: Thomas is being observed to determine if a referral for possible ADHD evaluation is appropriate.

Target Behavior	Frequency of Occurrence	Total
Calls out of turn	|||||||||||||	13
Moves out of seat	||||||	6
Distracts others (e.g., drops things, moves the desk, touches others)	||||||||||	10
Makes unnecessary noises (e.g., taps desk, hums)	|||||||	7
Off task (e.g., not working; does not start assignment)	|||||||||||||||	15

Tentative conclusion: Additional observations across content area classes are recommended.

listen carefully for strategies they used or neglected. I sometimes get insights into what a particular student offered this group; I get ideas for topics for future science lessons and projects or minilessons on time management, breaking up a topic into "chunks," and so on. I also have students complete their own growth and process reflections, giving insight into what they felt went well and what areas their groups collectively and individually struggled with. My field notes, combined with the student perspective, provides a behind the scenes perspective of thinking processes and missed learning opportunities.

Informal assessment strategies are useful to teachers during parent–teacher conferences for discussing a student's strengths and weaknesses. They also help build an ongoing record of progress that may be motivating for students to reflect on and useful for their other teachers in planning lessons in different subjects. These "short cycle" assessments provide quick checkpoints for student comprehension that are generally tied tightly to content and instructional practices. (Supovitz, 2012, p. 5)

Many students want to establish a personal rapport with their teachers. They may talk of myriad subjects, seemingly unrelated to the unit. It is often during this informal chatter, however, that a teacher finds out about the students' backgrounds, problems, and interests. This type of conversation, in which a teacher assumes the role of active listener, can provide suggestions about topics for future lessons and materials and help the student's voice emerge. These moments serve not only as informal collections about learning style and interests for motivation, but also provide something traditional assessments are unable to do—yield opportunities to build connections that, in turn, translate to student motivation and resilience. Students can't truly grow if they don't believe their teacher is invested in their growth.

Discussion, both casual and directed, is also an integral part of assessment. Try to be available, both before and after class, for discussions about general topics, lessons, and assignments; seeing the whole learner is a holistic form of assessment that can pay dividends toward student achievement. For an assessment of reading comprehension, nothing replaces one-on-one discussion of the material, whether before, during, or after the actual reading. Finally, encourage students to verbalize their positive and negative feelings about the class itself as well as about topics, readings, and content area activities. Box 4.1 discusses how one teaching team sought to integrate a disciplinary literacy approach into its assessment practices.

MyLab Education **Self-Check 4.1**

MyLab Education **Application Exercise 4.1:**
Using Authentic Formative and Summative Assessments to Support Content Area Instruction

---

Portfolio Assessment in a Digital Age

4.2   Describe how portfolios can be used to assess student learning in content areas.

A valuable trend that occasionally swings in and out of mandated curricula is portfolio assessment. Portfolios can be a powerful tool for educators because of the unique opportunity they provide to assess patterns in students' academic progress, reflective thinking, and achievement over time (Chang, Liang, & Chen, 2013). Portfolios encourage the integration of different types of summative and formative assessments, which allows teachers to incorporate intervention and enrichment as needed. In addition, the combination of technology and student access to online publishing provides a unique opportunity for real-time publication and comprehensive synthesis of reading, writing, responding, and analyzing. Electronic portfolios, sometimes referred to as e-portfolios or digital portfolios, allow students to organize information, highlight skills, and represent their work

Box 4.1 Disciplinary Literacy

Using Assessments to Teach What Matters

A team of eighth-grade social studies teachers is charged with cooperatively planning its assessments. The teachers are in the process of transitioning to a disciplinary literacy approach to content area teaching and learning and are struggling to reach consensus on how best to assess their students' understanding of concepts presented in class. More importantly, they must collectively address the misconceptions and areas of stagnant growth that the data highlights. Previously, their instructional methods were traditional lectures and note taking, interspersed with some creative and group learning strategies, such as dioramas and plays. For these interactive activities, rubrics were used to assess students' participation; however, multiple-choice questions, with an occasional essay, were the predominant assessment tools. Some of the teachers favored this traditional approach because it provided a summative grade and mirrored the requirements that students encountered on mandated high-stakes assessments.

To be prepared to think like historians, students have worked to learn and use content-specific vocabulary, deconstructed texts to compare primary documents, and written reports to show their findings and conclusions based on the texts they have read. They have worked with small groups and kept a log to remind themselves of conversations, student participation, and great student-generated questions. The students have worked as partners to replicate the academic world of the historian and in these partnerships have created articles, compiled into a class journal. In one class, the students worked according to a rubric that guided their critical thinking. The teacher assessed their writing according to how the students first deconstructed the text and then how they used those ideas to comment on the habits and lifestyles of the aristocracy prior to the French Revolution. Within their writing, students used vocabulary effectively and practiced writing in a style that was indicative of historians, based on mentor texts they had read. The next step for these teachers was to consider additional assessment tools that would be an effective match for disciplinary literacy learning. They also sought to support colleagues who were accustomed to traditional assessment methods and who were not entirely convinced that a change in this area was needed. These teachers moved their practice from a teaching, assessment, and review cycle to a more purposeful cycle of concept presentation, application, demonstration, and feedback loop, where learning and practice are continuous and feedback is used to highlight what students are doing well and what changes need to be made to carry them towards mastery.

Linking Theory to Practice

Part of an effective content classroom includes the manner in which students are assessed and how those assessments are used to guide instruction. Assessments should be created with an intention of providing the teacher with information about how the students are learning, how they are thinking about the information, and how they are applying information outside of the textbook context. It is essential that teachers leverage the benefits of both formative and summative assessment "to focus not only on how to best measure students' needs, but also on how to measure and analyze classroom implementation/processes" (Glover et al., 2019, p. 67).

Formative assessments are shorter assessments, which may be used on a daily basis, that are intended to provide the teacher with a better understanding of how the students are analyzing and applying the concepts presented. Summative assessments typically follow a unit of study. They provide an opportunity for students to "show what they know" and engage in assessments that are more comprehensive. While formative assessments occur in the moment and are integrated in an ongoing cycle, summative assessments occur "at the end," and often teachers give these assessments as the final demonstration of mastery for a unit or concept. However, both types are instrumental in planning instruction while ensuring that each student has an opportunity to succeed in mastering the concepts essential to the content area.

Following these guidelines, using assessments to effectively plan instruction works directly to support the implementation of the concepts embedded in disciplinary literacies. The purpose behind disciplinary literacy is to help reinforce the reading, writing, and communication skills needed for students to successfully participate in the respective disciplines. As such, assessments should focus on how students are thinking, the vocabulary they are using, and how they are processing information, critically communicating, and problem solving according to the norms of the discipline (Harlen, 2005). Effective assessments should then be built to help students form and practice those mind-sets that will serve them well as they work toward mastery.

This allows for the use of assessment that moves beyond the traditional summative multiple-choice and essay-based tests. When effectively created and used to better understand student learning practices, assessments should be part of the learning process (Fang & Pace, 2013). Too often, assessments are stand-alone tools that have little to do with the daily life of the student. Students learn how to "cram" for a test, only to forget the information the following day. In disciplinary literacy classrooms, however, assessments can be reworked as tools of learning, preparing students for the real-world applications of the discipline (Saltmarsha & Saltmarsha, 2008).

To create an effective assessment, one must first highlight the overall focus of instruction. Disciplinary literacy suggests the following skills, knowledge, and attitudes may be the focus of classroom instruction:

- Vocabulary and how it is used contextually

- Skills needed to comprehend and deconstruct text

- Skills, social practices, and attitudes needed to participate effectively in each respective discipline

- Overall issues and themes related to critical thinking, moving students away from looking for one right answer

- Writing practices and an understanding of which genres are most appropriate to each discipline

Thinking back to the two types of assessments, students should be given both formative and summative opportunities to engage in authentic tasks that help them demonstrate and practice what they are learning. Here are several ideas for formative assessments. Remember, their purpose is to gauge on a daily basis how students are "forming" their ideas and practicing their skills associated with the content as they use vocabulary and learn to interact with text.

- **Concept Mapping**
  Through a concept map of learned material, the student moves his or her invisible thinking process to a tangible product that illustrates his or her connections and comprehension. The goal is to have students "map" a concept, including content-specific vocabulary, and key elements of instruction in a way that visually organizes and demonstrates relationships and meaning among content. These maps can be used for whole-class creation to give a snapshot of understanding, small-group creation to see collective thinking, or as individual assessments of student thinking both in the moment and over time.

- **Exit and entrance slips**
  Unlike traditional slips that test knowledge, these slips can be used to help reinforce contextual vocabulary usage. Learning the language of each discipline is an essential component of understanding how to communicate within each content area.

- **Student quick writes**
  Chapter 9 provides several different short writing strategies that can be used to help gauge student knowledge. These quick writes, which may be written in "tweet" form or on the back of an index card to ensure brevity, can be completed at the beginning of the day to better understand what students remember or at the end of the day to evaluate what they have learned. In addition, they can be used as summary "check-ins" that can support mastery and retention of concepts.

- **Student metacognition journals**
  Metacognition journals employ questions that make students more aware of the thought processes they use as they read and how those processes affect their interaction with the text. Metacognition journals may be structured through writing prompts that allow the students to gauge the hows and whys of their thinking. These tables and prompts might include questions such as:

  - How difficult was this section?
  - What strategies did you use to better understand the text, and why did you choose them?

- Is there anything you might change to make the strategies easier for you to use?
- Look at your writing. In what ways does it reflect the work of a scientist?
- Think about the reading. How did it help you better understand the concepts we talked about in class? What can you do if you still have questions?
- Think about our activity. How did it help you better understand the text? What can you do if you still have questions?
- Name one thing you did today that reflects the work of a scientist. Explain why.
- How comfortable are you "thinking like a scientist"? What are some things you may need help on to feel more comfortable?
- Tell me more about your thinking process when solving the problem.
- What obstacles did you face in creating your answer, and what did you do to overcome gaps in your thinking?

Summative assessments should be planned to allow the students to stretch out in their thinking. They should enable the students to summarize what they have learned, show a depth of understanding, and practice critical thinking skills. Here are a few examples:

- Inquiry-based projects
- Deconstructing and evaluating text sources
- Discipline-specific reports, such as those that analyze and discuss debates, archaeology digs, science labs, plays, and writing pieces
- Long-term writing projects that show a development in thought
  - Project-based learning that addresses real-world issues and utilizes content-specific processes to draw conclusions and create arguments

The challenge when planning assessments is to make them meaningful instructional tools. As a teacher implementing disciplinary literacy practices into classroom instruction, one should focus the assessments on ensuring that all students are forming habits of thought rather than retaining disparate pieces of information. When working with teachers who have different educational philosophies, it may be challenging to convince them that logs and projects have just as much weight as their multiple-choice tests. However, when assessments are effectively connected to and are used to guide instruction, they do serve to help teach what matters.

(Waters, 2007). Unlike blogs and random posts, which are considered personal spaces for expression, e-portfolios are artifact and standard driven that, when implemented and maintained correctly, can be valuable tools for learning that reinforce complex thinking, self-monitoring, and writing skills while providing educators a way to meet the endless requirements of standardized testing proficiency and teaching demands to create innovative environments.

As a global, balanced practice in gathering information about students, portfolio assessment is a powerful concept that has immediate appeal and potential for accomplishing the following purposes:

- Providing and organizing information about the nature of students' work and achievements

- Encouraging student management of learning and expectations as well as reflection and thematic analysis

- Involving students themselves in reflecting on their capabilities and making decisions about their work

- Using the holistic nature of instruction as a base from which to consider attitudes, strategies, and responses

- Assisting in the planning of appropriate instruction to follow

- Showcasing work mutually selected by students and teacher

- Revealing diverse and special needs of students as well as talents

- Incorporating multiliteracies and social technologies that students use outside of the classroom

- Displaying multiple student-produced artifacts over time

- Integrating assessment into the daily instruction as a natural, vital part of teaching and learning

- Expanding both the quality and the quantity of evidence by means of a variety of indicators

- Providing an alternative to the standard paper-and-pencil assessment routines

Portfolios are vehicles for ongoing assessment; and although they may seem challenging to implement, once developed, they provide teachers with an overview of a student's skills and growth. As teaching and learning become more digitized and data collection more scrutinized, many educators are looking toward forms of technology-enabled assessments (TEAs) to enhance their practice and engage students in both summative and formative assessment (Deneen et al., 2018, p. 487). Portfolios allow teachers and students to monitor both learning outcomes and processes. Students can engage in self-monitoring their progress, strengths, and weaknesses; problem solve; and work to achieve goals (Chang, Liang, & Chen, 2013). As such, portfolios lend themselves to instruction in content areas ranging from math and science to English, history, and health education. Though the content of a portfolio is tailored to a subject, the goal and production of the portfolio remain consistent. A benefit that encourages cross-curricular opportunities, the use of portfolios encourages integration and vertical alignment throughout students' school days.

Though teacher assignments and support define the creation of the portfolio, teachers and students collaboratively choose the significant pieces incorporated into student portfolios. Selections represent processes and activities more than products; student assessment is truly focused on the learning rather than the outcome. The feedback opportunities provided by a portfolio allow the learning process to be ongoing—with teacher and student input guiding the continuation of best practices and correcting misconceptions and incorrect thinking that obstructs the path towards mastery. A distinct value underlying the use of portfolios is a commitment to students' evaluation of their own understanding and personal development. In addition, electronic portfolios allow students to critique and "teach" through response and interaction with their peers' portfolios. By providing a more in-depth and thoughtful assessment than can be gleaned from on-demand tests alone, digital portfolios demonstrate student growth from novice to master (Deneen et al., 2018

p. 488). In addition to serving as a resource for student and teacher collaboration, digital portfolios have the "capacity to generate formative, student-regulated continuous engagement" (Deneen, 2013).

Adapting Portfolios to Content Area Classes

Through individual adjustments, portfolios can be adapted to serve different learning needs across the content areas. Techniques such as rubric evaluation, self- and peer responses, observing, and use of parent and teacher feedback provide helpful sources of information about students in the classroom. The use of portfolios is, in many ways, a more practical method of organizing this type of information, in addition to providing an opportunity that pushes students to publish their work and take agency over their learning. While, in some cases, portfolios have earned a reputation for being high maintenance, electronic portfolios make student assessment over time easier for teachers because of their holistic and self-motivating nature. With digitized work, teachers are able to identify examples from a portfolio and adapt them into meaningful, instructional content (Waters, 2007).

Once students take ownership for their portfolio development, the continuous adding and revising of their portfolios incorporate themselves into the daily routines of the classroom. For example, students may begin a math course by saying things such as, "What are we learning this for anyway? It's got nothing to do with me and my life." As opportunities are provided for functional application in realistic situations, student comments and attitudes may change over time to, "I never realized how the things I am doing in class connect to my life and world!" Additionally, students may view their portfolio as another form of social networking within the school day. Responses and reviews of other portfolios provide interconnectedness to students' use of the Internet and natural affinity for technology.

Much more than a folder for housing daily work, a record file, or a grab bag, a portfolio is a comprehensive profile of each student's progress and growth. As emphasis on global competitiveness and standards-based instruction sharpens, teachers must find ways to actively encourage "integrative, holistic, student-centered learning across academic and cocurricular domains" (Kehoe & Goudzwaard, 2015, p. 350). With the incorporation of the Internet and website building, the portfolio itself can be completely electronic. The transition from paper-and-pencil portfolios to digitally designed formats allows student collections to become a place for reflection and growth, not just a collection of artifacts (Hicks et al., 2007). Student portfolios can become an exploration of learning, extending outside the realm of standard paper activities and incorporating additional tools of learning and enjoyment, including artistic visuals, music, and video production. Professional associations have endorsed the use of portfolios. For example, if you are preparing to teach a math class, whether it's arithmetic, algebra, or trigonometry, the National Council of Teachers of Mathematics (NCTM) offers assessment guidelines to help teachers to decide with students the types of student work-products that should be part of a portfolio. Box 4.2 outlines a procedure for implementing portfolios.

Melissa, a secondary English teacher, experimented with e-portfolios as a comprehensive evaluation tool for literacy and writing development. Here's how she described the process of implementation that she followed:

> I viewed e-portfolio development to incorporate technology and student multiliteracies with state- and county-mandated content and researched-based instruction. Once a skeptic of the portfolio, the integration of standards-driven instruction and teaching evidences for student success had me searching for a method to assess students and collect data in a holistic, ongoing manner. The logistics of traditional portfolios didn't align with my practice, the

organization and filing of the students' papers seemed daunting, and the shuffling of folders and wasted time spent on portfolio development made the understanding of portfolios as an assessment tool nearly impossible. Once I incorporated students' technology skills with the portfolio concept, I was able to see the benefit of the portfolio and even found grading and "paperwork" benefits as well.

To begin implementing e-portfolios in my class, I followed certain steps:

- In order to identify a proper outlet for student e-portfolio and publishing, I started with a general Google search and then focused on researching websites and technologies that were freely available and user friendly. Both commercial portfolio software and website creation sites offer pros and cons that must be considered in relation to student needs and available technology. Though this process and the initial setup of the student portfolios were a bit time consuming, it was time well spent. Once the student websites to house their portfolios were established and the process of implementing the portfolios was completed, the portfolios themselves became almost entirely student driven and self-sufficient.

- I explained the concept of portfolios and discussed why they were important. I emphasized to students their role as a writer and publisher to the Internet world. Students were provided examples of e-portfolios to aid their understanding of acceptable artifacts. I also compared their electronic portfolio to their pages on social media sites and referenced the "upkeep" of their learning and examination as a tool for exploration, where layers are peeled away to reveal new meaning. Similar to interactive notebooks or day planners with which the students were already familiar, we discussed as a class digital portfolio organization and the basic elements that must be included. Finally, I encouraged students to utilize one another. Peer and self-generated texts became outlets for understanding and analysis. Student self-maintenance was the driving force—choice and freedom fit within the parameters of their portfolio creation.

- Next, I explained the purposes of our portfolio: to describe a portion of students' work over the quarter, showing how it has improved and how they've grown; to reflect on and evaluate their own work in writing and literacy; and to compile a body of work that can travel with them indefinitely. As a class, we also discussed the usefulness of analysis and reliability—understanding what is significant and owned versus what is plagiarized and unreliable. For those students who were graduating or applying to further their education, I explained the importance of the "live" portfolio as a reference for their work and accomplishments. In addition, I explained the portfolio as an activity in global connectedness and the students' role as writer, thinker, creator, and evaluator. The goal of our discussion was to have the students see the opportunity to have agency over their work and learning.

- Then we discussed the requirements for our portfolio: to create work and explore literature, literacy, writing, and skills development as an integrated process; to incorporate all levels of learning as well as venture outside of the classic paper trail of thinking; to incorporate writing as well as multimedia, art, and audio as a means of analysis, response, and understanding; to post only the best work that each student has done; to respond and reflect not only on a student's own creation but also the portfolios and work of others; to add pieces that also conform to standard writing and reading expectations; and, at the end of the school year, to evaluate students' overall progress and development.

- I gave examples of the kinds of contributions that would be incorporated: writing, reflections (both self and peer), research findings and sources, projects, videos (both individual creation and those found to connect to student learning), responses to writing prompts, visuals, and audio. In addition, I kept a linked portfolio and posted assignments, classmate examples, and potential prompts for those students who were struggling.

- Finally, we discussed the need for continued updating of portfolio websites and the importance of responding to each other's work. Guidelines were given for posting frequency and topics. All student essays and submitted writing needed to be uploaded to a blog page attached to the student's website portfolio. All documents and materials that were not created solely by the student required citations or references to illustrate the fact that it was not the student's own work. Students were given examples and a brief tutorial for setting up their webpages. Class time was allocated for students to set up their portfolios. Students were advised that portfolios would be graded periodically for content and growth.

Incorporating electronic portfolios is a continuous process for both students and the instructor. To fully utilize portfolio development as part of planning and assessment, teachers must first define the learning purpose and work toward integration of authentic learning activities (Lewis, 2017, p. 73). As the teacher gains a better understanding of technology and potential uses and assignments, the student expectations and portfolios will need to be adapted accordingly. While the lack of paper files is a bonus, the incorporation of the Internet has pros and cons. Plagiarism, copyright violations, and Internet guidelines must be explained so students understand the consequences and procedures. Additionally, student incorporation of their social literacies with formal learning may require an adjustment period. Regardless, the electronic portfolio has benefits beyond its classroom application. Not only are digital records of achievement maintained by the students themselves, but also the revision of portfolio material can be as easy as a click of the computer mouse (Lam, 2011). Additionally, grading, growth, and comprehension can be monitored in a more precise, less stressful process. Student ownership and response, teacher accessibility, and concrete learning artifacts make the electronic portfolio a tool to try. Figure 4.2 depicts the scoring rubric that Melissa used to assess her students' e-portfolios.

Box 4.2 Evidence-Based Best Practices

Steps in the Implementation of Portfolios

To get started implementing the portfolio assessment process, certain logical steps must be taken and certain decisions need to be made:

1. *Discuss with your students the notion of portfolios as an interactive vehicle for assessment.* Explain the concept and show some examples of items that might be considered good candidates for the portfolio. Provide some examples from other fields, such as art and business, where portfolios have historically recorded performance and provided updates.

2. *Specify your assessment model.* What is the purpose of the portfolio? Who is the audience for the portfolio? How much will students be involved? Purposes, for example, may be to showcase students' best work, to document or describe an aspect of their work over time (to show growth), to evaluate by making judgments using either certain standards agreed on in advance or the relative growth and development of each individual, or to document the process that goes into the development of a single product related to a unit of study.

3. *Decide what types of requirements will be used, approximately how many items, and what format will be appropriate for the portfolio.* Furthermore, will students be designing their own portfolios? Or will they have a uniform look? Plan an explanation of portfolios for your colleagues and the principal; also, decide on the date when this process will begin.

4. *Consider which contributions are appropriate for your content area.* The main techniques for assessing students' behavior, background knowledge, attitudes, interests, and perceptions are writing samples, video records, conference notes, tests and quizzes, standardized tests, pupil performance objectives, self-evaluations, peer evaluations, daily work samples, and collections of written work (such as vocabulary activities, graphic organizers, concept maps, inquiry/research projects, and reports).

Figure 4.2 Electronic Portfolio Rubric

	1 Not Demonstrated	2 Developing	3 Proficient	4 Accomplished	5 Distinguished
Artifacts					
Selected Artifacts	Artifacts are unconnected to skills and objectives; selection is based on convenience.	Artifacts demonstrate targeted skills and objectives on the basic level.	Artifacts clearly demonstrate targeted skills and objectives.	Artifacts clearly demonstrate targeted skills and objectives; purposeful selection illustrates deeper understanding and reflection.	Artifacts clearly demonstrate extensive understanding of targeted skills and objectives; purposeful selection illustrates reflection and mastery.
Variety of Artifacts	All artifacts are of similar form and quality.	Artifacts vary in form, but quality is similar	Artifacts vary in form and demonstrate growth over time.	Artifacts vary in form and quality; consistent growth is evident.	Artifacts vary in form and quality; consistent growth is evident, and content illustrates clear growth and development.
Mechanics	Spelling and punctuation distract from the content; editing is not evident.	Spelling and punctuation errors are present but do not distract from the content.	Spelling and punctuation errors are minor; editing efforts are demonstrated.	There are few to no spelling and punctuation errors; editing resulted in revisions that worked.	Spelling, punctuation, and editing resulted in a work that is ready for publication.
Reflections					
	No reflection on work is evident; reflections don't include areas of growth or areas of continued effort.	Reflections are vague or repetitive; reflections may include areas of growth but don't describe areas of continued effort.	Most of the reflections include specific reactions, areas of growth, and recognized areas of continued effort.	All reflections are specific to selected artifacts; reactions include a clear understanding of areas of growth and noted weakness.	All reflections include detailed reactions that are descriptive and insightful; clear understanding of growth and areas of weakness are noted, and goals are set for future work.
Multimedia Elements					
Collaboration	There is no connection between student work and peer/audience influences; comments are not posted.	Connections between student work and peer/audience influence are limited.	Connections between student work and peer/audience influence are demonstrated in student's revisions and reflections.	Connections between student work and peer/audience influence are demonstrated in student's revisions, reflections, and posted elements to extend concepts.	Connections between student work and peer/audience influence are strongly linked to student's revisions, reflections, and posted elements to extend concepts; clear connections are drawn between targeted concepts and external information.
Graphics, Links, and 21st-Century Elements	There are no elements that contribute to understanding of goals; multimedia use is inappropriate and distracting.	Some elements that contribute to understanding of goals are present, but multimedia use is basic and limited.	Elements that contribute to understanding of goals are present; multimedia use is complex and illustrates connections.	Elements contribute to understanding of goals and demonstrate complex thinking; multimedia selection is purposeful and complex.	Elements clearly demonstrate understanding of goals and make complex connections between objectives; multimedia selection is purposeful, complex, and creative.
Publishing Elements					
Organization	There is no organization; portfolio is simply a random collection of student work.	Portfolio organization is limited; student work generally illustrates progressive growth and understanding.	Portfolio is organized with thought and demonstrates progressive growth and understanding.	Portfolio organization is well thought out; collection demonstrates progressive growth and understanding, and order choice is specific to objectives.	Portfolio organization shows extensive understanding of growth and progression; order choice demonstrates clear connections between objectives and student reflections.
Formatting	Text is difficult to read, navigation is confusing, and use of formatting tools is not evident.	Text is difficult to read, navigation is basic, and better use of formatting tools is needed.	Text is generally easy to read, navigation allows for accessibility, and formatting tools are used.	Text is easy to read, navigation is well thought out, and creative use of formatting tools is present.	Text is appropriately selected for maximum impact, navigation is well planned, and creative use of formatting tools makes for maximum effectiveness.

Figure 4.2 (*Continued*)

	1 **Not Demonstrated**	2 **Developing**	3 **Proficient**	4 **Accomplished**	5 **Distinguished**
Citations	Multimedia is not cited and/or citations are not correctly formatted.	Some of the multimedia used is cited with accurate and correct citations.	Most of the multimedia is cited with accurate and correct citations.	All multimedia is cited with accurate and correct citations.	All multimedia and content in the student portfolio is accurate and correctly cited.
Formal Language	Portfolio is casual, and social networking elements are present.	Portfolio uses basic formal language with little social networking elements.	Most of the portfolio utilizes formal writing and differs from social networking elements.	Formal writing is used throughout the portfolio; social networking elements are not present.	Advanced formal writing and vocabulary are utilized; clear distinction between social networking and portfolio creation is evident.

Figure 4.3 A Personal Reflection for Science

Experiment:

They're All Wet—Determine what effect soaking seeds has on the time it takes them to sprout. In a group of four, develop an experiment using the scientific procedure. Evaluate your group from a scientific and cooperative point of view.

Reflection:

I selected the experiment "They're All Wet" as my best work in science for a number of reasons.

1. My group worked very well together. Everyone was assigned a job (reader, recorder, speaker, organizer), and everyone got to talk.

2. We wrote a sound hypothesis and design for our experiment because we took our time and we thought about the process.

3. We kept very good records of our observations, and then everyone participated in telling about them.

4. Even though our experiment did not prove our hypothesis, I learned many things from this experiment (see above).

Next time maybe my results will support my hypothesis, but I did learn the proper way to conduct an experiment.

Portfolio contributions can take many forms. Fifth-grade teacher Cherrie wanted to experiment with portfolios as an assessment tool for writing and science. An example of a portfolio contribution made by one of Cherrie's students is a personal reflection on an experiment done in science class (see Figure 4.3).

Checklists and Check-Ins

Informal assessment techniques, such as checklists, check-ins, and content area reading inventories (discussed later in this chapter), are different from natural, open-ended observation. They often consist of categories or questions that have already been determined; they impose an a priori classification scheme on the observation process. A checklist is designed to reveal categories of information the teacher has preselected. When constructing a checklist, you should know beforehand which reading and study tasks or attitudes you plan to observe. Individual items on the checklist then serve to guide your observations selectively.

The selectivity that a checklist offers is both its strength and its weakness as an observational tool. Checklists are obviously efficient because they guide your observations and allow you to zero in on certain kinds of behavior. But a checklist can also restrict observation by limiting the breadth of information recorded, excluding potentially valuable raw data. Figure 4.4 presents sample checklist items that may be adapted to specific instructional objectives in various content areas.

In addition to checklists, observations, logs, and inventories, various forms of check-ins should be considered part of the portfolio assessment repertoire. There are several

Figure 4.4 Sample Checklist Items for Observing Reading and Study Behavior

Reading and Study Behavior	Fred	Pat	Frank	JoAnne	Jerry	Courtney	Mike	Mary
Comprehension								
1. Follows the author's message	A	B	B	A	D	C	F	C
2. Evaluates the relevancy of facts								
3. Questions the accuracy of statements								
4. Critical of an author's bias								
5. Comprehends what the author means								
6. Follows text organization								
7. Can solve problems through reading								
8. Develops purposes for reading								
9. Makes predictions and takes risks								
10. Applies information to come up with new ideas								
Vocabulary								
1. Has a good grasp of technical terms in the subject under study								
2. Works out the meaning of an unknown word through context or structural analysis								
3. Knows how to use a dictionary effectively								
4. Sees relationships among key terms								
5. Becomes interested in the derivation of technical terms								
Study Habits								
1. Concentrates while reading								
2. Understands better by reading orally than silently								
3. Has a well-defined purpose in mind when studying								
4. Knows how to take notes during lecture and discussion								
5. Can organize material through outlining								
6. Skims to find the answer to a specific question								
7. Reads everything slowly and carefully								
8. Makes use of book parts								
9. Understands charts, maps, tables in the text								
10. Summarizes information								

Grading Key: **A** = always (excellent)
B = usually (good)
C = sometimes (average)
D = seldom (poor)
F = never (unacceptable)

advantages to using a variety of different formative check-in strategies to glean information about where students are in the learning process. First, students and teachers interact in collaborative settings. Second, an open-ended question format is conducive to the sharing of students' own views. Third, these strategies help to reveal to what extent students are in touch with their internal disposition toward reading subject matter material.

Some examples of formative assessments that act as pulse points for learning include class polls, 3-2-1 check-ins, and opportunity sticks. With each of these strategies, teachers can quickly discover what students think and how students' perceptions compare across learning levels.

Poll the Class

An easily implemented strategy, posing a question and polling the class gives teachers a quick formative way to identify student proficiencies or struggles. A powerful way to have student answers displayed and explored, polling either digitally or manually presents their answers, allows for comparison of responses put in the context of common group characteristics, and can be useful in securing baseline data about students' learning mastery.

CLASSROOM SNAPSHOT Fourth-grade teacher Angela utilizes a poll of the class to see mathematics mastery for adding decimals and decimal placement. After teaching the concept, Angela created a short activity via Plickers, a website that allows for instant class poll results. Having already assigned students numbers and printed off polling cards, Angela created seven questions and had students work independently on each question, showing their answers via their cue cards after each problem. Through the Plickers site (https://get.plickers.com/), the student poll results populated and demonstrated key areas of mastery and questions that required review. At the end of the activity, students reviewed their results both as a class and reflected on their contributions to overall class results.

3-2-1 Check-In

In 3-2-1 check-ins, teachers are not only requesting students to demonstrate mastery and summarize but also are looking for student reflection and insight for next steps for learning. This strategy asks students to present 3 things they learned, 2 connections they've made either with the content or across concepts, and 1 question that they still have regarding the lesson. Adaptations in the format and questions asked can be made, but the ultimate goal is a combination of mastery demonstration, connection to content and learning, and reflection on thinking and cognition.

CLASSROOM SNAPSHOT Utilized in a middle school robotics class, the 3-2-1 strategy was implemented as an exit ticket following an introductory lesson on coding. First, the teacher asked students to list 3 new things they learned during the class—this allowed them to pull from vocabulary and concepts, as well as acting as a review for the new content. Next, the teacher asked for 2 challenges that the students experienced while learning about coding. Finally, the teacher requested students generate 1 question they had after learning the new material or that emerged during the lesson and remained unanswered. The teacher then used this info to guide discussion and make clarifications during the subsequent coding lessons.

Opportunity Sticks

An exercise in randomization, opportunity sticks are simply a way to hold all students accountable for learning and speaking. For this strategy, teachers write student names individually on Popsicle sticks or individual notecards. After posing a question, reviewing a concept, or teaching new material, the teacher can randomly check in on students to see if comprehension and application is at the desired and planned level. Opportunity sticks are an easy way to formatively assess student learning, engage students, provide an opportunity for all voices to be heard, and allow freedom for feedback from both the teacher and other learners.

CLASSROOM SNAPSHOT Opportunity sticks used in a high school math classroom not only hold all students accountable for their learning, but also provide a good pulse point of where class comprehension is at any given time. Throughout the class period, the teacher pulled sticks for answers to questions during warm up review, minilesson questioning, and brief check-ins requesting students to repeat back concepts in their own words. To switch up the pressure and monotony of calling one student name and waiting for an answer, the teacher randomly picked more than one stick at a time and asked several students to rapid fire their answers. In addition, the instructor called on students one at a time, picking sticks after the initial response and having those students agree or disagree with the answers previously given. Finally, the teacher peppered opportunity stick answers with purposeful calling on students for either management or comprehension support.

A Framework for Strategy Implementation, Data Collection, and Instructional Decision Making

While data collection and formative assessment can drive classroom practice and student outcomes, just as important are the strategies used to collect the data and the interpretation and implementation of the findings. Not only is it important to know what students know, but it is of equal value to use that information to determine future implications for instruction and mastery. For true data-driven instruction to occur, practitioners must not only consider the what, but also the way (method), the why, and the what next. To implement a mastery learning cycle, teachers must teach, assess, data dive, plan, implement, and retest to ensure intended goals were met.

1. Teaching Cycle: What, why, and how is content taught?

   While planning practices frequently encourage teachers to think about content standards, essential questions surrounding concepts, and the activities that will help support knowledge acquisition, it is important for teachers to also process the reasons behind the skills and standard choices they are making during their planning process. In addition, practitioners need to reflect on the instructional strategies that best fit their plans and purposefully incorporate evidence to monitor student understanding. Furthermore, considering strategic assessments to address both individuals and groups prior to ever teaching the first lesson ensures that instruction will lead students to make clear and consistent connections, as well as provide plans that build upon each other with assessment "check-ins" tied to learning objectives.

2. Assessment: Does teaching translate to learning?

   Part of assessment that is often overlooked is the need for teachers to frequently and consistently utilize multiple purposefully planned evidences to monitor student understanding and progress. Not only must teachers carefully plan collection data points to "know what students know," but they also must consider what format of assessment makes the most sense for specific content standards, concepts, student progress, and point in the teaching cycle. Useful assessments not only provide evidence of student learning, but also act as points of feedback to guide student thinking and correct student misconceptions. Often, simply asking the question, "What am I looking for" or "How do I know if they know it?" can guide planning and assessment creation. Assessment strategies must be varied; using everything from class discussion to formal quizzes provides targeted support to improve both individuals and the group. By incorporating purposeful assessment that aims to see if teaching has translated to student mastery of concepts, teachers can get helpful glimpses into the strengths and weaknesses of the learners with which they work.

3. Data Analysis: What do the data show?

   While "data dives" encourage teachers to delve deep into assessment results to analyze differences in whole-class performance and identify patterns of learning, purposeful processes for data analysis help support comprehensive investigation of student thinking. First, teachers should be very clear during the planning of assessments to identify how each assessment question or inquiry represents a specific standard. For example, some teachers will have the standard or objective in parentheses next to the question number on the assessment. Next, teachers should frame their analysis around the guiding questions of "What do the data tell you?" and "How will I respond?" These questions become the bridge between where students currently are and the next steps to move them forward in their learning journey. Teachers engage in this analysis process looking at the percentage of students who reached mastery and at the percentage of students who have not yet reached mastery. The data provide an overall snapshot of student proficiency and also of teacher effectiveness.

Teachers should then move into an item analysis where each question and answer choice are reviewed for patterns of mastery or misconception. During this time, teachers must reflect regarding the skills students need to understand in order to demonstrate mastery on the assessment items. In addition, after looking over the items, teachers should prioritize which concepts must be retaught. For example, special consideration must be given when 50% or more of the students get any item wrong. With these items it's important to investigate not only the skills needed to correctly answer the question, but also identify if students chose the same wrong answer or if any trends in answers are present. The goal is to "see" student thinking through their assessment choices and results. It is these discoveries that then guide teacher support of complete student mastery.

4. Reteaching: What is the plan?

Knowing what students know or don't know is only helpful if it aids in the formulation of a plan for further growth. After the data dive, a reteach, remediation, enrichment cycle must be developed, with the goal being to correct misconceptions, reteach missed content, and encourage continuation of points of mastery. Though many teachers do a sweeping study session prior to an assessment or review assessment answers following item analysis reflection, the reteaching cycle must be purposeful, and both students and teachers must be held accountable for whether the reteaching translated to greater growth or mastery. If a test is given on a Friday, data analysis should be conducted within days and areas of mastery and reteaching should be identified. Next, teachers must purposefully plan out the process, literally building reteaching and support for mastery of missed concepts into their daily plans. For example, if a formative check-in demonstrates a missed skill must be retaught, the teacher must purposefully and practically incorporate the reteaching of that previously taught concept just as if it is new information that needs to be presented. Similar to the initial planning process, teachers should identify how long it will take to reteach the concept and what strategies and materials would best support student comprehension, this time with consideration given to how it was taught previously. The teacher should then carefully form a reteach cycle in which both old and new concepts are woven together. In this sense, "review" is unnecessary, as continuous assessment, analysis, reflection, and reteaching becomes an instructional cycle, based on data analysis.

5. Accountability: When is the retest?

Teachers support students' mastery of content. Each reteaching cycle must have a set assessment date following the initial assessment analysis and reteaching process. To continue with the example from above, if an assessment is given on a Friday, and a reteach cycle is planned to begin the following Wednesday, a retest date to identify the effectiveness of the reteach must be planned to again determine teaching effectiveness and identify whether mastery has been reached. Without this accountability piece, reteaching becomes general practice rather than data-driven instruction. These reteach assessments can come in the form of parallel assessments (the same format as the initial assessment regarding content and rigor) or in the form of a cumulative assessment where "old" concept questions are rotated into or given a section on the assessment of the "new" concepts. Regardless of the method, setting a retest date commits both teachers and students to mastering the content. It provides a point of accountability and opportunity.

6. **Outcomes:** How to continue supporting prior and new instruction?

Reflecting on teacher effectiveness and student mastery can be intimidating, but data dives and clear reteaching processes can move assessments from simple opportunities for students to demonstrate right or wrong answers to moments of growth and reflection on what has "not yet" been mastered. Though there are many ways to reteach, practitioners must consider strategy selection not only based on what the data is saying students need, but also on the practicalities of pacing and available time to reteach. These moments for data-driven instruction during the daily lesson include but are not limited to warm-ups, do-nows, closure, exit tickets, small-group instruction, and centers. Using assessment data to inform instructional decisions and applying assessment strategies to reinforce learning equips students to comprehend content area material.

Rubrics and Self-Assessments

Students need to play a role in the assessment of their own literacy products and processes. Teachers who want to help students get more involved in assessment invite them to participate in setting goals and to share how they approach the assignment and the assessment. In their discussion on activating students, Lyon et al. (2019) discuss the need for student agency in the formative assessment process. Students are not just the source of data, but they, too, should use data to engage in the process of reflecting on and analyzing their own learning.

Rubrics are categories that range from very simple and direct to comprehensive. Rubrics provide students with detailed, consistent guidelines about the expectations for their papers or projects. Some are designed to help individual students self-assess; often, they are designed to be used by small groups or by an individual student and teacher. In Figure 4.5, a basic rubric, sometimes referred to as a *holistic rubric*, serves the dual purpose of involving each student in evaluating the group's work on an inquiry project involving the Internet and in self-evaluating. This type of scoring rubric provides a list of criteria that correspond to a particular grade or point total.

Figure 4.5 Rubric for Self-Evaluation

Sixth-Grade Inquiry Project

Name: _____

Directions: Evaluate your performance in each of the following categories. Feel free to make comments about areas of this project in which you believe you were successful and areas in which you thought you could improve.

Content	Points Possible	Points Earned	Comments
Selection of topic and identification of subtopics	5		
Planning and organization of project	10		
Annotated bibliography of print resources: thoroughness and focus (minimum 4)	20		
Annotated bibliography of Web resources: thoroughness and focus (minimum 4)	20		
Effective use of time in the computer lab	5		
Presentation of findings to classmates	15		

More detailed types of rubrics include *analytic rubrics* and *weighted trait rubrics*. Analytic rubrics break down the total score for an assignment into separate traits on which the assignment will be evaluated. Weighted trait rubrics, although similar to analytic rubrics, assign higher values to some traits than to others. The weighted trait rubric shown in Figure 4.6 was developed in a seventh-grade life science class by the teacher and her students for a unit on exploring the five senses. The teacher gave the students copies of the rubric in advance, so they could monitor themselves. With a scale of 0 to 3, students were graded individually and as part of a group by their teacher and by themselves. Note that 70% of the total grade was based on their individual scores, whereas 30% was based on the group score. A rubric such as this can be time consuming to develop. Rubrics containing less detail and those developed in partnership with students may take less time to construct. They surely help involve students in monitoring their own learning in an authentic, meaningful way that takes the guesswork out of assessment.

MyLab Education
Video Example 4.3:
Criteria for Evaluation
Watch this video to learn more about developing assessment tools, such as rubrics and checklists.

MyLab Education **Self-Check 4.2**

MyLab Education **Application Exercise 4.2:**
Using e-Portfolios as an Assessment Tool

Figure 4.6 Detailed Rubric for an Inquiry Project on the Five Senses

	Group Evaluation	Individual Evaluation
3	• Worked well together every day • Thoroughly completed the lab activity • Developed a well-organized, very neatly presented handout that combined all group members' work, including at least one visual aid • Worked independently on most days	• Used at least four sources, including one website and one traditional source; correctly listed the sources • Thoroughly answered the assigned question • Came up with and answered thoroughly two related questions • Participated in an experiment and engaged in a thoughtful reflection around that experiment • Cooperated with and helped group members every day
2	• Worked well together most days • Completed the lab activity with some effort • Developed a well-organized, fairly neatly presented handout that combined all group members' work; may or may not have included a visual aid • Worked independently on some days	• Used at least three sources, including one website and one traditional source; listed the sources • Thoroughly answered the assigned question • Came up with and tried to answer two related questions • Participated in an experiment and engaged in a thoughtful reflection around that experiment
1	• May or may not have worked well together • Completed the lab activity • Developed a handout that combined all group members' work; did not include a visual aid • Did not work independently	• Used at least two sources; listed the sources • Answered the assigned question • Came up with and tried to answer one related question • Participated in an experiment and engaged in a reflection around that experiment • Cooperated with and helped group members some days
0	• Did not work well together • Did not complete the lab activity • Did not develop a handout that combined all group members' work • Did not work independently	• Used fewer than two sources • Did not answer the assigned question • Did not come up with any related questions • May have participated in an experiment but did not reflect on that experiment • May or may not have cooperated

Grading Scale

• 70% of your grade is based on your individual score
• 30% of your grade is based on the group score

Final Score	Letter Grade
2.5–3.0	A
2.0–2.4	B
1.4–1.9	C
0.6–1.3	D
Below 0.6	F

Assessing Text Complexity

4.3 **Define text complexity and compare the ways in which it can be measured.**

Text complexity is determined by analyzing *qualitative components* such as levels of meaning, structure, and knowledge demands; *quantitative components* such as readability measures and other scores of text complexity; and *reader-task components*, such as motivation, knowledge, and experiences, and task variables such as purpose and questions (CCSS, 2010; Hiebert, 2011). Content area texts can pose a multitude of challenges for students, even for those who are proficient readers. The vocabulary in content area texts tends to be unfamiliar to students but is essential for comprehension. It is often in what Beck, McKeown, and Kucan (2013) termed Tier 3: low frequency and content specific. Additionally, content area texts contain grammatical metaphors, when authors use word meanings and word order in a way that is unfamiliar to students. Connections between concepts may be subtle, making the text difficult for students to understand (Fang & Pace, 2013).

Evaluating texts and assessing students' interactions with texts are crucial tasks for content area teachers and students—and they call for sound judgment and decision making. One of the best reasons we know for making decisions about the quality of texts is that the assessment process puts you and students in touch with the texts they read. One source of information to consider is publisher-provided descriptions of the design, format, and organizational structure of the textbook along with grade-level readability designations. Another information source is your acquired knowledge of and interactions with the students in the class. A third is your own sense of what makes the textbook a useful tool. A fourth source is student perspective, so that instructional decisions are not made from an isolated teacher's perception of the students' perspectives. To complement professional judgment, several measures can provide you with useful information: content area comprehension inventories and readability formulas such as Lexile levels, the cloze procedure, and a content area framework for student analysis of reading assignments. The first order of business, then, if content area reading strategies are to involve students in taking control of their own learning, is to find out how students are interacting with the text.

Content Area Reading Inventories

Teacher-made tests provide another important indicator of how students interact with text materials in content areas. A teacher-made **content area reading inventory** (CARI) is an alternative to the standardized reading test. The CARI is informal. As opposed to the standard of success on a norm-referenced test, which is a comparison of the performance of the tested group with that of the original normative population, success on the CARI test is measured by performance on the task itself. The CARI measures performance on reading materials actually used in a course. The results of the CARI can give a teacher some good insights into *how* students read course material.

Administering a CARI involves several general steps. First, explain to your students the purpose of the test. Mention that it will be used to help you plan instruction and that grades will not be assigned. Second, briefly introduce the selected portion of the text to be read and give students an idea or direction to guide silent reading. Third, if you want to find out how the class uses the textbook, consider an open-book evaluation; but if you want to determine students' abilities to retain information, have them answer test questions without referring to the selection. Finally, discuss the results of the evaluation individually in conferences or collectively with the entire class.

A CARI can be administered piecemeal over several class sessions so that large chunks of instructional time will not be sacrificed. The bane of many content area instructors is spending an inordinate amount of time away from actual teaching.

A CARI elicits the information you need to adjust instruction and meet student needs. It should focus on students' abilities to comprehend text and to read at appropriate rates of comprehension. Some authorities suggest that teachers also evaluate additional competency areas, such as study skills: skimming, scanning, outlining, taking notes, and so forth. We believe, however, that the best use of reading inventories in content areas is on a much smaller scale. A CARI should seek information related to basic reading tasks. For this reason, we recommend that outlining, note taking, and other useful study techniques be assessed through observation and analysis of student work samples.

Teachers estimate their students' abilities to comprehend text material at different levels of comprehension by using inventories similar to the one shown in Figure 4.7 for American history. The teacher wanted to assess how students responded at literal

---

Figure 4.7 Sample Comprehension Inventory in American History

General directions: Read pages 595–600 in your textbook. Then look up at the board and note the time it took you to complete the selection. Record this time in the space provided on the response sheet. Close your book and answer the first question. You may then open your textbook to answer the remaining questions.

STUDENT RESPONSE FORM

Reading time: _____ min.   _____ sec.

I.   *Directions:* Close your book and answer the following question: In your own words, what was this section about? Use as much space as you need on the back of this page to complete your answer.

II. *Directions:* Open your book and answer the following questions.

   1. To prevent the closing of banks throughout the country, President Roosevelt declared a national "bank holiday."
      a. True   b. False

   2. The purpose of the Social Security Act was to abolish federal unemployment payments.
      a. True   b. False

   3. The National Recovery Administration employed men between the ages of 18 and 25 to build bridges, dig reservoirs, and develop parks.
      a. True   b. False

   4. President Roosevelt established the Federal Deposit Insurance Corporation to insure savings accounts against bank failures.
      a. True   b. False

III. *Directions:* Answers to these questions are not directly stated by the author. You must "read between the lines" to answer them.

   1. Give an example of how FDR's first 100 days provided relief, reform, and recovery for the nation.
      _____

   2. How is the Tennessee Valley Authority an example of President Roosevelt's attempt to help the poorest segment of American society?
      _____

   3. How did the purpose of the Civil Works Administration differ from the purpose of the Federal Emergency Relief Act?
      _____

IV. *Directions:* Answers to these questions are not directly stated by the author. You must "read beyond the lines" to answer them.

   1. If FDR had not promoted his New Deal program through his fireside chats, do you think it would have been successful? Why or why not?
      _____

   2. Why did FDR's critics fear the New Deal? Do you think their concerns were justified? Why or why not?
      _____

   3. Which New Deal program would you call the most important? Why?
      _____

(getting the facts), inferential (making some interpretations), and applied (going beyond the material) levels of comprehension. At this time, you can also determine a measure of reading rate in relation to comprehension.

While students read the material and take the test, the teacher observes, noting work habits and student behavior, especially of students who appear frustrated by the test. The American history teacher whose inventory is illustrated in Figure 4.7 allowed students to check their own work as the class discussed each question. Other teachers prefer to evaluate individual students' responses to questions first and then to discuss them with students during subsequent class sessions. Figure 4.8 shows how an art history teacher used a CARI before beginning a unit on art in the 20th century. He used the results to guide his subsequent instruction. Information you glean from a CARI will help you organize specific lessons and activities. You can decide on the background preparation needed, the length of reading assignments, and the reading activities when you apply your best judgment to the information you have learned from the assessment.

Reading Rates

To get an estimate of students' rates of comprehension, follow these steps:

1. *Have students note the time it takes to read the selection.* This can be accomplished efficiently by recording the time in 5-second intervals by using a "stopwatch" that is drawn on the board.

2. *As students complete the reading, they look up at the board to check the stopwatch.* The number within the circle represents the minutes that have elapsed. The numbers along the perimeter of the circle represent the number of seconds.

Figure 4.8 Content Area Reading Inventory (CARI) — Art History

In preparing to teach a unit on art in the 20th century, a ninth-grade art history teacher wanted to see what his students already knew about this topic and whether they could connect artists' names with the work they produced. He showed them photos of three paintings and asked them the following questions.

1. Have you seen any of these paintings? Tell me where you remember seeing them.
2. Can you name the artist of each painting? How did you know?
3. Can you put the paintings in order, starting with the one that was painted first to the one that was painted last?
4. What do you know about the following terms?
   a. Cubism
   b. Fauvism
   c. Art Deco
   d. Dadaism
5. List artists who you think are from the 20th century. What do you know about them?
6. What political and social events do you think influenced art in the 20th century?
7. List any paintings you know of from the 20th century.
8. What were artists rejecting in the 20th century?

The results helped him organize his instruction. Students were able to recognize a few paintings but had a hard time attributing each painting to an artist. They named several artists, but many of the artists they named were not of the 20th century. A few students had heard of the terms Art Deco and Cubism, but none of the students recognized the terms Dadaism and Fauvism. Students had a grasp of some 20th-century events, so the teacher used that prior knowledge as a starting point for his instruction. As the unit study progressed, students applied their growing knowledge of art in the 20th century to organize a timeline of important 20th-century events, as well as 20th-century artists and the works they created. This process and graphic organizer helped the students to see how world events influenced and were reflected by art and art movements.

3. *Later, students or the teacher can figure out the students' rates of reading in words per minute.* For example:

Words in selection: 1,500
Reading time: 4 minutes 30 seconds
Convert seconds to a decimal fraction. Then divide time into words.

$$\frac{1,500}{4.5} = 333 \text{ words per minute}$$

4. *Determine the percentage of correct or reasonable answers on the comprehension test.* Always evaluate and discuss students' rates of reading in terms of their comprehension performance.

Information you glean from a CARI will help you organize specific lessons and activities. You can decide on the background preparation needed, the length of reading assignments, and the reading activities when you apply your best judgment to the information you have learned from the assessment.

Readability

There are many readability formulas that classroom teachers can use to estimate textbook difficulty. The more common readability formulas used today are quick and easy to calculate; many are already calculated in advance by the text publisher. These formulas typically involve a measure of sentence length and word difficulty to determine a grade-level score for text materials. This score supposedly indicates the reading achievement level that students need to comprehend the material. Because of their ease, readability formulas are used to make judgments about materials. These judgments are global and are not intended to be precise indicators of text difficulty.

Keep in mind that readability measures don't account for the experience and knowledge that readers bring to content material. They are not designed to tap the variables present in readers. Our purpose, interest, motivation, and emotional state as well as the environment that we're in during reading contribute to our ability to comprehend text. While readability measures can provide one measure of guidance when selecting texts, teachers must take care not to discourage students from using a variety of texts, both easier and more challenging, that can potentially add to their enjoyment and understanding of content area concepts (Fang & Pace, 2013). Box 4.3 explains how one teacher, Brian, responded to diverse reading levels in his middle school language arts class.

Box 4.3 Voices from the Field

Brian, Middle School Language Arts Teacher

Challenge

A novel study is an essential part of the English language arts curriculum at the middle and secondary education levels. It is a time when students can learn about various reading strategies and literary devices as well as develop a passion for reading. However, when the diverse reading abilities within a classroom are not considered, the entire unit can become a disaster. In my first year of teaching, I planned a novel study focused on one specific text. At the time, I was confident that the novel study would be a platform for rich discussion, analysis, and critique. Unfortunately, the unit had become a platform for disengagement and frustration. For many students, the text used was too complex and far from understandable, preventing them from engaging in meaningful dialogue and identifying important literary concepts within the text. Other students, however, felt that the novel was too easy, resulting in them reading ahead and ultimately lacking the engagement needed for planned activities. Although some students really enjoyed the book, the overall vision for the study was compromised, in part, because of my struggle to address the diverse reading levels of students within my classroom. I became overwhelmed by the challenge of determining how to lead a successful novel study in a classroom of diverse learners.

Strategy

After seeking the advice of more experienced colleagues, I decided to give a thematic novel study a try, in the hopes that it would be an effective approach for meeting the diverse reading levels of students in my class. A thematic novel study would allow several books, at a variety of reading levels, to be taught at the same time. A common theme would essentially provide the link between concurrent novels in the classroom and allow struggling students to access higher-order thinking and discussion with their advanced counterparts. In this approach, students are able to comfortably read at their individual reading levels, use literary devices within text, and have a voice within the learning environment.

Once a theme for the novel study is established, books on a variety of reading levels can be selected. Next, a reading assessment can be administered. I used the Gates-MacGinitie reading assessment to identify students who needed individual diagnosis or special instruction. This tool assesses students on comprehension and vocabulary, with the final score on each section being translated into a specific grade level. Each grade level score can then be translated into a Lexile score, which is used to help determine the most appropriate book for a given student. Once reading levels are determined, students can then be matched with one of the unit's novels that is an appropriate match for his or her reading level. The reading assessment tool can also be used for pre- and post-testing, which can be used to measure growth over time or monitor instructional effectiveness.

In one of my classes, two novels became the focus of our novel study: *The Hunger Games* by Suzanne Collins and *The Girl Who Fell from the Sky* by Heidi Durrow. Students reading below grade level read *The Hunger Games*, while students reading at or above grade level read *The Girl Who Fell from the Sky*. Although these books are completely different in plot and reading level, they are closely connected by theme and essential questions. For example, questions that linked the books included: Does society influence your actions and mind-sets? Are the decisions caretakers make for children always in the children's best interest? Is there ever a situation where death is the best option? Does your environment shape your identity? Whole-class discussions and instruction opportunities were made possible through these questions. Students were able to voice their insights on these topics, using examples from the novel they were reading. If a student disagreed with a statement made from someone reading another novel, they would communicate their opposing argument using examples from their issued book. Having students read different novels heightened the overall level of critical thinking and created a curiosity on the part of students about the novel they had not read, increasing their appetite for more reading after the unit was over.

Reflection

A thematic novel study, in my experience, has produced positive academic results among diverse learners. Whole-class instruction and discussion were facilitated by the connectedness of students to the common themes of their novels. Using a reading assessment tool prior to reading helped me to better understand the diverse reading abilities of my students. The assessment allowed me to successfully match students with novels so that they could be active participants throughout the novel study. Students were engaged, grasped complex concepts, and participated enthusiastically in class discussions. In fact, in-depth discussions about the different novels created an atmosphere in which students declared that the other novels were must-reads, asking to read their neighbor's book. I believed that the increased excitement about reading was due, in part, to the fact that students were able to read something that they understood. This was the first time all of my students were able to speak in-depth and knowledgably about their novels. The unit was so powerful. Many students did not even realize they were predicting, clarifying, connecting, visualizing, questioning, and evaluating in their discussions. When students are appropriately matched with a novel on their grade level, confusion, frustration, and boredom are minimized. As a result, reading becomes a leisure activity and not an unbearable task.

LEXILE LEVELS In recent years, the Lexile framework has become a commonly used measure of text complexity. Many publishers have defined Lexile measures for the books they produce, while newspapers and magazine articles available through commonly used periodic databases frequently include Lexile text measures.

Lexile text measures are intended to assist teachers in selecting reading materials that are at an appropriate level of difficulty for their students. Lexile text measures are written as a number followed by the letter *L*. The Lexile scale ranges from below 200L for beginning reader texts to above 1700L for advanced texts. Lexile ranges have recently been realigned to match the text complexity grade bands established in the Common Core State Standards. The new emphasis on increasing text complexity intends to support students as they "stretch" to develop advanced reading skills and apply those skills to more challenging texts. Lexile measures are not intended to be prescriptive for specific grade levels, and guidelines for levels vary among sources. General guidelines for grade-level current bands and stretch bands are:

Grade Band	Current Lexile Band	Stretch Lexile Band
K–1	n/a	n/a
2–3	450L–725L	450L–790L
4–5	645L–845L	770L–980L
6–8	860L–1010L	955L–1155L
9–10	960L–1115L	1080L–1305L
11–CCR	1070L–1220L	1215L–1355L

It is important to remember that a Lexile measure is not intended to reflect the quality or content of any printed text, nor can a Lexile measure take into account the background knowledge that students bring to a text. A Lexile measure can, however, help teachers to consider how content area reading materials correspond to students' reading levels so that a compatible match between the two can be made.

MyLab Education **Self-Check 4.3**

MyLab Education **Application Exercise 4.3:**
Engaging Students with Appropriate Texts

Looking Back Looking Forward

Assessing students and texts is a process of gathering and using multiple sources of relevant information for instructional purposes. Two major approaches to assessment prevail in education today: a formal, high-stakes one and an informal, authentic one. Pressure from policy makers and other constituencies has resulted in the adoption of standards-based instruction, specifying goals and objectives in subject areas and grade levels. Hence, student performance on state-mandated tests must also be considered by teachers who need to make instructional decisions based on their students' content literacy skills, concepts, and performance.

An informal, authentic approach is often more practical in collecting and organizing the many kinds of information that can inform decisions, including (1) students' prior knowledge in relation to instructional units and text assignments, (2) students' knowledge and use of reading and other communication strategies to learn from texts, and (3) assessment of materials. The use of portfolios and careful observation and documentation of students' strengths and weaknesses as they interact with one another and with content-specific material sheds light on the *why* as well as the *what* in teaching and learning.

In this chapter, the key terms, major purposes, and legitimate uses of standardized tests were presented. Contrasts were drawn between formative data collection and testing. As teachers engage learners in a process of portfolio development and formative assessment, they make adaptations appropriate for their subject matter and consider student mastery as a continuous process. Suggestions for assessing students' background knowledge included portfolios, and instructionally based strategies. Purposeful data collection that not only aims to identify areas of student need but also demonstrates student thinking processes helps both teachers and students assess performance, behavior, and perspectives. For insights into how students interact with text material and a measure of performance on the reading materials used in a course, teacher-made content area reading inventories were suggested.

Assessing the difficulty of text material requires both professional judgment and quantitative analysis. Text assessment considers various factors within the reader and the text—the exercise of professional judgment being as useful as calculating a readability formula. Teachers, therefore, must be concerned about the quality of the content, format, organization, and appeal of the material. Procedures for assessing text difficulty included content area comprehension inventories and readability formulas such as Lexile levels.

How do teachers incorporate instructional practices and strategies into lessons *before*, *during*, and *after* assigning texts to read? In the next chapter, we explore the design of content literacy lessons and units of study. These lessons and units bring students and texts together in content learning situations.

eResources

Go to the website for the International Literacy Association and select "Get Resources" to access the "What's Hot Report." Read and discuss current policy initiatives that have the potential to affect literacy education.

Also on the International Literacy Association website, go to the link for "Get Resources," then to "Position Statements." Read the 2018 position statement, "Improving Digital Practices for Literacy, Learning, and Justice: More Than Just Tools." Discuss the issues and recommendations raised in that document.

Go to the website for the National Assessment of Educational Progress. There you will find information about NAEP scores and current assessment trends. Discuss these scores and trends in the context of other types of assessments used or required in your school.

Chapter 5
Planning Instruction for Content Literacy

Written in collaboration with Lina Soares, Ph.D.

Roman Kosolapov/Shutterstock

 ## Chapter Overview and Learning Outcomes

After reading this chapter, you should be able to:

5.1 Outline the process for teaching and supporting students as they master new strategies.

5.2 Explain the B–D–A framework and include typical activities for each stage of this type of lesson.

5.3 Describe the different components of a well-designed unit.

5.4 Describe the different strategies for cooperative learning.

5.5 Explain the characteristics of students and tasks that guide choosing an effective strategy for collaborating.

Organizing Principle

Instructional planning brings students and texts together in ways that support content literacy and learning.

Planning is essential, whether fighting a war, leading a country, running a business, or teaching a class of middle or high school learners. When Dwight Eisenhower was asked what the key to victory was during the Normandy invasion of World War II, he minimized the product of planning—the battle plan—noting that "plans are nothing; planning is everything." It was the strategic planning that went into the lead-up to the invasion—the process of thinking through the actions needed for victory—that made the difference between success and failure. Thinking through objectives, activities, unintended consequences, and strategic alternatives in case something goes wrong is key to a well-managed classroom where the focus is on learning. A lack of planning can have short- and long-term damaging results. Without a plan in the classroom, you not only lose instructional time and classroom management, but you also sacrifice student engagement, motivation, and learning, all of which can be difficult to retrieve.

Likewise, the key to content literacy and learning is the forethought that goes into planning *instructional frameworks* that support thinking and learning with text. Engaged learning is the result, quite often, of well-planned lessons and units of study. Someone in the world of business once said that 90% of your results come from activities that consume 10% of your time. When this saying is applied to an instructional context, the time teachers take to plan engaged learning environments is time well spent. Planning appropriate frameworks for instruction includes the thinking through of text-centered lessons and units of study revolving around what students need to learn, strategies and activities that will facilitate learning, and texts that serve as vehicles for learning. With one-to-one technology initiatives promoting computer and smartphone integration into lesson plans and causing competition for student attention and focus, planning is survival. The organizing principle of this chapter underscores the planning of active text learning environments in content area classrooms: Instructional planning brings students and texts together in ways that support content literacy and learning.

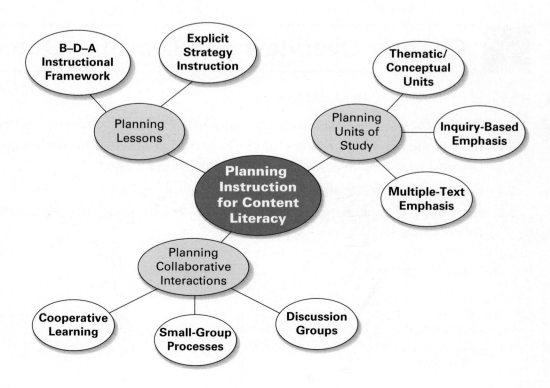

Frame of Mind

1. How can content area teachers plan and design instruction so that students will actively engage in literacy- and subject-related activities?
2. What planning components are involved in explicit strategy instruction?
3. What is involved in designing a text lesson based on a B–D–A instructional framework?
4. How does designing a unit of study help teachers plan a variety of instructional activities that connect literacy and learning as well as explore the interrelatedness of content?
5. How do teachers create an inquiry/research emphasis within units of study?
6. How can teachers incorporate collaborative/cooperative learning activities within lessons and units of study?
7. How are guided discussions different from reflective discussions?

Content literacy has the potential to play an important role in the academic lives of children and adolescents. In order to plan instruction effectively, a teacher needs to be aware of the *explicit* and *functional* dimensions of content literacy. The explicit aspects of content literacy emphasize direct instruction in the development of skills and strategies that enable students to comprehend what they are reading. Instruction is explicit in the sense that teachers overtly engage in the teaching of procedures to develop students' understanding and use of strategies. In a schoolwide curriculum, the primary responsibility for explicit strategy instruction often falls on the shoulders of reading/language arts teachers and literacy specialists. Yet classroom teachers also have a responsibility to show students how to learn with discipline-specific texts, especially those students who struggle with literacy tasks in an academic context. As more rigorous teaching objectives and initiatives for literacy across content areas grow, all teachers are encouraged to incorporate reading strategies within their core instruction to support student literacy growth.

As crucial as explicit strategy instruction may be to students' literacy development, another equally important dimension of content literacy is the functional nature of strategy use in content areas. Functional instruction emphasizes the application of strategies needed to learn from a variety of print and digital sources of information. When the functional aspects of content literacy are operating in the classroom, the teacher is able to integrate literacy and learning in a seamless fashion. To the casual observer in a content area classroom, the functional use of strategies would be difficult to categorize as a "strategy lesson." What the observer might conclude, however, is that the teacher used a variety of instructional activities and strategies that actively engage students in learning the content under study.

Explicit Strategy Instruction

5.1   Outline the process for teaching and supporting students as they master new strategies.

It's hard to use an instructional strategy effectively if teachers aren't truly familiar with what the strategy is meant to do and why. When building this metacognition of strategies, there are three levels of knowledge necessary for both teachers and students to be successful: declarative, procedural, and conditional knowledge (LaJoie, 2008; McKeown, Beck, & Blake, 2009; Pilonieta, 2010).

- Declarative knowledge accounts for teachers' and students' understanding of strategies. Before we can hope to effectively implement any strategy, it is important that all parties understand what a strategy is and the skills it is meant to support. If teachers are hoping to build vocabulary, it is unlikely they will achieve results with a strategy meant to support fluency.

- Procedural knowledge refers to teachers' and students' aptitude to execute strategies. Any time students are learning a new strategy or adapting one in a new way, they have little prior knowledge and will require explicit instruction. Teachers need to explain and model the new strategy, often several times or in a variety of ways, before students will be confident and successful at implementing the strategy independently.

- Conditional knowledge is often the last to develop and refers to the ability to determine and select strategies that are most appropriate and effective for the content and task at hand. This requires teachers to know about the intricacies of the content to be studied as well as the abilities of the students. In order to adequately support student learning and develop the metacognitive skill that allows students to self-select and employ strategies, teachers need to plan based on student characteristics and appropriately scaffold instruction. For example, if students are struggling with the difficulty of the textbook, choosing a strategy that requires them to read independently will most likely lead to frustration. In contrast, using a strategy, such as jigsaw groups (which you will learn about later in this chapter), that allows students to discuss what they read and work collaboratively with classmates, they will more likely be engaged and comprehend more of what they are reading.

Students use strategies to support learning only when they have the appropriate materials, the teacher has created an instructional scenario that prompts and scaffolds proper use, and students are well-versed in both content and strategy expectations (Waters & Kunnmann, 2009). With these ideals in mind, it is up to the teacher to create the most conducive conditions for learning.

When texts serve as tools for learning in content area classrooms, teachers have a significant role to play. That role can be thought of as "instructional scaffolding." Content-literate students know how to learn with texts independently. Yet many students have trouble handling the conceptual demands inherent in text material when left to their own devices to learn. A gap often exists between the ideas and relationships they are studying and their prior knowledge, interests, attitudes, cultural background, language proficiency, or reading ability. Instructional scaffolding allows teachers to support students' efforts to make sense of texts while showing them how to use strategies that will, over time, lead to independent learning. (See Box 5.1 for additional ideas on how to support all learners.)

Used in construction, scaffolds serve as supports, lifting up workers so that they can achieve something that otherwise would not have been possible. In teaching and learning contexts, scaffolding means helping learners to do what they cannot do at first. Instructional scaffolds support text learners by helping them achieve literacy tasks that would otherwise have been out of reach. Instructional scaffolding provides the necessary support that students need as they attempt new tasks; at the same time, teachers model or lead the students through effective strategies for completing these tasks. Providing "necessary support" often means understanding the diversity that exists among the students in your class, planning active learning environments, and supporting students' efforts to learn with texts. All learners will benefit from explicit, scaffolded instruction in the use of literacy strategies.

Strategy instruction helps students who struggle with text become aware of, use, and develop control over learning strategies (Nash-Ditzel, 2010). Explicit teaching provides an alternative to "blind" instruction. In blind instructional situations, students are taught what to do, but this is where instruction usually ends. Although directed to make use of a set of procedures that will improve reading and studying, students seldom grasp the rationale or payoff underlying a strategy. As a result, they attempt to use the strategy with little basis for evaluating its success or monitoring its effectiveness. Explicit instruction, however, attempts to show students not only *what* to do, but

Box 5.1 RTI for Struggling Adolescent Learners

Planning, Implementing, and Differentiating Strategies to Meet the Needs of All Learners

Trying to meet the needs of the diverse population in your class can often seem an overwhelming task, but with policies and measures such as Response to Intervention (RtI) and the Individuals with Disabilities Education Act of 2004, it is imperative that teachers find effective ways to scaffold learning to support the development of all students.

When teaching students strategies to support content learning, there are several ways in which you can differentiate both instruction and practice to provide effective scaffolding. Offering flexible grouping opportunities allows teachers to cluster students based on needs and gives students opportunities to work with students of heterogeneous abilities (Tomlinson & Moon, 2013). Once students are placed in temporary heterogeneous groups, teachers can offer instruction that is specifically tailored to the learning needs of the small group. This may include extended intensive practice with strategies or materials, adapted resources, or additional support in transferring strategy knowledge to a variety of situations

(Ehren, Deshler, & Graner, 2010). When students are placed in groups with students of varied abilities, they can work with and learn from each other.

Another way of implementing strategies while adapting to the different learning abilities and needs in your classroom includes accommodations to the product associated with the strategy (McMackin & Witherell, 2010). While all students may be working on a collaborative activity, the accountability task can be modified to match the abilities of the students: reports may be shorter, students may be allowed to use word processing programs to correct spelling and grammar, or the number of supporting resources may be fewer to allow students with lower reading levels to be successful within the same time limits as the rest of the class.

Overall, strategy instruction supports all students in every content area. With proper planning, teachers can provide whole-class instruction on methods that support content while supporting students with diverse learning needs.

also *why, how,* and *when.* Dewitz, Jones, and Leahy (2009) offer that direct instruction in comprehension can be successful when teachers explicitly teach and model strategies, followed by guided practice and independent practice with a focus on when and how strategies can be used during the reading process. In addition, explicit strategy instruction can help students independently transfer skills and strategies to unique scenarios (Fuchs et al., 2003) and other content areas (Alger, 2009). As Figure 5.1 shows, explicit strategy instruction has several components: *awareness and explanation, modeling and demonstration, guided practice,* and *application.* By way of analogy, teaching students to be strategic readers provides experiences similar to those needed by athletes who are in training. To perform well with texts, students must understand the rules, work on technique, and practice. A coach (the teacher) is needed to provide feedback, guide, inspire, and share the knowledge and experiences that she or he possesses in the same way literacy coaches support teachers.

Figure 5.1 Instructional Model for Explicit Strategy Instruction

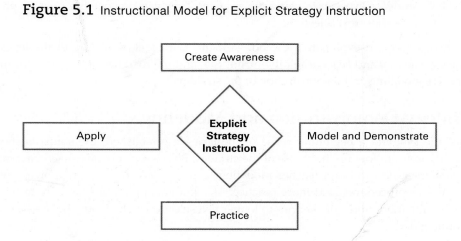

Strategy Awareness and Explanation

To begin the awareness and explanation stage of explicit strategy instruction, first conduct an informal assessment of students' ability to use a literacy strategy. As discussed in Chapter 4, formative assessments are becoming more prevalent in today's classrooms as a means for planning suitable instruction and often are developed by schools or districts to ensure appropriate pacing and equity throughout classrooms. Students should think of the assessment as a "tryout" rather than as a test of their ability to use the strategy. Assessment gives the teacher an opportunity to determine the degree of knowledge that students have about a strategy under discussion. Moreover, it yields insight into how well the students use a strategy to handle a reading task. For these reasons, assessing the use of a strategy should occur in as natural a context as possible. Assessment can usually be accomplished within a single class period if these steps are followed:

1. *Assign students a text passage of approximately 500 to 1,500 words.* The selection should take most students 10 to 15 minutes to read.

2. *Direct students to use a particular strategy.* For example, suppose the strategy involves writing a summary of a text selection. Simply ask students to do the things they normally do when they read a passage and then write a summary of it. Allow adequate time to complete the task.

3. *Observe the use of the strategy.* Note what students do. Do they underline or mark important ideas as they read? Do they appear to skim the material first to get a general idea of what to expect? What do they do when they begin actually constructing the summary?

4. *Ask students to respond in writing to several key questions about the use of the strategy.* For example: What did you do to summarize the passage? What did you do to find the main ideas? Did you find summarizing easy or difficult? Why?

During the awareness step, a give-and-take of ideas takes place between teacher and students. As a result, students should recognize the rationale and process behind the use of the strategy. It is important to first discuss the assessment. Teachers should use their observations and students' reflective responses to the questions for this purpose. Continue the strategy discussion with the following activities:

- Lead a discussion of why the strategy is useful. What is the payoff for students? How does it improve learning?

- Engage in a discussion that explains the rules, guidelines, or procedures for being successful with the strategy.

- Have students experience using the strategy. They can practice the rules or procedures on a short text selection.

Awareness and explanation provide students with a clear picture of the learning strategy. The *why* and *how* are solidly introduced, and the road has been paved for more intensive modeling and demonstration of the strategy.

Strategy Demonstration and Modeling

Once the *why* and a beginning sense of the *how* are established, the students should receive careful follow-up in the use of the strategy. Follow-up sessions are characterized by demonstration through teacher modeling, explanations, practice, reinforcement of the rules or procedures, and more practice. The students progress from easy to harder practice situations and from shorter to longer text selections. The following activities are recommended:

- *Use a SMART Board, chart, Microsoft PowerPoint presentation, or overhead transparency to review the steps students should follow.*

- *Demonstrate the strategy.* Walk students through the steps. Provide explanations. Raise questions about the procedures.

- *As part of a demonstration, initiate a think-aloud procedure to model how to use the strategy.* By thinking aloud, the teacher shares with the students the thinking processes he or she uses in applying the strategy. Thinking aloud is often accomplished by reading a passage out loud and stopping at key points in the text to ask questions or provide prompts. The questions and prompts mirror the critical thinking required to apply the strategy. Once students are familiar with the think-aloud procedure, encourage them to demonstrate and use it during practice sessions. In Chapter 7, we explain in more detail the role that think-alouds play in modeling strategies.

Guided Practice

Use trial runs with short selections from the textbook, trade book, or other reference materials. Debrief the students with questions after each trial run: Did they follow the steps? How successful were they? What caused them difficulty? Have them make learning log entries. Often, a short quiz following a trial run shows students how much they learned and remembered as a result of using the study strategy.

The practice sessions are designed to provide experience with the strategy. Students should reach a point where they have internalized the steps and feel in control of the strategy.

Strategy Application

The preceding components of strategy instruction should provide enough practice for students to know *why*, *how*, and *when* to use the study strategies that have been targeted by the teacher for emphasis. Once students have made generalizations about strategy use, regular class assignments should encourage its application. Rather than assign for homework a text selection accompanied by questions to be answered, frame the assignment so that students will have to apply the strategies they are learning. Repeated practice with strategies will also allow students multiple exposures to content, strengthening their comprehension of both strategies and material and leading to students' ability to independently apply methods. This repetition also allows teachers opportunities to provide immediate and meaningful feedback to students about their understanding of material and strategy use (Blachowicz et al., 2006).

MyLab Education **Self-Check 5.1**

MyLab Education **Application Exercise 5.1:**
Differentiating Strategies in Content Area Instruction

Planning Lessons

5.2 Explain the B–D–A framework and include typical activities for each stage of this type of lesson.

A lesson usually revolves around all of the students in a class reading the same text. Sometimes lessons require differentiation or elements of blended learning that support individualized instruction. Text-centered lessons provide a blueprint for action, and planning in advance of actual practice is simply good common sense. Planning is not only essential because learners respond well to structure, but it also aids student engagement and classroom management. When reading text, learners need to sense where they are going and how they will get there. Lessons should be general enough to include all students and flexible enough to allow the teacher to react intuitively and spontaneously when a particular plan is put in actual practice. In other words, lessons shouldn't restrict decisions about the instruction that is in progress; instead, they should encourage flexibility and change.

Lesson Plan Formats

Lesson plan formats vary from school district to school district. However, a comprehensive lesson plan undoubtedly will be aligned with standards (sometimes referred to as *benchmarks* in some local and state curricular guides) within a particular content area at a particular grade level. Moreover, a comprehensive lesson plan not only will address the standards in a discipline but also will include instructional goals or objectives, essential questions, assessment, instructional strategies and activities, instructional materials and resources, and technology. What questions do teachers need to consider when planning lessons?

- *Standards (benchmarks).* What local, state, or national standards will be addressed? Common Core State Standards are available for reading and math and make accommodations for other content areas. In addition, many states have additional or supplementary objectives for some content areas or special populations.

- *Instructional goals.* What will students need to know and be able to do? What knowledge, attitudes, skills, and strategies will students gain from participation in the lesson?

- *Essential questions.* What "big" questions will generate discussion about the topic under study? What questions will be asked to help students focus on important aspects of the topic?

- *Instructional strategies and activities.* What instructional practices, strategies, and activities will be used in the lesson? How will the learning environment support collaborative interactions among students and active engagement in the topic?

- *Instructional materials and resources.* What textbook assignments, trade books, newspaper and magazine articles, reference materials, electronic texts, and so on, will students need to engage in learning?

- *Academic language.* What important vocabulary words need to be taught to enhance content understanding? What learning supports will be used to teach the content-specific vocabulary words?

- *New literacies.* How will the use of new literacies support student learning? How will technology and media extend and enhance the lesson?

- *Assessment.* What assessment tools will be needed to evaluate student learning? Will students engage in self-assessment?

Throughout Part I of this book, we have discussed various instructional practices, strategies, and activities to engage students in reading content area text materials. These content literacy practices and strategies fit nicely within the strategy awareness and explanation section of the lesson plan format we just described. Teachers can plan lessons in what we call a B–D–A instructional framework.

B–D–A Instructional Framework

What a teacher does *before reading, during reading,* and *after reading* (B–D–A) is crucial to active and purposeful reading. The **B–D–A instructional framework** can help teachers incorporate instructional strategies and activities into lessons involving content literacy and learning. A lesson doesn't necessarily take place in a single class session; several class meetings may be needed to achieve the objectives of the lesson. Nor do all the components of a

Figure 5.2 B–D–A Instructional Framework

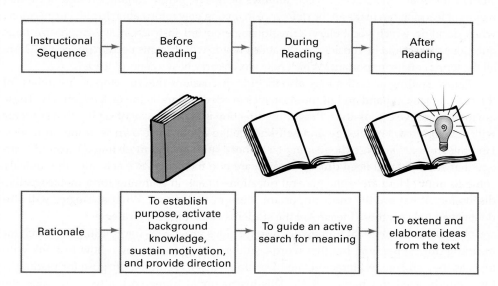

B–D–A lesson necessarily receive the same emphasis in any given reading assignment; the difficulty of the material, students' familiarity with the topic, and your judgment all play a part when you decide on the sequence of activities you will organize. What the structure of a B–D–A instructional framework tells you is that readers need varying degrees of guidance. As we show throughout this book, there are before-reading, during-reading, and after-reading activities that support students' efforts to construct meaning. The components of a B–D–A instructional framework can be examined in Figure 5.2.

BEFORE-READING ACTIVITIES   A B–D–A-centered lesson that includes activity and discussion before reading reduces the uncertainty that students bring to an assignment. Before-reading activities get students ready to read, to approach text material critically, and to seek answers to questions they have generated about the material. The before-reading dimension of a lesson, which is explained in Chapter 6, has also been called the *prereading* phase of instruction. During this instructional phase, a teacher often emphasizes one or more of the following: (1) motivating readers, (2) building and activating prior knowledge, (3) introducing key vocabulary and concepts, and (4) developing metacognitive awareness of the task demands of the assignment and the strategies necessary for effective learning.

A key factor related to motivation is activating students' interest in the text reading. However, concerning how to motivate students, we must first raise a fundamental question: Why should students be interested in this lesson? A teacher may even wish to consider whether he or she is interested in the material! If teachers are going to be models of enthusiasm for students, then the first step is to find something in the material about which to get really excited. Enthusiasm—it is almost too obvious to suggest—is contagious. Another consideration is the relevance of the material to students' lives, both in school and beyond. Relating material as building blocks for future learning can help students understand the purpose and practicality of new material. It is also helpful to explain the importance of new knowledge to possible life and career opportunities for students to appreciate the application of this content in their futures and to encourage the generalization of skills across time and space. As well as being a crucial component to student motivation and engagement, this is an essential element of the Common Core State Standards.

Building and activating prior knowledge for a lesson and presenting key vocabulary and concepts are also essential to preparation before reading. In making decisions related to prior knowledge, it's important to review previous lessons in light of present material. What does

MyLab Education
**Video Example 5.1:
Curiosity and Interest in Science**
Notice how a middle school science teacher arouses curiosity and interest prior to reading.

MyLab Education
Response Journal 5.1
Reflecting on your school experience, how did some of your teachers create interest in text readings in the before-reading phase of a text lesson?

MyLab Education
Video Example 5.2:
Engagement
Watch how a high school teacher engages students in reflection by activating prior knowledge.

yesterday's lesson have to do with today's? Will students make the connection to previously studied material? Sometimes several minutes of review before forging on into uncharted realms of learning can make all the difference in linking new information to old. Furthermore, when deciding which vocabulary terms to single out for instruction, we emphasize three questions that should be considered: What key words will students need to understand? Are all the terms equally important? Which new words carry heavy concept loads?

Before-reading activities may also include discussions that develop an awareness of the reading task at hand and of the strategies needed to handle the task effectively. These are metacognitive discussions. Providing direction is another way of saying that students will develop task knowledge and self-knowledge about their own learning strategies. Helping students analyze the reading task ahead of them and modeling a learning strategy that students will need during reading are two metacognitive activities that quickly come to mind. Here are some general questions to ask in planning for a metacognitive discussion: What are the most important ideas in the lesson? What strategies will students need to learn these ideas? Are the students *aware* of these strategies?

A B–D–A instructional framework also includes provisions for guiding the search for meaning during reading. In other words, students need to be shown how to think with texts as they engage in literacy-related learning, such as setting a purpose for reading, a topic emphasized in Chapters 6–10. This instructional framework also encourages the incorporation of technology and multimedia to support learning before, during, and after interaction with a text. Pop culture, videos, music, and games can be incorporated to the B–D–A framework and connected to literacy to strengthen student understanding and meet the needs for digital elements in lesson planning.

DURING-READING ACTIVITIES   Teachers easily recognize the important parts of a text assignment. Most students don't. Instead, they tend to read every passage in every chapter in the same monotonous way. Each word, each sentence, each paragraph is treated with equal reverence. No wonder a disconnect often exists between the text and the reader.

The disconnect between text and reader is especially noticeable in content areas where readers must interact with highly specialized and technical language. Nowhere, for example, is content literacy more challenging for students than in the reading of mathematics texts. Math texts are tersely written in highly condensed language. Students must perceive and decode mathematical symbols, construct meanings for specialized and technical vocabulary and concepts, analyze and interpret relationships, and apply interpretations to the solution of problems.

Study how two mathematics teachers adapt the B–D–A instructional framework to scaffold reader–text interactions during reading. The first teaches prealgebra classes in a middle school. The students have studied linear equations and are preparing to learn the procedures in order to solve a system of linear equations graphically. The ultimate objective is for the students to find the answer to a system of linear equations by graphing and to know that for an ordered pair to be a solution, it must satisfy two linear equations simultaneously. During the before-reading phase of the lesson, the teacher shows a YouTube video clip on how to graph a system of equations using the slope intercept form and the students are asked to explore the following questions: How do I find the slope intercept form? How do I solve a system of linear equations graphically? The questions tap into the students' prior knowledge and their conceptions (some naive, some sophisticated) of linear equations.

As part of the lesson, the teacher asks the students to use their math journals to write definitions of several terms associated with linear equations: slope intercept form, system of equations, y-intercept, ordered pair, point of intersection. The students' definitions are discussed as the teacher builds on what they know to arrive at a set of class definitions of the terms. He then pairs the students in "study buddy" teams and asks them to use what they already know about linear equations to read the assigned section from the textbook to build an understanding of how to solve systems of linear equations graphically. The study buddies read the text section and complete the selective reading guide illustrated in Figure 5.3.

Figure 5.3 Using a Selective Reading Guide in Math

Before reading, think about the ways in which we have defined *a system of linear equations* in class discussion. Now compare our definitions with the one in the book. Develop in your own words a definition of *a system of linear equations* based on what you know and what you have read.

System of linear equations:

Now read and define other key terms in this section.

Slope intercept form:

y-intercept:

Order pair:

Point of intersection:

In your own words, write the steps to converting a standard linear equation to a slope intercept form.

_____

_____

Explain why the solution of a system of linear equations has to be an ordered pair that satisfies both equations simultaneously.

Explain. Why is the point of intersection a solution?

_____

Example 1. Put the following linear equations in slope intercept form and then graph to find a solution.

$$y = 3x - 2$$
$$y - 3 = -2x$$

Example 2. Is the ordered pair (1, 3) a solution to the system of linear equations? Solve by inspection.

$\{= - + 4$

$= 3$

*Explain*_____

Example 3. Is the ordered pair (5,-1) a solution to the system of linear equations? Solve by inspection.

*How do you know?*_____

You're on your own!

Complete problems 1–31 with your "study buddy."

Together, the "study buddies" discuss the assigned material as they work through the guide. Selective reading guides, as we suggest in Chapter 10, are one way of engaging students in reading by providing a "road map" to the important concepts in the material.

The second teacher, a high school mathematics teacher, also adapts the B–D–A framework to guide students' engagement with the text and to help them make important connections between reading and mathematics. When she first started teaching, she noticed with some dismay that students almost never read the text. Nor did they talk about mathematics with one another. Therefore, she makes a conscious effort to incorporate literacy and cooperative learning principles whenever instructional situations warrant them.

One such situation occurred when her students were studying the concepts of ratio, proportion, and percentage. The focus of the lesson was a section that dealt with the development of scale drawings as an application of proportion. She initiated the lesson by having students take five minutes to write admit slips, a writing-to-learn strategy we introduce in Chapter 9. Admit slips are students' "tickets of admission" to the lesson. The teacher can use them in a variety of ways to find out what students are feeling and thinking as they begin the class period.

The teacher triggered admit slip writing with the prompt: "If you had a younger brother or sister in the sixth grade, how would you describe a scale drawing in words that he or she would understand?" Using a collaborative website such as Tricider, Edmodo, or Edublog set up in advance by the teacher, the students wrote freely for several minutes until instructed to "wind down" and complete the thoughts on which they were working. The teacher and students reviewed the admit slips posted by the class and shared a few of the students' descriptions that highlighted teaching objectives. The discussion that followed revolved around the students' conceptions of scale drawings and what it means to be "in proportion."

The teacher then formed four-member cooperative groups to guide students' interactions with the text section on scale drawings. Each team was assigned to draw a scale model of the recreation room in its "dream house." First, the teams had to decide what facilities would be included in the recreation room. Once they developed the list of facilities, the team members read the text section and discussed how to develop a scale that would fit all of the facilities into the space provided for each team at the chalkboard. The lesson concluded with the teams describing their scale drawings. The teacher then asked the students to regroup and develop a list of the important ideas related to scale models.

Figure 5.4 Post-reading Activity for a Southwest Asia Lesson

I. *Directions:* An economist, a theologian, an historian, and a geographer all feel competent to speak on any of the following topics. Who is really best qualified? Who is the specialist in each field? On the blank line preceding each topic, place the letter of the correct specialist.

A. Economist
B. Theologian
C. Historian
D. Geographer

_____1. The region holds over half the world's oil reserves.

_____2. The belief that Muhammad is the prophet of Allah.

_____3. The Fertile Crescent between the Euphrates and Tigris Rivers.

_____4. The five basic beliefs of all Muslims.

_____5. Desalinization is needed for large-scale farming.

_____6. A house of worship for Jews.

_____7. The country of Persia became Iran in 1935.

_____8. The lowest point on the Earth's surface.

_____9. The Suez Canal was built to allow commercial trading.

_____10. The Wailing Wall is a sacred site.

_____11. Kurds are the largest ethnic group without a homeland.

_____12. The first monotheistic religion.

_____13. Mountains and deserts are predominant landforms.

_____14. Arabs of Southwest Asia believe they are descendants of Abraham.

_____15. The modern state of Israel was created in 1948.

II. *Directions:* Pretend you are the economist, the theologian, the historian, or the geographer. Write a "guest editorial" for the local newspaper revealing your professional attitude toward women in the workplace.

AFTER-READING ACTIVITIES Guidance during reading bridges the gap between students and text so that students learn how to distinguish important from less important ideas, perceive relationships, and respond actively to meaning.

Ideas encountered before and during reading may need clarification and elaboration after reading. Post-reading activities create a structure that refines emerging concepts. For example, a social studies teacher who was nearing completion of a unit on Southwest Asia asked her students to reflect on their reading by using the activity in Figure 5.4. The writing prompt in part II of the after-reading activity is based on an instructional practice called RAFT, which we describe in Chapter 9. The writing and follow-up discussion refined and extended the students' thinking about the ideas under study. The questions "Who is really best qualified?" and "Who is the specialist in each field?" prompted students to sort out what they had learned. The teacher provided just enough structure by listing topics from various facets of Southwest Asian culture to focus students' thinking and help them make distinctions.

Activities such as the one in Figure 5.4 extend thinking about ideas encountered during reading. Writing activities, study guides, and other after-reading practices are springboards to thinking and form the basis for discussing and articulating ideas developed through reading.

Examples of B–D–A-Centered Lessons

How teachers adapt the B–D–A instructional framework depends on the students in the class, the text that they are studying, and the kinds of activities that will be reflected in the lesson. Following are some examples of text-centered lessons in different content areas at different grade levels. As you study these lessons, notice how the teachers adapt the B–D–A framework in their lessons.

MIDDLE SCHOOL PHYSICAL EDUCATION CLASS Middle school students were assigned a text on cardio fitness. The text explained the two different types of cardiorespiratory exercise (aerobic and anaerobic) and the examples of physical activity associated with each as well as the benefits or lack thereof. The teacher's objectives were to (1) involve students in an active reading and discussion of the text and (2) engage in aerobic and anaerobic exercises to understand why one is more beneficial to cardiorespiratory health. Study how he planned his instructional activities in Figure 5.5.

HIGH SCHOOL FRENCH CLASS By way of contrast, study how a high school French teacher taught Guy de Maupassant's short story "L'Infirme" to an advanced class of language students. The story is about two men riding in a train. Henry Bonclair is sitting alone in a train car when another passenger, Revalière, enters the car. This fellow traveler is disabled, having lost his leg during the war. Bonclair wonders about the type of life he must lead. As he looks at the disabled man, Bonclair senses that he met him a few years earlier. He asks the man if he is not the person he met. Revalière is that man. Now Bonclair remembers that Revalière was to be married. He wonders if he got married before or after losing the leg or at all. Bonclair inquires. No, Revalière has not married, refusing to ask the girl to put up with a "deformed" man. However, he is on his way to see her, her husband, and her children. They are all very good friends. The French teacher formulated five objectives for the lesson:

1. To teach vocabulary dealing with the concept of "infirmity"
2. To foster students' ability to make inferences about the reading material from their own knowledge
3. To foster students' ability to predict what will happen in the story in light of the background they bring to the story
4. To foster students' ability to evaluate their predictions once they have read the story
5. To use the story as a basis for writing a dialogue in French

Figure 5.5 B–D–A Activities in a Middle School Physical Education Class

I. Before Reading

    A. Before introducing the text, determine what students now know about cardiorespiratory health.

        1. What are the positive effects that cardiorespiratory exercise has on the heart?

        2. What is the difference between aerobic and anaerobic exercise, and what are some examples of physical activity for each form?

        3. Why is one form better for cardiorespiratory health?

    B. Connect students' responses to these questions to the text assignment. Introduce the passage and its premise.

    C. Form small groups of four students each, and direct each group to participate in the following situation:

    Pretend that you are trying to come up with a new school-wide cardio-fitness plan for students at your school, and you want to present your idea to the school's faculty to get their support. You decide to enlist your eighth graders in your project to create a workout for all students in the school to get in some cardiorespiratory exercises quickly and at no cost for expensive equipment. What are some creative and efficient ways they can accomplish this task?

    Tech-Savvy Solution: Have students view a short cardio-fitness video to predict the aerobic versus anaerobic exercises based on the exercises shown. *Note:* Always do a preview prior to student viewing to ensure the video is appropriate for student viewing and to avoid having the video blocked by school software.

    D. Have the students share their group's predictions and write them on the board.

II. During Reading

    A. Assign the selection to be read in class.

    B. During reading, direct students to note the similarities and differences between their ideas on the board and what they read about cardiorespiratory health.

Tech-Savvy Solution: If the text is being read on a laptop or device in a PDF file, encourage students to annotate as they read, using the editing tools through their PDF reader software. Students may underline similarities, star newly gained info, and highlight points they think are important for understanding.

III. After Reading (Day 2)

    A. Discuss the previous day's reading activity. Have the students compare what they learned about the positive effects cardiorespiratory exercise has on the heart to their initial ideas before reading. How many of the students' initial ideas were similar to the benefits mentioned in the text? How many were different? Have the students differentiate between aerobic exercise and anaerobic exercise and share which form of exercise is better for cardio fitness and why.

    B. Extend students' understanding of cardiorespiratory health. Set up stations on the football field that differentiate between aerobic and anaerobic exercises. Divide the class into groups of four students. Each group is responsible for testing each of the exercises as they move from station to station and measure:

        1. The ability of students to correctly and carefully execute the cardio-fitness skills mentioned in the reading (aerobic and anaerobic)

        2. Measure their heart rates to determine which skill provided the greatest cardio exercise

Conduct the experiment during lunch time. The students will make notes and take them back to the classroom. Each group's discoveries will be discussed in class.

Tech-Savvy Solution: Incorporate a smartphone fitness app to track students' fitness results, including calories burned and best overall workout.

Two of the activities used in the French teacher's plan, the *graphic organizer* and the *inferential strategy,* are explained in depth in later chapters. The steps in the activities section of the lesson plan are outlined in Figure 5.6.

These lesson activities all have the same underlying purpose. Each provides a set of experiences designed to move readers from preparation to engagement with the text to extension and elaboration of the concepts in the material under study. How teachers plan instructional activities for content literacy lessons varies by grade level and the sophistication of the students. The same is true of developing plans for a unit of study. In the next section, we go beyond designing and planning lessons to decisions related to thematic learning involving multiple literacy experiences.

MyLab Education Self-Check 5.2

MyLab Education Application Exercises 5.2:
Using the Before-During-After (B-D-A) Framework in a Content Area Classroom

Figure 5.6 A B–D–A Lesson in a High School French Class

I. Before Reading

A. Begin the lesson by placing the title of the story on the board: "L'Infirme." Ask students to look at the title and compare it to a similar English word (or words). Determine very generally what the story is probably about (a disabled person).

B. Introduce key words used in the story by displaying a *graphic organizer:*

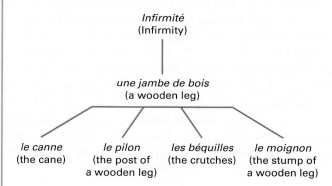

C. Use the *inferential strategy.* Ask and discuss with the class the following three sets of questions. Have the students write down their responses.

1. *Vous avez peut-être vu quelqu'un qui est très es-tropié à cause de la perte d'une jambe ou d'un bras. Qu'est-ce qui traverse votre esprit? De quoi est-ce que vous vous demandez?*
    (You may have seen someone who is very disabled because of the loss of a leg or an arm. When you see such a person, what crosses your mind? What do you wonder about?)

2. *Dans l'histoire, Bonclair voit ce jeune infirme qui a perdu la jambe. Qu'est-ce que vous pensez tra-verse son esprit?*
    (In the story, Bonclair sees this disabled young man who has lost his leg. What do you think crosses his mind?)

3. *Quand vous voyez quelqu'un qui a l'air vague-ment familier, qu'est-ce que vous voulez faire? Qu'est-ce que vous faites? Quels sont souvent les résultats?*
    When you see someone who looks vaguely familiar, what do you want to do? What do you do? What are often the results?)

4. *Dans cette histoire, Bonclair se souvient vaguement qu'il a fait la connaissance de cet infirme. Prédites cequ'il fera et prédites les résultats.*
    (In this story, Bonclair remembers vaguely having met this disabled. Predict what he does and the results.)

5. *Imaginez que vous êtes fiancé(e) à un jeune homme ou à une jeune femme. Puis vous avez un accident qui vous rend estropié(e). Qu'est-ce que vous*

feriez? Voudriez-vous se marier? Pourriez-vous compter sur l'autre de vous aimer encore?
    (Imagine that you are engaged to a young man or woman. Then you have an accident that leaves you disabled. What would you do? Would you still want to marry? Could you still expect the other to love you?)

6. *Dans notre histoire, Revalière a eu un accident juste avant son marriage. Prédites ce qu'il fera et ce qu'il comptera de la jeune fille. Prédites les résultats.*
    (In our story, Revalière has had an accident just before his marriage. Predict what he did and what he expected of the young woman. Predict the results.)

Tech-Savvy Solution: Have students Google image search the story title and predict the plot based on the visuals generated. *Note:* Always do a Google image search prior to student participation to ensure avoidance of inappropriate images that may not be filtered by school software.

II. During Reading

A. Assign the reading, instructing the students to keep in mind their prior knowledge and predictions.

B. Ask them to note possible changes in their predictions.

Tech-Savvy Solution: Use the smartphone app Word Lens to aid with text translation for struggling students or English Learners.

II. After Reading

A. After the reading, conduct a follow-up discussion with students. Relate their predictions to what actually happened, noting how our background knowledge and experience of the world lead us to think along certain lines.

B. Have the class form groups of four with at least one male and one female in each group. Establish the following situation:

Une jeune fille vient d'être estropiée dans un accident de na-tation. Son fiancé lui a téléphoné. Il veut lui parler. Qu'est-ce qu'il veut lui dire? On frappe à la porte. C'est lui.

(A young lady was recently disabled in a swimming accident. Her fiancé has called her. He wants to talk to her. What does he want to talk about? There is a knock at the door. It is he.)

1. Think together, drawing on your past knowledge or experience of situations like this. Write a 15- to 20-line group dialogue in French between the young lady and her fiancé. What might he have to tell her? How might she react?

2. Select a male and female student to present the group's dialogue to the class.

Tech-Savvy Solution: Have students use the Vocaroo web-site to record their dialogue and share the link on the class webpage or via student e-mails.

Planning Units of Study

5.3 Describe the different components of a well-designed unit.

Units of study organize instruction around objectives, activities, print and nonprint resources, and inquiry experiences. A unit may be designed for a single discipline or may be interdisciplinary, integrating two or more content areas. In middle schools, where content area teachers are teamed in learning "communities" or "families," opportunities abound to develop interdisciplinary units. Interdisciplinary units require coordination and cooperation by all of the content area teachers teamed within a learning community. Team planning helps students make connections not otherwise possible among many knowledge domains and provides students with multiple exposures to new information, leading to deeper understanding and long-term retention (Kamil, 2003). For example, a middle school teaching team organized an interdisciplinary unit around the theme of "Ancient Civilizations of the Americas." Team members developed a four-week unit in which 130 seventh graders were "born" into the Mayans, Incas, or Aztecs. The students assumed the role of cultural anthropologists to explore what the three ancient civilizations had in common culturally, economically, politically, geographically, and technologically. The teachers provided many opportunities for the students to actively process the information—both emotionally and intellectually.

Components of a Well-Designed Unit

The unit of study is a planning tool that includes (1) a title reflecting the theme or topic of the unit, (2) the major concepts to be learned, (3) the texts and information sources to be studied by students, (4) the unit's instructional activities, and (5) provisions for assessing what students have learned from the unit.

CONTENT OBJECTIVES *Content analysis* is a major part of teacher preparation in the development of a unit of study. Content analysis results in the *what* of learning—the major concepts and understandings that students should learn from reading the unit materials. Through content analysis, the major concepts become the objectives for the unit. It doesn't matter whether these content objectives are stated in behavioral terms. What really matters is that you know which concepts students will interact with and develop. Therefore, it's important to decide on a manageable number of the most important understandings to be gained from the unit. This means setting priorities; it's impossible to cover every aspect of the material that students will read or to which they will be exposed.

A unit on spatial relationships for a high school art class provides an example of how a teacher planned content objectives, activities, and materials. First, she listed the major concepts to be taught in the unit:

- Humans are aware of the space about them as functional, decorative, and communicative.
- Space organized intuitively produces an aesthetic result, but a reasoned organization of space also leads to a pleasing outcome if design is considered.
- Occupied and unoccupied space have positive and negative effects on mood and depth perception.
- The illusion of depth can be created on a two-dimensional surface.
- The direction and balance of lines or forms create feelings of tension, force, and equilibrium in the space that contains them.
- Seldom in nature is the order of objects so perfect as to involve no focal point, force, or tension.

INSTRUCTIONAL ACTIVITIES AND TEXT RESOURCES The high school art teacher then developed the activities and identified the texts to be used in the unit (see Figure 5.7). As you study the figure, keep in mind that some of the text-related activities suggested are explored later in this book.

The actual framework of units will vary. For example, you might organize a unit entirely on a sequence of lessons from assignments in a single textbook. This type of organization is highly structured and is even restrictive in the sense that it often precludes the use of various kinds of other literature rich in content and substance. However, a unit of study can be planned so that the teacher will (1) use a single textbook to begin the unit and then branch out into multiple texts and differentiated activities, (2) organize the unit entirely on individual or group inquiry and research, or (3) combine single-text instruction with multiple-text activities and inquiry.

Figure 5.7 Activities and Texts

Text-Related Activities	Texts
1. Graphic organizer	Graham Collier, Form, Space, and Vision
2. Vocabulary and concept bulletin board	
	Chapter 3, Collier
3. Prereading	Chapters 6 and 7
4. Prereading	Chapters 6 and 7
	Chapter 11
5. Art journal	Chapter 3
6. K-W-L	Chapters 6 and 7
	Chapter 11
7. Vocabulary exercise	H. Botten, Do You See What I See?
8. Vocabulary exercise	H. Helfman, Creating Things That Move
9. Vocabulary exercise	D. McAgy, Going for a Walk with a Line
	L. Kaumpmann, Creating with Space and Construction
10. Student's choice (list of projects for research study)	G. Le Freure, Junk Sculpture
	J. Lynch, Mobile Design
11. Hands-On Ink dabs Straw painting Dry seed arrangement Cardboard sculpture Positive-negative cutouts Perspective drawing Large-scale class sculpture Mobiles Space frames	Calder's Universe

Displays of artist's works with questionnaires to be filled out about them |
12. Filmstrip	
13. Field trip to studio of a sculptor	
14. Field trip to museum	
15. Learning corner	

Branching out provides the latitude to move from a single-text lesson to independent learning activities. The move from single to multiple information sources exposes students to a wide range of texts that may be better suited to their needs and interests. By interacting with multiple texts and a variety of authors, students are exposed to a wider range of styles, formats, and vocabulary, which in turn can raise their comprehension of content and increase their vocabulary through repeated and diverse exposure to new words. By engaging with multiple texts on the same topic, students also build valuable critical thinking skills as they learn to assimilate information from several sources, which often provide small vignettes of information or possibly conflicting data (National Council of Teachers of English [NCTE], 2004, 2006) (see Figure 5.8). As mentioned previously, technology and multimedia must be considered when planning. With teachers being encouraged to promote 21st-century skills and critical thinking, unit planning must acknowledge digital realities and complex multiliteracies.

Unit planning simply provides more options to coordinate a variety of information sources. In single-discipline units, B–D–A activities become an integral part of unit teaching.

Figure 5.8 "Branching Out" in a Thematic Unit: Using a Wide Range of Texts

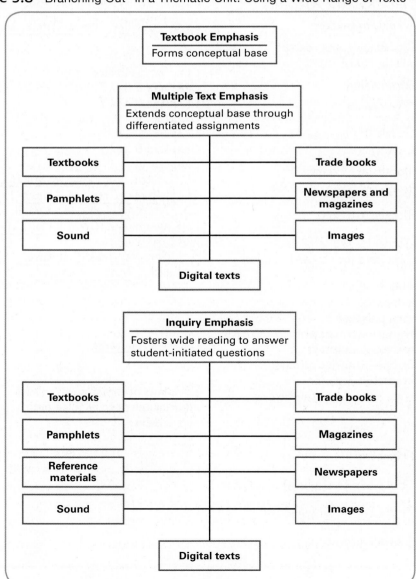

Listing texts and resources is an important part of the planning process for a single-discipline unit. One reason a unit is so attractive as a means of organization is that the teacher can go beyond the textbook—or, for that matter, bypass it. A wide array of literature, both narrative and informational, gives students opportunities for an intense involvement in the theme or topic under study. Trade books, digital texts, pamphlets, periodicals, reference books, newspapers, and magazines are all potential alternative routes to acquiring information.

Moreover, the Internet has become a valuable planning resource for teachers in the development of units. You can access many useful ideas for integrating digital texts into units of study.

An Inquiry/Research Emphasis in Units of Study

Gathering, organizing, and sharing information are crucial to both academic success and success in our information-rich society. Inquiry should, therefore, play a major role in learning important content, and the process of inquiry should be woven into thematic units of study. Students generate research questions based on their interests and developing knowledge of issues and topics. Next, they seek answers to those questions by exploring a variety of sources such as texts, artifacts, and people. Then, they evaluate and organize the information they have found so that their findings can be communicated in ways appropriate to their purpose and audience (International Reading Association and National Council of Teachers of English [IRA/NCTE], 1997). Research continues to be an important part of the Common Core State Standards, represented in all four of their English language arts strands, as well as in literacy in content area strands (National Governors Association Center for Best Practices, 2010).

How teachers guide inquiry/research projects is the key to a successful unit. The process of inquiry, like the process of writing that we describe in Chapter 9, works best when it occurs in steps and stages. Each stage of an inquiry/research project requires careful support by a teacher. In Box 5.2, we outline the stages and procedures for guiding inquiry/research.

When teachers simply assign and evaluate research reports, students often paraphrase whatever sources come to hand rather than actively pursuing information that they are eager to share with others. Genuine inquiry is an opportunity to build critical thinking skills and is always a messy endeavor characterized by false starts, unexpected discoveries, changes in direction, and continual decision making. Too much guidance can be as dangerous as too little.

In an in-depth study of two middle school research projects, Rycik (1994) found that teachers may lose their focus on genuine inquiry as they establish procedures for guiding all students to complete a project successfully. The teachers in the study were very concerned with providing sufficient guidance, so they broke down their projects into a series of discrete steps (such as making note cards) that could be taught, completed, and evaluated separately. As the projects moved forward, the teachers gradually came to believe that mastering the procedure for each step was the primary outcome of the project, even more important than learning content information.

Rycik (1994) concluded that inquiry should not be confined to one big research paper because teachers cannot introduce and monitor the wide range of searching, reading, thinking, and writing skills that students need to complete such projects. Good researchers, like good writers, must learn their craft through frequent practice in a variety of contexts. This means that students should research from a variety of sources and express their findings for a variety of audiences in a variety of forms. Some recommendations for integrating research into the classroom routine include the following:

- *Make identifying questions and problems as important in your classroom as finding answers.*

- *Provide frequent opportunities to compare, contrast, and synthesize information from multiple sources.*

- *Present findings of research in a variety of products and formats,* including charts, graphs, and visual or performing arts.
- *Discuss possible sources for information* presented in the class or for answering questions posed by the teacher or students (e.g., personal interviews, diaries, experiments).

The teacher must carefully plan inquiry-centered projects, giving just the right amount of direction to allow students to explore and discover ideas on their own. The research process isn't a do-your-own-thing proposition; budding researchers need structure. The trick is to strike a balance between teacher guidance and student self-reliance. A research project must have just enough structure to give students (1) a problem focus, (2) physical and intellectual freedom, (3) an environment in which they can obtain data, and (4) feedback situations in which to report the results of their research.

Box 5.2 Evidence-Based Best Practices

Procedures for Guiding Inquiry/Research Projects

I. Raise questions, identify interests, organize information.
  A. Discuss interest areas related to the unit of study.
  B. Engage in goal setting.
    1. Arouse curiosities.
    2. Create awareness of present levels of knowledge.
  C. Pose questions relating to each area and/or subarea.
    1. "What do you want to find out?"
    2. "What do you want to know about?"
    3. Record the questions or topics.
    4. "What do you already know about?"
  D. Organize information; have students make predictions about likely answers to gaps in knowledge.
    1. Accept all predictions as possible answers.
    2. Encourage thoughtful speculations in a nonthreatening way.

II. Select materials.
  A. Use visual materials.
    1. Trade books
    2. Magazines, catalogs, directories
    3. Newspapers and comics
    4. Indexes, atlases, almanacs, dictionaries, readers' guides, computer catalogs
    5. Films, slides
    6. Online videos, television programs
    7. Digital texts: CD-ROMs, website documents, online articles and databases, webinars, virtual field trips
  B. Use nonvisual materials.
    1. Audio files
    2. Recorded music or talk
    3. Radio programs or webcasts
    4. Field trips
  C. Use human resources.
    1. Interviews
    2. Letters
    3. On-site visits
    4. Discussion groups
    5. E-mail
    6. Listservs

  D. Encourage self-selection of materials.
    1. "What can I understand?"
    2. "What gives me the best answers?"

III. Guide the information search.
  A. Encourage active research.
    1. Reading
    2. Listening
    3. Observing
    4. Talking
    5. Writing
  B. Facilitate with questions.
    1. "How are you doing?"
    2. "Can I help you?"
    3. "Do you have all the materials you need?"
    4. "Can I help you with ideas you don't understand?"
  C. Have students keep records.
    1. Learning log that includes plans, procedures, notes, and rough drafts
    2. Book record cards
    3. Record of conferences with the teacher

IV. Consider different forms of writing.
  A. Initiate a discussion of sharing techniques.
  B. Encourage a variety of writing forms.
    1. Essay or paper
    2. Lecture to a specific audience
    3. Case study
    4. Story: adventure, science fiction, another genre
    5. Dialogue, conversation, interview
    6. Dramatization through scripts
    7. Commentary or editorial
    8. Thumbnail sketch

V. Guide the writing process.
  A. Help students organize information.
  B. Guide first-draft writing.
  C. Encourage responding, revising, and rewriting.
  D. "Publish" finished products.
    1. Individual presentations
    2. Classroom arrangement
    3. Class interaction

A Multiple-Text Emphasis in Units of Study

The literature-based movement in elementary schools serves as a prototype for the use of trade books in middle and high school classrooms. In addition, technology makes it possible to access and explore information sources through digital programs, electronic books, and the Internet. Internet inquiries and WebQuests provide excellent instructional frameworks for inquiry-centered learning. Although textbooks may be used to provide an information base and digital textbooks can be convenient, the foundation for individual and group inquiry into a theme or topic is built on students' use of multiple information resources, both print and nonprint. Trade books (see Chapter 11) and digital texts, as we explained in Chapter 2, are geared to students' interests and inquiry needs.

Say that in a middle grade classroom, students are engaged in a thematic unit on meteorology. What might you observe over several weeks? For starters, the teacher may conduct several whole-class lessons at the beginning of the unit using the textbook to develop a conceptual framework for individual and **group investigation**. As the weeks progress, however, whole-class activity is less prevalent.

Instead, small groups work on research projects or in discussion teams about weather history using *Blizzard! The Storm That Changed America* (2000) by Jim Murphy, *Isaac's Storm: A Man, a Time, and the Deadliest Hurricane in History* (1999) by Erik Larson, *The Perfect Storm: A True Story of Men Against the Sea* (1997) by Sebastian Junger, and *The Johnstown Flood* by David McCullough (1968). Individual students are also working on inquiries into weather forecasting with books such as Alan Watt's *Instant Storm Forecasting* (2009) and Mark Breen's *The Kids' Book of Weather Forecasting* (2000), while other students are reading excerpts from Frederick Lutgen's *The Atmosphere: An Introduction to Meteorology* (1979).

In addition, the students are conducting research online by tapping into the rich information resources on the Internet. Several students investigate the websites of the National Oceanic and Atmospheric Administration (NOAA), the National Weather Service, and Weather Spark. Others explore software programs: Extreme Weather (Layered Earth), Weather and Atmosphere (TeachEngineering), and Flip Out Over Weather (Digital Wish). One or two students navigate the pages of electronic reference books, such as Grolier's New Book of Popular Science (Grolier). Others access online libraries and digital journals, while some investigate documentaries and popular videos.

Toward the end of the unit, the class completes culminating activities, which may involve panel discussions, report writing, and oral presentations in which individuals or groups share knowledge gleaned from the various activities and texts. Tasks like this address standards related to reading, writing, speaking and listening. In this class, what you would observe is that everyone has something to contribute and information is gleaned from multiple access points.

Active learning environments within units of study integrate whole-class, small-group, and individual learning activities. Whole-class presentation is an economical means of giving information to students when the classroom context lends itself to information sharing. A whole-class activity, for example, may be used to set the stage for a new thematic unit. The unit introduction, discussion of objectives, and background building can all take place within whole-class structure when the teacher must take on the primary role as content expert. However, the chief drawback of whole-class presentation is that it limits active participation among students. Although whole-class interaction provokes discussion to an extent, it cannot produce the volume of participation necessary to engage students in active learning situations. A viable alternative supported by a substantial body of research lies in the use of collaborative interactions between teacher and students and among students. These **collaborative interactions** are grounded in the principles underlying cooperative learning and small-group processes. Box 5.3 offers suggestions for supporting English Learners in understanding content area concepts.

Box 5.3 Supporting English Learners

Content literacy can be particularly difficult for English Learners (ELs). ELs are not only learning how to use English to comprehend subject-matter content and the unfamiliar technical language presented in classroom texts; they must also learn the basic language needed to comprehend the content-specific vocabulary and language structures that are used to make inferences, draw conclusions, and ask questions. In light of these challenges, we agree with Echevarria, Vogt, and Short (2017): there is a need for content area teachers to implement strategies that build on content-specific knowledge and also take into account the linguistic differences of ELs.

As previously discussed within the chapter, building and activating prior knowledge is essential for EL students. It is equally important for teachers to be familiar with what their EL students already know in order to make the important connections between the new content to be learned and the EL's background knowledge. In addition, classroom teachers need to provide effective scaffolding to support EL students as they try to make sense of texts and learn new content topics. Because scaffolds serve as supports, the following instructional scaffolds are recommended for EL students:

- Hands-on manipulatives: Manipulatives can include a variety of things, from colored tiles and blocks in math and food web charts and microscopes in science to maps and globes in social studies. Manipulatives provide the concrete means for EL students to engage in learning new content.

- Realia: Objects from real life, such as money, photos, and food items, can be used to help EL students connect to their personal lives. Such objects can be held, smelled, and observed to build comprehension within content literacy.

- Visuals: Visual aids include photographs, illustrations, film, charts, and art, to name a few, that will help EL students build background knowledge. Visuals help EL students grasp important concepts in content area classrooms, reducing the demands of possible auditory information overloads.

- Graphic organizers: Graphic organizers are another visual source that allows EL students to organize new information into smaller "chunks" and tap into background knowledge.

- Group Work: Group work takes on many shapes and forms but works especially well with EL students. The process of interacting and collaborating with native English-speaking students helps EL students understand essential academic vocabulary and comprehend key concepts.

- Outlines: Teacher-prepared outlines provide the scaffolding support EL students need and further serve as a review tool throughout a learning segment.

MyLab Education **Self-Check 5.3**

MyLab Education **Application Exercise 5.3:**
Supporting English Learners in Content Area Units

Planning Collaborative Interactions

5.4 Describe the different strategies for cooperative learning.

Cooperative learning allows groups of students to pursue academic goals through collaboration in classroom instructional activities. The goals of cooperative learning, therefore, are to foster collaboration in a classroom context, develop students' self-esteem in the process of learning, encourage the development of positive group relationships, and enhance academic achievement (Johnson, Johnson, & Holubec, 2008; Webb, 2008). Cooperative groups facilitate active participation and should be a primary form of classroom organization when teachers bring students together to comprehend texts. The National Reading Panel's review of research on text comprehension identifies cooperative learning as a scientifically supported comprehension strategy (NRP, 2000). We agree with Duke and Pearson (2002), however, who view cooperative learning as an "instructional medium" that facilitates reading comprehension rather than an individual instructional strategy. Within the learning environment created by cooperative groups, students produce more ideas, participate more, and take greater intellectual risks. A cooperative group, with its limited audience, provides more opportunity for students to contribute ideas to a discussion and take chances in the process. The students can try out ideas without worrying about being wrong or sounding dumb—a fear that often accompanies risk taking in a whole-class situation.

Cooperative Learning

Engaged learners are socially interactive. Bringing learners and texts together in social collaboration to engage in discussions may be achieved through **cooperative learning groups**.

Many variations on cooperative group learning are possible, but cooperative learning is not as simple as student grouping. Instead, cooperative groups are focused and purposeful; every student in a cooperative group contributes to the common goal, and many times roles are defined, with each student responsible for a portion of the group success. Several cooperative grouping patterns work well within the context of content literacy practices and text-related discussions. The cooperative groups described in the following sections give you a feel for how students might collaborate in their interactions with texts and with one another as they extract and construct meaning to make sense out of what they are reading.

JIGSAW GROUPS Interdependent team learning with texts may be achieved through *jigsaw groups* (Aronson & Patnoe, 1997). Jigsaw teaching requires students to specialize in a content literacy task that contributes to an overall group objective. **Jigsaw groups** are composed of students divided heterogeneously into three- to six-member teams. Each student on a team becomes an expert on a subtopic of a theme or topic about which the class is reading. Not only is the student accountable for teaching the other members of the group about his or her subtopic, but he or she is also responsible for learning the information other group members provide during the jigsaw discussions. This strategy is beneficial for all students, but especially hesitant readers and learners, because the text or information is "chunked" into more manageable pieces that are less overwhelming.

For example, a science teacher in a middle school engages students in a thematic unit on the atomic theory. As part of the unit of study, he divides the class into three large groups, and the groups are further divided into groups of Aristotle, Dalton, Thomson, Millikan and Chadwick, Rutherford, and Bohr. Each student within each group will be assigned to become an expert on a particular topic related to the group's atomic theorist: time period, model development, major discovery, and illustration of the atomic model. Once each student has his or her assigned topic, he or she will move from station to station to initially conduct research individually and then come together to present with other "experts" working on the same topic. Each group will be given questions about its topic to guide its collaborative research. Students will also be given time to gather information and gain familiarity about their topic, so they can present to the class at the end. Once completed, the first set of experts regarding the *time period* of their atomic model will present the information they gathered, one by one, in front of the class, after which the next group of experts on *model development* will do the same, followed by the group of experts on *major discovery* and *illustration of the atomic model*. Each of the expert groups has a variety of resource materials and texts made available by the teacher to help them explore and clarify their subtopics. When the members in each of the expert groups complete their tasks, they return to their jigsaw teams to teach and share what they have learned. As each jigsaw member presents his or her findings, the other members listen and take notes in preparation to construct a timeline on the development of the atomic model. As a culminating activity, each group will then present their timelines and together provide additional information it has gathered regarding its atomic model, such as a biographical sketch on the theorist, a description of the experiment to develop the atomic model, and contributions to atomic knowledge. Students must submit their work for assessment and will be graded on their participation as well as the work they have gathered (see Figure 5.9.)

The purpose of a jigsaw group is for the kids to learn how to work together, take responsibility for the topic they are individually assigned, and learn more about their solar system in a way that's fun for them. Strategic grouping could also be incorporated, such as grouping a very bright student with a student who needs a lot of support. Though there are a variety of different grouping methods, the overall purpose of cooperative learning is to encourage student collaboration and success.

A theater teacher also finds jigsaw to be useful in involving students in collaborative guided discovery into the four styles of modern theater. The class is divided into four heterogeneous groups. Each group is assigned one of four theatrical genres: Melodrama, Realism, Absurdism, and Dadaism. Within their groups, each student chooses a subcategory on which he or she would like to focus research: key elements and philosophies of

Figure 5.9 Note-Taking Protocol for Atomic Theory Jigsaw

Theorist	Period	Model Development	Major Discovery	Model Illustration
Aristotle				
Dalton				
Thomson				
Millikan & Chadwick				
Rutherford				
Bohr				

the genre, the development of the genre (What caused the movement? How did it evolve from the other artistic movements of its time?), the lasting effects of the genre (What type of impact has the style had on art, culture, and society? Is it still felt today?), the audience reaction (How was the genre first received by audiences and critics?), and the playwrights associated with the genre and their major works.

Once research is completed, groups discuss their findings and work together to create a cohesive presentation for the class. In this way, all students will be exposed to all four genres as well as become experts on their subcategory. It's important to note that while subcategories are being researched, students may enter discussions with other students researching the same subcategory. This would prompt a comparison of the genres. (See Figure 5.10.)

STUDENT TEAMS ACHIEVEMENT DIVISIONS (STAD)   Student teams lend themselves well to content area learning situations that combine whole-class discussion with follow-up small-group activity. The originator of **Student Teams Achievement Divisions (STAD)** groups, Robert Slavin (1988; 1994), emphasizes the importance of achieving team learning goals but also recognizes that individual performance is important in cooperative groups.

STAD groups work this way: The teacher introduces a topic of study to the whole class, presents new information, and then divides the class into heterogeneous four-member groups of high-, average-, and low-achieving students to engage in follow-up team study. The goal of team study is to master the content presented in the whole-class discussion. The team members help each other by discussing the material, problem solving, comparing answers to guide material, and quizzing one another to ensure that each member knows the material. The students take periodic quizzes, prepared by the teacher, following team study. A team score is determined by the extent to which each member of the team improves over past performance. A system of team awards based on how well students perform individually ensures that team members will be interdependent for learning.

After providing background on the area, a social studies teacher planning a unit on the Age of Exploration divided the class into heterogeneous teams of four students. Each

Figure 5.10 Note-Taking Protocol for Modern Theater Genre Jigsaw

	Melodrama	Realism	Absurdism	Dadaism
Key elements and philosophies of the genre				
The development of the genre (What caused the movement? How did it evolve from the other artistic movements of its time?)				
Lasting effects of the genre (What type of impact has the style had on art, culture, and society? Is it still felt today?)				
Audience reaction (How was the genre first received by audiences and critics?)				
Playwrights associated with the genre and their major works				

team was to work together and use maps and other research materials to identify and understand the discoveries and terms associated with the period of exploration during the 1400s–1500s: *Bartolomeu Dias, Vasco da Gama, Christopher Columbus, Vasco Núñez de Balboa, Ferdinand Magellan, Hernando Cortes,* and *Francisco Pizarro.* For each of these explorers, teams had to exhibit their knowledge on the reasons for exploration, the country for whom the explorer traveled, map the associated exploration route and discoveries, and determine the date of significance related to historical developments at the time. In addition, each team had to complete a short quiz on the Age of Exploration. Through this process, teams were able to guide their own learning through the structured support of the strategy (see Figure 5.11).

LEARNING CIRCLES   Johnson et al., (2008) underscore the importance of positive interdependence through a cooperative learning model. Similar to STAD, learning circles mesh whole-group study with small-group interactions and discussion. Learning circles may comprise two to six members of varying abilities who come together to share text resources and help each other learn. All of the content literacy activities that we present in this book can be adapted to the type of interdependent learning teams that are suggested by Johnson and colleagues. However, cooperative groups don't run by themselves. You must plan for the success of positive interdependence by teaching students how to use collaboration skills to work interdependently in teams and then facilitating the group process as students engage in discussion and interaction.

Johnson et al. (2008) suggest 18 steps for structuring learning circles, some of which include specifying content objectives, deciding on the size of the group, assigning students to groups, arranging the room, planning instructional activities and guide material to promote interdependent learning, explaining the academic task, explaining the criteria for success, structuring the division of labor within the groups, structuring individual accountability and intergroup cooperation, monitoring students' behaviors, teaching the skills of collaboration, providing task assistance as needed, evaluating student learning, and assessing how well the teams functioned.

Group brainstorming, prediction, problem solving, mapping, and study strategies, all of which are discussed in Part Two, are easily woven into the fabric of cooperative learning circles. Coming to a group consensus on a variety of discussion tasks is an important outcome in cooperative learning groups. Students need to be shown how to engage cooperatively in consensus building as they decide what conclusions they can or cannot support as a result of their interactions with texts and one another.

GROUP INVESTIGATION   As we explained earlier in this chapter, students can be combined in teams of two to six to collaborate on inquiry topics that interest them within the context of a thematic unit and the major concepts of study. Each group selects a topic and cooperatively plans the inquiry in consultation with the teacher. Each research team, for example, decides how to investigate the topic, which tasks each member will be responsible for, and how the topic will be reported. The groups then conduct the investigation, synthesize their findings into a group presentation, and make their presentation to the entire class. The teacher's evaluation includes individual performance and the overall quality of the group presentation. Examples include the following:

- In Figure 5.12, study how an American history teacher in high school sets up a group investigation project on the Civil War.
- One math teacher showed the relevant applications of trigonometry by creating groups to investigate how different careers use these math skills. Students were placed in groups of three and asked to conduct research on the Internet on the career of their choice. Each member of the group was given a role:

  Math expert: Find concepts and theories that are relevant to the chosen career. Examples include the Pythagorean Theorem, trigonometric functions, and the Law of Sines.

  Researcher: Find applications of trigonometry in the chosen career.

  Graphic designer: Responsible for finding pictures, graphs, and diagrams that illustrate how trigonometry is used in the chosen career.

- After students completed their research, groups presented their findings to the class. (See Figure 5.13.)
- In Figure 5.14, study how a middle school science teacher creates a fictitious contest to encourage students to complete a group investigation project on the Earth's ecosystems.

MyLab Education **Self-Check 5.4**

MyLab Education **Application Exercise 5.4:**
Grouping Students for Collaborative Learning in Content Area Classes

---

Figure 5.11 A STAD Project for a Unit on the Age of Exploration

Teach: Students will be given material to research the Age of Exploration. Students will go over notes in class and divide up into groups of four. Important topics discussed are reasons for exploration and for what European country, dates, ocean routes and intended destinations, discoveries, and the historical significance.

Team Study: Teams will come together and use maps and other research materials to identify and understand the terms listed below. Map identification is important along with dates, the historical facts, concepts, and the significance.

Bartolomeu Dias, Vasco da Gama, Christopher Columbus, Vasco Núñez de Balboa, Ferdinand Magellan, Hernando Cortés, Francisco Pizarro

Quiz:

What happened in Constantinople that caused the Europeans to begin exploration by sea?

What were the 3 Gs that led to European exploration?

Who led the Portuguese exploration that reached the Cape of Good Hope?

Who led the Portuguese exploration that rounded the Cape of Good Hope to reach India?

Which explorer landed in Hispaniola and is often credited for discovering America?

Who was the first European to sail around the globe?

Who was the Spanish explorer who conquered the Incas?

What two countries dominated the Age of Exploration?

What did Cortés actually find and then conquer?

Who was the first explorer to see the Pacific Ocean?

Figure 5.12 A Group Investigation Project for a Unit on the Civil War

Directions: Congratulations! You have been chosen to anchor the new series *TimeLine.* This show features the same type of in-depth interview as *NightLine,* except you have a time machine. You can go back in time and interview someone from the Civil War. To prevent changing the future, here are the rules:

1. Work in pairs. Both of you will do research and write the interview. Decide who will be the interviewer and who the interviewee. Decide on a historical interview date.

2. Your interviewee may be an actual historical figure (e.g., Ulysses S. Grant), or you may create a fictional eyewitness to a historical event (e.g., Surrender at Appomattox).

3. Your research must be based on at least two sources, only one of which may be an encyclopedia. A bibliography must be included in the written interview turned in after the presentation.

4. Presentation

   a. Introduce the interviewee and briefly tell why this person is important or interesting.
   b. Your questions must stay within your time frame.
   c. The interviewee's answers must be reasonable and based on historical facts from your research.
   d. You are encouraged to include visual aids: pictures, cartoons, maps, props, and costumes.
   e. The interview should last no less than 4 minutes and no more than 10 minutes.

Here is a list of possible subjects, or you may choose your own.

Abraham Lincoln	Jefferson Davis	Andrew Johnson	Salmon P. Chase
Robert E. Lee	Ulysses S. Grant	"Stonewall" Jackson	William T. Sherman
David Farragut	Belle Boyd	Harriet Tubman	John Wilkes Booth
Mathew Brady	Walt Whitman	Frederick Douglass	Richmond
Mark Twain	*Uncle Tom's Cabin*	Underground Railroad	Fort Sumter
Battle of Gettysburg	Confederate soldier	Emancipation Proclamation	Sojourner Truth
Union soldier	Elizabeth Cady Stanton		

Figure 5.13 A Group Investigation Project for a Unit on Right Triangles and Trigonometry

Description of the strategy: The idea of this group investigation is to show students that trigonometry is important in "real life." The group investigation requires groups of students to show how different careers use trigonometry. For this investigation, students will spend time in the computer lab. Students will be separated by the teacher into heterogeneous groups of three. The teacher will choose a leader of the group. Each group will select a career that uses trigonometry, such as an engineer, crime scene investigator, or construction worker. Once students have chosen a career, they will need to obtain teacher approval. Students will decide what their role will be in this investigation. The three roles are as follows:

Math expert: Find concepts and theories that are relevant to the chosen career. Examples include the Pythagorean Theorem, trigonometric functions, and the Law of Sines.

Researcher: Find applications of trigonometry in the chosen career.

Graphic designer: Responsible for finding pictures, graphs, and diagrams that illustrate how trigonometry is used in the chosen career.

The teacher provides a list of helpful websites to the students. After students have completed their research, the individuals within the group will meet to discuss how they would like to present the information to the class. The group leader will organize the discussion and handle any disagreements within the group. Creativity is encouraged. The presentation will be done as a group, with each student focusing on his role in the investigation. A detailed description of the required presentation will be provided to the students with an attached rubric for individual and group assessments.

To make sure that all students stay focused and understand the activity, the teacher will circulate throughout the classroom and computer lab to check on students' progress. Also, it may be helpful to have poster board, markers, rulers, scissors, and glue available to students for use in their presentations.

Figure 5.14 A Group Investigation Project for a Unit on the Earth's Ecosystems for a Middle School Science Class

This group investigation activity will allow students the opportunity to select an ecosystem that appeals to them and assemble with classmates who share a similar interest. Students will then form a collaborative research group that will ideally consist of between two and six students. As the instructor, I will meet with each research group to discuss the ecosystem it has selected and present it with project guidelines (see below). As inquiry begins, each group will be responsible for deciding how it will investigate its ecosystem. Additionally, each group will be accountable for self-assigning roles for conducting research, agreeing on how to unify its findings, and selecting a formal presentation format. Research will culminate with group presentations to the class, which will be evaluated based upon the quality of the presentation as well as the contributions of each group member.

Group Investigation Project: The Earth's Ecosystems

To enrich our unit study of population dynamics, I have created a group investigation project centered on the following ecosystems:

Forest	Grasslands
Desert	Tundra
Fresh Water	Marine Water

Students will select an ecosystem that appeals to them and assemble with classmates who share a similar interest. I will meet with each group and provide it with the following guidelines:

Project Guidelines

Condé Nast Traveler is seeking entries from middle school students throughout the region to create an informative and eye-catching advertisement featuring the Earth's ecosys-

tems. Advertisements can be exhibited in any format (e.g., a poster, a brochure, a flier, a pamphlet, a booklet) and must include the following:

- Fauna: Describe two native animals and their adaptations needed to survive (include pictures).
- Flora: Describe two native plants and their adaptations needed to survive (include pictures).
- Symbiotic relationships: Detail two organisms, identify the type of symbiosis, and explain the role each organism plays in the relationship.
- Average daily temperatures along with a seasonal temperature graph
- Average daily precipitation along with a seasonal precipitation graph
- Topography
- Geographical location depicted on a world map
- Three recreational activities for visitors
- Appropriate clothing for visitors to pack
- Three fascinating facts about the biome
- Three exciting pictures capturing the essence of the biome
- If applicable, a brief description of any endangered or threatened species within the biome

Your advertisements must contain all the required information while being factually and grammatically correct. Keep in mind, you are promoting new *Condé Nast Traveler* travel packages to the "Earth's ecosystems," so make your final product resourceful and artistically appealing to potential tourists. The advertisement selected as the winner will be featured in all *Condé Nast Traveler* offices to supplement the company's new travel packages. Good luck!

Small-Group Processes

5.5   Explain the characteristics of students and tasks that guide choosing an effective strategy for collaborating.

Small-group learning is complex, and learners need modeling of how to operate in cooperative teams. Students must know how to work together and how to use techniques they have been taught. The teacher, in turn, must know about small-group processes. The practical question is: How will individual students turn into cooperative groups? Anyone who has ever attempted small-group instruction in the classroom knows the dilemma associated with the question. Many conditions can confound team learning if plans are not made in advance; teachers must scaffold instruction around such matters as the size, composition, goals, and performance criteria of small groups and the division of labor within a group.

GROUP SIZE   The principle of "least group size" operates whenever you form learning teams. A group should be just large enough to include all the skills necessary to solve a problem or complete a task. A group that's larger than necessary provides less chance for individual participation, lower levels of engagement, and greater opportunity for conflict. If too many students are grouped together, there's bound to be a point of diminishing returns. The group size for content area reading should range from two to six members (depending, of course, on the type of reading task). Because most small-group activities involve discussion, three- or four-member groups are probably best.

GROUP COMPOSITION   Homogeneous grouping is often not necessary for discussion tasks. Both intellectual and nonintellectual factors influence a small group's performance, and the relationship between intelligence and small-group performance is often surprisingly low. Experiential and social background, interests, attitudes, and personality contribute greatly to the success of a cooperative group. Grouping solely by reading or intellectual ability shortchanges all students and robs discussion of diversity.

Students who struggle with reading shouldn't be relegated to tasks that require minimal thinking or low-level responses to content material. There is no quicker way to initiate misbehavior than to put students who find reading difficult together in a group. People learn from one another. A student whose background is less extensive than other students' can learn from them. The student who has reading difficulties needs good readers as models. Furthermore, the student who has trouble reading may in fact be a good listener and thinker who will contribute significantly to small-group discussion. Comparatively, the advanced reader not only can exercise fluency skills and articulate concept but also must master comprehension prior to discussion with group members. This opportunity for flexible grouping also allows teachers to strategically place students in order to best meet their individual needs for a particular task (Strickland, 2009; Tomlinson, 2006).

GROUP GOALS AND TASKS   Group learning is goal oriented. How the goals and the paths to task completion are perceived affects the amount and quality of involvement of the team members. If group goals are unclear, members' interest quickly wanes. Goals must also be directly related to the task. The conditions of the task must be clearly defined and must be understood by the individual members of the group.

Therefore, you should explain the criteria for task performance. For example, when students work with reading guides, such as those that are suggested in this book, they should attempt to adhere to such criteria as the following:

- *Each student should read the selection silently and complete each item of the guide individually or with others in the group,* depending on the teacher's specific directions.

- *Each item should be discussed by the group.*

- *If there is disagreement on any item, a group member must defend his or her position using textual evidence and show why there is disagreement.* This means going back into the selection to support one's position.

- *No one student should dominate a discussion or boss other members around.*

- *Each member should contribute something to each group discussion.*

- As students work on literacy activities in their groups, the teacher can facilitate performance by reinforcing the criteria that have been established.

TEAM BUILDING IN COOPERATIVE LEARNING   Groups lack cohesiveness when learning is not cooperative but competitive and when students aren't interdependent in learning but work independently. However, since the 1970s, social scientists and instructional researchers have made great strides in understanding the problems of the competitive classroom. Researchers (Johnson & Johnson, 2009a; Slavin, 2013) have studied the practical classroom applications of cooperative principles of learning. The bulk of their research suggests that cooperative small-group learning has positive effects on academic achievement and social relationships. **Positive interdependence** can be achieved through a variety of schemes in which students are rewarded for their individual and collaborative effort (Johnson & Johnson, 2009b; Vacca, Lapp, & Fisher, 2011). For example, a social studies teacher attempted to have students adhere to discussion behaviors during their interactions in small groups. (These discussion behaviors were basically the same as those we discussed under performance criteria.) Each small group earned a performance grade for discussing text assignments in a 6-week thematic unit. Here's how the group members earned their grades:

- The teacher observed each member in the group to monitor the use of the desired discussion behaviors.

- On Fridays, each group earned a color reward worth a given number of points: green = one point, blue = two points, black = three points, and red = four points. The color that a group earned was based on how well it had performed according to the criteria for discussion.

- Each member of the group received the color (and the points that went with it) that the whole group earned. Therefore, if one or two members of the group did not use the appropriate discussion behaviors, the entire group got a lower point award.

- The color for each student in the class was noted on a learning incentive chart.

- Each week, the small groups changed composition by random assignment.

- The points attached to each color added up over the weeks. When the unit was completed, a specific number of points resulted in a performance grade of A, B, C, or D.

What happened as a result of the reward system? On the Monday of each week that students were randomly assigned to new groups, they immediately went to the learning incentive chart to check the color received the previous week by each of the other members in their new group. Motivation was high. Group pressure caused individual students who had not received high points the previous week to concentrate on improving their performance in the new group.

GROUP ROLES AND DIVISION OF LABOR   If cooperative groups are to be successful, members must divide the work of the group and understand their different roles within the group. Therefore, consider specifying complementary and interconnected responsibilities that the group must undertake to accomplish a joint task. Johnson and Johnson (2009a) define several roles, which may vary by the nature of the task, for example:

- *Leader:* The group leader facilitates the work of the group. Leadership skills include *giving directions* (reviewing instructions, restating the goals of the group, calling attention to time limits, offering procedures on how to complete the task most effectively), *summarizing* aloud what has been read or discussed, and *generating responses* by going beyond the first answer or conclusion and producing a number of plausible answers from which to choose. Guiding statements for the leader include "Let's hear from _____ next" or "I know we'd like to hear more about that, but let's refocus on our task."

- *Reader:* The reader in the group is responsible for reading the group's material aloud so that the group members can understand and remember it. Guiding statements for the reader include "I'm having trouble reading, can everyone hear me?" or "Let me pause here so we can identify what's important."

- *Writer-recorder:* The writer-recorder records the responses of the group on paper, edits what the group has written, and makes sure the group members check this work for content accuracy and completeness. Some guiding statements to ensure recorder effectiveness include "I heard you say _____ . Is that correct?" or "How would you like me to write that down?"

- *Checker:* The checker makes sure the group is on target by checking on what is being learned by the members. The checker, therefore, may ask individuals within the group to explain or summarize the material being discussed. Some guiding statements for the checker include "Can you say that in a different way?" or "You stated _____ . Can you give more details about that?"

- *Encourager:* The encourager watches to make sure that all the members in the group are participating and invites reluctant or silent members to contribute. Some suggested guided questions for the encourager include "We've heard a lot from; what are your thoughts, _____ ?" or "Let's go around the group and get input from everyone."

MyLab Education
Response Journal 5.2
What is your reaction to the point system that the social studies teacher used to create positive interdependence among the small groups in his class? How might this system be implemented in your own classroom?

If students are to understand the roles and the responsibilities of each role, you will need to develop in them a knowledge and an awareness of each. Discuss each role, demonstrate appropriate behavior and responses, role-play with students, coach, and provide feedback during actual group discussions.

Planning Discussions

Many of the instructional strategies and alternatives in this book are necessarily tied to discussion of one kind or another. Discussion allows students to respond to text, build concepts, clarify meaning, explore issues, share perspectives, and refine thinking. But effective discussions don't run by themselves. For a discussion to be successful, a teacher has to be willing to take a risk or two.

Whenever you initiate a discussion, its outcome is bound to be uncertain, especially if its purpose is to help students think critically and creatively about what they have read. Often a teacher abandons discussion for the safety of recitation, in which the outcome is far more predictable. A text discussion, however, should be neither a quiz show nor, at the opposite end of the continuum, a bull session. Yet when discussions aren't carefully planned, students often feel an aimlessness or become easily threatened by the teacher's questions. Both being quizzed about text material and simply shooting the bull are apt to close doors on active text learning.

Different purposes for text discussion lead to the use of different types of discussions by content area teachers. *Guided discussions* and *reflective discussions* provide varying degrees of structure for students to talk about text as they interact with one another (Wilen, Ishler, Hutchison, & Kindsvatter, 2004).

GUIDED DISCUSSION   If your aim is to develop concepts, clarify meaning, and promote understanding, the most appropriate discussion may be *informational*. The main objective of an informational discussion is to help students grapple with issues and understand important concepts. When the discussion task is information centered, teachers use a *guided discussion*.

In a guided discussion, a teacher provides a moderate amount of scaffolding as he or she directs students to think about what they have read through the use of questions and/or teacher-developed guide material. Because the emphasis is on content understanding and clarification, it is important to recognize the central role of the teacher in a guided discussion. Your responsibilities lie in asking questions, in probing student responses when clarifications are needed to extend thinking, in encouraging student questions, and in providing information to keep the discussion on course. The potential problem, however, is domination of the discussion. Alvermann, Dillon, and O'Brien (1988, p. 31) caution that, when overused, this role "can result in a discussion that more nearly resembles a lecture and frequently may confuse students, especially if they have been encouraged to assume more active roles in discussion."

A guided discussion can easily take a *reflective turn*. When teachers consciously shift gears from guided discussion to reflective discussion, their roles in the discussion shift, as explained in the section below.

For example, Creech and Hale (2006, p. 23) explain that discussion can be an important component of an inquiry approach in science classrooms, as teachers model their own problem-solving processes for students: "I model talking aloud about my own thinking processes and encourage students to 'think aloud' about how they make sense of what they are doing. Through this instructional conversation, students learn the *text* includes labs, data, and their own work and that *reading* is an active problem-solving process."

One example of a structured format for guided discussions is the Paideia Seminar that seeks to integrate critical literacy skills with social interaction around a text (Roberts & Billings, 2011). First, students must prepare for a discussion by reading and considering the chosen text and preparing questions or comments for the group discussion. Students then enter into

MyLab Education
Video Example 5.3: Engaging Students Through Discussion
This video shows how an eighth-grade science teacher engages students in group discussion.

a guided dialogue about the text and their perceptions and reaction to it. During this time, the teacher and students pose prompts or questions to the group to further the conversation. Once the discussion is complete, teachers prepare an opportunity for students to apply their understanding of the text. Paideia Seminars provide opportunities for students to collaborate to better understand content while building intellectual and social skills (Robinson, 2006).

REFLECTIVE DISCUSSION   A reflective discussion is different from a guided discussion in several respects. The purpose of a reflective discussion is to require students to engage in critical and creative thinking as they solve problems, clarify values, explore controversial issues, and form and defend positions. A reflective discussion, then, presumes that students have a solid understanding of the important concepts they are studying. Without a basic knowledge and understanding of the ideas or issues under discussion, students cannot support opinions, make judgments, or justify and defend positions. This type of instruction provides a forum to reflect the diverse perspectives in the classroom (Brookfield & Preskill, 2005).

The teacher's role during a reflective discussion is that of participant. As a participant, you become a group member so that you can contribute to the discussion by sharing ideas and expressing your own opinions: "Teachers can guide students to greater independence in learning by modeling different ways of responding and reacting to issues, commenting on others' points of view, and applying critical reading strategies to difficult concepts in the textbooks" (Alvermann et al., 1988, p. 31).

Creating an Environment for Discussion

Discussion is one of the major process strategies in the content area classroom. Because many of the strategies in this text revolve around discussion of some sort, we offer several suggestions for creating an environment in which discussion takes place, whether in small groups or in the whole class. In today's digital world, it is important to also consider virtual discussion. While the tenets of good discussion apply regardless of the format, virtual discussions are becoming an additional outlet for content area teachers and are not limited to the hours of the school day.

ARRANGE THE CLASSROOM TO FACILITATE DISCUSSION   Arrange the room so that students can see each other and huddle in conversational groupings when they need to share ideas. A good way to determine how functional a classroom is for discussion is to select a discussion strategy that does not require continuous question asking. For example, brainstorming involves a good mixture of whole-class and small-group discussion. Students need to alternate their attention between the board (where the teacher or another student is writing down all the ideas offered within a specified time) and their small groups (where they might categorize the ideas) and back to the front of the room (for comparison of group categories and summarization). If students are able to participate in the various stages of brainstorming with a minimum of chair moving or other time-consuming movements, to see the board, and to converse with other students without undue disruption, the room arrangements are adequate or conducive to discussion.

ENCOURAGE LISTENING   Encourage a climate in which everyone is expected to be a good listener, including the teacher. Let each student speaker know that you are listening. As the teacher begins to talk less, students will talk more. Intervene to determine why some students are not listening to each other or to praise those who are unusually good role models for others. Accept all responses of students positively.

Try starting out with very small groups of no more than two or three students. Again, rather than use questions, have students react to a teacher-read statement (e.g., "Political primaries are a waste of time and money"). In the beginning, students may feel constrained to produce answers to questions to satisfy the teacher. A statement, however, serves as a possible answer and invites reaction and justification. Once a statement is given, set a timer or call time by your watch at two-minute intervals. During each interval, one student in the group may agree or disagree *without interruption*. It is important for students to respectfully consider the perspectives of classmates, so after each group member has an opportunity to respond, the group summarizes all dialogue, and one person presents this summary to the class (Larson, 2000).

ESTABLISH A GOAL FOR DISCUSSION   Establish the meaning of the topic and the goal of the discussion: "Why are we talking about railroad routes, and how do they relate to our unit on the Civil War?" Also, explain directions explicitly, and don't assume that students will know what to do. Many of the content area reading strategies in this book involve some group discussion. Frequently, strategies progress from independent, written responses to sharing to comparing those responses in small groups and then to pooling small-group reactions in a whole-class discussion. Without the guidance of a teacher who is aware of this process, group discussion tends to disintegrate.

FOCUS THE DISCUSSION   Keep the focus of the discussion on the central topic or core question or problem to be solved. Teachers may begin discussions by asking a question about a perplexing situation or by establishing a problem to be solved. From time to time, it may be necessary to refocus attention on the topic by piggybacking on comments made by particular students: "Terry brought out an excellent point about the Underground Railroad in northern Ohio. Does anyone else want to talk about this?" During small-group discussions, one tactic that keeps groups on task is reminding them of the amount of time remaining in the discussion.

Keeping the focus is one purpose for which teachers may legitimately question to clarify the topic. They may also want to make sure that they understood a particular student's comment: "Excuse me, would you repeat that?" Often, keeping the discussion focused will prevent the class from straying away from the task.

AVOID SQUELCHING DISCUSSION   Give students enough think time to reflect on possible answers before calling on someone or rephrasing your question. Moreover, try to avoid answering your own question. (One way to prevent yourself from doing this is to resist having a preset or "correct" answer in your own mind when you ask a question beyond a literal level of comprehension.) Do not interrupt students' responses or permit others to interrupt students' responses. Do, however, take a minute or two for you or a student to summarize and bring closure to a group discussion just as you would in any instructional strategy. Never underestimate the importance of providing appropriate time for students to develop their responses before sharing with the class. Some students may take longer to fully consider how they'd like to respond to questions or prompts. Others may be hesitant to share or lack confidence in their response, so consider allowing students to share ideas with a partner before presenting them to the class. This collaboration allows them to clear up any misunderstandings and gather peer support before engaging the whole group.

Both guided and reflective discussions may be conducted with the whole class or in small groups. A small-group discussion, whether guided or reflective, places the responsibility for learning squarely on students' shoulders. Because of the potential value of collaborative student interactions, we underscore the invaluable contribution of small-group discussions. Small-group learning opportunities help learners contribute ideas to a discussion and take chances in the process. The students can try out ideas without worrying about being wrong or sounding dumb—a fear that often accompanies risk taking in a whole-class situation. Although allowing students to work in small groups may require teachers to allow students to self-direct learning, accountability measures can be put in place to ensure engagement. Each group member can take on a role (as mentioned in the Group Roles and Division of Labor section above) within the group to facilitate and record the group's work. In addition, the teacher may want to develop an open-ended assignment that all groups can complete that will outline their thoughts during the discussion and that will allow the teacher to review all students' work after circulating to facilitate the activity during class.

> MyLab Education **Self-Check 5.5**
> MyLab Education **Application Exercise 5.5:**
> Dividing the Labor of Group Work in Content Area Classes
> ✓ Check Your Understanding

Looking Back Looking Forward

Planning is essential for content literacy and learning. It helps teachers to think through the goals, activities, texts, and strategies necessary to support students' learning with text. It also allows teachers to prepare to differentiate instruction for students who may struggle with content or skills. For example, the planning that goes into explicit strategy instruction helps teachers model and show students how to use literacy strategies to learn and provides an opportunity for students to apply this knowledge in a supportive setting, leading to student success. Components of an explicit strategy instructional framework include awareness and explanation, modeling and demonstration, guided practice, and application.

In addition, B–D–A instructional frameworks help teachers to plan instructional activities at critical periods within the reading and discussion of a text that has been assigned to the whole class. This particular lesson structure focuses on what students do *before*, *during*, and *after* reading to facilitate text comprehension. A unit of study, however, helps teachers to organize instructional activities around inquiry projects and multiple texts. Unit planning gives the teacher much more latitude to coordinate resource materials and activities. Unit activities can be organized around the whole class, small groups, or individuals. An effective content classroom, organized around text lessons and units of study, thrives on collaborative interactions between teacher and students and among students. These interactions are grounded in the principles of small-group processes, cooperative learning, and discussion.

In the next chapter, our emphasis turns to kindling student interest in text assignments and preparing students to think positively about what they will read. The importance of the role of prereading preparation in learning from text has often been neglected or underestimated in the content area classroom. Yet prereading activity is in many ways as important to the text learner as warm-up preparation is to the athlete. Let's find out why.

eResources

Access useful ideas for content literacy lesson plans in English/Language Arts by visiting the following sites:

Reading Rockets: The website offers teachers with multiple reading strategies for a diverse range of readers. Each strategy has a page of information devoted to its implementation. Handouts and videos are provided, as well as scholarly references to theories associated with each strategy.

Newsela: The website provides teachers with informational texts that are aligned to text level and reading skill. Multiple topics are offered that will appeal to students' interests. Teachers can create text sets and classwork assignments and quizzes to share with their students.

Access useful ideas for content literacy lesson plans in science by visiting the following sites:

ExploreLearning Gizmos: ExploreLearning is a community-created resource center that was developed to enhance the science classroom through the use of online labs. This site allows classroom teachers to utilize hands-on labs for science inquiry projects when cost constraints or setting up actual labs are impractical.

EdPuzzle: EdPuzzle is a great resource that offers videos for students to watch at home or in school to build scientific conceptual understanding on a content topic.

STEMscopes: STEMscopes is a one-stop resource center that is aligned to the 5E science model. The website provides tiered reading sources, videos, hands-on labs, and multiple interdisciplinary materials that teachers can use for remediation and enrichment.

PBS LearningMedia: This website contains science lessons and supporting materials for engaging students in science discovery.

Understanding Science: This website was developed by UC Berkeley and is a companion to the Understanding Evolution website. The site focuses on the nature of science as a practice and the process skills that underpin the 5E and 3D model for teaching and learning.

Access useful ideas for content literacy lesson plans in math by visiting the following sites:

National Council for Teachers of Mathematics: If they are a member, teachers can access a wide variety of math lessons that are implementation-ready across grade levels.

Desmos: Desmos is a graphing tool that math teachers can use to support student learning. The website offers teachers ready-made activities to support learners in Grades 6–12.

Access useful ideas for content literacy lesson plans in social studies and history by visiting the following sites:

Library of Congress Digital Collections: The website is a clearinghouse of primary sources for American history that offers print, photos, and music that students can use to understand the story of America.

Stanford History Education Group: The website is a resource center that provides document-based lessons and assessments that teach students to think like a historian.

iCivics: The website was founded by Justice Sandra Day O'Connor to engage students in meaningful civics education. The site offers a number of games that students can play to learn about constitutional law and individuals' rights.

Federal Resources for Educational Excellence (FREE): The website is maintained by the U.S. Department of Education, offering a variety of resources in support of important historical figures in U.S. history.

Content literacy lesson plans can be accessed for inquiry projects and cooperative learning in your subject area by exploring:

Lesson Planet: The website offers teachers ready-made lesson plans, instructional materials, and videos, as well as information articles for any content topic.

Edutopia: Edutopia is a website founded by the George Lucas Educational Foundation and features a wealth of resources for all content areas that have been implemented in successful K–12 schools.

Education World: This website provides teachers with lesson plans, worksheets, WebQuests, and multiple resources for technology integration.

Part II Instructional Practices and Strategies

Chapter 6

Activating Prior Knowledge and Interest

Syda Productions/Shutterstock

Chapter Overview and Learning Outcomes

After reading this chapter, you should be able to:

6.1 Explain how self-efficacy affects literacy development and what teachers can do to support self-efficacy and engagement in learning within a discipline.

6.2 Describe the value of activating curiosity and interest in content and explain how each of the strategies mentioned builds this type of engagement.

6.3 Explain how predicting and questioning can support comprehension during content area reading.

Organizing Principle

Activating prior knowledge and generating interest create an instructional context in which students will read with purpose and anticipation.

Learning happens. Most people outside the fields of cognitive psychology and education probably give little thought to how it happens or why it happens. Learning is rooted in what we already know. Cognition—the process of knowing—is an active process that takes place in the brain. From a content literacy perspective, the essence of cognitive readiness is to prepare students to make connections between what they know and what they will learn. It is impossible to learn without prior knowledge.

Getting students cognitively ready to learn with text is no easy task. Teachers occasionally are perplexed by the behaviors of students who can acquire content through lecture and discussions but appear neither *ready* nor *willing* to read to learn. Readiness is a state of mind, a mental preparation for learning, a psychological predisposition; but readiness also entails an emotional stake in the ideas and concepts under scrutiny and a willingness on the part of the students to *want* to engage in learning. Students *will* want to read when they have developed a sense of confidence in their ability to use reading to learn. Confident readers connect what they already know to what they are learning. They generate interest in the reading task at hand, even when the text is inherently dry or difficult. Preparing students to think purposefully about what they will read is implicit in the organizing principle for this chapter: Activating prior knowledge and generating interest create an instructional context in which students will read with purpose and anticipation.

Frame of Mind

1. Why do prereading strategies that activate prior knowledge and raise interest in the subject prepare students to approach text reading in a critical frame of mind?
2. How can meaningful learning be achieved with content area reading?
3. Why is it important for students to have some degree of choice over what they read?
4. How and why does a prediction strategy, such as use of an anticipation guide, facilitate reading comprehension?
5. Why is it important for content area teachers to develop a self-efficacy for teaching reading in their discipline?

"Why can't we just read like in other classes? Why do we always have to think about what we read?" complained an irritated high school junior in his history class. The teacher, who uses and adapts many of the instructional strategies suggested in this book, was momentarily caught off guard by the student's questions. But rather than dismiss them as the rantings of a malcontent, he turned the student's questions into a positive event by initiating a brief discussion about what it means and what it takes "to read like a historian."

The discussion was aimed at building and reinforcing students' concepts of reading as an active search for meaning—a process that, from a historian's perspective, involves detecting bias, analyzing and verifying information, inferring cause and effect, and thinking critically about ideas presented in text. Much of what transpired during the discussion boiled down to this: Active readers think *about* text, think *with* text, and think *through* text. "Historians," the teacher explained with more than a little enthusiasm, "actively search for meaning in everything they read, and that's what I expect from each of you."

Although the classroom incident just described is one of countless little dramas that occur daily in the context of teaching, for us it typifies two of the most powerful realities of content literacy: First, that many students are passive participants when it comes to reading to learn; and second, that caring and knowledgeable teachers can make a difference in the way students approach reading and learn with texts.

For many passive readers, learning with text remains a mysterious process. For most teachers, reading just happens, particularly when there is a strong purpose or a need to read in the first place. However, a great deal of uncertainty pervades reading for many students. The reading process remains a mystery to students who believe they have limited control over their chances of success with a reading assignment.

You can do a great deal to reduce the lack of control and the uncertainty that students bring to text learning situations. You can take the mystery out of learning with texts by generating students' interest in what they are reading, convincing them that they know more about the subject under study than they think they do, helping them actively connect what they do know to the content of the text, and making them aware of the strategies they need to construct meaning.

The challenge content area teachers face with reading to learn is not necessarily related to students' inability to handle the conceptual demands of academic texts. What students can do and what they choose to do are related but different instructional matters. Therefore, you need to create conditions that not only allow students to read effectively but also motivate them to want to read purposefully.

Self-Efficacy and Motivation

6.1 **Explain how self-efficacy affects literacy development and what teachers can do to support self-efficacy and engagement in learning within a discipline.**

When students engage in content literacy activities, some feel confident in their ability to achieve success with reading and writing tasks. Others feel unsure and uncertain. Confident learners exhibit a high level of *self-efficacy* in content literacy situations; unsure learners, a low level. **Self-efficacy** refers to an "I can" belief in self that leads to a sense of competence. Bandura (1986, p. 391) explains that self-efficacy refers to "people's judgment of their abilities to organize and execute courses of action required to attain designated types of performance." Self-efficacy is not concerned with the skills and strategies students bring to content literacy situations, but rather it focuses on students' estimations of their ability to apply whatever skills and strategies they bring to literacy learning. As Alvermann (2001) explains, self-efficacy contributes to the development of students' literacy identities. Before they can become lifelong readers, students must first view themselves as competent and capable readers.

Self-efficacy and motivation are interrelated concepts. If students believe, for example, that they have a good chance to succeed at a reading task, they are likely to exhibit a willingness to engage in reading and to complete the task. Guthrie and Wigfield's (2000) model of reading engagement calls for instruction that underscores the importance of students' motivation in addition to their growth in conceptual knowledge, their use of comprehension strategies, and their social interaction in the classroom. The National Institute for Literacy (2007) explains that students who are motivated readers share several characteristics: They perceive that they have some level of control over their reading; they apply appropriate strategies to make complex reading tasks more manageable; and they display a high level of engagement in their reading experiences.

MyLab Education
Response Journal 6.1
Think about your own self-efficacy as a learner. In which subject, if any, in your academic background have you judged yourself unable to succeed? How has low self-efficacy in the subject affected academic performance?

Box 6.1 Evidence-Based Practices

Supporting English Learners: The Intersections of Literacy and Culture

As we have discussed throughout this chapter, every student brings to school their own experiences. We also know that teachers bring their experiences as well. Reading can conjure, for some, images of sitting on a warm lap and being read to by a parent or caregiver. For others, however, reading brings to mind a whirlwind of words on a page that make little sense. Purcell-Gates (2013) writes that "whatever children learn about print before they enter school is shaped by the literacy traditions in their community" (p. 72). Students take these experiences with them as they engage in formal school instruction. We encourage teachers to consider their own relationship with literacy and how their perceptions of literacy are connected to their own families and cultures.

Reflection can occur through the development of a literacy autobiography in which teachers are asked to narrate ten moments in their lives that developed their literate selves. We encourage them to think broadly about these "literacy moments." For example, teachers might write about singing with family members, reading the text in video games, or learning another language. In this way, teachers can think about the books, the moments, and the lived experiences that shaped their literate selves. By first recognizing their own literacy practices, teachers can acknowledge how these practices influence their teaching and begin to seek out new ways to support students, particularly those of different languages and cultures (Bedard, Horn, & Garcia, 2011).

We then encourage teachers to ask their students to perform a similar activity. It is important for students to recognize themselves as having literacy identities. Students can, for example, be encouraged to form literacy identities by creating lists of places they, or others, read or interact with written language. One way to do this is to give them a handout with the alphabet written out in boxes. Then for each letter, they must fill that box with items they read. For example, the letter A may contain the words: autobiography, address book, assignments for school, etc. Often students give examples that the teacher had not thought of. This is a way to learn about how reading and writing are used in students' homes and communities and to allow students to see how often they engage in reading—even if they do not read a novel a night.

Keep in mind that English Learners' literacy levels vary, just like their language levels. If a student is literate in their first language, they can often transfer many of the reading skills they use in their first language to the reading of English. Understanding literacy activities in any language subsequently helps promote literacy in English. In addition, strong oral storytelling traditions also support literacy learning in later years (Peregoy & Boyle, 2017). To support English Learners' self-efficacy for reading in English, encourage students to make the connections between the skills they use in their first language in the home and their learning of the English language in school. Once students make these connections, the teacher should create safe reading environments that encourage students to explore and expand their literacy activity repertoire. Peregoy and Boyle (2017) encourage teachers of English Learners to use strategies, such as pictures, graphs, and dramatization, that offer cues to meaning, and to incorporate peer support to help beginners navigate informational text. Additionally, teachers are encouraged to remember another key element to supporting English Learners in reading instruction, which is "to state clearly to your students why you want them to read a particular passage and what they will do with the information later" (p. 387).

When we think about our authentic literacy practices, we always read for a purpose. Whether we are reading to follow the instructions on a recipe, to know which door to use as the exit, or to go on an adventure with Alice through the looking glass, we read already knowing our purpose. While making your purpose clear is important for all students, it is particularly important to designate the objective of reading for English Learners so that they know what to pay attention to when reading and why they're being asked to read. This clear purpose, along with other techniques for activating prior knowledge such as those described in this chapter, can help English Learners to better understand content area concepts. As teachers continue to work with diverse populations, it is important that they reflect on their own experiences, learn from their students' experiences, and then create meaningful instruction that is derived with the strengths and needs of the students in mind.

By the time they enter middle school, students' motivation to read—particularly motivation that comes from their own authentic interests and desires to explore topics through reading—often declines. For struggling readers, this decline in motivation is often compounded by the assessment and grouping practices common in middle and secondary schools. The problem of aliteracy—when an individual can read but chooses not to do so—has been found to continue into later adolescence and even into adulthood. Sarroub and Pernicek (2016) suggest that reluctant reading cannot be attributed to one single factor. Instead, a multitude of factors, including negative experiences with literacy learning and narrow definitions of literacy and what it means to be literate, contribute to reluctant reading, especially among boys.

Despite the proliferation of social networking, texting, and messaging outlets, nearly half of all older adolescents read no books at all for pleasure (Institute of Education Sciences, 2011). By fostering a learning environment that is response centered, teachers can provide students with critical opportunities to explore texts, construct meaning, and make personal connections to content area topics. Box 6.1 supports additional ways in which teachers can support the development of self-efficacy and motivation for reading, particularly among English Learners.

Students' motivation for reading and learning with texts increases when they perceive that text is relevant to their own lives and when they believe that they can generate credible responses to their reading of the text (Ford-Connors et al., 2015). Research suggests that, unlike out-of-school reading experiences, in-school reading is often perceived to be uninteresting to many students. One study found that even students who were identified as avid readers outside of school were not necessarily engaged in school reading experiences (Wilson & Kelley, 2010). One factor found to inhibit students' motivation to read centered on their belief that they rarely control what they read during the school day (Daniels & Steres, 2011). A relevant curriculum, engaging instructional strategies, and a school culture that fosters wide reading can help to engage students in reading across the curriculum. Box 6.2 discusses how teachers can apply a disciplinary literacy approach to familiarizing students with content area vocabulary and text perspective. Students have been found to be more enthusiastic about in-school reading when the texts used are accessible and interesting and when they have a choice in the selection of the text (Lapp & Fisher, 2009).

With the rise of multiliteracies, reading now takes place not only in traditional print form but on screens, through hyperlinks, and even within digital games. What counts as "reading" need not be limited to fictional texts or novels but rather expanded to include comics, graphic novels, documents, such as sports statistics, and, of course, nonfiction. Mackey (2014) suggests that students must receive guidance to choose appropriate text selections. She recommends that teachers talk with students about how texts were chosen for use in the classroom and, in cases where texts were selected by a school or district level committee, the process through which those decisions were reached. Using complex and challenging texts that are engaging and accessible to students can increase literacy outcomes across content areas (Lupo et al., 2017).

While adolescents might not always feel comfortable talking about their out-of-school reading with peers, it is helpful to offer a neutral forum through which students can share reactions to and suggestions about texts beyond the classroom. Within the classroom, the teacher can consider students' varied reading abilities and interests and make accessible a wide range of texts that will appeal to those needs and levels (Morgan & Wagner, 2013).

Bruner (1970, 1990), a pioneer in the field of cognitive psychology, suggested that the mind doesn't work apart from feeling and commitment. Learners make meaning when they exhibit an "inherent passion" for what is to be learned. How people construct meaning depends on their beliefs, mental states, intentions, desires, and commitments. Likewise, Eisner (1991) calls on us to celebrate thinking in schools by reminding us that

**MyLab Education
Video Example 6.1:
Engagement**
Watch this video to learn about how to actively engage students in content area learning.

Box 6.2 Disciplinary Literacy

Thinking Before Reading: Using Vocabulary to Help Students Prepare to Read

Preparing for reading is a vital step to help build comprehension in each content area. What students do before they read often helps them better connect with and understand what they read. Typically, activities such as asking *what do we already know* through a KWL chart or previewing a chapter through titles, subtitles, and text features can help readers get an idea of what they will read. This previewing activates schema, prompts effective questioning, and generally prepares students to add purpose to their reading by helping them become more active readers. Such strategies can be used effectively in any content class and tend to grow with the students as they move from grade to grade.

However, when content is being taught with an emphasis on teaching its disciplinary literacies, text is used more as a conduit to help students think, write, problem solve, and express understanding about larger ideas in the content. Following the tenets of disciplinary literacy, the goal is not only to teach students to read and understand text, but to acquire thinking habits of each respective discipline, learning to think like a professional in each field. The focus, then, of activities in the classroom moves beyond understanding text to understanding practices, vocabulary, and thinking habits inherent to each discipline. When students work with text they must employ the ability to engage in practices that are inherent to the field or discipline itself. For example, in a science classroom, it is more important to teach students to deconstruct a text in the same way a scientist might than employ strategies to understand the text (Fang & Coatoam, 2013). When students prepare to read from a disciplinary literacy perspective, they would ask themselves questions such as:

- Why would a scientist read this text?

- What task does this text facilitate in the science lab?

- What information does this text provide to a scientist?

- What is the genre of this text, and how does it relate to the overall problem the scientist is trying to solve?

- Who wrote this text, and how does the author's background help support the credibility of this document?

While all these questions are essential to developing the mind-set of the discipline, before students can successfully deconstruct a text, they must understand the vocabulary of the discipline. Not only do students need to know the language of a discipline, but they need to know how that language is used. Understanding disciplinary language allows students to ask and answer these essential questions using language that exemplifies what it means to be a professional in the field. Consider the metaphor of a child trying to gain entrance to a secret club. In order to get into the club, the child must first know the secret word. Once the child gains entrance, he works quickly to learn the language of the club members. To truly be

an insider, the child must learn, replicate, and communicate through secret handshakes, insider jokes, and the use of language that is unique to the world of the club. Disciplinary language works in a similar way. To truly *be* a scientist, one must first speak and write like a scientist to gain true acceptance into the field of science. Thus, to prepare students to read, teachers must help them learn to use the words most important to their discipline.

Choosing vocabulary words is perhaps the most challenging step of the preparation. When thinking about a discipline, there are just so many words that one might argue are important to understanding the field. The first suggestion is to narrow down the words that are necessary to best understand the text itself. Those words may come from the text or may be outside words that help build a greater understanding of the concepts of the text. For example, in a science classroom, it may help to teach students Latin and Greek roots. This may help them categorize words, sort concepts, and better understand how terms work together (Boyd, Sullivan, Popp, & Hughes, 2012).

Think as well about the words that are important contextually and that lend themselves to providing a greater understanding of the practices in the professions (Carpenter, Earhart, & Achugar, 2014). Consider a word like *environment*. In language arts, environment is connected to setting. To think like a fiction writer, a student would want to develop the setting, analyzing how it interacts with the characters and plot to best tell a story that the reader can visualize. In a science classroom, the concept of environment may be studied as it is affected by human interaction, disease, or animal habitats. Environmental factors must be detailed in a way that other scientists can understand and replicate rather than visualize. In a social studies classroom, environment might be understood as a background that is affected by the interaction of people and events. The idea of environment may also take on more of a political hue as students use it to inspire action. In a mathematics class, environment may be broken down as a geometric concept to be studied, planned, and segmented according to a formulaic arrangement of shapes.

Students should also be familiar with words that are essential to understanding and participating in practices in the profession (Carpenter et al., 2014). Students will not be able to complete tasks if they are unaware of how to interpret the steps of the directions. Taking apart directions and illustrating the verbs and nouns, which explain what to do, are ideal prereading activities. These prereading vocabulary practices can be conducted through authentic, real-world activities that help students retain and correctly use vocabulary. Learning to use, understand, and contextually place vocabulary is an essential prereading step. Choice of vocabulary may be based on words that help them understand content, process, or context. Helping students become insiders through vocabulary will help them read actively with success.

brains may be born, but minds are made. Schools do not pay enough attention to students' curiosity and imagination. As a result, students disengage from active participation in the academic life of the classroom because there is little satisfaction to be gained from it. Given the current policy emphasis on accountability and adequate yearly progress as measured by high-stakes assessments (discussed in Chapter 4), teachers often find themselves torn between seeking to increase students' interest in content area subjects by supporting their motivation to learn and simply trying to fulfill externally imposed, and even arbitrary, achievement targets.

Nevertheless, effective teachers understand the importance of taking the time to make their subject areas relevant to students. In exploring matters of the mind, cognitive activity cannot be divorced from emotional involvement. Meaningful learning with texts occurs when students reap satisfaction from texts and a sense of accomplishment from reading. As Ivey and Fisher (2005, p. 8) explain, "Teachers who understand their students' backgrounds, prior knowledge, interests, and motivations are much more likely to make the connections that adolescents crave."

Teachers can support students' motivation for reading by setting clear goals and expectations for reading; providing students with access to a variety of reading materials; and, when possible, allowing students a level of choice in selecting the texts they read (Brozo & Flyny, 2007; Guthrie & Davis, 2003). Teachers can also give students opportunities to interact with one another through shared reading experiences, and they can guide students in learning how to evaluate their own understanding of a text (Wigfield, 2004; Reed, Schallert, Beth, & Woodruff, 2004).

Two of the most appropriate questions that students can ask about a text are "What do I need to know?" and "How well do I already know it?" The question "What do I need to know?" prompts readers to activate their prior knowledge to make predictions and set purposes. It gets them thinking positively about what they are going to read. "How well do I already know it?" helps readers search their experience and knowledge to give support to tentative predictions and to help make plans for reading.

As simple as these two questions may seem on the surface, maturing readers rarely *know enough* about the reading process to ask them. "What do I need to know?" and "How well do I already know it?" require *metacognitive awareness* on the part of the learners. However, these two questions, when consciously raised and reflected on, put students on the road to regulating and monitoring their own reading behavior. It is never too early (or too late) to begin showing students how to set purposes by raising questions about the text.

As students ready themselves to learn with texts, they need to approach upcoming material in a critical frame of mind. Instructional scaffolding should make readers receptive to meaningful learning by creating a reference point for connecting the given (what one knows) with the new (the material to be learned). A frame of reference signals the connections students must make between the given and the new. They need to recognize how new material fits into the conceptual frameworks they already have. In Box 6.3, Drew, a mathematics coach, works with a fifth-grade teacher to activate her students' knowledge for and interest in the concepts of area and perimeter. Conceptual conflicts are the key to creating motivational conditions in the classroom. Should students be presented with situations that take the form of puzzlement, doubt, surprise, perplexity, contradiction, or ambiguity, they will be motivated to seek resolution. Why? The need within the learner is to resolve the conflict. As a result, the search for knowledge becomes a driving motivational force. When a question begins to gnaw at a learner, searching behavior is stimulated; learning occurs as the conceptual conflict resolves itself.

Box 6.3 Voices from the Field

Drew, Mathematics Coach

Challenge

During a unit on area and perimeter, a fifth-grade classroom teacher, Mrs. Little, and I posed a real-world mathematical task to students to allow them to explore these concepts more deeply. Here is the task they were given:

> You have 12 yards of fencing to build a rectangular cage for your rabbit. Which dimensions give you the most space inside the cage?

Students often struggle with solving these types of mathematical tasks for a couple reasons: They struggle to read and make sense of the mathematical situation, and, sometimes, they don't know where to begin. In this case, students struggled to distinguish between the concepts of perimeter (the amount of fencing) and area (the space inside).

Strategy

To support the students, Mrs. Little and I spent time at the beginning of the lesson activating their prior knowledge by asking them about real-life examples of area and perimeter. We posed questions such as:

- If we needed to build a fence, how would we determine how much fencing we would need?

- Can you think of other examples where we would need to figure out the distance around something?

- If we needed to put carpet down on the floor of a house, how would we determine how much carpet we would need?

- Can you think of other examples where we would need to figure out how much material we will need to cover a flat surface?

We posed the task to students and provided them with plastic square tiles to begin exploring the task. Initially, students connected the number 12 in the task with the need to grab 12 square tiles. Nearly every student did this and immediately made rectangles. Some students made a rectangle that was 6 tiles wide and 2 tiles tall, while others made one that was 4 tiles wide and 3 tiles tall. While both used 12 tiles, neither rectangle had a perimeter of 12.

Seeing this misconception, Mrs. Little and I revisited students' understanding of perimeter by asking them a few questions:

Mrs. Little: Do we know the amount of fencing that we have or the space that we have inside of our pen?

Lisa: We have 12 yards of fencing.

Mrs. Little: So, if we think about fencing, will the amount of fencing be the distance around the rectangle or the space inside?

Oscar: Fencing will go around, so we need to find the distance on the outside of the rectangle.

Polly: If we know that we have 12 yards of fencing, how can we use our tiles to help us?

Jimmy: We can look at the rectangles that we made and then count the distance around each shape.

Mrs. Little: Go ahead and do that.

As students counted the distance around, they realized that neither rectangle had a perimeter of 12 units. Rather, the $6 \cdot 2$ rectangle had a perimeter of 16 units, and the $4 \cdot 3$ rectangle had a perimeter of 14 units. Students were confused about how to find a rectangle with a perimeter of 12 units. Mrs. Little asked, "How can we find a rectangle that has a perimeter of 12?" Students started to manipulate the 12 tiles and counted the perimeter of their representations. No students were able to find a rectangle that used 12 tiles and also had a perimeter of 12.

Mrs. Little then asked, "Do we have to use exactly 12 tiles, or can we use a different number?" The students all responded, "A different number."

When Mrs. Little asked why that was the case, Samuel commented, "The only thing given to us is that the fencing or perimeter had to be 12. The number of tiles could be different."

Students worked for the next 15 minutes making rectangles out of their tiles that had a perimeter of 12. The teacher then asked students to share their solutions on the SMART Board by drawing a picture of their rectangle and writing the dimensions. The use of a visual helped struggling students to make sense of their classmates' answers. Table 1 shows the students' solutions.

During the discussion, Mrs. Little had made Table 1 on the SMART Board and asked students to talk with their table groups about observations that they had. Tyrone mentioned, "There are two rectangles that have an area of 5 and two that have an area of 8." After Mrs. Little asked him to explain the difference between the two rectangles that had an area of 5, Tyrone said, "One rectangle is 5 by 1 and the other is 1 by 5. When we draw them, they have the same dimensions, but one is just twisted around." Tyrone drew a visual up on the SMART Board of the two rectangles to match his explanation.

Lastly, the entire class was able to explain that the pen with the largest amount of space was a 3 by 3 rectangle, which students called a square. The discussion of this part of the task allowed students to discuss the relationship between squares and rectangles.

Reflection

This lesson allowed fifth-grade students to build on their prior knowledge of fencing and carpets to explore a real-world mathematical task about the area and perimeter of rectangles. The use of guiding questions at the beginning of the lesson using real-life examples of area and perimeter provided a foundation that was revisited later in the lesson to address misconceptions. Also, the use of concrete manipulatives (plastic square tiles) and drawings helped students to connect the mathematical concepts to representations of those concepts. By having the opportunity to create pictorial representations, students were able to better grasp the difference between area and perimeter and successfully complete the task.

State Standards for mathematical practice emphasize the need for teachers to build upon students' prior knowledge to help them make sense of the mathematical situations that are embedded in tasks and problems. This task is an example of how students' prior knowledge of fencing and carpeting helped them explore area and perimeter.

Table 1

Width	Length	Area
5	1	5
4	2	8
3	3	9
2	4	8
1	5	5

MyLab Education **Self-Check 6.1**

MyLab Education **Application Exercise 6.1:**
Supporting Self-Efficacy in a Content Area Classroom

Curiosity and Interest

6.2 **Describe the value of activating curiosity and interest in content and explain how each of the strategies mentioned builds this type of engagement.**

Activating curiosity and activating interest are closely related instructional activities. Curiosity gives students the chance to consider what they know already about the material to be read. Through your guidance, they are encouraged to make connections and to relate their knowledge to the text assignment. And further, they will recognize that there are problems—conceptual conflicts—to be resolved through reading. Curiosity helps students raise questions that they can answer only by giving thought to what they read. Box 6.4 explains how an assistant principal coached a high school economics teacher to effectively activate students' background knowledge and generate interest in finding out more about topics in this discipline. Some have cautioned that prereading strategies should not undermine students' ability to think through and critically analyze the text for themselves. As Sandler and Hammond (2012/2013, p. 59) explain, "Providing too much information up front in prereading activities can undermine the student's ability to figure out the text for himself." However, when used appropriately, prereading strategies can serve to pique students' curiosity and connect their prior knowledge to new material to be learned.

Box 6.4 Voices from the Field

Derrick, High School Assistant Principal

Challenge

Mr. Austin, an applicant for a teaching position in our Business Education department, had a great interview! We talked content, student-centered classrooms, learning strategies, and the infusion of technology to make his students 21st-century learners. I was confident that he was going to be the one who turned our Business Education department around and created demand for the courses. I had a particular hope for Mr. Austin because he would be teaching the Principles of Business course that I had taught before becoming an assistant principal. Over the course of the first quarter, I would pass through his class and see him

teaching his heart away, or at least doing a lot of talking. His students were compliant because they really liked him as a person. I heard his first formal observation was fair, but not the *spectacular* that I had hoped. I conducted my second formal observation of his Principles of Business class and was stunned. This couldn't have been the guy I talked to last June in his interview. Students were doing round-robin reading in the textbook for most of the class. Students struggled with the vocabulary and when asked questions about the content had little to offer. In our postobservation conference, I discovered something worse. Mr. Austin was struggling and was considering quitting. Students were trying to do the work, but their grades were horrible. Our new semester was soon to begin and Mr. Austin would have a new set of students for the Principles of Business class in the spring.

Strategy

In our conversation at the postobservation conference, I tried to tap back into the discussions we had in his interview, particularly what it means to truly have a student-centered classroom. Many courses are, by their nature, difficult to make student centered. Principles of Business, however, isn't one. Students bring knowledge of businesses in their role as a consumer. Mr. Austin and I had to develop a way for their perspective and background knowledge to play a role in the class. Our first task, then, was to create *critical consumers*. To mentor Mr. Austin, I tapped into his own background knowledge by engaging him in a discussion of his first college economics class:

Me: Mr. Austin, do you remember your college econ class?

Mr. Austin: Vaguely, why?

Me: What is the basic problem of economics?

Mr. Austin: Hmm...

Me: Scarcity, remember?

Mr. Austin: Oh, yeah... needs and wants.

Me: Yup... there are unlimited wants with limited what?

Mr. Austin: Resources... yeah, I remember.

Me: Yes... and scarcity forces choice... so we have the three basic economic questions, remember them?

Mr. Austin: Umm... one, what to produce? Ah... what were the others?

Me: (1) What to produce? (2) How to produce it? and (3) For whom?

Mr. Austin: Yeah... that was it.

Me: That is the start of *thinking economically*. So, let's extend the questions to: (1) What is the product? (*What is the producer's purpose?*), (2) How is it made? (*Is it a good, service, or both?*), and (3) Who is the audience? (*Who would buy this?*)

With the three economic questions, students have a tool for reflecting on prior knowledge as a consumer. They can now become critical consumers. The teacher can provide active and critical homework assignments, such as analyze three television commercials using the three questions as a template. Once students become comfortable with that exercise, they can extend it by examining why particular commercials come on during certain television shows. Once their critical consumer mind is activated, they can better read texts. They can use their phones, via the Flipboard news app, to read brief articles on consumer products, technology, and companies with which they have a personal relationship like Apple, Samsung, and so on. The personal connection, we both agreed, increases the commitment to reading. Mr. Austin, while understanding this task, then asked, "But not all of my topics are directly consumer oriented. A lot of it is based on the perspective of business owners, government, and workers. That is where it gets hard."

He was right. So, our next task would also be to help students acquire multiple perspectives, such as producers, sellers, regulators, and workers, to aid their understanding in the content. I described to him a project I did many years ago, when technology was very limited. It was called the Virtual Mall. I created a blueprint of a nearby mall on a large white sheet of bulletin board paper and posted it on my wall. I marked the square footage of available plots. Students could form groups of from one to three people as a business organization. I gave students two choices: They could be producers or sellers. Those who chose sellers had to acquire a plot for their store. Producers, once sellers described their business type, would decide the type of product they would manufacture. For example, when multiple groups chose to sell athletic shoes, the producers would choose the brand of shoe to manufacture. Student groups had to produce advertisements to gain demand, and the quality of advertisement determined the number of customers who visited the store each week. Each group used teacher-made spreadsheets to calculate its sales and revenues based on its demands. To find out its demand, the group had to read the *Robinson News*, a fictitious news article I created. The news article also detailed other events affecting the businesses based on the weekly topics of the course. For example, on the topic of production cycle, the cost of raw goods for certain producers would go up and force producers to either increase their prices or lose money. When discussing labor, groups would have to react to federal laws on minimum wage that happened to pop up in the news. The activity, especially the readings, lasted the duration of the semester, evolved with the topics of the course, and infused the vocabulary of the course. The active learning and critical thinking required throughout this project served to motivate students to apply and extend their prior knowledge.

Reflection

When students are not connected to the content, there is little value that can be found in long readings related to the subject. Further, trying to overcome vocabulary and familiarity with terms in a text while trying to learn material makes comprehension, and even motivation, that much more difficult. Mr. Austin was able to adapt this activity to his comfort level, integrate more current technology, and use more multimedia to motivate students. The *Austin News*, an electronic newsletter, kept students steadily anticipating what would happen next. Students were looking ahead to upcoming topics and trying to predict what might happen in the *Austin News*, which helped to give Mr. Austin more ideas to add.

Whether it is business education, social studies, or science, every discipline has a method by which students can become investigators of the subject. Using that method as a guide and creating relevant student relationships to the content, can increase student efficacy and content area knowledge. Mr. Austin's case was no different. Starting with activating prior knowledge, students were able to become critical consumers of the products they see and buy in the world between home and school. With an engaging activity that encouraged a disciplinary literacy mind-set, students were able to move from critical consumers to critical producers and sellers and see problems from another perspective.

Creating Story Impressions

Using story impressions is an instructional strategy that arouses curiosity and allows students to anticipate story content. Although teachers use story impressions with narrative text, they may also be used to create "text impressions" in content areas other than English language arts.

The **story impressions** strategy (McGinley & Denner, 1987) uses clue words associated with the setting, characters, and events in the story to help readers write their own versions of the story prior to reading.

Fragments from the story, in the form of clue words and phrases, enable readers to form an overall impression of how the characters and events interact in the story. The clue words are selected directly from the story and are sequenced with arrows or lines to form a descriptive chain. The chain of clue words triggers impressions about the story. Students then write a "story prediction" that anticipates the events in the story.

The story impression example in Figure 6.1 was developed in preparation for students' reading of Jonathan Swift's classic, *Gulliver's Travels*. Based on the terms listed in the story chain, the students generated their prediction. Similarly, the example in Figure 6.2 shows how a high school Spanish teacher, Mr. Roundy, used the story impression strategy with his Spanish class. Mr. Roundy chose a story that he thought many of his students may have heard when they were children: *La princesa y el guisante* (*The Princess and the Pea*). He selected 10 words directly from the text and asked students to predict what might happen in the story based on their understanding of the words listed. Figure 6.2 shows the story impression his students created in preparation for their reading of *La princesa y el guisante*. After students had read the author's version of the story, Mr. Roundy had them compare and contrast their story impression predications with the text as the author wrote it.

Establishing Problematic Perspectives

Creating problems to be solved or perspectives from which readers approach text material provides an imaginative entry into a text selection. For example, the teacher's role in creating problematic perspectives is (1) providing the time to discuss the problem, raising questions, and seeking possible solutions before reading and then (2) assigning the reading material that will help lead to resolution and conceptual development.

Figure 6.3 shows a problematic perspective created by a teacher when her physical education class was studying nutrition. The teacher, knowing that her students often talked about watching competitive cooking shows, thought she would draw upon the idea of competition as she introduced this problematic perspective. Her goal was to have

**MyLab Education
Video Example 6.2:
Curiosity and Interest in Science**
Watch this video to learn how to encourage student-generated questions.

Figure 6.1 Story Impression for *Gulliver's Travels*

Classroom Artifact	
Story Chain	**Story Prediction**
shipwrecked little people politics corruption giant science useless immortal talking horses insane morals	After being shipwrecked with a bunch of little people, a traveler, whose interest in politics was obvious but whose past was filled with corruption, decided to live off his giant bank account. He believed that science was useless and had failed him. Knowing he wasn't immortal, he decided to survive his ordeal by talking to sea horses, making people believe that he was insane. That way, he thought, they might not pay attention to his questionable morals.

Figure 6.2 Story Impression for *La princesa y el guisante*

Classroom Artifact

Story Chain	Story Predication
principe (prince) *verdad* (truth) *mundo* (world) *encontrar* (to find) *deseo* (desire) *tempestad* (storm) *lluvia* (rain) *ropa* (clothes) *cama* (bed) *cuerpo* (body)	Creo que el Príncipe llega a su casa y encuentra que su esposa, la Princesa, no está y que toda su ropa ha sido dejada en su cama. Él anda por el mundo tratando de buscar lo que su corazón anhela, la Princesa, pero nadie le dice la verdad sobre donde ella está. Creo que la lluvia lo va a cojer. (I think that the Prince comes home to find that his wife, the Princess, is missing and all of her clothes have been left on the bed. He is out in the world trying to find his heart's desire, the Princess, but no one will tell him the truth about where she is. I think that the Prince is going to be caught in a rainstorm.)

the students connect food to nutrients. After the "competition," the students submitted their menus for review. This is one example of the winning breakfast:

> *Orange and strawberry juice made from the orange slices which were hard to squeeze so we added the strawberries: Vitamin C, some fiber, carbohydrates*

> *Scrambled eggs, smoked salmon, and cheese sandwich served on a bagel: Protein, calcium, fiber, carbohydrates, and omega-3*

Figure 6.3 Problematic Perspective: Physical Education

- You must plan three meals: breakfast, lunch, and dinner.
- You must use only the food in your center.
- You must plan the meals, making sure to include the nutrients listed on the meal tags.
- You have 30 minutes to plan, and you will work with a partner. One of you should be in charge of the food slips

- and the other should be in charge of the nutrient slips.
- Hint #1: You may want to match the food with the nutrients before you begin.
- Hint #2: Many foods contain multiple nutrients. Make sure to be thorough in your matching.
- For extra credit, you may approximate the calories for each meal.

Meal Tags

Breakfast	Lunch	Dinner
Your breakfast must contain:	Your lunch must contain:	Your dinner must contain:
Protein	Vitamin A	Protein
Calcium	B vitamins	Fiber
Vitamin C	Fiber	Fat
Fiber	Fat	Vitamin D
Omega-3	Iron	B vitamins
Carbohydrates	It cannot contain protein.	It cannot contain vitamin C.

Food Slips

Eggs	Cow's milk	Soy milk
Butter	Greek yogurt	Hamburger meat
Sliced ham	Sausage	Bacon

Food Slips

Steak	Chicken legs	Smoked salmon
Bagels	White Bread	Wheat crackers
Oatmeal	Strawberries	Orange slices
Spinach	Canned tomatoes	Refried beans
Cheddar cheese	Iceberg lettuce	Avocado
Corn	Grapes	Tofu
Brown rice	Chicken stock (used to make soup)	Potatoes
Carrots	Lemons	Sugar

Nutrient Slips

Calcium	Protein	Fat
Fiber	Omega-3	Iron
Vitamin A	B vitamins	Vitamin C
Vitamin D	Carbohydrates	

Creating a perspective, a role, for the student is one way to engage students in reading. Students in these roles find themselves solving problems that force them to use their knowledge and experience. A high school teacher created a perspective for students before assigning a reading in an automotive technology class. Students were presented with the following scenario: "You are the only mechanic on duty when a four-wheel-drive truck with a V-8 engine pulls in for repair. The truck has high mileage, and it appears that the problem may be a worn clutch disc. What tools do you think you will need to complete the repair? What procedures would you follow?"

In preparation for reading William Golding's book *Lord of the Flies*, an English teacher set up a perspective in which students' curiosity was aroused and their expectations of the story raised:

> *Imagine that you and your fellow classmates are stranded on an island after your plane has crashed. You cannot find the pilot and must make some important decisions. What actions will you take once you have an opportunity to process the situation?*

The class considered the orienting question. After some discussion, the teacher initiated the activity in Figure 6.4. The students formed small groups, and each group was directed to come to a consensus on the activities it would choose.

In a middle school mathematics class studying how to double, reduce, and find equivalent fractions, the teacher posed the problematic perspective presented in Figure 6.5. In response to the problem, one group's members listed the following as their action steps:

1. We must know how many teaspoons are in a cup and in a tablespoon.

2. We need to know if we buy a bag of flour how much of it there is. We need to know this for all our ingredients.

3. We must decide how many times we need to make this recipe. We think we just need to double it because one recipe makes five dozen, which is 60 cookies. We have to feed 100 kids, so double should be enough.

4. We have a question. Should we convert the fractions for our measuring cups first or should we double the recipe first?

Figure 6.4 Problematic Perspective in an English Class

Imagine that your plane crashes, leaving you and the other passengers stranded on an island. From the list below, which activities would you choose to do to try to ensure your survival?

_____	1. Elect a leader.
_____	2. Create a communication device.
_____	3. Devise a survival plan with the whole group.
_____	4. Create a rescue strategy.
_____	5. Gather tools for hunting.
_____	6. Build a shelter.
_____	7. Explore the island.
_____	8. Relax and try to have fun on the island.
_____	9. Build a fire.
_____	10. Gather wood.
_____	11. Create rules or laws.
_____	12. Purify water for drinking.
_____	13. Simply wait for rescue.
_____	14. Create fishing equipment.

Figure 6.5 Problematic Perspective in a Mathematics Class

We have a problem. Principal Sims has requested that we bake cookies for the entire grade level class of 100 students! However, the recipe she gave us is full of confusing fractions; and to top that off, we only have one 1/4 cup, 1 teaspoon, and two 1-cup measuring cups. To the best of your ability, figure out the following:

1. Convert all fractions so that you can use the measuring cups available.

2. Double or triple or quadruple the recipe (you must decide) so that each student can have at least one cookie. (It's OK if you have cookies left over; the teachers will eat them.)

3. Create a shopping list so we buy only the ingredients we need.

But before you begin, look at the recipe and plan your action steps. Make sure to get these checked off before you begin your calculations.

Principal Sims's Super Cookies

Makes about five dozen average-size cookies

4-1/4 cups of flour

1-1/4 cups granulated sugar

8 tablespoons of packed brown sugar

28 teaspoons of softened butter

8/4 teaspoons of vanilla

3 eggs

1 tablespoon of baking soda

2/4 teaspoon of salt

23 tablespoons of chocolate chips

Guided Imagery

Students' ability to visualize what they are reading is an important component for developing comprehension. **Guided imagery** allows students to explore concepts by creating mental images (Deshler et al., 2001). Samples (1977) recommends guided imagery, among other things, as a means of:

- Building an experience base for inquiry, discussion, and group work
- Exploring and stretching concepts
- Solving and clarifying problems
- Exploring history and the future
- Exploring other lands and worlds

Figure 6.6 shows a guided imagery example used by Ms. Maas with her sixth-grade middle school science students. As she explained, "My state standards require that my students describe ways in which organisms interact with each other and with nonliving parts of the environment and investigate factors that determine the growth and survival of organisms." To introduce the concept of symbiosis, Ms. Maas created a guided imagery exercise to help her students visualize and comprehend the importance of a commensal relationship within the marine environment. She presented her students with the text shown in Figure 6.6. After her students read and had time to think about the text, she initiated a whole-group discussion prompted by the following questions:

1. What do you think symbiosis means?

2. What were the two species illustrated in this visual exercise, and how did the partners affect one another?

3. Can a symbiotic relationship affect the two partners differently?

4. Did the relationship result in:
   a. Both partners benefiting (mutualism)
   b. One partner benefiting while the other partner was neither helped nor hurt (commensalism)
   c. One partner benefiting while the other partner was harmed (parasitism)

5. Can you think of any other symbiotic relationships found in nature?

Figure 6.6 A Guided Imagery Illustration

Close your eyes… start moving your body… you are a remora fish swimming through the balmy 83-degree waters of the Coral Sea off the northeast coast of Australia. As the cumulus clouds float overhead, intermittent rays of sunlight filter through the turquoise seawater to reveal the vivid colors of the Great Barrier Reef. You encounter danger everywhere as you constantly search for food and shelter. As you swim gracefully past huge outcrops of pink brain coral, you face a venomous red-and-white-striped lionfish and a blue-ringed octopus. You are quickly growing more tired of swimming and need to find your next meal fast. You decide to venture cautiously away from the protection of the reef. As you swim, you come face to face with a school of poisonous box jellyfish. You dive down, swimming hard and fast to avoid their enormous tentacles. Up ahead in the deep water, you confront the ocean's top predator: a great white shark. Despite being tired and hungry, you swim eagerly *toward* the shark, knowing this is exactly what you have been waiting for: your next free meal and free ride! You catch up with the shark and quickly attach yourself onto the underside of his body with your large, suckerlike mouth. Now you can finally rest from swimming and relax from the dangers of the ocean, knowing you are more protected attached to the shark than swimming alone in the vast ocean. All of a sudden, you sense you're moving through the water faster. The great white shark is now tailing a school of mackerel. He quickly darts into the mass of fish, devouring several fish in one bite. Ah, at last: your free meal. You swiftly release your grip from the shark's body and gulp up the uneaten scraps of food left behind. As the shark continues to thrash about and consume more, you find yourself quickly becoming full and satisfied. You speedily reattach yourself to the shark's body so as not to miss the ride or any other free meals along the way.

By introducing the concept of symbiosis through this guided imagery exercise, Ms. Maas was able to arouse her students' interest about the topic, activate their background knowledge, and motivate them to want to continue learning about these unique and vital relationships that exist in nature. Guided imagery provided an instructional option to help students connect what they see in their mind's eye to what they will study. The content area teacher assessed students' prior knowledge of and interest in a topic to be studied through an authentic instructional practice. Box 6.5 describes an additional instructional strategy, PreP, to assess students' prior knowledge within an instructional context, and to motivate them to learn more about a topic of study.

Content area teachers assess students' prior knowledge of and interest in a topic to be studied through authentic instructional practices. In Box 6.5, teacher Brian Williams explains how he used multimedia as a tool to activate students' prior knowledge and to prepare investigate a complex social topic.

Box 6.5 PreP Procedure

Evidence-Based Practices

Brainstorming is a key feature of the prereading plan (PreP), which may be used to estimate the levels of background knowledge that students bring to the text assignments.

Before beginning the PreP activity, the teacher should examine the text material for key words (which represent major concepts to be developed), phrases, or pictures and then introduce the topic that is to be read, following the three-phase plan outlined by Langer (1981, p. 154):

1. *Initial associations with the concept.* In this first phase, the teacher says, "Tell anything that comes to mind when…" (e.g., "you hear the word *Congress*"). As each student tells what ideas initially came to mind, the teacher jots each response on the board. During this phase, the students have their first opportunity to find associations between the key concept and their prior knowledge. When this activity was carried out in a middle school class, one student, Bill, said, "Important people." Another student, Danette, said, "Washington, DC."

2. *Reflections on initial associations.* During the second phase of PreP, the students are asked, "What made you think of… [the response given by a student]?" This phase helps the students develop awareness of their network of associations. They also have an opportunity to listen to each other's explanations, to interact, and to become aware of their changing ideas. Through this procedure, they may weigh, reject, accept, revise, and integrate some of the ideas that came to mind. When Bill was asked what made him think

of important people, he said, "I saw them in the newspaper." When Danette was asked what made her think of Washington, DC, she said, "Congress takes place there."

3. *Reformulation of knowledge.* In this phase, the teacher says, "Based on our discussion and before we read the text, have you any new ideas about ____ [e.g., "Congress"]?" This phase allows students to verbalize associations that have been elaborated or changed through the discussion. Because they have had a chance to probe their memories to elaborate on their prior knowledge, the responses elicited during the third phase are often more refined than those from the first. This time, Bill said, "Lawmakers of America," and Danette said, "The part of the U.S. government that makes the laws."

Through observation and listening during PreP, content area teachers will find their students' knowledge can be divided into three broad levels. On one level are students who have *much* prior knowledge about the concept. These students are often able to define and draw analogies, make conceptual links, and think categorically. On the second level are students who may have *some* prior knowledge. These students can give examples and cite characteristics of the content but may be unable to see relationships or make connections between what they know and the new material. On the third level are students who have *little* background knowledge. They often respond to the PreP activity by making simple associations, often misassociating with the topic.

Box 6.6 Voices from the Field

Brian, English Teacher

Challenge

Incorporating a novel study into the curriculum was a challenge for me as a first-year English teacher. In a novel study, I had to create a unit with a text as the focal point of teaching and learning, covering various literacy concepts while aligning text content with course objectives. It is imperative to have a strong start to any novel study to maximize student engagement and learning, but this is where I fell short! I thought to introduce a text, I only needed to do an author study, delving deeply into an author's life and body

of work, and give a summary of the text to motivate students to read. Through this strategy, it was my hope to get students to critically evaluate the author's style of writing, make connections between their work and life, and find similarities between their experiences and that of the author. However, this was found to be an insufficient approach: I had to do more. Unfortunately, I lacked a toolbox of skills and innovative strategies that would capture student interest in reading selected novels. I had to become creative in helping my students make a connection to the author and his work; otherwise, I would risk causing some of the students to lose focus of their overall goal of reading the text and thinking deeply about how it relates to them and our unit of study. After much reflection, I knew that activating prior knowledge and igniting student interest would be what strengthened their desire to become active participants in their learning. This, in turn, would support positive academic outcomes and achievement of curriculum standards.

Strategy

After exploring variety of strategies, I found the use of multimedia to be an effective tool to activate students' prior knowledge and interest. In this strategy, teachers are charged with sharing a thought-provoking video clip, audio recording, or photo with students that is related to their course text or objective. After that, students should be asked to write, draw, or talk about the multimedia presentation to share their thoughts about what they had just seen or heard. This activity can be done as a whole class, small group, or partner activity. This strategy allows students to think freely about a subject or topic without being guided by the teacher. It also gives the learners an opportunity to tap into familiar events and/or lived experiences related to the topic under study. A teacher may spark student thinking with a broad prompt. A nonguiding prompt could be, "What comes to your mind when you look at this photo?" or "How does this video make you feel?" Ultimately, this tool works to spark student interest, activate prior knowledge, and build a foundation for the learning of new material.

Putting the Strategy to Work

In my second year of teaching, given the controversial topic of guns in America, I decided to teach a unit on the effects of guns in our community. Todd Strasser's *Give a Boy a Gun* was a major novel within the unit, a story of the events that led up to a school shooting by two teenage males. The goal of this unit was for students to examine the effects of guns while simultaneously covering curriculum standards. Specifically, I wanted students to develop sociopolitical consciousness, critically analyzing and evaluating a real-world issue and taking steps to solve the identified problem. However, before beginning the unit, I had to activate prior knowledge and spark student interest. I knew, if I did not, the context of the reading and the unit concepts would be somewhat of a challenge for students to grasp.

To build a connection between the content and my students, I projected a picture of a gun on the board. As students gazed at the object, I asked them to take 5 minutes to silently and independently write everything that came to mind. Students began to quickly jot their thoughts and feelings about the image as soon as I started the timer. As time expired, I saw several hands shoot up in the air. My students were eager to share what they had written with their peers and me. I wanted to give everyone an opportunity to share, so I instructed students to share within their groups. As I walked around the classroom, I heard amazing dialogue about a variety of topics related to guns. I heard discussions about gun laws, guns in popular movies and video games, memories of hunting with family members, and violence in the community. Every student had had an experience with a gun, whether directly or indirectly. More importantly, every student was intrigued by the topic and wanted to know what was coming next in the lesson. This was my cue to introduce the major theme of our unit and the novel we were going to read for the next couple of weeks. Students were drawn to the unit because of their relationship with the topic, whether a fond memory or a passionate dislike. Either way, students wanted to contribute and learn more because of a simple activity that enabled them to think deeply about a lived experience related to the main topic.

Reflection

The use of multimedia as a tool to activate students' prior knowledge proved to be successful in my unit on the effects of guns in our community. The projected photo of a gun was simple, yet impactful. As a result, students were able to recount their experiences, communicate their points of view, and use their prior knowledge as a basis for future learning throughout the unit. It was great to see how the individualized perspectives, shared understandings, and differences in opinion on the topic of guns trickled into unit activities and discussions. Student interest in guns and what they meant to the community, based on class dialogue, heightened the level of engagement and investment in the classroom as we navigated the text and course concepts. Students even capitalized on their prior knowledge and used it as a building block for their final projects in the unit. For example, the student who took pride in hunting with his grandfather advocated for a restriction of certain guns in a letter to the senator, a girl whose boyfriend was robbed at gunpoint on schoolgrounds started a petition for increased school surveillance, and a few students wrote a letter to the superintendent to advocate for increased counseling services for those affected by gun violence. While there are a plethora of strategies to activate prior knowledge and student interest, I encourage educators to consider multimedia as an effective option.

MyLab Education **Self-Check 6.2**

MyLab Education **Application Exercise 6.2:**
Fostering Student Engagement in a Content Area Classroom

Making Predictions

6.3 **Explain how predicting and questioning can support comprehension during content area reading.**

Prediction strategies activate thought about the content before reading. Students must rely on what they know through previous study and experience to make educated guesses about the material to be read. You can facilitate student-centered purposes by creating anticipation about the meaning of what will be read.

Anticipation Guides

An **anticipation guide** is a series of statements to which students must respond individually before reading the text. Their value lies in the discussion that takes place after the exercise. The teacher's role during discussion is to activate thought. As students connect their knowledge of the world to the prediction task, you must remain open to a wide range of responses. Draw on what students bring to the task but remain nondirective in order to keep the discussion moving.

Anticipation guides may vary in format but not in purpose. In each case, the readers' expectations about meaning are raised before they read the text. Keep these six guidelines in mind in constructing and using an anticipation guide:

1. *Analyze the material to be read.* Determine the major ideas—implicit and explicit—with which students will interact.
2. *Write those ideas in short, clear declarative statements.* These statements should in some way reflect the world in which the students live or about which they know. Avoid abstractions whenever possible.
3. *Put these statements in a format that will elicit anticipation and prediction.*
4. *Discuss the students' predictions and anticipations before they read the text selection.*
5. *Assign the text selection.* Have the students evaluate the statements considering the author's intent and purpose.
6. *Contrast the readers' predictions with the author's intended meaning.*

Adapting Anticipation Guides in Content Areas

A science teacher began a weather unit by introducing a series of popular clichés about the weather. He asked his students to anticipate whether the clichés had a scientific basis (see Figure 6.7). The before-reading discussion led the students to review and expand their concepts of scientific truth. Throughout different parts of the unit, the teacher returned to one or two of the clichés in the anticipation guide and suggested to the class that the textbook assignment would explain whether there was a scientific basis for each saying. Students were then directed to read to explore those explanations.

A health education teacher raised expectations and created anticipation for a chapter on the human immunodeficiency virus (HIV) and AIDS. Rather than prepare

Figure 6.7 Anticipation Guide for Clichés About Weather

Directions: Put a check under "Likely" if you believe that the weather saying has any scientific basis; put a check under "Unlikely" if you believe that it has no scientific basis. Be ready to explain your choice.

Likely	Unlikely	
_____	_____	1. Red sky at night, sailors' delight; red sky at morning, sailors take warning.
_____	_____	2. If you see a sunspot, there is going to be bad weather.
_____	_____	3. When the leaves turn under, it is going to storm.
_____	_____	4. If you see a hornet's nest high in a tree, a harsh winter is coming.
_____	_____	5. Aching bones mean a cold and rainy forecast.
_____	_____	6. If a groundhog sees his shadow, six more weeks of winter.
_____	_____	7. Rain before seven, sun by eleven.
_____	_____	8. If a cow lies down in a pasture, it is going to rain soon.
_____	_____	9. Sea gull, sea gull, sitting on the sand; it's never good weather while you're on land.

written statements, she conducted the anticipatory lesson as part of an introductory class discussion. She raised curiosity about the topic by asking students to participate in a strategy known as the "every-pupil response." She told the students that she would ask several questions about becoming infected with HIV. Students were to respond to each question by giving a "thumbs up" if they agreed or a "thumbs down" if they disagreed. The class had to participate in unison and keep their thumbs up or down. After each question, the students shared their reasons for responding thumbs up or thumbs down. The questions were framed as follows: "Is it true that you can contract HIV by:

- Having unprotected sex with an infected partner?"
- Kissing someone with HIV?"
- Sharing needles with an HIV-infected drug user?"
- Sharing a locker with an infected person?"
- Using a telephone after someone with HIV has used it?"
- Being bitten by a mosquito?"

The verbal anticipation guide created lively discussion as students discussed some of their preconceived notions and misconceptions about HIV and AIDS.

Mathematics teachers also have been successful in their use of anticipation guides. In a precalculus class, the teacher introduced the activity shown in Figure 6.8 to begin the trigonometry section of the textbook. She created the anticipation guide to help students address their own knowledge about trigonometry and to create conceptual conflict for some of the more difficult sections of the chapter they would be studying.

Finally, a 10th-grade English teacher developed an anticipation guide for Elie Wiesel's book *Night*. She used the anticipation guide in Figure 6.9. She adapted the anticipation guide format by asking students, before reading, to discuss their responses to a series of statements about the Holocaust. After reading *Night*, the students were then asked to revisit their original responses to the statements on the guide and to consider whether their reading confirmed or refuted their prereading responses. For the post-reading discussion, the teacher placed a blank version of the anticipation guide on an overhead projector so that the students, as a class, could discuss how their knowledge and beliefs had changed because of their reading of *Night*.

Figure 6.8 Anticipation Guide for Preconceived Notions About Trigonometry

Directions: Put a check under "Likely" if you believe that the statement has any mathematical truth. Put a check under "Unlikely" if you believe that it has no mathematical truth. Be ready to explain your choices.

Likely	Unlikely	
_____	_____	1. Trigonometry deals with circles.
_____	_____	2. Angles have little importance in trigonometry.
_____	_____	3. Sailors use trigonometry in navigation.
_____	_____	4. Angles can be measured only in degrees.
_____	_____	5. Calculators are useless in trigonometry.
_____	_____	6. Trigonometry deals with triangles.
_____	_____	7. Trigonometry has no application in the real world.
_____	_____	8. Radians are used in measuring central angles.
_____	_____	9. Trigonometry has scientific uses.
_____	_____	10. Radians can be converted to degrees.

Figure 6.9 Anticipation Guide for *Night*

Directions: Read each of the following statements and, in the Before Reading column, place a plus (+) if you agree with the statement and a minus (–) if you disagree. Be prepared to support your responses during our class discussion. Later, after learning about the Holocaust, you will complete the After Reading column to see if any of your initial responses have changed. You'll be asked to discuss why you confirmed or changed your ideas from your before-reading responses.

Before Reading	Statement	After Reading
_____	The Holocaust took place only in Germany.	_____
_____	The Jews had plenty of time to escape, so they could have avoided being sent to a concentration camp.	_____
_____	Jews were targeted because of their religion.	_____
_____	Other countries did not know what was happening to the Jews.	_____
_____	People in concentration camps were killed only if they broke a law.	_____
_____	Life in the concentration camps wasn't so bad for those who were too old or too young to work.	_____
_____	Survivors of the Holocaust just want to forget about what happened.	_____
_____	Jews were the only target of Hitler and the Nazis.	_____
_____	The Holocaust took place between WWI and WWII.	_____
_____	The term *Holocaust* was developed by the Jewish prisoners while they were at the camps.	_____

Imagine, Elaborate, Predict, and Confirm (IEPC)

Many students, particularly those who struggle with reading, have difficulty creating mental images as they read (Lenihan, 2003). The **imagine, elaborate, predict, and confirm (IEPC)** strategy encourages students to use visual imagery to enhance their comprehension of a text selection. Figure 6.10 shows how a social studies teacher used the IEPC strategy to help her students understand Theodore Taylor's book *The Cay*. Wood and Taylor (2005) explain the steps in implementing the IEPC strategy:

Figure 6.10 IEPC Chart for *The Cay*

I	E	P	C
Being stranded on a desert island; feeling afraid Feeling suspicious of the person with whom you are stranded; wondering if he is going to harm you Being frustrated at not being able to see and not being able to do anything about it Seeing the dark rain clouds gather; wondering how long the storm will last and how strong it will be How will Phillip and Timothy survive?	Phillip and Timothy must have been terrified, especially after their boat was torpedoed. They must have been lonely, starving, exhausted. Phillip was White. Timothy was Black. Phillip had been taught that Black people were inferior. Will he overcome his prejudice? Phillip has lost his sight. He must feel helpless and angry because he is now dependent on Timothy. The wind is blowing furiously; waves are crashing on the shore; everything is soaked and flooded; it's hard to see or to walk.	Phillip and Timothy will learn to live together on the island. Timothy will help Phillip. Phillip will learn not to judge people by the color of their skin. Timothy and Phillip will survive the hurricane, and they will be rescued and returned to civilization. Phillip will learn how to adjust to his blindness, and Timothy and Phillip will remain friends.	Phillip disliked Timothy but had to rely on him. Timothy took care of Phillip; Phillip learned to respect and care about Timothy. Phillip learns through Timothy's actions toward him that racism is wrong; he regains his sight, both physically and emotionally. Timothy dies in the hurricane protecting Phillip. Phillip holds Timothy's hand until he dies. Phillip is able to live because of what Timothy taught him.

1. *Select a text passage or introduction to the text that contains content appropriate for developing imagery.* In the IEPC example illustrated in Figure 6.10, the teacher read a brief synopsis of the text to the students, which introduced them to the basic setting of the story and to the conflict that would develop in its plot.

2. *Imagine.* Have students close their eyes to imagine a scene from the book or text they are going to read. Encourage them to use experiences by thinking about the feelings, sights, smells, and tastes that they associate with the topic. Their images may emanate from the title of the text, a picture from the passage, or a passage read by the teacher. Ask students to share their images with a partner or with the group and to record their images in the I column of the IEPC chart. Students who were preparing to read *The Cay* imagined what it might be like to be stranded on a desert island with only one other person, whom they disliked or distrusted. They imagined the frustration that might result from being blind.

3. *Elaborate.* Once the students have heard initial responses from their classmates, ask them to think of additional details associated with the scene they have visualized. Ask questions that will prompt them to elaborate on the original images they described. Record their responses in the E column of the IEPC chart. The students preparing to read *The Cay* elaborated on their initial images by talking about what might have led to the dislike and distrust between the boy and the elderly man who were stranded on the island. They also elaborated on what it might feel like to experience a hurricane on the island, as the characters did in the story.

4. *Predict.* Have the students use their initial images and elaboration of those images to make predictions about the text they are going to read. Record those predictions in the P column of the IEPC. As Figure 6.11 shows, students offered a range of predictions about what might happen as *The Cay* unfolded and about how the characters might respond to their difficult predicament.

5. *Confirm.* During and after reading, encourage students to recall their predictions. Were they able to confirm their predictions, or have they modified their predictions based on what they have learned from reading the text? Record their confirmations

Figure 6.11 IEPC Chart for a Science Unit on Disease

Imagine	Elaborate	Predict	Confirm
Imagine you are a disease. What do you think your daily life would be like?	Write five questions you might ask a disease. Explain why each question is important.	Predict five things you think you will learn in the text. You can include vocabulary that might be important to this topic.	After you have read the text, look at the I, E, and P boxes. Pick five questions that you can answer according to the text.
I think my life would be hot and sweaty. I think I would be working all the time and never stop for lunch or anything. I think I would always have to be on the lookout for medicines that could slow me down or even stop me. But the biggest thing I would have to be ready for is to jump to the next person to keep my life going.	1. What do you do to people? 2. How do you spread? 3. Can you be stopped? 4. Where did you start? 5. How can I avoid you?	1. We will learn how disease is spread. 2. We will learn how to stop disease. 3. We will learn the meaning of infectious. 4. We will learn about what disease does to the human body. 5. We might learn about the CDC, which studies disease.	1. Disease is spread in all different ways. Some disease is spread through blood and other bodily fluids, and other disease is spread through the air. 2. Some diseases are really bad because they kill the host. When the host is dead, they have to look for a new place to live. 3. A synonym for infectious is contagious. 4. Some diseases are spread through human contact with wild animals. 5. Sometimes diseases are dormant, which means they don't do anything for a long time.

and modifications, using a different color marker for each, in the C column of the IEPC chart. As they read *The Cay*, the students looked carefully for passages and clues that would help them to identify which of their predictions were accurate and which needed to be modified. After reading the story, the students confirmed that their prediction that Phillip would learn not to judge people by the color of their skin proved to be accurate. In contrast, they recognized that their prediction that the characters would survive the storm together did not match what actually happened in the story.

In another example, a science class was preparing to read a text about the spread of disease. Before students read, their teacher introduced an IEPC chart to help them access what they already knew about the subject and to heighten their awareness of how they processed questions and information. She provided a thinking prompt in each category, which seemed to help her students come up with more relevant ideas. Figure 6.11 shows how one student used the IEPC chart to access what he already knew about disease, helping him better understand the text.

Question Generation

Teaching students to generate their own questions about material to be read is an important prereading instructional goal. Teachers need to intentionally select strategies that will engage students in expressing their perceptions and developing understanding of text topics (Cook-Sather, 2002). Neufeld (2005) suggests that, before reading a text, students ask and answer questions that will help them to read with a purpose, to recognize major characteristics of the texts, to activate their prior knowledge, and to make predictions about what they are about to read. By providing opportunities for students to generate questions and seek answers to those questions, teachers can support students in becoming strategic readers. In the following sections, we examine several instructional strategies for engaging students in asking questions for reading.

Active Comprehension

Teachers can use an **active comprehension** strategy when they *ask questions that beget questions in return*. You might, for example, focus attention on a picture or an illustration from a story or book and ask a question that induces student questions in response: "What would you like to know about the picture?" In return, invite the students to generate questions that focus on the details in the picture or its overarching message.

Or you might decide to read to students an opening paragraph or two from a text selection, enough to whet their appetites for the selection. Then ask, "What else would you like to know about _____?" Complete the question by focusing attention on some aspect of the selection that is pivotal to students' comprehension. It may be the main character of a story or the main topic of an expository text.

Active comprehension questions not only arouse interest and curiosity, but also draw learners into the material. As a result, students will read to satisfy purposes and resolve conceptual conflicts that they have identified through their own questions.

ReQuest

ReQuest, sometimes called reciprocal teaching, was originally devised as a one-on-one procedure for a remedial instructional context. Yet this strategy can easily be adapted to content area classrooms to help struggling readers think as they read. ReQuest encourages students to ask their own questions about the content material under study. Self-declared questions are forceful. They help students establish reasonable purposes for their reading. Manzo, Manzo, and Estes (2001) suggest the following steps for implementing the ReQuest strategy:

1. *Both the students and the teacher silently read the same segment of the text.* For students who have difficulty comprehending, Manzo recommends reading one sentence at a time. It can also be helpful to divide a longer, more complex text into smaller, more

manageable sections. Then students and teacher can pause at the end of each small section and implement the ReQuest procedure. It is also helpful to inform the students before they begin reading that they will be asking the teacher questions about the text after they have read it.

2. *The teacher closes the book and is questioned about the passage by the students.*

3. *Next there is an exchange of roles.* The teacher queries the students about the text.

4. *On completion of the student–teacher exchange, the students and the teacher read the next segment of the text, pausing at the predetermined stopping point.* Steps 2 and 3 are then repeated.

5. *Students stop questioning and begin predicting.* At a suitable point in the text, when the students have processed enough information to make predictions about the remainder of the assignment, the exchange of questions stops. The teacher then asks prediction questions: "What do you think might happen in the remainder of the text? What has the author said or implied that makes you think so?" Divergent thinking is encouraged.

6. *Students are then assigned the remaining portion of the text to read independently.*

7. *The teacher facilitates a follow-up discussion of the material.*

Although the steps for ReQuest were devised for one-on-one instruction, they can be adapted for the content area classroom where students struggle with texts.

The ReQuest strategy can be modified. For example, consider alternating the role of questioner after each question. Doing so will involve more students in the activity. Once students understand the types of questions that can be asked about a text passage, you might also try forming ReQuest teams. A ReQuest team composed of three or four students can compete with another ReQuest team. The teacher's role is to facilitate interaction between the teams.

Our own experiences with ReQuest suggest that students may consistently ask factual questions to stump the teacher or other students. Such questions succeed because the teacher is subject to the same restrictions imposed by short-term memory as the students. That you miss an answer or two is healthy—after all, to err is human.

However, when students ask only verbatim questions because they don't know how to ask any others, the situation is less effective. Some students don't know how to ask questions that will stimulate interpretive or applied levels of thinking. The teacher's role as a good questioner during ReQuest is to model asking different types of questions. Box 6.7 shows how a civics and economics teacher used ReQuest with her class of predominantly English Learners.

Box 6.7 Evidence-Based Best Practices

ReQuest Procedure

In a civics and economics class, a teacher applied the ReQuest strategy to help English Learners understand the different branches of government in the United States. She related their understanding of the U.S. government to that of their native countries.

1. *Both the students and the teacher silently read the same segment of the text.* The teacher and the English Learners read a section of the text about the structure of the U.S. government that outlined the three branches of government: legislative, judicial, and executive.

2. *The teacher closed the book and was questioned about the passage by the students.* The teacher encouraged students to make connections between the information in the

text and their experiences with the governments of their native countries. She was prepared to answer questions about the information presented in the reading as well as to assimilate this information with students' existing knowledge of alternative government structures. For example, one student from Mexico noted that, although Mexico has a president, presidential elections in that country are held every six years rather than every four years, as they are in the United States. He went on to point out that there is no opportunity for reelection of a president in Mexico as there is in the United States.

3. *Next, there was an exchange of roles.* The teacher then asked students questions about the text and encouraged

them to make comparisons between the U.S. government and those of the countries with which they were familiar. For example, the teacher asked students to compare the civil liberties protected by the U.S. Constitution with those that are protected by the governments of their native counties. A student from Mexico referenced the individual and social rights established in the Constitution of Mexico and made comparisons to amendments in the U.S. Constitution.

4. *On completion of the student–teacher exchange, the class and the teacher read the next segment of the text.* Steps 2 and 3 were repeated.

5. *The teacher invited students to make predictions.* At this point in the lesson, the civics and economics teacher asked questions such as, "Now that we know how laws are created, what changes in legislation do you think might lie in the future?"

6. *Students were assigned a subsequent portion of the text to read silently.*

7. *The teacher facilitated a follow-up discussion of the material.*

MyLab Education **Self-Check 6.3**

MyLab Education **Application Exercise 6.3:**
Using Anticipation Guides to Increase Engagement in Content Area Classes

---

Looking Back Looking Forward

Meaningful learning with texts occurs when students experience a sense of satisfaction with text and a feeling of accomplishment. In this chapter, the roles that self-efficacy and motivation play in purposeful learning were emphasized. Although some students may be skilled in reading and knowledgeable about the subject, they may not bring that skill and knowledge to bear in learning situations. It takes motivation, a sense of direction and purpose, and a teacher who knows how to create conditions in the classroom that allow students to establish their own motives for reading. One way to arouse curiosity about reading material is to encourage students to make connections among the key concepts to be studied. Another is to create conceptual conflict. Students will read to resolve conflicts arising from problem situations and perspectives and will use guided imagery to explore the ideas to be encountered during reading.

To reduce any uncertainty that students bring to reading material, you can help them raise questions and anticipate meaning by showing them how to connect what they already know to the new ideas presented in the text. The questions students raise as a result of predicting will guide them into the reading material and keep them on course. Anticipation guides, ReQuest, and self-questioning are strategies for stimulating predictions and anticipation about the content.

In the next chapter, we explore ways to guide reading comprehension in the curriculum. A classroom teacher who encourages student engagement in reading brings learners and texts together to explore and construct meaning.

---

eResources

Learn about ways to engage students in social networking about books by Googling "Goodreads." This site offers opportunities to search book databases, rate and review books, create virtual book clubs, and generate reading lists.

Chapter 7
Guiding Reading Comprehension

Written in collaboration with Lina Soares, Ph.D.

Goodluz/Shutterstock

Chapter Overview and Learning Outcomes

After reading this chapter, you should be able to:

7.1 Describe the ways in which teachers can model comprehension strategies and explain how each supports students' comprehension.

7.2 Explain how each of the strategies guide comprehension as students interact with text, from before reading support to after reading reflection.

7.3 Describe how each of the reading guides scaffolds students' understanding during reading.

Organizing Principle

Teachers guide students' reading by (1) modeling how to read, think, and learn with texts and (2) scaffolding instruction in the use of comprehension strategies that allow students to learn with text in meaningful ways.

Teachers have observed how some students approach the reading of academic text: They read as fast as they can—eyes skimming over words, fingers flipping through the pages—to glean bits of information here and there in a mad dash to finish the reading assignment! How many times have teachers received one- or two-word answers in response to thoughtful questions about assigned text? Superficial reading of academic text, more often than not, is devoid of thinking and learning.

Effective teachers, of course, always hope for more from their students. They set the bar high by challenging learners to develop ways of thinking that are essential for comprehending text and developing core concepts in a discipline. Through the instructional support they provide, teachers can build students' confidence and competence as readers by showing them how to use comprehension strategies to think deeply about text.

Today, reading in most classrooms includes a blend of traditional printed texts as well as reading with e-readers and other digital devices. While digital reading requires many of the same processes as traditional print reading, it also requires that students know how and when to access information from the different sources available. When navigating digital texts, the reader's purpose guides the choices they make as they search for information and make decisions about which resource options to retrieve (Cardullo et al., 2012). Whether the reading involves traditional or digital texts, active, engaged reading always involves a dialogue between the reader and the text. As we learned in the previous chapter, engaged readers are motivated, knowledgeable, strategic, and socially interactive. They have much to contribute to the dialogue that takes place in the mind as they interact with texts to construct meaning. Yet in today's diverse classrooms, students may have trouble handling the conceptual demands of difficult text. How does a content area teacher guide comprehension in ways that model thinking strategies and engage and sustain students in discipline-specific learning, especially if the ideas encountered during reading are complex?

Earlier, we studied how activating prior knowledge before, during, and after reading is a critical instructional component of content literacy lessons. In this chapter, we extend the dialogue on reading comprehension as we explore strategies to think and learn with text. As

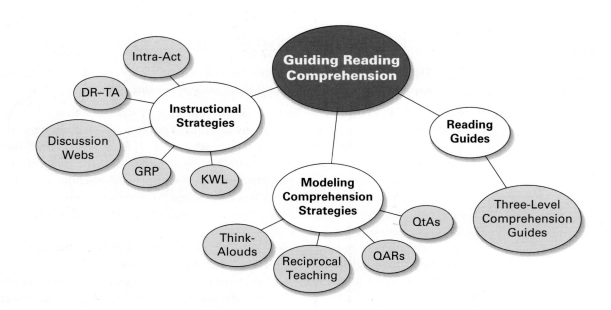

the organizing principle for this chapter highlights: Teachers guide students' reading by (1) modeling how to read, think, and learn with texts and (2) scaffolding instruction in the use of comprehension strategies that allow students to learn with text in meaningful ways.

Frame of Mind

1. How do think-alouds, reciprocal teaching, QARs, and QtAs model reading/thinking/learning strategies for students as they interact with texts in a discipline?
2. Describe the procedures associated with each of these literacy-related instructional strategies: KWL, KWHL, directed reading–thinking activity (DR–TA), guided reading procedure (GRP), intra-act, and discussion web. How do these instructional strategies support thinking and learning with text? Which of these strategies may be particularly useful when adapted to your content area?
3. Why and when should teachers use reading guides?
4. How can you engage your students in close reading of texts within your discipline?

Although metaphors come and go, one that has been around since the ancient Greeks is as powerful today as it was centuries ago. In Plato's *Theaetetus,* written more than 2,000 years ago, Socrates is asked to explain what it means to think. He responds to his questioner by explaining that when the mind is thinking it is merely talking to itself, asking questions and answering them. Thinking is a conversation. It is a dialogue that you have with yourself in your mind. When a reader engages in a dialogue with text, the conversation metaphor puts an incredibly complex process—reading—into the context of what happens inside the minds of readers. Texts make it possible to bring readers and authors together in content area classrooms. There is a catch, however. Thinking with texts requires students to participate actively in the conversation.

A conversation works only when participants are involved and interacting with one another. Everyday conversations, for example, involve an exchange of ideas between two or more parties—a give-and-take dialogue—around topics of mutual interest and relevance. Learning conversations in content area classrooms have similar characteristics, unless they break down or never get started. Dialogues easily turn into monologues when the transmission of information becomes more important than the sharing of ideas among students, teachers, and texts. Guiding the learning conversations that occur between the reader and the text is the subject of this chapter.

MyLab Education
Response Journal 7.1
What is your reaction to Socrates's explanation of what it means to think?
When you were a student, how helpful were worksheets in comprehending a text assignment?

Modeling Comprehension Strategies

7.1   Describe the ways in which teachers can model comprehension strategies and explain how each supports students' comprehension.

Students who struggle with text are usually unaware of strategies that will help them more effectively comprehend and make meaning. Content area teachers typically have more content to cover than time in which to teach it all. It is understandable, then, that some teachers view comprehension instruction as an added burden. Comprehension instruction can, however, support, rather than distract from, the teaching of content area concepts. Students' comprehension has been found to improve when teachers explain and model comprehension strategies that can aid students in their reading of content area texts (Biancarosa & Snow, 2004; Ness, 2009).

Currently, the practice of close reading, recommended in the Common Core State Standards for English Language Arts (CCSS-ELA) (National Governors Association, 2010), is noted as an important comprehension tool. Close reading encourages students to read and reread a text in order to understand it and to draw logical inferences from it. Using short but relevant text selections, close reading asks students to focus on what is explicitly stated by the author, to make inferences from the key details presented, and to support conclusions and inferences with evidence that is directly in the text (Fisher & Frey, 2014). Often, close reading requires multiple readings and discussions over multiple lessons. Teachers can support close reading discussions by asking text-dependent questions that focus on key issues that are explicitly presented as well as on text structure and the meaning for the text (Shanahan, 2015).

In this section, we explain additional research-based practices that provide explicit instruction in the use of comprehension strategies. Teachers from various disciplines can, with some modification, incorporate *think-alouds, reciprocal teaching, question–answer relationships (QARs)*, and *questioning the author (QtA)* into their instructional routines to show students how to read, think, and learn with discipline-specific texts.

Using Think-Alouds to Model Comprehension Strategies

In think-alouds, teachers make their thinking explicit by verbalizing their thoughts while reading orally. The think-aloud strategy helps readers clarify their understanding of reading and their understanding of how to use strategies. Students will more clearly understand the strategies after a teacher uses think-alouds because they can see how a mind actively responds to thinking through trouble spots and constructing meaning from the text (Fisher, Frey, & Lapp, 2011).

There are five basic steps to follow when using think-alouds. First, select passages to read aloud that contain points of difficulty, ambiguities, contradictions, or unknown words. Second, while orally reading and modeling thinking aloud, have students follow silently and listen to how trouble spots are thought through. Third, have students work with partners to practice think-alouds by taking turns reading short, carefully prepared passages and sharing thoughts. Fourth, have students practice independently. Encourage them to monitor the strategies they use when reading and to reflect on the degree to which they made predictions, formed mental images, recognized analogies that connected to what they read, or used a reading strategy to support their comprehension when the text did not make sense to them. Finally, to encourage transfer, integrate practice with other lessons and provide occasional demonstrations of how, why, and when to use think-alouds. Five points can be made during think-alouds:

1. Students should develop hypotheses by making predictions.

2. Students should develop images by describing pictures forming in their heads from the information being read.

3. Students should link new information with prior knowledge by sharing analogies.

4. Students should monitor comprehension by verbalizing a confusing point.

5. Students should regulate comprehension by demonstrating strategies.

Let's look at how each of these points can be modeled in a middle school earth science class.

DEVELOP HYPOTHESES BY MAKING PREDICTIONS   Teachers might model how to develop hypotheses by making predictions from the title of a chapter or from subheadings within the chapter. Suppose you were teaching with an earth science text. You might say, "From the heading 'How Minerals Are Used,' I predict that this section will tell about things that are made out of different minerals." The text continues:

> Some of the most valuable minerals are found in ores. An **ore** is a mineral resource mined for profit. For example, bauxite (BAWK-sight) is an ore from which

aluminum is taken. Iron is obtained from the ore called hematite (HEE-muh-tight). Bauxite and hematite are metallic minerals.

Metallic minerals are metals or ores of metals. Gold, iron, and aluminum are examples of metals. Metals are important because of their many useful properties.

One useful property of many metals is malleability (mal-ee-uh-BIL-uh-tee). **Malleability** is the ability to be hammered without breaking. Malleability allows a metal to be hammered into thin sheets.

DEVELOP IMAGES To model how to develop imaging, at this point you might stop and say, "I have a picture in my head from a scene I saw in a movie about the Old West. I see a blacksmith pumping bellows in a forge to heat up an iron horseshoe. When the iron turns a reddish orange, he picks it up with his tongs, and he hammers. The sparks fly, but slowly the horseshoe changes shape to fit the horse's hoof." The text continues:

> Another property of many metals is ductility (duk-TIL-uh-tee). **Ductility** is the ability to be pulled and stretched without breaking. This property allows a metal to be pulled into thin wires.

SHARE ANALOGIES To model how to link new information with prior knowledge, you might share the following analogies. "This is like a time when I tried to eat a piece of pizza with extra cheese. Every time I took a bite, the cheese kept stretching and stretching into these long strings. It is also like a time when I went to the county fair and watched people make taffy. They got this glob of candy and put it on a machine that just kept pulling and stretching the taffy, but it never broke." The text continues:

> Metals share other properties as well. All metals conduct heat and electricity. Electrical appliances and machines need metals to conduct electricity. In addition, all metals have a shiny, metallic luster.

MONITOR COMPREHENSION To model how to monitor comprehension, you can verbalize a confusing point: "This is telling me that metals have a metallic luster. I don't know what that is. I'm also confused because I thought this section was going to be about things that are made out of different minerals. This is different from what I expected."

REGULATE COMPREHENSION To model how to correct lagging comprehension, you can demonstrate a strategy: "I'm confused about what *metallic luster* means, and I don't know why the authors are talking about this when I expected them to talk about stuff made out of minerals. Maybe if I ignore the term *metallic luster* and keep on reading, I'll be able to make some connections to what I expected and figure it all out." The text continues:

> Very shiny metals, like chromium, are often used for decorative purposes. Many metals are also strong. Titanium (tigh-TAY-nee-um), magnesium (mag-NEE-zee-um), and aluminum are metals that are both strong and lightweight. These properties make them ideal building materials for jet planes and spacecraft.

"Oh, they're talking about properties of metals that make them especially good for making certain things, like aluminum for jets, because it is strong and lightweight. Now I understand why they're talking about properties. I'll bet chrome and chromium are just about the same, because I know chrome is the shiny stuff on cars. I think *metallic luster* must mean something like shiny, because chromium reminds me of chrome."

Similarly, when preparing to teach a middle school science unit on popular dynamics, Ms. Maas developed a think-aloud activity for one portion of that unit on "the water cycle." She realized that it was important for students to understand and comprehend the continuous movement of matter through both living and nonliving parts of an ecosystem. The continuous movement, or cycling of matter, is vital to sustain life on Earth.

Following the guidelines listed above, she described her implementation of the water cycle think-aloud:

> I presented my students with a text related to the water cycle. To begin our think-aloud activity, I modeled my hypothesis by saying, "From the title, I'm thinking this text is going to focus on water moving between streams, lakes, and oceans since water covers nearly 75% of the Earth's surface." As I proceeded with the lesson, students began reading the text and quickly realized that it pertained to water cycling through the ecosystem either as a liquid on land or as a vapor in the atmosphere. They encountered words such as *precipitation, condensation,* and *evaporation.* As they continued to read, I encouraged them to develop a mental image of a street in the summer after a rainstorm (precipitation) and the steam rising (evaporation) off the pavement. As we continued to read and learn more about the water cycle, I helped them to create analogies. For example, I compared this cycling of water through an ecosystem to water flowing across a water wheel. The energy created by the water turned the wheel just like energy (sun) drove the water cycle. As we continued to read, we encountered statements and questions that proved confusing, for example, questions such as "If water follows a continuous cycle, why do we need to conserve water?" or "If water becomes polluted, does it stay polluted forever since it remains in a constant and continuous cycle?" As we completed our reading of the text, I encouraged the students to "think aloud" to support their comprehension of the material. By effectively modeling and implementing think-alouds, I hope to provide my students with one more effective comprehension strategy to further their understanding and appreciation of the content material.

Think-alouds are best used at the beginning of lessons to help students learn the *whats* and *hows* of constructing meaning with text. The next teaching strategy, *reciprocal teaching,* is an excellent follow-up to think-alouds. **Reciprocal teaching** helps students learn how to apply the strategy learned during a think-aloud so that they can understand the author's message.

Using Reciprocal Teaching to Model Comprehension Strategies

When using reciprocal teaching, you model how to use four comprehension activities (generating questions, summarizing, predicting, and clarifying) while leading a dialogue (Palincsar & Brown, 1984). Then students take turns assuming the teacher's role. A key to the effectiveness of this strategy is adjusting the task demand to support the students when difficulty occurs. That is, when students experience difficulty, you provide assistance by lowering the demands of the task. As the process goes on, you slowly withdraw support so that students continue learning. When planning a reciprocal teaching lesson, there are two phases. The first phase has five steps:

1. Find text selections that demonstrate the four comprehension activities.

2. Generate appropriate questions.

3. Generate predictions about each selection.

4. Locate summarizing sentences and develop summaries for each selection.

5. Note difficult vocabulary and concepts.

In the second phase, decisions are made about which comprehension activities to teach based on the students' needs. It also helps determine students' present facility with the activities so that you are prepared to give needed support during the process. Once students are familiar with more than one strategy, reciprocal teaching can be used to model the decision-making process about which strategy to use.

MyLab Education
Video Example 7.1
Dimensions of
Comprehension
Watch this video to learn about the dimensions of comprehension.

Using Question–Answer Relationships (QARs) to Model Comprehension Strategies

Question–answer relationships (QARs) make explicit to students the relationships that exist among the type of question asked, the text, and the reader's prior knowledge. In the process of teaching QARs, you help students become aware of and skilled in using learning strategies to find the information they need to comprehend at different levels of response to the text (Raphael, 1984, 1986; Raphael & Au, 2005). Raphael explains the answers to questions can be found in different places:

- *In the Text—Right There:* The words used in the question and the words used for the answer can usually be found in the same sentence.

- *In the Text—Think and Search:* The answer is in the text, but the words used in the question and those used for the answer are not in the same sentence. You need to think about different parts of the text and how ideas can be put together before you can answer the question.

- *In Your Head—Author and You:* The answer is not in the text. You need to think about what you know, what the author says, and how they fit together.

- *In Your Head—On Your Own:* The text got you thinking, but the answer is inside your head; it is not directly answered by the author. You need to think about what you already know about the topic in order to answer the question.

The procedures for learning QARs can be taught directly to students by literacy specialists and can be reinforced by content area specialists. Keep in mind, however, that students may come to your class totally unaware of what information sources are available for seeking an answer, or they may not know when to use different sources. In this case, it is worth several days' effort to teach students the relationship between questions and answers. It may take up to three days to show students how to identify the information sources necessary to answer questions. The following steps, which we have adapted for content area situations, are suggested for teaching QARs:

1. *Introduce the concept of QARs.* Show students a description of the four basic question–answer relationships. We recommend a chart that can be positioned in a prominent place in the classroom. Students may then refer to it throughout the content area lessons. Point out the two broad categories of information sources: "In the text" and "In your head."

2. *Begin by assigning students several short passages from the textbook.* (These should be no more than two to five sentences in length.) Follow each reading with one question from each of the QAR categories on the chart. Then discuss the differences between a "right there" question and answer, a "think and search" question and answer, an "author and you" question and answer, and an "on your own" question and answer. Your explanations should be clear and complete. Reinforce the discussion by assigning several more short text passages and asking a question for each. Students will soon begin to catch on to the differences among the four QAR categories.

3. *Continue the second day by practicing with short passages.* Use one question for each QAR category per passage. First, give students a passage to read along with questions *and* answers *and* identified QARs. Why do the questions and answers represent one QAR and not another? Second, give students a passage along with questions and answers; this time, they have to identify the QAR for each. Finally, give students passages, decide together which strategy to use, and have them write their responses.

4. *Review briefly on the third day.* Then assign a longer passage (75 to 200 words) with up to six questions (at least one each from the four QAR categories). First, have students work in groups to decide the QAR category for each question and the answers for each. Next, assign a second passage, comparable in length, with five questions for students to work on individually. Discuss their responses either in small groups or with the whole class.

5. *Apply the QAR strategy to actual content area assignments.* For each question asked, students decide on the appropriate QAR strategy and write out their answers.

Once students are sensitive to the different information sources for different types of questions and know how to use these sources to respond to questions, variations can be made in the QAR strategy. For example, you might have students generate their own questions to text assignments—perhaps two for each QAR strategy. They then write down the answers to the questions as they understand them, except that they leave one question unanswered from the "think and search" category and one from the "on your own" or "author and you" category. These are questions about which the student would like to hear the views of others. During the discussion, students volunteer to ask their unanswered questions. The class is invited first to identify the question by QAR category and then to contribute answers, comments, or related questions about the material. Figure 7.1 shows how a physical education teacher applied the QAR strategy as she prepared her students to attempt to run a mile.

Figure 7.1 QAR—Physical Education

Diane, a physical education teacher, was preparing her sixth-grade students to attempt to run their first mile. She wanted to increase their understanding of the importance of being physically fit and to inspire those students who were less than enthusiastic about this upcoming assignment. As a before-reading activity, she gave the students a list of questions that related to the short story they were going to read. She asked the students to work in small groups, using the QAR categories, to predict where they thought the answer to each question would be found. Then the students read a short story that she had created titled *Out of Breath*:

Out of Breath

Sandy had just finished her mile run. Her heart was racing, sweat poured down her back, and she fought to catch her breath. She hated running and couldn't believe some people actually did this for fun. If it was up to her, no middle school kid would ever have to endure this torture again. That afternoon, after she got all cooled off and was back in class, her teacher announced that they would have a special speaker. A small woman walked in the room. She was wearing brightly colored clothes and a headband that shouted with bright pink. The teacher told them that Ms. Sally Lane was here to talk to them about her life. Ms. Lane was born with severe asthma. So much so that she couldn't take a fast walk, let alone run without wheezing and gasping for air. It seemed, she told the class, that she was in the hospital for an attack at least once a week. So for most of her childhood, she sat quietly and watched the other children play. Then in college, everything changed. She happened by a flier advertising a medical study taking place on campus. They were looking for people who suffered from asthma who might be willing to try a new, experimental treatment. Ms. Lane, who had tried everything, excitedly scribbled the number down and called as soon as she got home. She went to the first meeting and tried not to get her hopes up. A young man explained the procedures and told the small group about the potential harms. But all Ms. Lane heard was the potential to once and for all be done with asthma.

As it turns out, Ms. Lane was one of the lucky few who the treatment helped. She went an entire month without so much as a cough, so the next month she thought she would try to walk, and again—all month—no attack. She never even imagined running, but she was walking so fast at the end of the month that a slow jog wasn't really out of the question. The morning of her first run, she had to admit, breathing was tough, but she wasn't about to quit. Little by little she got faster and ran longer, and the running came easier. Before she knew it

(continued)

Figure 7.1 *(continued)*

she was running 5K and 10K races with ease. With her best friend she decided to set the ulti-mate goal: run a marathon in her hometown that would benefit asthma sufferers. She trained and worked hard and even suffered an attack, but she never gave up. She just kept running. By the time the marathon came around, she felt ready. She felt like she was flying as the start-ing gun sounded and she leaped into the crowd of runners. She was doing great until mile 10. Then she felt her old nemesis return. So she slowed down and took deep, careful breaths. She would not let it stop her. Even if she walked the rest of the way, she would finish the race. After walking for about a mile, she felt revived and ready to go, so she kicked up her legs and started to run. She finished the marathon with a time better than 56% of the other runners. That didn't matter as much to her as the fact that she worked through her fears and finished.

Sandy listened to her story and felt ashamed. Sure, the mile had been hard, but there was nothing keeping her from doing it. She felt inspired by Ms. Lane to do her best and work through any problems she might have. Nothing would ever get the best of her again.

After reading the short story, the students checked to see if their original predictions about where answers to questions would be found were correct. They recategorized the questions according to where they now believed the answers would be found and dis-cussed those answers together in preparation for their own attempt to run a mile. One group, for example, categorized the questions in the chart shown below:

In the Book	In My Head
Right There:	**Author and Me:**
What did Ms. Lane do when she thought she might have an asthma attack during the race?	How would you feel if you were Sandy?
	Where did Ms. Lane go for her treatment?
Why is running an important theme in this story?	
Think and Search:	**On my own:**
How do you know the treatment was effective?	Why did Sandy change?
	Describe the health issues Ms. Lane suffered.
What did Ms. Lane do when she thought she might have an asthma attack during the race?	

A second variation involves discussions of text. During question-and-answer ex-changes, preface a question by saying, "This question is *right there* in the text," or "You'll have to *think and search* the text to answer," or "You're *on your own* with this one," or "The answer is a combination of the *author and you.* Think about what the author tells us and what we already know to try and come up with a reasonable response." Make sure that you pause several seconds or more for "think time." Think time, or "wait time," is critical to responding to textually implicit and schema-based questions.

Once students are familiar with QARs, they can be used in combination with a vari-ety of interactive strategies that encourage readers to explore ideas through text discus-sions. Figure 7.2 shows how a high school English teacher applied a variation of the QAR strategy as she prepared her students to answer questions after reading Roald Dahl's *Lamb to the Slaughter.*

Questioning the Author (QtA)

Questioning the author (QtA) is a comprehension strategy that models for students the importance of asking questions while reading. Beck, McKeown, Hamilton, and Kucan (1997) devised the QtA strategy to demonstrate the kinds of questions students need to ask in order to think more deeply and construct meaning about segments of text as they read. Good readers act on the author's message. If what they are reading doesn't make sense to them, they generate questions about what the author says and means. When stu-dents struggle with text, however, they often do not have a clue about generating ques-tions, let alone interacting with the author of text.

Figure 7.2 QAR High School English

Jane, a high school English teacher, develops students' awareness of QARs using an excerpt from Roald Dahl's *Lamb to the Slaughter*. As a before-reading activity, she gave the students a list of questions that related to the excerpt they were going to read. Using the QAR categories, she asked the students to work in small groups to predict where they thought the answer to each question would be found. After reading, Jane asked her students to answer a set of questions about the excerpt and to identify the QAR associated with each question: *right there, think and search, on your own,* and *author and you.*

Lamb to the Slaughter

Mary Maloney is a devoted housewife. Mary is also six months pregnant. Her husband, Patrick Maloney, is a police detective who arrives home every evening at 5:00 p.m. and Mary has a drink waiting for him because she understands how tired he is. Mary is a doting wife and takes care of Patrick in an almost suffocating way!

As a rule, the couple eat out on Thursday evenings but on one particular Thursday night, Patrick does not want to go out. Instead, he tells Mary he has some disturbing news he needs to share with her. Patrick talks to Mary and at the end of his conversation he tells her that she will be looked after financially. Mary is bewildered and appears mad after she hears his news, but she still decides to cook him dinner and goes down to the basement freezer and gets a leg of lamb.

When Mary returns to the kitchen, she hits Patrick on the back of the head with the frozen lamb and he passes out and dies instantly. Mary is flustered but she decides to cover up the murder and puts the lamb in the oven to cook. While the lamb is cooking, she goes to the store and acts as if nothing has happened. Upon returning home, Mary finally calls the police in a tearful manner.

The police arrive to investigate, and Mary tells the police that when she arrived home from the store, she found her husband dead on the floor. She portrays a state of shock and to convince the police, the lamb is cooked so Mary pleads with the police to eat the lamb and offers that Patrick would have wanted them to have dinner. As Mary and the detectives eat the lamb, one detective states, "I bet the murder weapon is right here under our noses!" Mary listens and quietly chuckles to herself.

1. *Question:* Where did Mary go to get the leg of lamb?
   Answer: _____
   QAR: _____
2. *Question:* Why is Patrick offering to give Mary money?
   Answer: _____
   QAR: _____
3. *Question:* Why did Mary have the detectives eat the lamb?
   Answer: _____
   QAR: _____
4. *Question:* Why did Mary use the leg of lamb to hit Patrick instead of something else?
   Answer: _____
   QAR: _____
5. *Question:* Why did Mary kill Patrick?
   Answer: _____
   QAR: _____
6. *Question:* Why was Mary giggling at the end of the story?
   Answer: _____
   QAR: _____

The QtA strategy shows students how to read text closely as if the author were there to be challenged and questioned. QtA places value on the quality and depth of students' responses to the author's intent. It is important that students keep their minds active while reading as they engage in a dialogue with an author. Good readers monitor whether the author is making sense by asking questions such as, "What is the author trying to say here?" "What does the author mean?" "So what? What is the significance of the author's message?" "Does this make sense with what the author told us before?" "Does the author explain this clearly?" These questions are posed by the teacher to help students "take on" the author and understand that text material needs to be challenged.

Through QtA, students learn that authors are fallible and may not always express ideas in the easiest way for readers to understand. QtA builds metacognitive knowledge by making students aware of an important principle related to reading comprehension: *Not comprehending what the author is trying to say is not always the fault of the reader.* As a result, students come to view their roles as readers as "grappling with text" as they seek to make sense of the author's intent.

PLANNING A QTA LESSON   Planning QtA lessons for narrative or informational texts involves a three-stage process that requires the teacher to (1) identify major understandings and potential problems with a text prior to its use in class, (2) segment the text into logical stopping points for discussion, and (3) develop questions, or *queries*, that model and demonstrate how to "question the author." Box 7.1 examines the planning process.

When using QtA to comprehend stories, pose *narrative queries*. Through the use of narrative queries, students become familiar with an author's writing style as they strive to understand character, plot, and underlying story meaning. The following queries help students think about story characters: "How do things look for this character now?" "Given what the author has already told us about this character, what do you think the author is up to?" Understanding the story plot can be accomplished with queries such as these: "How has the author let you know that something has changed?" "How has the author settled this for us?"

Box 7.1 Evidence-Based Best Practices

Steps in a QtA Lesson

1. Analyze the text
   - *Identify major understandings and potential problems that students may encounter during reading.*
   - *Read the text closely and note the author's intent, the major ideas and themes, and any areas or potential obstacles in the material that could affect comprehension.*
   - *Reflect on your own comprehension as you read the text.* Note any passages that you reread or pause to think about, knowing that these sections will most likely be problematic for students.

2. Segment the text
   - *Determine where to stop the reading to initiate and develop discussion.* The text segments may not always fall at a page or paragraph break. You may want to stop reading after one sentence to ask a question.

3. Develop questions
   - *Plan questions that will help students respond to what the author says and means.* These generic questions prompt students' responses to the text and encourage them to dig deeper and make sense of what they are reading. The following question guide will help you frame initiating and follow-up questions at different points in the lesson. Initiating questions at the beginning of the reading draw students' attention to the author's intent, whereas follow-up queries focus the direction of the discussion and assist students

as they integrate and connect ideas. Follow-up questions help students determine why the author included certain ideas.

QtA Question Guide

Initial questions at the beginning of the lesson:

- What is the author trying to say?
- What is the author's message?
- What is the author talking about?

Follow-up questions during reading help students make connections and inferences about the text:

- This is what the author says, but what does it mean?
- How does this text segment connect with what the author has already said?

Follow-up questions during reading help students with difficulties and confusion with the way the author presents information:

- Does the author make sense here?
- Did the author explain this clearly?
- What's missing? What do we need to find out?

Follow-up questions during reading clarify misinterpretations or make students aware that they made an inference (reinforce QARs):

- Did the author tell us that?
- Did the author say that, or did you "think and search" to get the answer?

GUIDING THE QTA DISCUSSION Beck and colleagues (1997) recommend the use of a variety of "discussion moves" to guide students:

- *Marking:* Draw attention to certain ideas by either paraphrasing what a student said or by acknowledging its importance with statements such as "Good idea" or "That's an important observation."

- *Turning back:* Make students responsible for figuring out ideas and turning back to the text for clarification.

- *Revoicing:* Assist students as they express their ideas; filter the most important information and help students who are struggling to express their ideas by rephrasing their statements.

- *Modeling:* Think aloud about an issue that is particularly difficult to understand, one that students are unable to reach without assistance.

- *Annotating:* Provide information that is not in the text so that students can understand the concepts fully.

- *Recapping:* Summarize the main ideas as a signal to move on in the lesson. Recapping can be done by either the teacher or the students.

The thoughtful use of questions is vital for classroom discussion. As learners actively explore and clarify meaning, guide the discussion as you progress from one text segment to the next. Students can also be encouraged to formulate their own questions as they read a text in order to raise questions as they read, to monitor their comprehension, and to identify gaps that may exist in their expectations for the reading and the actual text. Following is one way to encourage students to ask questions as they read:

1. *Have students listen to or read a portion of the text from the beginning of a selection.*

2. *Ask students to write five to ten questions that they think will be answered by the remainder of the selection.*

3. *Discuss some of the questions asked by the students before reading. Write the questions on the board.*

4. *Have students read to determine whether the questions are answered.*

5. *After reading, ask the students to explain which questions were answered, which weren't, and why not.*

6. *Discuss with students the similarities and differences between their expectations of the reading and the actual text.*

MyLab Education **Self-Check 7.1**

MyLab Education **Application Exercise 7.1:**
Implementing a QtA in a Content Area Classroom

Instructional Strategies

7.2 Explain how each of the strategies guide comprehension as students interact with text, from before reading support to postreading reflection.

Strategies presented in this chapter teach students how to approach reading material with an inquisitive mind. Many of the instructional strategies presented here form a bridge between teacher-initiated guidance and independent learning behavior by students. When selecting strategies to use, first consider the content you plan to teach. Then consider implementing strategies that could best support your presentation of content area material as well as your students' active involvement in approaching your discipline like a professional—historian, mathematician, writer, and so on—who works in that discipline (Gillis, 2014).

In this section, we describe several instructional strategies that engage students in reading, guide their interactions with texts, and help them to clarify and extend meaning. The instructional strategies that follow include (1) *KWL*, which stands for What do you **K**now? What do you **W**ant to know? What did you **L**earn?; (2) *discussion webs*; (3) *guided reading procedure (GRP)*; (4) *intra-act*; and (5) *directed reading–thinking activity (DR–TA)*. Note the differences as well as the similarities of various instructional strategies emphasized in this section. Each can be adapted to serve different content area material. Think about the kinds of adaptations you will have to make with each instructional strategy to meet the needs of your content area. Box 7.2 examines adaptations you can make for English Learners (ELs).

Box 7.2 Supporting English Learners

Strategies presented in this chapter have been found to improve the content area reading skills of students while promoting higher levels of reading comprehension. English Learners (ELs) can also benefit from explicit instruction of the strategies presented along with additional supports to maximize the learning outcomes for students with limited English proficiency. Some additional supports can include:

- *Increased modeling of thinking:* Since ELs are simultaneously developing their reading and thinking skills, it is important that teachers working with ELs spend significant time modeling their thinking skills. Strategies such as think-alouds, reciprocal teaching, Question–Answer Relationships (QARs), and Questioning the Author (QtA) are important strategies to increase the reading comprehension skills of ELs. The use of these strategies in classrooms with ELs provides teachers with multiple modes where they can model their thinking while providing ELs with essential explicit instruction in effective thinking to increase comprehension.

- *Providing alternate texts:* Provide ELs with alternate texts to practice effective reading comprehension strategy use. Alternative texts can include text that is shorter in length or text with simple text structure (Peregoy & Boyle, 2013). Navigating a long piece of complex text can be a difficult task for students who are proficient in English and a monumental task for students working toward mastery of a new language. Providing ELs with a shorter, simply structured piece of text to practice specific reading comprehension skills allows ELs to focus on developing these strategies without the obstacle of a longer complex piece of text.

- *Increased discussion of strategy use:* Learning a new strategy along with a new language requires increased time for discussion (Fairbairn & Jones-Vo, 2010). ELs should be provided with extended time to discuss their understanding of reading comprehension strategies and the appropriate use of these strategies in order gain a high level of understanding that can develop into effective independent implementation of strategy use.

- *Provide time for practice with peers:* Providing time for students to discuss and practice reading comprehension strategies in small groups or with a peer allows ELs to practice their skills in a more comfortable environment. Often ELs are hesitant to share their thinking in a whole-class environment. Allotting time for students to share their thinking, to engage in discussions, and to practice developing reading comprehension skills in a smaller setting is crucial for EL's literacy development.

- *Provide students with visuals:* ELs benefit from the use of visuals along with strategy instruction (Herrell & Jordan, 2016). Visual images provide ELs with nonlinguistic representations of concepts that can increase ELs understanding and improve comprehension. Visual scaffolds can include photographs, drawings, maps, realia, and videos that promote vocabulary and concept understanding while increasing reading comprehension.

- *Use sentence frames:* Reading and the development of reading comprehension skills is a highly cognitive process often developed within the framework of class discussions. To assist ELs in becoming active participants of class discussions around strategy use, teachers can provide ELs with sentence frames (Gunning, 2019). Sentence frames provide ELs with a strong scaffold that they can use to craft and share their thinking. For example, teachers using the KWL strategy can provide ELs with sentence frames to use during instruction which can include:
  One thing I already knew about (the subject) was _____.
  One thing I would like to know about (the subject) is _____.
  One thing I learned about (the subject) was _____.

- *Using examples to increase understanding:* Introduce reading comprehension strategies through examples. When introducing reciprocal teaching, provide examples of appropriate questions, predictions, and summaries. When introducing Question–Answer Relationships (QARs), provide ELs with examples of questions for all four questions types. When introducing discussion webs, provide examples of completed graphic displays. ELs greatly benefit from being provided with concrete examples that they can use as a guide when in the process of mastering a new comprehension strategy.

- *Providing explicit vocabulary instruction:* Identify vocabulary words that may be difficult for ELs but are essential for strategy use. Provide explicit instruction to aid in the understanding of those vocabulary words. Providing ELs with simple definitions of vocabulary specific to each reading comprehension strategy supports successful use of new reading comprehension strategies. For example, teachers using the directed reading–thinking activity (DR–TA) with a short story or other narrative material would provide explicit vocabulary instruction of the words: setting, events, and plots.

The KWL Strategy

KWL is an instructional strategy that engages students in active text learning. The strategy begins with what students *know* about the topic to be studied, moves to what the students *want to know* as they generate questions about the topic, and leads to a record of what students *learn* as a result of their engagement in the strategy. Follow-up activities to KWL include discussion, the construction of graphic organizers, and summary writing to clarify and internalize what has been read.

KWL may be initiated with small groups of students or the whole class. When they develop confidence and competence with the KWL strategy, students may begin to use it for independent learning.

PROCEDURES FOR KWL   Here's how the KWL strategy works.

1. *Introduce the KWL strategy in conjunction with a new topic or text selection.* Before assigning a text, explain the strategy. Donna Ogle (1992, p. 271), the originator of KWL, suggests that dialogue begin with the teacher saying:

   > It is important to first find out what we think we know about this topic. Then we want to anticipate how an author is likely to present and organize the information. From this assignment we can generate good questions to focus on reading and study. Our level of knowledge will determine, to some extent, how we will study. Then, as we read we will make notes of questions that get answered and other new and important information we learn. During this process some new questions will probably occur to us; these we should also note so we can get clarification later.

   In the process of explaining KWL, be sure that students understand *what* their role involves and *why* it is important for learners to examine what they know and to ask questions about topics that they will be reading and studying.

   The next several steps allow you to model the KWL strategy with a group of learners or the entire class. Some students will find it difficult to complete the KWL strategy sheet on their own. Others will avoid taking risks or revealing what they know or don't know about a topic. Others simply won't be positively motivated. Modeling the KWL strategy reduces the initial risk and creates a willingness to engage in the process. Students who experience the modeling of the strategy quickly recognize its value as a learning tool.

2. *Identify what students think they know about the topic.* Engage the class in brainstorming, writing their ideas on the board or on an overhead transparency. Use the format of the KWL strategy sheet as you record students' ideas on the chalkboard or transparency. It's important to record everything that the students *think* they know about the topic, including their misconceptions. The key in this step is to get the class actively involved in making associations with the topic, not to evaluate the rightness or wrongness of the associations. Students will sometimes challenge one another's knowledge base. The teacher's role is to help learners recognize that differences exist in what they think they know. These differences can be used to help students frame questions.

3. *Generate a list of student questions.* Ask, "What do you want to know more about? What are you most interested in learning about?" As you write their questions on the whiteboard or SMART Board, recognize that you are again modeling for students what their role as learners should be: to ask questions about material to be studied.

   When you have completed modeling the brainstorming and question-generation phases of KWL, have the students use their own strategy sheets to make decisions about what they personally think they know and about what they want to know more about. Students, especially those who may be at risk in academic situations, may refer to the example you have modeled to decide what to record in the first two columns.

MyLab Education
Video Example 7.2
KWL and Vocabulary

Watch this video to hear Donna Ogle explain the connection between KWL and vocabulary learning.

4. *Anticipate the organization and structure of ideas that the author is likely to use in the text selection.* As part of preparation for reading, have students next use their knowledge and their questions to make predictions about the organization of the text. What major categories of information is the author likely to use to organize his or her ideas?

The teacher might ask, "How do you think the author of a text or article on _____ is likely to organize the information?" Have students focus on the ideas they have brainstormed and the questions they have raised to predict possible categories of information. As students make their predictions, record these on the board or transparency in the area suggested by the KWL strategy sheet. Then have students make individual choices on their own strategy sheets.

5. *Read the text selection to answer the questions.* As they engage in interactions with the text, the students write answers to their questions and make notes for new ideas and information in the L column of their strategy sheets. Again, the teacher's modeling is crucial to the success of this phase of KWL. Students may need a demonstration or two to understand how to record information in the L column.

Debrief students after they have read the text and have completed writing responses in the L column. First, invite them to share answers, recording these for the group to see. Then ask, "What new ideas did you come across that you didn't think you would find in the text?" Record and discuss the responses.

6. *Engage students in follow-up activities to clarify and extend learning.* Use KWL as a springboard into postreading activities to internalize student learning. Activities may include the construction of graphic organizers to clarify and retain ideas encountered during reading or the development of written summaries.

KWL EXAMPLES In Christa's U.S. history class, students were beginning a study of the Vietnam War. Christa realized that her students would have little, if any, prior knowledge of and attitudes toward the Vietnam War, even though it's still part of our national consciousness. The students, in fact, were acutely aware of the war from recent popular movies and also from relatives who had participated in it.

However, Christa realized that although students might know something about the Vietnam War, they probably had little opportunity to study it from the perspective of historians. This, then, was Christa's objective as a teacher of history: to help students approach the study of the Vietnam War—and understand the social, economic, and political forces surrounding it—from a historian's perspective.

Therefore, Christa believed that the KWL strategy would be an appropriate way to begin the unit. She believed that it would help students get in touch with what they knew (and didn't know) about the Vietnam War and raise questions that would guide their interactions with the materials they would be studying.

Christa began KWL knowing that her students were familiar with its procedures, having participated in the strategy on several previous occasions in the class. Following the six steps, the class as a whole participated in brainstorming what students knew about the war and what they wanted to know. Christa recorded their ideas and questions on an overhead transparency and encouraged students' participation by asking such questions as, "What else do you know? Who knows someone who was in the war? What did he or she say about it? Who has read about the Vietnam War or seen a movie about it? What did you learn?"

As ideas and questions were recorded on the transparency, Christa asked the students to study the K column to anticipate categories of information that they might study in their textbook and other information sources that they would be using: "Do some of these ideas fit together to form major categories we might be studying?" She also asked the students to think about other wars they had studied—World Wars I and II, the U.S. Civil War, and the American Revolution: "When we study wars, are there underlying categories of information on which historians tend to focus?"

On completion of the whole-class activity, Christa invited her students to complete their strategy sheets, recording what they knew, what they wanted to find out more about, and what categories of information they expected to use.

Then, for homework, she assigned several sections from a textbook covering the Vietnam War and asked students to work on the L column on their own. Figure 7.3 shows how one student, Clayton, completed his strategy sheet.

As part of the next day's class, Christa asked the students to work in groups of four to share what they had found out about the war. They focused on the questions they had raised as well as on new ideas they had not anticipated. When the groups completed their work, Christa brought the class together. She directed students to open their learning logs and write a summary of what they had learned from participating in KWL. Students used the L column on their strategy sheets to compose the summary. Clayton's summary is shown in Figure 7.4.

In Christa's class, the learning logs serve as history notebooks in which students can record what they are learning using a variety of writing-to-learn activities. (We explain learning logs and their uses more fully in Chapter 11.)

A high school math teacher adapted the KWL strategy to support his students' study of the Fibonacci numbers. Fibonacci numbers (a famous sequence of numbers that have been shown to occur in nature) are the direct result of a problem posed by a 13th-century mathematician, Leonardo of Pisa, on the regeneration of rabbits. The teacher used a math text from an enrichment unit to clarify and extend students' understanding of the Fibonacci numbers. The text selection, "Mathematics in Nature," illustrates the properties of the Fibonacci numbers and requires students to determine the relationships between these numbers and various phenomena in nature—for example, the leaves on a plant, the bracts on a pinecone, the curves on a seashell, or the spirals on a pineapple.

MyLab Education
Video Example 7.3
Using K-W-L in 8th Grade Math
Watch this video to see how one teacher used KWL in an eighth-grade mathematics class.

Figure 7.3 Clayton's KWL Strategy Sheet on the Vietnam War

K—What I Know	**W**—What I Want to Know	**L**—What I Learned and Still Need to Learn
U.S. lost war protest marches and riots movies made in 1960s jungle fighting POWs guerrilla fighting North and South fighting each other U.S. soldiers suffered the wall in Washington	Why did we go to war? Why did we lose? How many soldiers died? Who helped us? Who was president during war? On whose side were we?	Gulf of Tonkin Resolution made it legal for war but was not legally declared French helped U.S. Nixon withdrew troops because of fighting at home Lottery used to draft soldiers Antiwar movement at home 55,000 Americans died plus thousands of innocent people Kennedy, Johnson, and Nixon were the presidents Fought war to stop communism

Categories of Information I Expect to Use

A. cause
B. results
C. U.S. involvement
D. type of fighting
E.
F.
G.

Figure 7.4 Clayton's Summary in His Learning Log

We fought the Vietnam War to stop communism. The U.S. Congress passed the Gulf of Tonkin Resolution, which said it was OK to go to war there, but the war was never declared a war — it was only called a conflict. The French and South Vietnamese people helped us, but it didn't matter. 55,000 Americans died fighting. People protested in the United States. Nixon withdrew the troops because of pressure to end the war at home.

Before initiating the KWL strategy, the teacher used three props (a toy rabbit, a plant, and a pineapple) to arouse students' curiosity and to trigger their responses to the question, "What do these items have to do with mathematics?" After some exploratory talk, he then asked students, "What do you know about mathematics and nature?" The strategy sheet in Figure 7.5 illustrates the reader–text interactions that occurred as the teacher guided students through the steps in KWL.

KWL can also be adapted to include other relevant categories. KWHL—what I know, what I want to know, how I can find the information I need, and what I learned—is one common variation to the original KWL strategy. Figure 7.6 shows an application of KWHL in a health class.

The teacher used this strategy to activate students' prior knowledge about different types of macromolecules and to introduce them to some of the basic vocabulary associated with this topic. While the standard course textbook was the starting point for research to complete the KWHL chart, students were encouraged to consider other sources that they might use to help them learn more about this topic.

Figure 7.5 A KWL Strategy Sheet in a Math Class

K—What I Know	**W**—What I Want to Know	**L**—What I Learned and Still Need to Learn
planetary motion spirals 4 seasons landscaping geometric designs multiplying populations phases of the moon	What does a pineapple have to do with math? How are growth patterns in plants related to math? How is mathematics specifically related to nature? Where do bees fit?	Pineapples have hexagons on the surface that are arranged in sets of spirals. These spirals are related to Fibonacci numbers. Fibonacci numbers are found in leaf arrangements on plants. The rate that bees regenerate males is related to Fibonacci numbers. Who is this Fibonacci guy? What's the big deal about the "golden ratio"?

Categories of Information
I Expect to Use
A. Animals
B. Plants
C. Solar System
D. Laws of Nature
E.
F.
G.

Figure 7.6 A KWHL Strategy Sheet in a Health Education Class

Macromolecule	What do we **know**?	What do we want to find out?	How we find out what we want to learn?	What did we learn?
Proteins	• something you can eat • part of the body	• what this has to do with health	• textbook • Internet • health magazine	• proteins are made up of amino acids
Lipids				
Polysaccharides				
Nucleic acids				

Discussion Webs

Discussion webs encourage students to engage the text and each other in thoughtful discussion by creating a framework for them to explore texts and consider different sides of an issue in discussion before drawing conclusions. Donna Alvermann (1991) recommends discussion webs as an alternative to teacher-dominated discussions.

The strategy uses cooperative learning principles that follow a think–pair–share discussion cycle (McTighe & Lyman, 1988). The discussion cycle begins with students first thinking about the ideas they want to contribute to the discussion based on their interactions with the text. Then they meet in pairs to discuss their ideas with a partner. Partners then team with a different set of partners to resolve differences in perspective and to work toward a consensus about the issue under discussion. In the final phase of the discussion cycle, the two sets of partners, working as a foursome, select a spokesperson to share their ideas with the entire class.

The discussion web strategy uses a graphic display to scaffold students' thinking about the ideas they want to contribute to the discussion based on what they have read. The graphic display takes the shape of a web. In the center of the web is a question that is central to the reading. The question is posed in such a way that it reflects more than one point of view. Students explore the pros and cons of the question in the No and Yes columns of the web—first in pairs and then in groups of four. The main goal of the four-member teams is to draw a conclusion based on their discussion of the web.

PROCEDURES FOR THE DISCUSSION WEB   Alvermann (1991) suggests an integrated lesson structure for the discussion web strategy that includes the following steps:

1. *Prepare your students for reading by activating prior knowledge, raising questions, and making predictions about the text.*

2. *Assign students to read the selection and then introduce the discussion web by having the students work in pairs to generate pro and con responses to the question.* The partners work on the same discussion web and take turns jotting down their reasons in the Yes and No columns. Students may use key words and phrases to express their ideas and need not fill all of the lines. They should try to list an equal number of pro and con reasons on the web.

3. *Combine partners into groups of four to compare responses, work toward consensus, and reach a conclusion as a group.* Explain to your students that it is OK to disagree with other members of the group, but they should all try to keep an open mind as they listen to others during the discussion. Dissenting views may be aired during the whole-class discussion.

4. *Give each group 3 minutes to decide which of all the reasons given best supports the group's conclusion.* Each group selects a spokesperson to report to the whole class.

Figure 7.7 Discussion Web for *A Skin I'm In*

YES	Question	NO
Char and the others made fun of her for doing schoolwork	Should Maleeka have entered the writing context?	Maleeka is good at writing
Miss Saunders will think she won		Writing is something she shares with her father
Her boyfriend might not like her if she's smart	**Conclusion**	She can be someone else when she's writing
She's not sure that she will win the contest	Maleeka should have entered the contest because it shows what a good writer she is	She could win the prize
She doesn't want anyone to know what she has been writing about		Maleeka can do something she enjoys (writing)

5. *Have your students follow up the whole-class discussion by individually writing their responses to the discussion web question.* Display the students' responses to the question in a prominent place in the room so that they can be read by others.

The level of participation in discussion web lessons is usually high. The strategy encourages students' individual interpretations of what they are reading and also allows them to formulate and refine their own interpretations of a text in light of the points of view of others. As a result, students are eager to hear how other groups reached a consensus and drew conclusions during whole-class sharing. The strategy works well with informational or narrative texts and can be adapted to the goals and purposes of most content area subjects.

DISCUSSION WEB EXAMPLES English Language Arts (ELA) teachers use discussion webs as a comprehension strategy to engage students in critical thinking by having students analyze different sides of an issue before drawing a final conclusion. Study the discussion web in Figure 7.7 that an ELA middle grades teacher created for his class after his students read Sharon Flake's *The Skin I'm In,* winner of the 1999 Coretta Scott King – John Steptoe Award for New Talent. The book tells the story of Maleeka, a seventh grader in an inner-city school, who is torn between winning the approval of street-smart peers and pursuing her own academic capabilities. In this illustration, the question posed in the discussion web, "Should Maleeka have entered the writing contest?," invites students to consider the dilemma Maleeka faces as she works to resolve these conflicts.

Mathematics teachers might use the discussion web to help students consider relevant and irrelevant information in word problems. Study the discussion web in Figure 7.8 that a mathematics teacher created for his class. Note the adaptations he made to the traditional discussion web. In this illustration, the students worked in pairs to distinguish relevant and irrelevant information in the word problem. They also considered prior knowledge that was needed to solve the problem. When they had completed the discussion web, students then formed groups of four to solve the problem.

A dance teacher used the discussion web strategy as a tool to collaboratively assess students' efforts at choreography. Each group's members performed their original dance as their classmates observed. After all the groups had performed, the teacher created a discussion web, pictured in Figure 7.9, on the whiteboard. The central question for this discussion web was, "Did the group's choreography fit the concept the group intended to showcase?" The discussion web invited "yes" statements that explained choreographic elements that supported the group's intended concept as well as "no" statements that offered suggestions for improving the dance. Following each discussion, groups were encouraged to use the feedback they had received from the discussion web to revise their original routine.

Figure 7.8 Discussion Web for a Mathematics Word Problem

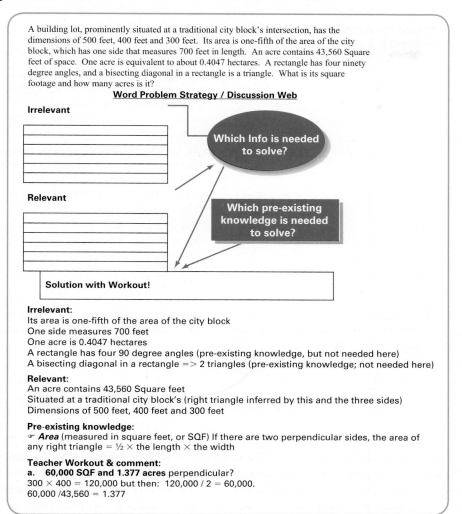

A building lot, prominently situated at a traditional city block's intersection, has the dimensions of 500 feet, 400 feet and 300 feet. Its area is one-fifth of the area of the city block, which has one side that measures 700 feet in length. An acre contains 43,560 Square feet of space. One acre is equivalent to about 0.4047 hectares. A rectangle has four ninety degree angles, and a bisecting diagonal in a rectangle is a triangle. What is its square footage and how many acres is it?

Word Problem Strategy / Discussion Web

Irrelevant

Which Info is needed to solve?

Relevant

Which pre-existing knowledge is needed to solve?

Solution with Workout!

Irrelevant:
Its area is one-fifth of the area of the city block
One side measures 700 feet
One acre is 0.4047 hectares
A rectangle has four 90 degree angles (pre-existing knowledge, but not needed here)
A bisecting diagonal in a rectangle => 2 triangles (pre-existing knowledge; not needed here)

Relevant:
An acre contains 43,560 Square feet
Situated at a traditional city block's (right triangle inferred by this and the three sides)
Dimensions of 500 feet, 400 feet and 300 feet

Pre-existing knowledge:
☞ **Area** (measured in square feet, or SQF) If there are two perpendicular sides, the area of any right triangle = ½ × the length × the width

Teacher Workout & comment:
a.   **60,000 SQF and 1.377 acres** perpendicular?
$300 \times 400 = 120,000$ but then: $120,000 / 2 = 60,000$.
$60,000 / 43,560 = 1.377$

Figure 7.9 Discussion Web for a Dance Class

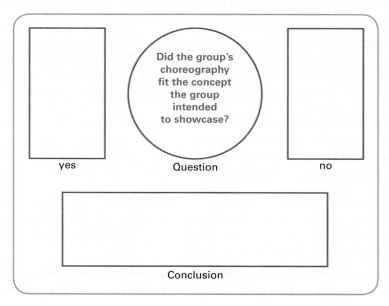

Did the group's choreography fit the concept the group intended to showcase?

yes   Question   no

Conclusion

Figure 7.10 Discussion Web for a Social Studies Class

YES	Should President Truman have dropped the atomic bomb on Japan?	NO
Too many innocent lives would be lost.		It was estimated that the proposed Operation Olympic would have cost as many Japanese casualties as the dropping of the bomb would have caused as well as many more American casualties in the Pacific Theater.
The cities of Hiroshima and Nagasaki could have been lost forever.		With the willingness of the Japanese to use mass suicide in the form of kamikaze pilots on Okinawa and people jumping to their death in Saipan, it was clear that extreme measures were needed to end the war.
Almost 60 cities had been destroyed already in Japan as a result of the war; they might have surrendered in time if we could just have been patient.		Firebombing had already killed 100,000 people in Tokyo, and Imperial Japan still showed no sign of surrender. An atomic bomb may have been the only way of getting the Japanese to surrender.
The only reason we really wanted to drop the bomb was because we wanted to justify spending about $2 billion on its development.	**Conclusion** Dropping the atomic bomb on Hiroshima and Nagasaki was the lesser of two evils for the United States as well as for Japan. No American lives were lost during the dropping of the bombs, and fewer Japanese lives were lost than would have been lost in Operation Olympic. The dropping of the bomb also protected America's political interests.	The bomb halted the war so quickly, which impressed the Soviet Union so much that it didn't request joint occupation of Japan.

Social studies teachers might use a discussion web to help students consider different perspectives on an issue or event. The discussion web in Figure 7.10 asked students to consider whether President Truman's decision to drop the atomic bomb on Japan in an effort to end World War II was correct. Working in small groups of four to five, students deliberated that decision from political, ethical, and strategic perspectives. The discussion web illustrates some of the main points that they considered when trying to achieve consensus on the question posed to them.

Guided Reading Procedure (GRP)

The **guided reading procedure (GRP)** emphasizes close reading (Manzo, 1975; Manzo, Manzo, & Thomas, 2009). It requires that students gather information and organize it around important ideas, and it places a premium on accuracy as students reconstruct the author's message. With a strong factual base, students will work from a common and clear frame of reference. They will then be in a position to elaborate thoughtfully on the text and its implications.

PROCEDURES FOR GRP Here's how the GRP works.

1. *Prepare students for reading.* Clarify key concepts; determine what students know and don't know about the particular content to be studied; build appropriate background; and give direction to reading.

2. *Assign a reading selection.* Assign 500 to 900 words in the middle grades (approximately five to seven minutes of silent reading); 1,000 to 2,000 words for high school (approximately ten minutes). Provide general purpose to direct reading behavior. For example, "Read to remember all you can."

3. *As students finish reading, have them turn their books facedown.* Ask them to tell what they remember. Record it on the board in the fashion in which it is remembered.

4. *Help students recognize that there is much that they have not remembered or have represented incorrectly.* Simply, there are implicit inconsistencies that need correction and further information to be considered.

5. *Redirect students to their books and review the selection to correct inconsistencies and add further information.*

6. *Organize recorded remembrances into some kind of an outline.* Ask guiding, nonspecific questions: "What were the important ideas in the assigned reading? Which came first? What facts on the board support it? What important point was brought up next? What details followed?"

7. *Extend questioning to stimulate an analysis of the material and a synthesis of the ideas with previous learning.*

8. *Provide immediate feedback, such as a short quiz, as a reinforcement of short-term memory.*

A GRP EXAMPLE   Eighth graders were assigned a reading selection from the music education magazine *Pipeline*. The selection, "Percussion—Solid as Rock," concerns the development and uses of percussion instruments from ancient to modern times.

The teacher introduced the selection by giving some background. She then began a guided discussion by asking students to remember as much as they could as they read the assignment silently. The teacher recorded the collective memories of her students on a whiteboard so that they could be seen by the group. Then she asked, "Did you leave out any information that might be important?" Students were directed to review the selection to determine whether essential information was missing from the list on the screen. The teacher also asked, "Did you mix up some of the facts on the list? Did you misrepresent any of the information in the author's message?"

These questions are extremely important to the overall GRP process. The first question—"Did you leave out any information that might be important?"—encourages a review of the material. Students sense that some facts are more important than others. Further questioning at this point will help them distinguish essential from nonessential information. The second question—"Did you mix up some of the facts on the list?"—reinforces the importance of selective rereading and rehearsal because of the limitations imposed by short-term memory.

Next, the teacher asked the class to study the information recorded on the whiteboard. The teacher directed the students to form pairs and then assigned the following task: "Which facts on the whiteboard can be grouped together? Organize the information around the important ideas in the selection. You have five minutes to complete the task."

Once students completed the task, the teacher encouraged them to share their work in whole-group discussion. Their groupings of facts were compared, refined, and extended. The teacher served as a facilitator, keeping the discussion moving, asking clarifying questions, and provoking thought. She then initiated the next task: "Let's organize the important ideas and related information. Let's make a map." Figure 7.11 shows what the students produced.

Outlining the mass of information will make students aware of the text relationships developed by the author. In Chapter 10, we explore several outlining procedures, such as **semantic mapping**, which help students produce the author's main ideas in relation to one another. Producing the author's organizational structure leads to more efficient recall at a later time and lays the groundwork for interpreting and applying the author's message. Once this common framework is developed, your questioning should lead to more divergent and abstract responding by the students.

In the example above, the discussion "took off" after the outline was completed. The teacher asked several reflective questions that helped students associate their previous experiences and beliefs about drumming to the content under discussion. Cognitive performance centered on evaluation and application as students linked what they knew to what they were studying.

Figure 7.11 Semantic Map of "Percussion—Solid as Rock"

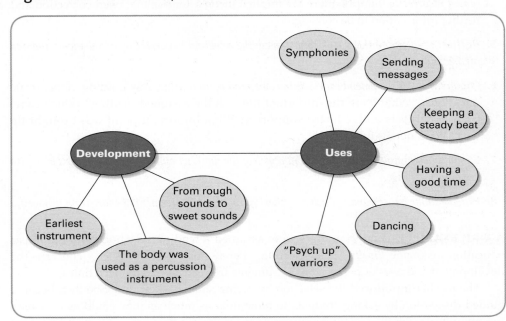

The final suggested step in the GRP is a short quiz, mainly to demonstrate in a dramatic way how successful the students can be with the reading material. The quiz should be viewed as positive reinforcement, not an interrogation check. Most of the students in this class earned perfect or near-perfect scores on the quiz—and this is as it should be. In Box 7.3, Rebecca, a middle school reading specialist, explains how she used the GRP with a group of students who were reading below grade level.

Box 7.3 Voices from the Field

Rebecca, Middle School Reading Specialist

Challenge

As a reading specialist, I work with variety of grade levels in small-group settings. Oftentimes, finding appropriate reading comprehension strategies to use with my students can be challenging. Most of the students I serve are below grade level in reading. Choosing texts to grab and sustain attention is difficult with the sixth-grade students in my reading group, all males reading at least one year below grade level. I knew it was essential to model how to read, think, and learn with texts as described in the guiding reading procedure. After several attempts at selecting books and passages for the students to read, I decided to arrange conferences to discuss their perspectives of reading. I often heard them make comments such as "I'm not a good reader" or "I hate reading." I also suspected an overall theme of low self-esteem within the group. I needed to find a text that interested the students and then select a strategy that would help to make the text comprehensible. In thinking about genres, I assumed that the students would enjoy fiction and mysteries; however, these types of texts did not come up in my conversations with them at all! Most described enjoyment in reading about a

variety of nonfiction topics such as sports, weather, animals, and even current events. Where I found the biggest interests, however, was through the conversations I heard the boys having among themselves. They seemed excited discussing a poster in a sixth-grade classroom of comic book heroes. Their enthusiasm convinced me to choose Sandler's (2013) *How a Comic Book Is Made*. I finally found the hook I needed!

Strategy

In the interest of increasing comprehension skills, the guided reading procedure was a perfect fit for the text and the students. The GRP requires students to collect information and organize it around significant points in the reading. We started with a discussion to generate background knowledge using questions such as: Who is your favorite comic book hero? Describe his or her powers and abilities. How do you access comics: Online? Hard copy of books? TV?

The text was laid out in a sequential manner, which was convenient for this strategy. We started by reading about the "idea" behind a comic. On the first day, after reading a short section aloud, students turned their books over and we talked about the major points in this segment. We used journals to do a "quick write," and we discussed details that were missed. We continued in this manner, going through the process and steps of creating a comic. We discussed the key people involved, such as the penciler, the inker, the editor, the letterer, and the actual author who writes the story. On the second day, after completing the reading, students were asked to review their journal entries and to revise their original responses. I gave them choices for arranging information, such as a timeline, chart, or summary. On the third day, partners read one another's writing to suggest details and provide feedback. I used the last day for a quick assessment, having students create a short four-panel comic with illustrations and writing. Students enjoyed adding speech bubbles and text with selected heroes such as "Captain Spark," "Flyboy," and "Thunderman." They worked with a partner to share ideas and then independently completed their own cartoon. This strategy allowed students time to close read and to discuss, write, reflect, and revisit text to support their comprehension of it. The students showed enthusiasm that I hadn't seen in a while with reading!

Reflection

The use of the GRP with my small group of struggling readers was a success. The strategy allowed the students to apply skills, such as collaborating, reflecting, analyzing, listening, and speaking, aligned with the Common Core. Their written product reflected their comprehension of the text. A key difference between this reading strategy and others that are similar such as a KWL chart and RCRR (read, cover, remember, retell) is that the GRP allows for the teacher to interject questions and responses to students' writing throughout the lesson. While the strategy itself is teacher guided, the students have multiple opportunities to work collaboratively and independently. When reaching struggling readers, I think text choice is just as critical as strategy selection. The GRP allows a time for students to talk about their reading and ask questions. I shared this strategy with my team of reading teachers so the GRP can be incorporated into our literacy routine.

Intra-Act

Intra-act lays the groundwork for reflective discussion. Pivotal to the intra-act strategy is the notion that students engage in a process of valuing as they reflect on what they have read. Hoffman (1979) suggests intra-act to provide readers with the opportunity to read critically by engaging in a process of valuing. The valuing process allows students to respond actively to a text selection with thought and feeling.

The intra-act procedure can be used with a variety of reading materials: content area text assignments, historical documents, newspaper and magazine articles, narratives, and poetic material. The procedure requires the use of small groups whose members are asked to react to value statements based on the content of the text selection.

PROCEDURES FOR INTRA-ACT   There are four phases in the intra-act procedure.

1. *Comprehension.* The comprehension phase promotes an understanding of the reading material to be learned. To begin this phase, the teacher follows effective prereading procedures by introducing the text reading, activating and building prior knowledge for the ideas to be encountered during reading, and inviting students to make predictions and speculate on the nature of the content to be learned. Building a frame of reference for upcoming text information is crucial to the overall success of the intra-act procedure.

2. Before inviting students to read the selection individually, the teacher forms small groups—intra-act teams—of four to six members. The teacher assigns a student from each group to serve as the team leader. The comprehension phase depends on the team leader's ability to initiate and sustain a discussion of the text. The team leader's responsibility is to lead a discussion by first summarizing what was read. The group members may contribute additional information about the selection or ask questions that seek clarification of the main ideas of the selection. The comprehension phase of the group discussion should be limited to seven to 10 minutes.

3. *Relating.* The team leader is next responsible for shifting the discussion from the important ideas in the selection to the group's personal reactions and values related to the topic. Many times, this shift occurs naturally. However, if this is not the case, members should be encouraged by the team leader to contribute their own impressions and opinions. Discussion should again be limited to seven to 10 minutes.

4. *Valuation.* Once group members have shared their personal reactions to the material, they are ready to participate in the valuation phase of the discussion. The teacher or team leader for each group distributes a game sheet. This game sheet contains a valuing exercise—a set of four declarative statements based on the selection's content. These value statements reflect opinions about the text selection and draw insights and fresh ideas from it. The purpose of the valuing exercise is to have students come to grips with what the material means to them by either agreeing (A) or disagreeing (D) with each statement. Figure 7.12 shows such a game sheet.

5. *Reflection.* The reflection phase of intra-act begins by scoring the game sheet. Group members take turns revealing how each responded to the four statements. As each member tells how he or she responded, the other members check whether their predictions agreed with that member's actual responses. During this phase, the teacher acts as a facilitator, noting how students responded but refraining from imposing a point of view on students. Instead, encourage students to reflect on what they have learned by discussing, supporting, and challenging one another's responses to intra-act statements.

Intra-act will require several classroom applications before students become accustomed to their roles during discussion. Repeated and extensive participation in intra-act will help students become fully aware of the task demands of the procedure. In the beginning, we recommend that on completion of an intra-act discussion, students engage in a whole-class discussion of the process in which they participated. Help students debrief: "What did we learn from our participation in intra-act? Why must all members of a group participate? How might discussion improve the next time we use intra-act?" Questions such as these make students sensitive to the purpose of the intra-act procedure (problem solving) and the role of each reader (critical analysis).

AN INTRA-ACT EXAMPLE   After students in a contemporary issues class read Lewin's (2008) article "Teenagers' Internet Socializing: Not a Bad Thing," four students, Jose, Adrian, Jordan, and Emily, met as a group to discuss their thoughts and impressions of the text. Jose, the group's team leader, began with a summary of the article and then gave his reactions. Jose stated, "The article suggested that time spent on the Internet is not as bad as some may believe. The Internet provides teens with technology and literacy skills needed in the 21st century."

Figure 7.12 Intra-Act Example

> **Teens and Technology: Is Internet Socializing a Bad Thing?**
>
> Name: _____
> Date: _____
> Total Score: _____
> Percentage of Correct Predictions: _____
>
> | | Jose | Adrian | Jordan | Emily |
> |---|---|---|---|---|
> | 1. The use of social websites is a waste of time. | A | A | A | A |
> | | D | D | D | D |
> | 2. Participation in social networking websites gives kids valuable skills, such as collaboration. | A | A | A | A |
> | | D | D | D | D |
> | 3. Participation in social networking websites develops kids' technical skills, like creating a webpage. | A | A | A | A |
> | | D | D | D | D |
> | 4. Social networking can be dangerous. | A | A | A | A |
> | | D | D | D | D |
> | 5. Through the use of social networking websites, students can learn from their peers. | A | A | A | A |
> | | D | D | D | D |

After some discussion about the key points of the article, the team leader shifted the conversation to elicit personal reactions and responses of the group in the relating phase. Jordan reacted to the article by stating, "I think technology is part of our world and we must embrace it. There are many different purposes and benefits of using social media. I use the Internet not only to communicate with my friends in a social way but also to study for tests, do research, and share ideas."

Adrian replied, "I agree that the Internet, if used appropriately, is a useful tool. We just need to inform our parents because they do not have as much experience and ongoing use with it. I've never talked with strangers online, only my friends; but my parents think that is a major problem with Internet use."

Emily joined the conversation by adding that she thought too much time spent on the Internet instead of face-to-face interaction reduced personal connections with others and negatively affected social skills.

When time for discussion was over, the valuation phase was initiated. Students were given a game sheet with these five value statements:

1. The use of social networking websites is a waste of time.

2. Participation in social networking websites gives kids valuable skills, such as collaboration.

3. Participation in social networking websites develops kids' technical skills, like creating a webpage.

4. Social networking can be dangerous.

5. Using social networking websites, students can learn from their peers.

Each student was asked to respond individually to the statements and then predict whether the other members of the group would agree or disagree with each statement. Each student completed his or her own intra-act game sheet. From the discussion, Jose was confident that Adrian would not agree with the first statement because she said that "I agree that the Internet, if used appropriately, is a useful tool." Similarly, he thought that Emily would agree because she thought too much time on the Internet could be problematic. He was also pretty sure that Jordan would disagree because he valued the role of technology in today's society. Jose used similar reasons to predict the group members' reactions to other statements.

As part of the reflection phase of intra-act, the group members shared what they learned. Jose found out that most of his predictions were accurate. He was surprised to find out that Adrian agreed somewhat with Statement 1, but she explained that "it's not always a waste of time, but when people use it to talk about other people and bully people on social networks, I think it is a waste of time and can have negative consequences." Others agreed with Adrian but thought that the use of the Internet did more good than harm. The debate was typical of the discussion that went on in all the groups as students worked out the ways in which ideas presented in the text fit in with their own attitudes and beliefs.

Social studies teachers might use the intra-act procedure to help students consider different perspectives on an issue or event from history. Study the intra-act in Figure 7.13 that an eighth-grade social studies teacher created for his class studying World War I while preparing to read the poems "The Call" by Jessie Pope and "Suicide in the Trenches" by Siegfried Sassoon. Before reading, students worked in small discussion groups to complete the intra-act chart; and after reading the poems, each group met again to reassess members' responses in light of the information in the poems. The intra-act chart illustrates some of the main points about human conflict in a time of war that the students considered when trying to achieve consensus on the questions posed to them.

Figure 7.13 Intra-Act Example

The Reality of War

Name: _____

Date: _____

Total Score: _____

Percentage of Correct Predictions: _____

Serving in World War I could have raised your social status.	A D	A D	A D	A D
Life in the trenches turned boys into men.	A D	A D	A D	A D
The speaker in "Suicide in the Trenches" is angry with civilians who did not serve in the war.	A D	A D	A D	A D
"The Call" more accurately depicts how World War I was for a solider.	A D	A D	A D	A D
"Suicide in the Trenches" is a tribute to parading soldiers at the end of war.	A D	A D	A D	A D

Directed Reading–Thinking Activity (DR–TA)

The **DR–TA** fosters critical awareness and thinking by engaging learners in a process that involves prediction, verification, interpretation, and judgment. Much like the QtA, the teacher guides the reading and stimulates thinking through the frequent use of open-ended questions such as "What do you think?" "Why do you think so?" "Can you prove it?" The learning environment for a DR–TA lesson is critical to its success as an instructional practice. The teacher must be supportive and encouraging so as not to inhibit students' participation in the activity. As a rule, avoid inhibiting participation by refuting students' predictions; encourage students to think divergently, using information that is stated or implied in the text to substantiate their predications or interpretations. Wait time is also important. When posing an open-ended question, it is not unusual to pause for 2, 3, 5, or even 10 seconds for students to respond. Too often, the tendency is to slice the original question into smaller parts. Sometimes a teacher starts slicing too quickly out of a sense of frustration or anxiety rather than because of students' inability to respond. Silence may very well be an indication that hypothesis formation or other cognitive activities are taking place in the students' heads. So wait—and see what happens.

To prepare for a DR–TA with an informational text, analyze the material for its superordinate and subordinate concepts. What are the relevant concepts, ideas, relationships, and information in the material? The content analysis will help you decide on logical stopping points as you direct students through the reading.

Figure 7.14 Potential Stopping Points in a DR–TA for a Story Line with One Episode

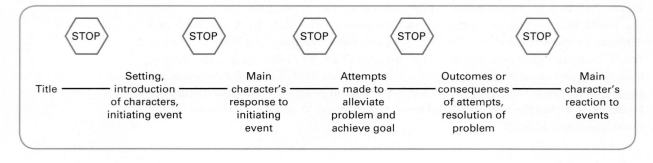

For short stories and other narrative material, determine the key elements of the story: the *setting* (time and place, major characters) and the *events in the plot* (the initiating events or problem-generating situation, the protagonist's reaction to the event and his or her goal to resolve the problem, the set of attempts to achieve the goal, outcomes related to the protagonist's attempts to achieve the goal and resolve the problem, the character's reaction).

Once these elements have been identified, the teacher has a framework for deciding on logical stopping points within the story. In Figure 7.14, we indicate a general plan that may be followed or adapted for specific story lines. Notice that the suggested stopping points come at key junctures in a causal chain of events in the story line. Each juncture suggests a logical stopping point in that it assumes that the reader has enough information from at least one preceding event to predict a future happening or event.

Figure 7.15 Excerpt of a DR–TA Transcript from a Biology Lesson on Plant Reproduction

Teacher–Student Interactions	Analysis of Lesson
I'D LIKE FOR YOU TO BEGIN BY SCANNING THE HEADINGS, SUBHEADINGS, PHOTOS, AND CAPTIONS IN THIS SECTION. THEN TELL ME WHAT YOU EXPECT TO FIND IN THIS SECTION. YOU KNOW IT IS ABOUT PLANT REPRODUCTION. WHAT ELSE DO YOU EXPECT TO LEARN?	The teacher directs students to preview a section of text about plant reproduction to activate prior knowledge and set a reading purpose.
S: It happens by bees.	The student's response is based on prior knowledge that she judges to be relevant.
WHY DO YOU SAY BEES?	The teacher encourages the student to elaborate on her response.
S: Well, I think because I know bees go from flower to flower.	The teacher probes the student for a more detailed response.
WHAT HAPPENS WHEN BEES GO FROM FLOWER TO FLOWER?	The teacher again scaffolds the student's response through questioning.
S: They get nectar from the flowers.	The teacher encourages other students to participate by asking them to analyze the student's hypothesis.
HOW DOES THAT HELP WITH PLANT REPRODUCTION?	
S: It helps spread the pollen from flower to flower.	
WHAT DOES POLLEN HAVE TO DO WITH PLANT REPRODUCTION?	
S: It allows them to reproduce asexually.	This student's response suggests that he is evaluating the other student's response.
DOES ANYONE AGREE OR DISAGREE?	
S: I think she is wrong.	
WHY?	The teacher probes for justification of the student's comment.
S: I think there are other ways for plants to reproduce.	The student offers a general statement.
CAN YOU ELABORATE?	The teacher asks for elaboration.
S: Well, I know that plants have both male and female parts, so they must reproduce sexually like humans do.	The student provides an explanation for his statement in terms of his prior knowledge.
ANYBODY ELSE?	The teacher does not point out the validity or lack of validity of either student's response. She recognizes that each student is thinking critically by tapping prior knowledge and connecting it with the new text. Students will then read on to determine clues to justify the concepts they have hypothesized. The teacher remains consistent as a facilitator of the discussion.
WELL, LET ME GIVE YOU THE FIRST PART OF THE TEXT TO READ AND DETERMINE IF YOUR PREDICTIONS ARE ACCURATE. I WANT YOU TO READ TO THE BOTTOM OF THE PAGE, AND THEN I WANT YOU TO GO TO THE TOP OF THE NEXT PAGE. IT WILL BE THE VERY TOP PARAGRAPH. COVER UP WHAT'S BELOW IT WITH YOUR PAPER. READ THAT FAR AND STOP.	
(Students read silently)	

In a high school biology class, students were engaged in a study of a textbook chapter on plant reproduction. Using a DR–TA framework, the teacher guided the students' interactions with the text material. Study an excerpt of the transcript from the beginning cycle of the DR–TA in Figure 7.15.

As you examine the transcript, note that teacher–student interactions are recorded in the left column of the box. The teacher's questions and comments are printed in capital letters, followed by the students' responses in lowercase letters. An analysis of the DR–TA lesson as it evolved is printed in the right column.

The transcript shows how the students used prior knowledge and text structure (discussed in Chapter 10) to anticipate the information that the text would reveal. As they shared what they expected to find, the students engaged in analyzing their pooled ideas. Their interactions with the teacher illustrate how a DR–TA instructional framework creates a need to know and helps readers declare purposes through anticipation and prediction making.

Once the purposes were established, the teacher assigned a section of the text chapter to be read. Although the students' predictions were amiss in the initial cycle of questioning, the teacher chose not to evaluate or judge the predictions. She recognized that as readers interact with the text, more often than not they are able to clarify their misconceptions for themselves.

MyLab Education **Self-Check 7.2**

MyLab Education **Application Exercise 7.2:**
Using Discussion Webs in Content Area Classes

Reading Guides

7.3 Describe how each of the reading guides scaffolds students' understanding during reading.

What exactly is a reading guide? It has sometimes been compared to a "worksheet"—something students complete after reading, usually as homework. But reading guides do more than give students work to do. Guides, like worksheets, may consist of questions and activities related to the instructional material under study. One of the differences, however, between a reading guide and a worksheet is that students respond to the questions and activities in the guide *as* they read the text, not after. A reading guide provides instructional support as students need it. Moreover, a well-developed guide not only influences content acquisition but also prompts higher-order thinking. In Box 7.4, see how a high school business teacher utilizes reading guides to scaffold his students' disciplinary literacy practices while learning the role of a project manager.

Guides help students comprehend texts better than they would if left to their own resources. Over time, however, text learners should be weaned from this type of **scaffolding** as they develop the maturity and the learning strategies to interact with difficult texts without guide material. With this caveat in mind, let's explore the use of one type of reading guide that scaffolds learning at different levels of understanding: three-level comprehension guides.

Recognizing the need to engage his students in an authentic business activity and acquire the language to communicate practices in a business context, one high school business teacher took on this challenge and sought to update his standardized curriculum. He began by choosing to focus on one career. He knew he could teach the "test elements" through a deep analysis of the career and thought this "semester in the life of a _____" concept might really appeal to his students. He wanted to focus on lesser-known business positions that were not on the top of his students' "what I want to be when I grow up" lists. Drawing upon the guidelines set forth by SEDL (Chauvin & Theodore, 2015), he revamped his high school business curriculum with three objectives in mind: 1) to elevate his students' content knowledge base through inquiry; 2) to encourage collaboration; and

Box 7.4 Disciplinary Literacy

Using Disciplinary Literacy with Project Planning in a Business Classroom

As we learned in Chapter 1, disciplinary literacy is becoming increasingly important in content classrooms due to the textual demands associated with discipline-specific content. As a reminder, each discipline requires students to read, write, think, and speak in order to acquire knowledge in the discipline itself (Shanahan & Shanahan, 2008). Thus, when students have opportunities to engage in specific discipline practices, they can begin to see themselves as engineers, mathematicians, scientists, poets and authors, and future entrepreneurs (Buehl, 2009). Put another way, teachers become the facilitators and scaffold learning so their students "develop the capacity to read disciplinary specific texts through an insider perspective" (Buehl, 2011, p. 10).

High school business classes provide an ideal setting for the application of disciplinary literacy. After all, the primary purpose of these classes should be to allow students to dip their toes into business practices to get a feel for their personal fit. Unfortunately, the purpose often gets lost in prolonged projects, outdated software applications, and job descriptions that no longer apply to real positions. The question then becomes: What

guidelines should content area classroom teachers consider when implementing disciplinary literacy practices and still teaching the content curriculum?

To assist classroom teachers, the Southwest Educational Development Laboratory (SEDL) provides recommendations or "insights" to consider when planning to initiate disciplinary literacy practices into their content areas (Chauvin & Theodore, 2015, p. 1):

1. Provide an approach to content instruction that cultivates the skills for 21st-century literacy: critical thinking, communication, collaboration, and creativity;
2. Take charge of designing authentic, real-word experiences and assessments;
3. Commit to a conceptual framework of learning by doing;
4. Provide opportunities for students to use inquiry, key habits of practice, and academic language; and
5. Implement ongoing, job-embedded professional development and collaboration by discipline with teachers as designers and facilitators.

3) to develop the academic language critical to the role of a project manager. The ultimate goal was to engage his students in one facet of a real-world business practice.

To begin, he chose the career path of the project manager. Not only does this job exist in almost every industry, but it also encompasses the basic skills necessary to be successful in the management of a business. He planned a 6-week project to be accomplished in three parts. For Part One, the students would conduct in-depth research on the knowledge, skills, and education required to be a project manager. During Part Two, the students would engage in actual project planning; and for Part Three, the students would prepare a presentation for an employer.

On day one, he had his business students scour the Internet for project manager job descriptions because he wanted his students to formulate an understanding of the words **project** and **project management**. It was essential that his students understand that every project is engineered by goal-minded individuals who are trained in leadership and management practices. Additionally, the students looked up college programs to identify the course of study associated with the training and development of a project manager. Over the course of 2 weeks, the students chose where they would ideally like to work and which salary was most appealing. Under the guidance of the teacher, they made their lists of required knowledge, skills, and education needed for project management that matched the job descriptions geographically and their preferences by salary for prospective employment.

To initiate Part Two, the teacher rolled out the sample project plan – the next great sneaker. To set the course for the project, he showed a power point on project management to highlight the essential project management techniques, the organizational, assessment, and software tools, and the project management process in order for his students to achieve the next great sneaker. In order for his students to fully understand the job of project management, he knew this could best be achieved if he created planning teams. He believed the jigsaw strategy (discussed in Chapter 5) would provide each member of the planning team the opportunity to become an expert. As a result, he divided his class into five teams, consisting of five members to a team, and each member of a team was assigned a critical element of the **five stages of project management**:

1. Project initiation – the member who defines the project

2. Project planning – the member who organizes how the project will be managed

3. Project execution – the member who describes how the work will be completed

4. Project monitoring and controlling – the member who monitors the progress of each stage

5. Project closing – the member who closes each stage of the project and is responsible for final approval

To scaffold learning, the teacher gave his business students reading guides with questions to guide their purpose for reading and to support their thinking and interaction with texts during reading, such as: Why is it important to develop a project charter? Why is it important to define the scope of a project? What are some of the risk factors that can impact a project? What is the difference between monitoring and controlling a project? What were the measures of success? Why is collaboration needed in project management? For the next 2 weeks, the students immersed themselves in multiple forms of information, viewed videos, and interviewed local project managers in their business community to understand the fundamental processes and job-related duties for their assigned role in project management.

For the third and final phase of the project, each project management team developed a video presentation targeted to the prospective employer they identified in Part One. From the viewpoint of a project manager, the teacher asked his students to feature the five stages of project management, allowing each member of a team to demonstrate his/her content knowledge and to articulate the language associated with the specific project stage. As a culminating activity, the teams shared their video presentations and, under the guidance of the teacher, completed the industry-standard SWOT analysis (Strengths, Weaknesses, Opportunities, and Threats). This allowed the students to rate their successes and opportunities in a manner that was compliant with real-world practices.

The result was an increased awareness into authentic business practices that often occur behind the scenes. The students saw that in order to produce the next great sneaker, a team of planners was essential to the success of the product. This class indeed succeeded in learning the specific vocabulary and concepts, but did so in a way that made sense with the real life language and practices of a project manager.

Comprehension Levels

Because reading is a thoughtful process, it embraces the idea of levels of comprehension. Readers construct meaning at various levels of thinking and conceptual difficulty (Herber, 1978). Figure 7.16 shows the different levels of comprehension.

At the *literal level*, students *read the lines* of the content material. They stay with print sufficiently to get the gist of the author's message. In simple terms, a literal recognition of that message determines what the author says. Searching for important literal information isn't an easy chore, particularly if readers haven't matured enough to know how to make the search or, even worse, haven't determined why they are searching in the first place. Most students can and will profit greatly from being shown how to recognize the essential information in the text.

Knowing what the author says is necessary but not sufficient in constructing meaning with text. Good readers search for conceptual complexity in material. They read at the *interpretive level—between the lines*. They focus not only on what authors say but also on what authors mean by what they say. The interpretive level delves into the author's intended meaning. How readers conceptualize implied ideas by integrating information into what they already know is part of the interpretive process. Recognizing the thought relationships that the author weaves together helps readers make inferences that are implicit in the material.

From time to time throughout this chapter, you have probably been trying to read us—not our words, but us. And in the process of responding to our messages, you

Figure 7.16 Levels of Comprehension

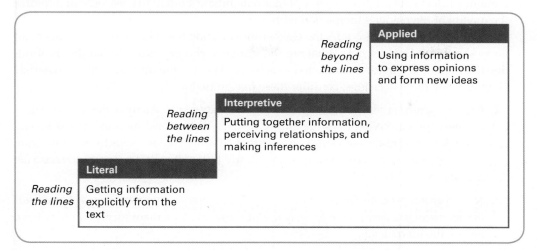

probably raised questions similar to these: "So what? What does this information mean to me? Does it make sense? Can I use these ideas for content instruction?" Your attempt to seek significance or relevance in what we say and mean is one signal that you are reading at the *applied level*. You are reading *beyond the lines*. Reading at the applied level is undoubtedly akin to critical reflection and discovery. When students construct meaning from text at the applied level, they know how to synthesize information—and to lay that synthesis alongside what they know already—to evaluate, question the author, think critically, and draw additional insights and fresh ideas from content material.

Three-Level Comprehension Guides

The levels-of-comprehension model that we have just introduced lends itself well to the development of guide material to engage students in reading. A three-level guide provides the framework in which students can interact with difficult texts at different levels of comprehension.

CONSTRUCTING THREE-LEVEL COMPREHENSION GUIDES Don't be misled by the apparent discreteness of comprehension levels. The term *levels* implies a cognitive hierarchy that may be more apocryphal than real. A reader doesn't necessarily read first for literal recognition, then interpretation, and finally application—although that may appear to be a logical sequence. Many readers, for instance, read text for overarching concepts and generalizations first and then search for evidence to support their inferences.

It is important to recognize that in reading, levels are probably interactive and inseparable. Nevertheless, the classroom teacher attempts to have students experience each aspect of the comprehension process as they read content material. In doing so, students adapt strategies as they interact with the material. They get a feel for the component processes within reading comprehension. They come to sense in an instructional setting what it means to make inferences, to use information as the basis for those inferences, and to rearrange or transform acquired understandings into what they know already in order to construct knowledge.

If guides were to be used with every text assignment every day, it would become counterproductive. One math teacher's evaluation of a three-level guide crystallizes this point: "The students said the guide actually helped them organize the author's ideas in their minds and helped them understand the material. I think the guide was successful, but I would not use it all the time because many of the assignments don't lend themselves to this type of activity." The three-level guide is only one instructional aid that helps students grow toward mature reading and independent learning.

**MyLab Education
Response Journal 7.2**
What do you think is the difference between responding to statements at different levels of comprehension versus responding to questions?

Finally, we urge you also to consider guides as tools, not tests. Think of each statement in a three-level guide as a prompt that will initiate student discussion and reinforce the quality of the reader's interaction with text.

Before constructing a guide, the teacher must decide the following: What important ideas should be emphasized? What are the students' competencies? What depth of understanding are the students expected to achieve? What is the difficulty of the material? Having made these decisions, consider these five guidelines:

1. *Begin construction of the guide at level II, the interpretive level.* Analyze the text selection, asking yourself, "What does the author mean?" Write down in your own words all inferences that make sense to you and that fit your content objectives. Make sure your statements are written simply and clearly (after all, you don't want to construct a guide to read the guide).

2. *Next, search the text for the propositions and explicit pieces of information needed to support the inferences you have chosen for level II.* Put these into statement form. You now have level I, the literal level.

3. *Decide whether you want to add a distractor or two to levels I and II.* We have found that a distractor maintains an active response to the information search, mainly because students sense that they cannot indiscriminately check every item and, therefore, must focus their information search more carefully.

4. *Develop statements for level III, the applied level.* Such statements represent additional insights or principles that can be drawn when relationships established by the author are combined with other ideas outside the text selection itself but inside the heads of your students. In other words, help students connect what they know already to what they read.

Figure 7.17 Three-Level Guide for a Health Lesson

I. Right There! What did the author say?

Directions: Place a check on the line in front of the number if you think a statement can be found in the pages you read.

_____ **1.** Every human being has feelings or emotions.

_____ **2.** Research workers are studying the effects on the body of repeated use of marijuana.

_____ **3.** You should try hard to hide your strong emotions, such as fear or anger.

_____ **4.** Your feelings affect the way the body works.

_____ **5.** You are likely to get angry at your parents or brothers or sisters more often than at other people.

II. Think and Search! What did the author mean?

Directions: Check the following statements that state what the author was trying to say in the pages you read.

_____ **1.** Sometimes you act in a different way because of your mood.

_____ **2.** Your emotional growth has been a continuing process since the day you were born.

_____ **3.** The fact that marijuana hasn't been proved to be harmful means that it is safe to use.

_____ **4.** Each time you successfully control angry or upset feelings, you grow a little.

III. On Your Own! Do you agree with these statements?

Directions: Check each statement that you can defend.

_____ **1.** Escaping from problems does not solve them.

_____ **2.** Decisions should be made on facts, not fantasies.

_____ **3.** Getting drunk is a good way to have fun.

5. *Be flexible and adaptive.* Develop a format that will appeal to you and your students. Try to avoid crowding too much print on the reading guide.

A THREE-LEVEL COMPREHENSION GUIDE EXAMPLE   The format of a three-level guide will vary from one content area to another. The classroom example that follows serves only as a model. As you study it, think of ways that you will be able to adapt and apply the three-level construct to your discipline-specific materials. A middle grade teacher constructed the three-level guide in Figure 7.17 as part of a health unit. Notice how she uses question–answer relationships (QARs) as cues to direct students' responses. Students completed the guide individually and then discussed their responses in small groups.

MyLab Education **Self-Check 7.3**

MyLab Education **Application Exercise 7.3:**
The impact of Supporting Disciplinary Literacy in Content Area Classrooms

---

Looking Back Looking Forward

Strategy-centered classrooms are places where students learn how to learn. Teachers support students' efforts to make meaning by guiding reading comprehension and modeling how to think and learn with texts. To this end, we explored several research-based comprehension strategies that show students how to be active, thoughtful readers: think-alouds, question–answer relationships (QARs), reciprocal teaching, and questioning the author (QtA). When these strategies are adapted to meet the textual and conceptual demands of a discipline, they not only model comprehension strategies but also engage learners in meaningful talk and discussion about the content under study.

Several comprehension-centered instructional strategies were also suggested to guide students' interactions with texts. These strategies are designed to help students clarify and extend meaning as they engage in reading. For example, KWL is a meaning-making strategy that engages students in active text learning and may be used with small groups of students or with an entire class. KWL is composed of several steps that help learners examine what they know, what they want to know more about, and what they have learned from reading; KWHL offers a variation on this strategy, asking students to also consider how they might find the information they need. The directed reading–thinking activity (DR–TA) was also described. DR–TA revolves around three guiding questions: (1) What do you think? (2) Why do you think so? (3) Can you prove it? The guided reading procedure (GRP) encourages close reading of difficult text, whereas the discussion web and intra-act strategies lay the groundwork for reflective discussion following the reading of text material.

In addition to comprehension strategies, teacher-prepared reading guides may also be used to guide reading. Three-level comprehension guides allow learners to interact with text, constructing meaning at different levels of thinking: literal, interpretive, and applied. In the next chapter, we focus on the building blocks of comprehension in a discipline: developing technical vocabulary and concepts. In particular, we examine the relationship between the vocabulary of a content area—its special and technical terms—and its concepts. How can a teacher help students to interact with the language of a discipline and, in the process, show them how to define, clarify, and extend their understanding of the concepts under study?

eResources

Explore topics on content area literacy presented on the Reading Rockets website. Consider how you might apply concepts presented there to enhance instruction in your discipline.

The National Reading Panel's focus on research-based strategies serves as a landmark in reading education. Review the panel's findings on text comprehension.

Use the keywords "QtA" or "questioning the author" and "KWL" or "KWL strategies" to search for these two powerful comprehension strategies. Consider how you might use these strategies in your content area. Reading Quest provides examples of how to apply strategies such as KWL and QtA in the discipline of social studies. If you teach social studies, consider how you might adapt these strategies for use in your classes.

Chapter 8
Developing Vocabulary and Concepts

Matej Kastelic/Shutterstock

Chapter Overview and Learning Outcomes

After reading this chapter, you should be able to:

8.1 Explain what teachers should consider when choosing terms for study.

8.2 Explain the importance of connecting new vocabulary to schema and describe strategies that support these connections.

8.3 Describe the strategies asking students to explore words in relationship to their context and to each other.

8.4 Describe the strategies students can use independently to build their vocabulary knowledge.

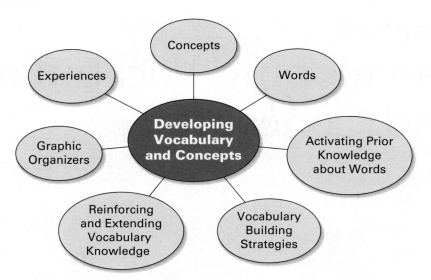

Organizing Principle

Teaching words well means giving students multiple opportunities to develop word meanings and learn how words are conceptually related to one another in the texts they are studying.

There is a strong connection between vocabulary knowledge and reading comprehension. If students are not familiar with most words they meet in print, they will undoubtedly have trouble understanding what they read. It has been suggested that words are the building materials students need to construct meaning as they read and learn with text. Technical vocabulary—words unique to a content area—is often unfamiliar to students but is particularly important for disciplinary thinking and learning. The more experience students have with unfamiliar words and the more exposure they have to them, the more meaningful the words will become.

Vocabulary is as unique to a content area as fingerprints are to a human being. A content area is distinguishable by its language, particularly the technical terms that label the concepts undergirding the subject matter. Teachers know they must do something with the language of their content areas, but they often reduce instruction to routines that direct students to look up, define, memorize, and use content-specific words in sentences. Such practices divorce the study of vocabulary from an exploration of the subject matter. Learning vocabulary becomes an activity in itself—a separate one—rather than an integral part of learning academic content. Content area vocabulary must be taught *well enough* to remove potential barriers to students' understanding of texts in content areas. The organizing principle underscores the main premise of the chapter: Teaching words well means giving students multiple opportunities to develop word meanings and learn how words are conceptually related to one another in the texts they are studying.

Frame of Mind

1. Why should the language of an academic discipline be taught within the context of concept development?
2. What are the relationships among experiences, concepts, and words?
3. How can a teacher activate what students know about words and help them make connections among related words?
4. How do graphic organizers help students anticipate and understand important concepts in content area texts?

5. How do activities for vocabulary and concept development help students refine their knowledge of special and technical vocabulary?

6. How can knowledge of word structure help students to understand word meanings?

Fridays always seemed to be set aside for quizzes when we were students, and one of the quizzes most frequently given was the vocabulary test: "Look up these words for the week. Write out their definitions and memorize them. Then use each word in a complete sentence. You'll be tested on these terms on Friday."

Our vocabulary study seemed consistently to revolve around the dull routines of looking up, defining, and memorizing words and using them in sentences. Such an instructional pattern resulted in meaningless, purposeless activity—an end in itself rather than a means to an end. Although there was nothing inherently wrong with looking up, defining, and memorizing words and using them in sentences, the approach itself was too narrow for us to learn words in depth. Instead, we memorized definitions to pass the Friday quiz—and forgot them by Saturday.

8.1 Explain what teachers should consider when choosing terms for study.

Having students learn lists of words is based on the ill-founded notion that the acquisition of vocabulary is separate from the development of ideas and concepts in a content area. Too often, teaching vocabulary means assigning a list of words rather than exploring word meanings and relationships that contribute to students' conceptual awareness and understanding of a subject. Once teachers clarify the relationship between words and concepts, they are receptive to instructional alternatives.

MyLab Education
Response Journal 8.1
What were some of your experiences with vocabulary instruction in content areas?

Selecting specific vocabulary words for meaningful, direct instruction from the plethora of potential words that might be studied in a subject area can be a challenge for teachers. As Ganske (2012, p. 211) explains, "Different situations require different levels of word knowledge." To provide guidance in selecting words on which to focus, Beck, McKeown, and Kucan (2013) categorize vocabulary words according to three tiers or levels:

> *Tier 1:* Tier 1 words are basic high-frequency and high-utility words that are commonly used in everyday language. Tier 1 might include words such as *friend, move, eat,* and *home.* Native language speakers typically don't require direct instruction to understand Tier 1 words.
>
> *Tier 2:* Tier 2 words are also high-frequency and high-utility words; however, words in this category are more commonly used by advanced or mature language users. Words such as *scalding, reprimand, clarify,* and *escapade* are examples of Tier 2 words. Vocabulary instruction is often needed in order for students to understand the meanings of these words.
>
> *Tier 3:* Tier 3 words are low-frequency words, but words that are needed to understand a content area material. Tier 3 words are part of the language of a subject area and, as the vocabulary demonstration in Figure 8.1 illustrated, unique and integral to each subject area. Examples of Tier 3 words include *Declaration of Independence, nucleus, quadratic equation,* and *palette.* Tier 3 words are those for which direct instruction is often required in content area classes.

Tier 3 words can be challenging when they are encountered in content material. Your participation in the demonstration in Figure 8.1 will illustrate why special and technical terms are likely candidates for vocabulary instruction in content areas. If your responses

Figure 8.1 Vocabulary Demonstration Words in Content Areas

Directions: In each of the nine blanks, fill in the name of the content area that includes all the terms in the list below:

1. _____
   - nationalism
   - imperialism
   - naturalism
   - instrumentalism
   - isolationist
   - radicalism
   - fundamentalist
   - anarchy

2. _____
   - forestry
   - ornithology
   - zoology
   - biology
   - entomology
   - botany
   - bacteriology
   - protista

3. _____
   - metaphor
   - allusion
   - irony
   - paradox
   - symbolism
   - imagery
   - simile

4. _____
   - prestissimo
   - adagio
   - larghetto
   - presto
   - allegro
   - largo
   - andante
   - tempo

5. _____
   - centimeter
   - milligram
   - deciliter
   - millisecond
   - kilometer
   - decimeter
   - kilogram
   - millimeter

6. _____
   - graffles
   - folutes
   - lesnics
   - raptiforms
   - cresnites
   - hygrolated
   - loors
   - chamlets

7. _____
   - trans fat
   - glycogen
   - monosaccharide
   - hydrogenation
   - enzymes
   - lyzine
   - cellulose

8. _____
   - octagon
   - hemisphere
   - decagon
   - hexagon
   - bisect
   - equilateral
   - quadrilateral
   - pentagon

9. _____
   - auricle
   - ventricle
   - tricuspid
   - semilunar
   - apex
   - mitral
   - aorta
   - myocardium

are similar to those of classroom teachers who have participated in this activity, several predictable outcomes are likely:

First, it is relatively easy for you to identify the content areas for several of the lists. Your knowledge and experience probably trigger instant recognition. You have a good working concept of many of the terms on these easy lists. You can put them to use in everyday situations that require listening, reading, writing, or speaking. They are your words. You own them.

Second, you probably recognize words in a few of the lists even though you may not be sure about the meanings of individual words. In lists 4 and 9, for example, you may be familiar with only one or two terms. Yet you are fairly sure that the terms in lists 4 and 9 exist as words despite the fact that you may not know what they mean. Your attitude toward these kinds of words is analogous to your saying to a stranger, "I think I've met you before, but I'm not sure." Several of the words from the lists may be in your "twilight zone"; you have some knowledge about them, but their meanings are a "bit foggy, not sharply focused." *Trans fat* in List 7 is a case in point for some of us who have heard the term used in television commercials and may even have purchased foods with trans fat at the supermarket. Nevertheless, our guess is that we would be hard-pressed to define or explain the meaning of trans fat with any precision.

Finally, in one or two cases, a list may have stymied your efforts at identification. There simply is no connection between your prior knowledge and any of the terms. You probably are not even sure whether the terms in one list really exist as words.

Which content area did you identify for List 6? In truth, the terms in this list represent nonsense. They are bogus words that were invented to illustrate the point that many of the content terms in textbooks look the same way to students that the nonsense words in List 6 look to you. You're able to pronounce most of them with little trouble but are stymied when you try to connect them to your knowledge and experience. Students are stymied this way every day by real words that represent the key concepts of a content area.

The words in these lists (except List 6) are actually taken from middle and high school textbooks. Just think for a moment about the staggering conceptual demands we place on learners daily as they go from class to class. Terminology that they encounter in content material is often outside the scope of their normal speaking, writing, listening, and reading vocabularies. Special and technical, Tier 3 terms often do not have concrete referents; they are abstract and must be learned through definition, application, and repeated exposure.

Your participation in this activity leads to several points about word knowledge and concepts in content areas. The activity is a good reminder that every academic discipline creates a unique language to represent its important concepts. This is why teaching vocabulary in content areas is too important to be incidental or accidental. Key concept words need to be taught directly and taught well.

Informational texts used in content area classes typically bring with them more challenging vocabulary demands than narrative or literary texts (Pearson, Hiebert, & Kamil, 2007). Providing students with direct instruction in vocabulary has been found to influence comprehension of text more than any other factor (Bromley, 2007). Students should not be left to their own devices or subjected to the vagaries of a look-up-and-define strategy as their only access to understanding the language of an academic discipline. Verbalizing a dictionary definition of a word and learning it by rote are quite different from encountering that word in a reading situation and constructing meaning for it based on conceptual knowledge and prior experiences.

In this chapter, we will show how to teach words effectively within the framework of subject matter learning. Teaching words well removes potential barriers to reading comprehension. Research has documented a strong link between vocabulary development and reading comprehension (National Reading Panel, 2000; Pressley, 2002a). Knowledge of word meanings, and the ability to use that knowledge effectively, contributes significantly to a student's reading and listening comprehension (Curtis & Longo, 2001). When teachers understand *how* students acquire knowledge of vocabulary concepts, vocabulary instruction can be effectively integrated within the context of subject area learning (Blachowicz, Fisher, Ogle, & Watts-Taffe, 2006).

Teaching words well involves helping students make connections between their prior knowledge and the vocabulary to be encountered in text and providing them with multiple opportunities to define, clarify, and extend their knowledge of words and concepts during the course of study

Box 8.1 Voices from the Field

Alyson, High School English Teacher

Challenge

As a high school English teacher, one important part of my routine is teaching vocabulary; however, I never gave much thought as to why or how vocabulary should be taught. I always felt it was to help students score higher on their ACT/SATs. A typical vocabulary lesson in my classroom would take place in the first 10 minutes of my class each day. Then the students would take a quiz on Friday. Often, I pulled words from online SAT vocabulary lists to help students learn words for all the standardized tests they were expected to take. I taught students these words by giving them synonyms they would have already known. Essentially, I was teaching students how to memorize word meanings, but I never asked students to take these words and apply them. I never asked students why it was important to learn these specific vocabulary words each week. My challenge became: How can I teach vocabulary in a meaningful way and not just a memorizing for a test way?

Strategy

When considering the diverse needs of learners in my classroom, including English Learners and special needs students, I realized that I had not been differentiating instruction or even giving them a rationale for studying these words. Students need context for why they are learning something in the classroom. They also need to know how this information can bring value to their lives. I decided to select words from the novels we were reading in class and to focus on an aspect or theme of a novel that connected to those words. In doing so, I wanted to bring attention to why an author chose specific words and how those choices influenced what the author communicated (Beck, McKeown, & Kucan, 2013).

Texts, such as *A Long Way Gone* by Ishmael Beah, *Night* by Elie Wiesel, *Macbeth* by Shakespeare, and *Siddhartha* by Hermann Hesse, became the basis for my vocabulary instruction. For example, when reading the novel *Siddhartha* by Hermann Hesse, I used a character study to examine how *Siddhartha* transforms from the beginning of the novel to the end. Since this theme is closely related to the theme in *Night* by Elie Wiesel, I focused on words that represented spirituality, which is one of the themes for *Siddhartha*. Below is a sample of the spirituality vocabulary chart.

Target Word	Summarized Story Context	Student-Friendly Explanation
Ablution (noun)	His fair skin was beginning to tan from the sun as he was bathing in the river and performing the sanctified **ablutions**, the sacred donations.	A religious act of washing one's body or part of the body; cleanse.
Atonement (noun)	As he was walking in the garden through the paths of flowers and the fig tree, sitting in the orchard of contemplation, washing his body daily in the bath **atonement**, surrendering in the dim shade of the mango forest, his gestures of perfect decency, everyone's love and delight, he still lacked all happiness.	To feel sorry for one's poor actions/sings. To feel remorseful for poor behavior.
Venerable (adj)	He began to question his **venerable** father and his other educators, that the astute Brahmans had already exposed to him the maximum and greatest of their wisdom, that they had already completed his education with their richness; however, he did not feel complete, his soul was not satisfied, the spirit was not tranquil, the heart was not fulfilled.	Given a great deal of respect for either age, wisdom, or character
Invocation (noun)	The ritual offerings and the **invocation** of the gods were magnificent, but was that it? Did the offerings give a joyful fortune?	Calling/conjuring for a god, deity, or higher power. The act of asking for help.
Contemplation (noun)	There he sat, completely enveloped in **contemplation**, reasoning, Om, then his spirit sent after the Brahman like an arrow.	Deep reflective thought; mediation.

Reflection

I always start class by focusing on vocabulary for the first 10 minutes of class, but I have made the change so that the vocabulary is centered on what students are currently reading. To help me with this transition I used Pearson and Gallagher's (1983) gradual release model. I did this in hopes that students would have more self-efficacy with growing their own vocabulary outside of my classroom. The goal for using the gradual release model was that in the beginning I picked more of the words and showed students where they are in the text. Then, once students had a solid understanding of why and how I picked the vocabulary words, I released this responsibility to them. I wanted this to be a process of releasing the choosing of words because I wanted the learning to become personalized for the students.

To begin, as a class we came up with a student-friendly definition based on the context clues. I aimed to choose two to three words a day. A typical warm-up would now look like:

1. Student enters the room and takes out their daybook.

2. Student creates a chart like above and writes the target word down from the board.

3. Student finds the word in the chapter we are going to read (they would be using skimming as a technique as well).

4. Once students find the sentence, they will then copy it down and attempt to underline context clues.

As my students became more comfortable with the process of picking vocabulary words, I started to release the work on to them. I let students work in groups to choose their own vocabulary words that related to our study. Since I teach *Siddhartha* in the middle of the school year, the chart above served as a model for my students. I made a few more entries with them as a class, but I began to release the decision making and problem solving to them. My goal was to support them in using word study as a meaningful strategy for understanding text, rather than as a seemingly disconnected English class activity. The next goal for my students is to have these newly learned words become a permanent part of their everyday language. To help them maintain their newly acquired vocabulary, I have them create individual dictionaries. Based on the vocabulary words we have discussed in class, students create entries for each word that include a student-friendly definition, two synonyms and two antonyms, a picture that represents or symbolizes the word, and a sentence that applies the word in context. The individual dictionaries serve as a resource to students as well as a note-taking opportunity that extends beyond looking up definitions on their phones. Vocabulary application strategies such as these spark students' interest about words and language and show students the importance of vocabulary terms beyond a single course or text.

Experiences, Concepts, and Words

Words are labels for concepts. A single concept, however, represents much more than the meaning of a single word. It may take thousands of words to explain a concept. However, answers to the question "What does it mean to know a word?" depend on how well we understand the relationships among direct experiences, concepts, and words.

MyLab Education
Video Example 8.1
Prior Knowledge and Vocabulary
Watch this video to see an example of the link between prior knowledge and vocabulary learning.

Learning the meaning of new terms by reading definitions is only minimally effective. Concepts are learned by acting on and interacting with the environment. Students learn concepts best through direct, concrete, purposeful experiences (Nagy, 1988; Wright & Cervetti, 2017). Learning is much more intense and meaningful when it develops through firsthand experience. However, in place of using direct experience, which is not always possible, students can develop and learn concepts through various levels of improvised or vicarious experience, which is often feasible in a classroom setting. The demands of vocabulary learning intensify in the middle and secondary grades as students are introduced to increasingly complex content area concepts. At this same stage, students' academic motivation often lags. It is essential, then, that students be given opportunities to study new concepts over time using a variety of methods (Lesaux, Harris, & Sloane, 2012). The comprehension of concepts can be fostered using strategies that encourage collaborative text-based discussions with teachers and peers (Fisher & Frey, 2014).

What Are Concepts?

Concepts create mental images, which may represent anything that can be grouped together by common features or similar criteria: objects, symbols, ideas, processes, or events. In this respect, concepts are similar to schemata. A concept hardly ever stands alone; instead, it is bound by a hierarchy of relationships. Therefore, we invent categories (or form concepts) to reduce the complexity of our environment and the necessity for constant learning. For example, every feline need not have a different name; each is known as a *cat*. Although cats vary greatly, their common characteristics cause them to be referred to by the same general term. Thus, to facilitate communication, we invent words to name concepts.

MyLab Education
Response Journal 8.2
What are some words related to your content area that didn't exist 10 years ago? One year ago? Why do you think these words are now in use?

Concept Relationships: An Example

Consider your concept for the idea of a *garment*. What pictures come to mind? Your image of the process of creating a garment might differ based on your experience with clothing, your interest level, or even your purpose for creating the garment. Maybe you base your idea on why you need the garment, how you will use it, or your skill level as a designer. Each student's experiences and understanding will vary as he or she takes on the task of understanding the process behind planning and making his or her own garment. Nevertheless, for any concept, we organize all our experiences and knowledge into conceptual hierarchies according to *class, example,* and *attribute* relationships. As part of the family and consumer science curriculum, students in an introductory apparel course learned that the concept of a *garment* is really made of a series of decisions that can be categorized according to the results of each decision. These relationships are shown in Figure 8.2.

Figure 8.2 A Concept Hierarchy Based on Class Relations—*Apparel*

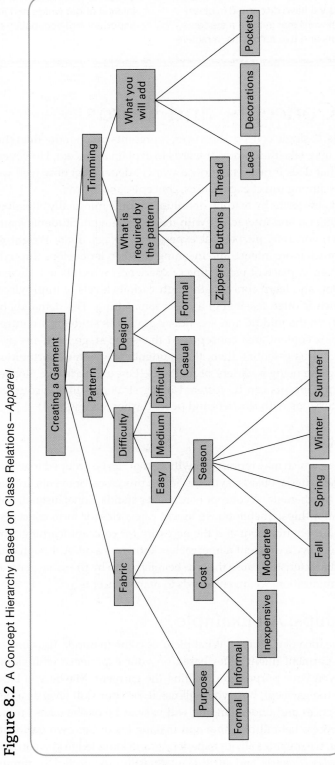

In any conceptual network, class relations are organized in a hierarchy consisting of superordinate and subordinate concepts. In Figure 8.2, the superordinate concept is creating a garment. *Pattern, trimming*, and *fabric* represent the three classes of decisions one will have to make when constructing a garment. They are in a subordinate position in this hierarchy. Each decision is then broken down into the smaller steps that must be considered to inform the larger class. These decisions are subordinate to their classes.

For every concept, there are examples. An *example* is a member of any concept being considered. Class–examples relations are complementary. For example, in order to decide on the season for which you will create your garment, you must weigh all four options: summer, spring, winter, and fall. When considering these subordinate levels, one must ask, "What do they have in common?" Obviously, each listed is a season, and the season would have an influential effect on the fabric choices one makes for the garment. This helps the learner focus on *relevant attributes,* the features, traits, properties, or characteristics common to every example of a particular group. In this case, the relevant attributes that are common to making a decision about fabric are that all examples listed are seasons. An attribute is said to be *critical* if it is a characteristic that is necessary for every class member to possess. An attribute is said to be *variable* if it is shared by some, but not all, examples of this class. Looking at making a fabric choice, we see that we will consider purpose, cost, and season. Their commonalities help us construct the garment in our mind and make appropriate choices so that the garment matches our needs. That is critical: All factors must affect our fabric choice. They also have variable characteristics. For example, *how* will they affect our fabric choice? Cost concerns a budget, purpose concerns how it will be used, and season concerns when it will be used.

This brief discussion illustrates an important principle: *Teachers can help students build conceptual knowledge of context terms and ideas by teaching and reinforcing the concept words in relation to other concept words*. This key instructional principle plays itself out in content area classrooms whenever students are actively making connections among the key words in a lesson or unit of study.

MyLab Education **Self-Check 8.1**

MyLab Education **Application Exercise 8.1:**
Choosing Vocabulary for Direct Instruction in a Content Area Classroom

---

Using Graphic Organizers to Make Connections among Key Concepts

8.2 Explain the importance of connecting new vocabulary to schema and describe strategies that support these connections.

At the start of each chapter, we have asked you to use a "chapter overview" to organize your thoughts about the main ideas in the text. These ideas are presented within the framework of a **graphic organizer**, a diagram that uses content vocabulary to help students anticipate concepts and their relationships to one another in the reading material. These concepts are displayed in an arrangement of key technical terms relevant to the important concepts to be learned.

Graphic organizers vary in format. One commonly used format to depict the hierarchical relationships among concept words is a "network tree" diagram. Keep in mind that network tree graphic organizers always show concepts in relation to other concepts. Let's take a closer look at how to construct and apply graphic organizers in the classroom.

A Graphic Organizer Walk-Through

Suppose you were to develop a graphic organizer for a text chapter in a high school psychology course. Let's walk through the steps involved.

1. *Analyze the vocabulary and list the important words.* The chapter yields several important words, including the following:

episodic memory	encoding	semantic memory
short-term memory	long-term memory	retrieval
sensory memory	storage	memory processes

2. *Arrange the list of words.* Choose the word that represents the most inclusive concept, the one superordinate to all of the others. Next, choose the words classified immediately under the superordinate concepts and coordinate them with one another. Then choose the terms subordinate to the coordinate concepts. Your diagram may look like Figure 8.3.

3. *Add to the scheme vocabulary terms that you believe the students understand.* You add the following terms:

flashbulb memories	explicit memory	organizational systems
echoic	riding a bicycle	tip-of-the tongue phenomenon
iconic	visual codes	schema
working memory	acoustic codes	

4. *Evaluate the organizer.* The interrelationships among the key terms may look like Figure 8.4 once you evaluate the vocabulary arrangement.

5. *Introduce the students to the learning task.* As you present the vocabulary relationships shown on the graphic organizer, create as much discussion as possible. Draw on students' understanding of and experience with the concepts the terms label. The discussions you will stimulate with the organizer will be worth the time it takes to construct it.

Figure 8.3 Arrangement of Words on Memory in a Psychology Test

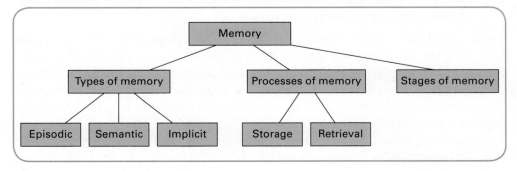

Figure 8.4 Arrangement of Words on Memory After Evaluation of Organizer

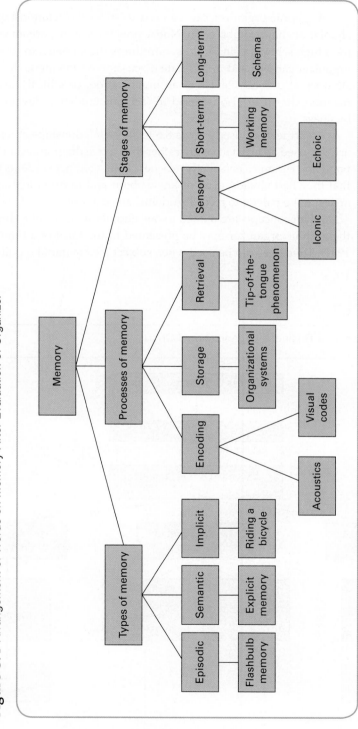

6. *As you complete the learning task, relate new information to the organizer.* This step is particularly useful as a study and review technique. The organizer becomes a study guide that can be referred to throughout the discussion of the material. Students should be encouraged to add information to flesh out the organizer as they develop concepts more fully.

A graphic organizer can be used to show the relationships in a thematic unit in a chapter or chapter subsection. Notice how the graphic organizer in Figure 8.5, developed for a high school business class, introduces the students to corporate infrastructure. This organizer can be used to facilitate discussion on the hierarchy of business roles, responsibilities at different levels of an organization, or ethical business practices. The organization chart can also be used to facilitate students' development of their own mock business.

An art teacher used Figure 8.6 to show relationships among types of media used in art. She used an artist's palette rather than a tree diagram. After completing the entries for paint and ceramics herself, the teacher challenged her students to brainstorm other media that they had already used or knew about and to provide examples; she used the open areas on the palette to record students' associations.

When concepts are related to one another in terms of a chronological or linear order, the graphic organizer may be presented in the form of a time line (Parker & Jarolimek, 1997). Time lines can be used when subject area material requires students to understand

Figure 8.5 A Graphic Organizer for a Business Organizational Chart

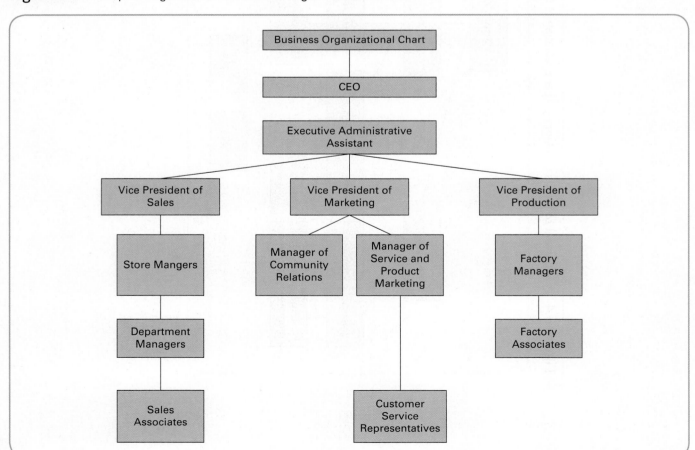

Figure 8.6 A Graphic Organizer for Types of Media in Art

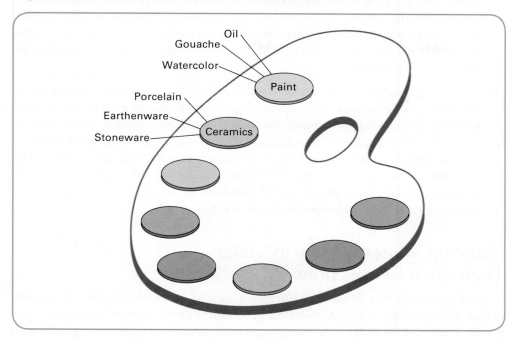

a sequence of events or the procedural order required to complete a given task. Figure 8.7 shows a time line used in an art history class to illustrate some of the major periods relevant to that content area.

Graphic organizers are easily adapted to learning situations in the elementary grades. For class presentations, elementary teachers often construct organizers on large sheets of chart paper or on bulletin boards. Still other elementary teachers draw pictures with words that illustrate the key concepts under study.

When used efficiently, graphic organizers have been found to be powerful learning tools for students whose achievement is below grade level or who are exhibiting learning issues (Guastello, Beasley, & Sinatra, 2000). Baxendell (2003) offers the following research-based suggestions for effectively implementing graphic organizers:

1. *Be consistent when implementing graphic organizers.* Students who struggle to learn content area material often benefit from routine and structure. Using standard and familiar models of graphic organizers can help to provide that structure. For example, when reviewing a science or social studies unit, a tree diagram may be used to organize key concepts. When explaining the steps needed to solve a mathematical equation, a flowchart may best outline the necessary procedures.

Figure 8.7 A Time Line for Art History

1200s–1300s	1400s–1500s	1600s–1700s	1800s	1900s
Individualism in Italian Art	Italian Renaissance	Baroque Period of Europe	Romanticism, Impressionism, Abstract Art	Modernism

2. *Use graphic organizers to coherently depict relationships between concepts.* For graphic organizers to be understandable, connections between concepts need to be clear and straightforward. Graphic organizers that are cluttered or disorganized can confuse, rather than clarify, concepts for students. To construct coherent graphic organizers, use clear labels to connect concepts and limit the number of ideas presented in any single graphic organizer.

3. *Seek creative ways to integrate graphic organizers across content areas and throughout different stages of a lesson or unit of study.* Graphic organizers can be used and adapted for different purposes within a single unit. They can, for example, be used before reading to activate students' background knowledge and illuminate misconceptions students may have about the topic to be studied. Graphic organizers can also be used during reading to clarify and synthesize concepts and after reading as a form of review. Encouraging students to incorporate illustrations into their graphic organizers can enhance their understanding of the content.

Showing Students How to Make Their Own Connections

Graphic organizers may be used by teachers to build a frame of reference for students as they approach new material. However, in a more student-centered adaptation of the graphic organizer, the students work in cooperative groups and organize important concepts into their own graphic representations.

To make connections effectively, students must have some familiarity with the concepts in advance of their study of the material. In addition, student-constructed graphic organizers presume that the students are aware of the idea behind a graphic organizer. If they are not, you will need to give them a rationale and then model the construction of an organizer. Exposure to teacher-constructed graphic organizers from past lessons also creates awareness and provides models for the instructional strategy.

To introduce students to the process of making their own graphic organizers, follow these steps:

1. *Type the key words and make copies for students.*

2. *Have them form small groups of two or three students each.*

3. *Distribute the list of terms and a packet of 3- by 5-inch index cards to each group.*

4. *Have the students write each word from the list on a separate card.* Then have them work together to decide on a spatial arrangement of the cards that depicts the major relationships among the words.

5. *As students work, assist as needed.*

6. *Initiate a discussion of the constructed organizer.*

Before assigning a graphic organizer to students, you should prepare for the activity by carefully analyzing the vocabulary of the material to be learned. List all the terms that are essential for students to understand. Then add relevant terms that you believe the students already understand and that will help them relate what they know to the new material. Finally, construct your own organizer.

The form of the student-constructed graphic organizer will undoubtedly differ from the teacher's arrangement. However, this difference in and of itself should not be a major source of concern. What is important is that the graphic organizer supports students' abilities to anticipate connections through the key vocabulary terms in content materials.

Activating What Students Know about Words

Graphic organizers may be used to (1) activate students' prior knowledge of the vocabulary words in a text assignment or unit of study and (2) clarify their understanding of concepts as they study text. From a strategy perspective, students need to learn how to ask the question "What do I know about these words?" When you use graphic organizers before reading or talking about key concepts, help the students build strategy awareness by exploring key terms before assigning text to read. In addition, consider the use of an informal assessment strategy known as knowledge rating (Blachowicz & Fisher, 2014), illustrated in Box 8.2.

Word Exploration

Word exploration is a *writing-to-learn* strategy that works well as a vocabulary activity. Before asking students to make connections between the words and their prior knowledge, a biology teacher asked them to explore what they knew about the concept of *natural selection* by writing in their learning logs.

A word exploration activity invites students to write quickly and spontaneously, a technique called *freewriting,* for no more than five minutes, without undue concern about spelling, neatness, grammar, or punctuation. The purpose of freewriting is to get down on paper everything that students know about the topic or target concept. Students write freely for themselves, not for an audience, so the mechanical, surface features of language, such as spelling, are not important.

Word explorations activate schemata and jog long-term memory, allowing students to dig deep into the recesses of their minds to gather thoughts about a topic. Examine one of the word explorations for the target concept *natural selection*:

> Natural selection means that nature selects—kills off or does away with—the weak so only the strong make it. Like we were studying in class last time, things get so competitive, even among us for grades, jobs, and so on. The homeless are having trouble living—they have no place to call home except the street and nothing to eat. That's as good an example of natural selection as I can think of for now.

The teacher then has several of the students share their word explorations with the class, either reading their texts verbatim or talking through what they have written, and notes similarities and differences in the students' concepts. The teacher then relates their initial associations to the concept and asks the students to make further connections: "How does your personal understanding of the idea of *natural selection* fit in with some of the relationships that you see?"

Brainstorming

An alternative to word exploration, brainstorming is a procedure that quickly allows students to generate what they know about a key concept. In brainstorming, the students can access their prior knowledge in relation to the target concept. Brainstorming involves two basic steps that can be adapted easily to content objectives: (1) The teacher identifies a key concept that reflects one of the main topics to be studied in the text, and (2) students work in small groups to generate a list of words related to the concept in a given number of seconds.

List–Group–Label

Notable educator and curriculum theorist Hilda Taba (1967) suggested an extension of brainstorming that she called "**list–group–label**." When the brainstorming activity is over and *lists* of words have been generated by the students, have the class form learning teams to *group* the words into logical arrangements. Then invite the teams to *label* each arrangement. Once the list–group–label activity is completed, ask the students to make predictions about the content to be studied. For example, you might ask, "How does the title of the text (or thematic unit) relate to your groups of words?" or "Describe why you decided to group certain words together on one list rather than place them on a different list."

A teacher initiated a brainstorming activity in her high school geometry class. The students, working in small groups, were asked to list in four minutes as many words as possible that were related to geometry. Then the groups shared their lists of geometry words as the teacher created a master list on the board from the individual entries of the groups. She also wrote three categories on the board—angles, shapes, and measures— and asked the groups to classify each word from the master list under one of the categories. Here's how one group organized some of the words from the master list:

Angles	Shapes	Measures
acute	polygon	circumference
right	trapezoid	protractor
obtuse	triangle	radius
	circle	area
	square	perimeter

Note that in this example, the teacher provided the categories. She recognized that students needed the additional structure to be successful with this task. Because of the activity, students were able to share what they knew with other members of the class and the teacher was able to identify gaps in students' understanding of concepts that could be addressed through subsequent readings and class discussions. Similarly, a social studies teacher used the list–group–label strategy during a unit study of Age of Enlightenment, an intellectual and philosophical movement that occurred throughout Europe in the 18th century. Students in her class had broad exposure to the topic from previous lessons. Next, she wanted to review their understanding of general topic concepts and begin to investigate those topics in depth. First, as a whole class, students brainstormed a list of words that came to mind as they recalled their previous reading about the Age of Enlightenment. Next, students worked in small groups to categorize the list of words based on commonalities. Finally, the whole class reconvened to discuss and reach consensus on the labels and words or phrases that corresponded to each label. Here is part of their final list:

Philosophers	Scientific Revolution	Political Theories
Voltaire	Telescope	Rationalism
Jean Jacques Rousseau	Laws of gravity	The Sovereign
John Locke	Sir Isaac Newton	The Social Contract
Thomas Hobbes	Scientific method	Reason

Word Sorts

Like brainstorming, word sorts require students to classify words into categories based on their prior knowledge. However, unlike brainstorming, students do not generate a list of words for a target concept. Instead, the teacher identifies the key words from the unit of study and invites the students to sort them into logical arrangements of two or more.

A word sort is a simple, yet valuable, activity. Individually or in small groups, students literally sort out technical terms that are written on cards or listed on an exercise sheet. The object of word sorting is to group words into different categories by looking for shared features among their meanings. There are two types of word sorts: the *open sort* and the *closed sort*. Both are easily adapted to any content area. In the **closed sort**, students know in advance of sorting what the main categories are. In other words, the criterion that the words in a group must share is stated. In a middle grade music class, students were studying the qualities of various "instrument families" of the orchestra.

Figure 8.8 Closed Sort for Musical Instruments

Strings (bow or plucked)	Woodwinds (single or double reed)	Brass (lips vibrate in mouthpiece)	Percussion (sounds of striking)
Violin	Flute	Trumpet	Timpani
Viola	Piccolo	Trombone	Bass drum
Cello	Oboe	French horn	Chimes
Harp	Clarinet		Xylophone
	Saxophone		Bells
	Bassoon		Triangle
			Snare drum

The music teacher assigned the class to work in pairs to sort musical instruments into four categories representing the major orchestral families: strings, woodwinds, brass, and percussion. Figure 8.8 represents the closed sort developed by one collaborative "think–pair–share" group. Similarly, Figure 8.9 shows how a social studies teacher applied a closed word sort to a unit on propaganda, and then extended that word sort strategy so that students could apply their understanding of the concepts they had studied.

Open sorts prompt divergent and inductive reasoning. No category or criterion for grouping is known in advance of sorting. Students must search for meanings and discover relationships among technical terms without the benefit of any structure.

Study how an art teacher activated what students knew about words associated with pottery making by using the open word sort strategy. She asked the high school students to work in collaborative pairs to arrange the following words into possible groups and to predict the concept categories in which the words would be classified:

jordan	lead	Cornwall stone	sgraffito
ball	chrome	cone	roka
antimony	slip	wheel	leather
cobalt	scale	bisque	hard
mortar	kaolin	stoneware	oxidation

Three categories that students formed were *types of clay, pottery tools,* and *coloring agents.* **Open word sorts** can be used before or after reading. Before reading, a word sort serves as an activation strategy to help learners make predictive connections among the words. After reading, word sorts enable students to clarify and extend their understanding of the conceptual relationships. For example, during a lesson on energy conservation and transfer, a science teacher began the lesson by asking students, "Who had heat in their home last night? How was the furnace able to make your home more comfortable?" This led students to begin thinking about energy transfer. Then, the teacher presented the students with the following words:

fuel	silver	warm air	embers
sparks	oxygen	copper	infrared waves
heat source	metals	light	kindling
gold	logs	firewood	

Before reading, the students tried, with mixed success, to make connections among the words. The open word sort served to activate their background knowledge and pique their interest in reading to learn more about this topic. After reading the text and discussing concepts related to energy transfer, the students revisited the open word sort. This time, they came to a consensus on the following categories for their word sort: *things a fire needs to burn; things a fire produces; fuels for a fire; good heat conductors.*

Figure 8.9 Closed Word Sort for a Social Studies Unit on Propaganda

This lesson focused on propaganda, covering how and why it is used, how it has developed over the years, and the various types of propaganda that are used. Vocabulary for this unit included various types of propaganda techniques that are used today. Students used a closed word sort to help them understand the connection between the terms as well as their purpose. Examples of vocabulary terms included:

A. **PLAIN FOLKS**—one of the common people

Examples: talking about growing up in small-town America; wearing boots and a cowboy hat while campaigning in Texas—anything to try to identify with the audience

B. **BANDWAGON**—everyone is supporting a candidate or a cause

Examples: posting a list of thousands of donors to your campaign on your website; claiming that the latest polls show you leading your opponent by 10 points

C. **TESTIMONIAL**—an important or famous person supports a candidate or a cause

Examples: A well-known musician sings at a campaign rally for a gubernatorial candidate

D. **NAME CALLING**—labeling as bad or not worthwhile

Examples: calling your opponent's plans "risky" or "wrongheaded"

E. **CARD STACKING**—presenting only those facts that are favorable to your side, by telling only either good things about your side or bad things about your opponent

Examples: listing recognitions you've received for your efforts as mayor; recounting 10 missed votes of your opponent

F. **GLITTERING GENERALITIES**—using broad, vague words and phrases that, while sounding nice, are not specific. This also involves the use of **slogans**.

Examples: campaign literature encourages support by saying: "Joe Smith, the time is now for leadership"; a candidate for school board claims to be for a quality education for all children and pledges to be fiscally responsible

G. **TRANSFER**—associating something or someone respected and approved of with a candidate or a cause—using objects, **symbols**, long-dead heroes.

Examples: appearing on stage before a very large American flag; mentioning former presidents in speeches, as in "I'm the only true Reagan Republican in the race."

Below is an example of how some of the terms were grouped in a closed word sort:

Encouraging a sense of identification with a person or cause:

plain folks, bandwagon, testimonial

Rejection and slanted analysis:

Name calling, card stacking

Using slogan and symbols:

Glittering generalities, transfer

Once propaganda techniques were defined and grouped, students were asked to apply these techniques by creating their own political ad using the following directives:

Create an ad for a mythical candidate for governor. This ad must use at least three propaganda techniques from those in today's lesson. Your ad may be a newspaper ad, a campaign flier or brochure, or the script for a radio or television ad.

What three propaganda techniques did you use in this ad? Circle the first propaganda technique used, underline the second technique used, and place large brackets around the third technique used. Then identify the techniques below:

- *First technique (circled):*
- *Second technique (underlined):*
- *Third technique (in large brackets):*

Knowledge Ratings

Text previewing strategies have been found to support students' comprehension (Bruns, Hodgson, Parker, & Fremont, 2011). As the procedure implies, **knowledge ratings** get readers to analyze what they know about a topic. The vocabulary list can be presented in a survey-like format that requires students to analyze each word individually, as in the three examples in Box 8.2.

Box 8.2 Evidence-Based Best Practices

Three Examples of Knowledge Ratings

Knowledge Rating from a Unit on Quadratic Functions and Systems of Equations in a High School Math Class

How much do you know about these words?

	Can Define	Have Seen/Heard	?
exponent	X		
intersection	X		
Domain			X
intercept		X	
Slope		X	
parabola			X
Origin		X	
Vertex		X	
irrationals	X		
Union		X	
coefficient		X	

Knowledge Rating from an Eight-Grade Language Arts Class on Poetry.

	I can define and use it.	I have heard it or read it.	I don't know this word.
Imagery			
Personification			
Alliteration			
Simile			
Metaphor			
Onomatopoeia			
Consonance			

Knowledge Rating from a High School Spanish I class.

Word	Meaning: I understand what it means in English	Speaking: I can pronounce it correctly	Listening: I can understand it when I hear it	Reading: I can understand it when I read it	Writing: I can use it to express an idea.
Descansar					
Ocupado					
Debido					
Jefe					
Empleo					
Trabajo					
Trabajar					

A follow-up discussion might revolve around questions such as these: Which are the hardest words? Which do you think most of the class doesn't know? Which are the easiest ones? Which will most of us know? Students should be encouraged within the context of the discussion to share what they know about the words. In this way, the teacher can assess and get some idea of the state of knowledge the class brings to the text reading or a larger unit of study.

These procedures are all a part of prereading preparation. Using one strategy, or two strategies in combination, can set the stage for students to read with confidence and engagement.

MyLab Education **Self-Check 8.2**

MyLab Education **Application Exercise 8.2:**
Using Graphic Organizers to Support Vocabulary Development in a
Content Area Classroom

Defining Words in the Context of Their Use

8.3 **Describe the strategies asking students to explore words in relationship to their context and to each other.**

Before considering a variety of extension activities that put students in the position of clarifying and refining their knowledge of words and concepts, consider strategies that permit text learners to define words in relation to the contexts in which they are used: the vocabulary self-collection strategy (VSS) and concept of definition (CD) procedure and problem-solving circles. By using a variety of instructional strategies for building content area vocabulary, teachers can help students to recognize when they do not understand a concept and to know how they might apply strategies to aid in their understanding of seemingly unfamiliar terms. Box 8.3 explains how problem-solving circles, a variation of literature circles commonly used in language arts, were applied in a mathematics class. Additionally, the VSS and concept of definition word maps (CD word maps) described in the following section are examples of instructional strategies that make students aware of and build learning strategies for defining words. Both activities invite students to use their texts to determine how words are defined in authentic contexts.

Box 8.3 Disciplinary Literacy

Using Problem-Solving Circles to Help Math Make Sense

Literacy skills are integral to mathematicians, but who can blame math teachers for being apprehensive about content area literacy? Too often, literacy in their classroom has included extra work that didn't really relate to their content. One math teacher in my school reported attending professional development that made literacy suggestions along the line of read-alouds, student research reports on famous mathematicians, and graphic organizers that had little to do with the actual discipline of math. What if teachers considered literacy as communication and thinking patterns, rather than simply reading and writing? This is the foundation of disciplinary literacy.

Math as a discipline can be broken down into eight general competencies that lead to a mastery of math concepts, practices, and general abilities (Hiltabidel, 2013):

1. Problem solving
2. Abstract and quantitative reasoning
3. Constructing arguments
4. Critiquing the arguments of others
5. Modeling/visualizing
6. Asking effective questions
7. Identifying, labeling, and categorizing
8. Understanding and using academic vocabulary

How does the math teacher teach these skills, all vital components of the discipline, while still teaching the curriculum? One middle school math teacher in our school found success in adapting literature circles, commonly used in English classes, to create problem-solving circles. The idea of problem-solving circles is based on the best practices of literature circles (Harvey, 2002). Literature circles provide students the opportunity to purposefully understand text by completing a task based on their roles. Students collaborate to build meaning and to reach consensus. To implement problem solving in mathematics, divide students into groups of four or five and assign each student a role from those listed below. Make sure students understand the responsibilities of their roles before they begin to problem-solve. You may want to model the roles or conduct a "fishbowl" where the students can watch an effective group implement the steps of problem solving. Next, provide each group with an authentic problem to solve, one that uses the concepts you are teaching. Then, as a group, using the skills of their roles, they will begin to solve the problem.

1. **Modeler**

    You will be responsible for modeling the problem. You may want to draw or make diagrams or charts to help your group *visualize* what is happening in the problem.

2. Questioner

You will be responsible for *questioning* your group members' interpretations of the problem, questioning their problem-solving techniques, and taking the problem itself apart.

3. Reader

You will be responsible for *reading* the problem, underlining words you don't know and words that might be essential to solving the problem. You should use your best reading techniques, such as chunking, highlighting, and practicing frequent checks of understanding.

4. Calculator

You will be doing the actual math. You are responsible for completing any *calculations*. You will work with your group to make sure all your calculations are done correctly. You should work to show all your work so that your group can explain its answers to another group.

Next, make vocabulary an integral part of students' daily practice. Teach the students to use word walls and personal dictionaries to understand what the problem is asking. Standards, texts, and Internet resources provide a starting point in building your own dictionary of terms. Websites such as Spelling City are helpful when building word banks.

The National Center for Educational Achievement (NCEA, 2009) highlights the following instructional components, all of which are supported within the tenants of disciplinary literacy, that support high achievement and authentic student success:

- Student engagement
- Inquiry-based instruction
- Cooperative learning
- Accessing students' prior learning
- Developing academic vocabulary

Thinking like a mathematician does not mean simply writing reports. It does not have to start with a read-aloud. Mathematicians are problem solvers and dynamic thinkers. They solve problems as they combine modeling, visualizing, critiquing, and questioning to analyze and evaluate the world around them. This is the foundation for implementing disciplinary literacy in a mathematics classroom.

Vocabulary Self-Collection Strategy

Vocabulary self-collection strategy (VSS) and vocabulary self-collection strategy plus technology (VSS+) promote the long-term acquisition of language in an academic discipline (Wolsey, Smetana, & Grisham, 2015). Students learn how to make decisions related to the importance of concepts and how to use context to determine what words mean. VSS has been found to be effective for teaching word meaning in context to students across ability levels (Harmon, Hedrick, Wood, & Gress, 2005) and for helping students to build independence as word learners (Ruddell & Shearer, 2002). The following steps may be used to begin the implementation of the vocabulary self-collection strategy:

1. *Divide the class into nominating teams of two to five students.* Together, the students on a nominating team decide which word to select for emphasis in the text selection. The teacher also nominates a word.

2. *Present the word that each team has selected to the entire class.* A spokesperson for each team identifies the nominated word and responds to the following questions:

   a. *Where is the word found in the text?* The spokesperson reads the passage in which the word is located or describes the context in which the word is used.

   b. *What do the team members think the word means?* The team members decide on what the word means in the context in which it is used. They must use information from the surrounding context and may also consult reference resources.

   c. *Why did the team think the class should learn the word?* The team must tell the class why the word is important enough to single out for emphasis.

The teacher first presents his or her nominated word to the class, modeling how to respond to the three questions. During the team presentations, the teacher facilitates the discussion, writes the nominated words on the board with their meanings, and invites class members to contribute additional clarifications of the words.

To conclude the class session, students record all the nominated words and their meanings in a section of their learning logs or in a separate vocabulary notebook. These lists may be used for review and study. Through the VSS, the teacher has a set of student-generated words that can be incorporated into a variety of follow-up vocabulary activities, as suggested in the next section.

Concept of Definition (CD) Word Maps

VSS provides opportunities to define and explore the meanings of words used in text readings. Many students, however, are not aware of the information that contributes to the meaning of a concept. Words in a text passage often provide only partial contextual information for defining the meaning of a concept.

Concept of definition (CD) word maps provide a framework for organizing conceptual information in the process of defining a word (Miller & Veatch, 2011; Schwartz & Raphael, 1985). Conceptual information can be organized by three types of relationships:

1. The general class or category in which the concept belongs
2. The attributes or properties of the concept and those that distinguish it from other members of the category
3. Examples or illustrations of the concept

CD word maps support vocabulary and concept learning by helping students internalize a strategy for defining and clarifying the meaning of unknown words. The hierarchical structure of a concept has an organizational pattern that is reflected by the general structure of a CD word map. In the center of the CD word map, students write the concept being studied. Working outward, they then write the word that best describes the general class or superordinate concept that includes the target concept. The answer to "What is it?" is the general class or category. Students then provide at least three examples of the concept as well as three properties by responding, respectively, to the questions "What are some examples?" and "What is it like?" Comparison of the target concept is also possible when students think of an additional concept that belongs to the general class but is different from the concept being studied. Figure 8.10 provides an example of a CD word map for the word *tiger*.

Figure 8.10 CD Word Map for the Word *Tiger*

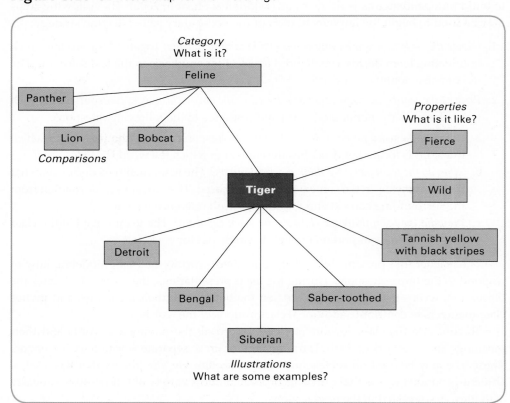

It is helpful to model CD word maps with students. This includes demonstrating the value of CD word mapping by connecting its purpose to how people use organizational patterns to aid memory and interpretation; introducing the general structure of a CD word map, explaining how the three probes define a concept, and walking students through the completion of a word map, and applying CD word mapping to an actual text selection.

Two caveats are relevant to CD word map instruction: CD word maps work best with concept words that function as nouns, but the procedure may be used, with some adaptation, with action words as well. A potential misuse of CD word maps occurs when teachers reproduce a general CD word map on the copier and expect students to define lists of words at the end of a text chapter. This is not the intent of CD word map instruction. Instead, students should internalize the process through demonstration and actual use, applying it as they need it for authentic text learning. Ultimately, the goal of CD word map instruction is to have students own the strategy of defining unknown words in terms of category, property, and example relationships.

MyLab Education
Video Example 8.2
Word Maps
Watch this video to learn about using word maps.

Reinforcing and Extending Vocabulary Knowledge and Concepts

As the vocabulary strategy interventions in this chapter suggest, using a single approach to vocabulary and concept development, such as a traditional dictionary definition approach, will not adequately meet the learning needs of all students. Adolescent learners require instruction that is responsive to both their learning needs and their developmental level (Fuchs, Fuchs, & Compton, 2010). Vocabulary instruction can be differentiated through the words chosen for study, application of definitions, and the teaching of relationships to underscore the context of more complex words (Vaughn et al., 2010). Some of the most successful strategies help students understand the importance of new vocabulary as it relates to their overall comprehension (Vaughn et al., 2010). It is important that teachers seek strategies that provide students with varied approaches to learning, using, and retaining new concepts while improving their overall comprehension (Duff, Fieldsend, Bowyer-Crane, & Hulme, 2008).

Students need many experiences, real and vicarious, to develop word meanings and concepts. They need to use, test, and manipulate technical terms in instructional situations that capitalize on reading, writing, speaking, and listening. In having students do these things, you create the kind of natural language environment that is needed to extend vocabulary and concept development. Various vocabulary extension activities can be useful in this respect. These activities should be completed individually by students and then discussed either in small groups or class. Through verbal interaction, students can exchange ideas, share insights, and justify responses in a nonthreatening context.

MyLab Education
Video Example 8.3
Secondary Science Vocabulary Strategies
Watch this video to learn about the importance of teaching concepts instead of simply memorizing definitions.

Semantic Feature Analysis (SFA)

Semantic feature analysis (SFA) establishes a meaningful link between students' prior knowledge and words that are conceptually related to one another. The strategy requires that you develop a chart or grid to help students analyze similarities and differences among the related concepts. As the SFA grid in Figure 8.11 illustrates, a topic or category (in this case, classifications of real numbers in an algebra class) is selected, words related to that category are written across the top of the grid and features or

Figure 8.11 Semantic Feature Analysis: Classification of Real Numbers

Determine which of these properties is found in the real numbers listed. Write Y (yes), N (no), or? if you are not sure.

	Whole Numbers	Natural Numbers	Integers	Rational Numbers	Irrational Numbers
Can be written as a fraction					
Include zero					
Can be a repeating decimal					
Can be negative					

properties shared by some of the words in the column are listed down the left side of the grid.

Students analyze each word, feature by feature, writing Y (yes) or N (no) in each cell of the grid to indicate whether the feature is associated with the word. Students may write a question mark (?) if they are uncertain about a feature.

A variation of a semantic feature analysis used in a computer science class is depicted in Figure 8.12. In developing this SFA, the teacher listed different types of web browsers down the left side of the grid. Words related to features that might be present in web browsers were listed across the top of the grid. Students were asked to use a plus sign (+) to indicate that a feature was present in a web browser or a minus sign (−) to indicate that a feature was not present. The teacher and her students revisited this SFA periodically throughout the course to update it as newer versions of some web browsers became available. Doing so led to class discussions on topics such as the marketing of web browsers, different ways that web servers ensure the security of customers who communicate and shop online, and technology's influence on the way people conduct everyday tasks such as information gathering, shopping, and bill paying.

As a teaching activity, SFA is easily suited to before- or after-reading instructional routines. If you use it before reading to activate what students know about words, recognize that they can return to the SFA after reading to clarify and reformulate some of their

Figure 8.12 A Semantic Feature Analysis for Computer Applications

Directions: Determine which of these properties is found in the web browsers listed.

	RSS Support	Support for Active X	Google Search from Toolbar	Tabbed Browsing	Pop-Up Blocking	Themes/ Skins
Firefox						
Internet Explorer						
Opera						
Safari						

initial responses on the SFA grid. In Box 8.4, "Voices From the Field," read how Tracy devised an effective SFA strategy for her biology class.

Categorization Activities

Vocabulary extension exercises involving categorization require students to determine relationships among technical terms much as word sorts do. Students are usually given four to six words per grouping and asked to do something with them.

Box 8.4 Voices from the Field

Tracy, Tenth-Grade Biology Teacher

Challenge

I noticed that students in my biology class seemed to have difficulty retaining information about specific concepts and vocabulary. Therefore, I wanted to incorporate strategies that would engage students more actively in learning important biology terms. In the past, I've had my students create vocabulary posters as part of their homework assignments. When studying the human body systems, students illustrated a given concept or term with a drawing, clip art, or a photo to help them remember the information. For example, when learning about the functions of the heart, some students represented this concept with an illustration of a pump, including a gasoline pump, bike pump, or even someone pumping iron. Students spent a lot of time on the assignment and enjoyed the activity, but they didn't seem to remember the concepts and the vocabulary.

Strategy

In order to help students process the connections between a given concept and its meaning, I continued to incorporate the homework assignment of illustrating the vocabulary word. However, this time, I asked students to add some written explanation of why they made their decision to illustrate the concept the way they did. For example, if a student used a balloon to illustrate the bladder, I would expect him or her to write something about how the bladder is like a balloon (i.e., because it can stretch and hold things). By writing to learn, I hoped that students would be able to add the information to their long-term memory. More recently, I used the semantic feature analysis as an informal assessment to see what students had learned so far about our topic of the excretory system. I began by creating a chart, shown below, with specific vocabulary, facts, and concepts chosen to summarize the topic we had been studying. I modeled the activity first by doing an example with my students. Then they continued independently by analyzing each concept and marking the column with a + or − to indicate if the words were conceptually related to one another.

Excretory System	Lungs	Skin	Kidneys	Liver
Excretes water				
Excretes urea				
Excretes carbon dioxide				
Excretes urine				

Reflection

After I enhanced the vocabulary illustration activity with a written component and incorporated the semantic feature analysis, students in my biology class were better able to create a meaningful link among concepts, their meanings, and their relationships to various body systems. Students' performance on a quiz showed that they consistently had a better recall and a better understanding of the terms and concepts. When we reviewed for the quiz, the students seemed more confident in their answers, where previously they tended to fish for the information and responses. Scores on the quiz itself improved compared with scores on previous quizzes. Even the typically struggling students scored 90% or above. Prior to using the semantic feature analysis as a learning tool, these students performed inconsistently on assessments with scores ranging from 70% to 100%. Now the majority were at a mastery level.

Students were engaged during the semantic feature analysis activity. They viewed it as a puzzle or game, and it was easy and fun for them to complete it. The novelty of the activity helped too. There was not a lot of writing, but they had to know the information in order to complete the activity successfully. Perhaps in the future, I will have students write a statement after completing the semantic feature analysis to explain their thinking and to tie all of the information together. I have also created a semantic feature analysis to review for the midterm exam. I hope that organizing and categorizing information will help students spark their memory and summarize the information learned in class.

Review for Midterm	Nervous System	Endocrine System
Carries electrical messages		
Carries chemical messages		
Carries messages on neurons		
Carries messages in blood stream		
Controls reactions to stimulus		
Involves brain and spinal cord		
Involves glands		
Message must jump over gap known as synapse		
Neurotransmitter must fit receptors on dendrite		
Involves hormones		
Involves receptors		
Involves target cells		
Hormones must fit receptor on target cell		
Involves neurotransmitters		
Involves dendrites		
Involves axons		
Message travels slower (minutes, hours, days)		
Message travels very fast (less than one second)		

That something depends on the format used in the exercise. For example, you can give students sets of words and ask them to circle in each set the word that includes the others. This exercise demands that students perceive common attributes or examples in relation to a more inclusive concept and to distinguish superordinate from subordinate terms. Following is an example from an eighth-grade social studies class.

Directions: Circle the word in each group that includes the others.

1. government
   council
   judges
   governor

2. throne
   coronation
   crown
   church

A variation on this format directs students to cross out the word that does not belong and then to explain in a word or phrase the relationship that exists among the common items, as illustrated in the following example.

Directions: Cross out the word in each set that does not belong. On the line above the set, write the word or phrase that explains the relationship among the remaining three words.

1. _____

    drama
    comedy
    epic
    tragedy

2. _____

    time
    character
    place
    action

Concept Circles

One of the most versatile activities we have observed at a wide range of grade levels is the concept circle. **Concept circles** provide still another format and opportunity for studying words critically—for students to relate words conceptually to one another. A concept circle may simply involve putting words or phrases in the sections of a circle and directing students to describe or name the concept relationship among the sections. The example in Figure 8.13 is from a middle grade science lesson.

In addition, you might direct students to shade in the section of a concept circle containing a word or phrase that *does not relate* to the words or phrases in the other sections of the circle and then identify the concept relationships that exist among the remaining sections (see Figure 8.14).

Finally, you can modify a concept circle by leaving one or two sections of the circle empty, as in Figure 8.15. Direct students to fill in the empty section with a word or two that relates in some way to the terms in the other sections of the concept circle. Students must then justify their word choice by identifying the overarching concept depicted by the circle.

Figure 8.13 The Concept Circle

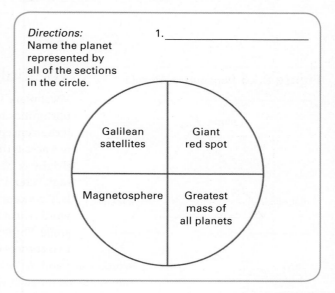

Figure 8.14 A Variation on the Concept Circle

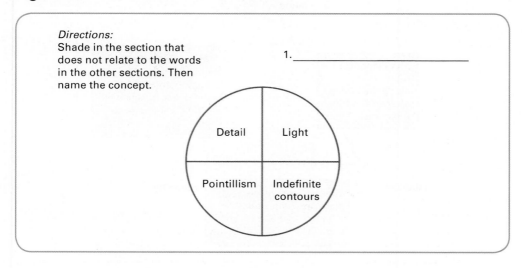

Figure 8.15 Another Variation on the Concept Circle

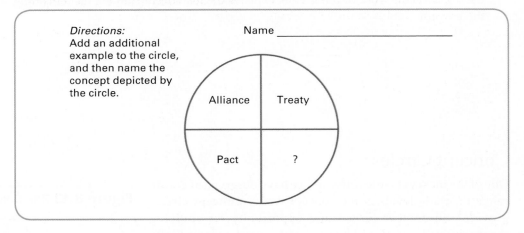

Figure 8.16 Vocabulary Triangle

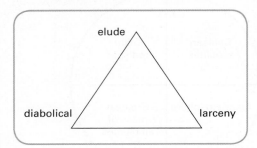

Vocabulary Triangles

Vocabulary triangles are another visual tool for providing students with opportunities to consider the relationships among word concepts and to apply those concepts in meaningful ways. Vocabulary triangles can be adapted for use across different content areas and for use with different levels of learners (Digby & Mayers, 1993). Figure 8.16 shows a vocabulary triangle used by a high school English teacher to help her students review and apply vocabulary concepts that had been discussed during their reading. She selected the words *elude, diabolical,* and *larceny* and placed each word in a corner of the triangle. Students were then asked to write sentences connecting the words from two corners of the triangle. Figure 8.17 shows how one student connected the words *elude* and *diabolical, diabolical* and *larceny,* and *larceny* and *elude,* creating a separate sentence for each word pair. By the time they had completed the triangle, students

Figure 8.17 Vocabulary Triangle with Paired Sentences

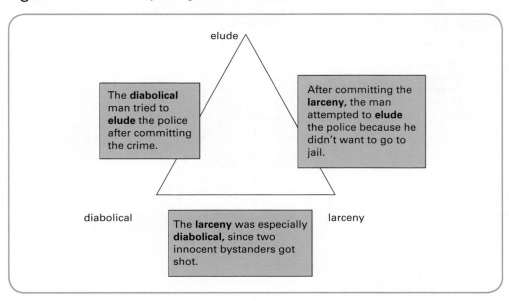

had applied each word twice in relation to another concept from their reading. Finally, as shown in Figure 8.18, students created one sentence that combined all three words from the triangle.

Magic Squares

The magic square activity is by no means new or novel, yet it has a way of reviving even the most mundane matching exercise. We have seen the magic square used successfully in elementary and secondary grades as well as in graduate courses. Here's how a **magic square** works. An activity sheet has two columns, one for content area terms and one for definitions or other distinguishing statements such as characteristics or examples (see Figure 8.19). Direct students to match terms with definitions. In doing so, they must take into account the letters signaling the terms and the numbers signaling the definitions. The students then put the number of a definition in the proper space (denoted by the letter of the term) in the "magic square answer box." If their matchups are correct, they will form a magic square. That is, the numerical total will be the same for each row across and each column down the answer box. This total forms the puzzle's "magic number." Students need to add up the rows and columns to check if they're coming up with the same number each time. If not, they should go back to the terms and definitions to reevaluate their answers.

The magic square exercise in Figure 8.19 is from a family and consumer studies class. Try it. Its magic number is 15. Analyze the mental maneuvers that you went through to

Figure 8.18 Vocabulary Triangle with Combined Sentence

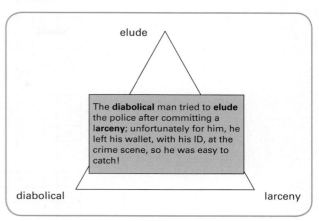

Figure 8.19 Magic Square: Analyzing Food Labels

Directions: Select the best answer for each of the terms from the numbered definitions. Put the number in the proper space in the magic square box. If the totals of the numbers are the same both across and down, you have found the magic number!

A. Serving size	**1.** Provides recommended dietary information for important nutrients, including fats, sodium, and fiber
B. Servings per container	
C. Calories	**2.** The nutrients listed first should be limited
D. Fat, cholesterol, sodium	**3.** How many portions are in a package
E. Fiber, vitamins	**4.** Eating enough of these nutrients can improve your health and help reduce the risk of some diseases and conditions
F. Trans fats, protein, and sugars	
G. Percent daily value	**5.** Provides a measure of how much energy you get from a serving of this food
H. 2,000	**6.** Recommendations for key nutrients but only for a 2,000-calorie daily diet
i. Footnote	**7.** Influences the number of calories and all the nutrient amounts listed on the top part of the label
	8. Recommended daily caloric intake
	9. Nutrients without a percent daily value

A	B	C
D	E	F
G	H	I

SOURCE: Information taken from the FDA website: www.cfsan.fda.gov/~dms/foodlab.html.

Figure 8.20 A Model of Magic Square Combinations

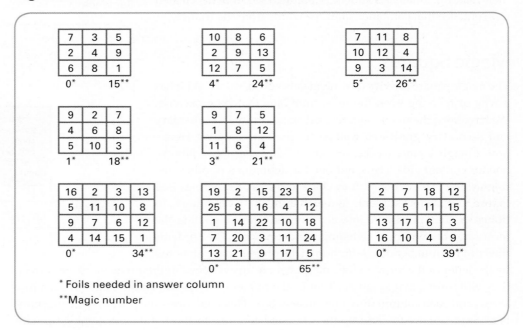

* Foils needed in answer column

**Magic number

determine the correct number combinations. In some cases, you undoubtedly knew the answers outright. You may have made several educated guesses on others. Did you try to beat the number system? Imagine the possibilities for small-group interaction.

Many teachers are intrigued by the possibilities offered by the magic square, but they remain wary of its construction: "I can't spend hours figuring out number combinations." This is a legitimate concern. Luckily, the eight combinations in Figure 8.20 make magic square activities easy to construct. You can generate many more combinations from the eight patterns simply by rearranging rows or columns (see Figure 8.21).

Notice that the single asterisk in Figure 8.20 denotes the number of foils needed so that several of the combinations can be completed. For example, the magic number combination of 18 requires one foil in the number 1 slot that will not match with any of the corresponding items in the matching exercise. To complete the combination, the number 10 is added. Therefore, when you develop a matching activity for combination 18, there will be 10 items in one column and nine in the other, with item 1 being the foil.

Figure 8.21 Variations on Magic Square Combinations

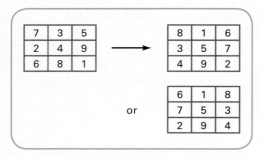

MyLab Education **Self-Check 8.3**

MyLab Education **Application Exercise 8.3:**
Using Multiple Strategies to Develop Content Area Vocabulary Knowledge

Vocabulary-Building Strategies

8.4 **Describe the strategies students can use independently to build their vocabulary knowledge.**

Showing learners how to construct meaning for unfamiliar words encountered during reading helps them develop strategies needed to monitor comprehension and increase their own vocabularies. Box 8.5 offers suggestions for supporting English Learners in

Box 8.5 Supporting English Learners

Strategies presented in this chapter promote students' vocabulary knowledge and reading comprehension. English Learners (ELs), with limited vocabulary knowledge, often struggle with reading comprehension. Approaches presented in this chapter can be effective for both native English speakers and ELs. The following suggestions can further support vocabulary development for ELs:

- *Be strategic with word choice:* English Learners and native English speakers will have differing vocabulary needs. This must be considered when choosing words for word study and vocabulary instruction. In addition, when choosing words to study, consider the English language proficiency of English Learners. A beginning English Learner will have different needs than an intermediate English Learner. Assessing ELs' word knowledge prior to instruction allows teachers to target specific vocabulary needs and provide vocabulary instruction that is most beneficial.

- *Increase time devoted to before-reading activities:* English Learners are likely to encounter many unknown words in reading selections and require increased time on before-reading activities that promote vocabulary and concept understanding. The focus of before-reading activities should be familiarizing ELs with key vocabulary and concepts (Herrell & Jordan, 2016). For example, before students read a selection on *camping*, the teacher should bring in pictures of a tent and other important objects used while camping and create a chart listing key information for each picture. English Learners should be provided with increased time to discuss and familiarize themselves with new vocabulary and concepts that are essential for their understanding of the text.

- *Use realia:* Realia, or concrete objects, can be used in the classroom to build background knowledge and promote vocabulary development. Blending realia into lessons that contain new or challenging vocabulary provides English Learners with opportunities to learn through their senses (Herrell & Jordan, 2016). Teachers should identify opportunities to include realia through a close examination of texts that will be used in the classroom to identify unfamiliar vocabulary and locate realia that will assist ELs in their understanding of new concepts.

- *Use manipulatives:* Manipulatives, or concrete devices that students can use to support learning, are important tools for English Learners. The use of manipulatives provides ELs with the opportunity to connect abstract concepts with concrete experiences (Echevarria, Vogt, & Short, 2010). For example, attribute blocks can be used to teach new vocabulary and concepts around shape, size, texture, and color.

- *Increase understanding of concepts using visual images:* Word sorts and graphic organizers can be an effective way for English Learners to view and construct relationships among words. The use of word sorts and graphic organizers with ELs should include words along with visual representations which support concept understanding for students who have a limited vocabulary (Gunning, 2006).

- *Personalize word study:* The use of vocabulary notebooks provides English Learners with the opportunity to focus on words and concepts specific to their individual language needs. As students encounter new words, they can add them to their vocabulary notebooks. Recorded words can include a written definition; student-created symbols or drawings to illustrate the meaning of the word; a sentence using the word, synonyms and/or antonyms for the word; or any other helpful information that provides the student with support for mastering word meaning. Vocabulary notebooks can become personal dictionaries, increasing interest and supporting understanding of new words and their meanings (Peregoy & Boyle, 2013).

- *Utilize students' native language:* English Learners can benefit from direct instruction of new vocabulary words and concepts in their native language. This can be a difficult task since most schools are not equipped to instruct in multiple languages. Another way to utilize students' native language is to examine cognates. Cognates are words that are similar between two languages. Spanish-speaking students can use their native language abilities to assist them in learning new vocabulary. For example, knowledge of the word *año* (year) can assist Spanish-speaking students in gaining an understanding of new vocabulary, such as *annual*. Helping English Learners make the connection between cognates provides ELs with a valuable tool for learning new vocabulary (Gunning, 2019).

- *Use dictionaries as a resource:* Dictionaries can be used as a resource that can provide both native English-speaking students and English Learners with valuable insight into the meaning of unknown words. Picture dictionaries, bilingual dictionaries, and monolingual dictionaries are three types of dictionaries that are most effective with English Learners (Peregoy & Boyle, 2013). Picture dictionaries can provide ELs with high-quality illustrations and diagrams. Bilingual dictionaries can be used with English Learners who are literate in their native language. ELs can look up a word in their native language and find it in English or look up a word in English and find it in their native language.

developing the vocabulary needed to comprehend content area concepts. Demonstrating how to use *context, word structure,* and the *dictionary* provides students with several basic strategies for vocabulary learning that will last a lifetime. With these strategies, students can search for information clues while reading so that they can approximate the meanings of unknown words. These clues often reveal enough meaning to allow readers who struggle with text to continue reading without "short-circuiting" the process and giving up because the text does not make sense.

You can scaffold the use of vocabulary-building strategies before assigning material to be read. If one or more words represent key concepts—and the words lend themselves to demonstration—you can model the inquiry process necessary to construct meaning. The demonstration is brief, often lasting no more than five minutes. There are three types of demonstrations that will make students aware of vocabulary-building strategies. The first is to model how to make sense of a word in the context of its use, the second involves an analysis of a word's structure, and the third combines context and word structure. Usually these demonstrations require the use of visuals, such as an overhead transparency or a whiteboard. After the brief demonstration, guide students to practice and apply the strategy that you just modeled so that they can become proficient in its use.

Using Context to Approximate Meaning

Constructing meaning from context is one of the most useful strategies at the command of proficient readers. Showing readers who struggle how to make use of context builds confidence and competence and teaches the inquiry process necessary to unlock the meaning of troublesome technical and general vocabulary encountered during reading. Using context involves using information surrounding a difficult word to help reveal its meaning. Every reader makes some use of context automatically. Strategy instruction, however, is needed when the text provides a *deliberate context* to help the reader with concept terms that are especially difficult. Often the text author will anticipate that certain words will be troublesome and will provide information clues and contextual aids to help readers with meaning. In these instances, students will benefit from a strategy that allows them to use the deliberate context to construct meaning.

The use of context is mostly a matter of inference. Inference requires readers to see an explicit or implicit relationship between an unfamiliar word and its context or to connect what they know already with the unknown term. It can't be assumed that students will perceive these relationships or make the connections on their own. Most students who struggle with text simply don't know how to use a deliberate context provided by an author. Three kinds of information are useful to struggling readers: *typographic, syntactic, semantic*, and *logographic* clues and cues.

TYPOGRAPHIC CLUES Typographic or format clues make use of footnotes, italics, boldface print, parenthetical definitions, pictures, graphs, charts, and the like. A typographic clue provides a clear-cut connection and a direct reference to an unknown word. Many students tend to gloss over a typographic aid instead of using it to spotlight the meaning of a difficult term. The teacher can rivet attention to these aids with minimal expenditure of class time.

For example, consider the way a science teacher modeled a strategy for revealing the meaning of the word *enzymes*, which was presented in boldface type in the text. Before assigning a text section titled "Osmosis in Living Cells," the teacher asked students to "turn to page 241." Then he asked, "Which word in the section on osmosis stands out among the others?" The students quickly spotted the word *enzymes*. "Why do you think this word is highlighted in boldface type?" he asked. A student replied, "I guess it must be important." Another student said, "Maybe because it has something to do with osmosis—whatever that is." The teacher nodded approvingly and then asked the students to see if they could figure out what *enzymes* meant by reading this sentence: "Chemical substances called **enzymes** are produced by cells to break down large starch molecules into small sugar molecules."

The science teacher continued the demonstration by asking two questions: "What are enzymes?" and "What do they do?" The students responded easily. The teacher concluded the walk-through with these words: "Words that are put in large letters or boldfaced print are important. If you pay attention to them as we just did, you will have little trouble figuring out what they mean. There are four other words in boldfaced type in your reading assignment. Look for them as you read and try to figure out what they mean."

SYNTACTIC AND SEMANTIC CLUES Syntactic and semantic clues in content materials should not be treated separately. The grammatical relationship among words in a sentence or the structural arrangement among sentences in a passage often helps clarify the meaning of a word.

Syntactic and semantic clues are much more subtle than typographic clues. Table 8.1 presents a summary of the most frequently encountered syntactic and semantic clues.

Help students visualize the inquiry process necessary to reveal meaning. For example, if a *definition clue* is used, as in this example from Table 8.1 ("Entomology is the study of insects, and biologists who specialize in this field are called entomologists") it may be appropriate first to display the term. During the modeling discussion, you can then show how *is* and *are called* provide information clues that reveal meaning for *entomology* and *entomologists*. A simple strategy would be to cross out *is* and *are called* in the sentence and replace them with equal signs (=):

> Entomology ~~is~~ = the study of insects, and biologists who specialize in this field ~~are called~~ = entomologists.

Table 8.1 Syntactic and Semantic Contextual Clues

Type of Clue	Explanation	Examples
Definition	The author equates the unknown word to the known or more familiar, usually using a form of the verb be.	*Entomology* **is** the study of insects, and biologists who specialize in this field **are called** *entomologists*. A *critical review* **is** an attempt to evaluate the worth of a piece of writing.
Linked synonyms	The author pairs the unknown word with familiar synonyms or closely related words in a series.	Kunta Kinte was the victim of **cruel, evil,** *malevolent,* and **brutal** slave traders. The senator from Connecticut possessed the traits of an honest and just leader: **wisdom, judgment,** *sagacity.*
Direct description: examples, modifiers, restatements	The author reveals the meaning of an unknown word by providing additional information in the form of appositives, phrases, clauses, or sentences.	*Example clue:* Undigested material, **such as fruit skins, outer parts of grain, and the string-like parts of some vegetables,** forms *roughage.* *Modifier clues:* Pictographic writing, **which was the actual drawing of animals, people, and events,** is the forerunner of written language. *Algae,* **nonvascular plants that are as abundant in water as grasses are on land,** have often been called "grasses of many waters." *Restatement clue:* A billion dollars a year are spent on *health quackery.* **In other words, each year in the United States, millions of dollars are spent on worthless treatments and useless gadgets to "cure" various illnesses.**
Contrast	The author reveals the meaning of an unknown word by contrasting it with an antonym or a phrase that is opposite in meaning.	You have probably seen animals perform tricks at the zoo, on television, or in a circus. Maybe you taught a dog to fetch a newspaper. **But learning tricks—usually for a reward—is very different from** *cognitive problem solving.* It wasn't a *Conestoga* like Pa's folks came in. **Instead, it was just an old farm wagon drawn by one tired horse.**
Cause and effect	The author establishes a cause-and-effect relationship in which the meaning of an unknown word can be hypothesized.	The *domestication* of animals probably began when young animals were caught or strayed into camps. **As a result, people enjoyed staying with them and made pets of them.** A family is *egalitarian* **when both husband and wife make decisions together and share responsibilities equally.**
Mood and tone	The author sets a mood (ironic, satirical, serious, funny, etc.) in which the meaning of an unknown word can be hypothesized.	A sense of *resignation* engulfed my thoughts as **the feeling of cold grayness was everywhere around me.** The *tormented* animal **screeched with horror and writhed in pain as it tried desperately to escape** from the hunter's trap.

*Italics denote the unknown words. Boldface type represents information clues that trigger context revelation.

A brief discussion will reinforce the function of the verb forms *is* and *are called* in the sentence.

The definition clue is the least subtle of the syntactic and semantic clues. However, all the clues in Table 8.1 require students to make inferential leaps. Consider one of the examples from the mood and tone clue: "The tormented animal screeched with horror and writhed in pain as it tried desperately to escape from the hunter's trap." Suppose this sentence came from a short story to be assigned in an English class. Assume also that many of the students would have trouble with the word *tormented* as it is used in the sentence. If students are to make the connection between *tormented* and the mood created by the information clues, the teacher will have to ask several effective clarifying questions.

The demonstration begins with the teacher writing the word *tormented* on the board. She asks, "You may have heard or read this word before, but how many of you think that you know what it means?" Student definitions are put on the board. The teacher then writes the sentence on the board. "Which of the definitions on the board do you think best fits the word *tormented* when it's used in this sentence?" She encourages students to support their choices. If none fits, she will ask for more definitions now that students have seen the sentence. She continues questioning, "Are there any other words or phrases in the sentence that help us get a feel for the meaning of *tormented*? Which ones?"

The inquiry into the meaning of *tormented* continues in this fashion. The information clues (*screeched with horror, writhed in pain, desperately*) that establish the mood are underlined and discussed. The teacher concludes the modeling activity by writing five new words on the board and explaining, "These words are also in the story that you are about to read. As you come across them, stop and think. How do the words or phrases or sentences surrounding each word create a certain feeling or mood that will allow you to understand what each one means?"

When modeling the use of context in Table 8.1, it's important for students to discover the information clues. It's also important for the teacher to relate the demonstration to several additional words to be encountered in the assignment. Instruction of this type can have a significant cumulative effect on student learning.

LOGOGRAPHIC CUES Logographs are visual symbols that represent a word. When paired with vocabulary instruction, logographs can become logographic cues (Beers, 2003) to support students' understanding of vocabulary concepts. Logographic cues are visual aids that students create to help them learn vocabulary concepts. On the front of a note card, students write the vocabulary word they are trying to learn; on the back of the note card, students write the definition in their own words as well as their own visual representation of the word based on its meaning. The visualization required in generating their own cue can help students to understand and retain vocabulary concepts and to make connections between their own image of a concept and its definition (Harvey & Goudvis, 2007). Logographic cues are particularly effective in content areas such as science because they help students to see abstract concepts, such as atoms and protons, in ways that make sense to them. By taking the time to think logically about a word and to create a visual representation for it, students are more likely to understand and remember its meaning.

Context-Related Activities

Readers who build and use contextual knowledge can recognize fine shades of meaning in the way words are used. They know the concept behind the word well enough to use that concept in different contexts. In the following sections, we suggest two ways to extend a student's contextual knowledge of content area terms.

MODIFIED CLOZE PASSAGES   Cloze passages can be created to reinforce technical vocabulary. However, the teacher usually modifies the procedure for teaching purposes. Every *n*th word, for example, needn't be deleted. The modified cloze passage will vary in length. Typically, a 200- to 500-word text segment yields sufficient technical vocabulary to make the activity worthwhile.

Should you consider developing a modified cloze passage on a segment of text from a reading assignment, make sure that the text passage is one of the most important parts of the assignment. Depending on your objectives, students can supply the missing words either before or after reading the entire assignment. If they work on the cloze activity before reading, use the subsequent discussion to build meaning for key terms and to raise expectations for the assignment. If you assign the cloze passage after reading, it will reinforce concepts attained through reading.

On completing a brief prereading discussion on the causes of the Civil War, an American history teacher assigned a cloze passage before students read the entire introduction for homework. See how well you fare on the first part of the exercise.

> What caused the Civil War? Was it inevitable? To what extent and in what ways was slavery to blame? To what extent was each region of the nation at fault? Which were more decisive—the intellectual or the emotional issues?
>
> Any consideration of the (1) of the war must include the problem of (2). In his second inaugural address, Abraham Lincoln said that slavery was "somehow the cause of the war." The critical word is "(3)." Some (4) maintain that the moral issue had to be solved, the nation had to face the (5), and the slaves had to be (6). Another group of historians asserts that the war was not fought over (7). In their view, slavery served as an (8) focal point for more fundamental (9) involving two different (10) of the Constitution. All these views have merit, but no single view has won unanimous support.
>
> *(Answers can be found on page 249.)*

OPIN   OPIN is a meaning-extending vocabulary strategy that provides another example of context-based reinforcement and extension. OPIN stands for *opinion* and also plays on the term *cloze*.

Here's how OPIN works. Divide the class into groups of three. Distribute exercise sentences, one to each student. Each student must complete each exercise sentence individually. Then each group member must convince the other two members that his or her word choice is the best. If no agreement is reached on the best word for each sentence, each member of the group can speak to the class for his or her individual choice. When all groups have finished, have the class discuss each group's choices. The only rule of discussion is that each choice must be accompanied by a reasonable defense or justification. Answers such as "Because ours is best" are not acceptable.

For example, an English teacher used the OPIN strategy as a way to introduce the vocabulary of dramas to her students, using terms such as *antagonist, protagonist, soliloquy, aside, parody, wit,* and *foil.* She presented the following statements and asked her students to choose the words that they believe best complete each sentence, providing a rationale to the other group members for their selections:

1. Ms. Dee obsessed over the recent events, the class now twice able to _____ her efforts.

2. She turned to confront her _____.

3. The student made the remark as an _____, not intending Ms. Dee to hear him.

4. Ms. Dee was not impressed by the intended _____ of the student during class.

5. Ms. Dee explained that the assignment was to be a _____ of what the play was about.

6. The students discovered the _____ was easy to understand.

7. Ms. Dee chose to stop the reading after the _____.

OPIN exercise sentences can be constructed for any content area. As part of a unit study on expressions and equations, students divided into small groups of three. They were provided with the following simple expressions and asked to identify equivalent expressions:

$$3(2 + x)$$
$$24x + 18y$$
$$x + y + x + y$$
$$15(x + 2)$$

First, each student attempted the task individually. Then he or she attempted to persuade the other members of the small group that the equivalent expression selected was the best choice. Each group shared its consensus, or lack thereof, with the class. Each equivalent expression was required to be accompanied by a reasonable explanation. The full class had the opportunity to discuss the thought process behind the selection of equivalent expressions. Below are correct equivalent expressions for the examples given:

$$3(2 + x) = 6 + 3x$$
$$24x + 18y = 6(4x + 3y)$$
$$x + y + x + y = 2x + 2y$$
$$15(x + 2) = 15x + 30$$

OPIN encourages differing opinions about which word should be inserted in a blank space. In one sense, the exercise is open to discussion; and as a result, it reinforces the role of prior knowledge and experiences in the decisions that each group makes. The opportunity to "argue" one's responses in the group leads not only to continued motivation but also to a discussion of word meanings and variations.

Word Structure

In addition to emphasizing context as a vocabulary-building strategy, showing learners how to approximate word meaning through word structure is another important aspect of vocabulary building. A word itself provides information clues about its meaning. The smallest unit of meaning in a word is called a *morpheme*. Analyzing a word's structure, *morphemic analysis,* is a second vocabulary-building strategy that students can use to predict meaning. When readers encounter an unknown word, they can reduce the number of feasible guesses about its meaning considerably by approaching the whole word and identifying its parts. When students use morphemic analysis in combination with context, they have a powerful strategy at their command. The relationship between morphology knowledge and vocabulary development appears to be reciprocal: Students who have acquired larger vocabularies tend to have a greater understanding of morphology, and building an understanding of morphology helps students to expand their vocabularies (Kieffer & Lesaux, 2007).

Student readers often find long words daunting. A long or polysyllabic word falls within one of four categories:

1. *Compound words made up of two known words joined together.* Examples: *commonwealth, matchmaker*

2. *Words containing a recognizable stem to which an affix (a prefix, combining form, or suffix) has been added.* Examples: *surmountable, deoxygenize, unsystematic, microscope*

3. *Words that can be analyzed into familiar and regular pronounceable units.* Examples: *undulate, calcify, subterfuge, strangulate*

4. *Words that contain irregular pronounceable units so that there is no sure pronunciation unless one consults a dictionary.* Examples: *louver, indictment*

Content vocabulary terms from categories 1 and 2 (compound words and recognizable stems and affixes) are the best candidates for instruction. You can readily demonstrate techniques for predicting the meanings of these words because each of their isolated parts will always represent a meaning unit.

In some instances, a word from category 3 may also be selected for emphasis. However, there is no guarantee that students will bring prior knowledge and experience to words that comprise the third category. Long phonemically regular words lend themselves to syllabication. Syllabication involves breaking words into pronounceable sound units or syllables. The word *undulate,* for example, can be syllabicated (un-du-late). However, the syllable *un* is not a meaning-bearing prefix.

Many words from category 3 are derived from Latin or Greek. Students who struggle with texts will find these words especially difficult to analyze for meaning because of their lack of familiarity with Latin or Greek roots. Occasionally, a word such as *strangulate* (derived from the Latin *strangulatus*) can be taught because students may recognize the familiar word *strangle.* They might then be shown how to link *strangle* to the verb suffix *-ate* (which means "to cause to become") to hypothesize a meaning for *strangulate.* Unfortunately, the verb suffix *-ate* has multiple meanings, and the teacher should be quick to point this out to students. This procedure is shaky, but it has some payoff.

Words from category 2 warrant instruction because English root words are more recognizable, obviously, than Latin or Greek ones. Whenever feasible, teach the principles of structural word analysis using terms that have English roots. Certain affixes are more helpful than others and knowing which affixes to emphasize during instruction will minimize students' confusion.

The most helpful affixes are the combining forms, prefixes, or suffixes that have single, invariant meanings. (See Appendix A.) Many other commonly used prefixes have more than one meaning or have several shades of meaning. Because of their widespread use in content terminology, you should also consider these variant-meaning prefixes for functional teaching. (See Appendix B for a list of prefixes with varying meanings.)

The tables of affixes are resources for you. Don't be misled into thinking that students should learn long lists of affixes in isolation to help in analyzing word structure. This approach is neither practical nor functional. We recommend instead that students be taught affixes as they are needed to analyze the structure of terms that will appear in a reading assignment.

For example, an English teacher modeled how to analyze the meaning of *pandemonium* before students were to encounter the term in an assignment from *One Flew Over the Cuckoo's Nest.* She wrote the word on the board—pan*demon*ium—underlining the English base word *demon,* and asked students for several synonyms for the word. Student responses included *witch, devil, monster,* and *wicked people.*

Then she explained that -*ium* was a noun suffix meaning "a place of." "Now let's look at *pan*. Sheila, have you ever heard of the Pan American Games? They are like the Olympics, but what do you think is a major difference between the Olympics and the Pan American Games?" Sheila and several students responded to the question. A brief discussion led the students to conclude the Pan American Games, like the Olympics, are a series of athletic contests; however, unlike the Olympics, only countries in North, Central, and South America and the Caribbean participate in the Pan American Games. The teacher affirmed the students' conclusions and noted that *Pan American* means, quite literally, "all the Americas." Further discussion centered around the word *panoramic*. Through this process, relating the known to the unknown, students decided that *pan* meant "all."

"Now, back to *pandemonium*. 'A place of all the demons.' What would this place be like?" Students were quick to respond. The demonstration was completed with two additional points. The teacher asked the class to find the place in *One Flew Over the Cuckoo's Nest* where *pandemonium* was used and read the paragraph. Then she asked them to refine their predictions of the meaning of *pandemonium*. Next the teacher discussed the origin of the word—which the English poet John Milton coined in his epic poem *Paradise Lost*. Pandemonium was the capital of hell, the place where all the demons and devils congregated—figuratively speaking, where "all hell broke loose."

Using the Dictionary as a Strategic Resource

The use of context and word structure are strategies that give readers insight into the meanings of unknown words. Rarely does context or word structure help learners derive precise definitions for key words. Instead, these vocabulary-building strategies keep readers on the right track so that they can follow a text without getting bogged down or giving up.

There are times, however, when context and word structure reveal little about a word's meaning. In these instances, or when a precise definition is needed, a dictionary, in either traditional print or electronic form, is a logical alternative and a valuable resource for students.

Knowing when to use a dictionary is as important as knowing how to use it. A content teacher should incorporate dictionary usage into ongoing plans but should avoid a very common pitfall in the process of doing so. When asked "What does this word mean?," the teacher shouldn't automatically reply, "Look it up in the dictionary."

To some students, "Look it up in the dictionary" is another way of saying "Don't bug me" or "I really don't have the time or the inclination to help you." From an instructional perspective, that hard-to-come-by teachable moment is lost whenever we routinely suggest to students to look up a word in a conventional or electronic dictionary.

One way to make the dictionary a functional resource is to use it to verify educated guesses about word meaning revealed through context or word structure. For example, if a student asks you for the meaning of a vocabulary term, an effective tactic is to bounce the question right back: "What do you think it means? Let's look at the way it's used. Are there any clues to its meaning?" If students are satisfied with an educated guess because it makes sense, the word need not be looked up. But if students are still unsure of the word's meaning, the dictionary is there.

When students go to a dictionary or an online vocabulary site to verify or to determine a precise definition, often they need supervision to make good decisions. Keep these tips in mind as you work on dictionary usage.

1. *Help students determine the "best fit" between a word and its definition.* Students must often choose the most appropriate definition from several. This poses a real dilemma for young learners. Your interactions will help them make the best choice of a definition and will provide a behavior model for making such a choice.

2. *If you do assign a list of words to look up in a dictionary, choose them selectively.* A few words are better than many. The chances are greater that students will learn several key terms thoroughly than that they will develop vague notions about many.

3. *Help students with the pronunciation key in a glossary or dictionary as the need arises.* This does not mean, however, that you will teach skills associated with the use of a pronunciation key in isolated lessons. Instead, it means guiding and reinforcing students' abilities to use a pronunciation key as they study the content of your course.

Vocabulary development is a gradual process, and students need multiple encounters with new words to grasp their meaning. Students who struggle with demanding text material will benefit from vocabulary-building strategies that make use of context clues, word structure, and appropriate uses of reference tools such as the dictionary.

MyLab Education **Self-Check 8.4**

MyLab Education **Application Exercise 8.4:**
Using Syntactic and Semantic Clues to Determine the Meaning of Unknown Words

---

Looking Back Looking Forward

A strong relationship exists between vocabulary knowledge and reading comprehension. In this chapter, we shared numerous examples of what it means to teach words well: giving students multiple opportunities to build vocabulary knowledge, to learn how words are conceptually related to one another, and to learn how they are defined contextually in the material that students are studying. Vocabulary activities provide students the multiple experiences they need to use and manipulate words in different situations. Conceptual and definitional activities provide the framework needed to study words critically. Various types of concept activities—such as semantic feature analysis, concept of definition word maps, word sorts, categories, concept circles, and magic squares— reinforce and extend students' abilities to perceive relationships among the words they are studying.

In the next chapter, we underscore the interrelationships between reading, thinking, and writing processes as we explore the role of writing in content area learning. The ideas presented in the chapter are intended to show how writing activity can and must go beyond "mechanical uses" in the content classroom.

Possible Answers to OPIN Exercises

English: 1. foil   2. antagonist   3. aside   4. wit   5. parody   6. protagonist   7. soliloquy

Science: 1. roots   2. radiation   3. rodents

Social Studies: 1. poverty   2. violence   3. Organize

Family and Consumer Studies: 1. absorbed   2. Soiled

Answers to Cloze Passage

1. cause   2. Slavery   3. Somehow   4. historians

5. crisis   6. Freed   7. Slavery   8. emotional

9. issues   10. interpretations

eResources

Discovery Education offers a site that allows users to create word puzzles. Search using keywords "discovery education + puzzle maker." Design a puzzle based on vocabulary words from a chapter of a content area text.

Seek out vocabulary-building strategies in your content area by using the keywords "vocabulary + lessons + (content area)" to conduct an Internet search. Many links will come up. Consider the value of each site and identify the best sites.

TeacherVision offers downloadable graphic organizers for immediate use. Search using keywords "TeacherVision + graphic organizers." Explore the Internet further for content-specific graphic organizers by using the keywords "graphic organizers + (content area)."

Chapter 9
Writing Across the Curriculum

Written in collaboration with Erin Donovan, Ph.D.

Shutterstock

⌄ Chapter Overview and Learning Outcomes

After reading this chapter, you should be able to:

9.1 Explain the purpose of writing to learn and how each of the WTL strategies support students content knowledge.

9.2 Describe the different types of academic journals and how they support students' interaction with text/content.

9.3 Describe the more formal process of writing in disciplines and explain how this writing should align with expectations of the subject matter.

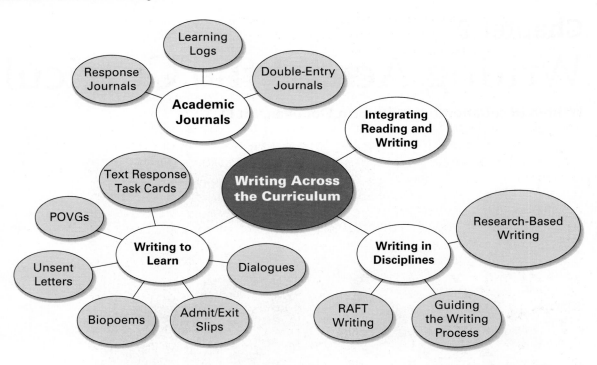

Writing activates learning by helping students to explore, clarify, and think deeply about the ideas and concepts they encounter in reading. Writing, thinking, and good old-fashioned hard work are tied together in ways that cannot be disentangled.

Whether today's students put pen to paper or create digital texts, *academic writing* can be an intimidating process at times, but it is also an indispensable tool for thinking and learning in content area classrooms. No wonder teachers use a variety of informal and formal writing activities to activate thinking and learning in their disciplines.

In other chapters, we have recommended instructional strategies that involve writing to support students' thinking and learning with all kinds of texts. In this chapter, we will highlight strategies that teachers can use to connect reading and writing in their content area classrooms. A classroom environment that supports reading and writing invites students to explore ideas, clarify meaning, and construct knowledge based both on the notions they bring to class as well as their interaction with the concepts presented in the text. When reading and writing are taught in tandem, the union influences content learning in ways not possible when students read without writing or write without reading. When teachers invite a class to write before, during, and after reading, they motivate students to use writing to think about what they will read and to think more deeply about the ideas they have read.

Sometimes reading and writing are taught in classrooms as if they bear little relationship to each other. The result has been to sever the powerful bonds for meaning-making that exist between reading and writing. There's little to be gained from teaching reading apart from writing. The organizing principle reflects this idea: Writing activates learning by helping students to explore, clarify, and think deeply about the ideas and concepts they encounter in reading.

Frame of Mind

1. Why emphasize writing to learn in content areas?
2. Why integrate writing and reading?
3. How might teachers create occasions for students to write to read and to read to write?
4. How can teachers use exploratory writing activities to motivate students to read and write?

5. How can teachers use journals to connect writing and reading?
6. How can teachers develop essay writing assignments through RAFT activities?
7. Why and how do teachers guide the writing process?

Students write often throughout the course of their daily routine. They text each other to make plans; they recommend restaurants and products online; they like and comment on the social media posts they read. Some students are in a state of self-expression that most teachers only dream of inspiring. The need to be heard and to connect is the primary point of social writing.

The social writing of adolescents, however, has not been without its controversies. There is a prevailing societal notion that texting, instant messaging, and posting on Facebook are diminishing adolescents' ability to use language effectively in their writing. Adults often cringe at the misuse of conjunctions and the abbreviated LOLs that permeate this form of expression. Regardless of the impact of social media writing, writing for social purposes is an integral part of students' lives today (Sweeny, 2010). Although many of today's adolescents do not identify social writing as "real writing," they do recognize the importance of academic writing in their school lives (Lenhart, Arafeh, Smith, & Macgill, 2008). Unfortunately, students often perceive academic writing tasks to be limited in scope; that is, short responses to homework questions (National Commission on Writing, 2003). It is the wise teacher who can connect the enthusiasm associated with social writing to the academic tasks of the classroom.

There are at least three good reasons for teachers to take a close look at the role of writing in content area classrooms. First, writing improves thinking. Second, it facilitates learning. Third, writing is closely connected to reading. Students in content literacy situations need varied and frequent experiences with writing and reading as tools for learning. As Cooper (2012) contends, writing is an essential tool for learning because it engages students in the texts they are reading while empowering learning. As a result, learners often have a greater depth of understanding when they write about what they are reading. Content area teachers usually have second thoughts about assigning writing in their classrooms because of preconceived notions of what the teaching of writing may entail. Teachers of every discipline share in the responsibility of showing students how to think and write as scientists, historians, mathematicians, and literary critics do. When students engage in writing as a way of knowing, they are thinking on paper or screens (Moore, Moore, Cunningham, & Cunningham, 2010).

Write to Read, Read to Write

There is no better way to think about a subject than to have the occasion to read and write about it. However, reading and writing don't necessarily guarantee improved thinking or learning. Students can go through the motions of reading and writing, lacking purpose and commitment, or they can work thoughtfully to construct meaning, make discoveries, and think deeply about a subject. One way to think about the reading–writing connection is that they both draw upon students' prior knowledge and cognitive processes (Lapp & Moss, 2012). In other words, reading and writing help us to understand what we already know; what we don't think we know but do know; and what we don't know until we have engaged in the process of meaning-making. Classrooms that integrate reading and writing lend encouragement to students who are maturing as readers and writers and provide instructional support so that readers and writers can play with ideas, explore concepts, clarify meaning, and elaborate on what they are learning.

Reading and Writing as Composing Processes

Reading and writing are acts of composing because readers and writers are involved in an ongoing, dynamic process of constructing meaning. Composing processes are more obvious in writing than in reading: The writer, initially facing a blank page or screen, constructs a text. The text is a visible entity and reflects the writer's thinking on paper. Less obvious is the "text"—the configuration of meanings—that students compose or construct in their own minds as they read.

Think of reading and writing as two sides of the same coin. The writer works to make a text sensible; the reader works to make sense from a text. As a result, the two processes, rooted in language, are intertwined and share common cognitive and sociocultural characteristics. Both reading and writing, for example, involve purpose, commitment, schema activation, planning, working with ideas, revision and rethinking, and monitoring. Both processes occur within a social, communicative context. Skilled writers are mindful of their content (the subject about which they are writing) and of their audiences. Skilled readers are mindful of a text's content and are also aware that they engage in transactions with its author. Skilled writers also understand the language and syntax that are not only suitable for their audience and purpose but also appropriate to the field for which they write (Fang & Coatoam, 2013). Box 9.1 explains how writing can bridge the comprehension gap for all students, not only for those who are skilled readers and writers.

The relationships between reading and writing have been a source of inquiry by language researchers since the mid-1970s (Close, Hull, & Langer, 2005). Several broad conclusions about the links between reading and writing can be drawn: Good readers are often good writers, and vice versa; students who write well tend to read more than those who do not write well; wide reading improves writing; and students who are good

Box 9.1 Writing with all Students

Writing can offer students a sense of self, freedom, expression, and acceptance that few other activities provide. Gifted students can use writing to explore topics outside of the prescribed curriculum. Gifted students may struggle to fit in socially or find themselves bored in a program that does not meet their needs. They excel when they are given options and creative avenues to format their sense of expression. An eighth-grade science teacher accomplished this sense of choice by providing writing extension topics that her students could use when they were done with assignments. These included researching, illustrating, organizing, and creating activities that introduced a fresh component of expression into the traditional science curriculum.

A social studies teacher was struggling to engage her gifted students. They simply weren't interested in completing the assignments she created. So, she allowed her students to create their own projects that could be done in class or at home. They could use these projects to sub out their daily assignments if they completed them by the due date. One of her students began a historical novel that he eventually self-published. Another student created a graphic flip book to illustrate one of the daily topics. Another group decided to outline a flipped history: if the Americans had not won their revolution. These writing activities increased the students' motivation to complete the required work they were assigned to prepare them for their grade level test. This use of writing engaged gifted students by encouraging them to explore history in the way that interested them the most.

Striving students may also benefit from writing. It is important to note that students who struggle with academic learning tasks typically find writing activities difficult to accomplish. Increasingly intensive instruction linked to specific skills and strategies is often needed before struggling learners can successfully complete independent writing activities. Often,

when students can write out their understanding of a reading or a topic, the teacher can begin to pinpoint where the student might have areas of misunderstanding. To promote their success, consider adjusting the length; and if you are assessing grammar, assess one element at a time that they have explicitly been taught. Let them include pictures and write in nontraditional formats such as bubble maps, outlines, or bulleted lists. Remember, the most important thing is their expression of understanding.

After you introduce these strategies, there may be students who continue to need support with expressing their thoughts through writing. Further accommodations might include explicit small-group or individualized-strategy instruction to produce abbreviated writing assignments. When students have difficulty writing, it is helpful to break down assignments into smaller, more manageable tasks. Teachers can modify the requirements of a writing assignment or divide writing prompts into a series of adapted steps, allowing struggling writers to focus on a single idea or concept. Striving writers also benefit from the use of computers to explore ideas as well as to check documents for spelling and grammar, allowing them to focus on content rather than proofreading. Voice recognition software supports students who face physical and cognitive challenges that impede their ability to write.

As we demonstrate in this chapter, writing-to-learn activities can also be used to support other types of literacy interventions. *Learning logs* can help students monitor their own comprehension and implement fix-up strategies when they encounter reading difficulties. *Exploratory writing* allows students to identify gaps between their prior knowledge and text content. Structured assignments such as *double-entry journals* allow students to process content from multiple perspectives or at multiple times to aid in comprehension.

readers and writers perceive themselves as such and are more likely to engage in reading and writing on their own.

Why connect reading and writing in instructional contexts? From a content literacy perspective, writing about ideas and concepts encountered in texts will improve students' acquisition of content more than simply reading without writing. When reading and writing are taught in concert, the union fosters problem solving and makes thinking and learning more powerful than if reading or writing is engaged in separately.

Reading and Writing as Exploration, Motivation, and Clarification

When teachers integrate writing and reading, they help students use writing to *think about what they will read* and to *understand what they have read*. Writing may be used as a motivational tool to catapult students into reading. It is also one of the most effective ways for students to understand something they have read. Teachers can put students into writing-to-read or reading-to-write situations because the writing process is a powerful tool for exploring and clarifying meaning.

Writers engage in a process of exploration and clarification as they go about the task of making meaning. They progress from exploring meaning to clarifying it as they continue to work with a piece of writing. A writer's first efforts are an initial attempt to think on paper or screen. The more writers work with ideas on paper or screen, the more they are able to revise, rethink, and clarify what they have to say about a subject.

Occasions to write on content subjects before reading and after reading create opportunities to learn content in concert with reading. Students who experience the integration of writing and reading are likely to learn more content, to understand it better, and to remember it longer. They are also more likely to connect what they read with their own experiences, thus increasing their motivation to write (Applebee & Langer, 2011). This is the case because writing, whether before or after reading, promotes thinking, but in different ways. Writing a summary after reading (see Chapter 10), for example, is likely to result in greater understanding and retention of important information. However, another type of writing—let's say an essay—may trigger the analysis, synthesis, and elaboration of ideas encountered in reading and class discussion.

The International Network of Writing Across the Curriculum Programs (INWAC), an informal community of teachers, researchers, and institutions who champion the development and use of writing strategies in content areas, identifies two major instructional components for disciplinary writing: writing to learn (WTL) and writing in disciplines (WID). Let's take a closer look at each component. How are they alike? How are they different?

MyLab Education
Response Journal 9.1
Why should exploratory writing be encouraged in content area classrooms?

MyLab Education
Video Example 9.1:
Connecting Reading and Writing
Study how a history teacher connects reading and writing in a unit on Vietnam.

Writing to Learn (WTL)

9.1 **Explain the purpose of writing to learn and how each of the WTL strategies support students content knowledge.**

Instructional activities that support WTL are, by their very nature, short and informal writing tasks. The writing that these activities produce is often tentative and unfinished. When students engage in WTL, they explore ideas and clarify what they are thinking about in relation to their content or subject matter. Before reading, WTL activities help students tap into prior knowledge and make connections between the "old" (what they already know) and the "new" (what they will be learning about). For example, many content area teachers combine a prereading activity such as brainstorming with five or so minutes of "quick writing" in which students write freely and spontaneously on what they know and on what they hope to learn from more in-depth reading and study. After reading, quick-writing activities such as *microthemes* are useful in helping students to summarize and extend their thoughts about a subject.

WTL should not be confused with *learning to write*. Students learn to write formally from the time they enter school and continue learning to write throughout their lives. Language arts and English teachers, entrusted with the primary responsibility for students' writing development, teach learners how to engage in the process of writing as a central component of learning to write. In this chapter, we discuss the content area teacher's role in guiding the writing process when students are engaged in more elaborate writing assignments, such as essays and research papers.

A variety of instructional activities may be used for WTL, including microthemes, point of view guides (POVGs), unsent letters, biopoems, text response task cards, and admit/exit slips. Having students write regularly in various kinds of journals is also an important component of writing to learn in content area classrooms.

Microthemes

More isn't necessarily better when getting students to think and learn by writing. In fact, brevity is the key to writing an effective *microtheme*. A microtheme is a brief piece of writing that results in a great deal of thinking (Knipper & Duggan, 2006). Think of microthemes as mini-essays. Teachers often require students to write a microtheme on one side of an index card or half-sheet of paper. A 5- by 8-inch index card is a lot less threatening for students than the prospect of writing a full-blown essay.

Microthemes can be assigned for a variety of purposes, including analyzing and synthesizing information and ideas encountered in reading, writing summaries, or taking a stand on an important issue. In a biology class, for example, students were involved in an ecological study of organisms in short-river communities along the western coast of Florida. One of the readings dealt with community relationships in the life of river turtles. As part of the unit, the teacher assigned a variety of WTL activities, including microthemes. One of the microthemes helped students to reflect on and synthesize information related to river turtle life. After much discussion of the topic, the teacher distributed index cards and assigned the following microtheme in the form of two questions: What relationships to other organisms does an adult river turtle have in this river community? How do these relationships differ from those of a young river turtle?

Before writing, students were asked to jot down notes and key points from the text and class discussions that they might use in the microtheme. Because words were at a premium, students had to be concise yet complete. Here's what Jaycee wrote on her index card:

> Adult river turtles have both direct and indirect relationships with other organisms in this river community. Direct relationships include eating many of the plants that grow in the river. Other organisms eat and live off the river turtle. Leeches suck on their blood like vampires while other animals eat the turtles' eggs. When there in the water river turtles can be food for certain fish, herons, and even a kind of snapping turtle. Indirect relationships are when turtles compete for a food source like tape grass with another organism. Young river turtles differ from adult river turtles. Young turtles can be carnivorous as well as herbivorous. They are also more likely to be eaten by preteters than adult turtles. When both young and adult turtles die they become food for decomposers that return all the substances in the turtles' body to the nonliving world.

Jaycee's microtheme is fact-laden and accurate in its description of direct and indirect relationships. Although she has some spelling errors (i.e., *preteters*) and grammatical miscues, these are to be expected in quick-writing activities. Jaycee and her classmates shared their microthemes in "study buddy" groups and had an opportunity to raise questions in a whole-class follow-up discussion. The teacher then gave students an opportunity to make content changes or add information to their index cards. Although a grade is not assigned to individual microthemes, the teacher has students save their themes to use as "study cards" for unit tests. Other teachers may choose to grade microthemes by assigning points based on a scale of 1 to 5, with 5 being rated as excellent.

Vocabulary can help students better understand and write about concepts presented in content classes. In a ninth-grade Introduction to Music Appreciation course, students were taught vocabulary that included the terms *dynamics, improvisation*, and *ensemble*. The teacher played several Miles Davis jazz pieces, explaining how each piece showed aspects of the terms the students learned. Then she played "All Blues" from Miles Davis's *Kind of Blue* and had the students write a microtheme so they, following her example, could show how the piece exemplified the use of dynamics, improvisation, and ensemble. The students were given an index card to express their thoughts. Samantha, a student who was struggling with the terms because this was her first music class, mentioned to the teacher how hearing the music and associating it with the terms really helped her. Her writing shows that she has more to learn about musical jargon, but she correctly defined the terms by matching them to what she heard. This is what she wrote on her index card:

> "All Blues" began as an <u>ensemble</u> piece because all the musicians played together. After the first part of the song, each musician played on their own. What I learned about jazz was that when people play solos the solos are <u>improvised</u>. This means that the notes are not written down. The musician plays what they think works best with the chords and the rhythms and they very often never play the same notes twice. Within the solos, the musicians changed the volume of their playing, which is known as <u>dynamics</u>. I thought Cannonball Adderley did the best job of changing his dynamics because he started off playing softly and then varied the volume of his playing. I thought with his dynamics he did a good job of letting his saxophone tell a story.

A new take on the microtheme idea is to have students "tweet" their responses. Using the 140-character limit based on the format of the popular Twitter website, students must encapsulate the ideas of their microtheme, choosing the most important details to highlight, within the 140-space limit. This may be done in simulation format, using an index card rather than the actual website, if technology is not available or if the website is not supported by the school district. This high-interest activity uses a format that many of the students may have experience using and supports their ability to summarize and focus their responses on the information that is most important.

This is an example of how a physical education teacher used tweeting for her nutrition unit. Each day the students tweeted a review on one healthy food they ate. In 140 characters they had to tell (1) what they ate, (2) one reason it was a healthy choice, and (3) why others might like it. Here is an example: #delishfiber Apples are full of fiber, very filling, low in calories, & give you lots of energy. I recommend them because they taste like fall in juice or full fruit form.

Finally, consider using the concept of memes. A meme is a pop-culturally developed and transmitted photo that is described by a caption. They are designed to capture a moment, concept, or emotion and, generally, are considered humorous. Memes have risen to celebrity status because when they are successful, they spread like wildfire. To transfer this idea into the academic realm, consider having the students focus on one idea and "sell" it to their fellow students. Teachers can host contests where the students vote on the most attention-getting idea. This also supports the evaluative level of thinking.

An English teacher used the concept of memes in her classroom to capture the idea of mood and tone. The students in her class read *To Kill a Mockingbird.* They each chose a character and a moment in the story that they felt helped shape the mood of the piece. They started by drawing the character. Drawing is one strategy to reinforce visualization strategies. Then the students wrote a short caption in the "meme style." The students shared their creations in small groups. Each meme was evaluated on its visual interest, impact of the caption, memorability, and connection to the story. The students had to justify their responses to the memes with passages from the text. This activity not only supported comprehension but also allowed the students to engage in peer analysis.

Point of View Guides (POVGs)

A point of view guide (POVG) connects writing to reading in a creative, nonthreatening manner (Wood, Lapp, Flood, & Taylor, 2008). POVGs are designed to trigger thoughtful reading and writing by having students "get inside the skin" of a character or a subject under study. Several key characteristics of POVGs include the following:

- POVGs are questions presented in an *interview* format that allow students to think about text from different points of view and perspectives.
- POVGs encourage *speculation, inferential thinking,* and *elaboration* by placing students in *role-play* situations.
- POVGs engage students in writing to learn by having them *actively contribute their own experiences* to the role.
- POVGs require *first-person* writing on the part of students as they respond to a situation.

POVGs can fit into a microtheme format or stand alone as a writing-to-learn activity. In the sample microtheme above, Jaycee's language is formal, textbooklike, and somewhat stilted. However, POVG writing usually results in more informal, playful language as students assume a role and write in the first person. Jaycee's biology teacher also adapts a microtheme format to include POVG-type responses. In the unit on turtle life in a river community, notice how the teacher switched from very academic questions in the microtheme example to a role-play situation:

> Situation: You are about to be interviewed as if you are a young river turtle living in a river community along the west coast of Florida.
> Question: As a young river turtle, what is your typical day like?

Before writing their responses on index cards, students are assigned to read the text and take notes. Notice how Jaycee's language changes as she assumes the role of a young river turtle:

> I get up in the morning thinking about the long day ahead of me. When I leave my veggie pad, the first thing I do is pick up the newspaper and check out the hatchery to see how the musk turtles are doing. They been having it rough lately. Then I go to the local restaurant where I feed on snails, worms, and water insects. As I make my way back to my pad I don't got any fears until I see my mom and dad chomping away at the only thing that will protect me later in life. Tape grass! At this point, I'm thinking, Is this good parental behavior? After a hard day's work, I go back home and dream of the day I become an adult. Will I do the same thing to my kids?

The structure of a POVG is easily adapted to learning situations in science, social studies, history, or English language arts. In a high school American history class, students are studying the Great Depression. They have been assigned to read about how farmers from the Great Plains fled to California during the Dust Bowl of the 1930s. The teacher's POVG establishes a situation for writing based on three questions:

> It's 1936. You were a farmer in Oklahoma during the Dust Bowl in which "the land just blew away." The bank foreclosed on your farm, and you and your family were forced to move west to California in search of work and a new life. You have been living in California for two years. You are about to be interviewed by

a writer from *Collier's Magazine*. First read the text and then write your responses fully for each of the questions in the first person.

1. What was it like when you reached California? Describe how you were treated.
2. What kind of farm work did you find in California? Was it different from what you expected in your former life as a farmer in Oklahoma?
3. Why did you give up migrant farming to move to a "shacktown" called "Okieville"? Describe what life was like for you and your family in Okieville.

A 10th-grade language arts class studied Joseph Campbell's *Hero with a Thousand Faces* to better understand the idea of archetype as expressed through the quest myth. The students' assignment was to write a quest myth of their own, but the teacher needed a way for his students to begin the brainstorming process. He provided the following POVG to help his students understand the mind-set of the hero.

You are a hero in the new world order. You must build a quest, find your friends and enemies, and generally save the world. Using what we learned, step into the mind of your hero and answer the following questions. Remember that you are answering as your hero and you must follow the rules of being a hero.

1. What is your main goal?
2. What is your main obstacle?
3. What will you need to survive?
4. How do you exemplify what it means to be a hero?

This is one student's response. He not only described his heroic attributes but included aspects of the hero's quest, demonstrating an understanding not only of the norms of the quest but also the idea of archetype.

1. Hello there, my name is Marty and my goal is simple: save the world. But I guess I should be a bit more specific because a hero always has a specific call to adventure that only he or she can answer. So, I have been called by a letter written in gold, disappearing ink to travel to the Nethersphere, dominate the wicked overlord who has enslaved the people, and save the princess who supposedly has the secret to world salvation. Have I mentioned that I only have two days? Have I mentioned that the princess is entrapped in a cell that is guarded by these spirits who can melt into your dreamscape, causing you to go insane? No big deal for a hero.
2. My main obstacle is my doubt. Like most heroes I always doubt whether I am the one who is actually the best person for the job. No matter how my mentor or allies might tell me otherwise, I just have a hard time believing I'm the guy. I mean, I'm the type of guy that always gets picked last for sports. How can I save the world?
3. I will need the advice of my mentors and my allies. Because I have such self-esteem issues they will be the ones who push me forward. I will also need to avoid the temptations of the quest that I am sure to find as I go along. I need to look for clues as I go because it seems like heroes always end up overlooking the things they will end up needing the most.
4. I am a hero because I am the only one who can solve the problem. I have some secret that will be revealed at the right time that rests only in me. I also represent a humble goodness that appeals to all people. Some people might call me an underdog, but in the end, I will have what it takes to help all people. I also, at the end at least, am willing to sacrifice myself for the good of all.

Unsent Letters

Like POVGs, the WTL activity known as *unsent letters* establishes a role-play situation in which students are asked to write letters in response to the material they are studying. The activity requires the use of imagination and often demands that writers engage in interpretive and evaluative thinking (Smith, 2002). In a middle school language arts class, students were reading the historical novel *Number the Stars* by Lois Lowry (1989). The story is about the Holocaust during World War II and is set in the city of Copenhagen during the third year of the Nazi occupation of Denmark. Lowry tells the story from the point of view of 10-year-old Annemarie Johansen. The plot revolves around Annemarie and her best friend, Ellen Rosen, who is Jewish and eventually escapes to Sweden with her family. The teacher invites her class to write an unsent letter from Annemarie to Ellen 20 years after the war ends. Here's what one student writes:

> Dear Ellen,
>   How is Sweden? I'm doing fine. I hope you are too. The war ended 20 years ago, but I am still heartbroken because of what the Nazis did. Remember that time when you were sleeping over and the Nazis barged in my apartment? I'm sorry I had to break your necklace, but I think it was worth it. I am married to a guy named Peter, not the Peter we know but another one. My name now is Annemarie Harrison. Do you like it? I have two kids, Ellen and Billy. I moved to America and live in a place called Vero Beach in Florida. It's so peaceful here. I wish it was like that back then, so you wouldn't have had to leave.
>   Sincerely your best friend,
>   Annemarie
>   P.S. Please write back!

An unsent letter is a nonthreatening way to have students demonstrate their knowledge about a topic under study. In a precalculus class, the teacher asked his students to write a friend an unsent letter describing what they have learned about right triangles. Here's what Max wrote to his buddy Nugget:

> Hey Nugget,
>   Right triangles are very easy to understand. If you have two legs of the triangle, you use the Pythagorean Theorem to find the hypotenuse ($a^2 + b^2 = c^2$). If you have one leg and the hypotenuse, you can find the second leg by plugging the number eight into the formula. You can also find the six trig. functions of the right triangle by using the lengths of the sides, or known angles, but you have to remember to put them in relation to r (which is the hyp.).
>   It's helpful to know about the properties of right triangles. Using them, you can find angles of depression and of elevation to objects above or below you. Unfortunately, sometimes they are confusing.

Biopoems

Unsent letters direct students' thinking with audiences in mind. **Biopoems**, by contrast, require students to play with ideas using language in a poetic framework. A biopoem allows students to reflect on large amounts of material within a poetic form. The biopoem follows a pattern that enables writers to synthesize what they have learned about a person, place, thing, concept, or event under study. For example, study the following pattern for a person or character:

MyLab Education
Response Journal 9.2
What is your reaction to the use of a biopoem as a writing-to-learn activity?

Line 1. First name

Line 2. Four traits that describe character

Line 3. Relative ("brother," "sister," "daughter," etc.) of _____

Line 4. Lover of _____ (list three things or people)

Line 5. Who feels _____ (three items)

Line 6. Who needs _____ (three items)

Line 7. Who fears _____ (three items)

Line 8. Who gives _____ (three items)

Line 9. Who would like to see _____ (three items)

Line 10. Resident of _____

Line 11. Last name

Biopoems help students to organize, review, and summarize what they have learned in a concise and creative manner. Following is an example of how a chemistry teacher adapted biopoems to the subject of the periodic table of elements.

The Periodic Table

Columns called families, rows called periods, arranged by atomic number

Mendeleev's child

Lover of electrons, protons, and neutrons

Who feels the heat caused by sodium in water, the lightness of argon, and the weight of platinum

Who needs all the attention I can give

Who fears computers, iPads, and TVs

Who gives gases, metalloids, and more information than I can remember

Who would like to tell us all about the world and likes it when more elements are added

Resident of my chemistry textbook of elements

A geometry teacher adapted the biopoem format for use in her class. Students were assigned to write a biopoem to describe the characteristics of a concept they were studying. Here's how one student described a trapezoid:

Trape

I've got two legs, two bases, and four angles.

My family includes sister Square and brothers Rhombus and Rectangle.

I need one pair of parallel sides and each pair of base angles to be congruent.

I fear two pairs of parallel sides and also fear only three sides to it.

I would like to see the pyramids in Egypt some day.

Resident of Polygon

Zoid

A science and physical education teacher teamed up to teach the impact of nutrients on the body. The science teacher provided the technical background of what nutrients did and how they interacted with the body. The PE teacher showed students which foods contained nutrients and how foods could be combined to provide a balanced diet. After receiving the information through notes and text sets, students teamed up to create a recipe book of nutrients. Each nutrient they chose was introduced through a biopoem. Here is an example from two boys who began their recipe compilation with calcium. They followed the format to create the following biopoem.

Line 1. First name

Line 2. Four traits that describe character

Line 3. Relative ("brother," "sister," "daughter," etc.) of _____

Line 4. Lover of _____ (list three things or people)

Line 5. Who feels _____ (three items)

Line 6. Who needs _____ (three items)

Line 7. Who fears _____ (three items)

Line 8. Who gives _____ (three items)

Line 9. Who would like to see _____ (three items)

Line 10. Resident of _____

Line 11. Last name

Calcium

Milk, yogurt, cheese, broccoli

Mother of bones and teeth

Lover of active bodies

Who feels strong as a mineral, soft as an element, and melted as ice cream

Who needs vitamin D, sunshine, and a kid who likes milk

Who fears lactose intolerance, soda, and water

Who gives strength, long lives, and good teeth

Who would like to see more broccoli, kale, and tofu being eaten

Resident of good health

Calcium

Another group chose vitamin C. The pair used the format but also played with language to give more personality to their chosen nutrient. The two students enjoyed having the chance to write expressively in their science class, a class where they were used to writing in a more technical manner.

Vivacious, viv-lovely, Viv C

Orangaciously, outrageously, citricity, curiosity

Sister to Vita A and Vita B

Lover of all that is Sunny and Funny and Deliciously Fresh Healthily Smooth

Who feels excited to open your eyes, brilliant in brightening your skin, illuminating to boost your immunity, and carefully considerate to your cardiovascular system

Who needs oranges and broccoli and cantaloupe and kiwis to explode into bodies

Who fears dark places where there is no sun and no fun, and closed mouths and hearts

Who gives health, hope, energy, and life

Who would like to see more jumping and pumping and running and sunning

Resident of the citroliciousness of citrus

Viv C Forlife

Biopoems, as you can see, help students to synthesize their learning as they play with ideas in a format that provides an alternative to prose writing.

Text Response Task Cards

When students read and write they often lack real purpose. They are provided a passage and a set of questions that essentially prompt them to look for key words and fill in the correct answer. These "end of the chapter" questions often act more as a copying activity than one that encourages high-level thinking. As mentioned, the combination of reading and writing helps students more clearly understand content and text while building their own understanding through reflective writing. But to be truly effective in practice, the combination must also be an authentic activity that involves the student beyond simply answering questions.

Text response task cards direct the students to respond to the text in a way that involves authentic practices of the discipline. This strategy builds on the idea of disciplinary literacy. Each card identifies a task that a person within each discipline would do as both a reader and a writer within the discipline. For example, in a math class, a task card may prompt a student to read a passage and then list the mathematical calculations needed to solve the main character's problem.

The strength of these cards is that they not only encourage students to write but do so in a way that uses the tone, language, and thinking skills of each respective content area. The idea behind these cards is versatile enough to allow them to be used as exit or entrance slips or as the writing prompts for microthemes. They can also be used in centers to help direct students' thinking and writing.

Here is an example from a seventh-grade science classroom. Working in groups, students were given videos that described environmental anomalies. They watched a video and then used the following to describe the information they observed. Working as a group, they moved from forming a question to inferring an answer and then checking their educated guess with the facts they were presented.

1. Think like a scientist. Write down one thing that you didn't understand.	2. Think like a scientist and look for facts that might help you explain what you don't understand.
3. Think like a scientist and make an inference based on the facts you found.	4. Think like a scientist and confirm or change your inference.

Here is an example from one of the groups, which watched a video about hot springs in Greenland.

1. We don't understand how there can be hot springs in Greenland. It's too cold.
2. We noticed volcanos and noticed steam coming from the springs (maybe they are heated underground, because the steam was rising). We noticed that there were glaciers and snow on the ground, but people were in the hot springs in their bathing suits, so it actually was cold outside and the water was actually warm.
3. These are our facts:
   - The springs are not heated by volcanos. But did you know that in Iceland the same thing happens, and they are heated by volcanic activity?
   - Three springs run together to create a pool big enough to bathe in.
   - They are naturally heated to 60 degrees.
   - They are heated by deep layers in the Earth that rub together, and they are the same temperature all year long.
4. We think the springs are heated by layers in the Earth that rub together. This makes them unique because other hot springs, like the ones in Iceland, are heated by volcanic activity. Our inference is supported by the graphic in the video that shows how the layers move and how that movement radiates heat, making the water warm enough to bathe in.

Task cards can be used in the classroom to help emphasize the idea of writing as "real" people do in each discipline in the "real" world. For example, in social studies, students need to learn how to write like a historian, using jargon and genre typically employed in historical writing. When historians write, they focus on important people, details that explain events, and contextual evidence that helps shape moments in history. On the other hand, when mathematicians write, they look for patterns, organize figures, and work to make categorical sense of things that don't belong.

The first set of task cards was used by a middle school social studies department to help add purpose to students' reading. When the students realized that

1. Think like a historian and pick an event or a moment in time.	**2.** Think like a historian and look for facts that might help explain the event you chose.
3. Think like a historian and see if you can put the events in chronological order.	**4.** Think like a historian and see if you can find an original (primary source) account of the event.

1. Think like a historian and find the opinion that represents one side of an event.	**2.** Think like a historian and find the opinion that represents the other side of an event.
3. Think like a historian and compare how the sides are alike.	**4.** Think like a historian and contrast how the sides are different.

1.
Think like a mathematician and look for any like terms or numbers you can group.

2.
Think like a mathematician and look for any patterns that might be useful.

3.
Think like a mathematician and look for different methods to organize your numbers.

4.
Think like a mathematician and think about what the opposite of the problem might look like.

1.
Think like a mathematician and think of a real-world problem.

2.
Think like a mathematician and write down what you would need to solve it.

3.
Think like a mathematician and write down any formulas you might use to solve it.

4.
Think like a mathematician and work through the problem telling WHY you got your answer.

they were doing what real people did in their job, it helped build the purpose behind the activity. It is always important to build the "why" of any assignment. One way to do this is to show how content area concepts are relevant in the professional world. Then, using reading and writing together to create greater meaning, the students wrote about what they read, according to the directions of the task cards.

The second set of task cards was used in a seventh-grade math classroom. The students worked in partner groups and each morning used the cards to problem solve. The cards directed the way they wrote and thought about numbers, their relationships, and the thought processes that may be necessary to solve the problems, organize the numbers, or use the formulas they were given.

This activity was also used in an Introduction to Business class in high school. The students chose a job and then researched the day-to-day functions of that job. Then, they broke down those functions and created five task cards. The tasks they chose included writing e-mails, creating graphs, researching, presenting data, buying and selling products, designing web pages, creating marketing slogans, and organizing data. They shared their task cards with a partner, who then did an abbreviated version of the described task. At the end of the activity, the students decided whether or not they would enjoy the job based on the tasks they were given.

Admit Slips and Exit Slips

Admit slips are brief comments written by students on index cards or half-sheets of paper at the very beginning of class. The purpose of the admit slip is to have students react to what they are studying or to what's happening in class. Students are asked to respond to questions such as:

What's confusing you about _____ ?

What problems did you have with your text assignment?

What would you like to get off your chest?

What do you like (dislike) about _____ ?

The admit slips are collected by the teacher and read aloud (with no indication of the authorship of individual comments) as a way of beginning class discussion. Admit slips build a trusting relationship between teacher and students and contribute to a sense of community in the classroom.

In an algebra class, where students had been studying complex numbers, the teacher asked the class to use admit slips to explain difficulties they had with one of their homework assignments. One student wrote, "I didn't know where to start." Several other students made similar comments. The teacher was able to use the written feedback to address some of the problems that students had with the assignment.

An *exit slip*, as you might anticipate, is a variation on the admit slip. Toward the end of class, the teacher asks students for exit slips as a way of bringing closure to what was learned. An exit slip question might require students to summarize, synthesize, evaluate, or project.

In the algebra class, exit slips were used toward the end of the class to introduce a new unit on imaginary numbers. The teacher asked students to write for several minutes as they reflected on the question "Why do you think we are studying about imaginary numbers after we studied the discriminant?" One student wrote, "Because the discriminant can be negative, and I didn't know what kind of a number $\sqrt{-1}$ was. I'm guessing it must be imaginary. Right?" The teacher was able to sort through the exit slip responses and use them to introduce the new unit.

The several minutes devoted to exit slip writing are often quite revealing of the day's lesson and establish a direction for the next class.

This can be done digitally through several different applications or websites. One favorite and very user-friendly site, known as Poll Everywhere, allows students to answer questions via their cell phones and displays their responses in graph form. This offers an informal source of assessment while providing a fun, student-driven way for whole-class interaction.

MyLab Education **Self-Check 9.1**

MyLab Education **Application Exercise 9.1:**
Using Point of View Guides (POVGs) in a Content Area Classroom

---

Academic Journals

9.2   Describe the different types of academic journals and how they support students' interaction with text/content.

Because journals serve a variety of real-life purposes, not the least of which is to write about things that are important to us, they have withstood the test of time. Artists, scientists, novelists, historical figures, mathematicians, dancers, politicians, teachers, children, athletes—all kinds of people—have kept journals. Some journals—diaries, for example—are meant to be private and are not intended to be read by anyone but the writer. Sometimes, however, a diary makes its way into the public domain and affects readers in powerful ways. Anne Frank, probably the world's most famous child diarist, kept a personal journal of her innermost thoughts, fears, hopes, and experiences while hiding from the Nazis during World War II. Having read her diary, who hasn't been moved to think and feel more deeply about the tragic consequences of the Holocaust?

Other journals are practical rather than personal in that writers record observations and experiences that will be useful, insightful, or instructive. In more than 40 notebooks, Leonardo da Vinci recorded artistic ideas, detailed sketches of the human anatomy, elaborate plans for flying machines, and even his dreams. Novelists throughout literary history have used journals to record ideas, happenings, and conversations that have served to stimulate their imaginations and provide material for their writing. Even in a professional sport such as baseball, it is not unusual for hitters to keep a log of their at-bats: who the pitcher was, what the situation was (e.g., runner on base or bases empty), what types of pitches were thrown, and what the outcome of each at-bat was.

Academic journals also serve a variety of purposes. They help students generate ideas, create a record of thoughts and feelings in response to what they are reading, and explore their own lives and concerns in relation to what they are reading and learning. Academic journals create a context for learning in which students interact with information personally as they explore and clarify ideas, issues, and concepts under study. These journals may be used as springboards for class discussion or as mind stretchers that extend thinking, solve problems, or stimulate imagination. All forms of writing and written expression can be incorporated into academic journal writing, from doodles and sketches to poems and letters to comments, explanations, and reactions.

MyLab Education
Response Journal 9.3
Why do people journal?

Three types of journals have made a difference in content literacy situations: *response journals*, *double-entry journals*, and *learning logs*. Each of these can be used in an instructional context to help students explore literary and informational texts. Teachers who use academic journals in their classes encourage students to use everyday, expressive language to write about what they are studying in the same way that they encourage students to use talk to explore ideas during discussion. When expressive language is missing from students' journal writing, the students do not experience the kind of internal talk that allows them to explore and clarify meaning in ways that are personal and crucial to thinking on paper or on screen. Intentionally teaching this expressive language, breaking it down as far as language and syntax, and providing mentor texts may help students access their inherent internal talk.

When writing in academic journals, students need not attempt to sound "academic," even though they are writing about ideas and information of importance in various disciplines. Like the writing activities previously discussed in this chapter, journal entries need to be judged on the writer's ability to communicate and explore ideas, not on the quality of handwriting or the number of spelling and grammatical errors in the writing. Journal writing underscores informal learning. It relieves teachers of the burden of correction so that they can focus on students' thinking, and it creates a nonthreatening situation for students who may be hesitant to take risks because they are overly concerned about the mechanics of writing (e.g., handwriting, neatness, spelling, and punctuation).

Journaling can be used as a teaching tool, allowing students to explore the vocabulary, language, and syntax of each content area. Teaching students to write in the style of their content discipline allows them to step into the shoes of those people working and writing in real-world jobs. This adds purpose to the journaling and can even lead to reflection, asking the students how they felt to be writing as if they were, say, a scientist or, perhaps, a historian or even a musician.

A sixth-grade class was studying ancient Egypt and mummification. The teacher built student knowledge by showing videos and providing text sets that allowed the students to explore the process and significance of mummification. After they completed their work with the texts, the students wrote a diary entry from the perspective of the mummified person. This is an excerpt from one student's journal:

> Well, I guess my time was up. I didn't know where I was at first, but I knew it wasn't good. The stink of natron woke me up and I knew I was in trouble. I knew natron was the chemical that was used to dry out bodies. Oh Jeez! I opened my eyes and saw my old body spread out on a slab. Sure, enough these weird guys were making me into a mummy. I could hardly watch as they pulled my brain out of my nose. I was glad they left my heart alone. All of my other organs went into these jars that were all painted up. I think I remember learning that they were called canopic jars. They were really pretty nice. Then they started stuffing me with some straw stuff. All that straw made me want to sneeze, but I wondered so long if I actually could sneeze that the feeling passed. They left me alone like that and I knew I had a while to wait. It would be 40 to 50 days before they came back to wrap me up. I sure thought the afterlife would have been more exciting than this. At least I still have my stuff to keep me company.

To bring this activity into the digital sphere, students can experiment with blogging or vlogging. A blog is a journal that usually focuses on one topic. It can include a daily diary, text, pictures, instructions, and recommendations. A vlog is a video version of this where the writer speaks into a camera instead of writing. To begin this activity, it is helpful to show students examples of effective and ineffective blogs/vlogs and allow them to develop a rubric that explains the characteristics of effective examples.

A sixth-grade science class used blogging to explore the weather. Each student was assigned a geographic region and then conducted research into the prevailing weather patterns. Students played the roles of reporters from the National Weather Service as they wrote about weather patterns and how weather impacted the daily lives of people in the region. They even included survival tips for regions prone to inclement weather. They followed two other students who represented different regions. The teacher followed the students and added additional comments and questions to encourage discussion and to promote understanding of weather-related concepts. Box 9.2 explains how mentor texts can be used to support writing across the disciplines.

Box 9.2 Writing Like a Thinker

Using Mentor Texts to Learn the Discipline of Writers

Several teachers were interviewed about how they used writing in their classrooms. As a group, the teachers spoke proudly about their commitment to a practice that included having their students write each day, reflecting upon their experience with texts. One teacher, however, seemed frustrated with the interview questions and said, "I teach science. I have always struggled with my own writing and certainly struggle with teaching writing. Maybe that's why I chose to teach science. I am just not sure what place writing as a discipline has in my classroom."

The sentiments of the teacher are justified and support the idea of teaching writing but doing so in a way that better supports the objectives of each content area. Understanding which skills are needed to write the documents within each content area, as well as understanding the purpose and audience to which the documents are written, can help content area teachers more effectively teach students to think like the writers within each field.

Teaching students the mechanics behind writing can be a challenge for teachers because of the scope of their content. Teaching writing as it interacts within a content area requires not only a depth of content knowledge but also an understanding of how and why writing is used in that content area. Often writing is misused and artificially inserted in content classes just to check off a proverbial box. For example, learning how to write a report about a famous scientist may teach students valuable research skills, but does it teach them disciplinary writing skills inherent to their field? That is doubtful. To teach writing in the content area effectively, one must begin with writing from the field itself.

Mentor texts have long been used in the language arts classroom to show writers how "real" writers go about their business. They provide a basis on which students can begin to structure their own voice, matching it to those that they read. Mentor texts embody the best practice of combining reading and writing to teach a concept (Gallagher, 2014). They can even be used as a type of co-teacher: a different voice that instructs the students in best practices. However, when this idea is transferred throughout the content areas, students must first be taught how to deconstruct these mentor texts before they can use those same concepts to construct their own.

The first step is the choice of texts. Carefully choose a text that not only shows the skills, language, use of audience, and voice that are inherent within the content but also is written at the reading level comfortable to your students. It should show a clear rationale behind why people write within each content area. For example, a scientist writes a lab report. Encourage your students to question the following:

- What is the purpose behind the report?
- Who will read the report?
- What language and tone are necessary to properly convey the intent of the report?
- What is the structure of the report?
- How is the information organized?
- What skills are needed to produce the report?

Regardless of your content area and the text chosen, deconstructing a text should begin with the following areas of inquiry:

- Language, including use of syntax
- Author's purpose
- Intended purpose of the document
- Audience
- Specialized vocabulary
- Organization
- Text features (Dorfman & Cappelli, 2009)

Teachers should encourage the students to explore the document, refining their thinking skills to understand the overall organization of the document and how that organization adds to its purpose. These mentor texts can help students develop their own essential questions, narrow their topics, and choose careful language that is appropriate for their respective content areas (Owles & Herman, 2014).

Remember that mentor texts should come from a variety of sources, including the teacher. Allowing students the opportunity to take the teacher's work apart, exposing even its weaknesses, empowers the students to critique their own work. Teachers may also want to give their students drafts in various stages of development so the students can better understand the process of creating the documents and how revision ultimately effects the final document (Pytash, Edmonson, & Tait, 2014). They might even develop their own process checklist to guide them as they write as well as rubrics to help them critique their work and the work of their peers.

Writers write for a purpose. Stephen King delights his audience with tales of horror and gore; manual writers help their audience use products with carefully constructed directions; teachers write lesson plans to clearly articulate their plans; and politicians write cautiously constructed speeches to portray their image and objectives. Regardless of what is written, "real" writing has a purpose. Helping students understand this purpose using mentor texts not only enables them to better understand the purpose and form of writing in a content area but also supports them in their efforts to write like a content area thinker.

Response Journals

Response journals create permanent records of what readers are feeling and thinking as they interact with texts. A response journal allows students to record their thoughts about texts and emotional reactions to them. Teachers may use prompts to trigger students' feelings and thoughts about a subject or may invite students to respond freely to what they are reading and doing in class. Prompts include questions, visual stimuli, read-alouds, or situations created to stimulate thinking. An earth science teacher, for example, might ask students to place themselves in the role of a water molecule as they describe what it's like to travel through the water cycle. Examine how Mike, a low-achieving ninth grader who didn't like to write, responded in his journal entry:

> My name is Moe, its short for Molecule. I was born in a cloud when I was condensed on a dust particle. My neverending life story goes like this.
>
> During Moes life he had a great time boncing into his friends. He grew up in the cloud and became bigger and heavier. Moe became so heavy that one night lightning struck and he fell out of his cloud as a raindrop. He landed in a farmer's field where this leavy plant sucked him up. Moe became a small section of a leave on the plant and their he absorbed sunlight and other things. One day a cow came by and ate Moes leave. He was now part of the cow.
>
> Well you can guess the rest. The farmer ate the cow and Moe became part of the farmer. One day the farmer was working in the field, he started sweating and thats when Moe escaped. He transpirated into the air as a molecule again. Free at last he rejoined a group of new friends in a cloud and the cycle went on.

Mike's teacher was pleased by his journal entry, mechanical errors and all. On homework questions, he usually wrote short, incoherent answers. In this entry, however, he interacted playfully with the information in the text and demonstrated his understanding of the water cycle.

In a high school senior elective psychology course, students were studying Sigmund Freud's theory of psychoanalysis. The teacher used a response journal format to help students apply the concepts of id, ego, and superego to real-life experiences. In their response journals, students were asked to respond to the following situation: As you enter the classroom, you notice a copy of the key to the test you are going to take. Your teacher is nowhere to be found. What are your id, ego, and superego telling you to do? What action will you take? Why? Here's what one student wrote:

> As I walk into the classroom and notice that my teacher isn't in the room, my Id tells me "quick memorize the key before she comes back, you know you didn't study for the test last night and this is the only way you are going to pass." My Ego tells to look at the key, but just make it look like I'm waiting for her at her desk when she comes back in—she won't think I looked at it. My Superego tells me it is wrong to cheat and even if I did get an A on the test I would feel guilty. I would never be able to look at her in the eye again. In the end I would probably look at the key so quickly on the desk (because I would be so nervous of getting caught) I wouldn't even notice any of the answers.

CHARACTER JOURNALS   Role-playing is an excellent prompt for response journal writing. A history or an English teacher may invite students to assume the role of a historical or fictional character and to view events and happenings from the character's perspective. In an American history class, for example, students may engage is historical character writing. In doing so, they keep journals of events that took place in American history from the perspective of a fictitious historical family that each student created. The families witness all the events that take place in American history and write their reactions to these events. The teacher scaffolds the journal writing assignment with the guidesheet shown in Figure 9.1. Study the guidesheet, and then read several entries from one student's journal in Figure 9.2.

Figure 9.1 A Guidesheet for Historical Character Journals

To help you develop your historical character, use the information that you have gained about the American colonies and your own background knowledge.

Who is your character?

1. What is your character's name? How old is your character? Is he or she married? (*Note:* How old were people when they married during his or her time?)

2. Who else is in your character's family? How old is each of these people? (*Note:* What happened to a lot of children during this time?)

3. Where does your character live?

4. What does your character do for a living? Is he or she rich or poor?

5. What religion is your character? What attitude does he or she have toward religion?

6. How much education does your character have?

7. Was your character born in the United States, Europe, or Africa? If he or she was born in Europe, in what country?

8. How does your character feel about people who are "different" in skin color, religion, social or economic class, or nationality?

   a. Skin color? (*Note:* This may depend on where he or she lives.)

   b. Religion?

   c. Social or economic class?

   d. Nationality?

9. How does your character feel about being part of a colony instead of living in an independent country?

SKETCHBOOKS IN ART   A high school art teacher incorporates a **sketchbook** into his courses to guide students' thinking and responses to what they are learning and studying in class. As an introduction to the sketchbook, the class discusses reasons for keeping a sketchbook, which the teacher adapted from a model used by McIntosh (1991):

- *What should you include in your sketchbook?* New ideas, sketches, concepts, designs, redesigns, words, notes from class, drawings to show understanding, reflections on the class, questions that you have, and new things you've learned.

- *When should you include entries in your sketchbook?* (1) After each class; (2) anytime an insight or a design idea or question hits you; (3) anytime, so keep the sketchbook handy and visible in your work area.

- *Why should you draw and write in your sketchbook?* (1) It will record your ideas you might otherwise forget; (2) it will record and note your growth; (3) it will facilitate your learning, problem solving, idea forming, research, reading, and discussion in class.

Figure 9.2 Historical Character Journal Entries

1770

My name is Victoria Black and I'm thirteen years old. We are a Protestant family and we attend church regularly. It's a social as well as religious occasion for us. We stay all day, and my mother gossips with all of the neighbors. I've made a few friends there, but usually I stay with my sister. I have long blond hair and sparkling blue eyes in my mother's words. I'm learning how to take care of the home and cook lately. My mother says it's important because soon enough I'll be married. I think she wants me to marry one of the boys from town whose father is a popular lawyer. I have an older sister Sarah who is fifteen and has just gotten married. My parents are Mathew and Elizabeth Black. They are becoming older, and mother has been sick lately. We worry very much for them and say prayers daily. We live on Mander Plantation in Trenton, Pennsylvania, where my father grows cotton and some tobacco. We have many indentured servants that we treat very nicely. I've become close with a couple of them. Usually when servants' time has expired my father will give them some land to start up their lives. Because we are more north we haven't any African slaves yet. My father is planning a trip out east to buy some slaves later this month. I'm still not sure if buying people is the right thing to do, but my brother told me he doesn't think they're real people. I don't know how my father feels on this. He must think it's alright. My father is very confused about what's going on with the British. He doesn't understand why the colonists think they even have a chance at fighting and winning with the British. He thinks the war will be over in no time.

1778

I'm married now to William Brown, a new lawyer for Pennsylvania. We have two children, Mary and Richard Brown. They are still both very young, Mary is six and Richard is four and I'm expecting another soon! William is for the Revolutionary War. He feels the Brits are not being sensible with their laws for us. The taxation has bothered us greatly. Each week we scramble for money. Even though William is a lawyer, it's still hard to get started and receive reasonable wages. The British have also gone too far with the quartering act. We had British soldiers knock on our door last week asking for food. William was outraged. He says we have to have a revolution and win if we want to survive and live happily. William said things are just going to get worse and worse. I don't think things could get any worse. I do worry about this war, for my brothers and William. Hopefully neither of them will be in the militia. We are already hearing of some battles, which sound awful. We are starting to go to church and pray every day now for our family and country.

1779–1781

William and my brothers are going to be in the militia. I'm very worried for them. William feels what he's doing is right for the country. We seem to be winning some of the battles, which is surprising. The women and children from our church gather every day and pray for our brothers and husbands. We all try our hardest to stay on our feet and have enough food for everyone. Some weeks it's difficult. We feel that all of our money is going to taxes. We pray that the end will be here soon. I had a baby boy. We named him Daniel Brown. It will be hard to raise these children alone. Before William goes to the militia, I'm going to visit my mother. She's dying and I'd like to say goodbye to her.

- *How should you write and draw entries in your sketchbook?* You can express yourself in sketches and drawings; in single words, questions, or short phrases; in long, flowing sentences; in designs and redesigns; in diagrams, graphs, and overlays; or in colors.

- *Remember, the sketchbook is yours, and it reflects how perceptive you are with your ideas and how creative you are in your thought processes!*

MATH JOURNALS   Math teachers use response journals in a variety of ways. They may invite students to write a "math autobiography" in which they describe their feelings and prior experiences as math learners. Rose (1989, p. 24) suggests the following prompt for a biographical narrative in math:

> Write about any mathematical experiences you have had. The narratives should be told as stories, with as much detail and description as possible. Include your thoughts, reactions, and feelings about the entire experience.

If students need more scaffolding than the prompt, Rose recommends having them complete and write elaborations on sentences, such as:

My most positive experience with math was _____

My background in math is _____

Figure 9.3 Journal Entry in Response to the Prompt "What Goes Through Your Mind When You Do a Proof?"

> *October 7*
>
> When I look at something I have to prove, the answer is always so obvious to me, I don't know what to write. This confuses me more because then I just write down one thing. Even though I understand it, no one else could. I don't use postulates & theorems because I have no idea which is which. So if you gave me a proof, I could probably prove it, but just not mathematically using big words.

I liked math until _____

Math makes me feel _____

If I were a math teacher, I'd _____

The content of math journals may also include exploratory writing activities, summaries, letters, student-constructed word problems and theorem definitions, descriptions of mathematical processes, calculations and solutions to problems, and feelings about the course. Examine, for example, the journal entries in Figures 9.3 and 9.4.

Double-Entry Journals (DEJs)

A **double-entry journal (DEJ)** is a versatile adaptation of the response journal. As the name implies, DEJs allow students to record dual entries that are conceptually related. In doing so, students juxtapose their thoughts and feelings according to the prompts they are given for making the entries. To create a two-column format for a DEJ, have students divide sheets of notebook paper in half lengthwise. Younger writers may need more room to write their entries than a divided page allows. As an alternative, they may find that it is easier to use the entire left page of a notebook as one column and the right page as the other column.

DEJs serve a variety of functions. In the left column of the journal, students may be prompted to select words, short quotes, or passages from the text that interest them or evoke strong responses. In this column, they write the word, quote, or passage verbatim or use their own words to describe what is said in the text. In the right column, the students record their reactions, interpretations, and responses to the text segments they have selected.

As part of a science unit on the solar system, for example, middle grade students used double-entry journals as an occasion to explore their own personal meanings for

Figure 9.4 Journal Entry in Response to the Prompt "Explain to Someone How to Bisect an Angle"

> *9/4*
>
> <u>How to Draw a Bisected Angle</u>
>
> Make an acute angle. Label it $\angle ABC$ — making Point A on one ray, B at the vertex, or point where rays meet, and C on the other ray. Now, with a compass, draw an arc of any measurement which will cross both rays. Next, use your compass to measure the distance between the two points you made by making the arc and keep the measurement locked on your protractor. Now, put the point of your compass on one of the arc points and make a slash in the middle of the angle. Do the same from the other dot on the other ray. The slash marks should cross in the center. Make a point where the slashes cross. Label it Point D. Draw a ray starting at Point B going through Point D. $\overrightarrow{BD}$ now bisects $\angle ABC$.

the concept of the solar system. In the left column, they responded to the question "What is the solar system?" In the right column, the students reflected on the question "What does it mean to you?" Study the entries that three of the students wrote in the left column. Then compare the three corresponding entries from the right column.

What Is the Solar System?	What Does It Mean to You?
It is eight planets, along with asteroid belts, stars, black holes, and so on.	The solar system is a mystery to me. I know the planets and stuff, but how did it come into being? Galileo had something to do with the solar system, but I'm not sure exactly what. I would like to find out more about it.
It is planets and stars. Earth is the third planet from the sun. It is the only planet with water. Stars are huge—many much greater than the sun in size.	The solar system reminds me of a white-haired scientist who is always studying the big vast opening in the sky. When I look at the sky at night I see tiny twinkling lights. People tell me that they're planets, but I think they're stars. I see constellations, but I don't recognize them. I am not a white-haired scientist yet.
The eight planets are not very interesting to me, and I won't bother to go through them. But I did memorize the order of the planets by this sentence: *My very eager mother just served us nachos.* Take the beginning letters to remind you of each planet.	When I think about what the solar system means to me, I think about an unknown universe, which could be much larger than we think it is. I start to think about science fiction stories that I have read, alien beings and creatures that are in the universe someplace.

In an eighth-grade language arts class, the teacher and his students were engaged in a unit on the Yukon and Jack London's *Call of the Wild*. As part of the core book study of London's classic novel about the adventures of a sled dog named Buck, the teacher arranged for a sled dog team demonstration by a group of residents who participate in dog sledding as a hobby. His class was excited by the demonstration, which took place on the school's grounds. The next day, students used double-entry journals to reflect on the experience. In the left column, they responded to the question "What did you learn from the demonstration?" In the right column, they reflected on the question "How did the demonstration help you better understand the novel?" Examine some of the students' entries in Figure 9.5.

Learning Logs

Learning logs are similar to online threaded discussions, which were explained in Chapter 2. Like threaded discussions, learning logs add still another dimension to personal learning in content area classrooms (Bangert-Drowns, Hurley, & Wilkinson, 2004). The strategy is simple to implement but must be used regularly to be effective. As is the case with response and double-entry journals, students keep an ongoing record of learning *as it happens* in a notebook. They write in their own language, not necessarily for others to read but to themselves, about what they are learning. Entries in logs influence learning by revealing problems and concerns.

There is no one way to use learning logs, although teachers often prefer allowing 5 or 10 minutes at the end of a period for students to respond to questions such as "What did I understand about the work we did in class today?" "What didn't I understand?" "At what point in the lesson did I get confused?" "What did I like or dislike about class today?" The logs can be kept in a box and stored in the classroom. The teacher then reviews them during or after school to see what the students are learning and to recognize their concerns and problems.

Students may at first be tentative about writing and unsure of what to say or reveal—after all, journal writing is reflective and personal. It takes a trusting atmosphere to open up to the teacher. However, to win the trust of students, teachers refrain from making judgmental or evaluative comments when students admit a lack of understanding of what's happening in class. If a trusting relationship exists, students will soon recognize the value of logs.

Figure 9.5 Entries from a Double-Entry Journal Assignment for *The Call of the Wild*

Classroom Artifact

What did you learn from the demonstration?	How did the demonstration help you better understand the novel?
I learned that although dogs just look big and cuddly they really can work. When people take the time they can teach their dog anything. Yet that saying also applies to life. **[Alex]**	I never realized how hard it was for Buck to pull the sled. It takes a lot of work.
It was excellent. I learned that the owners and the dogs were a family and extremely hard workers. I learned how hard a race could be and the risk involved. I'm glad I got to see the dogs and their personalities. **[Marcus]**	It proved to me how Buck needed to be treated with praise and discipline and equality. That way you get a wonderful dog and a companion for life.
I learned about how they trained their dogs and that they need as much or more love and attention as they do discipline. **[Jennifer]**	It helped me understand the book better because it showed how unique Buck is compared to the other dogs. Also what a dog sled looks like and what Buck might have looked like. It made the story come alive more.

Box 9.3 Evidence-Based Practices

Authentic Writing with English Learners

Daniel (2017) reminds writing instructors that English Learners benefit from authentic writing experiences that are connected to their experiences. For example, an eighth-grade science class engaged in a unit study on the spread of disease. One of their writing assignments was to imagine that they worked for the Centers for Disease Control and Prevention (CDC). Their task was to catalog and categorize the diseases, their symptoms, and their cures. This class included several Hmong students who had limited proficiency with English. The teacher created sight word cards and corresponding picture cards of disease symptoms. Capitalizing not only on the eighth-grade fascination with all things gruesome but also picture/word associations, the Hmong students worked with their English-speaking counterparts to learn the vocabulary as they matched the sight word cards with the pictures. Next, they worked in small groups to dramatize symptoms that corresponded to a disease. The experience of playing these roles helped all students to understand the nature of the diseases they were studying. This activity supports the best practices of peer-based learning, scaffolding, and vocabulary-based instruction.

Genre-based writing can be supported with templates that scaffold and support writing and comprehension (Ortmeier-Hooper, 2017). For example, a template for a beginning English Learner could include an illustrated vocabulary chart. A more advanced English Learner might benefit from a synonym or antonym chart to access higher-level vocabulary concepts. Point-of-view guides, learning logs, and summarization charts can also serve as templates. Templates allow English Learners to focus more on the *why* of their writing and less on the *how.* Templates are most effective when they support student engagement in both reading and writing.

MyLab Education **Self-Check 9.2**

MyLab Education **Application Exercise 9.2:**
Using Mentor Texts in Content Area Classrooms

Writing in Disciplines

9.3 Describe the more formal process of writing in disciplines and explain how this writing should align with expectations of the subject matter.

WTL activities, as we have shown, provide students with numerous informal opportunities to explore and clarify ideas and concepts. A second instructional component of academic writing—known as writing in disciplines (WID)—involves more formal, elaborate, and well-thought-out writing on the part of students. Although there are aspects of academic writing that cut across all disciplines, each discipline has its specific *writing forms, styles*, and *conventions* that students must consider and follow as they engage in WID assignments.

As important as a research paper is for learning, in most, if not all, disciplines, other forms of writing are also essential: position papers, progress reports, lab and field reports, interpretive essays, reviews, project proposals, and journal or newspaper articles. Table 9.1 provides an extensive listing of writing forms that are an integral part of WID writing assignments.

MyLab Education
Video Example 9.2: Writing in Science
In this video, observe how a science teacher engages students in problem solving and hypothesis writing.

Table 9.1 Some Discourse Forms for Content Area Writing

Category	Examples
Media	Stories or essays for local papers School newspaper stories Interviews Radio scripts TV scripts
Technology	Blogs Wikis Nings Google Docs Threaded discussion groups LISTSERVs Multimodal texts YouTube videos Internet projects WebQuests
Reviews	Books Films Television programs Documentaries
Letters	Personal reactions Observations Public/informational Persuasive To public officials To imaginary people From imaginary places

Table 9.1 Continued

Category	Examples
Position papers	National concerns Local issues School issues Historical problems Scientific issues
Business writing	Memos Résumés Technical reports Proposals
Opinion writing	Commentaries Editorials
Anecdotes and stories	From experience As told by others Of famous people Of places Of content ideas Of historical events
Creative writing	Plays Poems Songs and ballads Fantasy Adventure Science fiction Historical fiction Historical "you are there" scenes Children's books Dramatic scripts
Science notes	Observations Science notebooks Reading reports Lab reports
Visual	Poster displays Cartoons and comic strips Photos and captions Collages and montages Mobiles and sculptures How-to slides
Math	Story problems Solutions to problems Record books Notes and observations
Reference materials	Booklets Fact books or fact sheets Dictionaries and lexicons
Other	Requests Journals and diaries Biographical sketches Guess who/what descriptions Demonstrations Puzzles and word searches Prophecy and predictions Dialogues and conversations

RAFT Writing

The key to thoughtful writing begins with the design of the assignment itself. The teacher's primary concern should be how to make an assignment *explicit* without stifling interest or the spirit of inquiry. An assignment should provide more than a subject to write on. This is where RAFT can make a difference in students' approach to writing.

RAFT is an acronym that stands for *role, audience, form,* and *topic*. **RAFT** allows teachers to create *prompts* for many types of discipline-specific writing assignments (Holston & Santa, 1985). What constitutes an effective writing prompt for academic assignments? Suppose you were assigned one of the following topics to write on, based on text readings and class discussion:

- Batiking
- The role of the laser beam in the future
- Nuclear disarmament

No doubt, some of you would probably begin writing on one of the topics without hesitation. Perhaps you already know a great deal about the subject, have strong feelings about it, or can change the direction of the discourse without much difficulty. Others, however, may resist or even resent the activity. Your questions might echo the following concerns: "Why do I want to write about any of these topics in the first place?" "For whom am I writing?" "Will I write a paragraph? A book?" The most experienced writer must come to grips with questions such as these, and with even more complicated ones: "How will I treat my subject?" "What role will I take?" If anything, the questions raise to awareness the *rhetorical context*—the writer's *role,* the *audience,* the *form* of the writing, and the writer's *topic*—that most writing assignments should provide. A context for writing allows students to assess the writer's relationship to the subject of the writing (the topic) and to the reader (the audience for whom the writing is intended).

RESEARCH QUESTIONS A good writing activity, then, *situates* students in the writing task. Instead of asking students to write about how to batik, give students a RAFT.

> To show that you understand how batiking works, imagine that you are giving a demonstration at an arts-and-crafts show. Describe the steps and procedures involved in the process of batiking to a group of onlookers, recognizing that they know little about the process but are curious enough to find out more.

This example creates a context for writing. It suggests the writer's role (the student providing a batiking demonstration), the writer's audience (observers of the demonstration), the form of the writing (a how-to demonstration), and the topic (the process of batiking). RAFT writing prompts contrived situations and audiences in the context of what is being read or studied. However, they are far from trivial, nonacademic, or inconsequential. Instead, when students "become" someone else, they must look at situations in a nontraditional way. After writing, they can compare different perspectives on the same issue and examine the validity of the viewpoints that were taken.

Or take, as another example, the nuclear disarmament topic:

> The debate over nuclear disarmament has countries and people taking different sides of the argument. There are some who argue that nuclear proliferation will lead to nuclear war or nuclear terrorism. There are others who contend that the nuclear arms race is the only way to maintain peace in the world.
>
> You have been selected to write a position paper for the class in which you debate your side of the argument. Another student has been selected to defend an opposing position. The class will then vote on the more persuasive of the two positions. Once you have investigated the issue thoroughly, write a paper to convince as many classmates as possible that your position is the better one.

As you can see from the two examples, each creates a lifelike context, each identifies a purpose and an audience, and each suggests the writer's stance and a format—that is, a demonstration or a position paper. In each case, students will not necessarily assume that the teacher is the audience, even though ultimately the teacher will evaluate the written product. Box 9.4, "Voices From the Field," describes how Ashley, a middle school science teacher, adapts RAFT in her classrooms.

Box 9.4   Voices from the Field

Ashley, Eighth-Grade Lead Science Teacher

Challenge

Science teachers in my school struggle to incorporate writing into the curriculum. Although students need to understand how to write within a discipline, I noticed that my students preferred a kinesthetic approach to science rather than composing a lab report. That's when it clicked for me that I could combine the two approaches to help maximize learning opportunities for my students while helping them use writing in meaningful ways within the science discipline. By using the RAFT strategy (role, audience, form, and topic) and science experiments together, students were able to physically engage with the science concept first by conducting experiments. Later, they were able to write about them using the literacy strategy. Using this method allows students to develop a context for writing by first participating in a lab activity and then applying what they had learned through RAFT.

Strategy

Initially, my students were not thrilled with having another writing assignment outside of their language arts class. Other teachers were not as receptive to the idea either because they did not feel comfortable "teaching language arts" in their science classes. I figured the only way to create buy-in from both the teachers and students was to conduct a little experiment myself. I was teaching a unit on microbiology, and the students had just spent the last two classes refreshing their memories on parts of the cell. In previous years, most students had simply memorized the information to perform well on the test but had not retained the concepts. This year, my students engaged in an edible cell lab, which included Jell-O and other various treats to construct prokaryotic cells (cells with no nuclear membrane) and eukaryotic cells (cells with a true nucleus). Upon completion of the lab, I modeled for the students how to develop a RAFT writing activity based upon the cell experiment. My role was that of the nucleus, and my audience was the other parts of the cell. I used a memo format on the topic of controlling the processes of the cell. I took the position that there were some parts of the cell that were not doing their job, and as their boss, I put a memo in each of their boxes as a friendly reminder.

The students and teachers responded overwhelmingly well to the wit and humor I included in my memo, and the students were eager to begin their own RAFT scenarios even before I could finish the instructions. A rather creative response came from a student who chose the role of the endoplasmic reticulum. This particular part of the smallest living organism is responsible for moving material around the cell, so the student decided to use the customers of the UPS delivery service as the audience. The student created a set of instructions on how to track your package (cell material) as it is being delivered to its final destination. In another example, a student included the use of the mitochondria (role) speaking to an audience of gym members. The student created a recipe (format) describing how to use energy to get the best workout possible or, in cellular terms, release energy for other cell functions. I used this technique several times over the course of the year, and my students showed improvement in their class assignments, test scores, and, most importantly, their retention of the concepts.

Reflection

As with other strategies, RAFT is not without its limitations. Not every student showed an interest, and students who struggled with reading and writing in general found some frustrations with this technique as well. However, using the RAFT method in science classes was an innovative way to get students engaged in the writing process. I believe that this technique not only helped me grow as an educator, but it served as a reminder that, as teachers, we should constantly search for innovative strategies to help our students learn across the disciplines. I would advise other teachers to use this activity to differentiate based on students' ability levels. Some students may need more assistance with the writing process, so you might consider using leading statements where students are allowed to fill in the blank. Over time students can become more comfortable with this strategy and, with your guidance, continue to advance their knowledge of the technique and the class material. Additionally, some of the vocabulary terms can be quite difficult for students to understand, therefore making the RAFT process more complicated. I would advise other teachers to be sure that students are equipped with basic knowledge of relevant vocabulary concepts before proceeding with RAFT.

Research-Based Writing

Research projects pave the way for writing at every stage of the process, whether writing involves drawing up a project schedule, choosing a topic, formulating research questions, making an outline, taking notes, preparing a first draft, revising and editing, or completing the paper. Teachers who carefully plan research projects give just the right amount of direction to allow students to explore and discover ideas on their own. Research isn't a do-your-own-thing proposition. Novice researchers need structure. A research project must have just enough structure to give students (1) a problem focus, (2) physical and intellectual freedom, (3) an environment in which they can obtain data, and (4) guidance in writing and reporting the results of their research. Procedures for guiding research projects are explained in Chapter 5.

Ideally, research arises out of students' questions about the topic under study. A puzzling situation may arouse curiosity and interest. We recommend using questions such as the following to initiate research:

How is _____ different from _____? How are they alike?
What has changed from the way it used to be?
What can we learn from the past?
What caused _____ to happen? Why did it turn out that way?
What will happen next? How will it end?
How can we find out?
Which way is best?
What does this mean to you? How does this idea apply to other situations?

As a result of questioning, students should become aware of their present level of knowledge and the gaps that exist in what they know. They can use the questioning session to identify a problem. You might ask, "What do you want to find out?" During the planning stage of a research project, the emphasis should be on further analysis of each individual or group problem, breaking it down into a sequence of manageable parts and activities. The teacher facilitates by helping students to clarify problems. As students progress in their research, data collection and interpretation become integral stages of the inquiry. Students will need the physical and intellectual freedom to investigate their problems. They will also need an environment—a library or media center—where they will have access to a variety of informational materials, including print and electronic sources.

Students need guidance as they learn to organize the material that they find. They can become lost in a pile of copies and links as they begin their research. Digital sketchbooks can serve as an organizational tool. Think of Pinterest. Users organize ideas on boards and add links to each topic. Followers can help evaluate the sources and even point users to new sources. This tool, or one similar to it, can be used to help students organize information as they research content area topics. If Pinterest is unavailable, this same concept can be accomplished through the creation of a PowerPoint presentation or a Google Docs document. Students can share their presentations with a small group through e-mail and react in a manner similar to that of a Pinterest user. A Google Docs document can allow students to pool their collective knowledge on a shared document that is accessible to all members of a small group. Box 9.5 explains how an eighth-grade language arts teacher used vlogging as a disciplinary literacy tool to support multimedia story telling.

The teacher's role during data collection and interpretation is that of a resource. Your questions will help the students interpret data or perhaps raise new questions, reorganize ideas, or modify plans: "How are you doing? How can I help? Are you finding it difficult to obtain materials? Which ideas are giving you trouble?" This role is very similar to that of guiding the actual writing of the research project.

Guiding the Writing Process

Getting started with the actual writing of a paper or research report can be difficult, even terrifying. Waiting until the night before to write a paper is not good strategy! One of the teacher's first instructional tasks is to make students aware that the writing process occurs in stages. It's the rare writer who leaps in a single bound from an idea-in-head to a finished product on paper. The stages of the writing process may be defined broadly as *discovery, drafting, revising*, and *publishing*. Table 9.2 presents an overview of these stages.

These stages are by no means neat and orderly. Few writers proceed from stage to stage in a linear sequence. Instead, writing is a *recursive* process; writing is a back-and-forth activity. As teachers, we want to engage students in the use of discovery strategies

Box 9.5 Disciplinary Literacies

Using Disciplinary Literacy to Explore the Real-Life Tasks of a Multimedia Story Teller

Access to new technologies means that we spend an ever-increasing amount of time online. Interest-based formats encourage reading, writing, listening and viewing to gain information about the world around us. A "vlog" or "blog" is an increasingly popular media forum. A vlog is a video log in which the creator provides advice, information, or their opinion on a chosen subject. The blog serves this same function; however, it may intertwine elements such as graphics, directions, recipes or literacy references to tell a complete story. Effective vloggers can capture the interest and attention of an audience. Vlogging or blogging can serve as a helpful forum for the language arts teacher who is trying to engage students in meaningful writing projects.

Using a disciplinary literacy framework, Sam, an eighth-grade language arts teacher, decided to have his students identify the elements of a successful vlog or blog.

To begin, Sam had his students choose a lifestyle topic. Sam outlined the assignment as follows:

1. Choose a lifestyle topic. This should be something you are interested in because you will be watching, reading, and, eventually, creating your own work in this topic category.
2. Find five vloggers or bloggers that talk and write about this topic.
3. Write down the number of followers they have and provide a table of contents for at least 10 of their most popular topics.
4. Watch or read the vlogs or blogs and capture:
   a. What do they do well?
   b. How are they presenting information?
   c. Why does this appeal to you? Why would you follow them?
   d. What would you do differently? What would you add or take away?
   e. Describe the quality of their work. How do they make it look "professional"?
   f. What are some of the advertisers that support this commentator? Why do you think they do?
   g. How do they use instructions, storytelling, graphics, and/or other unique elements?

After the students completed this pre-assignment, they worked in groups to create a rubric. This rubric could be used by consumers of these genres to outline the quality of the vlog or blog. A potential vlogger or blogger could use it to guide their work. Ryan, a reluctant writer, uncharacteristically raised his hand to voice his choice. His chosen topic was auto repair. He explained to his teacher that he and his dad were working on an old Jeep that they bought for $600. They spent their weekends trying to take apart and put back together this collection of metal and parts to try to create a roadworthy vehicle. To aid them in their pursuits, they frequented YouTube. They had already created a list of their favorite commentators who had become their weekly virtual helpers. Ryan not only completed the pre-assignment but worked well with the group as they built out their comprehensive list. Sam emphasized that the rubric should help them plan their project and should serve as an assessment tool.

After the rubrics were complete, the students set to work on creating their own blog or vlog. Ryan worked with his dad and filmed three different segments of their work on the Jeep's transmission. Ryan wrote the text that accompanied each video and described their step-by-step repair process. He uploaded his videos to YouTube and was thrilled when he started to see his follower count rise. His videos were highly rated by his classmates, and several of them added their comments and followed what he did. All this happened in real time, reinforcing the impact of this authentic assignment. This writing assignment reinforced the higher-level thinking skills of evaluating, creating, and applying. It also supported publishing writing in an authentic space. Ryan and his class went through the genuine process of creating stories that were viewed and used beyond their classroom.

---

to explore and generate ideas and make plans before writing a draft; but once they are engaged in the physical act of composing a draft, writers often discover new ideas, reformulate plans, rewrite, and revise.

DISCOVERY: GETTING IT OUT   What students do before writing is as important as what they do before reading. Discovery strategies involve planning, building and activating prior knowledge, setting goals, and getting ready for the task at hand. In other words, discovery refers to everything that students do before putting words on paper for a first draft. The term *prewriting* is often used interchangeably with *discovery*, but it is somewhat misleading because students often engage in some form of writing before working on a draft.

Discovery is what the writer consciously or unconsciously does to get energized and motivated—to get ideas out in the open, to explore what to say and how to say it: What will I include? What's a good way to start? Who is my audience? What form should my writing take? Scaffolding the use of discovery strategies in a classroom involves any support activity or experience that motivates a student to write, generates ideas for writing, or focuses attention on a subject. Students can be guided to think about a topic in relation to a perceived audience and the form that a piece of writing will take. A teacher who

Table 9.2 Stages in the Writing Process

Discovery
Exploring and generating ideas
Finding a topic
Making plans (Audience? Form? Voice?)
Getting started
Drafting
Getting ideas down on paper
Sticking to the task
Developing fluency and coherence
Revising
Revising for meaning
Responding to the writing
Organizing for clarity
Editing and proofreading for the conventions of writing, word choice, syntax
Polishing
Publishing
Sharing and displaying finished products
Evaluating and grading

recognizes that the writing process must slow down at the beginning will help students discover that they have something to say and that they want to say it.

Getting started on the right foot is what the discovery stage is all about. Generating talk about an assignment or research project before writing buys time for students to gather ideas and organize them for writing. Discussion before writing is as crucial to success as discussion before reading.

DRAFTING: GETTING IT DOWN   The drafting stage involves getting ideas down on paper in a fluent and coherent fashion. The writer drafts a text with an audience (readers) in mind.

If students are primed for writing through discovery strategies, first drafts should develop without undue struggle. The use of in-class time for drafting is as important as allotting in-class time for reading. In both cases, teachers can regulate and monitor the process much more effectively. For example, while students are writing, a teacher's time shouldn't be occupied grading papers or attending to other unrelated tasks.

The drafting stage should be a time to confer individually with students who are having trouble using what they know to tackle the writing task. Serve as a sounding board or play devil's advocate: "How does what we studied in class for the past few days relate to your topic?" or "I don't quite understand what you're getting at. Let's talk about what you're trying to say."

REVISING: GETTING IT RIGHT   Revising a text is hard work. Student writers often think that *rewriting* is a dirty word. They mistake it for recopying—emphasizing neatness rather than an opportunity to rethink a paper. Good writing often reflects good rewriting. From a content area learning perspective, rewriting is the catalyst for clarifying and extending concepts under study. Revising text hinges on the feedback students receive between first and second drafts.

Teacher feedback is always important, but it's often too demanding and time-consuming to be the sole vehicle for response. It may also lack the *immediacy* that student writers need to "try out" their ideas on an audience—especially if teachers are accustomed to taking home a stack of papers and writing comments on each one. The "paper load" soon becomes unmanageable and self-defeating. An alternative is to have students respond to the writing of other students. By working together in "response groups," students can give reactions, ask questions, and make suggestions to their peers. These responses to writing-in-progress lead to revision and refinement during rewriting.

Once feedback is given on the content and organization of a draft, students can begin to edit and proofread their texts for spelling, punctuation, capitalization, word choice, and syntax. Accuracy counts. Cleaning up a text shouldn't be neglected, but student writers in particular must recognize that concern about proofreading and editing comes toward the end of the process.

MyLab Education
Video Example 9.3: The Writing Process: Revising
This video discusses the importance of writing as a process, with an emphasis on the revising stage.

PRODUCT: ALLOWING FLEXIBILITY   The process of writing, researching, drafting, and, ultimately, publishing should be the focus of student research. If the goal of a research project is to teach this process, then the idea of what the students will be writing may be up for debate. The idea of a multigenre project allows students to express their research through their choice of product. Romano (1995) wrote about multigenre products and suggested two different ways to use multigenre project assignments in the classroom. He suggested that students might choose their mode of expression through one product chosen from a list (similar to the discourse forms list) or express their research through several smaller projects, all thematically linked together. Giving students choice allows them flexibility, which increases student motivation and allows for more authentic responses.

This is an example taken from an eighth-grade physical education class: The student's research topic was vegetarian diets and their effect on health. The student completed her research and chose to express her findings through the creation of an interactive menu. Using PowerPoint and hyperlinks, she created a menu that allowed the reader to click on a vegetarian item and learn about its health benefits. She included a list of citations that allowed the reader to go directly to the article to learn more about the topic from the original author.

In a ninth-grade language arts classroom, students chose a fairy tale to research. They were to research its origins and then trace the changes in its presentation throughout its history. With each change they were to explain how the contextual issues of society influenced its presentation. The assignment indicated that they were to choose several different genres to express their findings. One student chose the fairy tale *Snow White*. She began with the Grimm version and created a documentary that was inspired by the Grimm brothers. They explained that their stories were meant as cautionary tales. When they spoke of Snow White, they did so only as a side note, choosing instead to emphasize their own work. This was intended to demonstrate the male dominance of their society. In her next genre, she wrote about the famous Disney cartoon version. Here she wrote an interview of the Snow White character, portraying her as a woman dependent on little men to take care of her and a prince to wake her from her long apple-induced sleep. Snow White was meant to symbolize the stereotypical women's roles in the '30s and '40s as dependent on men. Finally, she wrote about the modern film version. She created a graphic novel that featured Snow White as a strong woman and an inspired fighter. This depiction showed that modern women could fight for their own causes, reflecting the changes in society since the 1937 release of the Disney version.

Multigenre projects allow freedom of expression, but they also allow students the opportunity to explore various types of writing styles and genres. While still learning the research process, they can also learn, for example, the how-to of writing a blog, an article, or a dialogue as well as how to structure an interview. Using multigenre projects helps differentiate the research project, allowing success for all students.

PUBLISHING: GOING PUBLIC   When students put in the time and effort to edit, revise, and proofread, their writing deserves to be shared with others. The "publishing" stage of the writing process gives student writers an audience so that the writing task becomes a real effort at communication—not just another assignment to please the teacher. When the classroom context for writing encourages a range of possible audiences for assignments (including the teacher), the purposes and the quality of writing often change for the better. When students know that their written products will be presented publicly for others to read, they develop a heightened awareness of audience. Teachers need to mine the audience resources that exist in and out of the classroom. Some possibilities for sharing finished products include the following:

- Oral presentations to the class
- Class publications such as newspapers, magazines, anthologies, and books
- Room displays
- A secure class website for class members and parents
- A class newspaper or magazine
- A roundtable panel

MyLab Education **Self-Check 9.3**

MyLab Education **Application Exercise 9.3:**
Using the RAFT Strategy in Content Area Instruction

Looking Back Looking Forward

In this chapter, we focused on writing to emphasize the powerful bonds between reading and writing. Content area learning, in fact, is more within the reach of students when writing and reading are integrated throughout the curriculum. The combination of reading and writing in a classroom improves achievement and instructional efficiency. When students write in content area classrooms, they are involved in a process of manipulating, clarifying, discovering, and synthesizing ideas. They also practice the role of a content writer, understanding genre, language, jargon, and syntax inherent to each content area. The writing process, then, is a powerful strategy for helping students gain insight into course objectives.

The uses of writing have been noticeably limited in content area classrooms. Writing has often been restricted to noncomposing activities such as filling in the blanks on worksheets and practice exercises, writing one-paragraph-or-less responses to study questions, or taking notes. The role of writing in content areas should be broadened because of its potentially powerful and motivating effect on thinking and learning.

Because writing promotes different types of learning, students should have many different occasions to write. Students should participate in exploratory writing activities, journal keeping, and discipline-specific forms of writing. Informal writing activities, such as the unsent letter, place students in a role-playing situation in which they are asked to write letters about the material being studied. Additional activities include biopoems, microthemes, POVGs, text response task cards, and admit/exit slips. Journals, one of the most versatile writing-to-learn strategies, entail students' responding to text as they keep ongoing records of learning while it happens in a notebook or loose-leaf binder. When students use response journals, double-entry journals, or learning logs, they soon learn to write without the fear of making mechanical errors. Students should also engage in RAFT writing assignments that are task explicit. An explicit RAFT assignment helps students determine the role, the audience, and the form of the writing as well as the topic.

Moreover, writing should be thought of and taught as a process. When students develop process-related writing strategies, they will be in a better position to generate ideas, set goals, organize, draft, and revise. The writing process occurs in stages; it is not necessarily a linear sequence of events but more of a recursive, back-and-forth activity. The stages of writing explored in this chapter were defined broadly as discovery, drafting, revising, and publishing. Discovery-related writing strategies motivate students to explore and generate ideas for the writing, set purposes, and do some preliminary organizing for writing. As students discover what to write about, they draft ideas into words on paper or on the computer screen. Drafting itself is a form of discovery and may lead to new ideas and plans for the writer. Revising strategies help students to rethink what they have drafted, making changes that improve both the content and organization of the writing. Allowing choice of product type increases motivation and allows students to better understand use of genre. Publishing involves celebrating and displaying finished products. The next chapter examines what it means to study. Studying texts requires students to engage in purposeful independent learning activities. Organizing information, summarizing chunks of information, taking notes, and conducting and reporting inquiry-centered research are examples of learner-directed strategies.

eResources

The website MathStories contains thousands of story problems for enhancing critical thinking and problem-solving skills. Many of the problems are based on children's literature. Browse the site and, working in small groups, write your own story problems based on content area topics of interest.

Use the keywords "double-entry journal," "double-entry journal + classroom lessons," and "RAFT writing strategies" to complete a search of these powerful writing strategies. Consider how you might use these strategies in your content area. Of all the sites that come up in your searches, identify the sites with the most complete information and lessons.

Chapter 10
Studying Text

Written in collaboration with Erin Donovan, Ph.D.

Shutterstock

Chapter Overview and Learning Outcomes

After reading this chapter, you should be able to:

10.1 Define the different types of text structure and how knowledge of text structure can influence comprehension.

10.2 Explain how graphic organizers support students' understanding and retention of content knowledge.

10.3 Explain how the ability to summarize can aid students in understanding and remembering material from content area instruction.

10.4 Explain the different approaches for note taking and how they support comprehension.

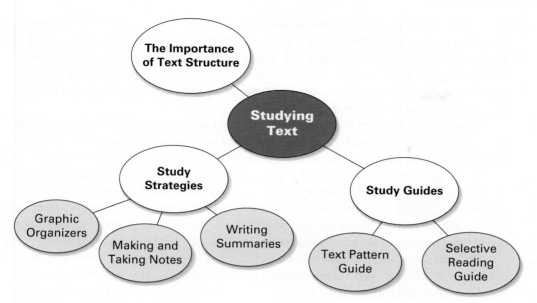

Organizing Principle

Studying text helps students make connections and think more deeply about ideas encountered during reading. Studying text is an active, persistent, demanding process that takes place inside the head. It requires not only concentrated effort but also reflective thinking. Through a growing array of technologies, including search engines and online texts, students have more information available to them than ever before. However, it is becoming increasing difficult for many students to discern relevant knowledge from less important details in the texts that they encounter. Thinking deeply and carefully about texts is an essential part of effective studying that can increase understanding of subject matter.

Students need to understand their reasons for studying text, whether their purposes involve acquiring, organizing, summarizing, or using information and ideas. They need to understand why they are learning content area concepts, and how those concepts can be applied beyond the classroom. Such connections can help to build a career-ready mind-set.

Studying text requires students to be strategic in their approach to text and topics. They need to be deliberate in their plans, conscious of their goals, and clear about how to apply strategies that will enable them to understand and remember both main ideas and supporting details. Putting study strategies to good use is directly related to students' knowledge and awareness of what it means to study. As they become more aware of studying text, students look for *structure*—how the important information and ideas are organized in text—in everything they read. The organizing principle suggests that one important aspect of studying text is to show students how to use the structure of ideas in text to their advantage: Studying text helps students make connections and think more deeply about ideas encountered during reading.

Frame of Mind

1. How is internal text structure different from external text structure?
2. How do graphic organizers help students make connections among important ideas?
3. What note-taking frameworks and procedures can you model for your students?
4. How can you show students how to summarize information?
5. What are study guides? How can you develop study guides using the levels-of-comprehension construct and text patterns?

The poster caught our attention immediately. It had just gone up on the bulletin board in Julie Meyer's classroom. "School Daze: From A to Z" defined significant school activities in the lives of students, each beginning with a letter of the alphabet. The entry for the letter *S* just happened to be the subject of this chapter. It read, "STUDY: *Those precious moments between texting, video games, movies, sports, food, personal grooming, and general lollygagging when one opens one's schoolbooks—and falls asleep.*"

Though some students might agree that studying is a quick cure for insomnia, few of us would deny that studying texts is one of the most frequent and predominant activities in schools today. The older students become, the more they are expected to learn with texts.

It's not uncommon to find a teacher prefacing a text assignment by urging students to "study the material." And some students do. They can study effectively because they know what it means to *approach* a text assignment: to *analyze* the reading task at hand, to *make plans* for reading, and then to *use strategies* to suit their purposes for studying. Students who approach texts in this way achieve a level of independence because they oversee their own learning.

Other students, less skilled in reading and studying, wage a continual battle with texts. Some probably wonder why teachers make a big deal out of studying in the first place. For them, the exhortation to "study the material" goes in one ear and out the other. Others try to cope with the demands of study, yet they are apt to equate studying texts with rote memorization, cramming "meaningless" material into short-term memory. Finally, some students have never been taught what studying looks like and have no frame of reference for the process that so many teachers demand. Too often, students are not aware of what it means to study, let alone how to use study strategies.

Today's students need to learn how to work smart. Working smart involves knowing when, and when not, to take shortcuts; it is knowing how to triumph over the everyday cognitive demands that are a natural part of classroom life. It also inevitably includes using technology. Technology can serve as a tool of inclusivity to assist with researching, problem solving, sharing, recruiting, providing feedback, and sharing outcomes (Howell, Minor, & Casimir, 2018).

MyLab Education
Response Journal 10.1
How is studying a text different from reading it?

Knowing how to work smart requires time and patience. Studying is a process that is learned inductively through trial and error and the repeated use of different strategies in different learning situations. And this is where teachers have a role to play. Through the instructional support you provide, students discover that some strategies work better for them than others in different learning situations.

The Importance of Text Structure

10.1   Define the different types of text structure and how knowledge of text structure can influence comprehension.

Authors impose structure—an organization among ideas—on their writing. Perceiving structure in text material improves learning and retention. When students are shown how to see relationships among concepts and bits of essential information, they are in a better position to respond to meaning and to distinguish important from less important ideas.

Educational psychologists from Thorndike (1917) to Kintsch (1977) and Meyer and Rice (1984) have shown that **text structure** is a crucial variable in learning and memory. Likewise, for more than 50 years, reading educators have underscored the recognition and use of organization as essential processes underlying comprehension and retention (Herber, 1978; Niles, 1965; Salisbury, 1934; Smith, 1964).

The primary purpose of many content area texts is to provide users with information Box 10.1 explains how primary documents can show students how historians use reading and writing in their discipline. To make information readily accessible, authors use external and internal structural features. *External text structure* is characterized by a text's overall instructional design—its format features. Its *internal text structure* is reflected by the interrelationships among ideas in the text as well as by the subordination of some ideas to others.

Box 10.1 Disciplinary Literacy

Studying Historical Text

History and social studies teachers often must contend with students who struggle to remain interested in their classes. Too often, students see history as a disconnected collection of facts and maps that have little to do with their day-to-day lives. Rita, a veteran social studies teacher, had many students who did not know how to study historical text. As one student once told her, "I don't like to study history. It's not like science. I get science. I just don't think I will ever get social studies." Rita talked to the student about why she liked science. It seemed that in science the student learned about things that potentially affected her life and just piqued her interest: diseases, parasites, epidemics, and other health-related issues. During a unit study of urban growth, the class read *Ghost Map* by Steven Johnson, a book that detailed the spread of cholera in London as that city grew as an urban power. After the unit was completed, the student asked Rita for more books detailing the history of disease. The student had finally found a way to connect social studies to her own interests. Connecting facts, providing relevant topics for in-depth study, and teaching students to approach topics with a historical mind-set comprise the foundation of disciplinary literacy in the social studies classroom.

In order to help more students study history, teachers like Rita must support their students in learning to think like historians. The first step may begin with changing the texts used in the classroom. The Library of Congress offers a free primary document search where a teacher can find pictures, letters, poems, songs, and documents. After the texts have been chosen, the teacher must show students how to study with purpose. One way to help students study text effectively is with various instructional strategies discussed in this chapter as well as previous chapters. Take, for example, the use of task cards, which were explained in Chapter 9. Each task card contains an explanation of a type of thinking that a historian does. The cards provide a purpose for studying text as the students sit down to examine the documents. Here are several examples of cards:

- Think like a historian and describe a picture by the grid system.
- Think like a historian and find words that we no longer use.
- Think like a historian and try to describe what type of person would have written this.
- Answer who they were, what they did for a living, and where would they live.

Rita implemented this system and was able to work one-on-one with a student as he studied a picture of Paul Revere. The student didn't recognize the picture, and it was unlabeled. He looked at the picture and held his task card directing him to use the grid system to describe the picture. The grid system is a way to break down a picture into small parts and analyze each part first before connecting it back to the meaning of the larger picture. Even with his task card, he was unsure of where to start his work. Rita worked with him to show him how to take the picture apart piece by piece, questioning each piece. Some of her prompts included: Why was he painted holding a silver mug? Why was he wearing such casual clothes? Why do you think he was posed that way? They were able to spend time talking through each question, understanding more about Paul Revere, and how deliberately subjects were posed to show status, employment, and wealth. At the end of the conversation, the student was able to connect his experience with the pictures he takes of himself on his cell phone—his "selfies." He explained how he carefully chooses his poses, always making sure his hat is tilted just right and his smile or pout fits the mood of the picture.

Rita also found that this approach benefited her gifted students. She noticed a student who was quickly completing the assignments with little thought or in-depth study. Rita worked with her to make sure she understood the process and was working toward the true purpose of the assignment. The student was using the "Think like a historian and tell me who would write this" task card and reading the lyrics for "Yankee Doodle." She had written, "A Yankee sang this to celebrate a victory." Rita stopped her work and helped her employ close-reading strategies, taking the song apart line by line. She looked up terms on her tablet that no longer meant what they once did. The student researched the date of the song and the name of the composer. She found out that the composer was British and the song was dated prior to the war. They talked about what America was like before the war, including how the relationship between the British and Americans changed. At the end of the discussion, her answer changed from an incorrect sentence to a page of thoughtful reflection that evidenced collaboration, problem solving, and close reading. She researched terms online, Googled information, and generally acquired a thorough understanding of the concepts she explored. In other words, she researched as if she were a historian.

Disciplinary literacy can be used to challenge students to approach texts as if they were historians. They learn that historians do not read documents line by line but rather read to complete tasks, using the document as information rather than letting the document guide their purpose. Disciplinary literacy also allows for different genres of text to be explored. We must remember that students are never going to like history if all they see is disconnected facts. Once they comprehend why history happened and how it relates to their modern life, then, historically speaking, history is not too bad.

External Text Structure

Printed and electronic texts contain certain format features—organizational aids—that are built into the text to facilitate reading. This book, for example, contains a *preface*, a *table of contents, appendixes*, a *bibliography*, and *indexes*. These aids, along with the *title page* and *dedication*, are called the *front matter* and *end matter* of a book. Of course, textbooks vary in the amount of front and end matter they contain. These aids can be valuable tools for prospective users of a textbook. Yet the novice reader hardly acknowledges their presence in texts, let alone uses them to advantage.

In addition, each chapter of a textbook usually has *introductory* or *summary statements, headings, graphs, charts, illustrations*, and *guide questions*. By learning how to attend to text features, students can identify the important information and increase their comprehension of the text (Bluestein, 2010).

Organizational aids, whether in electronic or printed texts, are potentially valuable—if they are not skipped or glossed over by readers. Headings, for example, are inserted in the text to divide it into logical units. Headings strategically placed in a text should guide the reader by highlighting major ideas.

Electronic text structure should be another addition to the standard course of study. Take social media profiles, for example. The most effective profiles begin and end with a message that is engaging and connects throughout the medium. The social media page itself has banners, titles, headings, and tags that not only build awareness of what others are doing but also provide structure to help users navigate the content (Alverman, 2010). As teachers build the "why," technology is a natural fit to demonstrate that text features do have purpose.

Within a text, authors use an internal structure to connect ideas logically in a coherent whole. Internal text structure might vary from passage to passage, depending on the author's purpose. These structures, or patterns of organization, within a text are closely associated with informational writing. Read Box 10.2 to learn how a high school reading specialist used several strategies to help build a student's understanding of text structure and, in turn, his understanding of texts in a world history course.

MyLab Education
Video Example 10.1: Using Text Structure to Aid Struggling Readers
Watch this video to learn how to use text structure to aid struggling readers.

MyLab Education
Response Journal 10.2
Why do some students ignore external organizational aids as tools for studying?

Box 10.2 Voices from the Field

Betsy, High School Reading Specialist

Challenge

I was asked to work with a ninth-grade student, Stephen, who was struggling in his world history class. No one seemed to know why he was struggling in this particular class. I met with Stephen and together we went through his notebook, assignments, and tests; and we discussed how the class was conducted. Stephen explained that the teacher generally went over the course material in a lecture format, and the students were supposed to "take notes." No specific structure or guidance was given for doing so. Students spent any remaining class time completing textbook readings and answering questions from an accompanying workbook.

My first inclination was to teach Stephen note-taking strategies so that he could gain the most from the teacher's lectures. However, when I reviewed his notes, they appeared to be sufficiently comprehensive and well organized. Additionally, I noticed that the assessments and assignments on which he had performed poorly appeared to be based primarily on the textbook readings. This observation led me to look at how Stephen approached informational text. I began by asking him to show me what he does when he begins to read a new chapter. I noticed that he simply opened the book to the chapter, settled in, and read through the entire chapter. Next, he opened the

workbook, read a question, and began flipping through pages to find the answer. He had difficulty with questions that required him to attend to specific text features, such as tables, maps, or illustrations. I concluded that what Stephen needed was to learn effective study strategies.

Strategy

In order to try to increase his comprehension of text, I decided to teach Stephen to notice and use text features using the text feature strategy from Boushey and Moser (2009). Using clear acetate sheets and Vis-à-Vis markers, we worked with one portion of the text as I modeled circling all of the text features, including headings, maps, illustrations, timelines, and tables. I also wrote brief notes on what I learned from each one of these figures. Next, I guided Stephen in applying the same procedure to a different portion of the text. Then he tried it on his own.

Once Stephen was independently attending to text features during a text preview as well as during reading, I wanted to teach him how to use the structure of the text to help him comprehend the main idea of each text section. Since he was not actually reading the headings, I decided to teach him a strategy for using those headings to aid his identification of important and interesting details. I taught him how to turn the heading of each section into a question. For example, if a heading reads "The Causes of the Russian Revolution," the reader turns the heading to the question, "What were the causes of the Russian Revolution?" Using sticky-note strips, I taught Stephen how to mark the parts of the following text that answered that question and only that question. I modeled two sections, then worked through a section with Stephen, and finally asked him to work through the next section on his own.

As Stephen's next class assessment was fast approaching, I introduced one last strategy: rereading. When reading dense informational text and trying to comprehend lengthy passages, students can sometimes lose meaning and be unable to identify where their understanding broke down. Chunking text into smaller parts and rereading those parts can be a helpful fix-up strategy.

Reflection

As Stephen completed the assignments related to the unit we worked on together, his grades steadily improved. I spoke with him after he received his unit test grade, and I asked him what had changed for him. Stephen told me that no one had ever told him that text features were that important and that the answers to questions can often be found there. He also told me he was surprised by how much it had helped to think about the headings and to use the "question strategy." He did say that, while he didn't really like to reread, he saw that is was important to try to remember to do so when something in the text didn't make sense.

The use of these strategies helped Stephen to improve his comprehension of informational text. It is often surprising to me how many middle and high school students have not been taught, or don't remember, the importance of attending to text features, especially headings. Informational texts can be difficult for students in so many ways. Providing them with strategies for identifying and understanding important concepts, and reinforcing those strategies across subjects and grade levels, can help to improve students' understanding of content area texts.

Internal Text Structure

Content area texts are written to inform. This is why exposition is the primary mode of discourse found in informational texts. This is not to say that some authors don't, at times, attempt to persuade or entertain their readers. They may. However, their primary business is to *tell, show, describe,* or *explain*. It stands to reason that the more logically connected one idea is to another, depending on the author's informative purpose, the more coherent the description or explanation is.

Skilled readers search for structure in a text and can readily differentiate the important ideas from less important ideas in the material. Research has shown that good readers know how to look for major thought relationships (Frey & Fisher, 2012). They approach a reading assignment looking for a predominant *text pattern* or organization that will tie together the ideas contained throughout the text passage.

Text patterns represent the different types of logical connections among the important and less important ideas in informational material. A case can be made for five text patterns that seem to predominate in informational writing: *description, sequence, comparison and contrast, cause and effect,* and *problem and solution*. The following sections contain descriptions and examples of these text structures.

DESCRIPTION   The description text pattern involves providing information about a topic, concept, event, object, person, idea, and so on (facts, characteristics, traits, features), usually qualifying the listing by criteria such as size or importance. This pattern connects ideas through description by listing the important characteristics or attributes of the topic under consideration. The description pattern is one of the most common ways of organizing texts. Here is an example:

> There were several points in the fight for freedom of religion. One point was that religion and government should be kept apart. Americans did not want any form of a national church as was the case in England. Americans made sure that no person would be denied his or her religious beliefs.

SEQUENCE   The sequence text pattern involves putting facts, events, or concepts into a sequence. The author traces the development of the topic or gives the steps in the process. Time reference may be explicit or implicit, but a sequence is evident in the pattern. The following paragraph illustrates the pattern:

The space shuttle program began in 1972 when NASA's intent to build a reusable space shuttle system was announced. The first shuttle orbital flight, *Columbia,* took place in 1981. Over the next thirty years, the space shuttle program flew 135 missions, concluding with the final mission, *Atlantis,* in 2011.

COMPARISON AND CONTRAST   The comparison and contrast text pattern involves pointing out likenesses (comparison) and/or differences (contrast) among facts, people, events, concepts, and so on. Study this example:

> Castles were built for defense, not comfort. In spite of some books and movies that have made them attractive, castles were cold, dark, gloomy places to live. Rooms were small and not the least bit charming. Except for the great central hall or the kitchen, there were no fires to keep the rooms heated. Not only was there a lack of furniture, but what was there was uncomfortable.

CAUSE AND EFFECT   The **cause and effect** text pattern involves showing how facts, events, or concepts (effects) happen or come into being because of other facts, events, or concepts (causes). Examine this paragraph for causes and effects:

> The fire was started by sparks from a campfire left by a careless camper. Thousands of acres of important watershed burned before the fire was brought under control. As a result of the fire, trees and the grasslands on the slopes of the valley were gone. Smoking black stumps were all that remained of tall pine trees.

PROBLEM AND SOLUTION   The problem and solution text pattern involves showing the development of a problem and one or more solutions to the problem. Consider the following example:

> The growing amounts of trash produced over the years and the limitations of landfills to handle that trash have been a serious concern in recent years. It is estimated that, on average, each American produces 4.5 pounds of trash per day, with approximately 67 percent of that being sent to landfills (Environmental Protection Agency, 2009). There are several concerns about landfill use, including the facts that not all materials decompose and dangerous chemicals can be leaked from landfills into the air and water. Recycling and composting offer helpful solutions to some of the problems of landfills. In addition to environmental benefits, recycling and composting can create new jobs.

Signal Words in Text Structure

Authors often showcase text patterns by giving readers clues or signals to help them figure out the structure being used. Readers usually become aware of the pattern if they are looking for the signals. A signal may be a word or a phrase that helps the reader follow the writer's thoughts.

Figure 10.1 shows signal words that authors often use to call attention to the organizational patterns just defined.

Awareness of the pattern of *long stretches* of text is especially helpful in planning reading assignments. In selecting from a passage of several paragraphs or several pages, teachers first need to determine whether a predominant text pattern is contained in the material. This is no easy task.

Informational writing is complex. Authors do not write in neat, perfectly identifiable patterns. Within the individual paragraphs of a text assignment, several kinds of thought relationships often exist. Suppose an author begins a passage by stating a problem. In telling about the development of the problem, the author *describes* a set of events that contributed to the problem. Or perhaps the author *compares* or *contrasts* the problem under consideration with another problem. In subsequent paragraphs, the *solutions* or attempts at solutions to the problem are stated. In presenting the solutions, the author uses heavy description and explanation. These descriptions and explanations are logically organized in a *sequence*.

The difficulty that teachers face is analyzing the overall text pattern, even though several types of thought relationships are probably embedded in the material. Analyzing

Figure 10.1 Signal Words and Phrases Used in Various Text Structures

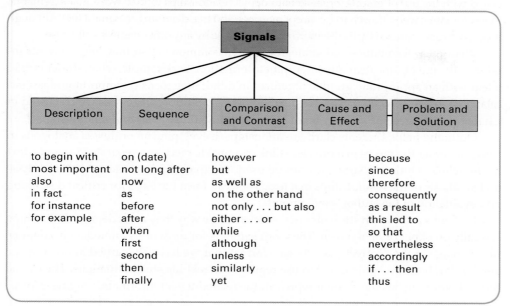

a text for a predominant pattern depends in part on how clearly an author represents the relationships in the text.

There are several guidelines to follow for analyzing text patterns. First, survey the text for the most important idea in the selection. Are there any explicit signal words that indicate a pattern that will tie together the ideas throughout the passage? Second, study the content of the text for additional important ideas. Are these ideas logically connected to the most important idea? Is a pattern evident? Third, outline or diagram the relationships among the superordinate and subordinate ideas in the selection. Use the diagram to specify the major relationships contained in the text structure and to sort out the important from the less important ideas.

Students must learn how to recognize and use the explicit and implicit relations in the text patterns that an author uses to structure content. When readers perceive and interact with text organization, they are in a better position to comprehend and retain information.

MyLab Education **Self-Check 10.1**

MyLab Education **Application Exercise: 10.1**
Supporting Students' Interactions with Texts in Content Area Classes

---

Graphic Organizers

10.2 Explain how graphic organizers support students' understanding and retention of content knowledge.

Graphic organizers are visual displays that help learners comprehend and retain *textually important information*. The research base for graphic organizers shows that when students learn how to use and construct graphic organizers, they are in control of a study strategy that allows them to identify what parts of a text are important, how the ideas and concepts encountered in the text are related, and where they can find specific information to support more important ideas (National Reading Panel, 2000). Graphic organizers can be used to support comprehension, promote oral sharing of information, assist in note taking, and encourage independent thinking (Lapp et al., 2014). Perhaps most importantly, they move students from receivers to innovators as students increase independent comprehension and organization.

An entire family of teacher-directed and learner-directed techniques and strategies is associated with the use of graphic organizers to depict relationships in text: word maps, semantic maps, semantic webs, flowcharts, concept matrices, and tree diagrams, to name a few. Although it is easy to get confused by the plethora of labels, a rose by any other name is still a rose.

What these techniques and strategies have in common is that they help students interact with and outline textually important information. For example, when students read a text with an appropriate graphic organizer in mind, they focus on important ideas and relationships. And when they construct their own graphic organizers, as we discussed in Chapter 8, they become actively involved in outlining those ideas and relationships.

Outlining helps students clarify relationships. Developing an outline is analogous to fitting together the pieces in a puzzle. Think of a puzzle piece as a separate idea and a text as the whole. Outlining strategies can be used effectively to facilitate a careful analysis and synthesis of the relationships in a text. They can form the basis for critical discussion and evaluation of the author's main points.

Problems arise when students are restricted in the way they must depict relationships spatially on paper or on a screen. The word *outlining* for most of us immediately conjures up an image of the "correct" or "classic" format that we have all learned at one time or another but have probably failed to use regularly in real-life study situations. The classic form of outlining has the student represent the relatedness of information in linear form:

I. Main Idea

    A. Idea supporting I
        1. Detail supporting A
        2. Detail supporting A
            a. Detail supporting 2
            b. Detail supporting 2

    B. Idea supporting I
        1. Detail supporting B
        2. Detail supporting B

II. Main Idea

This conventional format represents a hierarchical ordering of ideas at different levels of subordination. Roman numerals signal the major or superordinate concepts in a text section; capital letters, the supporting or coordinate concepts; Arabic numbers, the supporting or subordinate details; and lowercase letters, the subordinate details.

Some readers have trouble using a restricted form of outlining. Initially, at least, they need a more visual display than the one offered by the conventional format. And this is where graphic organizers can play a critical role in the development of independent learners.

To show students how to use and construct graphic organizers, begin by assessing how students usually outline text material. Do they have a sense of subordination among ideas? Do they have strategies for connecting major and minor concepts? Do they use alternatives to the conventional format? Make them aware of the rationale for organizing information through outlining. The jigsaw puzzle analogy—fitting pieces of information together into a coherent whole—works well for this purpose. Assessment and building awareness set the stage for illustrating, modeling, and applying the strategies. Box 10.3 outlines the steps used to build strategic knowledge and skills related to students' use of graphic organizers.

The New Outline of Brevity

Now more than ever, text is organized by its length rather than its content. However, this brevity can be used to organize ideas and build connections to what matters most. Using the Twitter format of 280 characters (revised as of 2017), students must choose to focus on the main concepts of the text. This can be used to build titles and tables of content, share main ideas, or outline the most prominent features of a character. In nonfiction, students must

Box 10.3 Evidence-Based Best Practices

Graphic Organizers

To introduce students to various kinds of graphic organizers that may be applicable to texts in your content area, the seminal article by Jones, Pierce, and Hunter (1988–1989) suggest some of the following steps:

1. *Present an example of a graphic organizer that corresponds to the type of outline you plan to teach.* For example, suppose that a text that students will read is organized around a cause and effect text pattern. First, preview the text with the students. Help them discover features of the text that may signal the pattern. Make students aware that the title, subheads, and signal words provide them with clues to the structure of the text. Then ask questions that are pertinent to the pattern—for example, "What happens in this reading?" "What causes it to happen?" "What are the important factors that cause these effects?"

2. *Demonstrate how to construct a graphic outline.* Suppose that math students have completed a reading about the differences between isosceles triangles and isosceles trapezoids. Show them how to construct a *Venn diagram* to map how they are alike and different. Next, refer to the comparison and contrast questions you raised in the preview. Guide students through the procedures that lead to the development of the Venn diagram: First, on an overhead transparency (or using a doc cam or SMART Board), present an example of a partially completed Venn diagram. Second, have students review the text and offer

suggestions to help complete the diagram. The accompanying graphic display shows a class-constructed rendering of a Venn diagram. Third, develop procedural knowledge by discussing when to use the Venn diagram and why.

3. *Coach students in the use of the graphic outline and give them opportunities to practice.* If other texts represent a text pattern that you have already demonstrated with the class, encourage students individually or in teams to construct their own graphic outlines and to use their constructions as the basis for class discussion. This step can also be done electronically, either collaboratively or individually, with students adding, revising, and reflecting as necessary.

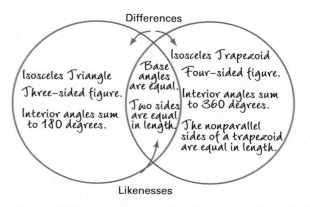

refine their ideas to expressing the impact of the climax, the end result or the focus of a thesis. What this does is push the idea of an outline into smaller points of focus. For struggling readers, this is an ideal strategy, as it allows them to point out what matters most. For gifted students, it pushes their sense of creativity, as they must learn to craft their ideas around a limited space of communication. Overall, it gives purpose to the idea of finding what matters most.

Using Graphic Organizers to Reflect Text Patterns

Students can be shown how to construct maps and other types of visual displays to reflect the text patterns authors use to organize ideas. Such organizers can provide a visual tool that illustrates the connections among concepts (Bulgren, Marquis, Lenz, Schumaker, & Deshler, 2009). According to Jones, Pierce, and Hunter (1988–1989, p. 21), "A fundamental rule in constructing graphic organizers is that the structure of the graphic should reflect the structure of the text it represents."

Jones and her colleagues recommend a variety of possible graphic organizer representations that reflect different text patterns. These "generic" outlines are illustrated in Appendix C. What follows are examples of how some of these outlines might be developed in content area classrooms.

COMPARISON AND CONTRAST MATRIX In addition to the Venn diagram and graphic organizers, a teacher can show students how a comparison and contrast pattern serves to organize ideas in a text using a matrix outline. A comparison and contrast matrix shows similarities and differences between two or more things (people, places, events, concepts, processes, and so on). Readers compare and contrast the target concepts listed across the top of the matrix according to attributes, properties, or characteristics listed along the left side. The first example was used by a music teacher (Figure 10.2). She wanted her

Figure 10.2 Comparison and Contrast Matrices for Music Theory

Part One:

Directions: In each box, write YES if the feature is present and copy the features from the piece. (See time signature box for an example.)

Musical Features	Piece A: "Für Elise" by Beethoven	Piece B: "Lately" by Stevie Wonder
Time signature	Yes 3/8	Yes 4/4
Key		
Treble clef		
Base clef		
How many measures are in each line? Is it a uniform number?		
Dynamic signs		
Chord symbols		
Eighth notes		
What instrument(s) is this written for?		

Part Two:

Directions: In each box, think about how the pieces are different. Answer the questions for each piece.

Musical Features	Piece A: "Für Elise" by Beethoven	Piece B: "Lately" by Stevie Wonder
Which piece is faster? Which is slower? How did you know?	Yes 3/8	Yes 4/4
Based on the key, which do you think would be easier to play on a piano? Why?		
Which piece looks easier to play based on the format of the sheet music? Why?		
Which piece would sound louder? How would you play these pieces differently? How do you know?		
Bonus question: How could you rewrite this piece so that other instruments might be able to play it? Which instruments would play this the best, based on the style and dynamics of the piece?		

students to compare the musical features of two very different compositions to better understand the commonalities that are inherent in all music. As well, she wanted to activate her students' critical thinking skills as they looked deeper into each composition to understand the differences between the pieces. After the students were done with the matrix, she played both pieces to aurally reinforce the similarities and differences.

PROBLEM AND SOLUTION OUTLINE   This graphic representation depicts a problem, attempted solutions, the result or outcomes associated with the attempted solutions, and the end result. It works equally well with narrative or informational texts to display the central problem in a story or the problem and solution text pattern. Figure 10.3 illustrates a problem and solution outline developed by students as part of a class reading of *Monster* by Walter Dean Myers. In studying characterization and plot, students were asked to evaluate the choices made by the main character in the story, Steve.

The book is written as a screenplay created by Steve to explain his experience awaiting trial for the murder of a store owner during a robbery, for which Steve may or may not have been serving as a lookout. Throughout the book, Steve reevaluates his decision to be at the store in the first place and struggles with the perception many have of him because of his possible participation in the robbery. The students completed a problem and solution outline to analyze the impact that Steve's choices may have had on his life. The teacher introduced the outline. Students worked in pairs to complete the outline and then shared their responses with the whole class.

NETWORK TREE   The network tree is based on the same principle as the graphic organizers introduced in Chapter 8 and used in the chapter organizers in this book. It represents the network of relationships that exists between superordinate concepts and subordinate concepts. It can be used to show causal information or to describe a central idea in relation to its attributes and examples. Notice how math students explored relationships in the quadratic formula by using the network tree illustrated in Figure 10.4.

Figure 10.3 Problem and Solution Outline for Walter Dean Myers's *Monster*

Problem	*Who* has the problem? Steve Harmon *What* was the problem? Should he be a lookout during the robbery, or should he stand up to his friends? *Why* was it a problem? If he stands up to his friends he could get beaten up; if he serves as the lookout, someone else could get hurt, and he could go to jail.

	Attempted Solutions	**Outcomes**
Solutions	Steve goes to the store but doesn't commit to being the lookout.	Steve ended up getting caught and going on trial.
	Steve claims he is not guilty during the trial.	Everyone wonders if he is innocent or just trying to get out of trouble.

	End Result Steve finds himself on trial for murder and is upset that everyone thinks he is a "monster" for getting involved in a robbery that results in murder. Even though he ends up being found not guilty, Steve knows some people will always believe he was guilty and that he made bad decisions.

Figure 10.4 Network Tree for the Quadratic Formula

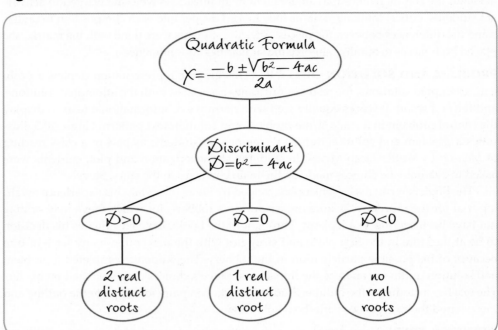

SERIES OF EVENTS CHAIN The series of events chain may be used with narrative material to show the chain of events that lead to the resolution of conflict in a story. It may also be used with informational text to reflect the sequence pattern in a text. It may include any sequence of events, including the steps in a linear procedure, the chain of events (effects) caused by some event, or the stages of something. Scientific and historical texts are often organized in a sequence pattern and lend themselves well to this type of graphic display. A science class, for example, might be asked to map the sequence of steps in the scientific method by using a series of events chain. After reading about the scientific method, students might make an outline similar to the one in Figure 10.5.

Figure 10.5 Series of Events Chain for the Scientific Method

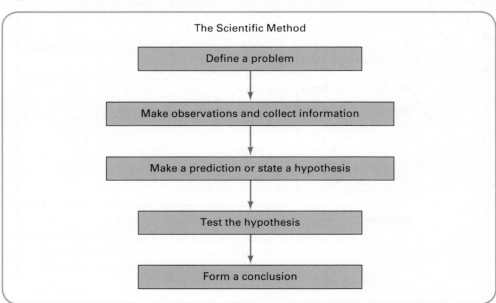

Figure 10.6 Series of Events Chain for an Excerpt from a Recipe Created in a Family and Consumer Science Class

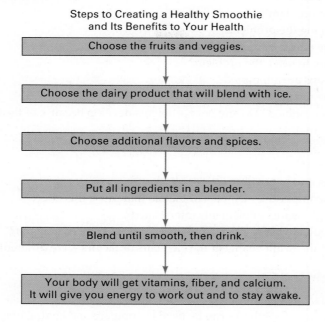

Steps to Creating a Healthy Smoothie
and Its Benefits to Your Health

| Choose the fruits and veggies. |

| Choose the dairy product that will blend with ice. |

| Choose additional flavors and spices. |

| Put all ingredients in a blender. |

| Blend until smooth, then drink. |

| Your body will get vitamins, fiber, and calcium. It will give you energy to work out and to stay awake. |

In a family and consumer science class, students learned not only how to make a recipe but the impact of healthy and nonhealthy food on their health. This idea of cause and effect worked well into a series of events chain. The teacher provided a list of possible ingredients to the students. They had to decide the order of the recipe and then researched what each ingredient offered their body. From that research, they created a series of events chain that showed the steps of the recipe as well as the impact of the food on their body. Figure 10.6 illustrates the work of one of the groups of students. They received ingredients intended for a smoothie. Other students received pizza ingredients, cookie ingredients, hummus ingredients, and sandwich ingredients. After they created their chain, they rated each recipe as healthy or unhealthy due to the impact it has on their energy, health, and caloric intake.

Appendix C illustrates additional types of graphic organizers that may be adapted to different content areas.

Using Questions with Graphic Organizers

Closely associated with the use of graphic organizers is an instructional scaffold that involves questioning. Graphic organizers and questions related to them go hand in hand. Buehl (1991), for example, lists the types of questions associated with the problem and solution, cause and effect, and comparison and contrast patterns.

Problem and Solution

1. What is the problem?
2. Who has the problem?
3. What is causing the problem?
4. What are the effects of the problem?
5. Who is trying to solve the problem?
6. What solutions are attempted?
7. What are the results of these solutions?
8. Is the problem solved? Do any new problems develop because of the solutions?

Cause and Effect

1. What happens?
2. What causes it to happen?
3. What are the important elements or factors that cause this effect?
4. How are these factors or elements interrelated?
5. Will this result always happen from these causes? Why or why not?
6. How would the result change if the elements or factors were different?

Comparison and Contrast

1. What items are being compared and contrasted?
2. What categories of attributes can be used to compare and contrast the items?
3. How are the items alike or similar?
4. How are the items not alike or different?
5. What are the most important qualities or attributes that make the items similar?
6. What are the most important qualities or attributes that make the items different?
7. In terms of the qualities that are most important, are the items more alike or more different?

Additional questions associated with graphic organizers are provided in Appendix C. There are many benefits to learning how to use and construct graphic organizers, not the least of which is that they make it easier for students to find and reorganize important ideas and information in the text.

Scripted questions are always a place to start, but the most effective questioning originates within the students. The concept of encouraging student-created questioning builds higher-order thinking skills. Additionally, if they can ask questions, knowing the components of a well-written question, they can also answer questions. Depka (2017) suggests that student-based questioning supports the learner's skill, imagination, and personal experiences. As well, students who ask and answer their own questions can more easily associate this process with real-world applications. Finally, when students write questions, they are more engaged in the classroom and eager to see the results of their work.

To build student questioning, start with a textual tour that focuses on what they want to know. As they read, teach them strategies to stop and jot when they find something that doesn't make sense or that might interest them beyond the black-and-white messages in the text. Teach them the question stems so they can choose which stem (who, what, when, where, or which) most clearly matches their intended question. Allow them to work with peers and share their work to build authentic practices that, again, mirror real-world group collaboration. These questions can become the basis of instruction and should play an active role as the class continues to interact with the text.

Semantic (Cognitive) Mapping

Another type of graphic display is the semantic, or cognitive, map. Maps are based on the same principles as graphic organizers. A popular graphic representation, often called a *semantic map* or a *cognitive map*, helps students identify important ideas and shows how these ideas fit together. Teachers avoid the problem of teaching a restricted, conventional outline format. Instead, the students are responsible for creating a logical arrangement among key words or phrases that connect main ideas to subordinate information. When maps are used, instruction should proceed from teacher-guided modeling and illustration to student-generated productions. A semantic map has three basic components:

1. *Core question or concept.* The question or concept (stated as a key word or phrase) that establishes the main focus of the map. All the ideas generated for the map by the students are related in some way to the core question or concept.
2. *Strands.* The subordinate ideas generated by the students that help clarify the question or explain the concept.
3. *Supports.* The details, inferences, and generalizations that are related to each strand. These supports clarify the strands and distinguish one strand from another.

Students use the semantic map as an organizational tool that visually illustrates the categories and relationships associated with the core question under study. To model and illustrate the use of a semantic map, a middle school social studies teacher guided students through the process. The class began a unit on the American industrial revolution. As part of the prereading discussion, four questions were raised for the class to consider: What do you think were the most important factors that impacted the American industrial revolution? How did they impact the industrial revolution? What did these factors have in common? How were they different?

Then, the teacher assigned the material, directing the students to read with the purpose of confirming or modifying their predictions about the impacting factors. After reading, the students formed small groups. Each group listed everything its members could remember about the factors on index cards, placing one piece of information on each card. On the SMART Board, the teacher wrote "Factors Surrounding the American Industrial Revolution" and circled the phrase. She then asked students to provide the main strands that helped answer the question and clarify the concept "What were the factors that impacted the American industrial revolution?" The students responded by contrasting their predictions to the explanations in the text assignment. The teacher began to build the semantic map on the SMART Board by explaining how the strands help students answer the questions and understand the main concepts.

Next, she asked the students to work in their groups to sort the cards they had compiled according to each of the strands depicted on the semantic map. Through discussion, questioning, and think-aloud probes, the class began to construct the semantic map shown in Figure 10.7. Some teachers prefer to distinguish the strands from supports through the use of lines or bolded text. Some teachers also find it helpful to use different colors to distinguish one strand from another. Another option is to incorporate technology into semantic mapping. There are many free websites that act as digital corkboards and allow students to generate, sort, and visually organize ideas and concepts.

With appropriate modeling, explanation, and experience, students soon understand the why, what, and how of semantic maps and can begin to develop maps by themselves. We suggest that the teacher begin by providing the core question or concept. Students can then compare and contrast their individual productions in a follow-up discussion. Of

Figure 10.7 Factors Surrounding the American Industrial Revolution

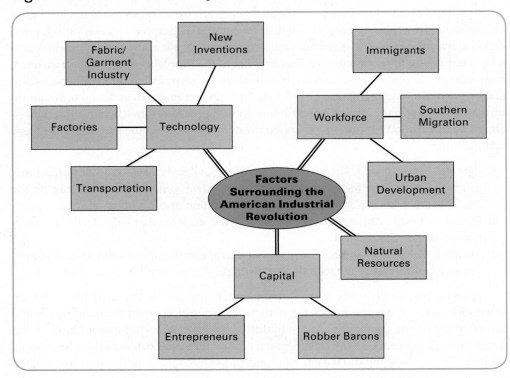

course, text assignments should also be given in which students identify the core concept on their own and then generate the structures that support and explain it. In addition to using graphic outlines, teachers can develop study guides (discussed later in this chapter) to help students discern text patterns.

A family and consumer science teacher wanted her students to understand the business behind their clothing brands. Semantic mapping fit her purpose because it would allow the students to draw meaning through appropriate use of questioning. She started the assignment by asking the students three questions: 1) Why do brands matter (if they do)? 2) Why do some clothes cost more than others? 3) What are the pros and cons of high-cost clothing? She wanted the students to learn how to support their ideas with different sources, so she provided the students with a blog, a podcast, a short video, and an article. As they worked in pairs, they used what they learned to develop their own answers to each question. One group used the blog to answer the first question:

Brands matter because according to the blog, they give designers a way to make their clothing unique. When designers brand their clothing, it creates demand because regardless of what the clothes look like, people want everyone to know they are wearing a certain brand. It can be a symbol of wealth, status or even politics.

The students then created their semantic maps to provide an argument that either supported or argued against high-cost brand clothing. Under each point, they supported their appeal with details from the textual sources. Here is an excerpt from one of the maps that argued against high-cost clothing:

Core concept: Clothes are too expensive.

Strand One: The money we spend on clothing doesn't go to the people who make the clothes.

Support: Article one tells us that the people who make clothes barely earn enough to survive. They work in horrible conditions and never see the glamourous side of fashion. When we are paying $50 for a t-shirt, they may see 50 cents of it. So when we are buying these overpriced pieces *of clothing, we are only making a bad situation worse. We are telling the designers who support these unfair labor practices, that it is ok. As consumers, we have to make our money count as our vote and start to vote for a fair paycheck for everyone.*

The semantic maps allowed the students to plan their approach by thoughtfully using research to support their opinions. Several of the groups changed what they originally wanted to argue based on what they learned. The class ultimately used the semantic maps to either plan a fashion business or plan a protest movement.

MyLab Education **Self-Check 10.2**

MyLab Education **Application Exercise: 10.2**
Using Graphic Organizers to Support Content Area Comprehension

---

Writing Summaries

10.3 Explain how the ability to summarize can aid students in understanding and remembering material from content area instruction.

Summarizing involves reducing a text to its main points. To become adept at summary writing, students must be able to discern and analyze text structure. If they are insensitive to the organization of ideas and events in expository or narrative writing, students will find it difficult to distinguish important from less important information. Good summarizers, therefore, guard against including information that is not important in the text passage being condensed. Immature text learners, by contrast, tend to *retell* rather than condense information, often including in their summaries interesting but nonessential tidbits from the passage. Good summarizers write in their own words but are careful to maintain the author's point of view and to stick closely to the sequence of ideas or events as presented in the reading selection (Friend, 2000/2001). When important ideas are not explicitly stated in the material, good summary writers create their own topic sentences to reflect textually implicit main ideas. Box 10.4 outlines the "rules" to follow in developing a well-written summary.

An eighth-grade English teacher used the summary strategy to help her students understand informational text. She placed four different articles around the classroom. These articles all focused on the same topic but provided different points of view. The students were divided into task teams. These task teams focused on the first two sections of the four-step process: highlighting vocabulary and identifying text structure. The vocabulary task team used context clues to define the vocabulary. Part of the process required that they explained how they came to their definition.

One group chose the word "dearth." This is how they defined it:

We think dearth means not much. We used the sentence before and after. The first one talked about that there's not very much clean water left. The sentence after said we should start conserving. We know that conserving means saving, so when we put that and the facts of the first sentence together, we came up with the idea that dearth means not much because we would have to save water.

The task groups defining text structure hunted for the following items:

Titles, subtitles, captions, pictures, italicized or bolded words. They created a map that showed how the article was organized. The teacher made sure that each article had a slightly different structure and that it contained enough features for the students to find.

Once each article included highlighted and defined text and a map of its text structure was created, each one of the task teams was assigned an article. They took the article and wrote a sentence completion activity for the next group to complete. One of the groups wrote the following:

Box 10.4 Evidence-Based Best Practices

Differentiating the Main Idea from the Details

When reading and writing expository text, students often find it difficult to differentiate the main idea from supporting details and to understand the relationship between the two. For example, a student may be able to identify the main idea in a subsection of a text but may not differentiate cause from effect or fact from opinion. Montelongo, Herter, Ansaldo, and Hatter (2010, p. 658) developed a four-part lesson cycle to help students make these types of connections when reading and writing expository text. As the authors explain, "Students must know the interrelationships among the topics, main ideas, and supporting details of paragraphs if they are going to comprehend and remember the important points the author is making." Montelongo, Herter, Ansaldo, and Hatter suggest the following instructional steps:

1. *Introduce vocabulary words.* Select vocabulary words that are essential for understanding the text. Use strategies, such as those described in Chapter 8, to engage students in understanding concepts rather than in memorizing definitions. Encourage students to focus on the context of the vocabulary words.

2. *Identify text structures.* Introduce, or revisit, the different types of internal text structures discussed in this chapter: description, sequence, comparison and contrast, cause and effect, and problem and solution. Work with students to help them identify the main idea and supporting details by identifying the signal words that correspond to the text structure of a particular passage.

3. *Practice using a modified sentence completion activity.* Provide the students with a fill-in-the-blanks worksheet-type page containing 10–12 sentences. Half of the sentences should be related to each other and, when placed in the correct order, form an expository paragraph. The remaining sentences should be unrelated to the topic at hand. Students should try to complete each sentence using an appropriate vocabulary word and then find the related sentences and assemble them into an expository paragraph. The resulting paragraph should contain one main idea and several supporting details. Montelongo, Herter, Ansaldo, and Hatter point out that, to complete this activity successfully, students will need to review all the sentences as opposed to simply identifying the first sentence as the one that states the main idea.

4. *Rewrite the text.* Ask students to rewrite the paragraph they assembled in the previous step using their own words. They may, for example, use their own synonyms in place of the author's words, or they may add their own supporting details to the text.

Water _____ is an important issue because we need to learn how to save our resources. (conservation)

Often water is _____ and can't be used to drink because it is unsafe. (polluted)

You can use your local _____ to find out the quality of water. After all, they were elected to make your life safer. (government)

Finally, the groups were given an article they hadn't worked with, and they rewrote what they considered to be the most important part of the text.

It is important to conserve water because frankly, we are running out. This is a major political issue that we don't hear enough about. We need to take the future in our hands and make sure we understand the quality of our water and what to do if it is not safe. As citizens, we can elect people who care, watch our own water use and make sure we know where to find information.

This activity was impactful because it was based on the effectiveness of peer learning, allowed the students to read multiple texts as they practiced different strategies, and provided a chance to ask and answer questions.

Using GRASP to Write a Summary

Teachers can show students how to summarize information through the guided reading procedure (GRP), as explained in Chapter 7. After students have read a text passage, they turn the books facedown and try to remember everything that was important in the passage. What they recall is recorded by the teacher on the whiteboard. Seize this opportune moment to show students how to delete trivial and repetitious information from the list of ideas on the board. As part of the procedure, the students are given a chance to return to the passage, review it, and make sure that the list contains all of the information germane to the text.

Figure 10.8 Details Remembered from an Article on the Planets

Students' First Recollections	Additions or Corrections
Ptolemy thought the planets orbited the Earth.	Orbited the Sun.
Kepler found that the planets orbited in a specific pattern.	Pattern is elliptical.
Nine planets in our solar system.	Currently, there are eight planets (Pluto was downgraded).
Planets consistently orbit the sun from a certain distance.	Order: Mercury, Venus, Earth, Mars, Jupiter, Saturn, Uranus, Neptune.
Mathematicians can calculate the movements of the planets.	Movement was previously thought to be controlled by gods. Movements based on geometry and based on pull of gravity.
Many planets have smaller bodies (moons) that orbit around them.	Moons orbit Mars, Jupiter, Saturn, Earth, Uranus, Neptune, and Pluto.

When this step is completed, the teacher then guides the students to organize the information using a graphic outline format. Here is where students can be shown how to collapse individual pieces of information from a list into conceptual categories. These categories can be the bases for identifying or creating topic sentences. The students can then integrate the main points into a summary.

Figure 10.8 shows how students in one science class adapted the GRP to summarize information they recalled from an article they read about planets. Following a model developed by Hayes (1989), the teacher modeled the development and writing of an effective summary by guiding students through a procedure called *GRASP* (*g*uided *r*eading and *s*ummarizing *p*rocedure). After following the initial steps of the GRP, the teacher recorded students' initial recollections of what they had read in the article on planets. Then, after they reread the article, students' additions and corrections to their first recollections were recorded.

The students then organized the information from these notes into the following categories: the planets, the movement of the planets, and changes in beliefs about the planets. These categories, along with the subordinate information associated with each, became the basis for writing the summary. The teacher walked the students through the summary-writing process as a whole class. First, the students were asked to contribute sentences to the summary based on the outline information that they had organized together. Then the teacher invited their suggestions for revising the summary into a coherent message. In schools that have one-to-one technology programs, real-time websites like Google Drive allow for class collaboration on one document, resulting in a summary that can be shared or published to the Internet. Figure 10.9 displays part of the completed summary, as revised by the class.

Figure 10.9 The Planet Summary, as Revised by the Students

While once Ptolemy thought that we had nine planets and they ~~circled~~ *orbited* around the Earth, we now know our solar system is a group of eight planets that ~~circle~~ *orbit* the sun in ~~a circle~~ *an ellipse*, called moons, . Some planets also have ~~things~~ smaller bodies moving around them.

Fixing Mistakes

Often the most effective way to teach what to do is to show what not to do. Provide students with two different summaries. There should be obvious issues with their format or their content. The most effective way to use this strategy is to focus on the one editing tip you want the students to master. In this case, focus on length. In a seventh-grade science class, the students focused on writing an effective findings report. The most important section of such a report is the summary. Their goal was to create a summary that highlighted the facts and showed the results. At first, the students drafted summaries that contained too much extraneous detail and focused on the students' personal experiences rather than the results of the experiment. Thinking like a scientist, the students are provided two summaries and asked to revise each of them in order to produce effective summaries:

Example One:

My partner and I combined baking soda and vinegar. I really didn't like how the vinegar smelled. I was nervous because I didn't know what would happen. He measured the stuff and then put it together and it foamed all over the place. I guess I would say the result was an explosion, but it didn't really explode, it just made a mess. I think we did it right.

Example Two:

The experiment combined baking soda and vinegar to see the result of two substances that create a reaction when they are combined. We combined equal parts of the soda and the vinegar and that combination created carbon dioxide. That gas is evident in the foamy effects of the combination.

As the teacher and students worked together to edit the sample summaries, they identified both points of praise and points in need of revision. As a next step, students could work independently or with a partner to look for the same elements, both effective and not effective, in their own writing.

Polishing a Summary

As you can see from the example above and the revised summary in Figure 10.9, a good summary often reflects a process of writing *and* rewriting. Teaching students how to write a polished summary is often a neglected aspect of instruction. When students reduce large segments of text, the condensation is often stilted. It sounds unnatural. We are convinced that students will learn and understand the main points better and retain them longer when they attempt to create a more natural-sounding summary that communicates the selection's main ideas to an audience—for example, the teacher or other students. Rewriting in a classroom is often preceded by a *response* to a draft by peers and teacher.

We dealt in much more detail with responding and revising in Chapter 9. Here, however, let us suggest the following:

- *Compare a well-developed summary that the teacher has written with the summaries written by the students.* Contrasting the teacher's version with the student productions leads to valuable process discussions on such subjects as the use of introductory and concluding statements; the value of connectives, such as *and* and *because*, to show how ideas can be linked; and the need to paraphrase—that is, to put ideas into one's own words to convey the author's main points.

- *Present the class with three summaries.* One is good in that it contains all the main points and flows smoothly. The second is OK; it contains most of the main points but is somewhat stilted in its writing. The third is poor in content and form. Let the class rate and discuss the three summaries.

- *Team students in pairs or triads and let them read their summaries to one another.* Student response groups are one of the most effective means of obtaining feedback on writing in progress.

- *In lieu of response groups, ask the whole class to respond.* With prior permission from several students, discuss their summaries. What are the merits of each one, and how could they be improved in content and form?

The real learning potential of summary writing lies in students' using their own language to convey the author's main ideas.

Using Digital Storytelling with ELs

Digital storytelling is a method of writing that focuses on a multimedia approach to telling a focused account (Crawley, 2015). It may include pictures, music, text, and narration, but the focus is on the story. English Learners often struggle to comprehend the message of a text and to translate and summarize that message into their own words. Digital storytelling can help ELs to summarize the content of the text. Students begin by translating their understanding into digital pictures. They can organize, rank, categorize, and order the pictures into a timeline that expresses their understanding. This can be used with text that has a conventional narrative structure or with one that describes a sequence of events. Next, they can verbally describe the digital picture they have created. This can be done through voice recording software and may help to eliminate the barrier of having to write what they are thinking. Finally, they can use keywords from the text to title each picture. This summarizing technique supports comprehension, an understanding of the main idea, and individualized expression. Philip and Garcia (2013) count this inclusivity as one of the main benefits of technology. In this open space, it is expression, rather than format, that is key.

MyLab Education **Self-Check 10.3**

MyLab Education **Application Exercise: 10.3**
Differentiating the Main Idea From the Details in a Content Area Text

---

Making Notes, Taking Notes

10.4 Explain the different approaches for note taking and how they support comprehension.

Effective study activities for acting on and remembering material involve making notes as well as taking notes. Notes can be written on study cards (index cards) or in a learning log that is kept expressly for the purpose of compiling written reactions to and reflections on text readings. In addition, the number of options for digital note taking is vast—students can utilize everything from a simple word processing document to online interactive binders.

Note making should avoid verbatim text reproductions. Instead, notes can be used to paraphrase, summarize, react critically, question, or respond personally to what is read. Whatever form the notes take, students need to become aware of the different types of notes that can be written and should then be shown how to write them.

Text Annotations

Text annotations describe the different kinds of notes students can write. Several are particularly appropriate for middle grade and secondary school students. For example, read the following passage. Then, study each of the notes made by a high school student, shown in Figures 10.10 through 10.13.

> The Bill of Rights was a compromise that helped support people's rights under the Constitution. It allowed the government to create new laws so that the Constitution could be flexible as the nation progressed. However, the Constitution itself would not change so it could maintain its original framework and intention. James Madison proposed the Bill of Rights and helped convince Congress to support the first nine amendments.

Under the First Amendment, people received freedom to speak against the government and assemble so that they might address issues they found unfair. As we will see with many of the amendments, while they propose freedom they also seek to limit and define the freedom. For example, you cannot yell "bomb" on an airplane, as that might impact the safety of the passengers on the flight.

The Bill of Rights also limits the power of government. It helps define what fair punishment is and when you or your home can be searched and tries to guarantee a fair trial while providing a lawyer to anyone who cannot afford one.

To date, there have been seventeen amendments added to the Constitution since the Bill of Rights was written. Some define voting rights, while others give the government a right to tax its people. Good or bad, the Bill of Rights provides a space for America to address new issues that may arise as times change and new needs must be met.

The *summary note*, as you might surmise, condenses the main ideas of a text selection into a concise statement. Summary notes are characterized by their brevity, clarity, and conciseness. When a note summarizes expository material, it should clearly distinguish the important ideas in the author's presentation from supporting information and detail. When the summary note involves narrative material, such as a story, it should include a synopsis containing the major story elements. Examine the example of a summary note from a student's note card in Figure 10.10.

The *thesis note* answers the question "What is the main point the author has tried to get across to the reader?" The thesis note has a telegramlike character. It is incisively stated yet unambiguous in its identification of the author's main proposition. The thesis note for a story identifies its theme. Study the example in Figure 10.11.

The *critical note* captures the reader's reaction or response to the author's thesis. It answers the question "So what?" In writing critical notes, the reader should first state the author's thesis, then state the reader's position in relation to the thesis, and, finally, defend or expand on the position taken. See Figure 10.12.

The *question note* raises a significant issue in the form of a question. The question is the result of what the reader thinks is the most germane or significant aspect of what he or she has read. See Figure 10.13.

Showing students how to write different types of notes begins with assessment; leads to awareness and knowledge building, modeling, and practice; and culminates in application. First, assign a text selection and ask students to make whatever notes they wish. Second, have the class analyze the assessment, share student notes, and discuss difficulties in making notes. Use the assessment discussion to make students aware of the importance of making notes as a strategy for learning and retention. Third, build students' knowledge for note making by helping them recognize and define the various kinds of text notes that can be written.

As part of a growing understanding of the different types of notes, students should be able to tell a well-written note from a poorly written one. Have the class read a short passage, followed by several examples of a certain type of note, one well written and the others flawed in some way. For example, a discussion of critical notes may include one illustration of a good critical note, one that lacks the note-maker's position, and another that fails to defend or develop the position taken.

Note-Taking Procedures

More than 50% of the material read or heard in class is forgotten in a matter of minutes. A system of taking and making notes triggers recall and supports retention. When students are

Figure 10.10 A Summary Note

> The Bill of Rights safeguards people's rights and allows the Constitution to be changed as needs change. Nine original amendments were part of the original Bill of Rights; seventeen more have been added.

Figure 10.11 A Thesis Note

> The Bill of Rights helps the Constitution to remain flexible while sticking to its roots. It protects the people and safeguards their rights but also limits freedoms in order to maintain safety and fairness.

learning how to take notes, modeling and practice should follow naturally from awareness and knowledge building. Teachers can guide students through the process of making and taking different types of notes by sharing their thought processes. For example, a teacher might show how a note is written and revised using a think-aloud procedure. Students can then practice note making individually and in peer groups of two or three. Peer-group interaction is typically nonthreatening and can lead to notes that can be duplicated, compared, and evaluated by the class with teacher direction.

Teachers can now vary not only how notes are taken but through what medium. Students often find taking notes on a laptop or digital notebook easier than writing the traditional longhand notes (Luo, Kiewra, Flanigan, & Peteranetz, 2018). Students can insert different text types, compile information more quickly, and even insert graphics, if appropriate. Providing this additional support also helps those students who complain about their "hands hurting" or who struggle with difficult-to-read handwriting. These notes can not only be easily taken but also can be saved in a way that ensures they won't get lost at the bottom of a school bag. Using OneNote is particularly impactful to students who struggle to organize their work. Files are automatically saved and dated as soon as they are created.

To facilitate the application of note-taking procedures to reading tasks across content areas, we suggest that students write notes regularly and in a variety of forms, such as learning logs, study cards, or on their computers. Note-taking procedures can take many forms. In this section, we highlight a few of those forms: reading logs, annotations, T-notes, and Cornell notes.

READING LOGS   Notes written in reading logs serve two purposes: They can aid students in organizing and synthesizing important information as they read a text, and they can serve as a tool for clarifying and reviewing text material. Gomez and Gomez (2007) suggest double-entry reading logs as note-making tools that can help students organize key details about complex topics and help teachers to gain information about student learning that can aid them in planning subsequent instruction. Students can, for example, use an argument/evidence double-entry reading log, shown in Figure 10.14, to distinguish main ideas or arguments found in a text from

Figure 10.12 A Critical Note

> The Bill of Rights helps the Constitution to remain flexible to address the changing needs of the American people. I think the Bill of Rights is a good start, but it really doesn't go far enough. The author lists the amendments that I think are necessary for anyone to live in a democratic society, but I know we still have problems. How are we enforcing the Bill of Rights? Many times, you hear of people being stopped and searched for reasons that may not be clear to them. I don't think that's what Madison intended when he first suggested this change to the Constitution.

Figure 10.13 A Question Note

> Has the Bill of Rights worked? The author lists several ways the Bill of Rights seems to have been effective. For example, it protects freedom of speech, limits the power of government, and works to ensure a fair trial. Without these basic rights protected, it would have been hard to ensure the pursuit of happiness as a reality for all Americans.

Figure 10.14 Argument/Evidence Double-Entry Reading Log

Main ideas or arguments from a text:	Evidence to support each main idea or argument:

Figure 10.15 Vocabulary/Concept Double-Entry Reading Log

Challenging terms from the text:	My interpretation of each term:

the evidence presented to support each main idea or argument. Similarly, a vocabulary or concept double-entry reading log, shown in Figure 10.15, can be used to help students identify those vocabulary concepts that they find difficult to understand. They can use the left-hand column of the double-entry log to list challenging terms and the right-hand column to write their interpretations of those terms. Later, following class discussions or additional readings that clarify these terms, students can revisit their double-entry logs by adding or revising the information they contain.

ANNOTATIONS   Annotations can be used as a cognitive literacy strategy across content areas to help students to understand text structure, identify and analyze important concepts, and communicate their understanding of those concepts (Pressley, 2006). Zywica and Gomez (2008) applied text annotation as part of their multiyear Adolescent Literacy Support Project. They found the strategy to be particularly useful when charts, graphs, and illustrations are frequently embedded in the text. The text annotation system they described was designed to help students to identify different components within a single text. As they read, students mark the text with annotation symbols that represent key concepts, questions, or transition points. Some of the text annotation symbols that students used as they read an article for a science class included the following:

- A rectangle around key content vocabulary
- A triangle around difficult or confusing words
- A double underline for main ideas or important points
- A single underline for supporting evidence
- An arrow for procedural words
- An asterisk for transition words ★
- A question mark for confusing information **?**

We recommend that teachers model the use of annotations and gradually introduce annotation symbols to students by selecting symbols that are most appropriate for organizing and understanding a particular text. Students should not be expected to use all of the annotation symbols at their disposal when reading a single text. As Zywica and Gomez remind us, the purpose of annotating text is to provide a framework to support students' understanding of concepts presented in a text, not to create busywork in addition to the reading. The text annotation procedure can be conducted as a whole-class activity, in which students take turns identifying various components of a text that is visible to the group through an overhead projector or whiteboard. Students can also work in pairs or in small groups to annotate a text and, in doing so, can deliberate about correctly identifying elements such as the main ideas and supporting evidence.

T-NOTES   T-notes provide a simple but effective framework for organizing information presented in texts. As Burke (2002) explains, teachers can adapt T-notes to help students compare and contrast concepts or to identify patterns across texts. The T-note example pictured in Figure 10.16 was used as a note-taking device for a middle school biology class. The teacher wanted to emphasize the focus terms associated with cell structure. She created her notes for two types of students. The first set of notes were most appropriate for her general education students. The students were supposed to find key words from the text and create a definition in their own words. She also had several English Learners in her class. They struggled with making sense of the text and often were lost when a textbook assignment was given. For those students, the teacher created notes that allowed them to highlight the best words to describe each term. These words were reinforced by the text to help them not only understand and define the terms but better utilize the format of the text itself. The following are examples from each type of student.

CORNELL NOTES   A tried-and-true note-taking procedure common in many schools is the Cornell system, developed by Walter Pauk in 1978. Cornell notes, as they are commonly called, can be used both as a note-taking procedure for recording important information during class lectures and as a study tool to review and extend concepts covered in class. Figure 10.17 shows the basic framework of Cornell notes. Students write details from a class lecture in the right-hand column. Soon after the lecture, students use the left-hand column to record questions or list key concepts that are based on the detailed notes they wrote during the lecture. Once students have had time to respond to those questions and to reflect on the material, they can use the space at the bottom of the page to write a summary statement, a synthesis of key points covered, or additional questions they need to address. Pauk and Ross (2007) recommend that students follow the sequence below when using Cornell notes:

1. *Record.* During a class lecture, record the important points addressed in the lecture in the right-hand column.
2. *Question.* As soon after the class as possible, use the left-hand column to develop questions about the material based on the notes you have written in the right-hand column.
3. *Recite.* Cover the notes you have taken during class and try to answer the questions you have written.
4. *Reflect.* Reflect on the material by asking and answering questions such as: How does this new information fit with what I already know? What new information have I acquired? Why is this information important?
5. *Review.* Spend time every week reviewing your notes. This consistent and sequential review of the material can help you to form connections and to analyze thoroughly the concepts presented. Consistent review can also aid in preparing for a unit assessment.

MyLab Education
Video Example 10.2: Summarizing
This video provides an overview on writing summaries.

Cornell notes have become a common note-taking format in many high school classes. An AP biology teacher took this concept to the next digital level. He was teaching the concept of cell biology and wanted his students to take sections of the topic and teach the topics to their classmates. To prep for the lesson, each student was assigned to use the Cornell note-taking technique to record the important information, write questions for their class, practice reading their notes, and reflect on the questions they might be asked about the material. The Cornell concept is based on reworking the information in a question and answer format. This employs high level thinking as the student thinks back from what they are learning and tries to reformat their knowledge into questions.

Here is a sample Cornell note process:

The student learned that the power station or brain of the cell is its mitochondria.

Figure 10.16 T-Note for Middle School Biology

T-Chart from an EL Student

Term	Key Words/My Sentence		
Cytoplasm	Thick Water Surrounded by cell membrane Surrounded by nucleus	Thin Solid	
Nucleus	Central Digests	Bottom Controls	
Cell membrane	Digests Produces	Separates Protects	Controls Arranges
Cell wall	Flexible Outside	Rigid Cellulose	Inside Bones
Mitochondria	Digests Produces Energy	Separates Protects RNA	Controls Arranges
Ribosome	Protein Translate	Separates RNA	Controls Energy
Vacuole	Stores Translates Survival	Separates Protects	Controls

T-Chart from a General Education Student

Term	Key Words/My Sentence
Cytoplasm	Thick, cell membrane, water, salts, protein The thick substance that is made of water, salts, and protein that is kept in place by the cell membrane.
Nucleus	Most important, central, activity, growth The most central and important part of a cell which controls all activity and growth.
Cell membrane	Separates and protects The cell membrane does two things. It separates and protects the cell.
Cell wall	Rigid and cellulose This is outside the cell wall and is made of rigid cellulose.
Mitochondria	Powerhouse, digestive, energy This is the powerhouse of the cell which creates energy through digestion.
Ribosome	Protein synthesis, translate RNA This does two things. It does protein synthesis and it translates RNA.
Vacuole	Storage, helps survive, stores waste This helps the cell survive by storing energy and waste.

Figure 10.17 Cornell Notes

Name _____   Date _____

Topic _____   Subject _____

| Questions or key concepts based on lecture notes or reading: | Important details from class lecture or reading: |

A summary statement, list of key points learned from the lecture or reading, or questions from your reflection that you still need to address:

The student then created the following note in Cornell format, using their own words to reformat:

What controls the cell?   The mitochondria

Cornell note taking is effective because it automatically puts information in a form that many students find easy to study. Students also are encouraged to write in their own words, which shows they can understand the concepts they are learning.

They were required to practice the lesson once before their "teaching time." The digital twist is that in each of the lessons, the notes and the questions would be taught through the flipped classroom model. This required the students to first create a blog showcasing their notes and questions and then turn that information into a video recording of their lesson. These videos were posted online and were available for all of the students to watch before going to class the following day. The students watched the videos, commented, asked questions, and provided feedback. This held the students accountable not only for watching the videos but also for responding to what they learned. The recorded videos prepared them for the hands-on learning that would take place during their class time. This innovative approach not only reinforced the concept of Cornell notes but provided a new way to learn, teach, and demonstrate understanding.

Study Guides

Note-taking procedures such as T-notes and Cornell notes can provide a study guide framework that helps students better comprehend texts. Over time, as students develop the maturity and the learning strategies to interact with difficult texts, the need for study guides is typically reduced. Until that time, however, study guides can provide students with support for navigating complex content area texts. In Chapter 7, we suggested the use of three-level comprehension guides for scaffolding learning at different levels of understanding. Text pattern guides and selective reading guides are also useful for helping students study difficult text.

Text patterns are difficult for some readers to discern, but once students become aware of the importance of organization and learn how to search for relationships in text, they are in a better position to use information more effectively and to comprehend material more thoroughly.

Text Pattern Guides

A study guide based on text patterns helps students perceive and use the major text relationships that predominate in the reading material. As you consider developing a study guide for text patterns, you may find it useful, first, to read through the text selection and identify a predominant pattern and, second, to develop an exercise in which students can react to the structure of the relationships represented by the pattern.

A middle school social studies teacher prepared a text pattern guide to help her students connect the reasons behind the temperance movement and how the movement claimed prohibition would solve societal issues. She organized this information into a problem/solution chart. Her overall goal was to help her students better understand how social problems can lead to social movements. The students read a brief passage and then filled out the following chart. Figure 10.18 is an example from one of her students.

The class read for two purposes: to see whether their predictions were accurate and to follow the cause and effect relationships in the material. First, the students read the selection silently; then, they worked in groups of four to complete the study guide.

A second example, the comparison and contrast study guide in Figure 10.19, shows how the format of a guide will differ with the nature of the material (in this case, narrative) and the teacher's objectives. Juniors in an English class used the study guide to discuss changes in character in the story "Split Cherry Tree."

Figure 10.18 Problem/Solution Guide for the Temperance Movement

Societal Problem	Proposed Solution
Violence in the home	If people didn't drink, they wouldn't be so violent with their wives and children because alcohol can change behavior.
Poverty	If people didn't spend so much money on alcohol, then they would have more money to spend on their family. The passage said sometimes men would take all their money to the bars while their families starved.
Living conditions	The water supply was dirty at this time. That's why a lot of people drank alcohol instead of water. They said if there was no alcohol, people might want to spend more money and time cleaning up the water supply.
Education	People didn't know how bad alcohol was. The Temperance Movement said that if people were educated on the bad effects of alcohol, they might not drink as much.
Economy and success of business	The Temperance Movement said that the economy would improve because there would be fewer people missing work and businesses would have less crime to deal with.
Crime	Crime would go down because people wouldn't make bad choices because they were drinking alcohol and there would be less need for them to steal because they needed money to buy alcohol.

Figure 10.19 Comparison–Contrast Study Guide for "Split Cherry Tree"

Directions: Consider Pa's attitude (how he feels) toward the following characters and concepts. Note that the columns ask you to consider his attitudes toward these things twice—the way he is at the beginning of the story (pp. 147–152) and the way you think he is at the end of the story. Whenever possible, note the page numbers on which this attitude is described or hinted at.

Characters and Concepts	Pa's Attitude at the Beginning of the Story	Pa's Attitude at the End of the Story
Punishment		
Dave		
Professor Herbert		
School		
His own work		
His son's future		
Himself		

Selective Reading Guides

Selective reading guides show students how to think with print. The effective use of questions, combined with signaling techniques, helps model how readers interact with text when reading and studying.

The premise behind the selective reading guide is that, though teachers understand how to process information from their own content area, students do not yet possess the necessary processing skills. A selective reading guide can help to guide students' reading of content area texts. Figure 10.20 illustrates how a selective reading guide was used by a marketing teacher in one Career and Technical Education (CTE) department as he guided his students toward developing consumer awareness and an understanding of a market economy. His selective

Figure 10.20 Selective Reading Guide for a Marketing Class

Chapter 20: Internet as Place

Page 365: Read the introduction. List the ways in which students can use the Internet to support their schoolwork.

Page 366: What is e-commerce? List several examples of businesses that rely on e-commerce.

Page 368: Use a Venn diagram to compare and contrast a dot-com business with a traditional business.

Pages 370–376: Skim the section on "The Internet as Retail Place." List both the positive and negative attributes of online shopping.

Page 376, Figure 29.9: The Better Business Bureau website illustrated in the text gives guidelines for responsible practices for online businesses. Based on your experiences with online shopping, what additional guidelines would you add to this list?

Page 376: The author states that many customers prefer to shop in traditional stores. Do you agree? Do you prefer to shop online or in traditional stores? Why?

Pages 379–381: Skim the section "Future of e-tailing." List the advantages and disadvantages of online shopping. Which do you think will have a more powerful impact on customers in the future?

Figure 10.21 A Reading Road Map

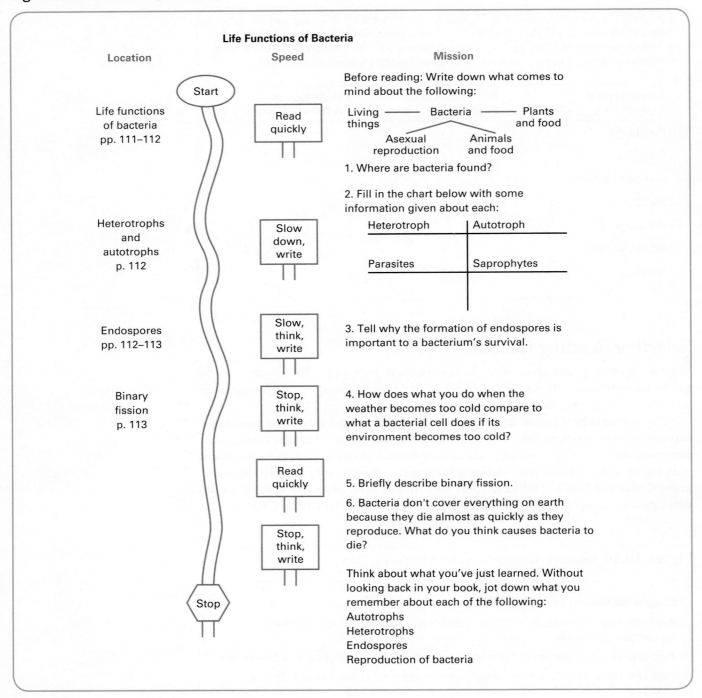

reading guide for a chapter from Clark, Sobel, and Basteri's text *Marketing Dynamics* uses both written questions and signals to help students in processing material from their text.

For struggling readers, teachers add a visual dimension to the guide. Study the guide in Figure 10.21, developed by a middle school science teacher. Notice how he guides students through the life functions of bacteria by using various kinds of cues, signals, and statements. The guide provides location cues to focus students' attention on relevant segments of text, speed signals to model flexibility in reading, and mission statements that initiate tasks that help students think and learn with texts.

Texted Reading Guides

An engaged classroom provides an opportunity to learn and practice in authentic ways. One way to do this is to encourage students to use technology that usually resides outside of the classroom, inside the classroom (Crawley, 2015). Texted reading guides are one way to allow students to use their texting skills academically. An activity that is best done in groups of two, texted reading guides can either be an e-mail exchange or, more ideally, a text exchange. The learners work together to text or e-mail each other their notes. Just like an outline, they should organize their writing so that, when read back, it can reflect the structure of the texts. This process starts with one reader texting a title and the other texting the main point. This continues until all the main points have been explored.

Here is an excerpt from an exchange about *The Outsiders*. The students were given the assignment to discuss how they felt about Ponyboy.

> Student One: *I like Ponyboy, but I think he is really naïve.*
> Student Two: *Why do you think that?*
> Student One: *I think he trusts people too much. Like when he is trusting his brothers to take care of everything. I think he looks at them like they can do no wrong. That is naïve. Don't you think.*
> Student Two: *Yes I guess, but they are also family. Sometimes you have to believe in something, right? If you can't believe in your family, what else do you have. I don't call that naïve, I call that loyal.*

Then the process begins again with a new title and new points. Not only does this assignment allow students to express their opinions and points of comprehension authentically, but also their conversation is saved digitally. They can look back at their notes to study, ask questions, and recall important points. They can read and revise it in real time, and through the revision, it becomes a living document.

MyLab Education **Self-Check 10.4**

MyLab Education **Application Exercise 10.4:**
Using Text Annotations in Content Area Classrooms

Looking Back Looking Forward

Teaching students how and why to study texts involves showing them how to become independent learners. In this chapter, we used the role that text structure plays to illustrate how you can teach students to use learner-directed strategies that involve constructing graphic organizers, writing summaries, and making and taking notes. We also emphasized the importance to connecting studying to authentic tasks and technologies.

Understanding how authors organize their ideas is a powerful factor in learning with texts. Because authors write to communicate, they organize ideas to make them accessible to readers. A well-organized text is a considerate one. The text patterns that authors use to organize their ideas revolve around description, sequence, comparison and contrast, cause and effect, and problem and solution. The more students perceive text patterns, the more likely they are to remember and interpret the ideas they encounter in reading as they connect them with their cultural backgrounds and life experiences.

Graphic organizers help students outline important information that is reflected in the text patterns that authors use to organize ideas. The construction of graphic organizers allows students to map the relationships that exist among the ideas presented in text. This strategy is a valuable tool for comprehending, retaining, and expressing information.

Students who engage in summarizing what they have read often gain greater understanding and retention of the main ideas in text. Students need to become aware of summarization rules and to receive instruction in how to use these rules to write and polish a summary.

Notes are part of another useful strategy for studying text. Making notes allows students to reflect on and react to important ideas in text.

In addition to the development of study strategies, teachers develop study guides to engage students in text comprehension and learning. With the use of guides, teachers provide instructional support to allow students to interact with and respond to difficult texts in meaningful ways. We explored and illustrated two types of guides: text pattern guides and selective reading guides. Text pattern guides help students to follow the predominant text structures in reading assignments. Selective reading guides show students how to think with text by modeling reading behaviors necessary to read effectively. How do teachers incorporate instructional practices and strategies into lessons *before, during,* and *after* assigning texts to read? In the next chapter, we explore the use of trade books in content literacy lessons and units of study. Trade books, like digital texts, are an alternative to textbooks.

eResources

Find more examples of graphic organizers by going to the Graphic Organizers Index.

Conduct your own Internet search using the keywords "semantic maps + lesson plans."

Go to the Lesson Planet website to explore semantic mapping.

Chapter 11
Learning with Multiple Texts

Written in collaboration with Jean Vintinner, Ph.D.

Shutterstock

Chapter Overview and Learning Outcomes

After reading this chapter, you should be able to:

11.1 Explain the importance of incorporating multiple texts, in addition to textbooks, into instruction.

11.2 Define the different types of trade books and articles and explain how each can support content area instruction.

11.3 Describe the different ways trade books can be incorporated into classroom practices.

11.4 Describe the different ways in which students can respond to what they read, including how each supports the comprehension of content knowledge.

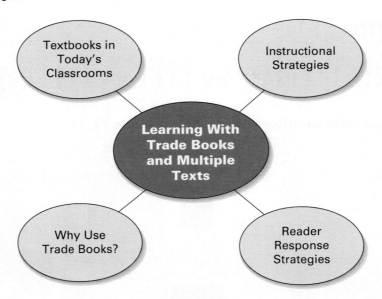

Organizing Principle

To build reading skills and subject area knowledge, students need access to a variety of texts that represent an alternative to the proverbial textbook.

Textbooks by themselves are not enough.

In Chapter 2, we discussed the important role that digital texts play in the academic and personal lives of students. In this chapter, the focus is on additional types of texts that provide alternatives to the textbook, including trade books and a wealth of fictional and informational texts that connect to curricular areas and learning objectives. Incorporating a variety of texts has the potential to motivate students with intense involvement in a subject and to develop in-depth understanding in ways not imagined a few years ago. Furthermore, by engaging students in active response to multiple texts, we heighten their interest and understanding of text content. For example, by introducing students to texts that reflect the contemporary realities of diverse cultures and classes, we increase their self-awareness and cultural understanding while increasing critical thinking and 21st-century skills. We also engage students whose cultures and realities may not be represented in textbooks alone. Should textbooks be abandoned? Certainly not. Our point in this chapter is to underscore the value of integrating a variety of texts and multimedia environments into the curriculum. Students need access to a collection of text resources that represent an alternative to the proverbial textbook.

Frame of Mind

1. Why use trade books to learn subject matter?
2. How can teachers create classroom libraries in content area classrooms?
3. What should the roles of self-selected reading and teacher read-alouds be in the content area classroom?
4. What are some ways that teachers can engage students in responding to the trade books and articles they read?
5. How can teachers involve students in inquiry-related activities?

Content area teaching often involves the use of one type of text—the textbook—often to the exclusion of other types of texts. Textbooks are more the rule than the exception in most classrooms. For many teachers, textbooks are classroom tools that serve as blueprints for learning content areas. In a standards-driven environment, they provide coverage of content in particular disciplines that may well appear on high-stakes tests of some kind, and they provide sequencing and pacing guides to help teachers stay on track to cover all material within the course. Time constraints in a standards-driven curriculum are real. Teachers feel enormous pressure to cover a certain amount of content in a specified period before students move on to the next chapter or unit of study. Teachers who operate under time constraints often view textbooks as efficient informational resources that support what students are studying and meet the objectives of a given course. When a textbook is the only source of information in a content area class, students come to connect the content of a subject with what are sometimes dull, lifeless textbooks. When the textbook becomes the curriculum, students are often disinterested in the subject and denied the range of perspectives and opportunities for critical thinking.

In order to nurture a culture of reading, students need exposure to a variety of texts in their classrooms as well as textbooks. In today's rapidly changing classrooms, learners are expected to read both print-based and electronic books, articles, and resources. Electronic books become commonplace in classrooms as schools transition from print-based books to e-books and e-textbooks. Students need exposure to texts, whether print based or digital in nature, that captivate them and capitalize on their interests. Readers need experience with multiple types of texts that let them see themselves represented in the content and satisfy their need to know about the world around them. In many ways, the content area classroom is the perfect place for students to connect with a multitude of texts because it affords students opportunities to build webs of meaning about a topic through a variety of sources. Through such experiences, students engage in meaning-making by evaluating information, connecting ideas across sources, comparing and contrasting information, and reflecting on meaning. In this chapter, we explore the role of multiple texts, with an emphasis on the use of trade books in the content areas.

MyLab Education
Response Journal 11.1
Based on your own school experiences, what do you believe are some of the problems associated with textbook-only instruction?

Why Use Trade Books and Multiple Texts?

11.1 **Explain the importance of incorporating multiple texts, in addition to textbooks, into instruction.**

Trade books, simply, are books created for a general audience rather than classroom instruction. They are rich in narrative and informational content and can provide a valuable complement to most textbooks. The language and structure of trade books is often less formal and more engaging to students. Trade books, in addition to other ancillary articles and resources, can transport students to different places and times in ways that textbooks cannot. Trade books and other nonfiction texts (Einstein, 2003) can also relate experiences and perspectives that may have been excluded in textbooks. Learning with multiple texts involves exposure to many different genres and forms, all of which are potential sources of information for the active learner. Teaching with a critical literacy framework (Luke, 2014) allows teachers to push students to evaluate what they read and to read the world (Freire, 1970/2000), and ultimately to learn about their place in this world. For example, a nonfiction or fiction trade book has the potential to be a magnifying glass that enlarges and enhances the reader's personal interactions with a subject. When teachers use textbooks and other texts in tandem, they help learners think critically about content and, perhaps more importantly, they also help them think about the larger questions of the world.

Recent national and state standards have emphasized the use of multiple texts assembled as *text sets*—books and articles related to a topic of study that are written at varying levels of text complexity—to help students understand the depth of the issues covered. This wealth of resources allows students of varying interests to learn from texts which are accessible and engaging. It can also allow students to remediate their understanding by reading several texts about a topic.

The use of multiple texts in the classroom can challenge and stimulate student thinking on a range of important issues with particular relevance to the world today, including immigration, globalization, mathematical concepts, scientific inquiry, and much more. Fang (2010), for example, contends that inquiry is the cornerstone of science and that science curricula should include the development of students' ability to access information, comprehend concepts, and produce science texts. Trade texts provide an ideal vehicle for accomplishing such goals. Of course, a science teacher, or any teacher for that matter, should not use trade texts just for the sake of avoiding the textbook. Schroeder, Mckeough, Graham, Stock, and Bisanz (2009) suggest that in a discipline such as science, teachers must first determine if trade texts match the goals of the curriculum and whether they support the goals of scientific literacy.

It is imperative that teachers place thought-provoking books and articles in the hands and minds of students. As Aidan Chambers (1973) notes, good literature both comforts and subverts. As adolescents seek to construct and establish their identities, trade books or articles with social justice themes may help give them a sense of agency and also help them empathize, which is a motivating factor needed for social change (Vogt et al., 2016). Furthermore, teachers need to acknowledge the power of trade books and guide students toward a more critical lens. According to critical literacy theorists (Luke, 2017; Bean & Moni, 2003; Foss, 2002), texts position the readers to assume a stance; in order to develop citizens and future leaders, teachers need to teach students how to think critically.

Today's trade books and articles can provide an effective complement to textbooks in virtually any subject. The best resources overcome many of the limitations of content area texts discussed in the previous section. They provide depth, considerate and accurate up-to-date information, material at a variety of reading levels, and motivation for learning. For example, high-quality trade books and articles can supply the depth of information that space limitations prevent textbooks from providing. Consider the brief textbook treatment of World War I you might find in a history text. Many outstanding trade books provide in-depth accounts of that event in history, such as *The First World War* (Keegan, 2003). Making a case for using picture books in secondary classrooms, *Faithful Elephants* (Tsuchiya, 1988) and *Passage to Freedom: The Sugihara Story* (Mochizuki, 2003) offer different perspectives on World War II, encouraging empathy and cross-cultural understanding. Trade books and articles can fulfill the need for story and provide the emotional dimension so lacking or one-sided in textbooks. Unlike textbooks, they move students' minds and their hearts.

In addition, trade books and articles, nonfiction titles in particular, often contain information that is written and organized in ways that make information more interesting and accessible. The best nonfiction books are more than "baskets of facts"; they speak to young readers personally through informal, engaging writing styles. Their clear, reader-friendly explanations of scientific principles or processes can be extremely helpful to students. In addition, authors of trade books and articles take enormous pains to ensure accuracy. In a speech in Columbus, Ohio, Jim Murphy explained that *each fact* in his award-winning nonfiction title *The Great Fire* (Murphy, 1998) was checked for accuracy at least three times. Similarly, authors of multicultural trade books cite deliberate and diligent research of a variety of sources in order to produce culturally authentic works (Loh, 2006).

Trade books and articles can help teachers differentiate instruction by meeting the range of reading levels in their classrooms. By using a variety of texts at different levels, teachers can match students with books they can read. Instead of having all students read the same textbooks, students can read a variety of different trade books about a particular topic. This allows teachers to give students books at their independent reading levels, a practice that has been associated with gains in achievement. Databases, such as EBSCO, allow teachers to find reading materials on a given topic or standard and filter the results based on variables such as text type or reading level. This allows students of all abilities to access materials related to course topics.

The reality is that many students do not know how to gain knowledge from informational texts because their school experiences have been limited to textbook-only reading. For some students, the only historic, mathematic, or scientific materials they will ever read are in textbooks. Nonfiction texts offer widely varying text structures, writing styles, and highly specific vocabulary, all of which can be challenging to readers. This type of text is typically less familiar to students than narrative and more difficult for them to read. Exposure to nonfiction text in content area classes gives students much-needed practice reading expository texts, which, unlike narrative, do not typically involve characters, plots, or settings. When teachers offer explicit and deliberate support in reading these nonfiction trade books and articles, students become more proficient in comprehension.

Trade books and articles help readers at all levels develop greater understanding of content-related concepts. Historical fiction titles, for example, provide a framework for remembering, understanding, and evaluating historical content. The same holds for content in science and other subject areas. Popular science books, both fact and fiction, provide background knowledge for science concepts covered in class and help students relate these concepts to their everyday lives.

Finally, trade books and articles have the power to motivate students to read more. The compelling visual qualities of today's nonfiction books make them many students' favorite out-of-school reading. Authors of nonfiction not only inform but also entertain. Consider, for example, *Phineas Gage: A Gruesome but True Story About Brain Science* (Fleischman, 2002). In 1848, Phineas Gage had a three-and-a-half-foot iron rod blasted through his head and survived. Despite his recovery, Gage's personality underwent a drastic transformation. He changed from a reliable, respected foreman to an unpredictable and temperamental man who eventually lost his job. The focus of the book is not simply on what happened to Gage but on what neurologists have learned and continue to learn today about the workings of the human brain. Because of its lively writing and extraordinary visuals, this amazing book provides background information about the human brain in a format sure to motivate even those students who have little initial interest in the topic. Recognizing the value of such texts, the Young Adult Library Services Association (YALSA) created the Excellence in Nonfiction award in 2010, which acknowledges quality nonfiction written for young adults, creating a list of engaging titles to incorporate into instruction.

Content knowledge support is not limited to nonfiction texts. Authors of fiction engage students through characters that remind readers of themselves and their peers. Many titles address students' emotional needs because they are written from the viewpoint of students. People of all ages and backgrounds are attracted to books that speak to them in some personal way. For many female students, for example, Ann Brashares's (2001) best-selling *Sisterhood of the Traveling Pants* collection speaks of the powerful bonds of friendship and its potential to transform lives. For males of any ethnicity, but especially Native American, Sherman Alexie's (2007) *The Absolutely True Diary of a Part-Time Indian* speaks of the trials and tribulations of forging multiple cultural identities. Some stories allow students to view contemporary events through the eyes of others, such as Angie Thomas's *The Hate U Give* (2017) whose protagonist is facing racial injustice. Today's young adult literature is more edgy than in the past and, one could argue, more representative of today's teens. Because of this, today's young adult books are likely to appeal to a wider audience than ever before; and as a result, teens will be more likely to read such books.

Capturing students' attention and promoting the habit of lifelong reading provide a major rationale for using trade books and articles. Of all the goals for literacy instruction, there is none more critical than creating students who read independently. Independent reading provides practice and pleasure and develops passion for books and learning. It affords students an opportunity to "get lost in a book"—to be so engaged in reading that one loses track of time, of place, of everything but the power of a text to transport

MyLab Education
Response Journal 11.2
Explain how incorporating multiple texts into instruction can help meet the needs of a variety of learners, specifically English Learners, struggling readers, and students performing above grade level.

MyLab Education
Video Example 11.1:
Using Informational Texts to Enhance Learning
The video provides an informative overview on using informational texts to enhance learning.

and transform us. Repeated experiences that involve true engagement with books help students develop a love of reading that may last a lifetime. When students are given opportunities to interact with quality trade books, they have a better chance of becoming lifelong readers. Textbooks alone cannot motivate students to continue their learning, particularly in the case of reluctant or academically diverse readers, who are often frustrated and defeated by textbooks in the first place. As Melissa, a high school English teacher, suggests in Box 11.1, there is no substitute for a good book.

Box 11.1 Voices from the Field

Melissa, High School English Teacher

Challenge

As an English teacher in a low-performing high school, I find it is important students buy into the idea that what they are doing is connected to their lives in some way, and it is essential that students feel they are working with a text that is part of "real-world" reading as opposed to the worksheet realm of textbook regurgitation. Because I am required by my school district to utilize designated texts and follow state standards in my lesson and unit planning, incorporation of trade books can seem like yet another element that must be present in my already overcrowded curriculum. However, the use of trade books allows for easy connections between nonfiction texts and literature and offers students the opportunity to read texts that have significance outside the classroom. Additionally, the identification, collection, and incorporation of trade books are deceivingly easy when approached with an open mind and willingness to adapt lessons to ensure student interest is increased and unmotivated learners are offered alternative access to literary concepts and understanding.

Strategy

One of my first steps was to streamline the skills I wanted students to master through my lessons. Instead of focusing on individual concepts that I would introduce through various means, I focused on planning units with trade books that allowed the collection of desired skills to be explored through novels, resulting in a deeper understanding of concepts. Instead of using short stories from the textbook to demonstrate various literary and writing devices, I had students identify elements as they developed throughout a novel, avoiding the choppy, disjointed approach that often results from textbook organization. This approach allowed for more holistic exposures to literature and stimulated identification of trends and developing elements over time. By making use of novels and texts outside of the textbook, I was able to cover the curriculum in a relevant context that permitted plenty of practice and encouraged generalization of skills beyond the English classroom.

The use of trade books also allows students to seek out their own texts related to the focus of the lesson. By providing students the opportunity to select supplemental texts that were relevant and interesting, I encouraged the students to take ownership of their learning and provided opportunities for them to become the "experts" in the class. Though textbooks provide related excerpts or articles that connect with the covered content, the incorporation of different forms of trade books not only can provide different lenses through which to view concepts and skills but also can allow students to explore aspects of the curriculum to which they have personal connections. While it was initially intimidating to incorporate student supplemental finds, I soon found that planning general activities became more enjoyable for the students because they were exploring texts in which they had an interest.

Though student choice was important, a large part of the standards is the incorporation of nonfiction texts and historical documents with the curriculum. Initially a challenge, it was this requirement that really illustrated the benefit of trade books. Trade books allowed me to present many facets of concepts and explore cross-curricular ideas within my one-subject classroom. Alternatively, students were exposed to texts and counterarguments that were timely and relevant to the skills being taught and their lives and community. By incorporating nonfiction accounts and historical perspectives, the students gained deeper insight and I was able to meet my necessary standards and objectives without completely overhauling previous lessons that also had value. Simple tweaks to my plans to recognize the place of trade books not only exposed the students to more nonfiction but also allowed students to mesh context and content in a way that made sense.

Reflection

Through the use of literature and multiple text types, I've been able to engage my typically unmotivated textbook learners in reading, writing, and thinking about a variety of texts that explore different concepts and perspectives. Providing students with short, engaging texts that built their background knowledge, stimulated discussion, and were relevant to the students' own lives prevented textbook "burnout" and encouraged proactive student behaviors. Throughout the process, I utilized the school librarian, various websites, and even some educational foundations to obtain funds to purchase trade books. I found that many trade books are accessible via donation sites like Swap.com, and many times single copies of books will be offered to schools for a small fee. As I increase my comfort level and build my understanding of the use of trade books, I continue to use the textbook less and less and incorporate multiple trade books with more and more frequency.

Learning with Trade Books and Articles

11.2 Define the different types of trade books and articles and explain how each can support content area instruction.

When students have opportunities to learn with trade books and articles, they are in a position to explore and interact with many kinds of texts, both fiction and nonfiction. Today's trade books are better than ever. They are written by authors in touch with the emotions and experiences of today's young people and address an enormous range of themes and genres. They present characters and events from virtually every ethnic and cultural group in accurate and meaningful circumstances and settings.

Today's trade books and articles offer teachers a variety of genres, ranging from easy-to-read titles using engaging formats to extremely sophisticated explorations of complex topics. Trade books and articles can serve the needs of every student in every academic area. The greatest challenge for teachers is deciding which resources to choose from the enormous selection available. Figure 11.1 provides a list of references to help teachers select good books for their classrooms.

Figure 11.1 Trade Book Selection Guide for Children and Adolescents

The ALAN Review (Assembly on Literature for Adolescents, National Council of Teachers of English). Published three times a year; articles and "Clip and File" reviews. Urbana, IL: National Council of Teachers of English.

Appraisal: Children's Science Books for Young People. Published quarterly by Children's Science Book Review Committee. Reviews written by children's librarians and subject specialists. Association for Library Service to Children. 2015.

The Newbery & Caldecott Awards: A Guide to the Medal and Honor Books. Chicago, IL: American Library Association. Provides short annotations for the winners and runners-up of ALA-sponsored awards.

Barr, C. (2013). *Best Books for High School Readers: Grades 9–12.* Englewood, CO: Libraries Unlimited. Lists 12,000 fiction and nonfiction titles, recommended in at least two sources and organized thematically.

Book Links: Connecting Books, Libraries, and Classrooms. Published six times a year by the American Library Association to help teachers integrate literature into the curriculum; bibliographies in different genres and subjects; suggestions for innovative use in the classroom.

Booklist. Published twice monthly by the American Library Association. Reviews of children's trade books and nonprint materials (video, audio, and computer software). Approximate grade levels are given; separate listing for nonfiction books.

Books for the Teenage Reader. Published annually by the Office of Young Adult Services, New York Public Library. Recommen-

dations from young adult librarians in the various branches of the New York Public Library.

Bulletin of the Center for Children's Books. Published monthly by Johns Hopkins University Press; detailed reviews and possible curriculum uses are noted.

Children's Books: Awards and Prizes. New York, NY: Children's Book Council. Award-winning titles as well as state "Children's Choice" awards for exemplary trade books.

Christenbury, L. (Ed.). (1995). *Books for You: A Booklist for Senior High Students* (11th ed.). Urbana, IL: National Council of Teachers of English. Provides annotations for both fiction and nonfiction written for students, organized into 50 categories.

Curriculum Center: Math Literature for Young Adults. An electronic list of young adult novels that incorporate math concepts.

Friedberg, J. B. (1992). *Portraying Persons with Disabilities: An Annotated Bibliography of Non-Fiction for Children and Teenagers* (2nd ed.). New Providence, NJ: Bowker. Provides comprehensive listings of nonfiction dealing with physical, mental, and emotional disabilities.

Goodreads. A "social catalog" of published works and reviews. This site allows readers to respond to literature and create groups within the site for conversations about books.

Gorman, M. (2003). *Getting Graphic: Using Graphic Novels to Promote Literacy with Preteens and Teens.* New York: Linworth Publishing. Provides an introduction to teaching with graphic novels and includes a bibliography of 50 graphic novels

(continued)

Figure 11.1 *(Continued)*

suitable for sixth grade as well as suggestions for using these books in the classroom.

Helbig, A., & Perkins, A. R. (2000). *Many Peoples, One Land: A Guide to New Multicultural Literature for Children and Young Adults.* Westport, CT: Greenwood Press. Provides an extensive listing of titles featuring African Americans, Asian Americans, Hispanic Americans, and Native Americans.

The Horn Book Magazine. Published six times a year by Horn Book, Inc.; articles by noted children's authors, illustrators, and critics on aspects of children's literature, including its use in the classroom. Nonfiction books are reviewed in a separate section.

International Reading Association. "Children's Choices," a list of exemplary, "reader-friendly" children's literature, is published every October in *The Reading Teacher.*

McClure, A. A., & Kristo, J. (Ed.). (2002). *Adventuring with Books: A Booklist for Pre-K–Grade 6* (13th ed.). Urbana, IL: National Council of Teachers of English. Summaries of hundreds of books arranged by genre and topic within content areas.

Miller-Lachman, L. (1992). *Our Family, Our Friends, Our World: An Annotated Guide to Significant Multicultural Books for Children and Teenagers.* New Providence, NJ: Reed Publishing. Comprehensive reference work includes 1,000 of the best English-language fiction and nonfiction multicultural books published since 1970. Each chapter introduces a culture, a map of the region, and an annotated list of books for preschool through Grade 12.

Notable Children's Trade Books in the Field of Social Studies. National Council for the Social Studies. Published yearly in the spring issue of *Social Education;* annotates notable fiction and nonfiction books, primarily for children in Grades K–8.

Outstanding Science Trade Books for Students K–12. National Science Teachers Association. Published each year in the spring issue of *Science and Children;* contains information consistent with current scientific knowledge; is pleasing in format; is illustrated; and is nonsexist, nonracist, and nonviolent.

Rand, D., & Parker, T. T. (2000). *Black Books Galore! Guide to Great African American Children's Books About Girls.* New York, NY: Jossey-Bass. Featuring 360 books arranged alphabetically by title, this book provides descriptions, notes awards, and spotlights well-known authors and illustrators.

Rosow, L. V. (1996). *Light'n Lively Reads for ESL, Adult and Teen Readers.* Englewood, CO: Libraries Unlimited. Books are arranged in 17 different thematic units. Each unit lists picture books, thin books, challenging books, book chapters and "strong passages," newspaper and magazine articles, and suggested activities related to each theme.

Schneider Family Book Award. These American Library Association awards are given annually to books for excellence in portraying the disability experience for children, middle grades readers, and young adults.

School Library Journal. Published by R. R. Bowker; articles on all aspects of children's literature, including its use in content areas; reviews by school and public librarians.

Totten, H. L., & Brown, R. W. (1995). *Culturally Diverse Library Collections for Children.* New *Teen Book Finder Database.* A database of all literature awarded one of the YALSA awards. This resource allows you to search based on title, award, year, genre, topic, or more.

We Need Diverse Books. A collections of book lists and resources to support diversity in children's literature.

MyLab Education
Video Example 11.2: Previewing Non-Fiction Texts
This video provides an informative overview on using informational texts to enhance learning.

NONFICTION BOOKS Nonfiction trade books have, in recent years, moved from the shadows into the spotlight of literary excellence. Nonfiction books, which include informational books and biographies, are not glorified textbooks. They connect with readers through writing that is strictly objective in tone and literal in content but that engages contemporary readers. These books contain elements of fiction that flesh out historical details and provide an element of entertainment. This form represents the kind of meaty material that entertains students at the same time it informs.

For many students, nonfiction is the literature of choice for out-of-school reading. Many students report a fascination with facts and a "need to know" that drives their reading choices. Despite its popularity, nonfiction seldom makes its way into content area classrooms. Because of this, nonfiction trade books are a largely untapped resource with great potential for motivating readers. By using nonfiction trade books in the classroom, teachers can bridge the gap between students' in- and out-of-school reading and capitalize on their interest in this genre. In Box 11.2, an art teacher uses biographies of famous artists to connect students' interests with course topics.

The wide array of nonfiction books available for the classroom can help teachers enliven classroom instruction in every content area. No single book will satisfy all readers, but teachers will find many titles that can spark student learning. Using nonfiction in the classroom can:

Box 11.2 Evidence-Based Best Practices

Appreciating Art and Artists Through the Use of Trade Books

Today's nonfiction trade books and articles offer teachers rich opportunities to involve students in learning about artists and analyzing their works. Art teacher Carole Newman has found many ways to create literacy activities that serve to extend student learning in her middle school art classes. One project that she typically involves her students in is the study of the lives and work of famous artists. This project combines reading, writing, and artistic expression. She begins this project by providing her students with a wide array of artists' biographies. These include books from the *Lives of the Artists* series, artists' biographies by Jan Greenberg and Diane Stanley, and many others. Some of the artists that students study include Diego Rivera, Frida Kahlo, Marc Chagall, Pablo Picasso, Jackson Pollack, Edgar Degas, Claude Monet, Georgia O'Keeffe.

Students identify an artist they wish to learn about and select and read a book about the artist's life. Students are required to identify five important facts about the artist's life and prepare an in-depth analysis of two of the artist's works. As part of this analysis, students record their observations about the works in a learning log. Finally, students create their own artwork, employing the style and media used by the artist under study. They share their findings through group presentations where they present information about the artists and their works as well as their original artistic creations.

- Deepen student knowledge of real people, places, and phenomena of the present and the past

- Provide in-depth, up-to-date information

- Help students see how knowledge in different domains is organized, used, and related

- Develop student familiarity with the language and vocabulary of a discipline

- Improve student comprehension of expository text, a skill required for survival in the Information Age

- Provide insights into contemporary issues of interest to teens that get little attention in textbooks

The range of topics available, the variety of formats, and the varying levels of difficulty make these books an indispensable resource for content area classrooms. Topics addressed in nonfiction trade books range from art to zoology. Formats range from encyclopedic treatments of topics like David Macaulay's (2008) *The Way We Work*, which describes the design and functions of the human body, to tightly focused, narrowly defined topics such as Karen Beil's (1999) *Fire in Their Eyes: Wildfires and the People Who Fight Them*.

There are outstanding biographies and autobiographies of all sorts of people, including rock stars (*John Lennon: All I Want Is the Truth* [Partridge, 2005]), writers (*e.e. cummings: A Poet's Life* [Reef, 2006]), athletes (Lance Armstrong and Sally Jenkins's [2001] *It's Not About the Bike: My Journey Back to Life*), composers (*This Land Was Made for You and Me: The Life and Songs of Woody Guthrie* [Partridge, 2002]), scientists (*Genius: A Photobiography of Albert Einstein* [Delano, 2005]), artists (*Chuck Close: Up Close* [Greenberg & Jordan, 1998]), and ordinary teens who find themselves in extraordinary situations (*A Long Way Gone: Memoirs of a Boy Soldier* [Beah, 2007], the tragic account of a former child soldier in Sierra Leone). There are books that recount real-life adventures, such as *Shipwreck at the Bottom of the World: The Extraordinary True Story of Shackleton and the* Endurance (Armstrong, 1998) and *Team Moon: How 400,000 People Landed Apollo 11 on the Moon* (Thimmesh, 2006). Other titles address contemporary issues of concern to people the world over, including world health crises, climate change, citizenship, and homelessness. There are collections of interviews written with young readers in mind, such as *Colors of Freedom: Immigrant Stories* (Bode, 2000), which presents the voices of teen immigrants from such places as Afghanistan, El Salvador, India, Cuba, and China. In addition, there are first-person accounts of teens who make disastrous mistakes, such as *Hole in My Life* (Gantos, 2002), about a teenager who discovered his passion for writing in prison and went on to become a beloved children's author. Figure 11.2 lists additional nonfiction titles useful for various content areas.

Figure 11.2 English-Language Nonfiction Trade Books for Content Area Classrooms

Science

Burns, L. G. (2007). *Tracking Trash: Flotsam, Jetsam, and the Science of Ocean Motion.* Boston, MA: Houghton Mifflin.

Dash, J. (2000). *The Longitude Prize.* New York, NY: Farrar, Straus & Giroux.

Delano, M. F. (2005). *Genius: A Photobiography of Albert Einstein.* Washington, DC: National Geographic.

Dendy, L. (2005). *Guinea Pig Scientists: Bold Self-Experimenters in Science and Medicine.* New York, NY: Henry Holt.

Dingle, A. (2007). *The Periodic Table: Elements with Style.* Boston, MA: Houghton Mifflin/Kingfishers.

Farrell, J. (2005). *Invisible Allies: Microbes That Shape Our Lives.* New York, NY: Farrar, Straus & Giroux.

Fleischman, J. (2002). *Phineas Gage: A Gruesome but True Story About Brain Science.* Boston, MA: Houghton Mifflin.

Giblin, J. (1995). *When Plague Strikes: The Black Death, Smallpox, AIDS.* New York, NY: HarperCollins.

Jenkins, S. (2002). *Life on Earth: The Story of Evolution.* Boston, MA: Houghton Mifflin.

Johnson, S. (2014). *How We Got to Now: Six Innovations that Made the Modern World.* New York, NY: Riverhead Books.

Pearce, F. (2007). *Earth Then and Now.* New York, NY: Firefly.

Sherman, J. (2018). *25 Women Who Thought of it First.* Mankato: Capstone Press.

Shetterly, M. L. & Freeman, L. (2018). *Hidden Figures: The True Story of Four Black Women and the Space Race.* New York, NY: HarperCollins.

Thimmesh, C. (2000). *Girls Think of Everything: Stories of Ingenious Inventions by Women.* New York, NY: Houghton Mifflin.

Thimmesh, C. (2006). *Team Moon: How 400,000 People Landed Apollo 11 on the Moon.* New York, NY: Houghton Mifflin.

Social Studies

Armstrong, J. (2002). *Shattered: Stories of Children and War.* New York, NY: Knopf.

Bartoletti, S. C. (2001). *Black Potatoes: The Story of the Great Irish Famine, 1845–1850.* Boston, MA: Houghton Mifflin.

Bitton-Jackson, L. (1997). *I Have Lived a Thousand Years: Growing Up in the Holocaust.* New York: Simon & Schuster.

Bode, J. (2000). *The Colors of Freedom: Immigrant Stories.* New York, NY: Franklin Watts.

Bryant, J. (2016). *Six Dots: A Story of Young Louis Braille.* New York, NY: Alfred A. Knopf.

Calabro, M. (1999). *The Perilous Journey of the Donner Party.* New York, NY: Clarion Books.

Cooper, M. (2002). *Remembering Manzanar: Life in a Japanese Relocation Camp.* New York, NY: Clarion Books.

Deem, J. M. (2005). *Bodies from the Ash: Life and Death in Ancient Pompeii.* Boston, MA: Houghton Mifflin.

Fleming, C. (2008). *The Lincolns: A Scrapbook Look at Abraham and Mary.* New York, NY: Schwartz & Wade Books.

Hoose, P. M. (2001). *We Were There, Too! Young People in U.S. History.* New York, NY: Farrar, Straus & Giroux.

Oppenheim, J. (2006). *Dear Miss Breed: True Stories of the Japanese American Incarceration During World War II and a Librarian Who Made a Difference.* New York, NY: Scholastic.

Raddatz, M. (2007). *The Long Road Home: A Story of War and Family.* New York, NY: Penguin.

Schanzer, R. (2004). *George vs. George: The American Revolution as Seen from Both Sides.* Washington, DC: National Geographic.

Weatherford, C. B. (2016). *Freedom in Congo Square.* New York, NY: Little Bee Books.

Art and Music

Beckett, W. (1999). *My Favorite Things: 75 Works of Art from Around the World.* New York, NY: Abrams.

Bryant, J. (2013). *A Splash of Red: The Life and Art of Horace Pippin.* New York, NY: Random House Children's Publishing.

Byrd, R. (2003). *Leonardo, Beautiful Dreamer.* New York, NY: Dutton.

Greenberg, J., & Jordan, S. (2004). *Andy Warhol: Prince of Pop.* New York, NY: Delacorte.

Greenberg, J., & Jordan, S. (1998). *Chuck Close: Up Close.* New York, NY: DK.

Grody, S., & Prigoff, J. (2007). *Graffiti LA: Street Styles and Art.* New York, NY: Harry N. Abrams.

Marsalis, W. (1995). *Marsalis on Music.* New York, NY: Norton.

Mühlberger, R. (1993). *What Makes a Monet a Monet?* New York, NY: New York Metropolitan Museum of Art/Viking.

Myers, W. D. (2006). *Jazz.* New York, NY: Holiday House.

Rosenstock, B. (2014). *The Noisy Paint Box: The Colors and Sounds of Kandinsky's Abstract Art.* New York, NY: Alfred A. Knopf.

Steptoe, J. (2016). *Radiant Child: The Story of Young Artist Jean-Michel Basquiat.* New York, NY: Little, Brown and Company.

Whitehead, K. (2008). *Art From Her Heart: Folk Artist Clementine Hunter.* New York, NY: G.P. Putnam's Sons.

Health and Physical Education

Armstrong, L., & Jenkins, S. (2001). *It's Not About the Bike: My Journey Back to Life.* New York, NY: Berkley Books.

Blumenthal, K. (2005). *Let Me Play! The Story of Title IX: The Law That Changed the Future of Girls in America.* New York, NY: Atheneum.

Canfield, J. (2000). *Chicken Soup for the Sports Fan's Soul: 101 Stories of Insight, Inspiration and Laughter in the World.* Deerfield, FL: HCI.

Chryssicas, M. K. (2007). *Breathe: Yoga for Teens.* New York, NY: DK.

Shivack, N. (2007). *Inside Out: Portrait of an Eating Disorder.* New York, NY: Simon & Schuster.

Thompson, L. A. (2015). *Emmanuel's Dream: The True Story of Emmanuel Ofosu Yeboah.* New York, NY: Schwartz & Wade Books.

Perhaps the greatest difficulty teachers face when selecting nonfiction for the classroom is deciding which books to choose from the large number available. An important point to keep in mind is that variety truly is the spice of life where reading and learning are concerned. No one book will satisfy all readers. The point of using nonfiction trade books in the classroom is to expose students to more than one point of view in a way that is both informational and readable. Although many nonfiction books sound like textbooks packaged in pretty covers, teachers can select quality books by considering the five As:

1. The **A**uthority of the author
2. The **A**ccuracy of text content
3. The **A**ppropriateness of the book for its audience
4. The literary **A**rtistry
5. The **A**ppearance of the book (Moss, 2003, pp. 123–124)

By following these five As, teachers can be assured that the texts they choose will present a factual representation of people and events in a way that is engaging for the age and ability of the students.

Classroom uses for nonfiction are limitless but are most often thought of in reference to student report writing or inquiry projects. Nonfiction trade books have many other excellent uses as well. For example, they can help students consider multiple perspectives related to a particular issue.

One interesting way to use nonfiction involves pairing fiction with nonfiction. Judy Hendershot involved her middle graders in reading the historical novel *Out of the Dust* (Hesse, 1997) as part of a social studies unit on the Depression. During this time, she read aloud the nonfiction title *Children of the Great Depression* (Freedman, 2005). Through this pairing of fiction with nonfiction, students developed a deeper understanding of the experiences of the children who suffered through the greatest economic downturn in American history. The first title exposes students to the harsh experiences of the female narrator during this time. The second provides a somewhat wider view, helping students understand the causes of the Depression as well as its impact on children across the country. This type of integrated instruction also allows teachers to deliver efficient instruction in multiple content areas, helping students make connections between subjects. This is crucial in schools that have dedicated a great deal of time to reading and math, much to the detriment of other subjects such as science, social studies, or the arts.

NONFICTION ARTICLES   Just as with nonfiction books, nonfiction articles can provide the same level of engagement. Students can find information on topics of relevance to them written by experts in the field or through firsthand accounts of others with similar interests. These articles cover the same topics, formats, and variety in readability, but do so in shorter texts. This brevity allows students to gather information more quickly and access a greater number of resources. These articles can also serve as mentor texts, supporting students as they learn to think, write, and discuss ideas within a given discipline. Nonfiction articles can also provide the most recent information on a topic, allowing students access to contemporary perspectives and knowledge.

In some cases, necessary scaffolding will require teachers to find appropriate nonfiction articles for students that align with curriculum objectives and reading abilities. Teachers can gather helpful resources and share them during instruction. As students develop critical literacy skills, teachers can guide students to find their own resources to further their understanding of course content, creating lifelong learners. Box 11.3 shows how a middle school psychical education teacher integrates trade books and articles into content area instruction.

PICTURE BOOKS   All too often, middle and high school teachers think of picture books as suitable only for the primary grades. However, the picture book format is broad and has, particularly recently, been adapted for students of all ages. Picture books encompass every genre and cover a wide range of subjects. They can be used to enhance instruction in every content area.

In picture books, art and text work together to tell a story. Picture books typically average around 32 pages in length, and their illustrations represent a wide range of media from original art to collage to cut paper. These books are works of art that can represent an area of study in and of themselves. Picture books are more than visual feasts, though; they contain the rich vocabulary and lyrical language characteristic of the finest literature. Picture books fall into five general categories: wordless books, picture books with minimal text, picture storybooks, illustrated books, and graphic nonfiction (Möller, 2015).

1. *Wordless books.* Illustrations tell the story completely; no text is involved. Tom Feelings's (1995) *The Middle Passage: White Ships/Black Cargo* portrays the cruel experience of slavery through powerful illustrations that transcend the need for words.
2. *Picture books with minimal text.* The illustrations in these books continue to tell the story, but words are used to enhance the pictures. *The Mysteries of Harris Burdick* (Van Allsburg, 1984) is an example of a book with minimal text.
3. *Picture storybooks.* Interdependent story and illustrations are central to the telling of the tale. *Show Way* (Woodson, 2005), which describes an African American family's tradition of making quilts originally designed as secret maps for runaway slaves, is an excellent example of a picture storybook in which illustration and text work together to create a seamless whole.
4. *Illustrated books.* These have more words than pictures, but the illustrations illuminate the text in important ways. A stunning example is Kadir Nelson's (2008) *We Are the Ship.* This amazing book was the 2008 winner of the Coretta Scott King Award, which recognizes an African American author and illustrator of outstanding books for children and young adults. Nelson, an extraordinary artist and storyteller, tells the story of the Negro Baseball Leagues from the 1920s to the 1940s. His breathtaking illustrations portray the forgotten players of that time with grace and strength.
5. *Graphic Nonfiction.* These texts are presented to resemble comic strips. The stories are represented in both pictures and text, including dialogue and narration (Schwarz, 2002). While graphic novels are fictional, these texts are autobiographical or expository and would be an engaging addition to content area studies. Spiegelman's (1986) *Maus: A Survivor's Tale* was originally presented in serial form and details the author's interviews with his father about his experience during the Holocaust. *Persepolis: The Story of a Childhood* (Satrapi, 2000) and *Persepolis: The Story of a Return* (Satrapi, 2004) detail the author's childhood in Iran during and after the Islamic Revolution and her move afterward. Readers can glimpse the daily life of a girl during this changing political and religious environment.

Many picture books suitable for middle and high school students are written to appeal to all age groups. Increasingly, however, picture books are written specifically with older readers in mind. Walter Dean Myers's (2002) *Patrol: An American Soldier in Vietnam* provides a vivid example of this trend. This unusual and gripping book combines mixed-media collages with a riveting poem about a young soldier's fear, confusion, and fatigue. Its in-depth focus and emotional content help readers connect with the realities of war for the typical foot soldier.

Picture books can scaffold student understanding of a range of topics through formats that intrigue rather than intimidate. Picture books provide students with background knowledge about people, places, events, and experiences, creating a context for new content learning. They can ground students in cognitive concepts critical for understanding a variety of content area subjects. Because picture books with a multicultural focus are increasing in availability, they can also provide rich opportunities for promoting cultural diversity and creating culturally responsive pedagogy (Souto-Manning, 2009).

Picture books are a particularly rich resource for struggling readers and English Learners. Illustrations aid comprehension, and the manageable length and limited

Box 11.3 Evidence-Based Best Practices

Linking Physical Education with Literacy Learning

Teacher Tona Wilson at Monroe Clark Middle School in San Diego makes literacy learning an integral part of her physical education classes. She uses read-alouds on a regular basis, for example, to teach students concepts related to health and physical education. She often reads aloud from books such as *Wilma Unlimited* (Krull, 2000) or *Chicken Soup for the Sports Fan's Soul* (Canfield, 2000). She regularly reads short newspaper and magazine articles about current events related to sports. These read-alouds provide a rich source for discussion and help students recognize the importance of health and physical education in their everyday lives.

Tona uses her strong knowledge of trade books related to sports to encourage her students to read in school and out of school. To become better acquainted with her students' sports-related interests, Tona has each student complete a survey about their sports-related preferences and extracurricular activities. This provides her with information that enables her to recommend particular titles to her students that relate to their interests in soccer, baseball, dance, or field hockey. She regularly consults with reading teachers at the school who provide assistance in locating books for students with particular interests.

Another literacy-related activity Tona involves her students in is a research project she calls "bioboards." Bioboards involve her students in using trade books and articles to research sports figures from the past or present. Students are required to locate information related to the person's life and (1) create a timeline of the sport figure's life, (2) identify great sports moments in his or her life, (3) research the schools the person attended and sports participation in school, and (4) create color pictures depicting selected events and write captions explaining each picture. Each student displays his or her information on an 11- by 17-inch board and presents it to the other members of the class.

As they learn about different types of games, students regularly engage in shared and guided reading activities that teach them about the history, rules, and methods of scoring. They then work with partners incorporating what they have learned about these games to create their own new games, such as racquetball soccer. In these and many other ways, Tona Wilson helps her students see the many values of literacy as they learn about health and physical education.

---

amount of print in picture books enhance their appeal to students for whom reading is a challenge. Because of their accessible format, picture books can motivate these students to read; and independent, enjoyable reading experiences can lead to reading that continues after the bell has rung, an important correlate to increased reading achievement.

Picture books lend themselves to use in virtually every content area. Math and science concepts can come alive though illustrated nonfiction picture books. *Go Figure! A Totally Cool Book About Numbers* (Ball, 2005) takes a lively look at the history of mathematics, number theory, logic, and more through puzzles and problems to solve. *Anno's Math Games II* (Anno, 1989) inspires critical analysis of the notion of sets and logical possibilities presented in the detailed illustrations. The science-related biography *The Man Who Made Time Travel* (Lasky, 2003) relates the story of John Harrison, who devoted 35 years of his life to solving the problem of tracking longitude in shipboard navigation. *Gregor Mendel: The Friar Who Grew Peas* (Bardoe, 2006) gives glimpses of the life and work of a man whose name is known to every biology student.

Picture books can also build bridges between the past and present. Many excellent titles focus on events surrounding World War II. In *Hidden Child* (2005), Isaac Millman describes his childhood in France as a Jewish boy hiding from the Nazis. *Home of the Brave* (Say, 2002) presents an enigmatic, haunting view of the internment of the Japanese during World War II. In *The Butter Battle Book* (1984), Dr. Seuss explores the illogical nature of war and poses the question "Which country will 'push the button' first?" *The War That Saved My Life* (Bradley, 2016), shows Ada's conflicted feelings as she leaves her home to stay away from war-torn London. When author and illustrator Peter Sís's (2007) teenage children asked him to describe his own youth, Sís responded with an extraordinary combination of graphic novel and picture book, *The Wall: Growing Up Behind the Iron Curtain*. Because words alone could not tell the story, he used period photographs, crosshatch drawings, and journal entries to describe the conflict between his need to pursue his creative instincts and the oppressive communist government in Czechoslovakia. The book provides a vivid portrayal of a world of darkness unimaginable to most of today's students and could give world history classes a personal glimpse of life under a totalitarian regime. Inspired as a child by the comic book *Martin Luther King and the Montgomery Story* (Hassler and Resnik, 1957), U.S. Congressman John Lewis worked with Andrew Aydin to create an autobiographical trilogy of graphic nonfiction texts reflecting a personal account of the civil rights movement. These novels, *March: Book One* (2013), *March: Book Two* (2015), and *March: Book Three* (2016), winners of several awards for literary achievement, have shared the experience of fighting for social justice and equality.

Illustrated picture books and graphic novels are useful in the English classroom as well. Bruce Coville's (1997) *William Shakespeare's* Macbeth provides an easy-to-read complement to Shakespeare's original work. A similar picture book adaptation of *The Necklace* (de Maupassant, 1993) is also available. Picture book versions of poems are increasingly popular and combine traditional texts with dramatic illustrations. The vivid illustrations in *The Cremation of Sam McGee* (Service, 1986), for example, provide an interesting visual counterpart to this tale of the Yukon during the Gold Rush. While these graphic representations are not meant to replace the works, they can provide struggling readers with a basic understanding of the plot on which they can build by reading the original story.

Illustrated books also deal with individuals who have made significant contributions to the arts. Kathleen Krull's *Lives of the Musicians: Good Times, Bad Times (and What the Neighbors Thought)* (1993) and *Lives of the Artists: Masterpieces, Messes (and What the Neighbors Thought)* (1995) give lighthearted, amusing glimpses of well-known musicians and artists. Each thumbnail sketch is only a few pages long, making them ideal for short read-alouds in music and art classes. Books focusing on individuals, such Jen Bryant's (2013) *A Splash of Red: The Life and Art of Horace Pippin* or Steptoe's (2016) *Radiant Child: The Story of Young Artist Jean-Michel Basquiat* provide greater depth of information on artists while still maintaining engaging visuals and minimal text.

These picture books and countless others can be integrated into different content areas. They can be used with older students as interesting schema builders, anticipatory sets to begin lessons, models for quality writing, motivators for learning, read-alouds, and springboards into discussion and writing. Figure 11.3 provides examples of picture books useful for content area classrooms at all grade levels.

FICTION BOOKS Fiction entices readers to interact with texts from a number of different perspectives that are impossible to achieve in nonfiction alone. Genres such as fantasy, traditional works (e.g., folktales, fables, and myths), historical fiction, and realistic fiction help readers step outside their everyday world for a while to consider a different subject or perspective. In doing so, readers learn to see the world through a different lens, a skill that is necessary for personal and societal change and development and an essential element of 21st-century skills.

For some students, fiction books are better bait than nonfiction books, since expository texts are perceived as too similar to textbooks. In search of new experiences, students tend to read books about protagonists who are the same age or older; rarely do they read books in which the protagonist is younger. Crossover novels, books that appeal to both teenagers and adults and that are marketed to both audiences (Hunt, 2007), have blurred the lines between young adult and adult literature. Crossover novels break from the tradition of young adult fiction through their (1) extended length, (2) sophisticated language, (3) unique narrative formats, (4) challenging vocabulary, (5) inclusion of adult characters, and (6) mature themes and topics. According to Hunt (2007), "The crossover novel requires more serious concentration from young readers and helps move them from the pleasures of light reading to the pleasures of literary reading."

Books such as Khaled Hosseini's (2007) *A Thousand Splendid Suns* and Anthony Doerr's (2014) *All the Light We Cannot See* are good examples of this trend. They demonstrate high standards of literary quality yet appeal to a young adult audience. In recognition of the appeal of the crossover phenomenon, the American Library Association now recognizes 10 adult books annually that have special appeal to teenage readers through its Alex Awards.

Figure 11.3 Picture Books for Middle and High School Classrooms

Aliki. (1999). *William Shakespeare and the Globe.* New York, NY: HarperCollins.

Bunting, E. (1994). *Smoky Night.* Ill. D. Diaz. Orlando, FL: Harcourt Brace.

Burleigh, R. (1997). *Hoops.* Ill. S. T. Johnson. San Diego, CA: Silver Whistle.

Chekhov, A. (1991). *Kashtanka.* Trans. R. Povear. Ill. B. Moser. New York, NY: Putnam.

Coville, B. (1997). *William Shakespeare's* Macbeth. Ill. G. Kelly. New York, NY: Dial.

de Maupassant, G. (1993). *The Necklace.* Ill. G. Kelly. New York, NY: Creative Editions.

Feelings, T. (1995). *The Middle Passage: White Ships/Black Cargo.* New York, NY: Dial.

Fox, M. (2000). *Feathers and Fools.* Ill. N. Wilton. San Diego, CA: Voyager.

Krull, K. (1993). *Lives of the Musicians: Good Times, Bad Times (and What the Neighbors Thought).* Ill. K. Hewitt. San Diego, CA: Harcourt Brace.

Krull, K. (1995). *Lives of the Artists: Masterpieces, Messes (and What the Neighbors Thought).* Ill. K. Hewitt. San Diego, CA: Harcourt Brace.

Krull, K. (1997). *Lives of the Athletes: Thrills, Spills (and What the Neighbors Thought).* Ill. K. Hewitt. San Diego, CA: Harcourt Brace.

Krull, K. (2000). *Wilma Unlimited: How Wilma Rudolph Became the World's Fastest Woman.* Ill. D. Diaz. San Diego, CA: Harcourt Brace.

Krull, K. (2003). *Harvesting Hope: The Story of Cesar Chavez.* San Diego, CA: Harcourt.

Lasky, K. (1994). *The Librarian Who Measured the Earth.* Ill. K. Hawkes. Boston, MA: Little, Brown.

Lasky, K. (2003). *The Man Who Made Time Travel.* Ill. K. Hawkes. New York, NY: Farrar, Straus & Giroux.

Lauber, P. (1996). *Hurricanes: Earth's Mightiest Storms.* New York, NY: Scholastic Press.

Lindbergh, R., & Brown, R. (1992). *A View from the Air: Charles Lindbergh's Earth and Sky.* New York, NY: Viking.

Lowe, S. (1990). *Walden.* Ill. R. Sabuda. New York, NY: Philomel.

Macauley, D. (1973). *Cathedral: The Story of Its Construction.* Boston, MA: Houghton Mifflin.

Macauley, D. (1998). *The New Way Things Work.* Boston, MA: Houghton Mifflin.

Maruki, T. (1980). *Hiroshima No Pika.* New York, NY: Lothrop, Lee & Shepard.

Myers, W. D. (2002). *Patrol: An American Soldier in Vietnam.* New York, NY: HarperCollins.

Garland, S. (1993). *The Lotus Seed.* Ill. T. Kiuchi. San Diego, CA: Harcourt.

Giblin, J. (1994). *Thomas Jefferson: A Picture Book Biography.* Ill. M. Dooling. New York, NY: Scholastic.

Golenbock, P. (1990). *Teammates.* Ill. P. Bacon. San Diego, CA: Harcourt Brace Jovanovich.

Goodall, J. (1979). *The Story of an English Village.* New York, NY: Atheneum.

Hoyt-Goldsmith, D. (1994). *Day of the Dead: A Mexican-American Celebration.* Ill. L. Migdale. New York, NY: Holiday House.

Igus, T. (1998). *I See the Rhythm.* San Francisco, CA: Children's Book Press.

Innocenti, R. (1985). *Rose Blanche.* San Diego, CA: Creative Editions.

Noyes, A. (1983). *The Highwayman.* Ill. C. Mikolaychak. New York, NY: Lothrop, Lee & Shepard.

Peacock, L. (1998). *Crossing the Delaware: A History in Many Voices.* Ill. W. L. Krudop. New York, NY: Atheneum.

Polacco, P. (1994). *Pink and Say.* New York, NY: Scholastic.

Price, L. (1990). *Aida.* Ill. L. & D. Dillon. San Diego, CA: Harcourt Brace.

Rappaport, D. (2001). *Martin's Big Words: The Life of Dr. Martin Luther King, Jr.* Ill. B. Collier. New York, NY: Hyperion.

Raschka, C. (1997). *Mysterious Thelonious.* New York, NY: Orchard.

Ryan, P. M. (2002). *When Marian Sang: The True Recital of Marian Anderson.* Ill. B. Selznick. New York, NY: Scholastic.

Rylant, C. (1984). *Waiting to Waltz: A Childhood.* Ill. S. Gammell. New York, NY: Bradbury.

Say, A. (2002). *Home of the Brave.* Boston, MA: Houghton Mifflin.

Service, R. (1986). *The Cremation of Sam McGee.* Ill. T. Harrison. New York, NY: Greenwillow.

Seuss, Dr. (1984). *The Butter Battle Book.* New York, NY: Random House.

Simon, S. (1990). *Oceans.* New York, NY: Morrow Junior Books.

Stanley, D. (1996). *Leonardo da Vinci.* New York, NY: Morrow.

Stanley, D. (2000). *Michelangelo.* New York, NY: HarperCollins.

Tsuchiya, Y. (1988). *Faithful Elephants: A True Story of People, Animals and War.* Trans. T. Kykes. Ill. Ted Lewin. Boston, MA: Houghton Mifflin.

Van Allsburg, C. (1984). *Mysteries of Harris Burdick.* Boston, MA: Houghton Mifflin.

Wisniewski, D. (1996). *Golem.* New York, NY: Clarion Books.

Yolen, J. (1992). *Encounter.* Ill. D. Shannon. San Diego, CA: Harcourt Brace Jovanovich.

One contributing factor to the increase in fiction reading could be the popularity of movie adaptations. Students tend to read books that have been made into movies. This is easily corroborated in major bookstores; following the release of the movies, bookshelves are stocked with copies of the original texts. Popular young adult books such as *Coraline* (Gaiman, 2006), *Holes* (Sachar, 1998), *Speak* (Anderson, 1999), *The Sisterhood of the Traveling Pants* (Brashares, 2001), *The Fault in Our Stars* (Green, 2012), *The Hate U Give* (Thomas, 2017), *Wonder* (Palacio, 2013), and *Simon vs. the Homo Sapiens Agenda* (Albertalli, 2015) and many more have been made into successful motion pictures. It is relevant to note that there have also been several occasions in which movies have been adapted into books, such as books that have extended the *Star Wars* universe. In the classroom, teachers can encourage critical discussions of the similarities and differences in plot and character development by studying the author's and the film director's decisions.

Currently, fantasy is a hot genre for teens. Stories about vampires, dragons, and superheroes never cease to engage and amaze young adult readers. Although fantasy seems an unlikely addition to the required reading list in a content area classroom, consider the possibilities for a moment. Jane Yolen's series *The Pit Dragon Trilogy* (1996), which takes place on a planet called Austar IV, provides young readers with much to consider about the need to improve and change modern social conditions. Nancy Farmer's (2002) *The House of the Scorpion*, set in a futuristic society, offers a profound perspective on cloning and immigration. We can see ourselves more objectively when we consider our lives from the distance of these stories. In this way, fantasy and science fiction books can serve as a springboard for deeper discussions about big ideas. Dystopian novels, such as the *The Hunger Games* series (Collins, 2008, 2009, and 2010) and the *Divergent* series (Roth, 2011, 2012, and 2013) offer teachers an opportunity to explore social and political structures while showing teenage protagonists working to change their worlds.

Poetry and drama provide fascinating insights into a myriad of topics. From Nikki Grimes's (2002) *Bronx Masquerade*, about urban high school students who share their writing in a poetry slam, to Naomi Shihab Nye's (2002) *19 Varieties of Gazelle: Poems of the Middle East*, these genres provide personal glimpses into the human experience. *A Wreath for Emmett Till*, Marilyn Nelson's (2005) moving tribute to the life of the African American boy who was the victim of a racially motivated murder in 1955, is an extraordinary work. This series of 15 sonnets is multilayered and unsparing in its honesty.

Poetry titles like *Big Talk: Poems for Four Voices* (Fleischman, 2000), *Joyful Noise: Poems for Two Voices* (Fleischman, 1988), and *Math Talk: Mathematical Ideas in Poems for Two Voices* (Pappas, 1993) have real performance potential in the secondary classroom. The poems in each of these titles were designed to be read aloud. English teachers might use these books as models for students to create their own poems in multiple voices. Poetry slams, too, can provide a motivating and interesting way to engage teens in writing and reading their own poetry.

Other texts provide classroom performance opportunities as well. Gary Soto's (1997) *Novio Boy: A Play* is a lighthearted story about young love in a Mexican American community, with realistic characters and familiar situations that students will identify with. Walter Dean Myers's *Monster* (2001) is presented as a screenplay and recounts the life-changing fallout of a young man being in the wrong place at the wrong time. For teachers who do not want to tackle group plays, Chamber Stephens's (2002) *Magnificent Monologues for Teens* provides single-character sketches covering a range of topics of interest to teens. Also, the 2007 Newbery winner *Good Masters! Sweet Ladies!: Voices from a Medieval Village* (Schlitz, 2007) offers a wide range of monologues from the perspectives of medieval youth.

Realistic fiction books run the gamut from problem realism, to sports stories, to mysteries, to adventure, to romance. Young adults have long gravitated toward titles about young people engaged in personal struggles; they like to read stories that reflect their trials and tribulations, real and perceived. For example, *The First Part Last* (Johnson, 2003), the second book in a trilogy, is a powerful novel that describes a teenage father struggling to raise an infant on his own. Renee Watson's (2017) *Piecing Me Together* tells the story of Jade as she struggles to find a way to move beyond the challenges she faces in her neighborhood and make a life for herself through her artwork. *When Zachary Beaver Came to Town* (Holt, 1999) is the poignant story of Toby, a boy in a small Texas town, who befriends Zachary, "the world's fattest boy," and discovers that his own problems are not as bad as they seem. *Jerk, California* (Friesen, 2008) describes a teenage boy who survives the torment of living with Tourette's syndrome and discovers the truth about his real father and a family he has never known.

The popularity and demand for "edgy" books, ones that address serious subjects such as sex, drugs, abuse, and so on, suggest that today's young people crave books that speak to them and not about them or for them. Teens want to read authentic stories about real dramas and traumas. *Go Ask Alice* (Anonymous, 1971) has compelled young readers for more than four decades with its story of a teen addict whose life is spiraling out of control. *Impulse* by Ellen Hopkins (2008) reveals the inner turmoil of three teens placed in a psychiatric hospital after failed suicide attempts. *Speak* by Laurie Halse Anderson (1999) is about a girl dealing with date rape. *Skud* (2004) by Dennis Foon addresses male violence, and *Paranoid Park* (2008) by Blake Nelson is about an accidental homicide. Award-winning novelist Jason Reynolds has eloquently dealt with these issues in many of his novels. In *Long Way Down* (2017), 15-year-old Will sets out to avenge the death of his brother and runs into several people who force him to question his actions. *Ghost* (2016) is the first in the *Track* series and features a middle school student who uses track to come to terms with family issues and determine the type of man he wants to be.

Realistic fiction is a perennial teen favorite. Historical fiction, while less popular, has the potential to give the past a pulse. Historical fiction can put a human face on history in ways that textbooks cannot. Through vicarious involvement in the lives of characters who never actually existed but who are placed in times and places that actually did, teens can participate in the most triumphant or the most terrible moments in history. Laurie Halse Anderson's (2000) *Fever 1793* is a dramatic account of a little-known historical event, the yellow fever epidemic in Philadelphia, and demonstrates how a young woman's strength of character helped her survive events that turn her world upside down. Markus Zusak's (2007) *The Book Thief* reveals a compelling story of Nazi Germany during World War II, as narrated by Death. Another extraordinary book set during the time of the Holocaust is *The Boy in the Striped Pajamas* (Boyne, 2006), the unlikely story of a friendship between two children in a concentration camp, one an inmate and one the child of the commandant. Rita Williams-Garcia's trilogy *One Crazy Summer* (2011), *P.S. Be Eleven* (2015), and *Gone Crazy in Alabama* (2016) shine a light on the civil rights movement through the eyes of the three young Gaither sisters. Set in the late 1960s, the sisters experience the movement of the Black Panther Party while spending the summer with their estranged mother in California. In the next novel, the girls return to Brooklyn with a better understanding of the world. In the final novel, we see the whole family return to Alabama and a varied perspective of racial relationships in the South. Through these three Gaither sisters, readers are able to get a glimpse of their experience during this troubled time. This is historical fiction at its best—moving stories of the power of family and friendship.

Many worthy works of fiction are found on the annual *Young Adults' Choices List*, sponsored by the International Literacy Association. This list reflects the book choices of teens themselves, including titles dealing with social and political issues, such as drunk driving, equal rights, racial injustice, death, and war. The host of fiction books available can do much to enhance and clarify the content curriculum. An author's ability to bring lifelike characters into sharp focus against a real-world setting results in compelling reading. Showing students how authors use different points of view toward history is explored in Box 11.4.

Books for Reluctant Readers

Meeting the needs of reluctant readers is a perennial challenge for all teachers. Now more than ever before, however, there are easy-to-read titles on a range of topics relevant to today's content area classroom. In addition to picture books, reluctant readers often respond positively to high-interest, low-ability books, short books (those with fewer than 100 pages), series books, and graphic novels.

Short but intriguing fiction titles such as *Stuck in Neutral* (Trueman, 2001) are sure to captivate those readers who do not readily connect with books. Shawn McDaniel, the main character and narrator of the story, has cerebral palsy and cannot walk, talk, or focus his eyes. As the story progresses, the reader comes to understand the strange world that Shawn inhabits, a world rich with experiences that he is unable to communicate to

Box 11.4 Evidence-Based Best Practices

Exploring Different Points of View Toward Historical Events

The use of trade books and articles can help expose students to a variety of perspectives in relationship to historical events. Students typically study world explorers as part of social studies at both the middle and high school levels. The use of multiple texts can offer perspectives about historical events beyond those provided in the textbook. By experiencing a wide variety of texts, students can reflect on the ways in which history is not only reported but also interpreted by writers. Consider, for example, the events surrounding Christopher Columbus's discovery of the New World. Trade books and articles from the historical fiction, nonfiction, and picture book genres provide dramatically different portrayals of that event and allow students to gather information to critically reflect on history.

Social studies teacher Robert Wells involves his students in examining these different points of view. He uses six different biographies and historical fiction titles for this lesson. Two of these are *Pedro's Journal* (Conrad, 1991), a fictionalized account of Columbus's voyage narrated by Pedro, a ship's boy who accompanied Columbus on his journey, and Jane Yolen's

Encounter (1992), an account of Columbus's arrival told from the point of view of a Taino Indian boy.

Robert divides students into groups based on the books they are reading and directs students to look at each book's account of the events of October 12, 1492. He focuses groups' reading, asking them to think about the following questions as they read: What are the events that take place as Columbus lands? What is the author's point of view toward Columbus? How does the author describe the native people Columbus meets? What is Columbus's attitude toward the natives?

After students have read their books, Robert leads the whole class in completing a data chart that compares the answers to the questions found in each of the books. The students then engage in a discussion about why the accounts of the same events are different. They reflect on the sources each author used to create the account as well as the reasons authors who consulted the same sources might provide different accounts. Through this discussion, students gain understanding of the idea of history as interpretation rather than fact.

others. As the story progresses, Shawn becomes increasingly concerned about his father's attitude toward him, and he panics when he begins to think that his father is considering killing him to stop his suffering. This moving book raises a number of issues related to euthanasia and is sure to provoke interesting discussions. In *A Monster Calls* (2011) by Patrick Ness, realistic fiction and fantasy meld as young Conor tries to come to terms with his mother's illness while dealing with nightly visits from the enigmatic Monster. The beautiful but haunting illustrations help pull the reader into the story as Conor tries to figure out why the Monster comes to him.

Dozens of other fiction and nonfiction titles can captivate reluctant readers. In *Thirteen Reasons Why* (Asher, 2007), Hannah, a teenage girl, sends her classmate a package of cassette tapes that explain her recent suicide. Clay, the narrator who is the last in a series of students Hannah has asked to review the tapes, and other teens within her circle of friends are forced to consider how their actions may have contributed to her death. Readers are able to see events from Hannah's perspectives as she explains her "reasons," but they can also gain insight from Clay as he hears the tapes and talks to his classmates to pull together what really happened. Series books continue to have great appeal for reluctant readers as students become familiar with a cast of characters and story lines and continue reading to learn what happens; fantasy and romance titles are particularly popular with teens who may not love to read. Fantasy novels allow readers to completely escape their everyday experiences and enter a completely different world. The *Star Wars, Cirque du Freak, Circle of Magic,* and *Young Wizards* series help satisfy teen interests in fantasy. The *Luxe* series, teen romance books set at the turn of the century, is popular with female teen readers. Reluctant readers are often drawn to the *Bluford High* series, which follows a collection of students in an inner-city high school as they face a variety of personal and academic challenges. Informational series such as Dorling Kindersley's *Eyewitness Books* are extremely appealing to students who enjoy reading about the real world.

Graphic novels are an incredibly rich resource for reluctant readers. Graphic novels employ sophisticated relationships among words and images that can promote critical thinking in ways that words alone cannot. They can be particularly useful for students who find it difficult to visualize what is happening in a text; the graphics support the text and help students get at the meaning. They can also be useful for those students who reject the texts typically found in classrooms. Students attracted to the highly stylized graphics will be drawn into the story. The unique combination of the visual and verbal may be the catalyst that turns a reluctant reader into a ravenous one. Finally, for students who are "Generation Visual" (Lyga, 2004)—that is, they spend most of their time "wired" in some way, whether playing video games or exploring social media—these books can provide a familiar visual format.

Graphic novels can engage students in both fictional and factual topics, particularly when they are as well written as Art Spiegelman's (1986) *Maus: A Survivor's Tale*. In this book, the story of the Holocaust is vividly told with the Nazis depicted as cats and the Jewish people as mice. Rather than detracting from the seriousness of the subject, the cartoon format lends force to the plight of the Nazis' victims. More recent graphic novels that are popular with students include *American Born Chinese* (Yang, 2008), which won the highly coveted Michael L. Printz award for young adult literature. This sophisticated text is made up of three individual plotlines: one focused on Chinese folk hero Monkey King; one focused on Jin Wang, an Asian American middle school student who doesn't fit in at school; and one focused on the plight of Danny, a teenager shamed by his Chinese cousin. Gareth Hinds's (2007) *Beowulf* uses full-color illustrations and mixed media to relate this legendary story to a modern audience. *Malcolm X: A Graphic Biography* (Helfer, 2006) describes the events of its subject's life with drama and conflict.

MyLab Education Self-Check 11.2

MyLab Education Application Exercise 11.2:
Linking Content Area Instruction with Literacy Learning

Instructional Strategies for Using Trade Books and Articles

11.3   Describe the different ways trade books can be incorporated into classroom practices.

A study of exemplary content area instruction found a key commonality among effective teachers: All of them used multiple texts with a range of formats and difficulty levels (Allington & Johnston, 2002). These teachers capitalized on the myriad uses for trade books and articles in the content area classroom and used them to enhance and extend students' content area literacy learning. This section will identify ways that teachers can organize students for literature study. Virtually all of these ways of using literature can enhance objectives for student learning in every content area.

Creating Classroom Libraries and Text Sets

Several key components are necessary to create a multitext content area classroom. First and foremost, content area teachers need to acquire books and articles related to their content area. These resources can be used to stock classroom libraries, both for large- and small-group reading and for individual inquiry. Locating texts for these purposes is always a challenge, but resourceful teachers have found that library book sales, garage sales, and book clubs such as Scholastic and Trumpet are good resources for obtaining inexpensive books. E-books are also a good option, as they are often less expensive than print versions and can be readily available both in the classroom and at home. Many public libraries offer instant access to a wide variety of e-books, allowing families and teachers to supplement their library. Databases such as Project Gutenberg offer access to texts within the public domain, offering readers many titles, both new and from the traditional canon of literature.

A classroom library is a critical component of a multitext classroom. By creating a classroom library of texts at a range of reading levels and in a variety of genres including picture books, poetry, historical fiction, biography, and informational, teachers increase students' access to books and help motive them to learn. Other resources, such as magazines and newspapers, are equally appropriate for inclusion in a content area classroom library. To meet the diverse reading needs and interests of today's students, as well as the variety of ways that trade books and articles can be used in the content area classrooms, classroom libraries should include a wide range of titles, addressing a variety of topics and reading levels. In addition, digital classroom libraries can be set up through class webpages or Google sites and include links to e-books and digital copies of texts.

What kinds of books might be found in a classroom library in an American history class? Good choices include survey books about history such as *A History of US* (Hakim, 1999), the highly acclaimed series by Joy Hakim that speaks directly to students about historical events using a conversational style. Historical fiction, for example Avi's (2008) *The Seer of Shadows*, combines history with a thrilling story, in this case, the Victorian obsession with the spirit world and a photographer who hatches a scheme to get rich quick by exploiting that obsession. Titles by authors such as Ann Rinaldi and Russell Freedman could add to this collection. The nonfiction *5,000 Miles to Freedom: Ellen and William Craft's Flight from Slavery* (Fradin & Fradin, 2006) uses photographs, letters, and newspaper accounts to document the true adventure of the Crafts as they escaped from slavery to freedom in the North. Easy-to-read picture book biographies, such as *The Amazing Life of Benjamin Franklin* (Giblin, 2000), also have a place in the classroom library. Hundreds of informational titles could round out such a collection, including books by renowned young adult authors like Jim Murphy and many others.

However, these titles, excellent as they are, might not appeal to less motivated students. Middle and high school students enjoy books with humor and comic books. For that reason, the teacher might consider *Cartoon History of the United States* (Gonick, 1991), a satirical vision of American history. The *Who Was?* series is a collection of illustrated biographies of people of historical or pop-culture significance. They present accurate information about the subjects in short texts combined with humorous illustrations to engage readers. Other amusing titles, including *So You Want to Be President?* (St. George, 2000) and *Explorers Who Got Lost* (Sansevere-Dreher, Dreher, & Renfro, 1994), debunk some of the myths about our presidents and famous explorers of the past. Magazines like *National Geographic World, Cobblestone*, or *Time for Kids* could round out such a collection.

In addition to a range of titles broadly related to a content area discipline, teachers will want to create text sets related more specifically to particular units of study within a content area. Text sets involve assembling a variety of titles that span a range of difficulty levels and include a range of resources, including books as well as other sources such as magazines, websites, newspaper articles, and so on. A sample text set related to the Civil War appears in Figure 11.4. These text sets can be used in myriad ways: for independent, self-selected reading, individual inquiry, or idea circles.

Sustained Silent Reading

Organized, systematic efforts to make independent reading central in the lives of students are essential. Such experiences can create adolescents who want to continue reading after the bell has rung and "read like a wolf eats," as author Gary Paulsen describes the ravenous hunger for books that consumes book lovers. All too often, in today's standardized test-driven culture, we forget the importance of independent reading. Hundreds of studies document the fact that the more time students spend reading, the higher their reading achievement. To encourage reading and demonstrate its importance, many secondary schools provide uninterrupted time for **sustained silent reading**, sometimes referred to as SSR time or DEAR (Drop Everything and Read). At one San Diego high school, a

Figure 11.4 Text Set on the Civil War

Picture Books

Ackerman, N. (1990). *The Tin Heart*. Ill. Michael Hays. New York, NY: Atheneum. This picture book describes the effect of the Civil War on the friendship of two young girls who live on opposite sides of the Mason-Dixon line.

Lyon, G. E. (1991). *Cecil's Story*. Ill. P. Catalanotto. New York, NY: Orchard. A picture book title that describes the apprehensions of a young boy whose father may need to leave home to serve in the Civil War.

Turner, A. (1987). *Nettie's Trip South*. Ill. Ron Himler. New York, NY: Macmillan. A young girl travels south during the 1850s and discovers first-hand the horrors of slavery.

Winter, J. (1992). *Follow the Drinking Gourd*. New York, NY: Dragonfly. Slaves escape to freedom through the lyrics of a folk song that provide directions for following the Underground Railroad.

Plays

Davis, O. (1978). *Escape to Freedom: A Play About Frederick Douglass*. New York, NY: Viking Penguin. This compelling play exposes young readers to the incredible life of Frederick Douglass.

Nonfiction

Armstrong, J. (2005). *Photo by Brady: A Picture of the Civil War*. New York, NY: Atheneum. Armstrong tells the fascinating story of the life of Brady and his indelible mark on history.

Fleming, T. (1988). *Band of Brothers: West Point in the Civil War*. New York, NY: Walker. Describes men who were friends and classmates at West Point and later served in the Civil War, often fighting against one another.

Lester, J. (1968). *To Be a Slave*. Ill. T. Feelings. New York, NY: Dial Press. Using the actual words of his subjects, Lester portrays life as it existed for slaves in this country.

Murphy, J. (1990). *The Boys' War: Confederate and Union Soldiers Talk About the Civil War*. New York, NY: Clarion Books. Diaries, letters, and original photographs tell the story of young boys who participated in the Civil War.

Folktales

Hamilton, V. (1985). *The People Could Fly*. Ill. L. & D. Dillon. New York, NY: Knopf. A collection of American Black folktales narrated in authentic dialect.

Nolen, J. (2005). *Big Jabe*. Ill. Kadir Nelson. New York, NY: Amistad. A tall tale about an African American baby who improves life for the slaves on a plantation.

Historical Fiction

Hahn, M. D. (2003). *Hear the Wind Blow*. New York, NY: Clarion Books. The story of a 13-year-old Virginia boy whose life is changed forever when a Confederate soldier he hides in his home is discovered by the Yankees.

Hansen, J. (1986). *Which Way Freedom?* New York, NY: Walker. Describes the life of an escaped slave who serves in the Civil War.

Hunt, I. (1964). *Across Five Aprils*. New York, NY: Follett. Describes how the Creighton family of southern Illinois struggled with the impact of the Civil War.

Reeder, C. (1989). *Shades of Gray*. New York, NY: Macmillan. Twelve-year-old Will Page, the orphaned son of a Confederate soldier, must live with his Uncle Jed, who refused to fight for the Confederacy.

Silvey, A. (2008). *I'll Pass for Your Comrade: Women Soldiers in the Civil War*. New York, NY: Atheneum. Describes the women who posed as men to fight in the Civil War and how they coped with daily life as soldiers in a world dominated by men.

Warren, A. (2009). *Under Siege: Three Children at the Civil War Battle for Vicksburg*. New York, NY: Farrar, Straus & Giroux. Uses primary sources to tell the story of children who survived this battle by living in a cave.

Websites

American Memory—Primary Source Photographs of the Civil War

The Civil War Home Page—Comprehensive Website Related to the Civil War

---

separate 25-minute period is allocated each day for sustained silent reading time. During this time, everyone—teachers, students, and even custodial workers at the school site—reads. Uninterrupted sustained silent reading time lets students practice reading and read for their own purposes and pleasure. Students self-select materials other than their textbooks. They can read books, magazines, or newspapers from home or obtain texts from the school or classroom library that relate to personal interests.

Providing access to a range of text types during sustained silent reading time can increase student motivation for reading because it involves letting students read about topics of interest to them. Silent reading of self-selected books is an effective way to promote the type of engaged reading that has been shown to increase achievement (Guthrie, Schafer, & Huang, 2001; Merga, 2018).

Simply providing time for SSR, however, may not be sufficient to ensure that students benefit from this time. Pilgreen (2000) identifies eight factors of SSR success: (1) access to books, (2) appealing books that address student interests, (3) classroom environments that encourage reading as a social activity, (4) encouragement from teachers and parents, (5) staff training in SSR, (6) reduce the use of tests of knowledge or book reports, (7) follow-up activities that can encourage further reading, and (8) distributed time to read that includes short periods of 15 to 20 minutes at least twice a week. Fisher (2004) argues that SSR programs should not consist of isolated instances in which certain teachers engage students in reading, but rather need to be schoolwide initiatives that represent a larger emphasis on staff development, collaboration between teachers and students, and effective administrative leadership.

Effective sustained silent reading programs have a number of benefits:

- They increase the amount of time students spend reading during the school day.
- They help students develop interest in a subject.
- They build knowledge that helps students read and learn more about a topic.
- They provide a basis for researching a particular topic.
- They familiarize students with different formats and genres used to report information that can be models for their own research and writing (Worthy, Broaddus, & Ivey, 2001).

Teacher Read-Alouds

Students in Maria's ninth-grade English class read excerpts from *The Diary of Anne Frank* (Frank, 1967) in their literature anthology every year. This year she decided to enrich her students' study of the diary by reading aloud the informational book *Anne Frank: Beyond the Diary* (van der Rol & Verhoeven, 1993). This visually appealing text contains background on the Frank family, including their move from Germany to Amsterdam, photographs of the diary itself, artifacts, maps of the "secret annex," and a heartbreaking primary source document—the Nazis' typewritten list of Frank family members targeted for arrest. Maria described her use of the book in the following way:

> Before my students start reading the diary, I read aloud Chapters 1 and 2. These chapters provide important background about Anne's life and information about Hitler's rise to power. I put the map of the "secret annex" that appears in the book on the document camera to give students a spatial understanding of the place where the Franks and the van Daans lived. Then my students read the diary. After they've completed their reading of the diary, I read chapters that describe how the Frank family was arrested and the later discovery of the diary. Finally, I read the section of the book that describes Anne's life after the arrest at the concentration camp at Bergen Belsen. After each reading, I passed the book around so that students could more closely examine the photographs. They were very interested in the book. I put several copies of the book in the classroom library, and several students read it on their own after reading the diary.

This example demonstrates several purposes that content area read-alouds can accomplish. First, **read-alouds** can provide important background information that enhances student understanding of assigned readings. Maria's use of the map of the secret annex, for example, helped students visualize the setting for Anne Frank's experiences. Secondly, the read-aloud extended and enhanced the content in the diary itself by describing the rest of Anne Frank's tragic story. Third, reading aloud can spur student interest in a topic. After hearing a book read aloud, students are much more likely to pick up books on this topic, and related ones, on their own. If the read-aloud is from a picture book, the illustrations can further support students' understanding by providing a visual representation of concepts and content.

Reading aloud is considered by many experts to be the single most important activity in developing student literacy ability, regardless of age. Reading aloud provides literary experiences in a supportive context and exposure to the various forms of written language, both narrative and expository. As students listen to literature, they subconsciously absorb its rhythms, structures, and cadences. Teachers can model these qualities during a read-aloud and support students' ability to mimic this rich reading internally while reading silently. Read-alouds give struggling readers access to information in the more difficult texts commonly used in content area classrooms; teachers can introduce and model the correct pronunciation of new content-specific words and elaborate on content through discussion. With digital access increasing, students can experience read-alouds both in and out of the classroom. Not only do many websites offer text-to-voice options, but teachers also have additional opportunities via the Web to incorporate technology that allows for "flipped" classrooms and prerecorded readings. In reverse, many educational websites offer transcripts of instructional videos, allowing students to view the content and refer to the transcript later to reinforce understanding.

In addition, read-alouds provide a way for teachers to demonstrate for students the mental processes used to make sense of what they are reading. These processes can become evident to students through many of the strategies described in this book, including think-alouds, directed reading–listening activities, and many others. Read-aloud experiences should go beyond brief isolated experiences during which the teacher reads and students listen. These "bigger" read-aloud experiences should be interactive, with students actively engaged in thinking, questioning, clarifying, and summarizing texts (Ivey, 2002). Teachers can build schema and develop metacognition while reading. Finally, read-alouds provide opportunities for response to literature that can lead to engagement and further understanding of content. These will be described in the following section.

Based on hundreds of read-aloud experiences, Barbara Erickson (1996) offers the following guidelines for middle and high school teachers who wish to incorporate reading aloud in their classes:

- Hold students' interest
- Stimulate discussion
- Reflect authors from many cultures
- Match the social and emotional levels of the listeners

Erickson also suggests that teachers prepare for read-alouds carefully by first practicing the work. She recommends that initial read-alouds last no longer than 15 minutes to capitalize on the active attention of students. Furthermore, she advocates using pictures and props to heighten student interest and increase understanding of text content.

Read-alouds can include books from a variety of genres, including poetry, short stories, fiction, nonfiction, magazine articles, or even plays. Sharon Creech's (2001) *Love That Dog* is a perfect read-aloud for an English class; it uses free verse to explore the ways that poetry helps a young boy express his grief about losing his beloved dog. Similarly, Jacqueline Woodson's (2014) *Brown Girl Dreaming* is an autobiography in verse. The text lends itself to both social studies and language arts as the author uses descriptive language in free verse to tell of her childhood in the 1960s, comparing her time in the South to her life in New York as she comes to realize her value as a writer. The poetic picture book *I See the Rhythm* (Igus, 1998) is an ideal music class read-aloud. This stunning book traces the history of African American music through dramatic visuals and rhythmic poetry. An outstanding read-aloud for a world history class studying ancient civilizations is *Bodies from the Ash* (Deem, 2005). This title provides fascinating glimpses of life in ancient Pompeii, based on the clues provided by the plaster-cast remains of the unfortunate men, women, and children who died there.

At the beginning of a science lesson, an excerpt from a book read aloud to the class or a picture book can provide an enjoyable preview of the lesson's contents. In this way, trade books play a supporting role by introducing a part of our perspective on the lesson that entices students to want to learn more. The verbal imagery of the text or the visual stimuli of picture books appeal to all age groups and should help to activate schemata that are crucial to further learning. For example, an excellent introduction to a study of the planets is Elaine Scott's (2007) *When Is a Planet Not a Planet? The Story of Pluto*. In this clearly written text, she outlines the history of the discovery of the planets and compares the work of scientists today with those of the past. Her explanation of modern-day scientists' skepticism surrounding Pluto's status as a planet and their development of new

definitions for the term provide current information about what constitutes of a planet and the existence of dwarf planets.

Read-alouds need not be cover to cover. Reading excerpts from books, magazines, newspaper articles, or webpages can sometimes be more effective than longer read-alouds. "Bits and pieces" read-alouds include reading picture captions from nonfiction titles to provide "sneak previews" of books. Short read-alouds focusing on biographical profiles from any of the Kathleen Krull *Lives of* books, for example, can provide an engaging way to interest students in artists, musicians, presidents, and so on.

Group Models for Studying Trade Books

As teachers become increasingly convinced of the value of using literature in content area classrooms, they will want students to experience literature in increasingly varied ways. They may decide that students can benefit from "breaking out" of the textbook to engage in reading trade books and articles, or they may use literature in connection with units of study. Many teachers use the additional time provided by block scheduling to engage students in reading and discussing trade books. One of the most challenging aspects of using literature in the classroom—whether fiction or nonfiction—is grouping students for instruction. The grouping pattern of choice depends on the teacher's and students' goals and purposes for using the literature. The following sections will explain four different grouping models that teachers might wish to use as they involve students in studying content-related literature.

WHOLE-GROUP/SINGLE-BOOK MODEL   Sometimes teachers want all students in a class to have a common reading experience centered on the same book. On these occasions, they may use a whole-group model in which all students read the same book. Science teacher Ken Blake wanted to extend his textbook's treatment of outer space and space travel. He decided to involve his students in reading *Team Moon: How 400,000 People Landed Apollo 11 on the Moon* (Thimmesh, 2006).

Because this was the first time he had used literature to supplement the textbook, he decided to use the whole-group/single-book model. He purchased 25 copies of the book, and each student read the book. Students then participated in large- and small-group discussions about a variety of topics, including the work of the astronauts during the flight and the discoveries they made as they explored the moon. Students also compared and contrasted information in their textbook to that found in this book. They considered the challenges posed by the expedition and debated the importance of sending astronauts for further explorations of the moon. This process increased students' understanding of content while building critical thinking skills in asking students to synthesize information from multiple sources, and it applied their learning to classroom discussion and debate.

SMALL-GROUPS/MULTIPLE-BOOKS MODEL   A second model for using literature is the small-groups/multiple-books model. With this model, students work in small groups to read different books related to a common theme. In using multiple texts, teachers can find resources that support different interests or perspectives on the topic, find materials that meet a range of reading levels, and supports students' competency with a variety of text types. Alan Trent used multiple copies of several fiction and nonfiction titles to supplement textbook content and enrich his students' study of the Civil War. Students formed groups based on their selection of one of four different books: *Hear the Wind Blow* (Hahn, 2003), *The War Within: A Novel of the Civil War* (Matas, 2001), *Fields of Fury: The American Civil War* (McPherson, 2002), and *The Boys' War: Confederate and Union Soldiers Talk About the Civil War* (Murphy, 1990). Students read and discussed each title in their small groups over a 2-week period. Using the jigsaw strategy, students then formed new groups in which they shared their information. They then shared the information obtained from one another with the larger group through creative extensions, including projects, dramatic presentations, and debates.

INDIVIDUAL INQUIRY MODEL   Individual inquiry is an increasingly popular method to involve students in research by letting them explore issues of personal interest related to the topic. As part of inquiry experiences, students generate ideas and questions and pose problems. Through their research projects, students investigate topics and collect, analyze, and organize information. Students later share this information through a project or report. By using several sources about the same topic, students can examine multiple points of view and evaluate the accuracy of information. Individualized projects also allow teachers to differentiate instruction based on student needs. Students can access texts at varying abilities or in different languages to allow them to comprehend content. By offering students autonomy in their choice of topics and resources, motivation and engagement are increased.

Inquiry projects can combine fiction with nonfiction. In an inquiry project with high school students, English teacher Joan Kaywell (1994) linked fiction and nonfiction books. Her class first generated a list of problems affecting today's teens, such as anorexia nervosa, stress, suicide, pregnancy, sexual abuse, and so on. The class narrowed the number of topics to five and formed inquiry groups based on each topic. At this point, each student in a group selected and read a different young adult novel related to the identified problem.

After reading their novels, students used nonfiction materials to conduct research about the problem posed in their novel. Each student found at least one nonfiction source and cited a minimum of ten facts related to the topic. Students then reconvened in small groups where they pooled these facts and selected 25 facts to be included in an information sheet about the problem. They discussed source credibility, recency, and relevancy of information as they narrowed down their lists. They then presented this information to the larger group.

Elizabeth Wein's *Code Name Verity* (2012) tells the story of two young women involved in the combat of World War II. While reading this thriller, students can investigate the politics and parties involved in World War II and the role women play in conflicts such as these. This type of interdisciplinary instruction allows teachers to capitalize on students' interest and support connections in learning.

MyLab Education **Self-Check 11.3**

MyLab Education Application Exercise 11.3:
Grouping Students for Studying Trade Books

Reader Response Strategies

11.4 Describe the different ways in which students can respond to what they read, including how each supports the comprehension of content knowledge.

Reader response refers to the way a person reacts to hearing or reading a piece of literature. It describes the unique interaction that occurs between a reader's mind and heart and a particular literary text (Hancock, 2007; Gillis, 2014). Reader responses are dynamic, fluid, and varied. Different readers construct different meanings from texts; no two readers interpret the same work in the same way.

Why should content area teachers be interested in responses to literature? Research suggests that students grow in several different areas when engaged in response-based activities:

- They develop ownership of their reading and their responses.
- They make personal connections with literature.

- They gain appreciation for multiple interpretations and tolerance for ambiguity.
- They become more critical readers and attain higher levels of thinking and richer understanding of literature.
- They increase their repertoire of responses to literature.
- They begin to view themselves as successful readers.
- They develop greater awareness of the literary quality of a work (Spiegel, 1998).

Involving students in response to literature can help content area teachers meet many important goals related to developing student thinking skills. Response activities can help to develop critical thinkers: Students who can examine different sides of an argument respond more thoughtfully to texts and more thoroughly understand the ways texts work.

Response-centered classrooms can help students grow in their understanding and appreciation of nonfiction just as surely as fiction. Teachers often assume that nonfiction literature will elicit only efferent responses, but studies have found that readers do respond aesthetically to nonfiction (Hancock, 2007). Effective teachers guide students' responses to biographies and informational books in ways that encourage students to appreciate both information in and experience of reading. By providing a supportive context and engaging activities that promote both oral and written responses, teachers can extend and deepen students' literary experiences with both nonfiction and fiction.

The rest of this chapter is devoted to examples of instructional strategies teachers can use to promote responses to literature. Strategies for promoting responses range from writing to drama to inquiry-driven idea circles. All of the strategies described are designed to help teachers encourage meaningful student responses, both aesthetic and efferent, to the excellent literature available today. Through reader response experiences, students can make personal connections between texts and their lives, reflect on what these books have to teach them, and deepen their involvement with literature.

Writing as a Reader Response

Writing in response to reading, whether fiction or nonfiction, allows learners to share their thoughts and feelings about a text. It can help students construct meanings of texts at the same time it improves writing fluency. Writing in response to nonfiction can evoke feelings and enhance learning of text content. As noted in Chapter 9, "writing to learn" can help students think about what they will be reading or reflect on what has been read. It can improve understanding of difficult concepts, increase retention of information, prompt learners to elaborate on and manipulate ideas, and help them gain insight into the author's craft. Notice in Figure 11.5 how a high school English teacher uses the RAFT writing-to-learn strategy to help students think more deeply about trade books and articles they have been reading related to a unit on Shakespeare's *Macbeth*. RAFT, as you recall from Chapter 9, is a strategy that helps students understand their role as writer, their audience, the format of their work, and the topic of their writing.

A variety of written response activities encourages students to think in different ways. This process also supports students' metacognition to recognize how much of the text they understand and areas in which they need clarification. Some response activities described in this section focus on helping students respond emotionally to texts, others on helping them process information or record what they have learned. Some of the activities are formal, while others are informal in nature.

REFLECTIVE WRITING One of the many excellent ideas presented in Stephanie Harvey and Anne Goudvis's (2017) *Strategies That Work* is the idea of asking students to use writing to reflect on the mental connections they make between the texts they are reading and their own lives. As students grow in sophistication, they develop the

Figure 11.5 RAFT Writing-to-Learn Strategy for *Macbeth* Unit

Role	Audience	Format	Topic
Writer	Readers of Bruce Coville's *William Shakespeare's* Macbeth	Narrative	Create text to accompany Coville's pictorial depiction telling the story of *Macbeth* from the perspective of one of the following characters: Macbeth, Lady Macbeth, or one of Banquo's future kings. Write original narrative using original dialogue from the play; text must match Coville's visuals.
Felance	Facebook readers	Facebook page	Construct a Facebook page as Felance that is read by the villagers in Macbeth's kingdom. Include residents' posts and friends' replies regarding Macbeth's rule and the events that occur as a result of his greed. Use Goodall's *The Story of an English Village* to ensure that you are writing to your audience and your inferences match the context of the time period.
TMZ celebrity reporter	Internet webpage readers	Online article	Plan a celebrity-style news article exposing the Macbeths and investigating the changes that occurred as a result of Macbeth's rule. Also comment on the murder and mayhem that marked his rise to power. Compare Alan Bold's *Scotland's Kings & Queens* historical accounts with Macbeth's actions and reign.
MTV director	Renaissance television viewers	Storyboard with script	Compose a newscast to be played on local MTV stations providing warnings about the Black Death and identifying symptoms and methods of prevention. In a "special report" illustrating connections to modern plagues, predict the effect of a new plague of your creation. Use Giblin's *When Plague Strikes: The Black Death, Smallpox, AIDS* to guide your work.
Artist	Globe Theater attendees	Symbolic artistic representation	Interpret the plot, theme, tone, and character emotions in Shakespeare's *Macbeth*. Using Aliki's *William Shakespeare and the Globe*, design a piece of symbolic artwork that would be present on the stage as scenery.

ability to recognize the mental connections they make between the texts they read and other texts as well as between the texts they are reading and the wider world. Harvey and Goudvis refer to these connections as *text-to-self, text-to-text*, and *text-to-world* connections, respectively, and are necessary for higher-order thinking during reading. It is possible for students to make these connections with books from any genre.

Text-to-self connections arise when readers feel personal connections with text events or characters' emotions. Harvey and Goudvis recommend using memoirs or realistic fiction to help students develop skills in making text-to-self connections because reader identification with characters can be particularly strong in these types of texts. Saying "It reminds me of ..." can prompt students to reflect on these types of connections.

Text-to-text connections involve connecting ideas across texts. The concept of *text* can be broadened here; students might connect text content to a work of art, movie, or song. These connections include comparing characters' personalities and actions, story events and plot lines, and lesson themes or messages in stories; finding common themes, writing styles, or perspectives in an author's work; and comparing the treatment of common themes by different authors. Teachers can present multiple versions of the same story or event and compare how the representations are similar or different and explore how the perspective of the author or artist influenced their writing.

Text-to-world connections are the most sophisticated connections students can make. With these types of connections, students reflect on the relationship between the content of the text and the wider world. This could include connections related to current or past world events, issues, or concerns. These connections support students' understanding of the relevance of content and encourages engagement by provoking students to question the cause and repercussions of events as they make comparisons to the text.

POST-IT NOTES   Harvey recommends that teachers use think-alouds and other text demonstrations to model for students how readers naturally create these connections. After this modeling occurs, students can begin to record the various kinds of connections on Post-it Notes as they read, jotting down words or phrases that explain the thoughts or feelings that occur to them as they read. As they read and record these connections, students can code text-to-self connections (T–S), text-to-text connections (T–T), and text-to-world connections (T–W). Students should not focus solely on recording and categorizing their connections but should reflect on how the connection has led them to a greater understanding of the text. These notes can serve as the basis for rich after reading discussions about the kinds of thinking students have done as they read. In addition, these notes can often evolve into longer written pieces.

Post-its are also an effective tool for posing questions during reading. According to Zywica and Gomez (2008), annotating text while reading supports comprehension. If students have questions or concerns as they read, they can quickly place the note directly next to the text. This allows students to go back after reading to see if their questions have been answered or if they need to do additional reading. By placing these notes in the text, students have quick and direct access to the information and can use these notes as the basis of inquiry or as a study tool.

Expository Texts as Models for Writing

Students need a variety of writing experiences in the classroom, including experience in writing nonnarrative texts. One way to involve students in informational writing is by having them use information trade books and articles as models or mentor texts for their own writing. These books can serve as models for brief, short-term writing experiences or extended, long-term experiences. Within content areas, they can provide examples for speaking within a discipline. Articles from science journals show how scientists communicate. Primary documents from history include language and structure reflective of that time. In order to communicate effectively in any discipline, students need exposure to how experts write.

The Important Book (Brown, 1949), though a picture book, can serve as a model for information writing in many content areas. Each paragraph of this book states an important characteristic or main idea about a common object. This trait is followed by supporting details that further enhance the description of the object and then a restatement of the main idea. Leslie Hughes, a middle school science teacher, used this text structure during a review of a unit on oceans. The teacher read the model to the class and provided students with the following text frame:

The important thing about _____ is _____.

Students then formed writing groups and were assigned particular topics related to oceans. They identified the main idea related to their topic and inserted it into the text frame. They provided supporting details and concluded the writing with a restatement of the main idea. An example of one student's effort follows:

The important thing about a tide pool is that it contains a community of plants and animals. Tide pools are left in rocky basins and shallow hollows as low tide causes ocean water to go back out to sea. These basins of sea water contain plants, crabs, periwinkles, and other plant and animal life. But the important thing about tide pools is that they contain a community of plants and animals.

Dozens of nonfiction books can provide models for inquiry-related writing. *My Season with Penguins: An Antarctic Journal* (Webb, 2000) is a field journal maintained by biologist Sophie Webb. This title could serve as a model for students' own field journals in a science class. Examples of books that model the use of interviews and oral history abound. One of the finest is *Oh Freedom! Kids Talk About the Civil Rights Movement with the People Who Made it Happen* (King & Osborne, 1997). This book was actually created by young people; the students interviewed friends, family members, and neighbors who told the story of the civil rights movement from their own perspectives. The result is an amazing oral history of that turbulent time. Teachers could involve students in conducting their own oral history interviews related to topics of study in a social studies class.

MyLab Education
Response Journal 11.3
Explain how writing in response to reading can build students' abilities to comprehend, develop, and refine social skills, using critical thinking skills.

Process Drama as a Heuristic

Responding to literature through drama provides a wealth of opportunities for enhancing student engagement in learning (Wells & Sandretto, 2017). *Process drama* experiences allow students to establish an imaginary world in which they experience fictional roles and situations. Process drama differs from other forms of drama in that it does not involve the use of scripts; instead, students themselves compose and rehearse episodes that continue over time, and audience is integral to the process (O'Neill, 1995). Like reading, drama requires that students make meaning based on the reading that they have done. However, with drama, this meaning-making takes on a visual component. That is, students externalize the visual images they create from a text and incorporate thought, language, and movement to demonstrate their learning. Through drama, they enter the world of the text, whether fiction or nonfiction, which lets students interact with, observe, and reflect on that world.

Students reshape learning obtained through print into a dramatic form. Dramatic activities encourage changes in student thinking and promote positive experiences with literature. Many struggling readers have difficulty creating mental images as they read. Dramatic activities scaffold this image making in a motivating and meaningful way.

These activities can generate interest and help students enter a text, seeing and feeling the emotions of the characters or experiencing the events described. By combining reading with dramatic experiences, teachers help students enhance their oral language skills through listening and speaking, thereby developing vocabulary and reading fluency. Dramatic activities encourage learners to listen for cues and learn to use their voices to convey emotion. In addition, they help students develop self-confidence and cooperative learning skills. Activities such as these benefit students who thrive when allowed to work collaboratively or who enjoy the kinesthetic action during learning and support extended engagement. These activities also offer a natural entry point into the world of writing; students can move from simply dramatizing the words of others to creating their own scripts that can be performed.

For many students, drama heightens understanding of the often dense and complex expository material found in today's nonfiction. It can enhance student understanding of both technical vocabulary and specific content-related concepts. It can motivate students to explore the content of these books more deeply. Most of all, it can bring abstract information to life, making it concrete and therefore comprehensible, which can be particularly helpful for struggling readers or English Learners.

Dramatic responses to literature have other benefits as well. Responses of this type require in-depth familiarity with the text to be dramatized. Generally, learners need repeated exposure to a text before they can formulate a response to it. This repeated exposure could be particularly beneficial for struggling readers, as it gives them a purposeful reason to reread the text to build comprehension and fluency.

IMPROVISATIONAL DRAMA Improvisational drama involves students in active response to literature and encourages them to use their imaginations. It is beneficial for students of all ages, many of whom find dramatic play extremely motivating. Improvisational responses to fiction and nonfiction help students mediate texts in ways that make them interesting, memorable, and comprehensible (Horowitz, 2017). When creating improvisational drama, teachers create structures that allow students to explore important themes found in the books they read. In one scene in *The Giver* (Lowry, 1993), for example, Jonas and the Giver talk about the fact that Jonas could be lost and that all his received memories could be released on people who have never experienced painful memories. In an improvisation based on this book, students could assume roles as members of the society and receive memories for the first time. They could describe this event and the feelings they experience as a result of it (Temple, Martinez, Yokota, & Naylor, 2005). Through this dramatic activity, students deepen their understanding of *The Giver* and the people whose lives it explores, and it encourages readers to gain an understanding of perspectives other than their own. Such experiences provide a nice change of pace in the classroom. Students not only enjoy these activities but also appear to retain much of the information presented as a result of the dramatizations.

Other more structured forms of dramatic response can sensitize students to expository text organization. For example, after reading *The Heart and Blood (How Our Bodies Work)* (Burgess, 1988), a middle grade teacher involved her students in a dramatic activity designed to demonstrate the sequence by which blood flows through the heart. One half of the class carried red sheets of construction paper to represent oxygenated blood, and the other carried blue to represent deoxygenated blood. Eight students then paired up to act as valve gatekeepers. Student desks were arranged in the shape of the heart, and stations represented the lungs and other body parts. Students moved around the room, simulating the flow of blood through the heart and other organs, then wrote about the activity in their learning logs (Moss, 2003).

PANTOMIME Pantomime is another form of response useful with content-related texts. It requires learners to communicate using their bodies without relying on verbal communication. Students might enjoy creating pantomimes in response to Aliki's (1983) *A Medieval Feast*. This particular book contains many scenes that students could pantomime, including depictions of turning boars on the spit, fencing fields, and sounding trumpets (Stewig & Buege, 1994). Nicholas Reeves's (1992) *Into the Mummy's Tomb* could stimulate dramatizations of the building of the pyramids, the burial of Tutankhamen, the process of mummification, or the purposes of the artifacts found in the tomb.

TABLEAU Tableau or snapshot drama is another motivational dramatic response activity. Tableaus are silent performances that involve three-dimensional representations. A tableau typically involves no movement, talking, or props, only gestures. Students freeze moments in time and demonstrate the physical or emotional relationships and character gestures or activities. Typically, teachers give students time to plan their tableau in small groups. Each group comes to the front of the class, and the teacher gives a "one, two, three, freeze" cue. The audience members then discuss the tableau, offering their interpretations of what they see.

This activity works extremely well with all kinds of texts, including poetry, fantasies, realistic fiction, biographies, and information books. For example, small groups could create tableaus related to selected poems from Cynthia Rylant's (1984) *Waiting to Waltz*. Or small groups of students could select and read different texts related to a common theme and select a scene to dramatize. Each person in the group would assume a role in the drama. After practicing, students could create their "frozen moments." The other students in the class could then attempt to identify the scene portrayed. Similarly, creating "frozen moments" in Matt de la Pena's *Last Stop on Market Street* (2015) would allow readers to explore themes related to social studies as readers learn about a community.

READER'S THEATER Reader's theater differs from process drama in that it involves oral presentation of a script by two or more readers. No props, costumes, or memorization of lines is required. Students must, however, read their parts fluently, with appropriate dramatic flair. Reader's theater is often used with folktales or narrative text but can be used with nonfiction as well.

Information books and biographies with dialogue are easily adapted to this format, but picture books, short stories, or excerpts from longer books can also be quite effective. The following guidelines can help teachers adapt nonfiction texts to a reader's theater script:

1. Select an interesting section of text containing the desired content.
2. Reproduce the text.

3. Delete lines not critical to the content being emphasized, including those that indicate that a character is speaking.
4. Decide how to divide the parts for the readers. Assign dialogue to appropriate characters. With some texts, it will be necessary to rewrite text as dialogue or with multiple narrators. Changing third-person point of view to first-person (*I* or *we*) can create effective narration.
5. Add a prologue to introduce the script in storylike fashion. If needed, a postscript can be added to bring closure to the script.
6. Label the readers' parts by placing the speaker's name in the left-hand margin followed by a colon.
7. After the script is finished, ask others to read it aloud. Students can then make revisions based on what they hear. Give students time to read and rehearse their parts (Young & Vardell, 1993).

An obvious next step is to involve students in selecting books from which they can develop their own reader's theater scripts. Through this activity, learners build comprehension, develop critical thinking skills, make decisions, work cooperatively, and practice the process of revision.

Idea Circles

Another excellent way for students to respond to trade books and articles is through the use of idea circles. **Idea circles** represent the small-group/multiple-text model of organizing the classroom for literature study. They involve students in small-group peer-led discussions of concepts fueled by reading experiences with multiple texts (Guthrie & McCann, 1996). Idea circles are an ideal way to promote peer-directed conceptual understanding of virtually any aspect of content area learning. This conceptual learning involves three basic ingredients: facts, relationships between facts, and explanations.

Idea circles not only engage students in learning about other subjects, but they also require engagement in a variety of literacy activities, including locating information, evaluating the quality and relevance of information, summarizing information for their peers, and determining relationships among information found in a variety of sources. They require that students build higher-order thinking skills by learning to integrate information, ideas, and viewpoints. In addition, they involve students in a variety of important collaborative processes, including turn taking, maintaining group member participation, and coaching one another in the use of literacy strategies (Guthrie & McCann, 1996).

Idea circles share some things in common with literature circles. Like literature circles, they involve three to six students in directed small-group discussions. Like literature circles, idea circles are peer led and involve student-generated rules. However, idea circles involve students in discussion surrounding the learning of a concept rather than a discussion centering on a single literary text. In literature circle discussions, students may have conflicting interpretations of a piece of literature. With idea circles, students work together to create a common understanding of a concept by constructing abstract understanding from facts and details. Another difference between literature circles and idea circles is in the use of texts. With literature circles, students all read and respond to a single text. With idea circles, each student may interact with a different text in preparation for the group discussion, allowing students to interact with texts at a variety of reading levels and formats. Then, during the discussion, students share the unique information that they have found. Furthermore, idea circle discussions require the use of informational, rather than literary, texts.

The teacher begins the idea circle experience by presenting students with a goal in the form of a topic or question. An example of a question might be "What is a desert?" Before the idea circle meets, students can either read extensively from relevant informational trade books or other nonfiction texts or read and discuss their findings concurrently. Information that students bring to the group comes from prior experiences and discussions with others as well as from their readings. In their groups, students exchange facts, discuss relationships among ideas, and offer explanations. As this linking together of facts continues, students create a conceptual framework around a topic or question. Individuals offer information, check it against the information found by others, and discuss topics more deeply. Students continually challenge one another regarding the accuracy and relevance of their information. Through this checking, students are encouraged to search for information, comprehend the texts being used, and synthesize information from multiple sources. When conflicts arise, students search their sources to clarify conflicting information, building their ability to use textual evidence to support claims. Teachers can vary the level of scaffolding through the amount of support they offer in providing texts. Ultimately, the group must weave together the important details that all students contribute.

GETTING STARTED WITH IDEA CIRCLES Here's how to use idea circles in your classroom:

1. Decide whether to engage the entire class in idea circles simultaneously or to start with a single team and gradually add more.
2. Identify appropriate topics of study. The topic should be interesting, explanatory, and expansive. In addition, the topic should contain natural categories or subtopics.
3. Set clear goals for what each group should accomplish during its discussion. Students may complete data charts, semantic maps, or other graphic organizers.
4. Provide students with a rich array of trade books and other resources at a variety of levels related to the topic under study.
5. Make sure students have read and learned about the topic before participating in the idea circle.
6. Post student-generated interaction rules so that students know how to function in their groups.

When used as part of a unit of study, idea circles are most effective when placed at the middle or end of a unit, since students already have some schema for the topic.

During a social studies exploration of the mound-building tribes in Ohio, teacher Ann Craig involved her students in an inquiry project using idea circles. She divided students into three different groups, with each assigned to study a different mound-builder tribe: the Hopewells, the Adenas, and the Fort Ancient. Ms. Craig focused student inquiry through questions like these: "What were some of the purposes of the mounds?" "Where did each tribe live in Ohio?" "Why are they no longer in existence?" Students consulted a variety of different sources, including trade books, textbooks, websites, and so on, to locate answers to these questions. Finally, the groups were reconfigured so that each contained an Adena expert, a Hopewell expert, and a Fort Ancient expert. The final product for the idea circle was for each group to complete a data chart comparing and contrasting each of the three tribes.

Using Technology to Respond to Literature

Today's students are technology savvy. They have grown up with immediate access to information. They memorized e-mail addresses before house addresses. Teenagers spend a great deal of time on the Internet communicating, networking, and gaming. As we stated in Chapters 1 and 2, teachers need to understand that these activities are acts of literacy. Students are reading and writing and critically thinking, even as they "play." To maintain student interest and to use what students already know, teachers can capitalize on students' digital immersion to further their learning and comprehension of texts. Teachers may even be able to raise the status of reading in the personal lives of students.

Students are forming book clubs (among other clubs) on social networks such as Facebook, Twitter, and Instagram. Such venues enable students from a variety of places to participate in online discussions about anything. The efficacy of book clubs relies on the contributions of members; as people negotiate thoughts, opinions, and interpretations, greater understanding is achieved. Teachers can set up an Internet community of readers and facilitate reading discussions that go beyond the classroom and allow students to connect with others who have similar reading interests. Per social networking norms, responses are brief and unedited, but the key here is content, not necessarily quality. Also, the comments are documented and can be saved for future analysis. In the classroom, teachers can ask students to elaborate and explicate. Allowing students to interact with other readers as a method of accountability is a welcome change from or addition to reading quizzes and point systems popular in many classrooms.

BLOGGING AND THREADED DISCUSSIONS Blogging about books and threaded discussions, as we discussed in Chapter 2, can also be effective. For example, two popular blogging sites for adolescents are LiveJournal and Blogger. As we saw in earlier chapters, many students write and read blogs on a daily basis. These blogs may not necessarily be about books, as people blog about anything and everything under the sun. However, teachers can encourage students to blog about books and their responses to books and also to read other people's blogs about books. Blogs also have space for comments and questions. Again, it is customary to write many short responses. The idea is to help students build momentum around reading and writing about reading. For this generation, it is often easier to build a sense of community via the Internet. Goodreads is an excellent tool for students to blog reactions to books while tracking what they've read. Goodreads allows students to rate books as well, letting classmates see lists of other books they may enjoy. While Goodreads is a public site, you can create groups within the site for specific classes or schools. As students often take their cues from peers, sharing sites such as these are a way to foster continued interest in reading.

The fan fiction sites are fascinating. Fan fiction is a phenomenon that was around long before the Internet; however, it is becoming a popular vehicle for young readers and writers. Essentially, fans write fictional pieces in the same vein as their idols and publish these pieces online. For example, *Harry Potter* fans have the opportunity to make up fiction about the famous magician; fans have written about Harry's married life with Ginny, his early years with the Dursleys, his inner monologues, and so on, in the manner of J. K. Rowling. In this manner, fans can fill in gaps, write from the perspective of secondary characters, and extend or elaborate on specific scenes. Fans can also write literary crossovers (e.g., Harry Potter in Dante's *Inferno*). Writing and reading fan fiction allows readers to focus on the aspects and characters they find most appealing and build on these stories.

There are rules for fan fiction. Fans cannot contribute pieces "out of canon," meaning fans must be true to the author or genre. Pieces generally include the following components: disclaimer, peer-review process (space for comments), rating, short commentary about context, and a request for reviews. True to their stage of development, adolescent fan fiction writers want approval and feedback. These writers are doing everything that we want them to do in the classroom: This process supports comprehension, as writers must build from what they know. They are negotiating and navigating texts, and they are writing and revising based on critical feedback. Why not make this a classroom assignment?

FILE SHARING Google Drive, Dropbox, OneDrive, and other file-sharing options is another great tool for encouraging collaborative writing. File sharing provides a cloud storage service for documents, photos, and videos. File-sharing users can also use these services to create and edit various types of files. The key to using these various Internet practices is to recognize that users, in this case our adolescent students, are seeking attention and collaboration by participating and contributing to a social and public network. Google Docs, for example, allows students to concurrently work on and to share a single document. All the members of a Google group have access to Google Docs and can actively view and make changes to a document in real time.

Technology allows us to extend learning beyond the four walls of the classroom; it also gives us an opportunity to connect with our students and to motivate them and for students to connect with each other. It provides students with choices about when and where they log in. As active members of their respective Internet communities, students experience pride of ownership in their writing and thoughts. Teachers do need to explain the advantages and disadvantages of making personal lives and thoughts public, as teenagers tend to forget that their published words have permanence.

MyLab Education **Self-Check 11.4**

MyLab Education **Application Exercise11.4:**
Using Idea Circles in a Content Area Classroom

Looking Back Looking Forward

As you can see, texts have the power to expand our vision; link us with people from the past, present, and future; and widen our vision of the world. The dialogue that is created between a text and its reader can be a powerful one—it can confuse or perplex us, unnerve us, move us to laughter or tears, or urge us to social action. It can satisfy our curiosity or make us see old ideas in completely new ways. By complementing textbook content with trade books and articles involving students in opportunities to respond to those texts, we can help to ensure that students view the work of the scientist, the historian, or the musician as more than just knowing the facts about a topic—recognizing that such work involves interpretation, reflection, and consideration of multiple points of view.

Trade books and articles in content area classrooms can extend and enrich information across the curriculum. Textbooks generally are unable to treat subject matter with the depth and breadth necessary to fully develop ideas and concepts and engage students in critical inquiry. Trade books and articles have the potential to capture students' interests and imagination in people, places, events, and ideas.

Whereas textbooks compress information, trade books and articles provide students with intensive and extensive involvement in a subject. Trade books and articles offer students a variety of interesting, relevant, and comprehensible text experiences. With trade books and articles, students are likely to develop an interest in and an emotional commitment to a subject. Trade books and articles are schema builders. Reading texts helps students generate background knowledge and provides them with vicarious experiences. Many kinds of trade books and articles, both nonfiction and fiction, can be used in tandem with textbooks.

Access to texts within the content area classroom helps ensure that students are exposed to content in a variety of formats. By creating classroom libraries, providing time for reading, and reading aloud to students, teachers increase the possibility that students will become lifelong readers.

By involving students in reading and responding to trade books and articles through writing, drama, and inquiry activities such as idea circles, teachers move students from the solitary act of reading to building community around texts through peer interaction. In sharing their responses to literature, whether written or oral, students learn to reflect more deeply on the meanings of texts and connect more personally to the texts that they read. They begin to see that reactions to texts are as varied as the students in a particular classroom and that by understanding each person's response to a text, we come to understand our humanity and ourselves more fully.

eResources

There are many websites that will help you locate books of interest to your students. Visit one of the following sites that provide useful information on children's literature: the Children's Literature Web Guide, the Young Adult Library Services Association's Teen Book Finder Database, and the Assembly on Literature for Adolescents Review (ALAN Review). Browse these sites for information relevant to your content area. Share your findings in small groups and discuss the ways teachers might use these sites.

Explore the various lessons for your own content area by searching the Web for lesson plans and resources for adolescent and young adult literature.

Appendix A

Affixes with Invariant Meanings

Affix	Meaning	Example
Combining Forms		
anthropo-	man	anthropoid
auto-	self	autonomous
biblio-	book	bibliography
bio-	life	biology
centro-, centri-	center	centrifugal
cosmo-	universe	cosmonaut
heter-, hetero-	different	heterogeneous
homo-	same	homogeneous
hydro-	water	hydroplane
iso-	equal	isometric
lith-, litho-	stone	lithography
micro-	small	microscope
mono-	one	monocyte
neuro-	nerve	neurologist
omni-	all	omnibus
pan-	all	panchromatic
penta-	five	pentamerous
phil-, philo-	love	philanthropist
phono-	sound	phonology
photo-	light	photosynthesis
pneumo-	air, respiration	pneumonia
poly-	many	polygon
proto-	before, first in time	prototype
pseudo-	false	pseudonym
tele-	far	television
uni-	one	unicellular
Prefixes		
apo-	separate or detached from	apocarpous
circum-	around	circumvent
co-, col-, com-, con-, cor-	together or with	combine
equi-	equal	equivalent
extra-	in addition	extraordinary
intra-	within	intratext
mal-	bad	malpractice
mis-	wrong	mistreatment

Affix	Meaning	Example
non-	not	nonsense
syn-	together or with	synthesis

Noun Suffixes

Affix	Meaning	Example
-ana	collection	Americana
-archy	rule or government	oligarchy
-ard, -art	person who does something to excess	drunkard, braggart
-aster	inferiority or fraudulence	poetaster
-bility	quality or state of being	capability
-chrome	pigment, color	autochrome
-cide	murder or killing of	insecticide
-fication, -ation	action or process of	classification, dramatization
-gram	something written or drawn	diagram
-graph	writing, recording, drawing	telegraph, lithograph
-graphy	descriptive science of a specific subject or field	planography, oceanography
-ics	science or art of	graphics, athletics
-itis	inflammation or inflammatory disease	bronchitis
-latry	worship of	bibliolatry
-meter	measuring device	barometer
-metry	science or process of measuring	photometry
-ology, -logy	science, theory, or study of	phraseology, paleontology
-phobia	fear	hypnophobia
-phore	bearer or producer	semaphore
-scope	instrument for observing or detecting	telescope
-scopy	viewing, seeing, or observing	microscopy
-ance, -ation, -ion, -ism, -dom, -ery, -mony, -ment, -tion	quality, state, or condition; action or result of an action	tolerance, adoration, truism, matrimony, government, sanction
-er, -eer, -ess, -ier, -ster, -ist, -trix	agent, doer	helper, engineer, countess, youngster, shootist, executrix

Adjective Suffixes

Affix	Meaning	Example
-able, -ible	worthy of or inclined to	debatable, knowledgeable
-aceous, -ative, -ish, -ive, -itious	pertaining to	impish, foolish, additive, fictitious
-acious	tendency toward or abundance of	fallacious
-est	most	greatest

Affix	Meaning	Example
-ferous	bearing, producing	crystalliferous
-fic	making, causing, or creating	horrific
-fold	multiplied by	fivefold
-form	having the form of	cuneiform
-ful	full of or having the quality of	masterful, useful, armful
-genous	generating or producing	androgenous, endogenous
-ic	characteristic of	seismic, microscopic
-less	lacking	toothless
-like	similar to	lifelike
-most	most	innermost
-ous, -ose	possessing, full of	joyous, grandiose
-wise	manner, direction, or positions	clockwise

Appendix B

Commonly Used Prefixes with Varying Meanings

Prefix	Meaning	Example
ab-	from, away, off	abhor, abnormal, abdicate
ad-	to, toward	adhere, adjoin
ante-	before, in front of, earlier than	antecedent, antediluvian
anti-	opposite of, hostile to	antitoxin, antisocial
be-	make, against, to a great degree	bemoan, belittle, befuddle
bi-	two, twice	biped, bivalve
de-	away, opposite of, reduce	deactivate, devalue, devitalize
dia-	through, across	diameter, diagonal
dis-	opposite of, apart, away	dissatisfy, disarm, disjointed
en-	cause to be, put in or on	enable, engulf
epi-	upon, after	epitaph, epilogue, epidermis
ex-	out of, former, apart, away	excrete, exposition
hyper-	above, beyond, excessive	hyperphysical, hypersensitive
hypo-	under, less than normal	hypodermic, hypotension
in-, il-, im-, ir-	not, in, into, within	inept, indoors
inter-	between, among	interscholastic, interstellar
neo-	new, young	neophyte, neo-Nazi
ortho-	straight, corrective	orthotropic, orthopedic
per-	through, very	permanent, perjury
peri-	around, near, enclosing	perimeter, perihelion
post-	after, behind	postwar, postorbital
pre-	before, in place, time, rank, order	preview, prevail
pro-	before, forward, for, in favor of	production, prothorax, pro-American
re-	again, back	react, recoil
sub-, sur-, sug-, sup-	under, beneath	subordinate, subsoil, substation
super-	above, over, in addition	superhuman, superlative, superordinate
syn-	with, together	synthesis, synchronize
trans-	across, beyond, through	transatlantic, transconfiguration, transaction
ultra-	beyond in space, excessive	ultraviolet, ultramodern
un-	not, the opposite of	unable, unbind

Appendix C

Graphic Organizers with Text Frames

Graphic organizers are visual illustrations of verbal statements. Frames are sets of questions or categories that are fundamental to understanding a given topic. Here we show nine "generic" graphic forms with their corresponding frames. Examples of topics that could be represented by each graphic form are also given. These graphics show at a glance the key parts of the whole and their relations, helping the learner to comprehend text and solve problems.

Used to describe a central idea: a thing (a geographic region), process (meiosis), concept (altruism), or proposition with support (experimental drugs should be available to AIDS patients). Key frame questions: What is the central idea? What are its attributes? What are its functions?

Spider Map

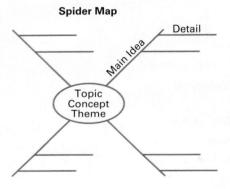

Used to describe the stages of something (the life cycle of a primate); the steps in a linear procedure (how to neutralize an acid); a sequence of events (how feudalism led to the formation of nation-states); or the goals, actions, and outcomes of a historical figure or character in a novel (the rise and fall of Napoléon). Key frame questions: What is the object, procedure, or initiating event? What are the stages or steps? How do they lead to one another? What is the final outcome?

Series of Events Chain

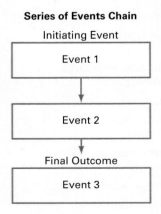

Used for time lines showing historical events or ages (grade levels in school), degrees of something (weight), shades of meaning (Likert scales), or ratings scales (achievement in school). Key frame questions: What is being scaled? What are the end points?

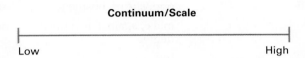

Used to show similarities and differences between two things (people, places, events, ideas, etc.). Key frame questions: What things are being compared? How are they similar? How are they different?

Compare/Contrast Matrix

	Name 1	Name 2
Attribute 1		
Attribute 2		
Attribute 3		

Used to represent a problem, attempted solutions, and results (the national debt). Key frame questions: What was the problem? Who had the problem? Why was it a problem? What attempts were made to solve the problem? Did those attempts succeed?

Problem/Solution Outline

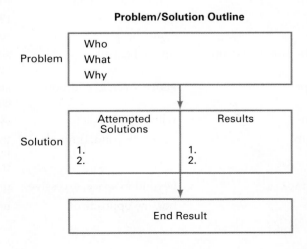

Used to show causal information (causes of poverty), a hierarchy (types of insects), or branching procedures (the circulatory system). Key frame questions: What is the superordinate category? What are the subordinate categories? How are they related? How many levels are there?

Used to show the causal interaction of a complex event (an election, a nuclear explosion) or complex phenomenon (juvenile delinquency, learning disabilities). Key frame questions: What are the factors that cause *X*? How do they relate? Are the factors that cause *X* the same as those that cause *X* to persist?

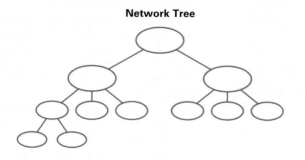

Network Tree

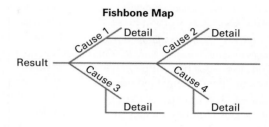

Fishbone Map

Used to show the nature of an interaction between persons or groups (European settlers and Native Americans). Key frame questions: Who are the persons or groups? Did they conflict or cooperate? What was the outcome for each person or group?

Used to show how a series of events interact to produce a set of results again and again (weather phenomena, cycles of achievement and failure, the life cycle). Key frame questions: What are the critical events in the cycle? How are they related? In what ways are they self-reinforcing?

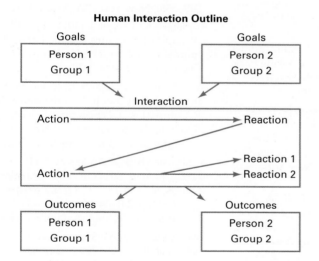

Human Interaction Outline

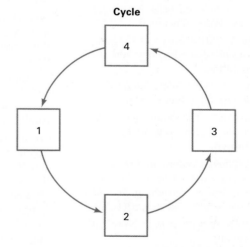

Cycle

Source: Copyright © 1988 North Central Regional Educational Laboratory. All rights reserved. Reprinted with permission of Learning Point Associates.

References

Abrams, S. (2000). *Using journals with reluctant writers: Building portfolios for middle and high school students.* Thousand Oaks, CA: Corwin Press.

Achieve. (2017). *Strong standards: A review of changes to state standards since the Common Core.* Retrieved from https://www.achieve.org/files/StrongStandards.pdf

Achugara, M., & Carpenter, B. (2012). Developing disciplinary literacy in a multilingual history classroom. *Linguistics and Education, 23,* 262–276.

Ackerman, N., & Hays, M. (Illustrator). (1990). *The tin heart.* New York, NY: Atheneum.

Adlit.org. (2008). Brian Selznick. Retrieved March 1, 2009, from www.adlit.org/transcript_display/19677

Ahearn, L. (2012). *Living language: An introduction to linguistic anthropology.* Singapore: Wiley-Blackwell.

Albertalli, B. (2015). *Simon vs. the homo sapiens agenda* (1st ed.). New York, NY: HarperCollins.

Alexander, P. (1986). *Silver Burdett biology.* Morristown, NJ: Silver Burdett.

Alexie, S. (2007). *The absolutely true diary of a part-time Indian.* New York, NY: Little, Brown.

Alger, C. (2009). Content area reading strategy knowledge transfer from pre-service to first-year teaching. *Journal of Adolescent & Adult Literacy, 53*(1), 60–69.

Aliki. (1983). *A medieval feast.* New York, NY: Crowell.

Aliki. (1999). *William Shakespeare and the Globe.* New York, NY: HarperCollins.

Allen, J. (2007). *Inside words: Tools for teaching academic vocabulary, grades 4–12.* Portland, ME: Stenhouse.

Allen, M. B. (2003). *Eight questions on teacher preparation: What does the research say?* Denver, CO: Education Commission of the States.

Alliance for Excellent Education. (2006). *Policy brief: Why the crisis in adolescent literacy demands a national response.* Washington, DC: Author.

Allington, R., & Johnston, P. H. (Eds.). (2002). *Reading to learn: Lessons from exemplary fourth-grade classrooms.* New York, NY: Guilford Press.

Allison, E., & Goldston, M. J. (2018). Modern scientific literacy: A case study of multiliteracies and scientific practices in a fifth grade classroom. *Journal of Science Education and Technology, 27*(3), 270–283.

Alsubaie, J., & Ashuraidah, A. (2017). Exploring writing individually and collaboratively using Google Docs in EFL contexts. *English Language Teaching, 10*(10), 10–30.

Alvarez, M. C. (1996). Explorers of the universe: Students using the World Wide Web to improve their reading and writing. In B. Neate (Ed.), *Literacy saves lives* (pp. 140–145). Herts, UK: United Kingdom Reading Association.

Alverman, D. (2010). *Adolescents' Online Literacies: Connecting Classrooms, Digital Media, and Popular Culture.* New York, NY: Peter Lang Inc.

Alvermann, D. E. (1991). The discussion web: A graphic aid for learning across the curriculum. *Reading Teacher, 45*(2), 92–99.

Alvermann, D. E. (2001). Reading adolescents' reading identities: Looking back to see ahead. *Journal of Adolescent & Adult Literacy, 44,* 676–690.

Alvermann, D. E., & Moore, D. W. (1991). Secondary school reading. In P. D. Pearson, R. Barr, M. L. Kamil, & P. Mosenthal (Eds.), *Handbook of reading research* (2nd ed., pp. 951–983). New York, NY: Longman.

Alvermann, D. E., Dillon, D. R., & O'Brien, D. G. (1988). *Using discussion to promote reading comprehension.* Newark, DE: International Reading Association.

Alvermann, D. E., Swafford, J., & Montero, K. M. (2004). *Content area literacy instruction for the elementary grades.* Boston, MA: Allyn & Bacon.

Ames, L. J. (1986). *Draw fifty cars, trucks, and motorcycles.* Garden City, NY: Doubleday.

Anderson, D. L. (1999). *Using projects in the mathematics classroom to enhance instruction and incorporate history of mathematics.* Paper presented at the National Council of Teachers of Mathematics annual conference, San Francisco, CA.

Anderson, L. H. (1999). *Speak.* New York, NY: Farrar, Strauss & Giroux.

Anderson, L. H. (2000). *Fever 1793.* New York, NY: Simon & Schuster.

Anderson, R. C., & Freebody, P. (1981). Vocabulary knowledge. In J. T. Guthrie (Ed.), *Comprehension and teaching: Research perspectives* (pp. 77–117). Newark, DE: International Reading Association.

Anderson-Inman, L., & Horney, M. (1997). Electronic books for secondary students. *Journal of Adolescent & Adult Literacy, 40*(6), 486–491.

Anno, M. (1989). *Anno's math games II.* New York, NY: Philomel.

Anonymous. (1971). *Go ask Alice.* New York, NY: Simon Pulse.

Applebee, A. N. (1991). Environments for language teaching and learning: Contemporary issues and future directions. In J. Flood, J. M. Jensen, D. Lapp, & J. R. Squire (Eds.), *Handbook of research on teaching the English language arts* (pp. 549–558). New York, NY: Macmillan.

Applebee. A., Langer, J. (2011). EJ extra: A snapshot of writing instruction in middle schools and high schools. *The English Journal, 100*(6), 14–27.

Armbruster, B. B. (2000). Responding to informative prose. In R. Indrisano & J. R. Squire (Eds.), *Perspectives on writing: Research, theory, and practice.* Newark, DE: International Reading Association.

Armbruster, B. B., & Anderson, T. H. (1985). Frames: Structure for informational texts. In D. H. Jonassen (Ed.), *Technology of text* (pp. 331–346). Englewood Cliffs, NJ: Education Technology Publications.

Armstrong, J. (1998). *Shipwreck at the bottom of the world: The extraordinary true story of Shackleton and the Endurance.* New York, NY: Crown.

Armstrong, J. (2002). *Shattered: Stories of children and war.* New York, NY: Knopf.

Armstrong, L., & Jenkins, S. (2001). *It's not about the bike: My journey back to life.* New York, NY: Berkley Books.

Aronson, E., & Patnoe, S. (1997). *The jigsaw classroom: Building cooperation in the classroom* (2nd ed.). New York: Addison Wesley Longman.

Aronson, M. (1998). *Art attack: A short cultural history of the avant-garde.* New York, NY: Clarion Books.

Artley, A. S. (1975). Words, words, words. *Language Arts, 52,* 1067–1072.

Asher, J. (2007). *Thirteen reasons why.* New York, NY: Penguin.

Atkin, S. B. (1993). *Voices from the fields: Children of migrant farmworkers tell their stories.* Boston, MA: Little, Brown.

Atwell, N. (1990). Introduction. In N. Atwell (Ed.), *Coming to know: Writing to learn in intermediate grades* (pp. xi–xxiii). Portsmouth, NH: Heinemann.

Atwell, N. (2014). *In the middle: A lifetime of learning about writing, reading, and adolescents* (3rd ed.). Portsmouth, NH: Heinemann.

Au, K. H., & Mason, J. M. (1981). Social organizational factors in learning to read: The balance of rights hypothesis. *Reading Research Quarterly, 17*(1), 115–152.

Avi. (2008). *The seer of shadows.* New York, NY: HarperCollins.

Baker, F. W. (2009). *State standards which include elements of media literacy.* Retrieved February 5, 2009, from www.frankwbaker.com/state_lit.htm

Baker, J. (1991). *Window.* New York, NY: Greenwillow.

Baker, L. (1991). Metacognition, reading, and science education. In C. M. Santa & D. E. Alvermann (Eds.), *Science learning: Processes and applications* (pp. 12–13). Newark, DE: International Reading Association.

Baker, L., & Brown, A. (1984). Cognitive monitoring in reading. In J. Flood (Ed.), *Understanding reading comprehension* (pp. 21–44). Newark, DE: International Reading Association.

Baker-Doyle, K. J. (2018). I, Pseudocoder: Reflections of a literacy teacher-educator on teaching coding as critical literacy. *Contemporary Issues in Technology and Teacher Education (CITE Journal), 18*(2).

Ball, D., & Forzani, F. M. (2010). Teaching skillful teaching. *Educational Leadership, 68*(4), 40–45.

Ball, D. L., & Forzani, F. M. (2011). Building a common core for learning to teach and connecting professional learning to practice. *American Educator, 35*(2), 38–39.

Ball, J. (2005). *Go figure! A totally cool book about numbers.* New York, NY: DK Children.

Ballard, R. D. (1988). *Exploring the Titanic.* New York, NY: Scholastic.

Bamford, R. A., & Kristo, J. V. (Eds.). (1998). *Making facts come alive: Choosing quality nonfiction literature K–8.* Needham Heights, MA: Christopher Gordon.

Bandura, A. (1986). *Social foundations of thought and action: A social cognitive theory.* Englewood Cliffs, NJ: Prentice Hall.

Bangert-Drowns, R. L., Hurley, M. M., & Wilkinson, B. (2004). The effects of school-based writing-to-learn interventions on academic achievement: A meta-analysis. *Review of Educational Research, 74,* 29–58.

Banks, A. B. (2008). *An introduction to multicultural education* (4th ed.). Boston, MA: Pearson.

Banks, J. A. (2001). *Cultural diversity and education: Foundations, curriculum, and teaching* (4th ed.). Boston, MA: Allyn & Bacon.

Barack, L. (2011). The Kindles are coming: Ereaders and tablets are springing up in schools–and librarians are leading the way. *School Library Journal, 57*(3), 58–60.

Bardoe, C. (2006). *Gregor Mendel: The friar who grew peas.* New York, NY: Abrams Books.

Barnes, D. (1995). Talking and learning in the classroom: An introduction. *Primary Voices K–6, 3*(1), 2–7.

Barnhouse, D. (2012, April 23). How testing is hurting teaching. *The New York Times.* Retrieved from http://www.nytimes.com

Barnitz, J. G. (1994). Discourse diversity: Principles for authentic talk and literacy instruction. *Journal of Reading, 37*(7), 586–591.

Barr, C. (2013). *Best Books for High School Readers: Grades 9–12.* Englewood, CO: Libraries Unlimited. Lists 12,000 fiction and nonfiction titles, recommended in at least two sources and organized thematically.

Barrentine, S. J. (1999). *Reading assessment: Principles and practices for elementary teachers.* Newark, DE: International Reading Association.

Barry, A. L., Gay, A. S., Pelkey, M. L., & Rothrock, K. (2017). What types of text are novice teachers choosing to teach mathematics? *Issues in the Undergraduate Mathematics Preparation of School Teachers, 3.*

Bartoletti, S. C. (2001). *Black potatoes: The story of the great Irish famine, 1845–1850.* Boston, MA: Houghton Mifflin.

Bartoletti, S. C. (2006). *Hitler youth: Growing up in Hitler's shadow.* New York, NY: Scholastic.

Barton, D., & Hamilton, M. (1998). *Local literacies: Reading and writing in one community.* London, UK: Routledge.

Bauman, K. (2018, August 8). New survey questions do a better job capturing mobile use. U.S. Census Bureau. Retrieved November 17, 2018, from https://www.census.gov/library/stories/2018/08/internet-access.html

Baxendell, B. W. (2003). Consistent, coherent, creative: The 3 C's of graphic organizers. *Teaching Exceptional Children, 35,* 46–53.

Bazalgette, C., & Buckingham, D. (2013). Literacy, media and multimodality: A critical response. *Literacy, 47*(2), 95–102.

Beach, R. W. (2011). Issues in analyzing alignment of language arts common core standards with state standards. *Educational Researchers, 40*(4), 179–182.

Beachum, F. (2018). The Every Student Succeeds Act and multicultural education: A critical race theory analysis. *Teachers College Record, 120*(13), 1–18.

Beah, I. (2007). *A long way gone: Memoirs of a boy soldier.* New York, NY: Farrar, Straus & Giroux.

Beals, M. P. (1995). *Warriors don't cry: A searing memoir of the battle to integrate Little Rock.* New York, NY: Washington Square Press.

Beaman, B. (1985). Writing to learn social studies. In A. R. Gere (Ed.), *Roots in sawdust: Writing to learn across the disciplines* (pp. 50–60). Urbana, IL: National Council of Teachers of English.

Bean, R. M. (2004). Promoting effective literacy instruction: The challenge for literacy coaches. *The California Reader, 37*(3), 58–63.

Bean, R. M., Cassidy, J., Grumet, J. E., Shelton, D. S., & Wallis, S. R. (2002). What do reading specialists do? Results from a national survey. *The Reading Teacher, 55*(8), 736–744.

Bean, T. W. (2001). An update on reading in the content areas: Social constructionist dimensions. *Reading Online, 5*(5). Retrieved October 5, 2005, from www.readingonline.org/articles/art_index.asp?HREF=handbook/bean/index.html

Bean, T. W., & Moni, K. (2003). Developing students' critical literacy: Exploring identity construction in young adult fiction. *Journal of Adolescent & Adult Literacy, 46*(8), 638–648.

Beatty, P. (1987). *Charley Skedaddle.* New York, NY: Morrow.

Beck, I. L., McKeown, M. G., Hamilton, R. L., & Kucan, L. (1997). *Questioning the author: An approach for enhancing student engagement in text.* Newark, DE: International Reading Association.

Beck, I. L., McKeown, M. G., & Kucan, L. (2002). *Bringing words to life: Robust vocabulary instruction*. New York, NY: Guilford Press.

Beck, I. L., McKeown, M. G., & Kucan, L. (2013). *Bringing words to life: Robust vocabulary instruction* (2nd ed.). New York, NY: Guilford Press.

Bedard, C., Horn, L. V., & Garcia, V. M. (2011). The impact of culture on literacy. *The Educational Forum, 75*(3), 244–258. doi:10.1080/00131725.2011.577522

Beebe, B. F. (1968). *African elephants*. New York, NY: McKay.

Beers, K. (2003). *When kids can't read, what teachers can do*. Portsmouth, NH: Heinemann.

Beers, K. (2013/2014). What matters most: Considering the issues and the conversations we need to have. *Journal of Adolescent & Adult Literacy, 57*(4), 265–269.

Beil, K. M. (1999). *Fire in their eyes: Wildfires and the people who fight them*. San Diego, CA: Harcourt Brace.

Belli, G. (2003). *The country under my skin*. New York, NY: Anchor Books.

Berger, M. (1986). *Atoms, molecules, and quarks*. New York, NY: Putnam.

Berman, I., & Biancarosa, G. (2005). *Reading to achieve: A governor's guide to adolescent literacy*. Washington, DC: National Governor's Association for Best Practices.

Berry, K., & Herrington, C. (2011). States and their struggles with NCLB: Does the Obama blueprint get it right? *Peabody Journal of Education, 86*, 272–290.

Betts, E. (1950). *Foundations of reading* (rev. ed.). New York, NY: American Book Company.

Bialostok, S. M. (2014). Metaphors that teachers live by: A cultural model of literacy in the era of new literacies. *Language and Education, 28*(6), 501–520.

Biancarosa, G., & Snow, C. (2004). *Reading next: A vision for action and research in middle and high school literacy*. Report to Carnegie Corporation of New York. Washington, DC: Alliance for Excellent Education. Retrieved June 25, 2007, from www.all4ed.org/publications/ReadingNext/ReadingNext.pdf

Bishop, R. S. (2003). Reframing the debate about cultural authenticity. In D. L. Fox & K. G. Short (Eds.), *Stories matter: The complexity of cultural authenticity in children's literature* (pp. 25–37). Urbana, IL: National Council of Teachers of English.

Bitton-Jackson, L. (1997). *I have lived a thousand years: Growing up in the Holocaust*. New York, NY: Simon & Schuster.

Blachowicz, C. (1986). Making connections: Alternatives to the vocabulary notebook. *Journal of Reading, 29*, 643–649.

Blachowicz, C., & Fisher, P. J. (2014). *Teaching vocabulary in all classrooms*. Boston, MA: Pearson.

Blachowicz, C. Z., Fisher, P. J. L., Ogle, D., & Watts-Taffe, S. (2006). Vocabulary: Questions from the classroom. *Reading Research Quarterly, 41*(4), 524–539.

Blakeslee, S. (2004). The CRAAP test. *LOEX Quarterly, 31*(3), 6–7. Available from http://commons.emich.edu/cgi/viewcontent.cgi?article=1009&context=loexquarterly

Bleich, D. (1978). *Subjective criticism*. Baltimore, MD: Johns Hopkins University Press.

Blohm, J. M., & Lapinsky, T. (2006). *Kids like me: Voices of the immigrant experience*. Boston, MA: Intercultural Press.

Bluestein, N. A. (2010). Unlocking text features for determining importance in expository text: A strategy for struggling readers. *The Reading Teacher, 63*(7), 597–600.

Blumenthal, K. (2005). *Let me play: The story of Title IX: The law that changed the future of girls in America*. New York, NY: Atheneum.

Bode, J. (1989). *New kids on the block: Oral histories of immigrant teens*. New York, NY: Franklin Watts.

Bode, J. (2000). *Colors of freedom: Immigrant stories*. New York, NY: Franklin Watts.

Boushey, G., & Moser, J. (2009). *The CAFÓ book: Engaging all students in daily literacy assessment and instruction*. New York, NY: Stenhouse.

boyd, d. (2014). *It's complicated: The social lives of networked teens*. New Haven, CT: Yale University Press.

Boyd, F., Sullivan, M., Popp, K., & Hughes, M. (2012). Vocabulary instruction in the disciplines. *Journal of Adolescent and Adult Literacy, 56*(1), 18–20.

Boykin, A. W. (1984). Reading achievement and the social-cultural frame of reference of Afro-American students. *Journal of Negro Education, 53*(4), 464–473.

Boyne, J. (2006). *The boy in the striped pajamas*. New York, NY: Fickling.

Braden, E. G. & Rodriguez, S. C. (2016). Beyond mirrors and windows: A critical content analysis of Latinx children's books. *Journal of Language and Literacy Education, 12*(2), 56–83.

Bradley, K. (2016). *The war that saved my life*. New York, NY: Dial Press.

Brashares, A. (2001). *Sisterhood of the traveling pants*. New York, NY: Delacorte.

Breakstone, J., McGrew, S., Smith, M., Ortega, T., & Wineburg, S. (2018). Why we need a new approach to teaching digital literacy. *Phi Delta Kappan, 99*(6), 27–32.

Britton, J. (1970). *Language and learning*. London, UK: Allen Lane.

Bromley, K. (2007). Nine things every teacher should know about words and vocabulary instruction. *Journal of Adolescent and Adult Literacy, 50*(7), 528–537.

Brookfield, S. D., & Preskill, S. (2005). *Discussion as a way of teaching: Tools and techniques for democratic classrooms* (2nd ed.). San Francisco, CA: Jossey-Bass.

Brown, A. L. (1978). Knowing when, where, and how to remember: A problem of metacognition. In R. Glaser (Ed.), *Advances in instructional psychology* (pp. 117–175). Mahwah, NJ: Erlbaum.

Brown, A. L., Bransford, J. W., Ferrara, R. F., & Campione, J. (1983). Learning, remembering, and understanding. In J. Flavell & E. Markham (Eds.), *Handbook of child psychology* (pp. 393–451). New York, NY: Wiley.

Brown, A. L., & Palincsar, A. S. (1982). Inducing strategic learning from texts by means of informed, self-control training. *Topics in Learning and Learning Disabilities, 2*, 1–17.

Brown, D. (1987). *Principles of language learning and teaching*. Englewood Cliffs, NJ: Prentice Hall.

Brown, M. W. (1949). *The important book*. Ill. L. Weisgard. New York, NY: Harper & Row.

Brown-Jeffy, S., & Cooper, J. E. (2011). Toward a conceptual framework for culturally relevant pedagogy: An overview of the conceptual and theoretical literature. *Teacher Education Quarterly, 38*(1), 65–84.

Brozo, W. G. (1989). Applying a reader response heuristic to expository text. *Journal of Reading, 32*, 140–145.

Brozo, W. G. (1990). Learning how at-risk readers learn best: A case for interactive assessment. *Journal of Reading, 33*, 522–527.

Brozo, W. G. (2017). *Content literacy for today's adolescents: Honoring diversity and building competence* (6th ed.). New York, NY: Guilford Press.

Brozo, W. G., & Flyny, E. S. (2007). Content literacy: Fundamental toolkit elements. *Reading Teacher, 61*(2), 192–194.

Brozo, W. G., & Tomlinson, C. M. (1986). Literature: The key to lively content courses. *Reading Teacher, 40*, 288–293.

Bruner, J. (1961). The act of discovery. *Harvard Educational Review, 31*, 21–32.

Bruner, J. (1970). The skill of relevance or the relevance of skills. *Saturday Review, 53*.

Bruner, J. (1986). *Actual minds, possible worlds*. Cambridge, MA: Harvard University Press.

Bruner, J. (1990). *Acts of meaning*. Cambridge, MA: Harvard University Press.

Bruner, J., Goodnow, J., & Austin, G. (1977). *A study of thinking*. New York, NY: Science Editions.

Bruns, M. K., Hodgson, J., Parker, D. C., & Fremont, K. (2011). Comparison of the effectiveness and efficiency of text previewing and preteaching keywords as small-group reading comprehension strategies with middle school students. *Literacy Research and Instruction, 50*, 241–252.

Bryant, J. (2013). *A splash of red: The life and art of Horace Pippin*. New York, NY: Random House Children's Publishing.

Buckley-Marudas, M. F. (2016). Literacy learning in a digitally rich humanities classroom: Embracing multiple, collaborative, and simultaneous texts. *Journal of Adolescent & Adult Literacy, 59*(5), 551–561.

Buehl, D. (1991). Frames of mind. *The Exchange: Newsletter of the IRA Secondary Reading Interest Group*, pp. 4–5.

Buehl, D. (2009a). *Classroom strategies for interactive learning* (3rd ed.). Newark, DE: International Reading Association.

Buehl, D. (2009b). Linking research to practice in disciplinary instruction: An interview by David Moore. *Journal of Adolescent and Adult Literacy, 52*(6), 535–537.

Buehl, D. (2011). *Developing readers in the academic disciplines*. Newark, DE: International Reading Association.

Bulgren, J. A., Marquis, J. G., Lenz, B. K., Schumaker, J. B., & Deshler, D. D. (2009). Effectiveness of question exploration to enhance students' written expression of content knowledge and comprehension. *Reading & Writing Quarterly, 25*, 271–289.

Bunting, E., & Diaz, D. (Illustrator). (1994). *Smoky night*. Orlando, FL: Harcourt Brace.

Burgess, J. (1988). *The heart and blood (How our bodies work)*. Englewood Cliffs, NJ: Silver Burdett.

Burke, J. (2002). *Tools for thought: Graphic organizers for your classroom*. Portsmouth, NH: Heinemann.

Burleigh, R., & Johnson, S. T. (Illustrator). (1997). *Hoops*. San Diego, CA: Silver Whistle.

Burnett, C., & Merchant, G. (2015). The challenge of 21st-century literacies. *Journal of Adolescent & Adult Literacy, 59*(3), 271–274.

Bushweller, K. (2017). Classroom technology: Where schools stand. Technology Counts, 2017. *Education Week, 36*(35).

Buss, F. (2002). *Journey of the Sparrows*. London, UK: Puffin.

Bustle, L. S. (2004). The role of visual representation in the assessment of learning. *Journal of Adolescent & Adult Literacy, 47*, 416–423.

Butler, S., Urrutia, K., Buenger, A., & Hunt, M. (2010). *A review of the current research on comprehension instruction*. National Reading Technical Assistance Center, RMC Research Corporation. Retrieved January 11, 2015, from www2.ed.gov/programs/readingfirst/support-/compfinal.pdf

Calabro, M. (1999). *The perilous journey of the Donner Party*. New York, NY: Clarion Books.

Calderón, M., & Minaya-Rowe, L. (2011). *Preventing long-term ELs: Transforming schools to meet core standards*. Thousand Oaks, CA: Corwin.

Calderón, M., Slavin, R., & Sánchez, M. (2011). Effective instruction for English learners. *The Future of Children, 21*(1), 103–127.

Calderón, M. E., & Minaya-Rowe, L. (2011). *Preventing long-term ELs: Transforming schools to meet core standards*. Thousand Oaks, CA: Corwin.

Camarota, S. (2012). *Immigrants in the United States: A profile of America's foreign-born population*. Washington, DC: Center for Immigration Studies.

Camp, G. (1982). *A successful curriculum for remedial writers*. Berkeley, CA: National Writing Project, University of California.

Campano, G. (2007). *Immigrant students and literacy: Reading, writing, and remembering*. New York, NY: Teachers College Press.

Canada, J. (2010). *Fist, stick, knife*. Saratoga Springs, NY: Beacon Press.

Canfield, J. (2000). *Chicken soup for the sports fan's soul: 101 stories of insight, inspiration and laughter in the world*. Deerfield, FL: HCI.

Cardullo, V., Zygouris-Coe, V. I., & Wilson, N. S. (2017). Reading nonfiction text on an iPad in a secondary classroom. *Journal of Research in Reading, 40*, 190.

Cardullo, V., Zygouris-Coe, V., Wilson, N. S., Craanen, P. M., & Stafford, T. R. (2012). How students comprehend using e-readers and traditional text: Suggestions from the classroom. *American Reading Forum Annual Yearbook* [Online], Vol. 32.

Carlo, M. S., August, D., McLaughlin, B., Snow, C. E., Dressler, C., Lippman, D. N., ... White, C. E. (2004). Closing the gap: Addressing the vocabulary needs of English-language learners in bilingual and mainstream classrooms. *Reading Research Quarterly, 39*(2), 188–215.

Carnoy, M., & Garcia, E. (2017). *Five key trends in U.S. student performance*. Economic Policy Institute, pp. 1–61. Retrieved from http://www.epi.org/files/pdf/113217.pdf

Carpenter, B., Earhart, M., & Achugar, M. (2014). Working with documents to develop disciplinary literacy in the multilingual classroom. *The History Teacher, 48*(1), 91–103.

Carr, E., & Ogle, D. (1987). K-W-L Plus: A strategy for comprehension and summarization. *Journal of Reading, 30*, 626–631.

Carter, B., & Abrahamson, R. F. (1990). *Nonfiction for young adults: From delight to wisdom*. Phoenix, AZ: Oryx Press.

Cassidy, J., & Cassidy, D. (2009, February/March). What's hot in adolescent literacy. *Reading Today, 26*(4), 1, 8, 9.

Castek, J., & Coiro, J. (2015). Understanding what students know: Evaluating their online research and reading comprehension skills. *Journal of Adolescent & Adult Literacy, 58*(7), 546–549.

Chadha, A. (2018). Virtual classrooms: Analyzing student and instructor collaborative experiences. *Journal of the Scholarship of Teaching and Learning, 18*(3), 55–71.

Chambers, D., Jones, P., McGhie-Richmond, D., Riley, M., May-Poole, S., Orlando, A. M., ... Wilcox, C. (2018). An exploration of teacher's use of iPads for students with learning support needs. *Journal of Research in Special Educational Needs, 18*(2), 73–82.

Chang, C., Liang, C., & Chen, Y. (2013). Is learner self-assessment reliable and valid in a web-based portfolio environment for high school students? *Computers and Education, 60,* 325–334.

Chang, I. (1991). *A separate battle: Women and the Civil War.* New York, NY: Scholastic.

Charlotte-Mecklenburg Schools. (2014). *English Language Learner (ELL) Services.* Retrieved from https://wearecms.edlioschool.com/apps/pages/index.jsp?uREC_ID=1407078&type=d&pREC_ID=1581315

Chauvin, R., & Theodore, K. (2015). Teaching content-area literacy and disciplinary literacy. *SEDL Insights, 3*(1), 1–10. Retrieved from https://www.sedl.org/insights/3-1/teaching_content_area_literacy_and_disciplinary_literacy.pdf

Chekhov, A., & Moser, B. (Illustrator). (1991). *Kashtanka.* (R. Povear, Trans.). New York, NY: Putnam.

Chen, S.-F. (2017). Modeling the influences of upper-elementary school students' digital reading literacy, socioeconomic factors, and self-regulated learning strategies. *Research in Science & Technological Education, 35*(3), 330–348.

Cherry, L. (2000). *The great kapok tree: A tale of the Amazon rain forest.* San Diego, CA: Harcourt.

Clark, B., Sobel, J., & Basteri, C. G. (2006). *Marketing dynamics.* Tinley, IL: Goodheart-Wilcox.

Clark, R. P. (1987). *Free to write: A journalist teaches young writers.* Portsmouth, NH: Heinemann.

Clary, D., Oglan, V., & Styslinger, M. (2008). *It is not just about content: Preparing content area teachers to be literacy leaders.* Retrieved February 12, 2009, from the Literacy Coaching Clearinghouse website, www.literacycoachingonline.org

Close, E. A., Hull, M., & Langer, J. A. (2005). Writing and reading relationships in literacy learning. In R. Indrisano & J. A. Paratore (Eds.), *Learning to write, writing to learn: Theory and research in practice* (pp. 67–79). Newark, DE: International Reading Association.

Cloud, N., Genesee, F., & Hamayan, E. (2009). *Literacy instruction for English language learners: A teacher's guide to research-based practices.* New York, NY: Heinemann.

Coiro, J. (2003). Reading comprehension on the Internet: Expanding our understanding of reading comprehension to encompass new literacies. *Reading Teacher, 56,* 458–464.

Coiro, J. (2012). The new literacies of online reading comprehension: Future directions. *Educational Forum, 76*(4), 412–417.

Coiro, J., & Moore, D. W. (2012). New literacies and adolescent learners: An interview with Julie Coiro. *Journal of Adolescent & Adult Literacy, 55*(6), 551–553.

Collins, A. (2017). *What's worth teaching? Rethinking curriculum in the age of technology.* New York, NY: Teachers College Press.

Collins, A., & Halverson, R. (2009). *Rethinking education in the age of technology: The digital revolution and schooling in America.* New York, NY: Teachers College Press.

Collins, J. L. (1997). *Strategies for struggling writers.* New York, NY: Guilford Press.

Collins, S. (2008). *The Hunger Games.* New York, NY: Scholastic.

Collins, S. (2009). *Catching fire.* New York, NY: Scholastic Press.

Collins, S. (2010). *Mockingjay.* New York, NY: Scholastic Press.

Common Core State Standards Initiative. (2010). *Common Core State Standards for English language arts & literacy in history/social studies, science, and technical subjects.* Washington, DC: CCSSO & National Governors Association.

Cone, M., & Wheelwright, S. (Photographer). (1992). *Come back, salmon: How a group of dedicated kids adopted Pigeon Creek and brought it back to life.* San Francisco, CA: Sierra Club Books for Children.

Congressional Digest. (1999, August–September). The federal role in education: 1999–2000 policy debate topic. *Congressional Digest, 193.*

Conley, M. (2008). Cognitive strategy instruction for adolescents: What we know about the promise, what we don't know about the potential. *Harvard Educational Review, 78*(1), 84–106.

Conrad, P. (1991). *Pedro's journal.* New York, NY: Scholastic.

Considine, B., Horton, J., & Moorman, G. (2009). Teaching and reading the millennial generation through media literacy. *Journal of Adolescent and Adult Literacy, 52*(6), 471–481.

Cook-Sather, A. (2002). Authorizing students' perspectives: Toward trust, dialogue, and change in education. *Educational Researcher, 31*(4), 3–14.

Cooney, T., Bell, K., Fisher-Cauble, D., & Sanchez, W. (1996). The demands of alternative assessment: What teachers say. *Mathematics Teacher, 89,* 484–487.

Cooper, A. (2012). Today's technologies enhance writing in mathematics. *The Clearing House, 85,* 80–85.

Cooper, M. (2002). *Remembering Manzanar: Life in a Japanese relocation camp.* New York, NY: Clarion Books.

Cope, B., & Kalantzis, M. (Eds.). (2000). *Multiliteracies: Literacy learning and the design of social futures.* London, UK: Routledge.

Cordero, K., Nussbaum, M., Ibaseta, V., Otaíza, M. J., & Chiuminatto, P. (2018). Read, write, touch: Co-construction and multiliteracies in a third-grade digital writing exercise. *Journal of Computer Assisted Learning, 34*(2), 162–173.

Cortés, S., García-Pernía, M. R., de la Fuente, J., Martínez-Borda, R., & Lacasa, P. (2018). Young creators in open spaces: Digital ethnography. *Digital Education Review, (33),* 185–202.

Coville, B., & Kelly, G. (Illustrator). (1997). *William Shakespeare's* Macbeth. New York, NY: Dial.

Crawley, S. (2015). Beyond digital stories: Crafting digital compositions for opinion writing. *Voices from the Middle, 23*(2), 49–55.

Creech, J., & Hale, G. (2006). Literacy in science: A natural fit, promoting student literacy through inquiry. *The Science Teacher, 73*(2), 22–27.

Creech, S. (1996). *Walk two moons.* New York, NY: HarperCollins.

Creech, S. (2001). *Love that dog.* New York, NY: HarperTrophy.

Crew, L. (1991). *Children of the river.* New York, NY: Laurel Leaf Press.

Cronin, M. K. (2014). The Common Core of literacy and literature. *English Journal, 103*(4), 46–52.

Crosby, C. (2018). Empowering English language learners and immigrant students with digital literacies and service-learning. *Reading Matrix: An International Online Journal, 18*(2), 38–58.

Crue, W. (1932, February). Ordeal by cheque. *Vanity Fair.*

Crutcher, C. (1989). *Athletic shorts.* New York, NY: Greenwillow.

Crystal, D. (2008a). *Txting: The Gr8 Db8.* Oxford, England: Oxford University Press.

Crystal, D. (2008b). Texting. *English Language Teaching (ELT) Journal, 62*(1), 77–83.

Cuero, K. K. (2010). Artisan with words: Transnational funds of knowledge in a bilingual Latin's narratives. *Language Arts, 87*(6), 427–436.

Cummings, C. (2012). Teacher created prescriptive interactive content (TCPIC), SAMR, and modernizing remediation in social science education. *Journal of Social Studies Research 2014 Conference Proceedings, 37*–39.

Cummins, J. (1981). The role of primary language development in promoting educational success for language minority students. In J. Cummins (Ed.), *Schooling and language minority students: A theoretical framework* (pp. 3–49). Los Angeles: Evaluation, Dissemination, and Assessment Center, California State University at Los Angeles.

Curry, J. (1989). The role of reading instruction in mathematics. In D. Lapp, J. Flood, & N. Farnan (Eds.), *Content area reading and learning: Instructional strategies* (pp. 187–197). Upper Saddle River, NJ: Prentice Hall.

Curtis, M. E., & Longo, A. M. (2001). Teaching vocabulary to adolescents to improve comprehension. *Reading Online, 5*(4). Retrieved August 8, 2005, from www.readingonline.org/articles/art_index.asp?HREF=curtis/index.html

Dahl, R. (1995). *Lamb to the slaughter.* New York, NY: Penguin Books.

Daniel, M. (2017). *English Learners at the Top of Their Class: Reading and Writing for Authentic Purposes.* New York, NY: Rowan and Littlefield.

Daniels, E., & Steres, M. (2011). Examining the effects of a school-wide reading culture on the engagement of middle school students. *Research in Middle Level Education, 35*(2), 1–12.

Daniels, H. (1994). *Literature circles: Voice and choice in book clubs and reading groups* (2nd ed.). York, ME: Stenhouse.

Danielson, C. (1996). *Enhancing professional practice: A framework for teaching.* Alexandria, VA: Association for Supervision and Curriculum Development.

Danzer, G. A. (2007). *The Americans: Reconstruction to the 21st century.* New York, NY: McDougall Littell.

Darling-Hammond, L. (2006a). Constructing 21st-century teacher education. *Journal of Teacher Education, 57,* 300–314.

Darling-Hammond, L. (2006b). *Powerful teacher education: Lessons from exemplary programs.* San Francisco, CA: Jossey-Bass.

Darling-Hammond, L., & Baratz-Snowden, J. (2005). *A good teacher in every classroom: Preparing the highly qualified teachers our children deserve.* San Francisco, CA: Jossey-Bass.

Dash, J. (2000). *The longitude prize.* New York, NY: Farrar, Straus & Giroux.

Davis, O. (1978). *Escape to freedom: A play about Frederick Douglass.* New York, NY: Viking Penguin.

de Ramirez, L. L. (2013). Communicating with the world: Connecting the language classroom to a global audience using Web 2.0 tools. *Learning Languages, 18*(2), 6–7.

Dean, Z. (2007). *The A-List.* New York, NY: Poppy.

Deem, J. M. (2005). *Bodies from the ash: Life and death in ancient Pompeii.* Boston, MA: Houghton Mifflin.

Deighton, L. (1970). *Vocabulary development in the classroom.* New York, NY: Teachers College Press.

de la Peña, M. (2015). *Last stop on market street.* New York, NY: G.P. Putnam's Sons, an imprint of Penguin Group (USA).

Delano, M. F. (2005). *Genius: A photobiography of Albert Einstein.* Washington, DC: National Geographic.

Delpit, L. (2006). Lessons from teachers. *Journal of Teacher Education, 57*(3), 220–231. doi:10.1177/0022487105285966

Delpit, L. D. (1988). The silenced dialogue: Power and pedagogy in educating other people's children. *Harvard Educational Review, 58,* 280–298.

de Maupassant, G., & Kelly, G. (Illustrator). (1993). *The necklace.* New York, NY: Creative Editions.

Deneen, C. C. (2013). Eportfolios in a higher education context: Preliminary findings on assessment and technology issues. *Journal of Information Systems Technology & Planning, 6,* 17.

Deneen, C., Brown, G., & Carless, D. (2018). Students' Conceptions of Eportfolios as Assessment and Technology. *Innovations in Education and Teaching International, 55*(4), 487–496.

Depka, E. (2017). *Raising the Rigor: Effective Questioning Strategies and Techniques for the Classroom.* Bloomington, IN: Solution Tree Press.

Deshler, D., Schumaker, B., Lenz, K., Bulgren, J., Hock, M., & Knight, J. (2001). Ensuring content-area learning by secondary students with learning disabilities. *Learning Disabilities Research and Practice, 16*(2), 96–108.

Dessen, S. (2006). *That summer.* New York, NY: Viking.

Dessen, S. (2009). *Lock and key.* New York, NY: Puffin.

Dewey, J. (1899/1980). *The school and society.* Carbondale: Southern Illinois University Press.

Dewitz, P., Jones, J., & Leahy, S. (2009). Comprehension strategy instruction in core reading programs. *Reading Research Quarterly, 44*(2), 102–126.

Diaz, C. F. (2001). *Multicultural education for the twenty-first century.* New York, NY: Longman.

Díaz-Rico, L. T. (2008). *Strategies for teaching English learners* (2nd ed.). Boston, MA: Pearson.

Díaz-Rico, L. T., & Weed, K. Z. (2002). *The crosscultural, language, and academic development handbook: A complete K–12 reference guide.* Boston, MA: Allyn & Bacon.

Digby, C., & Mayers, J. (1993). *Making sense of vocabulary.* Englewood Cliffs, NJ: Prentice Hall.

Dillon, S. (2005, August 23). Connecticut sues the U.S. over school testing [Electronic version]. *The New York Times.*

Doerr, A. (2014). *All the light we cannot see: a novel* (1st Scribner hardcover ed.). New York, NY: Scribner.

Dole, J. (2004). The changing role of the reading specialist in school reform. *The Reading Teacher, 57,* 462–471.

Donelson, K. L., & Nilsen, A. P. (1997). *Literature for today's young adults* (5th ed.). New York, NY: Longman.

Dorfman, L., & Cappelli, R. (2009). *Nonfiction mentor texts: Teaching information writing through children's literature, K-8.* Portsmouth, NH: Stenhouse.

Dowell, M. S. (2018). Toward a working definition of digital literacy. In M. Khosrow-Pour, D.B.A. (Ed.), *Encyclopedia of Information Science and Technology* (4th ed., pp. 2326–2335). Hershey, PA: IGI Global.

Draper, R. J. (2008). Redefining content area literacy teacher education: Finding my voice through collaboration. *Harvard Educational Review, 78*(1), 60–83.

Dreher, P. (2000). Electronic poetry: Student-constructed hypermedia. *English Journal, 90*(2), 68–73.

Duff, F., Fieldsend, E., Bowyer-Crane, C., & Hulme, C. (2008). Reading with vocabulary intervention: Evaluation of an instruction for children with poor response to reading intervention. *Journal of Research in Reading, 31*(3), 319–336.

Duffelmeyer, F. A., & Baum, D. D. (1992). The extended anticipation guide revisited. *Journal of Reading, 35*(8), 654–656.

Duffy, C. M. (2016, January 1). *The impact of flipped learning on student achievement in an eighth grade earth science classroom.* ProQuest LLC.

Duffy, G. G. (1983). From turn taking to sense making: Broadening the concept of reading teacher effectiveness. *Journal of Educational Research, 76*, 134–139.

DuFour, R., & Eaker, R. (1998). *Professional learning communities at work: Best practices for enhancing student achievement.* Reston, VA: Association for Supervision and Curriculum Development.

Duhaylongsod, L., Snow, C., Selman, R., & Donovan, M. S. (2015). Toward disciplinary literacy: Dilemmas and challenges in designing history curriculum to support middle school students. *Harvard Educational Review, 85*(4), 587–608.

Duke, N. K., & Pearson, P. D. (2002). Effective practices for developing reading comprehension. In A. E. Farstrup & S. J. Samuels (Eds.), *What research has to say about reading instruction* (3rd ed., pp. 205–242). Newark, DE: International Reading Association.

Duncan, A. (2010). *A Blueprint for reform: The reauthorization of the Elementary and Secondary Education Act.* Washington, DC: U.S. Department of Education.

Dunkle, C. (2012). *Leading the Common Core State Standards: From common sense to common practice.* Thousand Oaks, CA: Corwin Press.

Dyer, D. (1997). *Jack London: A biography.* New York, NY: Scholastic.

Durrow, H. (2010). *The girl who fell from the sky.* Chapel Hill, NC: Algonquin Books of Chapel Hill.

Davis, A., & McGrail, E. (2009). "Proof-revising" with podcasting: Keeping readers in mind as students listen to and rethink their writing. *The Reading Teacher, 62*(6), 522–529.

Eanet, M., & Manzo, A. V. (1976). REAP: A strategy for improving reading/writing/study skills. *Journal of Reading, 19*, 647–652.

Echevarria, J., & Graves, A. (2003). *Sheltered content instruction: Teaching English-language learners with diverse abilities* (2nd ed.). Boston, MA: Allyn & Bacon.

Echevarria, J., Vogt, M., & Short, D. J. (2008). *Making content comprehensible for English language learners: The SIOP model* (3rd ed.). Boston, MA: Allyn & Bacon.

Echevarria, J., Vogt, M., & Short, D. J. (2017). *Making content comprehensible for English Learners: The SIOP Model* (5th ed.). Boston, MA: Pearson.

Echlin, H. (2007). *Digital discussion: Take your class to the Internet.* Retrieved September 8, 2008, from www.edutopia.org/whats-next-2007-Blog

Education Week. (2014, November 14). *NCLB waivers: A state-by-state breakdown* [Map]. Retrieved from http://www.edweek.org/ew/section/infographics/nclbwaivers.html

Education Week Research Center. (2016). *The Education Week Tech Confidence Index: Teachers and Technology Use in the Classroom 2016.* Retrieved from https://www.edweek.org/ew/section/multimedia/education-week-tech-confidence-index-teacher-and.html

Educational Technology Standards for Students (2007). Washington, DC: International Society for Technology in Education. Available at http://www.iste.org/Libraries/PDFs/NETS-S_Standards.sflb.ashx

Edwards, P. (1967). *Equiano's travels: The interesting narrative of the life of Olaudah Equiano or Gustavus Vassa, the African.* New York, NY: Praeger.

Ehren, B. J., Deshler, D. D., & Graner, P. S. (2010). Using the content literacy continuum as a framework for implementing RTI in secondary schools. *Theory Into Practice, 49*(4), 315–322

Ehst, S.E., & Hermann-Wilmarth, J. M. (2014). Troubling the single story: Teaching international narrative through a critical literacy lens. *The ALAN Review, 41*(3), 24–30.

Einstein, C. (2003). *Activating comprehension: Non-fiction in the classroom.* EPS Update. Retrieved Nov. 1, 2018, from https://eps.schoolspecialty.com/EPS/media/Site-Resources/Downloads/articles/Nonfiction.pdf

Eisner, E. (1997). Cognition and representation: A way to pursue the American dream? *Phi Delta Kappan, 78*, 349–353.

Eisner, E. W. (1985). *The educational imagination: On the design and evaluation of school programs* (2nd ed.). New York, NY: Macmillan.

Eisner, E. W. (1991). The celebration of thinking. *Maine Scholar, 4*, 39–52.

Eisner, W. (2000). *New York: The big city.* New York, NY: DC Comics.

Environmental Protection Agency. (2009). *Municipal solid waste generation, recycling, and disposal in the United States: Detailed tables and figures for 2008.* Washington, DC: Office of Resource Conservation and Recovery.

Epstein, S., & Epstein, B. W. (1978). *Dr. Beaumont and the man with a hole in his stomach.* New York, NY: Coward McCann & Geoghegan.

Erickson, B. (1996). Read-alouds reluctant readers relish. *Journal of Adolescent & Adult Literacy, 40*(3), 212–215.

Evans, C. W., Leija, A. J., & Falkner, T. R. (2001). *Math links: Teaching the NCTM 2000 standards through children's literature.* Englewood, CO: Teacher Ideas Press.

Fadiman, A. (1997). *The spirit catches you and you fall down: A Hmong child, her American doctors, and the collision of two cultures.* New York, NY: Farrar, Straus and Giroux.

Fairbairn, S., & Jones-Vo, S. (2010). *Differentiating instruction and assessment for English language learners.* Philadelphia, PA: Caslon Publishing.

Faltis, C. J., & Coulter, C. A. (2004). *Teaching English learners and immigrant students in secondary schools.* Upper Saddle River, NJ: Pearson.

Fang, Z. (2010). Improving middle school students' science literacy through reading infusion. *The Journal of Educational Research, 103*(4), 262–273.

Fang, Z., & Coatoam, S. (2013). Disciplinary literacy: What you want to know about it. *Journal of Adolescent and Adult Literacy, 56*(8), 627–632.

Fang, Z., & Pace, B. G. (2013). Teaching with challenging texts in the disciplines: Text complexity and close reading. *Journal of Adolescent & Adult Literacy, 57*(2), 104–108.

Gallagher, K. (2014). Making the most of mentor texts. *Educational Leadership, 71*(7), 28–33.

Farmer, H. M., & Ramsdale, J. (2016). Teaching competencies for the online environment. *Canadian Journal of Learning and Technology, 42*(3).

Farmer, N. (2002). *The house of the scorpion*. New York, NY: Atheneum/Richard Jackson.

Farr, R., & Tone, B. (1998). *Assessment portfolio and performance* (2nd ed.). Orlando, FL: Harcourt Brace.

Farrell, J. (2005). *Invisible allies: Microbes that shape our lives*. New York, NY: Farrar, Straus & Giroux.

Featro, S. M., & DiGregorio, D. (2016). Blogging as an instructional tool in the ESL classroom. *TESL-EJ, 20*(1).

Feelings, T. (1995). *The middle passage: White ships, black cargo*. New York, NY: Dial.

Fichett, P., & Heafner, T. (2010). A national perspective on the effects of high-stakes testing and standardization on elementary social studies marginalization. *Theory and research in social education, 38*(1), 114–130.

Finn, P. (1999). *Literacy with an attitude: Educating working class students in their own self-interest*. Albany: State University of New York Press.

Fisher, D. (2004). Setting the "opportunity to read" standard: Resuscitating the SSR program in an urban high school. *Journal of Adolescent & Adult Literacy, 48*, 138–149.

Fisher, D., & Frey, N. (2003). Writing instruction for struggling adolescent readers: A gradual release model. *Journal of Adolescent & Adult Literacy, 46*, 396–405.

Fisher, D., & Frey, N. (2014). Student and teacher perspectives on a close reading protocol. *Literacy Research and Instruction, 53*, 25–49.

Fisher, D., & Frey, N. (2014). Content area vocabulary learning. *The Reading Teacher, 67*(8), 594–599.

Fisher, D., Frey, N., & ElWardi, R. (2005). Creating independent writers and thinkers in secondary schools. In R. Indrisano & J. A. Paratore (Eds.), *Learning to write, writing to learn: Theory and research in practice*. Newark, DE: International Reading Association.

Fisher, D., Frey, N., & Lapp, D. (2011). Coaching middle-level teachers to think aloud improves comprehension instruction and student reading achievement. *The Teacher Educator, 46*(3), 231–243.

Flack, O., Mang, C., & Woessmann, L. (2017). Virtually no effect? Different uses of classroom computers and their effect on student achievement. *Oxford Bulletin of Economics and Statistics, 80*(1), 1–38.

Flanigan, K., & Greenwood, S. C. (2007). Effective content vocabulary instruction in the middle: Matching students, purposes, words, and strategies. *Journal of Adolescent & Adult Literacy, 51*(3), 226–238.

Flavell, J. H. (1976). Metacognitive aspects of problem solving. In L. B. Resnick (Ed.), *The nature of intelligence* (pp. 38–62). Mahwah, NJ: Erlbaum.

Flavell, J. H. (1981). Cognitive monitoring. In P. Dickson (Ed.), *Communication skills*. Orlando, FL: Academic Press.

Flynt, E.S., & Brozo, W. G. (2008). Developing academic language: Got words? *The Reading Teacher, 61*(6), 500–502.

Fleischman, J. (2002). *Phineas Gage: A gruesome but true story about brain science*. Boston, MA: Houghton Mifflin.

Fleischman, P. (1988). *Joyful noise: Poems for two voices*. New York, NY: HarperCollins.

Fleischman, P. (2000). *Big talk: Poems for four voices*. New York, NY: Candlewick.

Fleming, T. (1988). *Band of brothers: West Point in the Civil War*. New York, NY: Walker.

Foon, D. (2004). *Skud*. Toronto, Canada: Groundwood Books.

Ford-Connors, E., Dougherty, S., Robertson, D. A., & Paratore, J. R. (2015). Mediating complex texts in the upper grades: Considering motivation, instructional intensity, and cognitive challenge. *Journal of Adolescent & Adult Literacy 58*(8), 650–659.

Foss, A. (2002). Peeling the onion: Teaching critical literacy with students of privilege. *Language Arts, 79*(5), 393–403.

Fought, C. (2005). *Do you speak American: Are dialects fading?* Retrieved from http://www.pbs.org/speak/ahead/mediapower/dialect

Fox, M., & Wilton, N. (Illustrator). (2000). *Feathers and fools*. San Diego, CA: Voyager.

Fradin, D., & Fradin, J. (2006). *5,000 miles to freedom: Ellen and William Craft's flight from slavery*. Washington, DC: National Geographic.

Frank, A. (1967). *Anne Frank: The diary of a young girl*. New York, NY: Doubleday.

Freedman, R. (1995). *Immigrant kids*. New York, NY: Puffin.

Freedman, R. (2000). *Give me liberty! The story of the Declaration of Independence*. New York, NY: Holiday House.

Freedman, R. (2005). *Children of the Great Depression*. New York, NY: Clarion Books.

Freeman, E. B., & Person, D. G. (1998). *Connecting informational children's books with content area learning*. Boston, MA: Allyn & Bacon.

Freire, P. (1970/2000). *Pedagogy of the oppressed*. New York, NY: Continuum.

Frey, N., & Fisher, D. (2012). If you want to help students organize their learning: Fold, think, and write with three-dimensional graphic organizers. In D. Lapp, & B. Moss (Eds.), *Exemplary instruction in the middle grades: Teaching that supports engagement and rigorous learning* (pp. 310–320). New York, NY: Guilford Press.

Friend, R. (2000–2001). Teaching summarization as a content area strategy. *Journal of Adolescent & Adult Literacy, 44*, 320–329.

Friesen, J. (2008). *Jerk, California*. New York, NY: Penguin.

Frost, Robert. (1915). *North of Boston*. New York, NY: Henry Holt and Company.

Fry, E. (1977). Fry's readability graph: Clarifications, validity, and extension to level 17. *Journal of Reading, 21*, 242–252.

Frydenberg, M., & Andone, D. (2016). Creating micro-videos to demonstrate technology learning and digital literacy. *Interactive Technology and Smart Education, 13*(4), 261–273.

Fuchs, L., Fuchs, D., & Compton, D. (2010). Rethinking response to intervention at middle and high school. *School Psychology Review, 39*(1), 22–28.

Fuchs, L. S., Fuchs, D., Prentice, K., Burch, M., Hamlett, C. L., Owen, R., . . . Jancek, D. (2003). Explicitly teaching for transfer: Effects of third-grade students' mathematical problem solving. *Journal of Educational Psychology, 95*(2), 293–305.

Fulton, M., & Porter, M. (2000). *Common state strategies to improve student reading*. Denver, CO: ECS.

Furman, L. R. (2017, December 6). STEM needs to be updated to STREAM. *Huff Post*. Retrieved from https://www.huffingtonpost.com/rob-furman/stem-needs-updated-to-str_b_5461814.html

Gagne, R. (1970). *The conditions of learning*. New York, NY: Holt, Rinehart, and Winston.

Gaiman, N. (2006). *Coraline*. New York, NY: HarperCollins.

Gallant, R. A. (1991). *Earth's vanishing forests*. New York, NY: Macmillan.

Gallo, D. R. (2007). *First crossing: Stories about teen immigrants*. Cambridge, MA: Candlewick Press.

Gambrell, L. B. (1980). Think-time: Implications for reading instruction. *Reading Teacher, 33*, 143–146.

Ganske, K. (2012). If you want students to learn vocabulary move beyond copying words. In D. Lapp, & B. Moss (Eds.), *Exemplary instruction in the middle grades* (pp. 205–224). New York, NY: Guilford Press.

Gantos, J. (2002). *Hole in my life*. New York, NY: Farrar, Straus & Giroux.

Garcia, E. (2002). *Student cultural diversity: Understanding and meeting the challenge* (3rd ed.). Boston, MA: Houghton Mifflin.

Garland, S., & Kiuchi, T. (Illustrator). (1993). *The lotus seed*. San Diego, CA: Harcourt.

Gay, G. (1995). A multicultural school curriculum. In C. A. Grant & M. Gomez (Eds.), *Making school multicultural: Campus and classroom* (pp. 37–54). Englewood Cliffs, NJ: Merrill/Prentice Hall.

Gay, G. (2000). *Culturally responsive teaching: Theory, research, and practice*. New York, NY: Teachers College Press.

Gee, J. P. (1996). *Social linguistics and literacies: Ideology in discourses* (2nd ed.). London, England: Falmer Press.

Gee, J. P. (2012). *Social linguistics and literacies: Ideology in discourses* (4th ed.). New York, NY: Routledge.

Geiger, A. (2018). *America's public school teachers are far less racially and ethnically diverse than their students*. Retrieved from http://www.pewresearch.org

Gere, A. R. (Ed.). (1985). *Roots in the sawdust: Writing to learn across the disciplines*. Urbana, IL: National Council of Teachers of English.

Gersten, R., & Jimenez, R. (1994). A delicate balance: Enhancing literature instruction for students of English as a second language. *Reading Teacher, 47*, 438–449.

Gess, A. H. (2017). STEAM education: Separating fact from fiction. *Technology and Engineering Teacher, 77*(3), 39–41.

Giblin, J. (2000). More than just the facts: A hundred years of children's nonfiction. *The Horn Book, 76*, 413–424.

Giblin, J. (2002). *The life and death of Adolf Hitler*. New York, NY: Clarion Books.

Giblin, J., & Dooling, M. (Illustrator). (1994). *Thomas Jefferson: A picture book biography*. New York, NY: Scholastic.

Giblin, J. C. (1995). *When plague strikes: The Black Death, smallpox, AIDS*. New York, NY: HarperCollins.

Giblin, J. C., & Dooling, M. (Illustrator). (2000). *The amazing life of Benjamin Franklin*. New York, NY: Scholastic.

Gibbons, P. (2002). *Scaffolding language scaffolding learning: Teaching second language learners in the mainstream classroom*. Portsmouth, NH: Heinemann.

Gillet, J., & Kita, M. J. (1979). Words, kids, and categories. *Reading Teacher, 32*, 538–542.

Gillis, V. (2014). Disciplinary literacy: *Adapt* not adopt. *Journal of Adolescent & Adult Literacy, 57*(8), 614–623.

Gilster, P. (1997). *Digital literacy*. New York, NY: Wiley Computer Pub.

Girard, B., & Harris, L. (2012). Striving for disciplinary literacy instruction: Cognitive tools in a world history course. *Theory and Research in Social Education, 40*, 230–259.

Glover, T. A., Kettler, R. J., Reddy, L. A., & Kurz, A. (2019). Formative Assessment Approaches to Inform Teacher Practices: Key Considerations. *Assessment for Effective Intervention, 44*(2), 67–68.

Goble, P. (1991). *I sing for the animals*. New York, NY: Bradbury.

Gokhale, A., & Machina, K. (2018). Guided online group discussion enhances student critical thinking skills. *International Journal on E-Learning, 17*(2), 157–173.

Goldman, S. (2012). Adolescent literacy: Learning and understanding content. *The Future of Children, 22*(2), 89–116.

Golenbock, P., & Bacon, P. (Illustrator). (1990). *Teammates*. San Diego, CA: Harcourt Brace Jovanovich.

Gomez, L. M., & Gomez, K. (2007). Reading for learning: Literacy supports for 21st century work. *Phi Delta Kappan, 89*(3), 224–228.

Gonick, L. (1991). *Cartoon history of the United States*. New York, NY: HarperCollins.

Goodall, J. (1979). *The story of an English village*. New York, NY: Atheneum.

Goodlad, J. (1984). *A place called school*. New York, NY: McGraw-Hill.

Goodman, K., & Goodman, Y. (1978). *Reading of American children whose language is a stable rural dialect of English or a language other than English*. Washington, DC: National Institute of Education. (ERIC Document Reproduction Service No. ED173754)

Goodrich, F., & Hackett, A. (2000). *The diary of Anne Frank: Play and related readings*. New York, NY: Dramatists Play Service.

Graham, S. (2005). Strategy instruction and the teaching of writing: A meta-analysis. In C. A. MacArthur, S. Graham, & J. Fitzgerald (Eds.), *Handbook of writing research*. New York, NY: Guilford Press.

Gray, W. S. (1925). *Summary of investigations related to reading* (Supplementary Educational Monographs, No. 28). Chicago, IL: University of Chicago Press.

Graziano, K. J., & Hall, J. D. (2017). Flipping math in a secondary classroom. *Journal of Computers in Mathematics and Science Teaching, 36*(1), 5–16.

Gredler, M. E., & Johnson, R. L. (2004). *Assessment in the literacy classroom*. Boston, MA: Pearson.

Green, J. (2012). *The fault in our stars* (1st ed.). New York, NY: Dutton Books.

Greenberg, J., & Jordan, S. (1998). *Chuck Close: Up close*. New York, NY: DK.

Greene, B. (1999). *Summer of my German soldier*. New York, NY: Puffin Books.

Greenlee-Moore, M. E., & Smith, L. L. (1996). Interactive computer software: The effects on young children's reading achievement. *Reading Psychology, 17*, 43–64.

Griffin, G. A. (1991). Interactive staff development: Using what we know. In A. Lieberman & L. Miller (Eds.), *Staff development for education in the '90s* (pp. 243–258). New York, NY: Teachers College Press.

Grimes, N. (2002). *Bronx masquerade*. New York, NY: Speak.

Grove, N. (1981, March). Wild cargo: The business of smuggling animals. *National Geographic, 159*, 287–315.

Gruenewald, M. M. (2005). *Looking like the enemy: My story of imprisonment in Japanese American internment camps*. Troutdale, OR: New Sage Press.

Guastello, E. F., Beasley, T. M., & Sinatra, R. C. (2000). Concept mapping effects on science content comprehension of low-achieving inner-city seventh graders. *Remedial and Special Education, 21*, 356–365.

Guilfoyle, C. (2006). NCLB: Is there life beyond testing? *Educational Leadership, 64*(3), 8–13.

Gunderson, L. (2007). *English-only instruction and immigrant students in secondary schools: A critical examination.* Mahwah, NJ: Erlbaum.

Gunderson, L. (2009, February). *Where are the English Language Learners?* Paper presented at English Language Learner Institute at the Annual Convention of the International Reading Association, Phoenix, AZ.

Gunning, T. G. (2006). *Closing the literacy gap.* Boston, MA: Pearson.

Gunning, T. G. (2010). *Creating literacy instruction for all students* (8th ed.). Boston, MA: Pearson.

Gunning, T. G. (2019). *Creating literacy instruction for all students.* Boston, MA: Pearson.

Gunter, G., & Kenny, R. (2008). Digital booktalk: Digital media for reluctant readers. *Contemporary Issues in Technology and Teacher Education (CITE Journal), 8*(1), 84–99.

Guth, N. D., & Pettengill, S. S. (2005). *Leading a successful reading program: Administrators and reading specialists working together to make it happen.* Newark, DE: International Reading Association.

Guthrie, J. T., & Davis, M. H. (2003). Motivating struggling readers in middle school through an engagement model of classroom practice. *Reading and Writing Quarterly, 19*, 59–85.

Guthrie, J. T., & Humenick, N. M. (2004). Motivating students to read: Evidence for classroom practices that increase reading motivation and achievement. In P. McCardle & V. Chhabra (Eds.), *The voice of evidence in reading research* (pp. 329–354). Baltimore, MD: Brookes.

Guthrie, J. T., & McCann, A. D. (1996). Idea circles: Peer collaborations for conceptual learning. In L. B. Gambrell & J. F. Almasi (Eds.), *Lively discusssions! Fostering engaged reading* (pp. 87–105). Newark, DE: International Reading Association.

Guthrie, J. T., & Wigfield, A. (1997). Reading engagement: A rationale for theory and teaching. In J. T. Guthrie &

A. Wigfield (Eds.), *Reading engagement: Motivating readers through integrated instruction* (pp. 1–12). Newark, DE: International Reading Association.

Guthrie, J. T., & Wigfield, A. (2000). Engagement and motivation in reading. In M. Kamil, P. Mosenthal, P. D. Pearson, & R. Barr (Eds.), *Handbook of reading research, Vol. III* (pp. 403–424). Mahwah, NJ: Erlbaum.

Guthrie, J. T., Schafer, W. D., & Huang, C. (2001). Benefits of opportunity to read and balanced instruction on the NAEP. *Journal of Educational Research, 94*, 145–162.

Hadaway, N. L., Vardell, S. M., & Young, T. A. (2002). *Literature-based instruction with English language learners.* Boston, MA: Allyn & Bacon.

Hahn, M. D. (2003). *Hear the wind blow.* New York, NY: Clarion Books.

Hakim, J. (1999). *A history of US.* New York, NY: Oxford University Press.

Hall, B. (2004). *Literacy coaches: An evolving role.* Retrieved October 21, 2006, from www.carnegie.org/reporter/09literacy/index.html

Halliday, M., & Hasan, R. (1976). *Cohesion in English.* London, England: Longman.

Halpern, D. F. (1998). Teaching critical thinking for transfer across domains: Dispositions, skills, structure training, and metacognitive monitoring, *American Psychologist, 53*(4), 449–455.

Halverson, Lisa R., Graham, Charles R., Spring, Kristian J., & Drysdale, Jeffery S. (2012). An analysis of high impact scholarship and publication trends in blended learning. *Distance Education, 33*, pp. 381–413. Retrieved from https://www.tandfonline.com/doi/full/10.1080/01587919.2012.723166

Hamilton, V. (1985). *The people could fly: American black folktales.* New York, NY: Knopf.

Hamilton, V. (1988). *In the beginning: Creation stories from around the world.* Orlando, FL: Harcourt Brace.

Hammond, Z. (2015). *Culturally responsive teaching and the brain: Promoting authentic engagement and rigor among culturally and linguistically diverse students.* Thousand Oaks, CA: Corwin.

Hancock, M. (2007). *A celebration of literature and response: Children, books, and teachers in K–8 classrooms* (3rd ed.). New York, NY: Prentice Hall.

Hancock, M. R. (1993). Exploring and extending personal response through

literature journals. *Reading Teacher, 46*, 466–474.

Hansen, J. (1986). *Which way freedom?* New York, NY: Walker.

Hansen, M., Levesque, E., Valant, J., & Quintero, D. (2018). *The 2018 Brown Center report on American education: How well are American students learning?* Retrieved from https://www.brookings.edu/wp-content/uploads/2018/06/2018-Brown-Center-Report-on-American-Education_FINAL1.pdf

Harlen, W. (2005). Teachers' summative practices and assessment for learning tensions and synergies. *The Curriculum Journal, 16*(2), 207–223.

Harmon, J. M., Hedrick, W. B., Wood, K., & Gress, M. (2005). Vocabulary self-selection: A study of middle-school students' word selections from expository texts. *Reading Writing Quarterly, 26*, 313–333.

Hamon, J. M., Wood, K. D., Hedrick, W. B., Vintinner, J., & Willeford, T. (2009). Interactive word walls: More than just reading and writing on the walls. *Journal of Adolescent & Adult Literacy, 52*(5), 398–408.

Hart, P. D., & Teeter, R. M. (2002). *A national priority: Americans speak on teacher quality.* Princeton, NJ: Educational Testing Service.

Harvey, D. (2002). *Literature circles: Voice and choice in book clubs and reading groups.* Portland, ME: Stenhouse.

Harvey, S. (1998). *Nonfiction matters: Reading, writing, and research in grades 3–8.* Portland, ME: Stenhouse.

Harvey, S., & Goudvis, A. (2000). *Strategies that work: Teaching comprehension to enhance understanding.* York, ME: Stenhouse.

Harvey, S., & Goudvis, A. (2007). *Strategies that work: Teaching comprehension for understanding and engagement.* York, ME: Stenhouse.

Harvey, S., & Goudvis, A. (2017). *Strategies that work: Teaching comprehension for understanding, engagement, and building knowledge.* Portsmouth, NH: Stenhouse.

Hassler, A. & Resnik, B. (1957). *Martin Luther King and the Montgomery story.* New York, NY: Fellowship of Reconciliation.

Hayes, D. A. (1989). Helping students grasp the knack of writing summaries. *Journal of Reading, 33*, 96–101.

Haynes, J. (2007). *Getting started with English language learners: How educators can meet the challenge*. Alexandria, VA: Association for Supervision and Curriculum Development.

Haynes, M. (2011). The federal role in confronting the crisis in adolescent literacy. *The Education Digest, 76*(8), 10–15.

Healy, M. K. (1982). Using student response groups in the classroom. In G. Camp (Ed.), *Teaching writing: Essays from the Bay Area writing project* (pp. 266–290). Portsmouth, NH: Boyton-Cook.

Heath, S. (1983). *Ways with words: Language, life, and work in communities and classrooms*. Cambridge, MA: Harvard University Press.

Heath, S., & Mangiola, L. (1989). *Children of promise: Literate activity on linguistically and culturally diverse classrooms*. Washington, DC: National Education Association.

Hedges, H., Cullen, J., & Jordon, B. (2011). Early years of curriculum: Funds of knowledge as a conceptual framework for children's interests. *Journal of Curriculum Studies, 43*(2), 185–205.

Heitin, L. (2009). *Grassroots professional development*. Retrieved February 5, 2013, from http://www.edweek.org/tsb/articles/2009/03/16/02timmons.ho2.html

Helfer, A. (2006). *Malcolm X: A graphic biography*. New York, NY: Farrar, Straus & Giroux.

Herber, H. L. (1964). Teaching reading and physics simultaneously. In J. A. Figurel (Ed.), *Improvement of reading through classroom practice. Proceedings of the 9th Annual Convention of the International Reading Association, 9*, 84–85.

Herber, H. L. (1970). *Teaching reading in content areas*. Englewood Cliffs, NJ: Prentice Hall.

Herber, H. L. (1978). *Teaching reading in content areas* (2nd ed.). Upper Saddle River, NJ: Prentice Hall.

Herrell, A. L., & Jordan, M. (2016). *50 strategies for teaching English language learners* (5th ed.). Boston, MA: Pearson.

Herrera, L. J. P., & Kidwell, T. (2018). Literature circles 2.0: Updating a classic strategy for the 21st century. *Multicultural Education, 25*(2), 17–21.

Herrera, S. G., & Murry, K. G. (2016). *Mastering ESL/EFL methods: Differentiated instruction for culturally and linguistically diverse (CLD) students*. Upper Saddle River, NJ: Pearson.

Herrera, S. G, Holmes, M. A., & Kavimandan, S. K. (2012). Bringing theory to life: Strategies that make culturally responsive pedagogy a reality in diverse secondary classrooms. *International Journal of Multicultural Education, 14*(3), 1–19.

Hesse, K. (1997). *Out of the dust*. New York, NY: Scholastic.

Hickam, H. (1998). *Rocket boys*. New York, NY: Delacorte.

Hicks, T. (2013). *Crafting digital writing: Composing texts across media and genres*. Portsmouth, NH: Heinemann.

Hicks, T., Russo, A., Autrey, T., Gardner, R., Kabodian, A., & Edington, C. (2007). Rethinking the purposes and processes for designing digital portfolios. *Journal of Adolescent & Adult Literacy, 50*(6), 450–458.

Hiebert, E. (2011). Using multiple sources of information in establishing text complexity. *Reading Research Report #11.03*. Santa Cruz, CA: TextProject, Inc.

Hiltabidel, J. (2013). Investigating thinking in math class. *Educational Leadership, 70*(4).

Hilton, J. T. (2016). A case study of the application of SAMR and TPACK for reflection on technology integration into two social studies classrooms. *Social Studies, 107*(2), 68–73.

Hinds, G. (2007). *Beowulf*. New York, NY: Candlewick.

Hobbs, R. (2007). *Reading the media: Media literacy in high school English*. New York, NY: Teachers College, Columbia University.

Hobbs, W. (1989). *Bearstone*. New York, NY: Atheneum.

Hoffman, J. V. (1979). The intra-act procedure for critical reading. *Journal of Reading, 22*, 605–608.

Hoffman, J. V., Au, K. H., Harrison, C., Paris, S. G., Pearson, P. D., Santa, C. M., . . . Valencia, S. W. (1999). High-stakes assessments in reading: Consequences, concerns, and common sense. In S. J. Barrentine (Ed.), *Reading assessment: Principles and practices for elementary teachers* (pp. 21–34). Newark, DE: International Reading Association.

Hofstede, G., Hofstede, G. J., & Minkov, M. (2010). *Cultures and organizations: Software of the mind*. New York, NY: McGraw-Hill.

Holston, V., & Santa, C. (1985). RAFT: A method of writing across the curriculum that works. *Journal of Reading, 28*, 456–457.

Holt, K. W. (1999). *When Zachary Beaver came to town*. New York, NY: Holt.

Homer, C. (1979). A direct reading-thinking activity for content areas. In R. T. Vacca & J. A. Meagher (Eds.), *Reading through content* (pp. 41–48). Storrs: University Publications and the University of Connecticut Reading-Language Arts Center.

Honey, M. (1999). *Bitter fruit: African American women in World War II*. Columbia: University of Missouri Press.

Hoose, P. M. (2001). *We were there, too! Young people in U.S. history*. New York, NY: Farrar, Straus & Giroux.

Hopkins, E. (2008). *Impulse*. New York, NY: Margaret K. McElderry.

Horowitz, R. (2017). Drama-Based Pedagogy: New Ways of Incorporating Drama into the Secondary Classroom. *Texas Association For Literacy Education Yearbook*, 99–111.

Hosseini, K. (2007). *A thousand splendid suns*. New York, NY: Riverhead.

Houston, R., Hudson, R., La Tour, N., Ellison, A., Sapp, J., & Davis, D. (2005). *Mighty times: The children's march*. Montgomery, AL: Teaching Tolerance.

Hoyt-Goldsmith, D., & Migdale, L. (Photographer). (1994). *Day of the Dead: A Mexican-American celebration*. New York, NY: Holiday House.

Huffaker, D. (2005). The educated blogger: Using weblogs to promote literacy in the classroom. *AACE Journal, 13*(2), 91–98.

Hunt, I. (1964). *Across five Aprils*. New York, NY: Follett.

Hunt, J. (2007). Redefining the young adult novel. *Horn Book*. 2007. Retrieved February 14, 2009, from www.hbook.com/magazine/articles/2007/mar07_hunt.asp

Hynd, C. R., McNish, M. E., Guzzetti, B., Lay, K., & Fowler, P. (1994). *What high school students say about their science texts*. Paper presented at the annual meeting of the College Reading Association, New Orleans, LA.

Igus, T. (1998). *I see the rhythm*. San Francisco, CA: Children's Book Press.

Imbriale, R. (2013). Blended learning. *Principal Leadership*, 13(6), 30–34.

Innocenti, R. (1985). *Rose Blanche*. San Diego, CA: Creative Editions.

Institute of Education Sciences. (2008). *Improving adolescent literacy: Effective classroom and intervention practices*. IES Practice Guide. Retrieved from https://dwlibrary.wested.org/mediacore-files/Adolescent%20Literacy/1.%20Overview%20&%20Tools/2119637-4413500-adlit_pg_082608-attachment.pdf

Institute of Education Sciences. (2011). *The nation's report card: Reading 2011*. Washington, DC: U.S. Department of Education.

International Literacy Association. (2018). *Improving digital practices for literacy, learning, and justice: More than just tools* [Literacy leadership brief]. Newark, DE: International Literacy Association.

International Reading Association. (1999a). *Adolescent literacy position statement*. Newark, DE: Author.

International Reading Association. (1999b). *High-stakes assessments in reading: A position paper of the International Reading Association*. Newark, DE: Author.

International Reading Association. (2005). *Standards for middle and high school literacy coaches*. Newark, DE: Author. Retrieved March 1, 2006, from www.reading.org/downloads/resources/597coaching_standards.pdf

International Reading Association. (2006). *Standards for reading professionals*. Retrieved July 6, 2006, from www.reading.org/styleguide/standards_reading_profs.html

International Reading Association. (2006). *Standards for middle and high school literacy coaches*. Newark, DE: Author.

International Reading Association. (2008). *Implications for reading teachers in response to intervention (RTI)*. Retrieved October 9, 2008, from www.reading.org/downloads/resources/rti0707_implications.pdf

International Reading Association. (2012). *Adolescent Literacy: A position statement of the International Reading Association*. Retrieved from https://www.literacyworldwide.org/docs/default-source/where-we-stand/adolescent-literacy-position-statement.pdf

International Reading Association & National Council of Teachers of English. (1997). *Standards for the English language arts*. Newark, DE: Author.

Ivey, G. (2002). Getting started: Manageable literacy practices. *Educational Leadership*, 60, 20–23.

Ivey, G., & Broaddus, K. (2001). "Just plain reading": A survey of what makes students want to read in middle school classrooms. *Reading Research Quarterly*, 36, 350–377.

Ivey, G., & Fisher, D. (2005). Learning from what doesn't work. *Educational Leadership*, 63(2), 8–15.

Izzo, A., & Schmidt, P. R. (2006). A successful ABC's in-service project: Supporting culturally responsive teaching. In P. R. Schmidt & C. Finkbeiner (Eds.), *ABC's of cultural understanding and communication: National and international adaptations* (pp. 19–42). Greenwich, CT: Information Age Publishing.

Jackson, R. (1975). *Inside hitting with Reggie Jackson*. Chicago, IL: Regnery.

James, F. (2004). *Response to intervention in the Individuals with Disabilities Education Act (IDEA) 2004*. Retrieved November 19, 2008, from www.reading.org/downloads/resources/IDEA_RTI/report.pdf

Jasper, K. C. (1995). The limits of technology. *English Journal*, 84(6), 16–17.

Jenkins, S. (2002). *Life on earth: The story of evolution*. Boston, MA: Houghton Mifflin.

Jitendra, A. K., & Gajria, M. (2011). Main idea and summarization instruction to improve reading comprehension. In R. E. O'Connor & P. F. Vadasy (Eds.), *Handbook of reading interventions* (pp. 198–219). New York, NY: Guilford Press.

Johnson, A. (2003). *The first part last*. New York, NY: Simon Pulse.

Johnson, D. D., & Pearson, P. D. (1984). *Teaching reading vocabulary* (2nd ed.). Fort Worth, TX: Holt, Rinehart, and Winston.

Johnson, D. W., & Johnson, F. (2009a). *Joining together: Group theory and group skills* (10th ed.). Boston, MA: Allyn & Bacon.

Johnson, D. W., & Johnson, R. T. (2009b). An educational psychology success story: Social interdependence theory and cooperative learning. *Educational Researcher*, 38(5), 365–379.

Johnson, D. W., Johnson, R., & Holubec, E. (2008). *Cooperation in the classroom* (7th ed.). Edina, MN: Interaction Book Company.

Johnson, D. W., & Steele, V. (1996). So many words, so little time: Helping college ESL learners acquire vocabulary-building strategies. *Journal of Adolescent & Adult Literacy*, 39, 348–357.

Johnson, E., Mellard, D. F., Fuchs, D., & McKnight, M. A. (2006). *Responsiveness to intervention: How to do it*. Lawrence, KS: National Research Center on Learning Disabilities.

Jones, B. F., Pierce, J., & Hunter, B. (1988–1989). Teaching students to construct graphic representations. *Educational Leadership*, 46(4), 20–25.

Kamil, M. (2003). *Adolescents and literacy: Reading for the 21st century*. Washington, DC: Alliance for Excellent Education.

Kang, H.-S. (2017). Comic book project as a tool for teaching multimodal argument and fostering critical thinking skills: Implications for the L2 writing classroom. *CEA Forum*, 46(2), 202–216.

Kanter, D. (2010). Doing the project and learning the content: Designing project-based science curricula for meaningful understanding. *Science Education*, 94(3), 525–551.

Kaplan, L. S., & Owings, W. A. (2003). The politics of teacher quality. *Phi Delta Kappan*, 84(9), 687–692.

Karchmer, R. A., Mallette, M. H., Kara-Soteriou, J., & Leu, D. J. (2005). *Innovative approaches to literacy education: Using the Internet to support new literacies*. Newark, DE: International Reading Association.

Karchmer-Klein, R., & Shinas, V. (2012). Guiding principles for supporting new literacies in your classroom. *Reading Teacher*, 65(5), 288–293.

Kauffman, D., Zhao, R., & Yang, Y.-S. (2011). Effects of online note taking formats and self-monitoring prompts on learning from online text: Using technology to enhance self-regulated learning. *Contemporary Educational Psychology*, 36(4), 313–322.

Kaywell, J. (1994). Using young adult fiction and nonfiction to produce critical readers. *The ALAN Review*, 21, 1–6.

Kazakoff, E. (2013). Toward a theory-predicated definition of digital literacy for early childhood. *Journal of Youth Development*, 9(1), 41–58.

Keegan, J. (2003). *The first world war*. New York, NY: Random House.

Kehoe, A. & Goudzwaard, M. (2015) ePortfolios, badges, and the whole digital self: how evidence-based learning pedagogies and technologies can support integrative learning and identity development. *Theory into Practice, 54*(4), 343–351.

Kelly, J. (2009). *The evolution of Calpurnia Tate*. New York, NY: Henry Holt.

Kennedy, B. (1985). Writing letters to learn math. *Learning, 13*, 58–61.

Kieffer, M. J., & Lesaux, N. K. (2007). Breaking down words to build meaning: Morphology, vocabulary, and reading, comprehension in the urban classroom. *The Reading Teacher, 61*(2), 134–144.

Kimbell-Lopez, K., Cummins, C., & Manning, E. (2016). Developing digital literacy in the middle school classroom. *Computers in the Schools, 33*(4), 211–226.

King, C., & Osborne, L. B. (1997). *Oh freedom! Kids talk about the civil rights movement with the people who made it happen*. New York, NY: Knopf.

King-Sears, M., Swanson, C., & Mainzer, L. (2011). TECHnology and literacy for adolescents with disabilities. *Journal of Adolescent & Adult Literacy, 54*(8), 569–578.

Kinney, J. (2007). *The diary of a wimpy kid*. New York, NY: Abrams Books.

Kintsch, W. (1977). On comprehending stories. In M. A. Just & P. A. Carpenter (Eds.), *Cognitive processes in comprehension* (pp. 360–401). Mahwah, NJ: Erlbaum.

Kirby, D., Liner, T., & Vinz, M. (1988). *Inside out: Developmental strategies for teaching writing* (2nd ed.). Montclair, NJ: Boynton/Cook.

Kist, W. (2000). Beginning to create the new literacy classroom: What does the new literacy look like? *Journal of Adolescent & Adult Literacy, 43*, 710–718.

Kist, W. (2003). Student achievement in new literacies for the 21st century. *Middle School Journal, 35*(1), 6–13.

Kist, W. (2005). *New literacies in action: Teaching and learning in multiple media*. New York, NY: Teachers College Press.

Kist, W. (2007). Vocabulary media journals: Finding multimedia to define words. In M. T. Christel & S. Sullivan (Eds.), *Lesson plans for creating media-rich classrooms* (pp. 23–29). Urbana, IL: National Council of Teachers of English.

Kist, W. (2010). *The socially networked classroom: Teaching in the new media age*. Thousand Oaks, CA: Corwin Press.

Kist, W. (2012). Middle schools and new literacies: Looking back and moving forward. *Voices from the Middle, 19*(4), 17–21.

Kitchen, B. (1993). *And so they build*. New York, NY: Dial.

Klein, A. (2016). The Every Student Succeeds Act: An ESSA overview. *Education Week, 114*–195. Retrieved from http://www.edweek.org/ew/issues/every-student-succeeds-act/

Klein, N. (2000). *No logo: Taking aim at the brand bullies*. New York, NY: Picador.

Knipper, K., & Duggan, T. (2006). Writing to learn across the curriculum: Tools for comprehension in content area classes. *Reading Teacher, 59*(5), 462–470.

Knobel, M., & Lankshear, C. (2014). Studying New Literacies. *Journal of Adolescent & Adult Literacy, 58*(2), 97–101.

Knoeller, C. P. (1994). Negotiating interpretations of text: The role of student-led discussions in understanding literature. *Journal of Reading, 37*, 572–580.

Koretz, D., & Barron, S. T. (1998). *The validity of gains in scores on the Kentucky Instructional Results Information System*. Santa Monica, CA: Rand.

Krishnan, J., Cusimano, A., Wang, D., & Yim, S. (2018). Writing together: Online synchronous collaboration in middle school. *Journal of Adolescent & Adult Literacy, 62*(2), 163–173.

Krogness, M. (1995). *Just teach me, Mrs. K: Talking, reading, and writing with resistant adolescent learners*. Portsmouth, NH: Heinemann.

Krucli, T. E. (2004). Making assessment matter: Using the computer to create interactive feedback. *English Journal, 94*, 47–52.

Krull, K. (2003). *Harvesting hope: The story of Cesar Chavez*. San Diego, CA: Harcourt.

Krull, K., & Diaz, D. (Illustrator). (2000). *Wilma unlimited: How Wilma Rudolph became the world's fastest woman*. San Diego, CA: Harcourt Brace.

Krull, K., & Hewitt, K. (Illustrator). (1993). *Lives of the musicians: Good times, bad times (and what the neighbors thought)*. San Diego, CA: Harcourt Brace Jovanovich.

Krull, K., & Hewitt, K. (Illustrator). (1995). *Lives of the artists: Masterpieces, messes (and what the neighbors thought)*. San Diego, CA: Harcourt Brace.

Krull, K., & Hewitt, K. (Illustrator). (1997). *Lives of the athletes: Thrills, spills (and what the neighbors thought)*. San Diego, CA: Harcourt Brace.

Kubey, R., & Baker, F. (1999, October 27). Has media literacy found a curricular foothold? *Education Week*. Retrieved August 27, 2008, from www.frankw-baker.com/edweek.htm

Ladson-Billings, G. (1994). *The dream-keepers: Successful teachers of African American students*. San Francisco, CA: Jossey-Bass.

Ladson-Billings, G. (1995). Toward a theory of culturally relevant pedagogy. *American Educational Research Journal, 32*, 465–491.

Ladson-Billings, G. (1999). Preparing teachers for diverse student populations: A critical race theory perspective. In A. I. Nejad & P. D. Pearson (Eds.), *Review of research in education 24*, 211–247. Washington, DC: American Education Research Association.

Ladson-Billings, G. (2006). "Yes, but how do we do it?" Practicing culturally relevant pedagogy. In J. Landsman & C. Lewis (Eds.), *White teachers, diverse classrooms* (pp. 33–46). Sterling, VA: Stylus Publishers.

Lajoie, S.P. (2008). Metacognition, self-regulation, and self-regulated learning: A rose by any other name? *Educational Psychology Review, 20*, 469–475.

Lam, R. (2011). The role of self-assessment in students' writing portfolios: A classroom investigation. *TESL Reporter, 43*(2), 16–34.

Landsman, J., & Lewis, C. W. (2006). *White teachers/diverse classrooms: A guide to building inclusive schools, promoting high expectations, and eliminating racism*. Sterling, VA: Stylus.

Langer, J. A., & Applebee, A. N. (2007). *How writing shapes thinking: A study of teaching and learning*. CO: WAC Clearinghouse Landmark.

Langer, J. A. (1981). From theory to practice: A prereading plan. *Journal of Reading, 25*, 152–156.

Langer, J. A., & Applebee, A. N. (1987). *How writing shapes thinking*. Urbana, IL: National Council of Teachers of English.

Langer, J. A., & Flihan, S. (2000). Writing and reading relationships: Constructive tasks. In R. Indrisano & J. R. Squire (Eds.), *Perspectives on writing: Research, theory, and practice*. Newark, DE: International Reading Association.

Langstaff, J. (1991). *Climbing Jacob's ladder*. New York, NY: Macmillan.

Lankshear, C., & Knobel, M. (2003). *New literacies: Changing knowledge and classroom learning*. Buckingham, UK: Open University Press.

Lankshear, C., & Knobel, M. (2006). *New literacies: Everyday practices and classroom learning*. Open University Press.

Lapp, D., & Fisher, D. (2009). It's all about the book: Motivating teens to read. *Journal of Adolescent and Adult Literacy, 52*(7), 556–561.

Lapp, D., & Flood, J. (1995). Strategies for gaining access to the information superhighway: Off the side street and on to the main road. *Reading Teacher, 48*, 432–436.

Lapp, D., & Moss, B. (2012). *Exemplary instruction in the middle grades*. New York, NY: Guilford Press.

Lapp, D., Fisher, D., Flood, J., & Cabello, A. (2001). An integrated approach to the teaching and assessment of language arts. In S. Hurley & J. V. Tinajero (Eds.), *Literacy assessment of second language learners* (pp. 11–26). Boston, MA: Allyn & Bacon.

Lapp, D., Wolsey, T., Wood, K., & Johnson, K. (2014). *Mining complex text: Using and creating graphic organizers to grasp content and share new understandings*. New York, NY: Corwin.

Larson, B. E. (2000). Classroom discussion: A method of instruction and a curriculum outcome. *Teaching and Teacher Education, 16*, 661–677.

Lasky, K., & Hawkes, K. (Illustrator). (1994). *The librarian who measured the earth*. New York, NY: Little, Brown.

Lasky, K., & Hawkes, K. (Illustrator). (2003). *The man who made time travel*. New York, NY: Farrar, Straus & Giroux.

Lesaux, N. K., Harris, J. R., & Sloane, P. (2012). Adolescents' motivation in the context of an academic vocabulary intervention in urban middle school classrooms. *Journal of Adolescents & Adult Literacy, 56*(3), 231–240.

Lauber, P. (1986). *Volcano: The eruption and healing of Mount St. Helens*. New York, NY: Bradbury Press.

Lauber, P. (1996). *Hurricanes: Earth's mightiest storms*. New York, NY: Scholastic.

Lawrence, L. (1985). *Children of the dust*. New York, NY: HarperCollins.

Lee, C. D. (2004, Winter/Spring). Literacy in the academic disciplines and the needs of adolescent struggling readers. *Voices in Urban Education (VUE)*, 14–19.

Lee, J., Grigg, W., & Donahue, P. (2007). *The nation's report card: Reading 2007* (NCES 2007-496). Washington, DC: National Center for Education Statistics, Institute of Education Sciences, U.S. Department of Education.

Lee, J. O. (2011). Reach teachers now to ensure common core success. *Phi Delta Kappan, 92*(6), 43–44.

Leent, L., & Mills, K. (2018). A queer critical media literacies framework in a digital age. *Journal of Adolescent & Adult Literacy, 61*(4), 401–411.

Leffland, E. (1979). *Rumors of peace*. New York, NY: Harper & Row.

Leland, C. H., & Harste, J. C. (1994). Multiple ways of knowing: Curriculum in a new key. *Language Arts, 71*, 337–345.

Lemon, N. (2015). *Revolutionizing arts education in K-12 classrooms through technological integration*. IGI Global.

Lenhart, A., Arafeh, S., Smith, A., & Macgill, A. (2008). *Writing, technology, and teens*. Washington, DC: Pew Internet and American Life Project.

Lenihan, G. (2003). Reading with adolescents: Constructing meaning together. *Journal of Adolescent & Adult Literacy, 47*(1), 8–12.

Lenters, K. (2006). Resistance, struggle, and the adolescent reader. *Journal of Adolescent and Adult Literacy, 50*(2), 136–146.

Lester, J. (1968). *To be a slave*. New York, NY: Dial Press.

Lester, J. D. (1984). *Writing research papers: A complete guide* (4th ed.). Glenview, IL: Scott Foresman.

Leu, D. J., Coiro, J., Castek, J., Hartman, D. K., Henry, L. A., & Reinking, D. (2008). Research on instruction and assessment in the new literacies of online reading comprehension. In C. C. Block, S. Parris, & P. Afflerbach (Eds.), *Comprehension instruction: Research-based best practices*. New York, NY: Guilford Press.

Leu, D. J., Leu, D. D., & Coiro, J. (2006). *Teaching with the Internet K–12: New literacies for new times* (4th ed.). Norwood, MA: Christopher-Gordon.

Leu, D. J., McVerry, J. G., O'Byrne, W. I., Kiili, C., Zawilinski, L., Everett-Cacopardo, H., & Forzani, E. (2011). The new literacies of online reading comprehension: Expanding the literacy and learning curriculum. *Journal of Adolescent & Adult Literacy, 55*(1), 5–14.

Leu, D. J., Jr. (1996). Sarah's secret: Social aspects of literacy and learning in a digital information age. *Reading Teacher, 50*, 162–165.

Leu, D. J., Jr. (2000). Literacy and technology: Deictic consequences for literacy education in an information age. In M. L. Kamil, P. M. Mosenthal, P. D. Pearson, & R. Barr (Eds.), *Handbook of reading research, 3*, pp. 743–770. Mahwah, NJ: Erlbaum.

Leu, D. J., Jr. (2002). The new literacies: Research on reading instruction with the Internet. In A. E. Farstrup & S. J. Samuels (Eds.), *What research has to say about reading instruction*, pp. 310–336. Newark, DE: International Reading Association.

Leu, D. J., Jr., & Leu, D. D. (2000). *Teaching with the Internet: Lessons from the classroom* (3rd ed.). Norwood, MA: Christopher-Gordon.

Levin, E. (1992). *If you traveled west in a covered wagon*. New York, NY: Scholastic.

Levin, E. (1996). *If your name was changed at Ellis Island*. New York, NY: Scholastic.

Levine, D. S. (1985). The biggest thing I learned but it really doesn't have to do with science... *Language Arts, 62*, 43–47.

Lewin, T. (2008, November 20). Teenagers' internet socializing not a bad thing. *The New York Times*. Retrieved from www.nytimes.com

Lewis, A. B. (2018). What does bad information look like? Using the CRAAP test for evaluating substandard resources. *Issues in Science and Technology Librarianship, 88*.

Lewis, C., Perry, R., Hurd, J., & O'Connell, P. (2006). Lesson Study Comes of Age in North America. *Phi Delta Kappan*. December 2006, 273–281.

Lewis, J., Aydin, A., & Powell, N. (2016). *March: Book three*. Marietta, GA: Top Shelf Productions.

Lewis, J., Aydin, A., Powell, N., & Ross, C. (2013). *March: Book one*. Marietta, GA: Top Shelf Productions.

Lewis, J., Aydin, A., Powell, N., & Ross, C. (2015). *March: Book two*. Marietta, GA: Top Shelf Productions.

Lewis, L. (2017). ePortfolio as pedagogy: Threshold concepts for curriculum design. *E-Learning and Digital Media, 14*(1–2), 72–85.

Li, G. (Ed.) (2009). *Multicultural families, home literacies, and mainstream schooling*. Charlotte, NC: Information Age Publishing.

Liang, J. K., Liu, T. C., Wang, H. Y., Chang, B., Deng, Y. C., Yang, J. C., . . . Chan, T. W. (2005). A few design perspectives on one-on-one digital classroom environment. *Journal of Computer Assisted Learning, 21*, 181–189.

Lin, G. (2007). *The year of the dog*. Boston, MA: Little, Brown.

Lindbergh, R., & Brown, R. (1992). *A view from the air: Charles Lindbergh's earth and sky*. New York, NY: Viking.

Linder, K. E. (2017). Fundamentals of hybrid teaching and learning. *New Directions for Teaching and Learning, 149*, 11–18.

Lipsky, D. K., & Gartner, A. (1997). *Inclusion and school reform: Transforming America's classrooms*. Baltimore, MD: Paul H. Brookes.

Literacy Research Association. (2013). LRA policy update: Teacher performance assessment systems. Retrieved from https://www.literacyresearchassociation.org/assets/doc/Websitedocs/lrapolicyalertteacherperformanceassessmentsystemsfinal.pdf

Little, H. B. (2018). Media literacy: A moving target. *Knowledge Quest, 47*(1), 16–23.

Llewellyn, C. (1991). *Under the sea*. New York, NY: Simon & Schuster.

Loh, V. (2006). Quantity and quality: The need for culturally authentic trade books in Asian American young adult literature. *The ALAN Review, 34*(1), 36–53.

Longo, C. (2010). Fostering creativity or teaching to the test: Implications for state testing on the delivery of science instruction. *The Clearing House, 83*(2), 54–57.

Louie, B. (2006). Guiding principles of teaching multicultural literature. *The Reading Teacher, 59*(5), 438–448.

Lowe, S. (1990). *Walden*. Ill. R. Sabuda. New York, NY: Philomel.

Lowry, L. (1993). *The giver*. New York, NY: Houghton Mifflin.

Lowry, L. (1989). *Number the Stars*. Boston, MA: Houghton Mifflin.

Lubniewski, K. L., McArthur, C. L., & Harriott, W. (2018). Evaluating instructional apps using the app checklist for educators (ACE). *International Electronic Journal of Elementary Education, 10*(3), 323–329.

Luke, A. (2014). Defining critical literacy. In J. Zacher Pandya & J. Avila (Eds.), *Moving critical literacies forward: A new look at praxis across contexts* (pp. 19–31). New York, NY & London, England: Routledge/Taylor & Francis Group.

Luke, A. (2017). No grand narrative in sight: On double consciousness and critical literacy. *Literacy Research: Theory, Method, and Practice, 66*(1), 157–182.

Luo, L., Kiewra, K. A., Flanigan, A. E., & Peteranetz, M. S. (2018). Laptop versus longhand note taking: Effects on lecture notes and achievement. *Instructional Science, 46*(6), 947–971.

Lupo, S. M., Strong, J. Z., Lewis, W., Walpole, S., & McKenna, M. C. (2017). Building background knowledge through reading: Rethinking text sets. *Journal of Adolescent & Adult Literacy, 61*(4), 433–444.

Lyga, A. W. (2004). *Graphic novels in your media center*. Colorado Springs, CO: Libraries Unlimited.

Lyon, C., Nabors Oláh, L. & Wylie, E.C. (2019). *Working toward integrated practice: Understanding the interaction among formative assessment strategies*. The Journal of Educational Research, doi:10.1080/00220671.2018.1514359

Lyon, G. E. (1991). *Cecil's story*. New York, NY: Orchard.

Ma, W. (2007). Dialoging internally: Participatory learning in a graduate seminar. In C. C. Park, R. Endo, S. J. Lee, & X. L. Rong (Eds.), *Asian American education: Acculturation, literacy development, and learning* (pp. 167–195). Charlotte, NC: Information Age Publishing.

Ma, W. (2008). Participatory dialogue and participatory learning in a discussion-based graduate seminar. *Journal of Literacy Research, 40*(2), 220–249.

Macaulay, D. (1973). *Cathedral: The story of its construction*. Boston, MA: Houghton Mifflin.

Macaulay, D. (1978). *Castle*. Boston, MA: Houghton Mifflin.

Macaulay, D. (1982). *Pyramid*. Boston, MA: Houghton Mifflin.

Macaulay, D. (1998). *The new way things work*. Boston, MA: Houghton Mifflin.

Macaulay, D. (2008). *The way we work*. Boston, MA: Houghton Mifflin.

MacGinitie, W. H. (1993). Some limits of assessment. *Journal of Reading, 36*, 556–560.

MacGinitie, W., MacGinitie, R., Maria, K., Dreyer, L., & Hughes, K. (2006). *Gates-MacGinitie reading tests* (4th ed.). Rolling Meadows, IL: Houghton Mifflin Harcourt-Riverside Publishing.

Mackay, H., & Strickland, M. J. (2018). Exploring culturally responsive teaching and student-created videos in an at-risk middle school classroom. *Middle Grades Review, 4*(1), 1–11.

Mackey, M. (2014). Learning to choose: The hidden art of the enthusiastic reader. *Journal of Adolescent & Adult Literacy, 57*(7), 521–526.

Maguire, K. (2001). *Governors find education bill faults*. Retrieved October 2002 from www.speakout.com/cgi-bin/edt/im.display.printable?client.id=speakout&story.id=10037

Malinowski, B. (1954). *Magic, science and religion and other essays*. New York, NY: Doubleday.

Manyak, P. C., & Bauer, E. B. (2009). English vocabulary instruction for English learners. *The Reading Teacher, 63*(2), 174–176.

Manzo, A., Manzo, U., & Estes, T. (2001). *Content area literacy: Interactive teaching for interactive learning*. New York, NY: Wiley.

Manzo, A. V. (1975). Guided reading procedure. *Journal of Reading, 18*, 287–291.

Manzo, U., Manzo, A. V, & Thomas, M. T. (2009). *Content area literacy: A framework for reading-based instruction* (5th ed.). Hoboken, NJ: John Wiley & Sons.

Marcaruso, P., & Walker, A. (2008). The efficacy of computer-assisted instruction for advancing literacy skills in kindergarten children. *Reading Psychology, 29*(3), 266–287.

Marsalis, W. (1995). *Marsalis on music*. New York, NY: Norton.

Martin, F., Wang, C., Petty, T., Wang, W., & Wilkins, P. (2018). Middle school students' social media use. *Educational Technology & Society, 21*(1), 213–224.

Martínez, R. (2010). Spanglish as literacy tool: Toward an understanding of the potential role of Spanish-English code-switching in the development of academic literacy. *Teaching of English, 45*(2), 124–149.

Martínez-Roldán, C., & Newcomer, S. (2011). "Reading between the pictures": Immigrant students' interpretation of the arrival. *Language Arts, 88*(3), 188–198.

Maruki, T. (1980). *Hiroshima no pika*. New York, NY: Lothrop, Lee & Shepard.

Marzano, R. J. (2003). *What works in schools: Translating research into action*. Alexandria, VA: Association for Supervision and Curriculum Development.

Massell, D., Kirst, M., & Hoppe, M. (1997). *Persistence and change: Standards-based reforms in nine states*. Consortium for Policy Research in Education, University of Pennsylvania, Graduate School of Education. Washington, DC: U.S. Department of Education.

Matas, C. (2001). *The war within: A novel of the Civil War*. New York, NY: Simon & Schuster.

Matthew, K. (1996). What do children think of CD-ROM storybooks? *Texas Reading Report, 18*, 6.

McCloud, S. (2006). *Making comics: Storytelling secrets of comics, manga, and graphic novels*. New York, NY: William Morrow.

McColl, A. (2005). Tough call: Is No Child Left Behind constitutional? [Electronic version]. *Phi Delta Kappan, 86*(6), 604–610.

McCrea, B. (2013). Off the shelves. *T.H.E. Journal, 40*(2), 30–33.

McDaniel, C. A. (2006). *Critical literacy: A way of thinking, a way of life*. New York, NY: Peter Lang.

McGinley, W. J., & Denner, P. R. (1987). Story impressions: A pre-reading/writing activity. *Journal of Reading, 31*, 248–253.

McIntosh, M. (1991, September). No time for writing in your class? *Mathematics Teacher*, pp. 423–433.

McKenna, M. C., & Robinson, R. D. (2006). *Teaching through text: Reading and writing in the content areas* (4th ed.). Boston, MA: Pearson.

McKeon, C. (2001). E-mail as a motivating literacy event for one student: Donna's case. *Reading Research and Instruction, 40*(3), 185–202.

McKeown, M., Beck, I., & Blake, R. (2009). Rethinking reading comprehension instruction: A comparison of instruction for strategies and content approaches. *Reading Research Quarterly, 44*(3), 218–253.

McKinley, R. (1978). *Beauty: A retelling of the story of Beauty and the Beast*. New York, NY: HarperCollins.

McLaren, P. (1989). *Life in schools: An introduction to critical pedagogy in the foundations of education*. New York, NY: Longman.

McLaughlin, M., & Overturf, B. (2012). The Common Core: Insights into the K–5 standards. *Reading Teacher, 66*(2), 153–164.

McLuhan, M. (1962). *The Gutenberg galaxy: The making of typographic man*. Toronto, Canada: University of Toronto Press.

McMackin, M., & Witherell, N. (2010). Using leveled graphic organizers to differentiate responses to children's literature. *New England Reading Association Journal, 46*(1), 49–54.

McPherson, J. (2002). *Fields of fury: The American Civil War*. New York, NY: Atheneum.

McTighe, J., & Lyman, F. T. (1988). Cueing thinking in the classroom: The promise of theory-embedded tools. *Educational Leadership, 45*(7), 18–24.

McVerry, J. G. (2007). Forums and functions of threaded discussions: Using new literacies to build traditional comprehension skills. *The New England Reading Association Journal, 43*(1), 17–22.

Meibaum, D. L. (2016). *An overview of the Every Student Succeeds Act*. Cayce, SC: Southeast Comprehensive Center at American Institutes for Research.

Merga, M. (2018). Silent reading and discussion of self-selected books in the contemporary classroom. *English in Australia, 53*(1), 70–82.

Merkley, D. M., & Jefferies, D. (2001). Guidelines for implementing a graphic organizer. *Reading Teacher, 54*, 350–357.

MetaMetrics (2008). *The Lexile framework for reading: FAQ*. Retrieved September 19, 2008, from www.lexile.com/DesktopDefault.aspx?view=ed&tabindex=6&tabid=18

Meyer, B. J. F., & Rice, E. (1984). The structure of text. In P. D. Pearson (Ed.), *Handbook of reading research* (pp. 319–352). New York, NY: Longman.

Miholic, V. (1994). An inventory to pique students' metacognitive awareness. *Journal of Reading, 38*(2), 84–86.

Mike, D. G. (1996). Internet in the schools: A literacy perspective. *Journal of Adolescent and Adult Literacy, 40*, 4–13.

Miller, M., & Veatch, N. (2011). *Literacy in content (LinC): Choosing instructional strategies to teach reading in content areas for students grades 5-12*. Boston, MA: Pearson.

Miller, T. (1998). The place of picture books in middle-level classrooms. *Journal of Adolescent and Adult Literacy, 41*(5), 376–382.

Millman, I. (2005). *Hidden child*. New York, NY: Farrar, Straus & Giroux.

Minor, C., Howell, L., & Casimir, A. (2018). Come with me: EdTech and the journey into better realities. *Voices from the Middle, 25*(4), 19–23.

Mochizuki, K. (2003). *Passage to freedom: The Sugihara story*. New York, NY: Lee & Low Books.

Moje, E., Overby, M., Tysvaer, N., & Morris, K. (2008). The complex world of adolescent literacy: Myths, motivations, and mysteries. *Harvard Educational Review, 78*(1), 107–154.

Moje, E. B. (2007). Developing socially just subject-matter instruction: A review of the literature on disciplinary literacy. In N. L. Parker (Ed.), *Review of research in education* (pp. 1–44). Washington, DC: American Educational Research Association.

Moje, E. B. (2008). Responsive literacy teaching in secondary school content areas. In M. W. Conley, J. R. Freidhoff, M. B. Sherry, & S. F. Tuckey (Eds.), *Meeting the challenge of adolescent literacy* (pp. 58–87). New York, NY: Guilford Press.

Moje, E. B., Ciechanowski, K. M., Kramer, K., Ellis, L., Carrillo, R., & Collazo, T. (2004). Working toward third space in content area literacy: An examination of everyday funds of knowledge and discourse. *Reading Research Quarterly, 39*(1), 38–70.

Moje, E. B., Young, J. P., Readence, J. E., & Moore, D. W. (2000). Reinventing adolescent literacy for new times: Perennial and millennial issues. *Journal of Adolescent & Adult Literacy 43*, 400–410.

Moll, L. (1994). Literacy research in community and classrooms: A sociocultural approach. In R. B. Ruddell & H. Singer (Eds.), *Theoretical models and processes in reading*. Newark, DE: International Reading Association.

Moll, L., Amanti, C., Neff, D., & Gonzalez, N. (1992). Funds of knowledge for teaching: Using a qualitative approach to connect homes and classrooms. *Theory into Practice, 31*(1), 132–141.

Moll, L. C. (2015). Tapping into the "hidden" home and community resources of students. *Kappa Delta Pi Record, 51*(3), 114–117, doi:10.1080/00228958.2015.1056661

Möller, K. J. (2015). Integrating graphic nonfiction into classroom reading and content area instruction: A critical literacy focus on selection issues. *Journal of Children's Literature, 41*(2), 52–59.

Montelongo, J., Herter, R. J., Ansaldo, R., & Hatter, N. (2010). A lesson cycle for teaching expository reading and writing. *Journal of Adolescent & Adult Literacy, 53*(8), 656–666.

Moore, D., Moore, S., Cunningham, P., & Cunningham, J. (2006). *Developing readers and writers in the content areas K–12*. Boston, MA: Allyn & Bacon.

Moore, D., Moore, S., Cunningham, P., & Cunningham, J. (2010). *Developing Readers and Writers in the Content Areas K–12* (6th ed.). New York, NY: Pearson.

Moore, D. W., Bean, T. W., Birdyshaw, D., & Rycik, J. A. (1999). *Adolescent literacy: A position statement for the Commission on Adolescent Literacy of the International Reading Association*. Newark, DE: International Reading Association.

Moore, M. T. (2004). Issues and trends in writing instruction. In R. Robinson, M. McKenna, & J. Wedman (Eds.), *Issues and trends in literacy education* (3rd ed.). Boston, MA: Allyn & Bacon.

Morgan, D. N., & Wagner, C. W. (2013). "What's the catch?" Providing reading choice in a high school classroom. *Journal of Adolescent & Adult Literacy, 56*(8), 659–667.

Morrell, E. (2013). 21st-century literacies, critical media pedagogies, and language arts. *Reading Teacher, 66*(4), 300–302.

Moss, B. (1995). Using children's nonfiction tradebooks as read-alouds (Teacher's notebook). *Language Arts, 72*, 122–126.

Moss, B. (2003). *Exploring the literature of fact: Children's nonfiction trade books in the elementary classroom*. New York, NY: Guilford Press.

Mraz, M. (2000). The literacy program selection process from the perspective of school district administrators. *Ohio Reading Teacher, 34*(2), 40–48.

Mraz, M. (2002). *Factors that influence policy decisions in literacy: Perspectives of key policy informants*. Ph.D. dissertation, Kent State University.

Mühlberger, R. (1993). *What makes a Monet a Monet?* New York, NY: Metropolitan Museum of Art/Viking.

Murnane, R., Sawhill, I., & Snow, C. (2012). Literacy challenges for the twenty-first century: Introducing the issue. *The Future of Children, 22*(2), 3–15.

Murphy, J. (1990). *The boys' war: Confederate and Union soldiers talk about the Civil War*. New York, NY: Clarion Books.

Murphy, J. (1992). *The long road to Gettysburg*. New York, NY: Clarion Books.

Murphy, J. (1998). *The great fire*. New York, NY: Clarion Books.

Murphy, J., Chang, J.-M., & Suaray, K. (2016). Student performance and attitudes in a collaborative and flipped linear algebra course. *International Journal of Mathematical Education in Science and Technology, 47*(5), 653–673.

Murray, D. M. (1980). Writing as process: How writing finds its own meaning. In T. R. Donovan & B. W. McClelland (Eds.), *Eight approaches to teaching composition* (pp. 80–97). Urbana, IL: National Council of Teachers of English.

Myers, W. D. (1991). *Now is your time!: The African-American struggle for freedom*. New York, NY: HarperCollins.

Myers, W. D. (2001). *Monster*. New York, NY: HarperCollins.

Myers, W. D., & Grifalconi, A. (Illustrator). (2002). *Patrol: An American soldier in Vietnam*. New York, NY: HarperCollins.

Nachowitz, M. (2018). Scaffolding progressive online discourse for literary knowledge building. *Online Learning, 22*(3), 133–156.

Nagy, W. E. (1988). *Teaching vocabulary to improve reading comprehension*. Newark, DE: International Reading Association.

Nash-Ditzel, S. (2010). Metacognitive reading strategies can improve self-regulation. *Journal of College Reading and Learning, 40*(2), 45–63.

National Assessment of Educational Progress (2009). *The nation's report card: Reading 2009*. Washington, DC: Author.

National Center for Educational Achievement. (2009). *Core practices in math and science: An investigation of consistently higher performing schools in five states*. Austin, TX: National Center for Educational Achievement.

National Center for Educational Statistics. (2007). *The nation's report card: Reading 2007*. Retrieved April 17, 2009, from www.nces.ed.gov/pubSearch/pubinfo.asp? pubid=2007496

National Center for Higher Education. (2018). *Fast facts: Computer and internet use*. Retrieved October 25, 2018, from https://nces.ed.gov/fastfacts/display.asp?id=46

National Commission on Writing. (2003). *The neglected R: The need for a writing revolution*. Retrieved from www.writingcommission.org

National Council of Teachers of English (NCTE). (2004). *A call to action: What we know about adolescent literacy and ways to support teachers in meeting students' needs*. Urbana, IL: Author. Retrieved July 7, 2007, from www.ncte.org/about/over/positions/category/literacy/118622.htm

National Council of Teachers of English (NCTE). (2006). *NCTE principles of adolescent literacy reform: A policy research brief*. Retrieved July 7, 2007, from www.ncte.org/library/NCTEFiles/Resources/PolicyResearch/AdolLitResearchBrief.pdf

National Council of Teachers of English. (2010). *The NCTE definition of 21st century literacies*. Retrieved December 2012 from http://www.ncte.org/positions/statements/21stcentdefinition

National Council of Teachers of Mathematics (NCTM). (2000). *Principles and standards for school mathematics*. Washington, DC: Author.

National Governors Association Center for Best Practices, Council of Chief State School Officers. (2010). *Common Core State Standards English Language Arts*. Washington, DC: National Governors Association Center for Best Practices, Council of Chief State School Officers.

National Governors Association Center for Best Practices, Council of Chief State School Officers. (2018). *Common Core Key Shifts in English Language Arts*. Retrieved from http://www.corestandards.org/other-resources/key-shifts-in-english-language-arts/

National Governors Association Center for Best Practices, Council of Chief State School Officers. (n.d.). *Common Core State Standards*. National Governors Association Center for Best Practices, Council of Chief State School Officers, Washington, DC. Retrieved September 30, 2014, from http://www.corestandards.org/read-the-standards/

National Institute for Literacy (2007). *What content-area teachers should know about adolescent literacy.* Washington, DC: National Institute of Child Health and Human Development (NICHD).

National Middle School Association. (2005). *Highly qualified: A balanced approach.* Retrieved September 28, 2006, from www.nmsa.org

National Middle School Association, National Association of Elementary School Principals, & the National Association of Secondary School Principals. (2004). *Highly qualified: A balanced approach.* Retrieved April 14, 2006, from www.nmsa.org/portals/o/pdf/about/position_statements/EdWeek.pdf

National Reading Panel. (2000). *Teaching children to read: An evidence-based assessment of the scientific research literature on reading and its implications for reading instruction* (National Institute of Health Pub. No. 00-4769). Washington, DC: National Institute of Child Health and Human Development.

National School Boards Association. (2006). *The next chapter: A school board guide to improving adolescent literacy.* Alexandria, VA: Author. Retrieved May 18, 2008, from www.nsba.org

Nazario, S. (2006). *Enrique's journey: The story of a boy's dangerous odyssey to reunite with his mother.* New York, NY: Random House.

Neal, J. C., & Moore, K. (1991). *The Very Hungry Caterpillar* meets *Beowulf* in secondary classrooms. *Journal of Reading, 35,* 290–296.

Neill, M. (2003). Leaving children behind: How No Child Left Behind will fail our children. *Phi Delta Kappan, 85*(3), 225–228.

Neilsen, L. (2006). Playing for real: Performative texts and adolescent identities. In D. Alvermann, K. Hinchman, S. Phelps, & S. Waff (Eds.), *Reconceptualizing the literacies in adolescents' lives* (pp. 5–28). Mahwah, NJ: Erlbaum.

Nelson, B. (2008). *Paranoid park.* New York, NY: Puffin.

Nelson, J. (1978). Readability: Some cautions for the content area teacher. *Journal of Reading, 21,* 620–625.

Nelson, K. (2008). *We are the ship: The story of Negro League baseball.* New York, NY: Hyperion.

Nelson, M. (2005). *A wreath for Emmett Till.* New York, NY: Houghton Mifflin Harcourt.

Ness, M. K. (2009). Reading comprehension strategies in secondary content area classrooms: Teacher use of attitudes towards reading comprehension instruction. *Reading Horizons, 49*(2), 143–166.

Ness, P. (2011). *A monster calls.* (1st U.S. ed.). Somerville, MA: Candlewick Press.

Netiquette Guidelines (retrieved April 26, 2012). Online Student Expectations. Available at http://blogs.lsc.edu/expectations/netiquette-guidelines/

Neufeld, J. (2010). *New Orleans After the Deluge.* New York, NY: Pantheon.

Neufeld, P. (2005). Comprehension instruction in content area classes. *Reading Teacher, 59*(4), 302–312.

Newcomb, N. (2007). Psychology's role in mathematics and science education. *Research Report.* Washington, DC: American Psychological Association:

Newell, G. (1984). Learning from writing in two content areas: A case study/protocol analysis. *Research in the Teaching of English, 18,* 205–287.

New London Group. (1996). A pedagogy of multiliteracies: Designing social futures. *Harvard Education Review 66*(1), 60–92.

New Media Consortium. (2005). *A global imperative: The report of the 21st century literacy summit.* Retrieved September 23, 2014, from http://www.nmc.org/pdf/Global_Imperative.pdf.

Nichols, S. L., & Berliner, D. C. (2007). *Collateral damage: How high-stakes testing corrupts America's schools.* Cambridge, MA: Harvard Education Press.

Nichols, W. D., Wood, K. D., & Rickelman, R. (2001). Using technology to engage students in reading and writing. *Middle School Journal, 32*(5), 45–50.

Nieto, S. (2002). *Language, culture, and teaching: Critical perspectives for a new century.* Mahwah, NJ: Erlbaum.

Nieto, S., & Bode, P. (2012). *Affirming diversity: The sociopolitical context of multicultural education.* Boston, MA: Pearson.

Niles, O. (1965). Organization perceived. In H. L. Herber (Ed.), *Developing study skills in secondary schools* (pp. 36–46). Newark, DE: International Reading Association.

Noden, H. R. (1995). A journey through cyberspace: Reading and writing in a virtual school. *English Journal 84*(6), 19–26.

Noden, H. R., & Vacca, R. T. (1994). *Whole language in middle and secondary classrooms.* New York, NY: HarperCollins.

North Carolina Department of Public Instruction (NCDPI). (2012). *Accountability and curriculum reform effort.* Retrieved from www.ncpublicschools.org/acre

Noyes, A. (1983). *The highwayman.* Ill. C. Mikolaychak. New York, NY: Lothrop, Lee & Shepard.

Nye, N. S. (2002). *19 varieties of gazelle: Poems of the Middle East.* New York, NY: HarperCollins.

Nye, R. (1968). *Beowulf: A new telling.* New York, NY: Hill.

Oakes, J., & Lipton, M. (2007). *Teaching to change the world.* Boston, MA: McGraw-Hill.

Oakley, G., & Jay, J. (2008). "Making time" for reading factors that influence the success of multimedia reading in the home. *The Reading Teacher, 62*(3), 246–255.

O'Brien, R. C. (1975). *Z for Zachariah.* New York: Atheneum.

Office of Educational Technology (2017). *Reimagining the role of technology in education: 2017 National Education Technology Plan update.* U.S. Department of Education. Retrieved November 5, 2018, from https://tech.ed.gov/files/2017/01/NETP17.pdf

Ogle, D. (1986). KWL: A teaching model that develops active reading of expository text. *Reading Teacher, 39,* 564–570.

Ogle, D. M. (1992). KWL in action: Secondary teachers find applications that work. In E. K. Dishner, T. W. Bean, J. E. Readence, & D. W. Moore (Eds.), *Reading in the content areas: Improving classroom instruction* (3rd ed., pp. 270–281). Dubuque, IA: Kendall-Hunt.

Ohio Department of Education. (2003). *Ohio administrative codes and rules links: Rule 3301-13-01.* Retrieved September 2003 from www.ode.state.oh.us/proficiency/rules.asp?pfv=True

Ohler, J. (2010). *Digital Storytelling in the Classroom: New Media Pathways to Literacy, Learning and Creativity* (2nd ed.). New York, NY: Corwin.

Oldfather, P., & Dahl, K. (1994). Toward a social constructivist reconceptualization of intrinsic motivation for literacy learning. *Journal of Reading Behavior, 26,* 139–158.

O'Neill, C. (1995). *Drama worlds: A framework for process drama.* Portsmouth, NH: Heinemann.

Ortmeier-Hooper, C. (2017). *Writing across Culture and Language: Inclusive Strategies for Working with ELL Writers in the ELA Classroom*. National Council of Teachers of English.

Overturf, B. J., Montgomery, L., & Holmes-Smith, M. H. (2013). *Word nerds: Teaching all students to learn and love vocabulary*. Portland, ME: Stenhouse.

Owles, C., & Herman, D. (2014). Terrific teaching tips: Using mentor texts to develop our readers and writers. *Illinois Reading Council Journal, 42*(4), 51–58.

Pacheco, B. (2017, January 1). *The impact of iPad multimodalities on the literacy skills of adolescent males identified as low-achieving readers*. ProQuest LLC.

Palacio, R. J. (2012). *Wonder*. Random House Children's Books.

Palincsar, A. S., & Brown, A. L. (1984). Reciprocal teaching of comprehension-fostering and comprehension-monitoring activities. *Cognition and Instruction, 1*(2), 117–175.

Palmer, R. G., & Stewart, R. A. (1997). Nonfiction trade books in content area instruction: Realities and potential. *Journal of Adolescent and Adult Literacy, 40*, 630–641.

Pandya, J. Z. (2012). Unpacking Pandora's box: Issues in the Assessment of English learners' literacy skill development in multimodal classrooms. *Journal of Adolescent & Adult Literacy, 56*(3), 181–185.

Papert, S. (1980). *Mindstorms: Children, computers, and powerful ideas*. New York, NY: Basic Books.

Pappas, T. (1993). *Math talk: Mathematical ideas in poems for two voices*. New York, NY: Wide World.

Paris, D. (2012). Culturally sustaining pedagogy: A needed change in stance, terminology, and practice, *Educational Researcher, 41*(3), 93–97.

Paris, S., & Meyers, M. (1981). Comprehension monitoring, memory, and study strategies of good and poor readers. *Journal of Reading Behavior, 13*, 5–22.

Parker, W. C., & Jarolimek, J. (1997). *Social studies in elementary education*. Upper Saddle River, NJ: Prentice Hall.

Parnall, P. (1984). *The daywatchers*. New York, NY: Macmillan.

Parnall, P. (1991). *Marsh cat*. New York, NY: Macmillan.

Parry, K. (1993). Too many words: Learning the vocabulary of an academic subject. In T. Huckin, M. Haynes, & J. Coady (Eds.), *Second language reading and vocabulary learning* (pp. 109–129). Norwood, NJ: Ablex.

Parsons, L. (2001). *Response journals revisited: Maximizing learning through reading, writing, viewing, discussing, and thinking*. Markham, Canada: Pembroke Publishers.

Partridge, E. (2002). *This land was made for you and me: The life and songs of Woody Guthrie*. New York, NY: Viking.

Partridge, E. (2005). *John Lennon: All I want is the truth*. New York, NY: Viking.

Patterson, N. G. (2000). Hypertext and the changing roles of readers. *English Journal, 90*(2), 74–80.

Pauk, W., & Ross, J. Q. O. (2007). *How to study in college*. Boston, MA: Houghton Mifflin Harcourt.

Paulsen, G. (1987). *Hatchet*. New York, NY: Viking Penguin.

Paulsen, G. (1989). *The winter room*. New York, NY: Harcourt Brace.

Paulsen, G. (1990). *Woodsong*. New York, NY: Macmillan.

Paulsen, G. (1995). *Nightjohn*. New York, NY: Laurel Leaf Press.

Payne, R., DeVol, P., & Smith, T. (2005). *Bridges out of poverty: Strategies for professionals and communities*. Highlands, TX: Aha! Process.

Peacock, L., & Krudop, W. L. (Illustrator). (1998). *Crossing the Delaware: A history in many voices*. New York, NY: Atheneum.

Pearce, D. L. (1983). Guidelines for the use and evaluation of writing in content classrooms. *Journal of Reading, 27*, 212–218.

Pearson, P. D. (1974–1975). The effects of grammatical complexity on children's comprehension, recall, and conception of certain semantic relations. *Reading Research Quarterly, 10*, 155–192.

Pearson, P. D., & Gallagher, M. C. (1983). The instruction of reading comprehension. *Contemporary Educational Psychology, 8*, 317–344.

Pearson. P. D., Hiebert, E. H., & Kamil, M. (2007). Vocabulary assessment: What we know and what we need to learn. *Reading Research Quarterly, 42*(2), 282–296.

Pearson, P. D., & Hoffman, J. V. (2011). Teaching effective reading instruction. In T. V. Rasinski (Ed.), *Rebuilding the foundation: Effective reading instruction for 21st century literacy* (pp. 3–33). Bloomington, IN: Solution Tree Press.

Pearson, P. D., & Johnson, D. (1978). *Teaching reading comprehension*. Fort Worth, TX: Holt, Rinehart and Winston.

Pearson, P. D., & Spiro, R. (1982). The new buzz word in reading as schema. *Instructor, 89*, 46–48.

Peregoy, S. F. & Boyle, O. (2008). *Reading, writing and learning in ESL: A resource book for K-12 teachers* (6th ed.). Boston, MA: Pearson.

Peregoy, S. F. & Boyle, O. (2017). *Reading, writing and learning in ESL: A resource book for K-12 teachers* (7th ed.). Boston, MA: Pearson.

Peregoy, S. F., & Boyle, O. F. (2001). *Reading, writing, and learning in ESL: A resource book for K–12 teachers* (3rd ed.). New York, NY: Longman.

Peregoy, S. F., & Boyle, O. F. (2008). *Reading, writing, and learning in ESL: A resource book for teaching K–12 English learners* (5th ed.). Boston, MA: Pearson.

Peregoy, S. F., & Boyle, O. F. (2013). *Reading, writing and learning in ESL: A resource book for teaching K-12 English Learners* (6th ed.). Boston, MA: Pearson.

Perie, M., Grigg, W., & Donahue, P. (2005). *The nation's report card: Reading 2005* (NCES 2006-451). Washington, DC: U.S. Department of Education.

Perrin, A. (2016). *Book reading 2016*. Pew Research Center, Washington, DC. Retrieved November 8, 2018, from file:///Users/dbtaylor/Downloads/PI_2016.09.01_Book-Reading_FINAL.pdf

Perrin, A. (2018, March 8). *Nearly one-in-five Americans now listen to audio books* [Blog post]. Retrieved November 28, 2018, from http://www.pewresearch.org/fact-tank/2018/03/08/nearly-one-in-five-americans-now-listen-to-audiobooks/

Pew Internet and American Life Study. (2006). *Internet penetration and access*. Retrieved August 28, 2008, from www.pewinternet.org/topics.asp?page=2&c=3

Pew Internet and American Life Study. (2008). *Home broadband 2008*. Retrieved August 28, 2008, from www.pewinternet.org/topics.asp?page=1&c=3

Pew Research Center. (2018). *Internet/ Broadband Fact Sheet*. Pew Research Center, Washington, DC. Retrieved November 27, 2018, from file:///Users/dbtaylor/Downloads/PI_2016.09.01_Book-Reading_FINAL.pdf

Philip, T., & Garcia, A. (2013). The importance of still teaching the iGeneration: New technologies and the centrality of pedagogy. *Harvard Educational Review, 83*(2).

Phillips, V., & Wong, C. (2011). Tying together the common core standards, instruction, and assessments. *Phi Delta Kappan, 91*(5), 37–42.

Pilgreen, J. (2000). *How to organize and manage a sustained silent reading program.* Portsmouth, NH: Heinemann.

Pilonieta, P. (2010). Instruction of research-based comprehension strategies in basal reading programs. *Reading Psychology, 31*(2), 150–175.

Pitcher, S. M., Martinez, G., Dicembre, E. A., Fewster, D., & McCormick, M. K. (2010). Literacy needs of adolescents in their own words. *Journal of Adolescent & Adult Literacy, 53*(8), 636–645.

Plucker, J. A., Spradlin, T. E., Cline, K. P., & Wolf, K. M. (2005). *Education policy brief: No Child Left Behind, Spring 2005 implementation update* [Electronic version]. Bloomington, IN: Center for Evaluation & Education Policy.

Polacco, P. (1994). *Pink and say*. New York, NY: Philomel.

Pradl, G. M., & Mayher, J. S. (1985). Reinvigorating learning through writing. *Educational Leadership, 42*, 4–8.

Preble, L. (2006). *Queen Geek series*. New York, NY: Berkeley.

Pressley, M. (2000). What should comprehension instruction be the instruction of? In M. Kamil, P. Mosenthal, P. D. Pearson, & R. Barr (Eds.), *Handbook of reading research, 3*, 545–562. Mahwah, NJ: Erlbaum.

Pressley, M. (2002a). Comprehension instruction: What makes sense now, what might make sense soon. *Reading Online, 5*(2). Retrieved October 3, 2005, from www.readingonline.org/articles/art_index.asp?HREF=/articles/handbook/pressley/index.htm

Pressley, M. (2002b). *Reading instruction that works: The case for balanced reading*. New York, NY: Guilford Press.

Pressley, M. (2006). *Reading instruction that works: The case for balanced instruction*. New York, NY: Guilford Press.

Price, L. (1990). *Aida*. Ill. L. Dillon & D. Dillon. San Diego, CA: Harcourt Brace.

Pruisner, P. (2009). Moving beyond No Child Left Behind with the merged model for reading instruction. *TechTrends, 53*(2).

Puentedura, R. R. (2009). SAMR: A contextualized introduction. Retrieved November 12, 2018, from http://www.hippasus.com/rrpweblog/archives/2013/10/25/SAMRAContextualizedIntroduction.pdf

Purcell, K., Buchanan, J., & Friedrich, L. (2013, July 16). *The impact of digital tools on student writing and how writing is taught in schools*. Washington, DC: Pew Research Center. Retrieved November 12, 2018, from http://pewinternet.org/Reports/2013/Teachers-technology-and-writing

Purcell-Gates, L. (2013). Literacy worlds of children of migrant farmworker communities participating in a migrant head start program. *Research in the Teaching of English, 48*(1), 68–97.

Purcell-Gates, V. (1995). *Other people's words: The cycle of low literacy*. Cambridge, MA: Harvard University Press.

Pytash, K. (2012). Engaging preservice teachers in disciplinary literacy learning through writing. *Journal of Adolescent & Adult Literacy, 55*(6), 527–538.

Pytash, K., Edmondson, E., & Tait, A. (2014). Using mentor texts for writing instruction in a high school economics class. *Social Studies Research and Practice, 9*(1), 95–106.

Rainey, E., & Moje, E. (2012). Building insider knowledge: Teaching students to read, write and think within ELA and across the disciplines. *English Education*, 71–90.

RAND Reading Study Group. (2002). *Reading for understanding: Toward an R&D program in reading comprehension*. Santa Monica, CA: Science and Technology Policy Institute, Rand Education.

Ransom, K. A., Santa, C. M., Williams, C. K., Farstrup, A. E., Au, K. H., Baker, B. M., et al. (1999). High-stakes assessments in reading: A position statement of the International Reading Association. *Journal of Adolescent and Adult Literacy, 43*(3), 305–312.

Raphael, T. E. (1984). Teaching learners about sources of information for answering comprehension questions. *Journal of Reading, 27*, 303–311.

Raphael, T. E. (1986). Teaching question–answer relationships. *Reading Teacher, 39*, 516–520.

Raphael, T. E., & Au, K. H. (2005). QAR: Enhancing comprehension and test taking across grades and content areas. *The Reading Teacher, 59*(3), 206–221.

Rappaport, D., & Collier, B. (Illustrator). (2001). *Martin's big words: The life of Dr. Martin Luther King, Jr*. New York, NY: Hyperion.

Raschka, C. (1997). *Mysterious Thelonious*. New York, NY: Orchard.

Ray, D. (1990). *A nation torn: The story of how the Civil War began*. New York, NY: Scholastic.

Readence, J. E. (2002). Adolescent literacy. In B. J. Guzzetti (Ed.), *Literacy in America: An encyclopedia of history, theory, and practice* (pp. 13–15). Santa Barbara, CA: ABC-CLIO.

Redd, M., & Webb, K. S. (2005). *African American English: What a writing teacher should know*. Urbana, IL: National Council of Teachers of English.

Reed, J. H., Schallert, D. L., Beth, A. D., & Woodruff, A. L. (2004). Motivated reader, engaged writer: The role of motivation in the literate acts of adolescents. In T. L. Jetton & J. A. Dole (Eds.), *Adolescent literacy research and practice* (pp. 251–282). New York, NY: Guilford Press.

Reeder, C. (1989). *Shades of gray*. New York, NY: Macmillan.

Reef, C. (2006). *e.e. cummings: A poet's life*. New York, NY: Clarion Books.

Reeves, N. (1992). *Into the mummy's tomb: The real-life discovery of Tutankhamun's treasures*. New York, NY: Scholastic/Madison.

Reinking, D. (1995). Reading and writing with computers: Literacy research in a post-typographic world. In K. A. Hinchman, D. J. Leu, Jr., & C. K. Kinzer (Eds.), *Perspectives on literacy research and practice* (pp. 17–33). Chicago, IL: National Reading Conference.

Reinking, D. (1997). Me and my hypertext: A multiple digression analysis of technology and literacy. *Reading Teacher, 50*, 626–643.

Reinking, D. (1998). Synthesizing technological transformations of literacy in a post-typographic world. In D. Reinking, M. McKenna, L. D. Labbo, & R. Kieffer (Eds.), *Handbook of literacy and technology: Transformations in a post-typographic world* (pp. xi–xxx). Mahwah, NJ: Erlbaum.

Reinking, D. (2003). Multimedia and engaged reading in a digital world. In L. Verhoeven & C. Snow (Eds.), *Creating a world of engaged readers*. Mahwah, NJ: Erlbaum.

Reis, S. M., & Renzulli, J. S. (2005). *Curriculum compacting: An easy start to differentiating for high-potential students.* Waco, TX: Prufrock Press.

Renyi, J. (1998). Building learning into the teaching job. *Educational Leadership, 55*(5), 70–74.

Resta, P., & Laferrière, T. (2007). Technology in Support of Collaborative Learning. *Educational Psychology Review, 19,* 65–83. doi:10.1007/s10648-007-9042-7

Reynolds, J. (2017). *Ghost.* New York, NY: Atheneum.

Reynolds, J. (2017). *Long way down.* New York, NY: Atheneum.

Reynolds, J. (2018). *Jason Reynolds Track series: Ghost; Patina; Sunny; Lu.* New York, NY: Atheneum.

Ribeiro, S. (2015). Digital storytelling: An integrated approach to language learning for the 21st century student. *Teaching English with Technology, 15*(2), 39–53.

Richardson, V. (2003). The dilemmas of professional development. *Phi Delta Kappan, 84,* 401–406.

Rico, G. L. (1983). *Writing the natural way: Using right-brain techniques to release your expressive powers.* Los Angeles, CA: Tarcher.

Ride, S., & Okie, S. (1986). *To space and back.* New York, NY: Lothrop, Lee & Shepard.

Riis, J. A., & Museum of the City of New York. (1971). *How the other half lives: Studies among the tenements of New York.* New York, NY: Dover.

Riley, P. (2016). iPad apps for creating in your general music classroom. *General Music Today, 29*(2), 4–13.

Roberts, P. (1985). Speech communities. In V. Clark, P. Escholz, & A. Rosa (Eds.), *Language* (4th ed.). New York, NY: St. Martin's Press.

Roberts, T. & Billings, L. (2011). *Teaching critical thinking: Using seminars for 21st century literacy.* Larchmont, NY: Eye On Education.

Robinson, D. (2006). *The Paideia Seminar: Moving Reading Comprehension from Transaction to Transformation* (Unpublished doctoral dissertation). The Faculty of the Department of Language Arts and Literacy of the Graduate School of Education, University of Massachusetts Lowell.

Roby, T. (1987). Commonplaces, questions, and modes of discussion. In J. T. Dillon (Ed.), *Classroom questions and discussion* (pp. 134–169). Norwood, NJ: Ablex.

Rodrigues, R. J. (1983). Tools for developing prewriting skills. *English Journal, 72,* 58–60.

Rodriguez, L. J. (1993). *Always running: La vida loca: Gang days in L.A.* New York, NY: Touchstone.

Rohmer, H. (Ed.). (1997). *Just like me: Stories and self-portraits by fourteen artists.* San Francisco, CA: Children's Book Press.

Rohmer, H. (Ed.). (1999). *Honoring our ancestors: Stories and pictures by fourteen artists.* San Francisco, CA: Children's Book Press.

Romano, T. (1995). *Writing with passion: Life stories, multiple genres.* Portsmouth, NH: Heinemann.

Rose, B. (1989). Writing and mathematics: Theory and practice. In P. Connolly & T. Vilardi (Eds.), *Writing to learn mathematics and science* (pp. 19–30). New York, NY: Teachers College Press.

Rose, S. A., & Fernlund, P. M. (1997). Using technology for powerful social studies learning. *Social Education, 13*(6), 160–166.

Rosenblatt, L. (1938/1995). *Literature as exploration.* (5th ed.). New York, NY: Modern Language Association.

Rosenblatt, L. M. (1982). The literary transaction: Evocation and response. *Theory into Practice, 21,* 268–277.

Roth, V. (2012). *Insurgent.* New York, NY: Katherine Tegen Books.

Roth, V. (2013). *Allegiant.* New York, NY: Katherine Tegen Books, an imprint of HarperCollins Publishers.

Rothenberg, C. (2009). English language learners in the secondary classroom. In S. R. Parris, D. Fisher, & K. Hendley (Eds.), *Adolescent literacy, field tested: Effective solutions for every classroom* (pp. 168–179). Newark, DE: IRA.

Ruddell, M. R., & Shearer, B. A. (2002). "Extraordinary," "tremendous," "exhilarating," "magnificent": Middle school at-risk students become avid word learners with the Vocabulary Self-Collection Strategy (VSS). *Journal of Adolescent and Adult Literacy, 45,* 352–363.

Rumelhart, D. E. (1982). Schemata: The building blocks of cognition. In J. Guthrie (Ed.), *Comprehension and teaching: Research reviews* (pp. 3–26). Newark, DE: International Reading Association.

Rupley, W. H., Blair, T. R., Nichols, W. D. (2009). Effective reading instruction for struggling readers: The role of direct/ explicit teaching. *Reading & Writing Quarterly, 25,* 125–138.

Ryan, C. (2018, August). *Computer and internet use in the United States: 2016.* U.S. Census Bureau. Retrieved November 17, 2018, from https://www.census.gov/content/dam/Census/library/publications/2018/acs/ACS-39.pdf

Ryan, P. M. (2000). *Esperanza rising.* New York, NY: Scholastic.

Ryan, P. M., & Selznick, B. (Illustrator). (2002). *When Marian sang: The true recital of Marian Anderson.* New York, NY: Scholastic.

Rycik, J. A. (1994). *An exploration of student library research projects in seventh grade English and social studies classes.* Unpublished doctoral dissertation, Kent State University.

Rylant, C., & Gammell, S. (Illustrator). (1984). *Waiting to waltz: A childhood.* New York, NY: Bradbury.

Sachar, L. (1998). *Holes.* New York, NY: Farrar, Strauss & Giroux.

Salisbury, R. (1934). A study of the transfer effects of training in logical organization. *Journal of Educational Research, 28,* 241–254.

Saltmarsha, D., & Saltmarsha, S. (2008). Has anyone read the reading? Using assessment to promote academic literacies and learning cultures. *Teaching in Higher Education, 13*(6), 621–632.

Samples, R. (1977). *The whole school book: Teaching and learning late in the 20th century.* Reading, MA: Addison-Wesley.

Sanders, T. (2004). *No time to waste: The vital role of college and university leaders in improving science and mathematics education.* Paper presented at the invitational conference of Teacher Preparation and Institutions of Higher Education: Mathematics and Science Content Knowledge, Washington, DC.

Sandler, M. (2013). *How a comic book is made.* Portsmouth, NH: Heinemann.

Sandler, S., & Hammond, Z. (2012/2013). Text and truth: Reading, student experience, and the Common Core. *Kappan, 94*(4), 58–61.

Sansevere-Dreher, D., Dreher, D., & Renfro, E. (1994). *Explorers who got lost.* New York, NY: Tor Books.

Santa, C. M., & Havens, L. T. (1991). Learning through writing. In C. M. Santa & D. E. Alvermann (Eds.), *Science learning: Processes and applications* (pp. 122–133). Newark, DE: International Reading Association.

Sarroub, L. K., & Pernicek, T. (2016). Boys, books, and boredom: A case of three high school boys and their encounters with literacy. *Reading & Writing Quarterly, 32*(1), 27–55.

Satrapi, M. (2000). *Persepolis: The story of a childhood.* New York, NY: Pantheon Books.

Satrapi, M. (2004). *Persepolis 2: The story of a return.* New York, NY: Pantheon Books.

Savignano, M. A. (2017, January 1). *Educators' perceptions of the substitution, augmentation, modification, redefinition model for technology integration.* ProQuest LLC.

Say, A. (1990). *El Chino.* Boston, MA: Houghton Mifflin.

Say, A. (2002). *Home of the brave.* Boston, MA: Houghton Mifflin.

Schlitz, L. A. (2007). *Good masters! Sweet ladies!: Voices from a medieval village.* New York, NY: Candlewick.

Schmar-Dobler, E. (2003). Reading on the Internet: The link between literacy and technology. *Journal of Adolescent & Adult Literacy, 47,* 80–85.

Schmidt, K. M., & Beucher, B. (2018). Embodied literacies and the art of meaning making. *Pedagogies: An International Journal, 13*(2), 119–132.

Schmidt, P. R. (1999a). KWLQ: Inquiry and literacy learning in science. *Reading Teacher, 52*(6), 789–792.

Schmidt, P. R. (1999b). Know thyself and understand others. *Language Arts, 76*(4), 332–340.

Schmidt, P. R. (2000). Teachers connecting and communicating with families for literacy development. In T. Shanahan & F. Rodriguez-Brown (Eds.), *National reading conference yearbook* (49th ed., pp. 194–208). Chicago, IL: National Reading Conference.

Schmidt, P. R. (2001). The power to empower. In P. R. Schmidt & P. B. Mosenthal (Eds.), *Reconceptualizing literacy in the new age of multiculturalism and pluralism* (pp. 389–433). Greenwich, CT: Information Age Publishing.

Schmidt, P. R. (2003). *Culturally relevant pedagogy: A study of successful in-service.* Paper presented at the annual meeting of the National Reading Conference, Scottsdale, AZ.

Schmidt, P. R. (2005a). Culturally responsive instruction: Promoting literacy in secondary content areas. *Adolescent Literacy.*

Naperville, IL: Learning Point Associates. Retrieved from www.learningpt.org

Schmidt, P. R. (Ed.). (2005b). *Preparing educators to communicate and connect with families and communities.* Greenwich, CT: Information Age Publishing.

Schmidt, P. R. (2008, December). *Secondary pre-service teacher preparation for culturally responsive literacy teaching.* Paper presented at the 58th Annual Meeting of the National Reading Conference, Orlando, FL.

Schmidt, P. R., & Finkbeiner, C. (2006). *ABC's of cultural understanding and communication: National and international adaptations.* Greenwich, CT: Information Age Publishing.

Schmidt, P. R., & Lazar, A. M. (Eds.). (2011). *Practicing what we teach: How culturally responsive literacy classrooms make a difference.* New York, NY: Teachers College Press.

Schmidt, P. R., & Ma, W. (2006). *50 literacy strategies for culturally responsive teaching, K–8.* Chicago, IL: Corwin Press.

Schoenbach, R., Greenleaf, C., Cziko, C., & Hurwitz, L. (1999). *Reading for understanding: A guide to improving reading in middle and high school classrooms.* San Francisco, CA: Jossey-Bass.

Scholastic. (2006). *The kids and family reading report.* Retrieved August 30, 2008, from www.scholastic.com/aboutscholastic/news/readingreport.htm

Scholastic. (2008). *The 2008 kids and family reading report.* Retrieved August 30, 2008, from www.scholastic.com/aboutscholastic/news/readingreport.htm

Schroeder, M., Mckeough, A., Graham, S., Stock, H., & Bisanz, G. (2009). The contribution of trade books to early science literacy: In and out of school. *Research in Science Education, 39*(2), 231–250.

Schumm, J. S., & Mangrum, C. T., II. (1991). FLIP: A framework for content area reading. *Journal of Reading, 35,* 120–124.

Schwartz, R. M., & Raphael, T. E. (1985). Concept of definition: A key to improving students' vocabulary. *Reading Teacher, 39,* 198–204.

Schwarz, G. (2002). Graphic Novels for Multiple Literacies. *Journal of Adolescent & Adult Literacy, 46*(3), 262–265. Retrieved from http://www.jstor.org/stable/40017133

Sciezka, J. (2005). *Guys write for Guys Read.* New York, NY: Viking.

Scott, E. (2007). *When is a planet not a planet? The story of Pluto.* New York, NY: Clarion Books.

Scott, L. M. (2013). Appropriating the language in urban classes via rap parties. *Journal of Adult and Adolescent Literacy, 56*(8), 633.

Selznick, B. (2007). *The Invention of Hugo Cabret.* New York, NY: Scholastic Press.

Sender, R. M. (1986). *The cage.* New York, NY: Macmillan.

Service, R., & Harrison, T. (Illustrator). (1986). *The cremation of Sam McGee.* New York, NY: Greenwillow.

Seuss, Dr. (1984). *The butter battle book.* New York, NY: Random House.

Shaffer, D. W., Nash, P., & Ruis, A. R. (2015). Technology and the new professionalization of teaching. *Teachers College Record, 117*(12).

Shanahan, T. (Ed.). (1990). *Reading and writing together: New perspectives for the classroom.* Norwood, MA: Christopher-Gordon.

Shanahan, T. (2014). Educational policy and literacy instruction: Worlds apart? *The Reading Teacher, 68*(1), 7–12.

Shanahan, T. (2015, February 2). *Shanahan on literacy: Examples of close reading questions.* [Blog post]. Retrieved from http://www.readingrockets.org/blog/examples-close-reading-questions

Shanahan, T., & Shanahan, C. (2008). Teaching disciplinary literacy to adolescents: Rethinking content-area literacy. *Harvard Educational Review, 78*(1), 40–59.

Shanklin, N. (2006). *What are the characteristics of effective literacy coaching?* Retrieved November 1, 2007, from www.literacycoachingonline.org

Shanks, A. Z. (1982). *Busted lives: Dialogues with kids in jail.* New York, NY: Delacorte.

Sharan, Y. (2010). Cooperative learning: A diversified pedagogy for diverse classrooms. *Intercultural Education, 21*(3), 195–203.

Short, K., Harste, J., & Burke, C. (1996). *Creating classrooms for authors and inquirers.* Portsmouth, NH: Heinemann.

Shulman, L. (1987). Learning to teach. *AAHE Bulletin,* 5–6.

Siciliano, J. (2001). How to incorporate cooperative learning principles in the classroom: It's more than just putting students in teams. *Journal of Management Education, 25*(1), 8–20.

Simon, S. (1990). *Oceans.* New York, NY: Morrow.

Singer, H. (1978). Active comprehension: From answering to asking questions. *Reading Teacher, 31,* 901–908.

Sís, P. (2007). *The wall: Growing up behind the iron curtain.* New York, NY: Farrar, Straus & Giroux.

Skinner, R. A., & Staresina, L. N. (2004). State of the states [Electronic version]. *Education Week, 23*(7), 97–99.

Slavin, R. E. (1988). Cooperative learning and student achievement. In R. E. Slavin (Ed.), *School and classroom organization.* Hillsdale, NJ: Erlbaum.

Slavin, R. E. (1994). *Using Student Team Learning* (4th ed.). Baltimore, MD: Johns Hopkins University, Center for Social Organization of Schools.

Slavin, R. E. (2013). Classroom applications of cooperative learning. In S. Graham (Ed.), *APA handbook of educational psychology.* Washington, DC: American Psychological Association.

Smith, D. B. (1973). *A taste of blackberries.* New York, NY: HarperCollins.

Smith, F. (1988). *Understanding reading* (4th ed.). Hillsdale, NJ: Erlbaum.

Smith, L. (2002). *Unsent letters: Writing as a way to resolve and renew.* San Francisco, CA: Walking Stick Press.

Smith, N. B. (1964). Patterns of writing in different subject areas. *Journal of Reading, 7,* 31–37.

Snow, K. (2017). Social media field trips: Using disruptive technologies without disrupting the system. *Journal of Educational Multimedia and Hypermedia, 26*(2), 193–209.

Soto, G. (1997). *Novio boy: A play.* San Diego, CA: Harcourt Brace.

Souto-Manning, M. (2009). Negotiating culturally responsive pedagogy through multicultural children's literature: Towards critical democratic literacy practices in a first-grade classroom. *Journal of Early Childhood Literacy, 9*(1), 50–74.

Sparks, S. (2018). NAEP: Gaps widen between high fliers and low scorers. *Education Week, 37*(28).

Spellings, M. (2005). *A highly qualified teacher in every classroom: The secretary's annual report on teacher quality, 2005.* Retrieved August 5, 2006, from www.title2.org/secReport05.htm

Spencer, S. L., & Vavra, S. A. (2009). *The perfect norm.* Charlotte, NC: Information Age Publishing.

Spiegel, D. L. (1998). Reader response approaches and the growth of readers. *Language Arts, 76,* 41–48.

Spiegelman, A. (1986). *Maus: A survivor's tale.* New York, NY: Pantheon Books.

Spivey, N. M. (1984). *Discourse synthesis: Constructing texts in reading and writing.* Newark, DE: International Reading Association.

St. George, J. (2000). *So you want to be president?* New York, NY: Philomel.

Staker, H., Horn, M. B., & Innosight Institute. (2012). *Classifying K–12 blended learning.* Innosight Institute.

Stanley, D. (1996). *Leonardo da Vinci.* New York, NY: Morrow.

Stanley, D. (2000). *Michelangelo.* New York, NY: HarperCollins.

Stanley, J. (1992). *Children of the dust bowl: The true story of the school at Weedpatch Camp.* New York, NY: Clarion Books.

Staples, S. F. (1991). *Shabanu: Daughter of the wind.* New York, NY: Random House.

Stecker, P. M., Fuchs, D., & Fuchs, L. S. (2008). Progress monitoring as essential practice within Response to Intervention. *Rural Special Education Quarterly, 27,* 10–17.

Stephens, C. (2002). *Magnificent monologues for teens.* New York, NY: Sandcastle.

Steptoe, J. (2016). *Radiant child: The story of young artist Jean-Michel Basquiat.* New York, NY: Little, Brown and Company,

Stewig, J. W., & Buege, C. (1994). *Dramatizing literature in whole language classrooms.* New York, NY: Teachers College Press.

Street, B. (1995). *Social literacies: Critical approaches to literacy in development, ethnography and education.* New York, NY: Longman.

Strickland, C. (2009). *Exploring differentiated instruction.* Alexandria, VA: Association for Supervision and Curriculum Development.

Su, L. (2009). *I love yous are for white people.* New York, NY: Harper Perennial.

Suid, M., & Lincoln, W. (1989). *Recipes for writing: Motivation, skills, and activities.* Menlo Park, CA: Addison-Wesley.

Supovitz, J. (2012). Getting at Student Understanding - The Key to Teachers' Use of Test Data. *Teachers College Record, 114*(11), 29.

Sutherland, Z., & Arbuthnot, M. H. (1986). *Children and books* (7th ed.). Glenview, IL: Scott Foresman.

Sweeny, S. M. (2010). Writing for the instant messaging and text messaging generation: Using new literacies to support writing instruction. *Journal of Adolescent and Adult Literacy, 54*(2), 121–130.

Taba, H. (1967). *Teacher's handbook for elementary social studies.* Reading, MA: Addison-Wesley.

Talib, S. (2018). Social media pedagogy: Applying an interdisciplinary approach to teach multimodal critical digital literacy. *E-Learning and Digital Media, 15*(2), 55–66.

Tan, S. (2007). *The arrival.* New York, NY: Arthur A. Levine.

Tarasiuk, T. J. (2010). Combining traditional and contemporary texts: Moving my English class to the computer lab. *Journal of Adolescent & Adult Literacy, 53*(7), 543–552.

Tate, B. P. (2017, January 1). *A case study of policies and procedures to address cyberbullying at a technology-based middle school.* ProQuest LLC.

Tatum, A. (2000). Breaking down barriers that disenfranchise African American adolescent readers in low-level tracks. In P. Mason & J. S. Schumm (Eds.), *Promising practices for urban reading instruction* (pp. 98–118). Newark, DE: International Reading Association.

Tatum, A. (2005). *Teaching reading to black adolescent males: Closing the achievement gap.* Portland, ME: Stenhouse.

Taylor, C. (2018). Proving in geometry: A sociocultural approach to constructing mathematical arguments through multimodal literacies. *Journal of Adolescent & Adult Literacy, 62*(2), 175–184.

Taylor, D. B. (2012). Multiliteracies: Moving from theory to practice in teacher education. In A. B. Polly, C. Mims, & K. Persichitte (Eds.), *Creating technology-rich teacher education programs: Key issues* (pp. 266–287). Hershey, PA: IGI Global.

Taylor, D. B., & Yearta, L. S. (2013). Putting multiliteracies into practice in teacher education: Tools for teaching and learning in a flat world. In R. Hartshorne, T. Heafner, & T. Petty (Eds.), *Teacher education programs and online learning tools: Innovations in teacher preparation* (pp. 244–263). Hershey, PA: IGI Global.

Taylor, T. (1969). *The cay*. New York, NY: Harcourt.

Tchudi, S., & Yates, J. (1983). *Teaching writing in the content areas: Senior high school*. Washington, DC: National Education Association.

Temple, C., Martinez, M., Yokota, J., & Naylor, A. (2005). *Children's books in children's hands: An introduction to their literature*. Boston, MA: Allyn & Bacon.

Thimmesh, C. (2000). *Girls think of everything: Stories of ingenious inventions by women*. Boston, MA: Houghton Mifflin.

Thimmesh, C. (2006). *Team moon: How 400,000 people landed Apollo 11 on the moon*. New York, NY: Houghton Mifflin.

Thoman, E., & Jolls, T. (2005). *Literacy for the 21st century*. Retrieved February 22, 2013, from www.medialit.org

Thomas, A. (2017). *The hate u give*. New York, NY: HarperCollins.

Thompson, W. I. (1981). *The time falling bodies take to light: Mythology, sexuality, and the origins of culture*. New York, NY: St. Martin's Press.

Thorndike, E. (1917). Reading and reasoning: A study of mistakes in paragraph reading. *Journal of Educational Psychology, 8*, 323–332.

Tienken, C. H. (2011). Common Core State Standards: An example of data-less decision making. *AASA Journal of Scholarship & Practice, 7*(4), 3–18.

Tierney, R. J. (1998). Literacy assessment reform: Shifting beliefs, principled possibilities, and emerging practices. *Reading Teacher, 51*, 374–390.

Tierney, R. J. (2002). An ethical chasm: Jurisdiction, jurisprudence, and the literacy profession. *Journal of Adolescent and Adult Literacy, 45*(4), 260–276.

Tierney, R. J., & Pearson, P. D. (1983). Toward a composing model of reading. *Language Arts, 60*, 568–580.

Tierney, R. J., & Pearson, P. D. (1992). A revisionist perspective on "Learning to learn from texts: A framework for improving classroom practice." In E. K. Dishner, T. W. Bean, J. E. Readence, & D. W. Moore (Eds.), *Reading in the content areas: Improving classroom instruction* (3rd ed., pp. 82–86). Dubuque, IA: Kendall/Hunt.

Tierney, R. J., & Shanahan, T. (1991). Research on reading-writing relationships: Interactions, transactions, and outcomes. In P. D. Pearson, R. Barr, M. Kamil, & P. Mosenthal (Eds.), *Handbook of reading research* (2nd ed., pp. 246–280). New York, NY: Longman.

Tierney, R. J., Carter, M. A., & Desai, L. E. (1991). *Portfolio assessment in the reading-writing classroom*. Norwood, MA: Christopher-Gordon.

Tobias, S. (1989). Writing to learn science and mathematics. In P. Connolly & T. Vilardi (Eds.), *Writing to learn mathematics and science* (pp. 47–61). New York, NY: Teachers College Press.

Tomlinson, C. (2003). Deciding to teach them all. *Educational Leadership, 61*(2), 5–11.

Tomlinson, C. (2006, April). An alternative to ability grouping. *Principal Leadership: Middle Level Edition, 6*(8), 31–32.

Tomlinson, C. A. (2017). *How to differentiate instruction in academically diverse classrooms*. Alexandria, VA: ASCD.

Tomlinson, C. A., & Moon, T. (2013). *Assessment and success in a differentiated classroom*. Alexandria, VA: Association for Supervision and Curriculum Development.

Tomlinson, C. A., & Strickland, C. A. (2005). *Differentiation in practice: A resource guide for differentiating curriculum, grades 9–12*. Alexandria, VA: Association for Supervision and Curriculum Development.

Topping, D. H., & McManus, R. (2002). *Real reading, real writing: Content area strategies*. Portsmouth, NH: Heinemann.

Toppo, G. (2001). *Education bill could affect funding*. Retrieved from www.speakout.com/cgi-in/udt/im.display.printable?client.id=speakout&story.id=9967

Torgesen, J. K., Houston, D. D., Rissman, L. M., Decker, S. M., Roberts, G., Vaughn, S., . . . Lesaux, N. (2007). *Academic literacy instruction for adolescents: A guidance document from the Center on Instruction*. Portsmouth, NH: RMC Research Corporation, Center on Instruction. Retrieved May 19, 2008, from www.centeroninstruction.org

Trueman, T. (2001). *Stuck in neutral*. New York, NY: HarperTempest.

Trumble, J., & Mills, M. (2016). Teaching with technology: Apps and social media for the urban literacy classroom. In L. M. Scott, & B. Purdum-Cassidy (Eds.), *Culturally affirming literacy practices for urban elementary students*, pp. 139–149. Lanham, MD: Rowman & Littlefield.

Tsuchiya, Y., & Lewin, T. (Illustrator). (1988). *Faithful elephants: A true story of people, animals and war* (T. Kykes, Trans.). Boston, MA: Houghton Mifflin.

Tucker, C. R. (2012). *Blended learning grades 4–12: Leveraging the power of technology to create student-centered classrooms*. New York, NY: Corwin.

Turner, A., & Himler, R. (Illustrator). (1987). *Nettie's trip south*. New York, NY: Macmillan.

Twenge, J. M., Martin, G. N., & Spitzberg, B. H. (2018). *Trends in U.S. adolescents' media use, 1976–2016: The rise of digital media, the decline of TV, and the (near) demise of print*. Psychology of Popular Media Culture. Retrieved November 24, 2018, from https://www.apa.org/pubs/journals/releases/ppm-ppm0000203.pdf

Ung, L. (2000). *First they killed my father: A daughter of Cambodia remembers*. New York, NY: Perennial Press.

United Nations Educational, Scientific and Cultural Organization (UNESCO). (2005). *Education for all: Literacy for life*. Retrieved from http://unesdoc.unesco.org/images/0014/001416/141639e.pdf

U.S. Census Bureau. (2010). 2010 U.S. Census. Retrieved from U.S. Census Bureau website: http://2010.census.gov/2010census/data

U.S. Department of Education (2001). *The No Child Left Behind Act of 2001*. Retrieved January 11, 2002, from www.ed.gov/offices/OESE/esea/NCLBexecumm.pdf

U.S. Department of Education (2009). *Race to the Top Program Executive Summary*. Retrieved from www.ed.gov/programs/racetothetop/executive-summary.pdf

U.S. Department of Education (2010). *A blueprint for reform: The reauthorization of the elementary and secondary education act*. Washington, DC: U.S. Department of Education.

U.S. Department of Education (2010). *Transforming American education learning powered by technology: National Education Technology Plan 2010 executive summary*. Washington, DC: Office of Educational Technology.

U.S. Department of Education (2011). National Center for Education Statistics, National Assessment of Educational Progress (NAEP), *Reading Assessments, NAEP Data Explorer*. Retrieved from http://ed.gov/nationsreportcard/

NDEHelp/WebHelp/welcome-to-the-NAEP-data-explorer-htm

U.S. Department of Education. (2015). *Every Student Succeeds Act*. Washington, DC: U.S. Department of Education.

U.S. Department of Education, National Center for Education Statistics. (2017). *The Condition of Education 2017 (NCES 2017–144)*, English Language Learners in Public Schools.

Vacca, J., Lapp, D., & Fisher, D. (2011). Real-time teaching. *Journal of Adolescent & Adult Literacy*, 54(5), 372–375.

Vacca, J. L., Vacca, R. T., Gove, M. K., Burkey, L., Lenhart, L., & McKeon, C. (2002). *Reading and learning to read* (5th ed.). Boston, MA: Allyn & Bacon.

Vacca, R. T. (1998). Literacy issues in focus: Let's not marginalize adolescent literacy. *Journal of Adolescent and Adult Literacy*, 41(8), 604–610.

Vacca, R. T. (2002a). Content literacy. In B. J. Guzzetti (Ed.), *Literacy in America: An encyclopedia of history, theory, and practice* (pp. 101–104). Santa Barbara, CA: ABC-CLIO.

Vacca, R. T. (2002b). Making a difference in adolescents' school lives: Visible and invisible aspects of content area reading. In A. E. Farstrup & S. J. Samuels (Eds.), *What research has to say about reading instruction* (3rd ed., pp. 184–204). Newark, DE: International Reading Association.

Vacca, R. T., & Padak, N. D. (1990). Who's at risk in reading? *Journal of Reading*, 33, 486–489.

Vacca, R. T., & Vacca, J. L. (2000). Writing across the curriculum. In R. Indrisano & J. R. Squire (Eds.), *Perspectives on writing: Research, theory, and practice* (pp. 214–232). Newark, DE: International Reading Association.

Valdés, G. (1996). *Con respeto: Bridging the distances between culturally diverse families and schools: An ethnographic portrait*. New York, NY: Teachers College Press.

Valdes, G., & Figueroa, R. A. (1994). *Bilingualism and testing: A special case bias*. Norwood, NJ: Ablex.

Van Allsburg, C. (1984). *The Mysteries of Harris Burdick*. Boston, MA: Houghton Mifflin.

Van Allsburg, C. (1990). *Just a dream*. Boston, MA: Houghton Mifflin.

van der Rol, R., & Verhoeven, R. (1993). *Anne Frank: Beyond the diary*. New York, NY: Viking.

Vardell, S. M., & Copeland, K. A. (1992). Reading aloud and responding to nonfiction: Let's talk about it. In E. B. Freeman & D. G. Person (Eds.), *Using nonfiction trade books in the elementary classroom: From ants to zeppelins* (pp. 76–85). Urbana, IL: National Council of Teachers of English.

Varga-Dobai, K. (2018). Remixing selfies: Arts-based explorations of funds of knowledge, meaning-making, and intercultural learning in literacy. *International Journal of Multicultural Education*, 20(2), 117–132.

Vaughn, S., Cirino, P., Wanzek, J., Wexler, J., Fletcher, J., & Denton, C. (2010). Response to intervention for middle school students with reading difficulties: Effects of a primary and secondary intervention. *School Psychology Review*, 39(1), 3–12.

Vick, H. H. (1998). *Walker of time*. Lanham, MD: Reinhart.

Vickery, J. R. (2017). *Worried about the wrong things: Youth, risk, and opportunity in the digital world*. Cambridge, MA: MIT Press.

Vogt, M. E., & Echevarria, J. (2008). *99 ideas and activities for teaching English learners with the SIOP model*. Boston, MA: Pearson.

Vogt, M. T., Chow, Y. P., Fernandez, J., Grubman, C., & Stacey, D. (2016). Designing a reading curriculum to teach the concept of empathy to middle level learners. *Voices from the Middle*, 23(4), 38–45.

Von Ziegesar, C. (2002). *Gossip girl*. New York, NY: Poppy.

Vygotsky, L. S. (1934/1986). *Thought and language*. Cambridge, MA: MIT Press.

Walker, B. J. (1991, February–March). Convention highlights reading assessment changes. *Reading Today*, 20.

Walls, J. (2006). *The glass castle: A memoir*. New York, NY: Scribner.

Walpole, S., & McKenna, M. (2004). Intervention programs. In *The literacy coach's handbook*. New York, NY: Guilford Press.

Walsh, K., & Snyder, E. (2004). *NCTQ reports: Searching the attic for highly qualified teachers*. National Council on Teacher Quality. Retrieved February 2005 from www.ctredpol.org/pubs/Forum 15November2004/WalshPaper.pdf

Wang, M. C., Reynolds, M. C., & Walberg, H. J. (1994–1995). Serving students at the margins. *Educational Leadership*, 52(4), 12–17.

Wang, S.-K., & Hsu, H.-Y. (2017). A design-based research capturing science teachers' practices of information and communication technologies (ICTs) integration using the new literacy framework. *Journal of Computers in Mathematics and Science Teaching*, 36(4), 387–396.

Waters, J. (2007). Making things easy. *T H E Journal*, 34(4), 26–33.

Waters, K. S., & Kunnmann, T. W. (2009). *Metacognition and strategy discovery in early childhood*. H. S. Waters, & W. Schneider (Eds.). *Metacognition strategy use & instruction* (pp. 3–22). New York, NY: Guilford Press.

Watson, R. (2017). *Piecing me together*. New York, NY: Bloomsbury.

Webb, N. M. (2008). Learning in small groups. In T. L. Good (Ed.), *21st century education: A reference handbook* (pp. 203–211). Los Angeles, CA: Sage.

Webb, S. (2000). *My season with penguins: An Antarctic journal*. Boston, MA: Houghton Mifflin.

Wein, E. (2012). *Code name verity*. New York, NY: Hyperion.

Weiss, M. J., & Weiss, H. S. (2002). *Big city cool: Short stories about urban youth*. New York, NY: Persea Books.

Wells, T., & Sandretto, S. (2017). "I'm on a journey I never thought I'd be on": Using process drama pedagogy for the literacy programme. *Pedagogies: An International Journal*, 12(2), 180–195.

Wenglinski, H. (2000). *How teaching matters: Bringing the classroom back into discussions of teacher quality*. Princeton, NJ: Educational Testing Service. Retrieved from www.ets.org/Media/ Education_topics/pdf/teamat.pdf

West, D. M. (2013). *Digital schools: How technology can transform education*. Washington, DC: Brookings Institution Press.

Wheeler, R. S., & Swords, R. (2006). *Code-switching: Teaching Standard English in urban classrooms*. Urbana, IL: National Council of Teachers of English.

Wiesel, E. (2006). *Night*. New York, NY: Hill and Wang.

Wigfield, A. (2004). Motivation for reading during the early adolescent and adolescent years. In D. S. Strickland & D. E. Alvermann (Eds.). *Bridging the literacy achievement gap, grades 4–12* (pp. 251–282). New York, NY: Teachers College Press.

Wilen, W., Ishler, L., Hutchison, J., & Kindsvatter, R. (2004). *Dynamics of effective secondary teaching* (5th ed.). Boston, MA: Allyn & Bacon.

Wilhelm, J. D. (2008). National Writing Project. *Navigating meaning: Using think-alouds to help readers monitor comprehension.* Retrieved from http://www.nwp.org/cs/public/print/resource/495

Wilkinson, L. E., & Silliman, E. R. (2000). Classroom language and literacy learning. In M. Kamil, P. Mosenthal, P. D. Pearson, & R. Barr (Eds.), *Handbook of reading research* (Vol. 3, pp. 337–360). Mahwah, NJ: Erlbaum.

Williams, B. (1995). *The Internet for teachers.* Foster City, CA: IDG Books Worldwide.

Williams-Garcia, R. (2011). *One crazy summer.* New York, NY: Amistad.

Williams-Garcia, R. (2015). *P. S. be eleven.* New York, NY: Amistad.

Williams-Garcia, R. (2016). *Gone crazy in Alabama.* New York, NY: Amistad.

Willinsky, J. (1990). *The new literacy: Redefining reading and writing in the schools.* New York, NY: Routledge.

Wilson, N. D. (2008). *100 Cupboards.* New York, NY: Bluefire.

Wilson, N. S., & Kelley, M. J. (2010). Are avid readers lurking in your language arts classroom? Myths of the avid adolescent reader. *Reading Horizons, 50*(2), 99–112.

Winter, J. W. (2018). Performance and motivation in a middle school flipped learning course. *TechTrends: Linking Research and Practice to Improve Learning, 62*(2), 176–183.

Wisconsin Historical Society. (2009). *Thinking like a historian.* Retrieved May 4, 2009, from www.wisconsinhistory.org/ThinkingLikeaHistorian

Wise, B. (2009, February). Adolescent literacy: The cornerstone of student success. *Journal of Adolescent & Adult Literacy, 52,* 369–375.

Wisniewski, D. (1996). *Golem.* New York, NY: Clarion.

Wolf, M. (2018). *Reader come home: The reading brain in a digital world.* New York, NY: Harper.

Wolfson, G. (2008). Using audio books to meet the needs of adolescent readers. *American Secondary Education, 36*(2), 105–114.

Wolk, S. (2010). What should students read? *Phi Delta Kappan, 91*(7), 8–16.

Wolsey, T. D. (2004). Literature discussion in cyberspace: Young adolescents using threaded discussion groups to talk about books. *Reading Online, 7*(4). Available at www.readingonline.org/articles/art_index.asp?HREF=wolsey/index.html

Wolsey, T. D., Smetana, L., & Grisham, D. L. (2015). Vocabulary plus technology: An after-reading approach to develop deep word learning. *The Reading Teacher, 68*(6), 449–458.

Wong, J. L. (2007). *Seeing Emily.* New York, NY: Amulet Books.

Wood, K. D. (2001). *Literacy strategies across the subject areas: Process-oriented blackline masters for the K–12 classroom.* Boston, MA: Allyn & Bacon.

Wood, K. D., Lapp, D., Flood, J., & Taylor, D. B. (2008). *Guiding readers through text: Study guides for new times* (2nd ed.). Newark, DE: International Reading Association.

Wood, K. D., & Taylor, D. B. (2005). *Literacy strategies across the subject areas* (2nd ed.). New York, NY: Allyn & Bacon.

Wood, K. D., & Taylor, D. B. (2005). *Literacy strategies across the subject areas: Process-oriented blackline masters for the K–12 classroom* (2nd ed.). Boston, MA: Allyn & Bacon.

Woodson, J. (2005). *Show way.* New York, NY: Putnam.

Woodson, J. (2014). *Brown girl dreaming.* New York, NY: Nancy Paulsen Books.

Worthy, J., Broaddus, K., & Ivey, G. (2001). *Pathways to independence: Reading, writing, and learning in grades 3–8.* New York, NY: Guilford Press.

Wright, T. S., & Cervetti, G. N. (2017). A systematic review of the research on vocabulary instruction that impacts text comprehension. *Reading Research Quarterly, 52*(2), 203–226.

Writing in the Disciplines. (2001). *Writing in the disciplines.* Retrieved June 2009 from www.cariboo.bc.ca/disciplines

Wynn, T., & Harris, J. (2012). Toward a STEM + arts curriculum: Creating the teacher team. *Art Education, 65*(5), 42–47.

Yang, G. L. (2008). *American born Chinese.* New York, NY: Square Fish Press.

Yelland, N. J. (2018). A pedagogy of multiliteracies: Young children and multimodal learning with tablets. *British Journal of Educational Technology, 49*(5), 847–858.

Yolen, J. (1996). *The pit dragon trilogy.* San Diego, CA: Magic Carpet/Harcourt Brace.

Yolen, J., & Shannon, D. (Illustrator). (1992). *Encounter.* San Diego, CA: Harcourt Brace Jovanovich.

Young, T. A., & Vardell, S. M. (1993). Weaving readers theatre and nonfiction into the curriculum. *Reading Teacher, 46,* 396–406.

Zhensun, Z., & Low, A. (1991). *A young painter: The life and paintings of Wang Yani.* New York, NY: Scholastic.

Zipin, L. (2009). Dark funds of knowledge, sleep funds of pedagogy: Exploring boundaries between lifeworlds and schools. *Discourse: Students in the cultural politics of education. 30*(3), 317–331.

Zoch, M., Myers, J., & Belcher, J. (2017). Teachers' engagement with new literacies: Support for implementing technology in the English/language arts classroom. *Contemporary Issues in Technology and Teacher Education (CITE Journal), 17*(1).

Zusak, M. (2007). *The book thief.* New York, NY: Knopf.

Zywica, J., & Gomez, K. (2008). Annotating to support learning in the content areas: Teaching and learning science. *Journal of Adolescent and Adult Literacy, 52*(2), 155–165.

Name Index

Subject Index

Note: Figures and tables are indicated by *f* and *t*.